STRAFVOLLZUGSLAGER DER SS UND POLIZEI

HIMMLER'S WARTIME INSTITUTIONS FOR THE DETENTION OF WAFFEN-SS AND POLIZEI CRIMINALS

STRAFVOLLZUGSLAGER DER SS UND POLIZEI

HIMMLER'S WARTIME INSTITUTIONS FOR THE DETENTION OF WAFFEN-SS AND POLIZEI CRIMINALS

STUART B. T. EMMETT

FONTHILL

Fonthill Media Language Policy

Fonthill Media publishes in the international English language market. One language edition is published worldwide. As there are minor differences in spelling and presentation, especially with regard to American English and British English, a policy is necessary to define which form of English to use. The Fonthill Policy is to use the form of English native to the author. Stuart T. B. Emmett was born and educated in London and now lives in the United Kingdom and therefore British English has been adopted in this publication.

Fonthill Media Limited
Fonthill Media LLC
www.fonthillmedia.com
office@fonthillmedia.com

First published in the United Kingdom
and the United States of America 2017

British Library Cataloguing in Publication Data:
A catalogue record for this book is available from the British Library

ISBN 978-1-78155-560-6

Typeset in 10pr on 13pt Adobe Caslon Pro
Printed and bound by CPI Group (UK) Ltd, Croydon, CR0 4YY

Foreword

My motive for writing *Strafvollzugslager der* SS *und Polizei* was nothing more complicated than to bring to the public's attention the story of the highly secretive correctional institutions of the *Waffen*-SS. It is a story begging to be told. Heinrich Himmler, a man obsessed with maintaining the elite image of his 'Black Corps', would not have wished us to turn the pages of this book, but the history of the *Strafvollzugslager* will be a welcome addition to the library of anyone interested in learning more about the secretive inner-workings of the *Waffen*-SS.

My interest in this subject was first stirred after reading Franz W. Seidler's *Die Militärgerichtsbarkeit der Deutschen Wehrmacht 1939–45*. In it, Seidler explained the history of the *Waffen*-SS prison institutions and revealed that the ranks of this fighting force, usually presented as an elite fighting formation, were plagued with similar levels of delinquency and criminality that existed in the other German military services. My desire to discover more about Himmler's prisons resulted in a seven year search for research material to form the basis of this work.

Stuart B. T. Emmett

CONTENTS

Acknowledgements

Particular thanks are due to Dr Thomas Beelitz, the Dolles and Flothmann families, Kurt Grawe, Gustav Mayer, Gregor Nagler for allowing me unprecedented access to their personal family archives. I extend a very special thanks also to John Moore for his equally invaluable and unselfish assistance.

Respect is also due to Christolph Anweder, Klaus Böhme, Jan Daniluk, Paweł Gut of Szczecin, George Jerome, Mike Constandy, Krzysztof Grynder, Nico Heitmann, Arno Huth, Jamie Keenan, Christoph Maier, Mike Melnyk, Roland Pfeiffer, Andreas Schulz, Tilman Taube, Stephen Tyas and Dieter Zinke

I am indebted to my researchers Benjamin Haas and Kristian Petschko and also thank Peter Grohl and *Frau* Schmidt of the Bundesarchiv Berlin and both James Webb and Thomas Wrensch from Nuremberg for their assistance.

This book is especially dedicated to Linda and my son Bryan for their unswerving support and encouragement during the researching and writing of this book.

Sources

The primary sources put to use for the writing of this book are declassified state and regional archives located in Britain, Germany and the USA. Brought together, they permit us to penetrate the secrecy surrounding the work of the *Strafvollzugslager der* SS *und Polizei* and the *Waffen*-SS front probation programme. First in equal importance was the microfilm records of the National Archives in Washington D.C. In particular the microfilm publication A3343—records of SS officers from Berlin document centre, series SSO, the D.C. NARA Washington Microfilm; T-580, roll 212-215, the records of the Army Staff (Record Group 319) investigative records repository (IRR) personal name files, 1939-1976, the records of the Central Intelligence Agency (Record Group 263). Secondly, but of no less importance are the records of the German National Archives (*Bundesarchiv*) and the German *Polizei* decrypts of the National Archives at Kew (London). These ULTRA messages, deciphered at the top secret Bletchley Park, were declassified in 1997 and are a rich, and until now unpublished record of wartime communications, originating to and from the SS and *Polizei* prisons. In addition to the sources mentioned above, I have gleamed a great deal of information from German state archives, veteran's families, published and un-published works and received assistance from a veritable host of historians and smaller archives.

Methodology

Conscious that it was my task to construct a work that no only built upon earlier non-English works, but also to surpass it, the presentation of this book is accomplished in five distinct parts. Prior to examining the prison institutions of the *Waffen*-SS, the following chapter systemically outlines the disciplinary punishment process of the pre-war SS, it explains the various forms of short detention penalties which was placed at the disposal of Heinrich Himmler's senior officers and explores the concentration camp imprisonment procedure for SS miscreants. Moving on to the wartime disciplinary regulations of the *Waffen*-SS, the planning and implementation of the SS and *Polizei* jurisdiction is then elucidated to enable an understanding of the procedures that were implemented to detain criminal and delinquent SS men. This chapter includes a description of the *Hauptamt* SS-*Gericht Amt* III (department III), the office which dealt with punishment, clemency and rehabilitation issues and this and ensuing chapters all contain punishment case studies as a method of explaining the penalty method.

To accomplish the story of Himmler's wartime prison system the second chapter is arranged in chronological order and examines the origins, development, structure and activities of the SS-*Straflager* Dachau, the first penal institution established by the head of the SS to incarcerate and re-educate his felons requiring punishment with hard labour. Quickly brought into being in the spring of 1940, this prison, designed on the military model, carried out its appointed task within the terrifying barbed wire fence of a Bavarian concentration camp. While awaiting their release its harrassed inmates were permitted little time to reflect on their crimes and undertook many hours of punishment drill and back breaking quarrying. Presenting an explanation of the prisons command organisation and describing the prisons ethos and day to day business, this chapter explains the inevitable expansion of this penal centre, which will come as no surprise given the continued rise in criminality within the *Waffen*-SS and *Polizei*.

In unprecedented detail and relying on the not insignificant memoirs of a 1942 visitor and former convicts testimonies, the third chapter, in chronological order, scrutinises the difficult and unique developmental and operational history of the infamous *Strafvollzugslager der* SS *und Polizei* Danzig-Matzkau and its branch prisons. Until now this prisons history has remained shrouded in mystery, but finally revealing its secrets, we discover that its environs had been initially conceived as a military garrison and then a refugee camp. Rising to become the largest largest penal institution in the *Waffen*-SS, Matzkau has become synonymous with Himmler's jurisdiction's punishment regime. Taking nine months to construct, this penal institution operated for only four years and upwards of 15,000 convicts passed through its electrified barbed wires fences to undertake many hours of daily punishment drill until permitted to return to the front. Explaining this institutions relationship with the SS judiciary, the convicts daily routine is also detailed and uniquely in any language, the 1943 brutality scandal that resulted in the death of one commandant and the trial of another officer for dereliction of his duties are revealed. Finally, the post-war court investigation of Matzkau's former commandants is disclosed.

Uniquely, the fourth chapter charts in great detail the civil and military careers of the SS Judges and Verification Officers, the men tasked with running the *Waffen*-SS prisons. Recruited directly from the courts service and entrusted with the day to day business of guarding the felons, Himmler commanded these old SS men, mostly Austrian by birth, to re-educate the criminals using punishment drill and labouring in essential work that aided the war effort. Detailed memoirs are presented in this chapter and where possible, the prison administrator's post-war fates are revealed. Each biography includes educational qualifications, discloses their length of SS and Nazi party membership and the receipt of primary awards, such as combat medals, the SA Sports Badge and the War Service Cross with Swords.

Given the close entwinement of the prisons and front probation punishment program, it is necessary to devote the fifth and final chapter to the appraisal of this alternative penalty to incarceration. Here, is explained the justification for establishing the front line probation units for the *Waffen*-SS and *Polizei*, a policy that was tentatively introduced in 1939. The punishment of felons with part-prison and front parolee sentences had become a central tenant of the SS and *Polizei* jurisdiction by late 1941 and those malefactors penalized with terms of imprisonment were expected to undertake some form of front probation on the hardest pressed sectors of the battlefield as part of their castigation. Usually assigned dangerous or unpleasant tasks at the front or in the rear echelon, these parolees performed military activities that were beyond those expected from the ordinary infantryman.

As a political organisation, SS ranks have no meaningful equivalent after 1933, when many members of the force acquired rank equivalence to those in use with the *Polizei* and *Wehrmacht*. In this book I have used their service ranks throughout and have included a detailed comparative table as an appendix at the end of this work. As far as possible I have also used military terminology, which was in common use at the time.

Books written in English about the Third Reich inevitably use some German vocabulary, clearly as some German words and concepts are onerous or impossible to translate into English. As far as possible I have retained German words that were in common usage at the time, particularly for SS and military organisations. Where necessary, an English translation is provided afterwards and to save space, abbreviations have been used where applicable. Non-English words are italicised unless in common usage, and unfamiliar German words may be viewed in the glossary at the end of the book. All place names are presented in English or as written by the German administration at that time. Individual terms are explained and translated in the glossary at the end of the book.

This book is not a political tract, it neither supports nor opposes the workings, political ambitions, or murderous policies of the SS and the Nazi party. It is not an apologia, it is written as a contribution to the historical understanding of the subject and it is my hope that this work goes some way to achieving a better understanding of the subject and assist future researchers in their endeavours. I welcome contact with other researchers and readers with additional information on this subject.

I take absolute responsibility, as is customary, for any errors, omissions or over-simplifications, but it is my hope that the rest of the material is enough to stimulate insight and new trains of thought into the study of the *Waffen*-SS penal colony.

Introduction

Despite a paucity of surviving records, this book, for the first time in the English language, seeks to document in detail the history of the *Strafvollzugslager der* SS *und Polizei* (punishment camps of the SS and police). These *Waffen*-SS penal institutions were established to incarcerate the SS leader's court prosecuted malefactors of his military and security apparatus in a prison environment that ensured their continued use to the regime. Scouring Europe for manpower to replace heavy losses and desiring the creation of new armed formations, Heinrich Himmler, who could ill-afford felonious troops to remain safe in jail while his disciplined troops risked their lives at the front, wished above all to return his ideologically sound, but malfeasant elements to the front where they would continue to aid the regime in its war aims. Naturally there were those felons whose crimes precluded their deployment at the front or they had been judged physically incapable of soldiering and for these criminals, the *Waffen*-SS leadership introduced a front probation process at the beginning of the conflict which by the defeat at Stalingrad in February 1943 had become a central tenant of the SS judiciary and isolated parolees in closed formations, or sent them to the Eastern and Balkan Fronts to participate in the battle against the partisans.

In the spring of 1945, the Second World War, unleashed by the German leader Adolf Hitler six years earlier, had entered its last dying gasps and its front lines had begun to disintegrate under intense Allied air and ground bombardment, the city of Munich, the birth place of the Nazi movement, found itself directly threatened from ground attack in April 1945. With the front lines facing imminent collapse and requiring immediate re-enforcement, a decision was taken, regardless of their crimes, to release from their cells the entire convict population of the SS-*Straflager* Dachau, the last remaining penal institution of the *Hauptamt* SS-*Gericht* (SS main office for legal matters), from this point described as the *HA* SS-*Gericht*. These former felons then re-attached their insignia to their uniforms, hefted their combat webbing and equipment on their backs and accepted weapons and ammunition before marching from Dachau in a vain endeavour to halt the Allied advance. The decision to release the malfeasant elements of Himmler's justice system marked the end of this unique penal colony's six year history.

Within the vast topic that is the history of the *Waffen*-SS is the account of the *HA* SS-*Gericht*, the wartime disciplinary institution tasked with the equal application of Himmler's wartime jurisdiction. Engaging in pre-war discussions with the *Reichsjustizministerium* (national finance ministry), the SS leader demanded legal parity with the *Wehrmacht* and argued that the civil and military jurisdictions had no understanding for the special relationship which existed between his men and the *Führer*, Adolf Hitler, or indeed had any comprehension of what the Nazi leader would demand from this relationship. Agreeing to his stipulations, the Minister for the Legal Defence commanded the establishment of an autonomous judiciary for the *Waffen*-SS on 17 October 1939 and Heinrich Himmler authorised the creation of the *HA* SS-*Gericht* in the summer of 1939. Announcing the necessary orders to establish a headquarters and courts, the SS leader neglected to request funds to inaugurate a *Waffen*-SS prison.

Given responsibility for prosecuting undisciplined *Waffen*-SS and *Polizei* in special deployment, the *HA* SS-*Gericht* also instituted legal proceedings against the salaried members of the *Reichsführung*-SS, those deployed with the training schools, the staff of the various HSSPF and their subordinate forces. The remit of the secretive *HA* SS-*Gericht* was gradually expanded to include almost the entire military and security forces under Himmler's command. These included non-German volunteers, those subordinate to the *Waffen*-SS, or *Polizei* in special circumstances, homosexuals of the *Allgemeine*-SS, associates of the SiPo-*und* SD from 9 April 1940 and the entire *Ordnungspolizei*. By the wars end virtually the entire uniformed police service, including non-German forces, the German Red Cross and a myriad of defence organisations, had become subject to the SS and *Polizei* jurisdiction.

From its inception, it was the task of the *HA* SS-*Gericht* from its inception and until its dissolution in late April 1945 to conduct court investigations, to indict defendants, conduct court-martials and ensure the balanced implementation of disciplinary and court punishments. To enable them to carry out this task, the organisation recruited its own judges and clerks and operated independent courts. A draconian legal process was a central facet of the Nazi regime's world vision and to enable its leadership to prosecute its territorial and racial objectives, Adolf Hitler supported the imposition of harsh sentences, including the death penalty. However, this punitive legal process was at odds with Himmler's own belief that the principles of SS comradeship dictated that his men always receive another chance to make amends for their indiscretions. In practice, the SS leader enforced far fewer capital punishments than the civil and military jurisdictions, preferring that his miscreants served a short incarceration and then atoned for their crimes at the front as parolees.

Taking its first steps towards its participation in the worldwide conflagration that became World War Two in September 1939, the senior commanders of the *Waffen*-SS, long experienced at punishing their delinquent troops with cell detention for short periods, began to incarcerate their court punished felons within civil and military jails.

Unfortunately Himmler, once his felons had served their sentences, they then faced expulsion from the SS or *Polizei* and were drafted into one of the other military services. The consequences of this imprisonment process became a cause of much regret for Himmler, who loathed to lose such ideological sound 'bayonet strength' and judging that his arrangement with the civil and military judiciaries had failed to satisfy his requirements, the SS leader engendered the *HA* SS-*Gericht* to establish their own penal institutions on ideological and practical grounds in the spring of 1940 and the first *Strafvollzugslager der* SS *und Polizei* was established inside the infamous KL Dachau. Selecting a handful of long-serving, ideologically-sound officers of the *HA* SS-*Gericht* to carry out the *Reichsführer*'s demand for an 'SS-suitable environment' these guards received orders to imposed a strict regime, but were to preserve the inmates' National Socialist conviction to enable their rotation back into the front line as useful soldiers. These tough old-timer *Waffen*-SS jailers watched over each hard labour felon until their sentence had been fully served, or they had been judged suitable for parole.[1]

Within a year of its opening, the SS-*Straflager* Dachau had expanded and begun accepting convicts punished with short prison sentences. The convict population quickly outgrew the Dachau jail environs and the construction of another, larger institution for prison felons was implemented near the city of Danzig by 1941. When opened in 1942, this penal colony alone was inducting and releasing approximately 500 inmates per month, the vast majority policemen from the various uniformed and plain clothes branches of this organisation who had been imprisoned for a myriad of disciplinary and criminal offences. [2]

Prior to establishing the SS-*Straflager* Dachau, and with the permission of the German leader, the *Waffen*-SS had experimented with a front parole program in 1939, but in the wake of the successful 1940 campaign, the *HA* SS-*Gericht* received full control of the entire parole process and initiated regulations which permitted convicts to serve mixed prison and parolee sentences. Having served a portion of the prison punishment, the felons were then assessed to determine their fitness to leave their cells for the front and those judged suitable to return to the battle for the remainder of their penalty. Depending on their arm of service, this probation phase could be served with dedicated parole units, at the front with the troops, or with security units dedicated to fighting partisans. All categories of delinquent and criminal were included this method and amongst their number were the incorrigibles and camp prisoners. The parolees were under no illusion that their re-admittance into the SS depended on their wounding or death. In the last months of the conflict, the head of the SS begun forgathering serious military and *Waffen*-SS criminals into the infamous *Oberf.* Oskar Dirlewanger's brigade, which was expanded into a field division that deployed on the Eastern Front in 1945.

It is my belief that this book is a first and there is probably no other text in the English language that embraces the entire imprisonment and parolee process of the *Waffen*-SS. It is my hope that the readers believe, as do I, that undertaking this effort has advanced our knowledge of the *Waffen*-SS.

Stuart B. T. Emmett
London 2016

1

Disciplinary Punishment of SS Men

For the SS to fulfil its basic requirement, the protection of the *Führer*, their loyalty could never be placed in doubt and from its inception, the first leaders of the SS and Heinrich Himmler led his organisation as though it were a quasi-military force and placed its disciplinary concerns in his own hands and in those of his senior officers. Demanding absolute SS-*Manneszucht* (discipline) from each man, the *Reichsführer* expected them to also obey the *Führer* and his officers at all times. Exhorting his subordinate officers to deal with all signs of wrongdoing with the greatest severity, the SS leader permitted the punishment of his miscreants in accordance with the penalties contained within the SA-*Dienstverordnung* (SA service orders). Imposing punishments in accordance with the 12 December 1933 general service regulations for the SA, these statutes permitted the imposition of fines, a loss of leave entitlement, strong and mild reprimands and a ban on the wearing of uniforms and awards. In certain circumstances, Himmler and his pre-war senior commanders incarcerated their undisciplined men in their homes, or in cells located on SS owned premises in accordance with paragraph §8 of the general service regulations of the SA. These regulations permitted mild arrest for up-to 30 days, intensified room arrest under guard for a period not exceeding two weeks' duration and intensified arrest for up-to fourteen days with bread and water rations. However, recognising that these punishments could only be accepted on a voluntarily basis, the SS leadership imposed them as an educational measure with the intention of correcting bad behaviour. Miscreants refusing to obey an arrest penalty risked certain expulsion from the organisation.

In the autumn of 1934 the SA disciplinary regulations had been superseded by the SS-*Diszipliarstraf- und Beschwerdeordnung*, or SS-DBO (disciplinary and complaints regulations of the SS) and this collection of statutes permitted the disciplinary superiors to impose similar confinement punishments to those already offered by the SA. The offender's immediate higher ranking officer was responsible for judging those who had committed infractions against discipline and he conducted a disciplinary punishment process that decided whether to impose an acquittal, lesser penalty, or if the infraction merited such a measure, introduce the SS-*Ehrenstrafe* (honour punishment) the route by which expulsion was achieved.[1]

Those committing two minor offences faced automatic expulsion and four options existed for this decision: honourable discharge, a dishonourable discharge, temporarily expulsion, and the ultimate penalty at Himmler's disposal was the permanent expulsion for all time. Outside of the official sanctions of these disciplinary regulations, the SS leader also imposed up-to two year alcohol bans for drunkenness. Overseeing the equal implementation of the disciplinary regulations from May 1931 was the SS.-*Gericht* (SS court) and this small disciplinary office reviewed disciplinary punishments, ensured the smooth running of the appeals/clemency process and supplied the *Reichsführer* with a specialist opinion reports for serious, or complicated punishments. In addition the SS.-*Gericht* supported the work of the *Schieds- und Ehrengerichtsordnung der* SS (arbitration and honour judiciary), the body tasked with settling disputes between SS men and members of other Nazi organisations.[2]

The increasing militarisation of the SS required the implementation of disciplinary procedures for the armed wing of Himmler's force which was indistinguishable from those in use with the military. Both military services were afflicted with the time honoured disciplinary problems which had troubled all armies throughout history and the SS leadership demanded the ability to impose disciplinary punishments to maintain the troops *Manneszucht*, which preserved the troops fighting ability. The ultimate sanction at the commander's behest was expulsion from military service and they achieved this via the *Ehrenstrafe*. This disciplinary process ensured that unruly elements were removed from the troop's ranks in an effort to preserve their orderliness (this demand required that Himmler and his disciplinary superiors punished the undisciplined for the smallest of infractions). As the country prepared for war it was agreed that SS troops would take part in the fighting and Himmler envisaged a need to publish disciplinary regulations for the SS-VT that corresponded to those in use with the military. Commanding the SS.-*Gericht* to prepare these ordinances for mobile troops in early 1938, the completed draft received Himmler's approbation and the SS-*Disziplinar- und Beschwerdeordnung für der Mobile Truppen* (disciplinary and complaints regulations of the SS for mobile troops) came into force on 9 November the same year. Its principle deviation from earlier versions were extended rights for the *Reichsführer* and the inclusion of a regulation, which exhorted all commanders to send important cases directly to Himmler to obtain his personal decision. Introduced for the SS-VT, their replacement units and its re-enforcements, the 1938 SS-DBO supplied the leadership and commanding officers with the authorisation to punish acts, or omissions which were against the basic beliefs and basic laws of the SS, which violated soldierly discipline and order, threatened comradely cohesion, caused injurious behaviour in and out of service and was judged to be dishonourable behaviour. Against all members of his force, without restriction, the *Reichsführer* was entitled to impose all disciplinary sanctions as an educational measure and the penalties included a simple warning, a strong warning, *Stubenarrest* (room arrest) for officers and *Unterführer mit Portepee*, *Gelinder Arrest* (mild arrest) was set aside for *Unterführer* and men and *Geschäfte Arrest* (intensified arrest) for *Unterführer* without *Portepee* and men. Other punishments included demotion of service rank, degradation, service admonitions, cautions and fines, punishment guard, punishment drill three times every two hours and restriction of leave entitlement.

The leader of a *Standarte*, which included KL commandants, *Sturme*, or an independent *Sturmbann* were entitled to impose a simple and severe warning to an officer and a simple and severe warning, room arrest for up to two weeks and mild arrest for up to two weeks for an *Unterführer mit Portepee*. These penalties were also available for use against miscreant *Unterführer ohne Portepee* and men. Penalties applying this category of offender also included *Verschäften Arrest* (intensified arrest) for up to ten days. The leaders of non-independent *Sturmbann* were authorised to impose five days room arrest against an officer, room arrest and mild arrest for up to four weeks against an *Unterführer mit Portepee*. The imposition of three weeks intensified arrest also existed for *Unterführer ohne Portepee* and men. Additionally, the leader of a *Standarte* or an independent *Sturmbann* was permitted to impose ten days' room arrest for officers and a demotion, or degradation for *Rttf.* and *Sturmmänner*.

Each officer equipped with disciplinary punishment powers was entitled to dismiss a subordinate from the service if obvious treachery existed, when they found clear evidence of cowardice, revealed an explicit denial of service, when the offender had insulted an SS officer on duty, had been caught red-handed committing an offence during a site inspection, had been libellous, or had committed a misdemeanour crime (these dismissals were reported to a higher authority). Considering the punishment, the disciplinary superior then had to determine whether the penalty was appropriate, consider the type of misbehaviour and judge the degree of risk his behaviour damaged the leadership. Officers convinced that their punishment authority had proved insufficient would then report the matter to a competent disciplinary superior. In cases of the serious violation of trust, severe criminal offences, or any act which would in its self was grounds for the offenders dismissal, the disciplinary superior had orders to arrest the culprit immediately and submit a detailed report to the SS-TV inspector general and SS-VT inspector respectively, to permit them to take the temporary measures they deem necessary against the perpetrator.

Their reports were immediately forwarded to the *Reichsführer* and this document included observations about the miscreants ideological stance and the consequences of the offenders behaviour on discipline and the security and reputation of the SS. Serious violation of trust, which included arranging a desertion, orchestrating a mutiny, spying for the enemy, cowardice, heavy guard misconduct, dereliction of duty, unauthorized leave, insubordination, incitement, sedition, plundering, devastation, thievery and robbery in the deployment area of the mobile forces. Offender's penalties were announced in a written punishment orders and details of the offence recorded in the unit punishment book (*strafbuch*). Commanding officers had responsibility for maintaining the punishment book and for ensuring that its contents remained confidential and kept under lock and key.

Those sentenced to a term of sharp arrest, served their punishment in arrest cells, sleeping on a hard bench and usually received only bread and water. After the start of the sentence, the offender was permitted reading material and every four days and on each of the consecutive four days a meal that was served to the troops in the barracks.

The punished were forbidden from sleeping between reveille and taps. If the punishment risked the offender's health then the penalty was suspended until a doctor permitted its enforcement. Those penalized with mild arrest were detained in a holding cell and provided with a soft couch (bed) and receiving the same food as those in the barracks, the punished were permitted to read between waking and taps. Served at the home of the punished, room arrest recipients were forbidden from leaving the premises, they catered for themselves and were monitored to ensure compliance. The consumption of tobacco and alcohol was strictly forbidden for those facing an arrest punishment and for those sentenced to a term of room arrest. If the enforcement of a mild and sharp arrest proved impossible, then the disciplinary superior had the authority to replace the punishment with a guard, or order the offender to perform arduous duties. Enforcing the degradation by the removal of badges of rank was not carried out in the presence of members holding a lesser grade in rank to the punished. The promotion of delinquents during the period of the punishment was forbidden and those opposed to the penalty's imposition had the right to appeal before its enforcement, but no later than seven days after the date of the complaint. Appeals were decided by the disciplinary superior of the officer who imposed the sentence. Assessing the Top of Formappeal justified, he was permitted to erase or amend the order. Finding against the complainant, the appeals officer could also increase of the punishment. Further appeals were forbidden.[3]

The 1938 edition of the disciplinary regulations permitted the disciplinary superiors to punish persistent delinquents with a six month detention in the Sachsenhausen *Erziehungssturm* (Education Company) which represents the first sign that Himmler intended the creation of penal institutions, specifically designed for the segregated detention of his delinquent troops.

Prior to the introduction of the *Reichsführer*'s jurisdiction in October 1939, the imprisonment of civil court punished malefactors and criminals of the SS was undertaken in civil institutions and certain categories' of offender were detained inside concentration camps and their number included those convicted for contravening paragraph §175 and treachery legislation.

1.1 Pre-war Concentration Camp Detention

From the inception of the SS, it became the practice of the *Reichsführer* to incarcerate certain categories of his reprobates inside the RSHA controlled concentration camps. Here, behind the forbidding barbed wire fences of the *Schutzhaftlager* (protective custody camps) the former bodyguards laboured, ate and slept alongside their political enemies as prisoners, with all the risks that this type of detention entailed. Established as extra-judicial penal institution in early 1933, the concentration camps formed part of the Nazi's avowed plan to dismantle the liberal Weimar state. In the wake of the *Reichstag* burning on 28 February 1933 the Nazi leadership announced the 'For the Protection of the People' edict and this legislation precipitated the creation of auxiliary *Polizei* forces across

Germany from loyal SA and SS men who then proceeded to arrest and detain prominent members of the left wing and liberal opposition in makeshift detention centres to prevent them voting in the March general elections. The subsequent parliamentary victory secured the Nazi's hold on power, parliamentary democracy was then abolished in Germany and an extension of the 28 February edict, legalised the protective detention of those the Nazi's perceived as enemies of the state in concentration camps without resorting to any form of due process. Initially envisaged as a temporary measure, the state of Prussia alone held 25,000 opponents under the protective detention, often in abysmal conditions, by the end of June 1933. Camps were often located in empty business properties and quickly became a byword of brutality and torture.[4]

It was the Nazi leaders' desire to both politically and socially forcibly unite the German people into a racially pure people's society which excluded those identified as not possessing German ancestry. Publishing a succession of edicts to isolate these groups from the population, the regime then initiated a program of detaining Jews, non-whites, Slav's and Gypsies in the concentration camps (the mentally ill were sterilised or secretly euthanized).[5] The number of German Jews detained in the camps rose exponentially as a direct consequence of this brutal policy and here, within the camps wire fences they found themselves especially at risk from the guard's brutality and murderous impulses.[6]

Quickly appreciating that the camps were to become a permanent feature of the regime, Himmler judged correctly that whoever controlled these institutions would create for himself an influential power base within the Nazi apparatus. Proceeding to establish hegemony over many of the camps, he ensured that they formed a permanent feature of the state's repression and provided free labour for his economic empire. Requiring a steady supply of inmates to enable their economic viability, the camps accepted those deemed persistent criminals who had served two prison sentences, the so-called asocial/habitual criminals, from 1937 to fulfil this requirement. Those judged 'harmful to the public's health' completed their prison term and the RSHA then obtained a protection detention order on their release date which permitted the prisoners camp detention for six months. In reality, virtually all of those detained in the concentration camps remained within their forbidding barbed wire fences for an indeterminate period and the protection detention order was routinely renewed every six months.[7]

Within each camp existed a headquarters and the camps administrative and service needs were located within its environs alongside the *Arrestgebäude* (detention building) a place of detention which was also known as the camp arrest. This building usually included cells to isolate prisoners and camp guards punished with arrest penalties. Pre- and wartime camp guards discovered engaging in improper relationship with inmates, or denounced for assisting them to avoid the camp censor, were then themselves at risk from becoming prisoners.[8]

With the *Reichsführer*'s approbation, the practice of detaining disgraced SS men in concentration camps in the pre-war period was undertaken against those who had been punished with a prison sentence by the civil courts for committing serious criminal illegal acts, such as a prosecution for the offence of racial pollution, political offences and contravening against paragraph § 175 RStGB and other sex crimes. Prior to their incarceration in the civil jails, these types of SS offender routinely faced the *Ehrenstrafe*, were expelled for all time and the RSHA then assessed whether the severity of their crime required the application of a protection detention order. Enforced once the prison sentence had been served, RSHA agents arrested the former SS man at the prison gates and then took him immediately to a concentration camp. Here, the new camp prisoner accepted a striped uniform with a triangular coloured badge, which categorised him in accordance to his offence: Red for political crimes, Green for criminals, Yellow for Jews and Pink for those prosecuted for contravening paragraph § 175. Unfortunately, it has never been accurately determined exactly how many disgraced SS men in the pre-war period were detained in the concentration camps.[9]

The former SS man's survival now depended on avoiding confrontation with prisoners and guards, obtaining a useful job in the camp, or fostering a life-saving relationship with those in a position of responsibility. For some, their only chance of survival was to become an informer or overseer. The author Heinz Höhne records that eleven pre-war SS officers found themselves incarcerated in camps as prisoners for refusing to sign their oath of loyalty and writing on this subject in 1938, Himmler acknowledged that he had imprisoned in camps those accused of political or paragraph § 175 offences (although amongst these were certainly those detained in the SS-*Erziehungssturm*).[10]

The camp survivor Paul Martin Neurath recalled that the KL Dachau held a former SS man who had been prosecuted for racial pollution in 1938. Wearing a black triangle on his prison garb, he appeared not to have suffered retribution from other prisoners. This same source recalled that another disgraced SS man named Azzoni was a prisoner and overseer in the KL Buchenwald and became notorious amongst the inmates for his overt anti-Semitism.[11]

In some circumstances, detention in the *Schutzhaftlager* had deadly consequences. The author G. J. Giles reports that two disgraced SS men found themselves incarcerated in camps for committing paragraph § 175 offences in the pre-war period. Interestingly, the first, had himself formerly guarded the barracks that held homosexuals. Denounced for engaging in a sexual relationship with a prisoner, he first served his court sentence and then found himself detained in the very same barracks he had once guarded. It is reported that both the guards and prisoners belaboured him when his identity was revealed.[12]

For another officer, his camp punishment had dire consequences: Accused of contravening paragraph § 175 RStGB, *Sta.* Hans v.Kobelinski, a *Blutorden* holder and former member of the SD, was court punished and on the grounds of his 'crime' and the head of SS ordered his demotion to the rank of SS-*Mann* and expulsion from the SS on 9 May 1936. Released from his goal sentence, the RSHA obtained a protection detention order for v.Kobelinksi in 1936 and incarcerated him in the KL Dachau as a prisoner. He would not survive this experience. The camp commandant reported that v.Kobelinksi had committed suicide on 29 August 1937.[13]

1.2 Emslandlager

Exercising his authority as the Prussian Interior Minister, Herman Göring commanded the creation of four concentration camps in the Emsland region in June 1933. An additional dimension to the emerging Prussian state penal system, these camps were designed to isolate from society those people that the Nazi leadership perceived to be enemies of the state. Commanded by *Polizei* civil servants, the guards were selected from local SA and SS units. Awakened before 6.00 a.m. in summer, the Emsland inmates marched for an hour to their moorland sites and laboured to reclaim wetlands according to pre-determined quotas. The guards' brutality and murderous activities in the Emsland camps resulted in the camps transfer in 1934 to the care of the *Reichsjustizministerium* (national justice ministry).[14]

Demanding that the very worst malefactors were removed from its ranks in an effort to preserve its military integrity, the pre-war military handed those judged military shameful to the *Reichsjustizministerium* for detention in the Emslandlager. This policy continued into the war years and those judged 'militarily unworthy' by military courts found themselves incarcerated in the Esterwegen Punishment Camp (VII) from 1 November 1939. In the first six months of the war, a small number of *Waffen*-SS felons were incarcerated inside Esterwegen. The introduction of the 17 October 1939 edict permitted the incarceration of certain categories of SS and *Polizei* offender in the *Straflager der Allgemeine Justiz* in Emsland (KL Esterwegen) and of this number, the SS and *Polizei* courts had judged 71 militarily unworthy.[15]

Here, in the Emsland the Nazi regime detained military convicts punished with life sentences, those convicted of committing high treason and serious criminal acts, severely disabled offenders and those suffering medical conditions that requiring long term treatment in a hospital (afflictions such as T.B. or sexual diseases). 91 per cent of the Emsland offenders had committed serious criminal act.[16]

In Esterwegen a 300-strong camp prisoner work commando worked on the peat farm (*Zuchthäuslerstrafkompanie*—Hard Labour Punishment Company) in others were employed in the military clothing factory making boots, uniforms and winter clothing. Each barracks slept between 80 and 120 inmates and included a wash room and toilet. Surviving images reveal that the inmates wore *kratchen* headgear, a military uniform stripped of insignia and a white rectangular badge with a number was attached to the prisoner's upper-left hand tunic breast. All convicts performed military exercises and undertook sporting activities. Punishments for the ill-disciplined included terms of sharp arrest and the wearing of handcuffs and leg irons. Persistent offenders found themselves placed in the *Strafkompanie* (Punishment Company) and performed hard tasks and extra drill. Around 4,500 convicts found themselves detained in the KL Esterwegen on 31 January 1943 and of their number, some 3,500 had been convicted by military courts and the remainder by civil courts.[17]

The *Chef HA* SS-*Gericht* identified 47 SS convicts in the KL Esterwegen during early 1942 and of these, 25 were transferred to the *Strafvollzugslager der* SS *und Polizei* Danzig-

Matzkau at the end of June 1942, leaving 22 SS convicts in Esterwegen to continue serving their *Zuchthaus* sentences (two convicts were identified as Buder and Ketterer).[18] Representing only 1.3 per cent of the total inmate population of Esterwegen on 2 January 1943, Himmler issued orders in May 1942 which commanded his remaining felons in Esterwegen to be detained in similar conditions to those found in his prisons. As a consequence of this order, these convicts had all transferred to Matzkau by 31 August 1943.[1]

1.3 SS-*Erziehungssturm*

The military determined the standard for handling undisciplined soldiers in the pre-war period and they actively segregated subversive and ill-disciplined soldiers from their ranks to preserve its *Manneszucht* and ensure the unity of the troops. This requirement and the need to re-educate miscreants for future deployment at the front, resulted in the military leadership commanding the creation of the *Sonderabteilung* (special battalion) in the troop training grounds in October 1936. The re-educated elements of the pre-war special battalion were returned to front units in September 1939, but those failing to qualify for continued military service found themselves branded militarily shameful and were detained as prisoners in concentration camps. Amongst these recalcitrant elements were those appraised militarily unworthy, the politically doubtful, paragraph § 175 offenders, quarter-Jews felons, habitual criminals, psychopaths, pacifists and those granted suspended death sentences. Demanding their segregation from the general prison population, the RSHA acceded to the military's request and arranged their detention in a separate penal institution within the concentration camp, which was known as the *Sonderabteilung Wehrmacht*, or SAW. Establishing this separate prison in the KL Sachsenhausen on 1 May 1938, the camp commandant selected barracks twelve for the military inmates incarceration and entered here, those convicts who had wilfully refused to conform to prison regulations and those, who due to the special nature of their offence, required incarceration in a camp in accordance to German law.[20]

Sonderabteilung Wehrmacht inmates were supervised by the infamous *Hscha.* Richard Bugdalle and he was assisted by *Oscha.* Martin Knittler and *Oscha.* Fritz Ficker.[21]

The *Sonderabteilung-Wehrmacht*:

> *Abteilung* I; *Erziehungssturm*, or re-education department. Located in the KL Sachsenhausen, this section held those expecting to serve a short sentence of up to six months.
>
> *Abteilung* II; *Besserungsabteilung*, or improvement department. Located in the KL Buchenwald, this section detained those who had little prospect of release.

Harassed by their guards, these military convicts, clothed in camp garb and adorned with the pointing upwards red triangle performed many hours of military drill and laboured for between ten to twelve hours each day; except on Sunday. A large number of SAW inmates were put to work with the 1. SS-*Baubrigade* at Neusollstedt and at the Nordhausen slave labour complex towards the end of the war. Here, they laboured in underground factories to construct V-2 rockets. One author estimates that between 600 and 1,000 military convicts passed through the SAW and an additional 1,000 joined them in the wake of the 20 July 1944 assassination attempt on Adolf Hitler.[22]

Given the military's demand that the SS-VT emulated their punishment processes, the *Reichsführer* commanded the creation of the SS-*Erziehungssturm* (education company) in the KL Sachsenhausen during July 1938 and this institution accepted SS malefactors who had committed the offences mentioned above, or had shamed the bodyguard, (henceforth, only persistent malfeasants and those imprisoned for § 175 RStGB offences found themselves detained in camps). Here, the head of the SS commanded the prison to offer its inmates in what he described as an 'SS suitable' re-education environment, which circumvented institutionalisation and turned malfeasant elements into useful soldiers for the regime's special mission. As a consequence of this demand, the SS guards imposed a proverbial short, sharp, shock regime on their charges and re-education consisted of a harsh regime of military drill, labouring and indoctrination lectures. Corporal punishments were imposed on miscreants in the form of beatings on the bottom with a birch or cane.

The camp commandant established this prison in barracks 57 and 58 within the small camp, located between the administration offices and the camp arrest, and its guards were selected from the camp staff.

The SS-*Erziehungssturm*:

> *Abteilung* I; *Erziehungssturm*. For the disobedient, those who resisted other forms of detention, or had committed light offences.
>
> *Abteilung* II; *Besserungsabteilung*. For expellees. Amongst their number were former camp guards, typically those who had shown favouritism towards prisoners.

The 1938 edition of the SS-DBO permitted disciplinary superiors to punish persistent delinquents with a period of up to six months detention in the *Erziehungssturm*. This penalty was reserved for offenders whose offence required a harsher penal punishment than that offered by sharp arrest, but had been judged an offending type that Himmler wished to spare complete expulsion. Prior to his entry to this prison, the offender was first handed to the care of the RSHA and their detention fixed for six months' duration.[23]

The camp prisoners come to refer to this institution as the *Knochensturm* (bone battalion) and detaining thirteen convicts at the end of 1938, this number had risen to 73 inmates by September 1939.[34] The former political prisoner, Harry Naujocks, recalled that the 'bone men' were greatly feared by the camp prisoners and their guards regularly set them on the camp inmates. This nickname had almost certainly derived from the cross-bones motif attached to their SS drill uniforms.[25]

Post-war, the former camp inmate and author, Szalet Leon, recalled that the *Erziehungssturm* inmates lived in accommodation similar to the other prisoners and ate the same food. They also occupied an important position in the camp hierarchy. 'The elite prisoners in the KL Sachsenhausen distributed food throughout the camp' observed Leon and given the general privation prevailing amongst the camp inmates, this was undoubtedly a privileged detail.[26]

A handful of *Erziehungssturm* inmates were selected for field probation with the *Verlorenen Haufen* (forlorn hope) of the *Totenkopfdivision* in the autumn of 1939. However, those inmates continuing to behave in an undisciplined fashion risked a transfer to the *Schutzhaftlager* as camp prisoners.[27]

Letters originating from the LSSAH *Ersatz-Bataillon* in Berlin reveal the nature of the offences committed by those sent to the *Erziehungssturm*: To enable them to become soldiers once again, the battalion commander, *Hstuf.* Emil Sator, ordered six persistent disciplinary offenders of his unit, men who had committed at least two offences and set a bad example to the new trainees in the battalion, to report to the *Erziehungssturm* for re-education on 5 March 1940.[28]

Assigned to the LSSAH *Ersatz-Bataillon*, *Uscha.* Franz Effland was denounced for lying about his duty hours on 11 October 1939, a violation of the principle of truthfulness and comradeship, and was punished with eight days' sharp arrest on 16 October 1939. Undeterred by this sentence, Effland returned six hours late to his barracks from leave on 2 February the same year and was then punished with fourteen days' sharp arrest on 15 February 1940. Aware that the usual disciplinary methods had proved non-effective and keen to prevent Effland's undisciplined behaviour influencing the other men in his unit, this miscreants commander ordered him to the *Erziehung- und Besserung-Kompanie* (education and improvement company) for eight weeks. Released from his sentence, Effland then accepted a period of front probation.[29]

Brought for trial before the SS- *und Polizei-Gericht* III, Berlin on suspicion of committing three cases of unauthorised absence from his barracks, the court judged *Scha.* Erich Stichnoth guilty of the charges and sentenced him to a four months' fortress detention on 20 January 1940 (case Nr. St. L. 1/1939). Returning to the LSSAH *Panzeraufklärungskompanie*, Stichnoth again ignored company orders forbidding the men from leaving the barracks and absented himself from the barracks on 1 February 1940. Returning to the LSSAH *Ersatz-Bataillon* the following day, his commander punished him with fourteen days' sharp arrest, but complaining that his subordinate had a bad attitude towards military service, *Hstuf.* Sator ordered Effland to spend six months' incarcerated in the *Besserungsanstalt* (Improvement Institution) on 5 March. Stichnoth accepted front probation at the conclusion of his sentence. In this next instance, *Rttf.* Fritz v.Sturm of the LSSAH *Ersatz-Bataillon* staff company received orders to report to the *Erziehungssturm* on 2 March 1940. Possessing a chequered disciplinary history, v.Sturm had been reported for drunkenness in uniform and had arrived 100 minutes late from leave on 6 September 1939. An eight day sharp arrest was imposed on v.Sturm on 5 January 1940, but learning little from this experience, he once again returned late from leave on 16 January. Judged with expressing a careless service performance, v.Sturm's commander penalized him with a three days' sharp arrest on 31 January 1940. Posted to the 3. *Reserve-Kompanie*, the indiscipline v.Sturm once again received numerous admonishments from his company commander, who expressed concern that his poor attitude would result in behaviour that would lead to further disciplinary offences. Labelled an unreliable soldier whose 'careless attitude' had resulted in his unsuitability, v. Sturm's superior then demanded his harshest punishment. On the grounds that the normal methods of disciplinary methods had failed to correct his attitude, v. Sturm was ordered to serve an eight week period of punishment in the *Erziehungskompanie* 'to permit the possibility of making him a useful soldier.' None of these three soldiers had returned to the LSSAH by 1 February 1941.[30]

The 1940 summer campaign in France and the Low Countries concluded, the LSSAH Regiment in Metz contacted the SS-PHA on 17 October 1940 to inform them that the SS leader had ordered the degradation and expulsion of 24 year-old *Oscha.* Erich Wiebezick and 27 year-old *Oscha.* Heinz Sander on 10 September 1940 and commanding their and benefits to be withheld, Himmler then commanded both delinquents to the *Erziehungssturm* and the RSHA were notified of this decision on 25 September 1940.[31]

The *Erziehungssturm* in the KL Sachsenhausen converted to the SS-*Arrest und Haftanstalt* (SS arrest and detention institution) around February 1941 and this institution detained offenders awaiting trial before the Berlin tribunal and those sentenced to short terms of arrest and *Gefängnis*. Himmler commanded the creation of a bomb disposal commando in the KL Sachsenhausen on 12 December 1941 and accepted into its ranks were those convicts suspected of using their jail sentences to evade service at the front. Inmates completing 25 of these highly dangerous bomb disposal missions were then permitted to return to the SS-*Straflager* Dachau as convicts to complete their jail sentence.[32]

In 1942 it was reported that there existed in the KL Sachsenhausen, the *Abteilung* Z (Department *Zuchthaus*) which was under the control of the camp commandant. Its inmates became the responsibility of the *HA* SS-*Gericht* from August 1941, but it is by no means clear what connection this institution had with the SS- *Arrest und Haftanstalt* Sachsenhausen. Operating in a similar fashion to the prison regime which had formally existed in the *Erziehungssturm*, its inmates were forbidden from sending and receiving mail. It is unlikely that two penal colonies for *Waffen*-SS felons existed concurrently in the KL Sachsenhausen and so the *Abteilung* Z is probably a reference to the SS- *Arrest und Haftanstalt*, which had by this time been placed under the direct supervisions of the Berlin tribunal.[33]

1.4 *Sondergerichtsbarkeit der* SS *und Polizei*

The military jurisdiction stood on the cusp of operating in war conditions when the *Reichsführer* demanded parity with and freedom from the interference of the civil jurisdiction. Himmler and the lawyers of the SS.-*Gericht* spent much of the late 1930s arguing that the civil and military judiciaries had no understanding for the special relationship that the SS man enjoyed with Adolf Hitler and insisted that the special tasks entrusted by the regime required the creation of an independent jurisdiction with which to punish their miscreants by their own kind in war time.[34]

The introduction of this separate judiciary received the German leader's approval in late 1938 and the SS-*Verfügungstruppe HA* SS-*Gericht* was established in Munich on 1 June 1939 to ensure the balanced application of military and civil law throughout Himmler's field forces. However, the newly created *HA* SS-*Gericht* did not undertake its operations until the Polish campaign had been successfully concluded. The *Verordnung für eine Sondergerichtsbarkiet in Strafsachen für Angehörige der SS und für die Angehörigen der Polizeiverbände bei besonderem Einsatz* (Decree Relating to a Special Jurisdiction in Penal matters for Members of the SS and for Members of Police units on Special Tasks) was finally published on 1 September 1939 and coming into force on 17 October the same year, its newly created courts took responsibility for the prosecution of full-time members of the SS under the command of the *Reichsführer*, HSSPF staff members, those serving with the field forces, including their replacement units, the SS cadet schools and *Polizei* units involved in special tasks. Excluded from their remit were members of the *Allgemeine*-SS; their criminals continued to face trial before civil courts. Facing court-martial before the responsible SS and *Polizei* courts were troops who had committed serious offences. Their number included those who had refused to conform to military life, persistent offenders and those indicted for crimes such as theft, rape, robbery or murder. By the spring of 1945 these courts numbered some 60 mobile, 40 static and branch-courts and to enable the *HA* SS-*Gericht* to carry out its appointed task, it recruited judges to chair court martials and conduct criminal and disciplinary investigations on behalf of the responsible court (investigation officers/*Gerichts*-SS-*Führer*).[35]

Established by a *Führer* edict within the framework of the wartime military jurisdiction, the *Reichsführer*'s judiciary was committed to adopting military legal practices for his field forces and exercised its authorisation powers in reference to the relevant sections of the military punishment statutes, or MStGB, the relevant paragraphs of criminal and civil law and punished delinquents with the full range of disciplinary penalties authorised by the existing disciplinary regulations. Commonly, an expulsion was imposed in conjunction with *Gefängnis* sentences of twelve months' duration or longer. Perpetrator-based law was the foundation of all judgments within the SS and *Polizei* jurisdiction and the trial of soldiers and policemen took place respecting the legal rights of the defendant. Advocates could be appointed to any part of court procedure, but were usually involved in the more important or serious of cases.[36]

There existed in October 1939 no specific penal code written specifically for the SS, but it appears to have been Himmler's intention to codify an SS-Law for his forces. Envisaging a simplified legal process, he demanded that its judgments accommodated the far more rigid ideological standards held by the SS than ordinary citizens and responsibility for legal interpretation was handed to the leadership. During sentencing his judges were heavily influenced by values such as absolute obedience and loyalty and therefore were expected to make rulings that conformed to the SS ethos and ideology. The *HA* SS-*Gericht* fixed these arguments into explicit guidelines that were published in regular memoranda. The 15 October 1941 and 1 August 1942 aide-memoire contained demands for judges to deliver an appropriate National Socialist version of law and in each punishable act the adjudicator had clear instructions to announce a quick 'SS suitable judgment' which conformed to the requirements of the organisation and the leaderships expectations. This command resulted in a re-definition of all criminal offences and evidence for these re-interpretation is evident in Himmler's elucidation of paragraph § 92 MStGB, which regulated the offence of military disobedience. Its interpretation became so broad within his jurisdiction, that virtually every violation of an order issued by the *Führer* or himself could be punished under this regulation. For example, those who did not observe the 'Command concerning ethnic self-esteem' were prosecuted for disobedience in accordance to paragraph § 92 MStGB, enabling the courts to impose a far more draconian punishment that that offered by civil law. In theory, an SS man engaging in sexual relations with a Jewess could be sentenced to death.[37]

Adolf Hitler delegated the authorisation powers of an army commander to the *Reichsführer* and for much of the war Himmler exercised the same powers of pardon and commutation of sentences as those held by the Reich Supreme Judge and the commanders of the three branches of the military. These rights were applied in the form of authorisation powers of a *Gerichtsherr* (chief lord justice) in accordance with paragraph § 4 I KStVO and as Hitler's representative, Himmler retained the final decision in all disciplinary and criminal cases, excluding capital punishments involving officers. The final decision in these cases remained with the *Führer*, but were conferred on Himmler in the latter half of the war. Cases involving the prosecution of generals were almost always confirmed by the Nazi leader.[38]

In particular, the SS leader reserved for himself the right to review and confirm all punishment cases involving officers and *Polizei* civil servants, he conserved for himself the right to dismiss any SS personnel with membership number below 15,000 (i.e. the old guard) and retaining the right to intervene in all cases involving Hungarian and Swiss nationals, the SS leader received the authority to command demotions, dismissals, or the reduction to the ranks of all officer's and was permitted to prescribe disciplinary punishments in connection to penal sentences passed by the his courts. Confirming all judgments concerning race crimes, especially sex offences committed by his troops with non-German women in the occupied regions of the USSR, very few cases escaped the scrutiny of the *Reichsführer*, or his legal representative and Himmler took a keen interest in almost every criminal and disciplinary case.[39]

The *Reichsführer* delegated his *Gerichtsherr* powers to his senior subordinates:

- *Chef des HA* SS-*Gericht*, (Himmler's deputy in legal affairs),
- The senior salaried members of the *Stab* RF-SS and full time *Höherer* SS- *und Polizeiführer*, or HSSPF, (who represented Himmler in the various military districts,

where they co-ordinated SS and *Polizei* units and deputised for the SS leader during appeals,

- SS-*Hauptämter* Chiefs,
- SS-*Verfügungstruppe* commanders,
- SS-*Totenkopfdivision* commander, including the independent SS-*Totenkopf-Infantrie* Rgt.,
- '*Polizeidivision*' commander and reserve battalions,
- *Waffen*-SS School commanders,
- The Inspector of the *Ordnungspolizei,*
- The Inspector of the *Sicherheitspolizei-und* SD, including *Sicherheitspolizei* Battalions deployed on special duties under SS-*Abschnitt* Weichel, Warthe, Nordost, Spree, Südost, West Rhine, Südost and *Protektorat* Böhmen-*und* Mähren and deployed in Poland,
- Commanders of independent SS units and members of the *Polizei* units in special deployment,
- *Stabsführer Allgemeine*-SS,
- Camp Commandants,
- *Grenzpoliziei der Sicherheitspolizei* deployed on special duties under SS-*Abschnitt* Weichel, Warthe, Nordost, Spree, Südost, West Rhine, Südost and Protectorate Böhmen-und Mähren and deployed in Poland,
- Independent units.

A small number of *Gerichtsherrn*, usually generals leading non-German formations, received the authority to pass judgment on capital offence cases.[40]

The SS leader devolved additional authorisation powers on the *HA* SS-*Gericht* chief on 19 February 1941 and throughout the war, Generals Scharfe and Breithaupt were Himmler's *de facto* direct deputies in all disciplinary affairs.[41]

The 17 October 1939 edict confirmed that the appropriate National War Courts Office for Himmler's jurisdiction was the *Oberste* SS- *und Polizei-Gericht* (Superior SS and Police court) and established in Munich, this chambers responsibilities were defined by paragraph §14 of the KStVO. Performing essential tasks of particular importance to this jurisdiction, the *Oberste* SS- *und Polizei-Gericht* was both a procedural and sitting court and aside from prosecuting those who had committed very serious crimes, it also heard defendant's appeals. The court's *Gerichtsherr* was Himmler and he delegated this task to General Paul Scharfe and then to General Franz Breithaupt. Only senior judges, possessing the rank of *Ostubaf.* were permitted to chair its sessions and the permanent chairmanship of this court was eventually linked to the management of the *HA* SS-*Gericht Amt* I (establishing this link effectively unified legal opinion and case law). Later, Adolf Hitler relinquished his right to confirm death sentences that had been imposed by this court.[42]

The *Kriegssonderstrafrechtsverordnung* of 17 August 1938 was adopted by Himmler's jurisdiction and it acknowledged that the *Führer-und Reichskanzler* was the *Oberster Gerichtsherr der Waffen*-SS *und Polizei* (superior high justice of the armed SS and Police) this legislation authorised to confirm and annul death sentences imposed against all officers. Courts' judgments referred to paragraph § 5a KStVO in those cases when the capital punishment was invoked against soldiers and civilians judged guilty of undermining the war effort.[43]

The KStVO established the regular court processes for the military judiciaries and Himmler's judiciary carried out its court processes in accordance to its directives. Initially, the tribunal's judgments did not include front probation sentences, but within months of the start of the conflict, most court punishments included probation time. The opinions of the responsible *Gerichtsherr*, the *HA* SS-*Gericht* and interested main offices were sought during the confirmation stage of the tribunal process to confirm, or amend sentences. The case file, along with the recommendations and mitigations was then forwarded to the SS-*Richter beim* RF-SS for his views and he then presented to Himmler to obtain his confirmation. Using the enclosed opinions, he would then confirm, order a re-trial, or amend the original sentence. The confirmation order was then returned to the *Gerichtsherr*, the *HA* SS-*Gericht* and the sentencing judge and the punishment was either carried out or amended. In an effort to speed up the process, the confirmation process was later in the war conducted by telex and telegram.[44]

For most of the war years, Himmler's legal secretary was the SS-*Richter beim* RF-SS, Horst Bender, and the vast majority of Himmler's legal decisions passed through his office from 12 May 1940. In addition, the SS-*Richter beim* RF-SS case workers produced specialist legal reports, they handled the investigation of all clemency decisions and liaised between the SS leader and the various legal military and civil agencies. A post of considerable responsibility, Bender would prove a central figure in the development of the SS jurisdiction and often he became involved in complicated legal policy decisions.[45]

In the late summer/early autumn of 1939 the ranks of Himmler's army accepted large numbers of draftees and other war recruits. The following year these were joined by ethnic-Germans and non-Germans in their hundreds of thousands and by the end of the war its ranks included troops from uniformed branches of the military, many of whom were not members of the Nazi party, nor sympathised with their ideology. Almost immediately, this dilution of the pre-war SS-VT witnessed a substantive rise in disciplinary and criminal cases, which some of its senior commanders blamed on the recruitment of ethnic-Germans, non-Germans and forced drafts.[46]

Less motivated men inducted into the *Waffen*-SS are known to have resisted their strict, no-nonsense discipline and their entry witnessed an exponential increase in the numbers of men requiring court punishments: two per cent of the total number of troops committed criminal and disciplinary offences between 1939 and 1941 and this figure doubled to four per cent in 1942. At the end of the war the percentage of offenders stood at six per cent of total strength.[47]

The highest disciplinary sanction of the SS jurisdiction was the death penalty and military regulations permitted the application of this punishment for offences that affected the solidarity and comradeship of the front line soldiers from 12 May 1933. It was applicable also for offences such as murder, desertion, undermining the war effort, plundering, theft, treasonable activities, escaping from prison and paragraph § 175 RStGB offences and those imposed in accordance with § 5a of the KSSVO from 17 October 1939. *Waffen*-SS troops were at far greater risk of incurring a capital punishment than soldiers of the military and this was in large part due to Himmler's insistence that paragraph § 92 MStGB was imposed for a wide-range of offences such as crimes such as cowardice, property offences, homosexuality and violations of discipline.[48]

For the war's entirety the *HA* SS-*Gericht Amt* III (clemency, sentencing and prisons) was responsibility for supervising the imprisonment and probation of offenders. Discussing their work in April 1965, the specialist *Leiter des Gerichtswesens* of the *Waffen*-SS and *Polizei* in the *HA* SS-*Gericht*, Dr Günther Reinecke, offered this opinion of its work:

> The *Amt* III *Strafvollstreckung und Gnadenwesen* was headed by the current *Oberlandesgerichtsrat* Dr Burmeister. This office was exclusively concerned with the implementation and carrying out of the judgments that had been imposed during the SS jurisdictional procedures. These judgments were announced in accordance to the regulations from the special jurisdiction which had been introduced for members of the *Waffen*-SS and the *Polizei* units found in deployment from October 1939.

Dr Reinecke contended that the relevant laws regarding the introduction of this special jurisdiction had been established in accordance to the October 1939 edict, which placed them on par with the military, and the SS judiciary had adopted in particular the ordinary legislative procedures and the primary provisions applicable to the military war punishment law and the provisions of the German criminal statutes. Dr Reinecke ended his statement by observing that special laws did not exist for the SS.[49]

Hauptamt SS-Gericht Amt III; Gnadenwesen, Strafvollstreckung & Strafvollzug

Amtschef:
Stubaf. Bruno Kegel (12.9.–21.8.1941).
Ostubaf. Günther Burmeister (provisionally 21.8.1941–8.8.1942).
Ostubaf. Günther Burmeister (8.8.1942–29.4.1945).

Hauptabteilung IIIa; *Gnadensachen*, (appeals & pardons):
Stubaf. Hermann Meder (early 1940–16.12.1942).

Hauptabteilung IIIb; *Strafvollstreckung, Strafvollzug*, (sentencing & prisons):
Stubaf. Wolfgang Walther (1.4.1940–29.4.1945).

Created in the spring of 1941, the *Hauptabteilung* D II *Beschwerde-und Gnadensachen*, (Department III complaints and pardon cases), soon to be known as the SS-*Rechtamt Amt*

III (SS Legal Department, Department III) dealt with pardons, rehabilitation, reprieves and the execution of sentences. Overseeing the implementation of clemency law for court-sentenced felons, its case workers compiled reports on the execution of court punishments and observed the conditions of jail and concentration camp imprisonment. The *Amt* IIIb inspected their own prisons from the spring of 1940 and collated behavioural and medical reports concerning prison inmates. The leader of the SS-*Straflager* Dachau and commandant of the *Strafvollzugslager der* SS *und Polizei* Danzig-Matzkau both reported directly to this office. The expansion of the SS-*Rechtamt*, *Amt* III was agreed on 24 March 1943 and it then became known simply as the *Amt* III. At any given time, two, or three case workers, all SS-*Richter*, were assigned to each of the two sub-departments and they forwarded specialist reports to the *Reichsführer* with recommendations about sentencing and probation. If the circumstances of the case merited it, reprieves and pardons were imposed by the *Amt* III before any prison time was served.[50]

The entire *Amt* III was initially located at Munich 33, Karlstraße 10, but during the late summer of 1944 its offices re-located entirely to the lakeside holiday resort of Prien am Chiemsee in Bavaria, commandeering space at the 'Hotel zum Chiemsee' and 'Hotel zum Kronprinzen'.[51]

Speaking on the issue of recording criminal statistics in 1965, Burmeister revealed that his department had not undertaken this task during his tenure as *Chef des Amt* III, but they did file case files in accordance the crime committed and these punishment folders were colour coded. Recalling that it took the *Gerichtsherr* took three months on average to confirm a decision in officer's cases, Burmeister called to mind that it took up to two years for a case to be fully resolved. He confirmed that those sentenced to death were sent to the SS-*Straflager* Dachau to await the confirmation of their punishment.[52]

1.5 Wartime *Disziplinarvorgesetzte* and *Arrest* Punishments

Fearing that troops engaged in their military, or police duties without discipline would fail at the decisive moment, it was incumbent on the *Disziplinarvorgesetzte* (disciplinary superior) to impose obedience and order on his troops. The disciplinary superior had existed within the SS since its inception and usually the direct commanding officer of the defendant, a battalion, regimental, divisional commander or *Chef Hauptämter* (Main Office Chief) and he maintained order by punishing wrongdoers in accordance with the wartime provisions statutes of the SS-DBO as authorised by paragraph § 16a KStVO. The 17 October 1939 edict permitted the disciplinary superior to punish malefactors with penalties that including arrest sentences. These powers were also extended to the *Gerichtsherrn* and to the SS-*Richter* of the *HA* SS-*Gericht*.[53]

In practice most disciplinary matters were disposed of by the competent senior disciplinary officer, either by direct action, or by courts martial. Full disciplinary powers were also attached to Heinrich Himmler personally in his person as the *Reichsführer* and he was competent to impose all disciplinary penalties permitted by the regulations (Adolf

Hitler, or his legal representative, took a personal interest in those rare cases of punishments from the rank of *Gruf.* and upwards). Officers performing the role of disciplinary superior were made aware of the great responsibility resting upon his shoulders. To avoid weakening his own authority, the SS leader expected the disciplinary superior to always intervene when an offence threatened discipline. The disciplinary superior imposed chastisements without recourse to the court processes when the facts of the case was sufficiently clear and the guilt of the offender clearly established then (officers were always judged in court). Disciplinary superiors failing to carry out a disciplinary non-judicial punishment against a criminal subordinate or report him to the court from weakness, or a misunderstanding of comradeship would themselves faced prosecution risked trial for misconduct.[54]

Adjudicating a light offence not covered by criminal law, the disciplinary superior considered the nature of the misconduct, assessed the offender's character and took into account his previous behaviour. This permitted the miscreants commander to ascertain whether a lecture, exhortation, or a warning was sufficient punishment, or whether a more severe sanction was appropriate. Deciding these issues, he ensured that his decision satisfied the needs of the criminal law and both matched the task of the jurisdiction and *Gerichtsherrn* in the maintenance of the troop's discipline. In some circumstances, the disciplinary superior could organise and oversee a *Standgericht* (summary court) and prosecute offenders himself. To enable him to carry out this task, the disciplinary superior exercised unconditional trust in his adjutant in his role as a *Gerichtsoffiziere* (legal officer). The *Gerichtsoffiziere* presented the results of his investigations to the disciplinary superior with either a recommendation to dismiss the charge, impose a disciplinary punishment, or initiate a court process against criminal offenders. Undisciplined assigned to a *Hauptämter* other than their own were usually investigated by the *Gerichtsoffiziere* of their own main office and those requiring a court trial when deployed away from their *Hauptämter* were customarily court-martialled by the SS- *und Polizei-Gericht* III, Berlin. In circumstances in which the offender's superior lacked the necessary experience, or doubted his right to punish, he was encouraged to seek sentencing advice from the competent *Gerichtsoffiziere*. To speed up the process and relieve the burden on the courts, the *HA* SS-*Gericht* authorised competent disciplinary superior to perform the role of principle disciplinarian for lighter types of crimes on 10 June 1940 (excluding the abuse of service powers). This edict provided the disciplinary superior with examples of minor crimes that he was competent to handle.[55]

Acknowledging in 1940 that there existed within the SS men with criminal records who did not empathize with the Nazi world vision, the *HA* SS-*Gericht* recommended that disciplinary superiors passed these cases directly to the courts. The conscientious disciplinary superior were encouraged to check whether it was sufficient to punish a soldier in an easier way and urged to take into account the interests of discipline when making his decision.[56]

The law providing a minimum sentence of one month in *Gefängnis* for an offence, unless a simple arrest for this punishment was unacceptable the disciplinary superior was authorised to judge this a light offence and impose a fortnight or three weeks' sharp arrest penalty. Demanding a punishment was always applied in these circumstances, the SS-*Richter beim* RF-SS considered the imposition of an arrest penalty as an alternative to a prison punishment a gross violation of the SS basic law (an offence against what he described as their 'particular sacredness'). Recommending an *Ehrenstrafe* and expulsion for those punished with a prison sentence for a criminal act which the court had determined made the offender unsuitable for continued military service, the SS-*Richter beim* RF-SS reminded those involved in punishing that the proper elucidation of the facts was a top priority to ensure a fast process in both disciplinary and criminal court proceedings. Determining the question of guilt by judicial interrogation of witnesses under oath and deciding that the facts of the case were insufficient to permit disciplinary action, the disciplinary superior would then submitted a factual report to the *Gerichtsherr*. Tasked with ensuring the uniform treatment of all crime, the disciplinary superior prosecuted criminal cases at all costs and regularity was demanded in all criminal proceedings to ensure the *Gerichtsherr* and his judges were not excluded from the process.[57]

Disciplinary superiors failing to report crimes to the *Gerichtsherr* were criminally liable for contravening paragraph § 92, 147a MStGB.[58] Determining that he was competent to impose a punishment in accordance to the provisions of the wartime SS disciplinary regulations and paragraph § 54 MStGB, the full range of SS-DBO penalties were available to the disciplinary superior (intensified arrest was only permitted for officers to the rank of *Hstuf.*).[59]

Arrest and room arrest was imposed for up to 42 days duration and intensified arrest sentences were enforced for up to fourteen days' duration. Those punished in this fashion lay upon a wooden bunk in silence for 22 hours and received a meal of 800 kg of bread and water each day (combinations of these punishments were not uncommon). Offences and punishments ordered by the disciplinary superior and *Gerichtsherr* was recorded in the unit punishment file and a copy placed inside the offender's service record. The undisciplined soldier returned to duty once the punishment had been served, but committing a second similar, or more serious offence would result in further penalties which included permanent expulsion and detention in the SS-*Erziehungssturm* from 1938.[60]

The *HA* SS-*Gericht* reviewed all disciplinary punishments imposed by the disciplinary superior and the *Reichsführer* retained the right to amend all original sentences. Himmler and his advocate dealt directly with arrest sentences exceeding six weeks duration and it is clear from my studies that both the head of the SS and Horst Bender appear to have read most, if not every officer case file and exercised a keen interest in significant other ranks cases. Confirming in writing the imposition of sharp room arrest for all officers of the *Waffen*-SS in 1942, Himmler commanded that these offenders were permitted two hours' exercise a day. Ordering the restrictive use of room arrest on 8 October 1942, the SS leader complained that this punishment had been imposed when he had decided that an intensified arrest penalty was suitable. Demanding that room arrest be considered an especially mild form of punishment, Himmler commanded his advocate consider whether an intensified arrest was appropriate prior to the penalty's implementation.[61]

Discussing the courts failure in January 1943 to impose intensified room arrest in accordance with paragraph § 23 MStGB, Himmler then instructed the courts to impose this penalty only in exceptional cases.[62]

At this time, the head of the SS voiced his concern that the punishment of room arrest was not implemented uniformly against officers and as a result of his disquiet, Himmler commanded General Breithaupt to investigate its random implementation. Reporting on this matter on 8 December 1944, the general revealed that he had personally examined all room arrests and had discovered no irregularities. Acknowledging that his sample was limited, Breithaupt gave orders for the *Amt* III to examine court-issued room arrest judgements and report any irregularities.[63]

Disciplinary punishments for the German pre-war police were identical to those imposed within the military. The edict establishing unity between the Reich and the state administration from 30 January 1934 authorised the centralisation of the German police and the newly created Reich and Prussian interior ministry became the overall supervisory and command centre for them. The *Gemeinde Polizei* (local police) were responsible for maintaining law and order in large towns and cities, the *Gendarmerie* had responsibility for rural districts. The motorised *Schutzpolizei*, composed of younger policemen, lived in barracks and deployed in large towns and cities. Collectively, the *Gemeinde* and *Gendarmerie* were known as the *Ordnungspolizei* (order police).[64]

The *Hauptamt Ordnungspolizei Amt Verwaltung und Recht*, (high office administration and legal office) had responsible for disciplinary concerns between 30 June 1936 and September 1943. Responsibility for these matters were then the purview of the *Hauptamt Ordnungspolizei Rechtamt* (main police legal office).[65] The service disciplinary process for the *Polizei* was regulated by the 'National Service Criminal Procedure' and undisciplined civil servants attached to the *Polizei* found themselves admonished in accordance to the civil service laws. *Polizei* committing acts of criminality faced punishment before the civil courts. Those *Polizei* committing crimes or serious disciplinary offences while deployed outside the 1938 German borders in the war years, then faced trial before the responsible SS and *Polizei* court in accordance to the provisions of the 17 October 1939 edict.[66]

Punishing *Waffen*-SS and *Polizei* malefactors with an arrest penalty, the disciplinary superior and SS and *Polizei* courts then required a cell to serve his sentence. To carry out his chastisement, the majority of barracks and SS-*Hauptämter* constructed cell blocks to detain undisciplined troops punished with short terms of arrest. Cell blocks consisted of either a small number of individual, or multiple chambers and a mixture of each. These cells also held those waiting trial and waiting for transport to a military or civil jail. The detention block at the Berlin-Lichterfelde consisted of around ten cells, all secured with heavy wooden doors. Both the Oranienburg and Stettin SS-*Sanitäts-Ersatz-Bataillon* oversaw the detention of medical service arrestees in rooms with locks.[67]

In 1934, Himmler selected the Hotel Prinz-Albrecht at Kreuzberg-Berlin, Prinz-Albrecht-Straße 9 to accommodate his headquarters and the security services that would later be known as the RSHA. Appropriating the former art school at Prinz-Albrecht-Straße 8 for the *Gestapo* headquarters, the SD leadership settled in the baroque

Prinz-Albrecht-Palais at Wilhelmstraße 102 and the security services constructed the so-called *Hausgefängnis* (house prison) in the cellar of these buildings. Composed of 30 individual cells and a common cell capable of holding 50 suspects, *Oberverwalter- und Ostuf.* Wilhelm Gogalla commanded over the *Hausgefängnis* from late 1943. During the war years, his cells also detained members of the *Waffen*-SS and *Polizei* awaiting disciplinary punishments or trial.[68]

1.6 *Untersuchungshaft*

The malfeasant elements of the *Waffen*-SS and *Polizei*, those accused of serious crimes, who had been judged at risk of flight, or whose freedom had the potential to undermine morale, were placed in *Untersuchungshaft* (remand custody) to await the conclusion of the court investigation or trial. The detention of remand prisoners took place in the SS-*Straflager* Dachau, the *Strafvollzugslager der* SS *und Polizei* Danzig-Matzkau, civil and RSHA cells, or cell blocks located within SS-*Hauptämter*.

In early August 1940 the SS-*Richter beim* RF-SS was presented with a draft copy of the fifth collection of draft edicts which contained recommendations for how to calculate exactly the time already served was deducted from the sentence. The sixth collection of edicts was delivered to the SS-*Richter beim* RF-SS for his opinions on 15 November 1940.[69]

The SS- *und Polizei Haftanstalt* at Berlin-Schöneburg, Grunwaldstraße 68 was established from at least March 1942 and placed under the supervision of the SS- *und Polizei-Gericht* III, Berlin, it detained offenders penalised with short sentences and held those awaiting trial before the Berlin tribunal.The SS-FHA seconded guards to this institution and it was ran by the senior SS-*Beurkundungsführer* of the Berlin tribunal. The *HA* SS-*Gericht* transferred ten newly-appointed *Beurkundungsunterführer* to the SS- *und Polizei-Gericht* III, Berlin on 7 February 1945 with orders to deploy at the SS- *und Polizeigefängnis* at Berlin.[70]

The SS and *Polizei* courts are known to have incarcerated remand prisoners in civil jails. The SS- *und Polizei-Gericht* XIV, Metz and the SS-*Sonderlager* Hinzert detained delinquent SS camp guards awaiting trial and those serving short prison sentences at the *Gefängnis* Trier at Altstadt Trier, Windstraße 6.

1.7 *Standort Arrestanstalt*

Felons awaiting trial, punished with sharp arrest, or sentenced to a term of *Gefängnis* of less than three months' duration were also detained in what was known as the SS-*Standort Arrestanstalt* (garrison arrest centre). These institutions are known to have been established in the grounds of SS-*Standort*, *Hauptämter* and within the *Gestapogefängnis*. Ensconced in the grounds of the SS-FHA at Berlin–Wilmersdorf, Kaiserallee 188, the

SS-*Standortarrestanstalten* detained up to 200 miscreants in a few wooden barracks. A similar detention camp was established for the WVHA in the wooden barracks of the former Organisation Todt work camp at Berlin–Schlachtensee on the Unter den Eichen and this institution held remand inmates and malefactors of the SS-*Hauptämter* sentenced to intensified arrest.[71]

Reporting that the SS-*Standortarrestanstalten* Berlin and the SS- *Arrest und Haftanstalt* Sachsenhausen were full to capacity in March 1942, the senior judge at the Berlin tribunal, *Stubaf.* Wolfgang Wetzling, complained that the chronic shortage of cells in the Berlin region had resulted in offenders serving their sentences at the Oranienburg medical battalion. As a consequence of this situation, the chief judge recommended a new prison was constructed in Berlin to detain remand prisoners. Concurring with Wetzling's assessment of the situation, Himmler commanded the creation of the *Standortarrestanstalt der Waffen-*SS- *und Polizei* Berlin (garrison arrest institution) and entrusted the *Chef* WVHA with undertaking the process of obtaining land to build an inconspicuous sharp arrest centre for 60 officers and men (in cells). Setting aside a budget of 1.5 million *Reichsmark* for its construction, *Gruf.* Pohl entrusted the search for a suitable spot to *Stubaf.* Karl Sesemann of the WVHA department C I. Discovering that no suitable land existed in central Berlin, a decision was then taken to seek a site in the capitals suburbs.[72]

A potential site in Babelsberg and the former Organisation Todt camp on the Unter den Eichen were both rejected in April 1942, (although later, this site did in fact become an SS-*Standortarrestanstalten*) and a little later, General Dr Kammler's proposal to use an empty building was vetoed by the *Reichsminister für Rüstung*, who forbad new building work in the centre of Berlin. Renewing their search, a site was finally discovered and purchased at Berlin-Lankwitz, Marienfelderstraße, near the Lichterfelde barracks on 16 October 1942. Plans were initiated on 16 December for the construction of a brick prison to detain 200 convicted and 200 remand inmates (awaiting trial or the results of an appeal) and in addition to these requirements, the head of the SS commanded accommodation be constructed for a guard company, workshops and a clinic.[73]

In discussions between Dr Kammler, *Ostubaf.* Burmeister, *Stubaf.* Ulrich Dümichen and the *Bau Inspektor der Waffen-*SS *und Polizei Reich-Nord* on 11 November 1942, it was agreed to build accommodation for 688 inmates and to complete the project by October 1943. An allied air-raid on Berlin seriously damaged the site on the night of 23/24 August 1943, but despite this set-back, work continued apace until the *Gauleiter* of Berlin, Joseph Goebbels, in his capacity as the defence leader for Berlin, forbad further construction on 8 January 1944 (a proposed expansion of the *Arrest- und Haftanstalt* at Sachsenhausen was rejected at this time). As a consequence of the Allied bombing the plans to expand detention space in Berlin for those requiring sharp arrest and remand was abandoned.[74]

Outside of the Reich borders, offenders were detained in former civil jails, watched over by *Waffen-*SS troops selected from reserve units or members of the SD. The Krakau garrison detained offenders in the *Sicherheits-Polizeigefängnis* on Ulica Montelupich and the SS-*Standortarrestanstalt* Brünn utilised a former civil prison for the detention of its miscreants. In late 1944 the SS-*und Polizei-Gericht* VI, Krakau, branch court Lublin reported that *Schützen* Jurij Huzelo had spent seven days in remand detention prior to his trial on 22 June 1944. Judged guilty of his offence, the *Gerichtsherr* confirmed Huzelo's sentence on 30 June, (St. L. XII 522/44). Serving his two month punishment at the *Gefängnis* Lublin from 30 June, Huzelo release from jail was ordered on 23 August 1944.[75]

In France, the chief judge of the SS- *und Polizei-Gericht* XXI, Paris *Stubaf.* Knote proposed and was refused permission to construct a prison in Paris in December 1942. Undaunted, he established the *Truppenarrestanstalt der* LSSAH near Paris for the incarceration of delinquent troops for up to three months' duration. The head of the SS proposed the building of a *Standort-Arrestanstalt der Waffen*-SS *und Polizei* (remand and arrest detention Centre) in Paris in January 1943 to detain both criminals and delinquents requiring short jail sentences. This plan was never realised and the prison never built. The failure of these plans and the concern about overcrowding in their own prisons led Breithaupt to write to Himmler in the first week of February 1944 to propose building a new prison in Alsace.[76]

The *Untersuchungshaft- und Arrestanstalt der* SS- *und Polizei* at Prague IV, Lorettoplatz 6 had been conceived in early 1944 and had opened by late July the same year. This institution detained *Gefängnis* convicts with sentences not exceeding three months' duration, those remanded into custody and troops punished with arrest penalties. Prior to the opening of the *Untersuchungshaft- und Arrestanstalt der* SS- *und Polizei* at Prague, those awaiting trial had been detained at the SS-*Kaserne* Heinrich Himmler in Prague-Rusin. Placing the *Untersuchungshaft- und Arrestanstalt der* SS *und Polizei* Prague under the direct supervision of the SS- *und Polizei-Gericht* VIII, the *Beurkundungsführer* of this court office was appointed its prison superior. The *HA* SS-*Gericht* refused to supply guards for the prison and it became the responsibility of the SS-*Wachbataillon* 2 to provide these men. The SS-*Standort* Prague physician held responsibility for the inmate's medical concerns.[77]

1.8 *Strafvollstreckungszüge*

The divisional field formations of the *Waffen*-SS confined remand and short sentenced felons in what was known as the *Strafvollstreckungszüge* (punishment sections). The author Franz W. Siedler asserts that the *Strafvollstreckungszüge* were established for the *Waffen*-SS in 1944, but pointedly, the writer David Raub Snyder observed that they were instituted for the divisions of the armed forces in 1942. In the absence of a central order for their establishment, it appears that the majority of Himmler's divisions operated *Strafvollstreckungszüge* from 1943.[78]

Conceived to retain short sentenced offenders within the division to enable at their release a quick re-absorption within the ranks, their commandant, a non-commissioned officer, usually appointed directly by the divisional commander, was responsible for arranging the detention of offenders serving arrest or *Gefängnis* sentences of between one day and three months' duration in suitable accommodation. He also organised the guard detail for those awaiting escort to prison. Recalcitrant inmates faced punishment exercises, food withdrawal and sharp arrest sentences. Cigarettes and home leave were permitted if a close family member was killed in an air attack. Its inmates were occasionally subordinated to the pioneer and the supply battalions to undertake particularly hard labouring tasks.

The 12th SS-*Panzergrenadier*-Division *Strafvollstreckungszüge* operated in 1943 and again from 9 February 1944 with staff provided by the SS-*Panzer-Artillerie*-Rgt. 12. In early 1944 the *Chefrichter* of the *Hitlerjugend* field court, *Stubaf.* Dr Denzel, published the following service regulations for the *Strafvollstreckungszüge* on 8 February 1944:

> The Service and Regulatory Enforcement of Imprisonment in the 12. SS-*Pz.Gren.*Div. *Hitlerjugend*.
>
> Service Regulations.
>
> 1.) The type of service.
> The sentence of the punished in the *Strafvollstreckungszüge* must be physically demanding and be served in harder and more severe conditions of life than that found in any other service in the army.
> Those with *Gefängnis* punishments are to mainly carry out their labour service under difficult conditions. Those with arrest punishments should in the first line conduct military training, but also labouring in difficult conditions is to be considered for them.
>
> 2.) Duration of the service.
> The duration of the service in general and in particular his work is regulated by the *Leiter des Strafvollstreckungszüge*. The working time, taking account of the severity of the sentence and work is generally 10–14 hours per day; the amount of the punishment is demanded to utmost of what can be done without compromising health. Sundays are to be considered work weekdays.
>
> 3.) Use.
> The *Strafvollstreckungszüge* prisoners use takes place where his work is requested. If possible, the prison is not to work directly together with other units. The leader of the prison will decide the execution of the order in accordance with ability.
>
> 4.) Accommodation.
> Accommodating those punished with *Gefängnis* is carried out in existing *Gefängnis* cells. The accommodation of those with arrest punishments is to be accomplished in a secure property, but under intensified supervision.
>
> 5.) Supervision and Surveillance.
> For reasons of law and order permanent supervision and surveillance must be undertaken during the deployment in the *Strafvollstreckungszüge*. Supervision is required when

bringing [the inmate] from accommodation to the free work deployment. The existence of the prisoner is to be checked at least every morning and every evening.

6.) Escape attempts and escapes.
During attempted and escape attempts the guards may warn and immediately to make use of their weapons. Every escape attempt and escape is to be reported immediately to the leader of the prison, he shall take immediate steps to recapture in the event of an escape. An escape action report should always be submitted to see if the punishment was insufficient.

II. Enforcement regulations.

7.) Purpose of the penal system.
The purpose of the penal system, in addition to retribution and deterrence is to provide a sustainable educational influence over the punished. The courts, relentless severity and benevolence must unite to form a meaningful whole.

8.) The behaviour of the punished.
The punished are committed to unconditional obedience. Each off-duty intercourse with other people as well as receiving the benefits from anyone else's performance is forbidden and may be punished in his place of accommodation.

9.) Carrying of weapons.
During their time in the prison the punished will carry no weapons. However, it is important to ensure that if a prison expects an enemy attack then the immediate arming of weapons can be carried out for combat use.

10.) Orders and decorations, as well are removed from the punished and stored while they remain in prison.

11.) Military pay.
The military pay must be reduced by the unit of the punished and kept safe for the intended recipient.

12.) Meals, alcohol and smoking.
Because of their strong physical demands the punished will receive the normal catering fare of the troops, however, no market goods, confectionary and special allocations are permitted. They may obtain other additional foodstuffs or even returned leavings. They may not procure other foodstuffs from other sources. Alcohol and smoking is forbidden.

13.) Organisation of leisure time.
Only the published newspapers or newsletters of the troops and likewise books with educational content will be made available during their free time. Lighting is given to them until 20.00hrs and entertainment games are prohibited.

14.) Letters and other postal services.
Weekly, the punished must submit all received letters or postcards. In urgent cases the leader of the *Strafvollstreckungszüge* may permit a further letters in accordance to the regulations, in particular in cases of death or damage from bombing in the family, or for the regulation of fixed-term legalities, business matters or the like.

All post is censored by the leader of the prison or examined by a subordinate commander specially commissioned by him for this purpose. All incoming and outgoing post must be submitted respectively. If there are concerns based on the examination, then the post office is to withhold sending. If there are concerns based on the examination, the post is not to be posted and the item will be handed back to the punished or to the sender respectively. Affix the reasons to those letters handed to the punished.

Permission is given by the leader of the *Strafvollstreckungszüge* and only in exceptional cases for packages, or other postal services to be sent to or received from the punished. Receiving food or drinks of any kind are not allowed. Rejected letters, other post and packages and not sent, or kept by the punished are retained until the punished is release. The leader of the *Strafvollstreckungszüge* will use his absolute discretion about the disposal of perishable goods that cannot be held until release.

On the orders of the *Strafvollstreckungszüge* leader the [convicts] are at dismissal exempted from taking home letters and other post which due to their content are held back even after the conclusion of the punishment. These are given to the sentencing court for the unit of the punished in order to measure the disciplinary process, or to enter in the criminal file.

15.) Visits and holidays.
Visiting the punished is prohibited, but in exceptional cases only the leader of the prison may approve visits.

The punished are prohibited from taking leave and can only urgent cases, e.g. granted by the *Gerichtsherr* in cases of death or damage from bombing. His whose decision shall immediately obtained through the divisional judge.

16.) Perks.
From time to time and for educational reasons the leader of the *Strafvollstreckungszüge* can grant the punished individual, for particularly good performances benefits such as the procurement of goods, confectionary, tobacco and other additional food, (but no alcoholic drinks), grant the writing of a letter, or special permission for a visit.

17.) Punishments while they belong in prison.
The leader of the *Strafvollstreckungszüge* can impose against the punished an immediate disciplinary imprisonment if he commits another offence during his sentence with the proviso that this penalty should be extended after the duration of the newly imposed sentence and the punished stay in the prison for no more than three months. The leader of the *Strafvollstreckungszüge* should inform the field court of his misconduct and the new punishment. The *Strafvollstreckungszüge* leader imposing a disciplinary punishment is immediately to think about the effect on that the imposed penalty will have on the unit of the newly released punished.

Signed; SS-*Stubaf.* Denzel.[79]

Only judicial-punished felons entered the *Strafvollstreckungszüge* and they reported for their penalty with a copy of the disciplinary punishment order, a medical certificate listing their long freedom from diseases and pests which confirmed their fitness for detention and ability to work. The field court also provided a list of the punished equipment and weapons, which included clothes and footwear, as well as soap, which was necessary for laundry washing. All convicts remained under guard at all times and the divisional court calculated the penalty (this represented the beginning of the punishment and suspension of the punishment). The *Strafvollstreckungszüge* sent the court any and all amendments to the end of the punishment, (e.g. leave or the new imposed penalty), and using this information the court then calculated a new punishment. Each court penalty contained a start and end date and the prison leader announced every change to the punishment if it affected the calculation of the sentence. If an objection was raised to the punishment, then the field court, or the disciplinary superior would re-examine the case and make an appropriate decision. Immediately on entry, the leader of the prison would instruct the inmate about the rules and regulations of service and removed the following items from his person: his identity papers, cash, weapons, medals, jewellery, matches, knives and all possessions that had the potential to form part of an escape plan or facilitate bribes. Retaining his wedding ring, the prisoner accepted a receipt for the confiscated items and the prison retained his property until the time of discharge.

Dismissed from the *Strafvollstreckungszüge* on the last penalty day, in as far as possible just prior to the onset of darkness to enable him to reach his unit on the same day, (i.e. if at the conclusion of the punishment occurred at 5.12.1943, at midnight, then the prison prepared for release on 4.12.1943). The prison was ordered to expedite their exit as quickly as possible those inmates released early as part of a clemency decision made by the court or *Gerichtsherr*. Prior to discharge, the prison leader was tasked with admonishing the convict about his wrongdoings and handed him his discharge certificate, on which the date of his discharge was certified. The former convict then accepted a return-receipt of his release acknowledgement, all letters and other post, which had been kept from him until his release (these also included non-posted and edited letters). On the day of release the entry receipt for those punished by the disciplinary superior were returned to the field unit along with a prison fitness report. These documents were then sent to the sentencing court-martial and the discharge letter indicated the date and reason for the dismissal, (whether by penal order, or an early dismissal on the basis of what clemency, or enforcement decision respectively). Offenders committing further acts of indiscipline in the prison had their details added to the discharge report. The prison recorded the full names of inmates, their rank, unit and court judgment or disciplinary punishment respectively and the date, reference number, type and length of sentence and the date of entry were recorded on the sentencing order.[80]

Strafvollstreckungszüge are known to have been were utilised by other field formations: It was noted in September 1943 that the LSSAH had created a prison under the direct command of the 1st SS-*Panzer-Pionier-Abteilung* at Castell Zibka, 1.5 km south-east of Borgoforte, (south of Verona), the SS- *und Polizei-Gericht* X, Den Haag established a *Strafvollstreckungsabteilung* in May 1944. For offenders serving a term of *Gefängnis* of less than three months' duration the 5th SS-*Panzer*-Division *Wiking* operated a *Strafvollstreckungszüge* in October 1944 (the divisional commander had attempted but failed to receive permission to create a *Strafvollstreckungszüge* for his division on 14.6.1941). The 32nd SS-*Freiwilligen-Grenadier*-Division *30. Januar* operated a *Strafvollstreckungszüge* in April 1945, and it may be safely assumed that at this time virtually every SS division operated these makeshift prisons.

1.9 Wartime Incarceration of SS Men in Concentration Camps

The 17 October 1939 edict authorised the incarceration of *Waffen*-SS and *Polizei* offenders in concentration camps as prisoners. This potentially life-threatening punishment was imposed by the *Reichsführer* and his *Gerichtsherrn* until the war's end and to enable their incarceration in the camps, the *Gerichtsherrn* first applied to the RSHA for a protection detention order which permitted the offenders incarceration for six months. Discovered engaging in an illicit affair with another staff member of the SS-*Junkerschule* Bad Tölz in August 1939, *Ostuf.* Rudolf Klaebe found himself degraded on 26 September 1939 and then taken immediately to the KL Flossenbürg as a camp prisoner. Held in isolation until January 1940, Klaebe then transferred to the Sachsenhausen *Erziehungssturm* to prepare for front probation with the *Totenkopfdivision*.[81]

Preparing for the attack in the west, one SS commander exercised his *Gerichtsherrn* authorisation powers to incarcerate a few delinquent soldiers inside the KL Buchenwald. Established from former camp personnel, SS-VT troops and draftees in late 1939, Becoming aware that incorrigibles had joined his force who were incapable of complying with the strict military discipline in late 1939, the infuriated *Totenkopfdivision* commander, *Gruf.* Theodore Eicke, frustrated that his men visited local bars against orders to become inebriated, then announced to his troops that future violations of the war court regulations would result in their trial. Cancelling three days' worth of leave passes, six men of the 14. / 2. SS-*Totenkopf-Infantrie*-Rgt. stole a truck that very same day and drove into Munich for an evening of drunken revelry. Later, that same evening the inebriated truck driver crashed the vehicle into a tram, causing its derailment and arriving on the scene, the *Polizei* came across the drunken group, laying in an unperturbed heap, completely oblivious to their predicament. When the incident was reported to Eicke, he angrily ordered the offenders paraded before the assembled division and commanded them stripped of their uniforms, ordered their heads shaved and when then dressed in concentration camp garb, he sent them all to the KL Buchenwald as prisoners. The following day, Eicke commanded the arrest and expulsion of a soldier requesting his discharge from active service. He too found himself sent the KL Buchenwald as a prisoner. Desperate to improve discipline; the *Totenkopf* commander disseminated a special order on 23 November 1939 which threatened execution by firing squad for anyone in the division found misusing divisional vehicles. When notified of Eicke's actions, Himmler announced his disapproval of his methods and fearing the effect of incarceration in a concentration camp would have on recruitment, he forbad Eicke from sending offenders to the camps in future without his express permission.[82]

The *HA* SS-*Gericht Amt* III determined that three grades of camp detention existed for its recalcitrant convicts: category I (KL Dachau and Sachsenhausen) with more food and better working conditions than category Ia. Category Ia (KL Buchenwald) with harsher conditions than category I and finally for those requiring the severest punishment for their crimes their existed category III (KL Mauthausen) providing harder work and less food than category I.[83]

Obtaining permission to transfer the miscreant to a camp, the *Amt* III had responsibility for determining the length of sentence and category of concentration camp in which to incarcerate them. To enable them to determine this decision the *Amt* III considered the nature of the crime, his character, education, previous convictions, service history and family background and those judged having a possibility of rehabilitation entered a category I camp and the incorrigibles found themselves detained in the KL Mauthausen. The *Amt* III decided the treatment each could expect inside the camps and adjudicated the number of letters and parcels each inmates received, how much money their relatives were permitted to send and whether visitors was authorised (applicants wrote directly to the *Amt* III for a final decision in this matter). Although the 17 October 1939 edict commanded clemency appeals not to determine probation, these pleas were sent directly to the SS leader and the *Amt* III.[84]

Among those sent to the notorious KL Mauthhausen were firemen from Vienna who had been convicted of undermining the war effort and treasonable offences. Here, they wore service uniforms stripped of insignia and initially lived in the camp arrest they were later detained in a wooden barracks inside the camp itself.[85]

Responsibility for seeking authorisation for attaining a protection detention orders from the RHSA for *Waffen*-SS and *Polizei* miscreants became the responsibility of the *Amt* III from 10 September 1942. All questions pertaining to the punishment of this category of camp prisoners were then referred to this office. Applying in writing to the locally responsible *Gerichtsherr* for a camp protection detention order, the convict's incarceration was only undertaken once the *Amt* III received this document from the RSHA. Former *Waffen*-SS and *Polizei* camp prisoners were usually detained in a separate *Abteilung* (section) and their clothing, work assignments, letter and packages, money orders and visits were regulated according to the rules governing camp inmates. Once transferred to a camp, copies of the convict's admission request, the sentencing letter, sentence confirmation letter, the *Gerichtsherr* sentencing decision and a directory containing a personal sheet, recording the camp name and grade selected for detention, was then sent to the responsible court. The responsible court, or *Amt* III requesting the release of the offender had to obtain the permission of the competent *Gerichtsherr*. Expressing his satisfaction with this decision, the court then proffered the release application to the *Amt* III and they passed this document to the RSHA to enable them to cancel the detention order and supply a release date. A new detention order was issued when the *Amt* III submitted an application to transfer badly behaved convicts to the camps. The RSHA required the permission of the *Amt* III to transfer former SS and *Polizei* prisoners to another camp and in the event of their death, the responsible court, or *Amt* III applied in writing to the RSHA to cancel the camp detention order.[86]

Interestingly the time spent detained in the concentration camps still counted towards the inmate's military obligations, including those convicted for undermining the war effort. The families of former SS or policemen prisoners dying in the camp from illness, or other causes were not entitled to any benefits, or pensions, these rights were forgone at the moment they became camp prisoners.[87]

It had become apparent during the fourth year of the war that an exponential rise in the number of men committing offences that required a camp punishment had occurred and as a consequence of this increase, Himmler and the *HA* SS-*Gericht* sought ways to ensure that this category of offender remained capable of undertaking front service, or remained free of the camps altogether. Speaking with the chief judge at the SS- *und Polizei-Gericht* IV, Danzig between 30 April and 2 May 1942, Burmeister then informed the *Reichsführer* that the sentencing of men to civil jails had been undertaken until that point in time for exceptional cases, such as habitual criminals and homosexuals and he now argued successfully for this category of criminal to be prosecuted solely by their jurisdiction and then sentenced to terms of imprisonment in a separate section within a concentration camp. All judges were notified of this change in policy.[88]

Writing in the autumn of 1942, the *HA* SS-*Gericht* commanded concentration camp punishment be reserved for those serving terms of *Gefängnis*, or *Zuchthaus* who had demonstrated their unwillingness to accept re-education in prison, or had been judged persistent rule breakers. These convicts were then ordered to engage in bomb disposal work until proving themselves worthy of returning to prison. Inmates serving terms of *Zuchthaus*, or *Gefängnis* with a loss of civil and honour rights and declared unworthy to bear arms also fell into this category. Reserving the right to transfer these offenders to a category I camps for safe keeping and work punishment, prior to the imposition of the punishment the *HA* SS-*Gericht* were duty bound to inform Himmler of cases in which he alone was entitled to determine whether the offender was mentally and physically fit for the transfer. From this time the *Amt* III undertook all sentence reviews and the *Gerichtsherrn* were forbidden to send felons directly to concentration camps. At this time a decision was taken to continue sending paragraph § 175 offenders to camps, but those judged 'moderate homosexuals' continued to serve their punishment in prisons and was employed in the German war industry until judged fit for front service. Seeking to limit the number of offenders punished with a concentration camp sentence, the *HA* SS-*Gericht* stipulated that troops and women employees who had committed petty crimes would no longer to face incarceration in a camp and to ensure that mistakes were avoided, each court was required to submit each request for a camp punishment to the reserve court first, to permit the tribunal to judge whether the felon was suitable for re-education (again, the SS leader retained the final decision). Turning his attention to non-German volunteers, the *Reichsführer* stipulated that unless they had committed a particularly heinous crime, the non-Germans, especially Dutch and Norwegian volunteers, were to be spared a concentration camp punishment. There were exceptions to this order; abolishing the Danish police force, 2,118 of its members were arrested on 19 September 1944 and then sent as prisoners to the KL Buchenwald and Neuengamme.[89]

Following negotiations between the RSHA and the *Reichsjustizministerium*, the SS-*Richter beim* RF-SS could report in October 1942 that it had been decided to transfer those offenders serving a term of eight years *Zuchthaus*, or greater in civil detention to their control and incarcerate them to concentration camps.[90]

Naturally there were exceptions to this agreement and Eastern volunteers appear to have been unaffected by this command. Writing to the KL Buchenwald on 21 April 1944, the SS- *und Polizei-Gericht* XX, Nikolajew reported that the Tiflis born section leader Gregorij Gromow had left the *Polizeigefängnis* Nikolajew for incarceration in the KL Buchenwald.[91]

In this instance, this offender's case led to a departure from the usual camp punishment regime for miscreant former SS and *Polizei* camp prisoners:

Name: Dr jur. Ewald Kimenkowski.
Last Rank: SS-*Hauptsturmführer*.
Born: 12.4.1891 in Berlin.
Died: 28.7.1944 in Sachsenhausen.
NSDAP-Nr.: (joined 1929).
Promotions:
3.8.1941 SS-*Hauptsturmführer der Reserve*.
Prewar Assignments:
Kavallerie Inspektorate in 1935.
OKH 1938–1939.
Generalkommando III, Berlin in the summer of 1939.
Wartime Assignments:
Waffen-SS from 1939.
SS-FHA in 1939.
Amt W.v.V. *Hauptamt* 1940 –1942.

Notes: Studying law at University, Kimenkowski passed his *Referendarexamen* and received a law doctorate. Participating in the Great War, Dr Kimenkowski suffered a heart attack in 1915, but he recovered and returned to military duties. Wounded in his right shoulder in 1917, he suffered severe nerve damage, but recovered and then served as a *Gerichtsoffizier* on Field Marshal Hindenburg's staff in Prussia. Remaining in military service after the war, Dr Kimenkowski established his own publishing house in Berlin and for twenty years his company promulgated books of a military nature. The propaganda ministry authorised Dr Kimenkowski to publish a biography about the late *Präsident* Hindenburg in the autumn of 1941. Reading a copy of the published book, the leader of the *Ordenskanzlei des Führers-und Reichskanzlers* and member of the *Stab Reichsführer*-SS, *Oberf.* Dr Heinrich Döhle, expressed his concern to Himmler that he had been libelled on 30 December 1941. Demanding Dr Kimenkowski's court-martial, the *Chef* SS-FHA then ordered the SS-*Richter*, *Stubaf.* Heinz Meurin of the SS- *und Polizei-Gericht* III, Berlin to investigate the affair. As a consequence of the judge's recommendation, Dr Kimenkowski found himself arrested and taken to Schöneberg prison where he was held in a small blacked-out cell measuring one metre wide with little light for three days (later, he complained that a guard assaulted him and his injuries resulted in his hospitalisation). Then transferred to a cell with three other SS officers, he whiled away the hour's playing cards and chess with his cell mates and his yard exercise consisted of walking in circles. Writing to his wife on 17 January 1942, Dr Kimenkowski laid the blame for the offending book passages on the shoulders of *Stubaf.* Werner Peterseim, an officer of the SS-FHA *Abt.* VI (press office) and former press officer for the LSSAH.

Despite his pleas for clemency, Dr Kimenkowski found himself arraigned before the courts martial of the SS- *und Polizei-Gericht* III on 18 February 1942, (case Nr. St. L. II 5/42) and judged guilty of the deliberate slander and libelling of Dr Döhle, the tribunal imposed a term of six years *Zuchthaus* and ordered Dr Kimenkowski's expulsion from the SS. The *HA SS-Gericht* agreed with the sentencing decision on 25 February and confirming the sentence on 15 April, the *Reichsführer* ordered *Stubaf.* Peterseim's case referred to the *Oberste* SS- *und Polizei-Gericht.* Transferred to a single cell in the KL Sachsenhausen, probably the SS- *Arrest- und Haftanstalt*, a little later, Dr Kimenkowski found himself incarcerated in the SS-*Straflager* Dachau. Writing to *Oberf.* Dr Döhle in early 1942, Dr Kimenkowski once again attempted to place the blame for the slander on Werner Peterseim. Dismissed from the SS on 20 June 1942, the Nazi party *Gau-Gericht* for Berlin ordered Dr Kimenkowki expulsion in August the same year. Failing to impress the prison leader, Dr Kimenkowski had proved unwilling, or unable to fulfil his work norm and blamed his lack of fitness on his Great War wounds. As a consequence of this situation, the prison leader ordered his medical examination to determine whether he should transfer to a civil jail. The results of this examination were passed to the SS-*Richter beim* RF-SS on 4 August 1942 along with a request that Himmler permit his transfer him to a concentration camp as a prisoner. Permission was granted on 2 September and Himmler banned Dr Kimenkowksi from applying for a reprieve for another year. Returning to the question of his reprieve on 13 February 1944, the SS-*Richter beim* RF-SS

(Dr Wehser) noted that the head of the SS had ordered his detention in the camp until the end of the war, but the pressing need to supply workers for the German war industry resulted in the proposal for Dr Kimenkowski to work under General Dr Kammler of the WVHA. Agreeing to this suggestion, the general commanded Dr Kimenkowski spend a week excavating tunnels for factories producing aircraft and top secret rocket engines at Nordhausen and proposed that an overseer watched over him to report on his progress. Alas, this decision came too late for Dr Ewald Kimenkowski. He had died in the KL Sachsenhausen on 28 July, reportedly from an infection caused by an abscess on a gland. Given the wide spread practice of falsifying camp prisoner hospital charts, equally, he may have died from abuse, neglect or privation.[92]

Despite the death of Dr Kimenkowski, the SS leader continued to express an interested in the Nordhausen labour proposal and had become interested in extending the practice to other category of former SS and *Polizei* camp prisoners. During discussions between Dr Kammler and the SS-*Richter beim* RF-SS (Dr Wehser) on 14 August 1944, the general wrote approvingly on this subject and proposed that these inmates was gathered together in the KL Sachsenhausen just prior to their work deployment. On 7 October the *Amt* III commanded that all former SS and *Polizei* prisoners judged unsuitable for front probation with the SS-*Sonderbrigade Dirlewanger* to be made available for Dr Kammler's projects in Mittelbau-Dora. As a consequence of this decision, the SS-*Straflager* Mittelbau-Dora was constructed inside the camp during late 1944 and a hundred *Wilfo-und Polizei Häftlinge* had arrived here by 1 November. 'The police prisoners were like any other camp inmates assigned to work, although the concentration camp administration seems to have ensured that they have no outside contact because of the strict secrecy provisions in the camp' wrote one camp survivor and the political division of the KL Dora reported their observations of these inmates in June 1944:

> [...]The following are gentle, each inmate admitted to the *Gestapo*-Weimar sub-camp Nordhausen today are former policeman. Their hair is short, not shorn off; the following prisoners are divided so that they cannot contact other inmates who would witness their secret tragedy. [...]

Four of these non-German prisoners hailed from Holland and Belgium. The first *Zuchthaus* military convicts joined them in *Dora* in November 1944 and were accommodated in a separate *Sonderlager*, located near the *lagerrevier*.[93]

Adolf Hitler gave his tacit approval for secret executions to take place in concentration camps and it is known that camp staff provided execution squads for the execution of SS men condemned to death by the *Gerichtsherr* or SS and *Polizei* courts. Recollecting post-war that he had participated in the execution of an SS officer during March 1945, *Uscha*. Heinrich Schäfer stated that he and other members of the camp staff had formed a ten-man execution squad and the condemned was stood before a sandbank, behind the chicken run, near the firing range. 'Long live Germany, which is better than you are!'

Shouted the condemned as *Ostuf.* Carl Heimann gave the execution squad the order to fire. Their grisly task completed, Heimann then issued each of the execution squad twenty cigarettes, three quarts of 'Schnapps' and 100 grams of meat.[94]

Non-German Camp Prisoners

Though the *Reichsführer* and the *HA* SS-*Gericht* appear to have made strenuous efforts to keep the malfeasant non-German elements of the *Waffen*-SS out of the concentration camps, it is clear that this punishment was imposed on this group. Their period of enlistment expired, the 130 volunteers of the SS-*Freiwilligen*-Legion *Niederlande* request to return to Holland in late 1941 was refused and the chief of staff for the *Kommandostabes* RF-SS personally conducted a parade of the dissenters on 7 January 1942 to inform them that their service to the *Führer* was essential and desertion, a clear case of neglect of duty, was punishable by death. The field court received notification of their dissent and handing the matter to the local SS and *Polizei* court, this tribunal received orders to punish the objectors' disobedience with a term of twelve months' *Gefängnis*. Obtaining Himmler's approbation, *Heerbanleider Hauptmann* a. D. Meulenberg interviewed the objectors in Graz and succeeded in persuading all but 13 of their number to take the oath and join the SS-*Freiwilligen-Panzergrenadier*-Brigade *Nederland* on 23 December 1943. Writing to the HSSPF *Nordwest* on 20 January 1944, Meulenberg warned that the protesters had threatened to desert if forced to accept a new oath or return to the front. Refusing their demand to join other formations for the duration of the war, the authorities placed the dissenters in detention on 8 February. Although convinced that the objectors were behaving shamefully and ridiculous, the HSSPF *Nordwest* and the SS-*Richter beim* RF-SS nevertheless tasked themselves with finding a solution to the problem and drafted a new oath together on 21 January. With Himmler's support, it was agreed to treat harshly those objectors who refused to take this pledge and treat them as doubters and shirkers. Discussing the issue with the Dutch Nationalist leader, Mussert, the SS leader to give special consideration for those refusing the oath on religious grounds.[95]

Ordering a suspension of the court's process against the Dutchmen on 1 March, the *Reichsführer* permitted the dissenters another opportunity to accept the new oath, but commanded those continuing to refuse to be stripped of SS insignia and transferred to the SS-Brigade *Nederland* as a deterrent to other would-be objectors and as cowards. Here, Himmler commanded them to perform menial tasks with the supply unit (it was left to the commander to decide when they had proven themselves). The head of the SS approved a new version of an oath of allegiance that had been drafted by the HSSPF *Nordwest* and the Dutch leader on 21 April, but presenting this version of the pledge to the dissenters, they once again refused to repeat the wording. Writing to the leader of the SS-*Grenadier-Ersatz-Bataillon* 11 at Graz, *Stubaf.* Rädcke, on 13 April, the commander of the *Nederland* complained that the first four Dutch objectors had arrived at his headquarters and had immediately protested their treatment as Russian prisoners of war for five months and expressed their unwillingness to fight in the SS. 'It is impossible for such men of the same blood to be assigned to the reserve services as an inferior type' bemoaned the brigade commander and given his unit was no prison, he could imagine no use for troops stripped of the death heads badge. Supported by his corps commander, the brigade leader suggested the objectors accepted the oath used by the other troops, but refusing this offer they then demanded a transfer to the Army or Navy. Given their attitude, all four dissenters returned to Graz with a recommendation that they face trial.[96]

When informed of the situation on 13 May, the SS-*Richter beim* RF-SS recommended that war effort employment was found for the group, which was better than that offered to Russian prisoners of war. Meanwhile, *Stubaf.* Rädcke received a strong warning for questioning the *Reichsführer*'s pledge order and sending the objectors to the front without taking the oath. Receiving orders to return to the front, Rädcke died in action at Tuchkalla on 28 October while leading the SS-*Gebirgsjäger*-Rgt. 11. His replacement, *Stubaf.* Bernhard Barthelt, received orders on 22 August to present the new oath to the dissenting Dutchmen and the SS-*Richter beim* RF-SS voiced his confidence on 18 October that he had seen the end of the affair. Bender's optimism would prove misplaced; in the first week of November he was informed that fourteen Dutch *Kreigsmarine* draftees in Graz had objected to taking the oath and had demanded a transfer to the Navy. A decision was then taken to deal firmly with these dissenters. Permitting those who had not volunteered for the SS to transfer to the Navy-although it was policy to assign all Germanic volunteers to the *Waffen*-SS-those continuing to refuse to take the oath was ordered to be detained in the *Sonderlager* Hinzert and the names of those judged a danger to the other volunteers was reported to Himmler (two survived the war and immigrated to Canada in the 1950s). Though no agreement existed with the *Großadmiral* to establish a separate Germanic marine reserve unit in Sennheim, the Navy and the SS-*Richter beim* RF-SS agreed to transfer those who had been brought to Graz under false pretences on 4 December and it was left it to the SS-FHA and the SS-*Hauptamt* to arrange their discharge from the *Waffen*-SS to the Navy.[97]

Polizei auxiliaries were also at risk of a concentration camp sentence: Writing to the SS- *und Polizei-Gericht* XX on 2 May 1944, the *Kommandantur der Ordnungspolizei* Lithuania informed the court that a Lithuanian soldier named Franas Bartkevicius had been incarcerated in the forced labour camp at Frawinnischnen on 17 March 1944.[98]

There is some evidence that former non-German SS and *Polizei* prisoners were released from concentration camp detention on the grounds of ill-health. Deserting from his *Polizei-Bataillon*, the Latvian policeman found himself apprehended in Riga on 13 January 1943 and while awaiting trial before the SS- *und Polizei-Gericht* XVI, Riga in September 1943, he languished in the *Zentralzuchthaus* Riga (central prison). Judged guilty of desertion, the court imposed a term of three years' *Zuchthaus* and declared him an enemy of the Reich. Later, detained in Danzig-Matzkau, this convict then found himself hospitalised in a concentration camp and on the grounds of his incapacity he left detention in March 1944 to work on a farm.[99]

1.10 *Entwöhnungsaufenhalt*

Concerned at the sudden reported increase of alcoholism within the ranks of the *Waffen*-SS and *Polizei*, the *Reichsführer* ordered the creation of an institution in July 1941 in which to detain officers who had faced a court process for an alcohol related offence. The WVHA provided the funding to establish the *Entwöhnungsaufenhalt* (drying-out accommodation) and negotiated its creation with the concentration camp inspector. The KL Buchenwald commandant received orders on 23 July 1941 to construct an assistance barracks and a sauna near his headquarters and he took command of the *Entwöhnungsaufenhalt*, which was also known as the *Entwöhnungslager* (drying-out camp). Staffed with non-commissioned officers from his staff, the commandant selected *Ustuf.* Kamilo v.Knorr-Krehan as the institutions leader on 2 August 1941.[100]

Construction of the *Entwöhnungsaufenhalt* had been accomplished on 25 October 1941 and the decision to send drunks to the drying out camp was taken at the discretion of the courts and Himmler, (he decided on the length of sentence). The convict's behaviour was monitored by the *HA* SS-*Gericht* and those ordered to this institution wore civilian clothing and an armband attached to the sleeve of their jackets denoted their status. The inmates wore gym kit for sports activities and observed a number of strict rules: The inmates were forbidden to drink alcohol, smoke cigarettes, buy goods from the camp canteen or receive food parcels from home. Eating a strict vegetarian diet with no spices, the inmates worked in the commandant's vegetable garden and this supplied their sustenance. The vegetables were cooked in the SS camp kitchen. If desired, the inmates purchased fruit and mineral water directly from v.Knorr-Krehan and participated in military exercises during summer, undertook tough sports activities, played football and horses were made available for riding and equestrian sports. The camp physician monitored the inmate's health and ordered therapies that included time in the sauna. Delinquent detainees were subject to the commandant's punishment in accordance with the disciplinary regulations, but those discovered drinking alcohol risked a court-martial for disobedience and imprisonment.[101]

The first detainees were *Gendareriemeister* Albert Reiher, who had been punished by the SS- *und Polizei-Gericht* XIV, Metz, (case Nr. St. K. II 57/1941), *Leutnant der Gendarmerie* Albert Schuster and *Leutnant der Gendarmerie* Jacob Hofmann who had both had been punished by the SS- *und Polizei-Gericht* II, Düsseldorf, (case Nr. St. L. II 102a-b/1941). *Ustuf.* Otto Friedrich had been commanded to the drying out camp by the SS- *und Polizei-Gericht* XII, Hamburg (case Nr. St. L. I 75/1941).[102]

Name: Otto Andreas Friedrich.
Last Rank: SS-*Untersturmführer*.
Born: 22.7.1908 in Hoheneich/Gmünd.
NSDAP-Nr.: 364.933 (joined 4.1.1931).
SS-Nr.: 270.268 (joined 1.6.1932).

Promotions:

9.11.1936	SS-*Oberscharführer der Allgemeine*-SS.
20.4.1939	SS-*Untersturmführer der Allgemeine*-SS.

Prewar Assignments:

SD-*Unterabschnitt Ost-Hannover* from 1.11.1936.

SD-*Oberabschnitt Nordwest* from 11.10.1937.

Bernau SD-*Schule* in 4.1939.

Referent SD-*Oberabschnitt Nordwest* HQ (Hamburg) in 1939.

Wartime Assignments:

Theologian affairs specialist with the SD-*Leitabschnitt Amt* II (Hamburg) from 1.9.1939.

SiPo and SD *Inspektor* (Hamburg) from 1.4.1941.

SD-*Oberabchnitt* Vienna on 5.5.1944.

Decorations & Awards:

0.0.19__	SS-*Zivilabzeichen* (Nr. 165.596).
0.0.19__	SA-*Sportsabzeichen in Bronze.*
0.0.19__	*Deutsches Reichssportabzeichen in Bronze.*
0.0.19__	SS-*Ehrenwinkel für alte Kämpfer.*
16.11.1940	*Totenkopfring der* SS.
0.0. 19__	*Dienstauszeichnung der* NSDAP *in Bronze.*
0.0.1938	*Die Medaille zur Erinnerung an den* 13. März 1938 (Austria)

Notes: Attending *Volksschule* for six classes, Friedrich obtained his *Abitur* from *Höhere Schule* and studied jurisprudence at university until passing passed his *Referendarexamen* in 1932. His political activities in his home region of Niederdonau resulted in his imprisonment for three weeks for the handling and illegal use of a weapon. Serving part of his imprisonment, Friedrich then fled Austria for Hamburg and continued his legal studies. The SD punished Friedrich with a strong warning for an unknown offence on 6 June 1937. Friedrich participated in the *Anschluss* of Austria on 12 March 1938 and married his fiancée Hermine S., (b. 5.11.1911 in Vienna) on 18 March the same year. They had two children up to the point when records ceased in May 1945. He continued to study law at university in the spring of 1939. Commanded to replace the duty officer for the Hamburg SD service building on Sunday, 23 February 1941, Friedrich received orders to supervise the guards from the guard house, but during his period of duty he left his post to visit a local bar and consumed two litres of beer and two schnapps. Returning to his post five hours later, his intoxication was reported to his commanding officer, *Stubaf.* Engel, who ordered Friedrich's arrest for three days and reported his act of neglect to the SD ID 2. A disciplinary process was then conducted against Friedrich for negligence and he found himself arraigned before the courts martial of the SS- *und Polizei-Gericht* XII, Hamburg on 29 May 1941 (case Nr. St. L. I 75/1941). Here, the court chairman, *Stubaf.* Dr Leo Ernst, was supported in his deliberations by *Ostuf.* Dr Friedrich Schlüter and *Ustuf.* Paul Christophersen and *Hstuf.* Kappe prosecuted the case. Judged guilty of his neglect of guard duty in contravention of paragraph § 141 Abs. 1 MStGB, the court imposed a term of three week *Stubenarrest* on Friedrich. Confirming the judgment on 12 August 1941, the *Reichsführer* chose not to deduct his three days in remand detention from his sentence on the grounds that his offence was a consequence of his excessive drinking. Commanding Friedrich's incarceration in the drying out camp for a period of three months, Himmler also imposed a ten year alcohol ban on him. Writing on 26 September 1941, Dr Reinecke explained that this command was not a punishment, but in Buchenwald, Friedrich was expected to engage in healthy sports activities and hard military training. Leaving the drying out camp, Friedrich returned to the SD. His family were evacuated to Breiteneich on 7 April 1944. The only significant effect that the drying out sentence appeared to have on Friedrich's career was his lack of promotion—he was not elevated beyond the rank of *Ustuf.*[103]

Demanding that the drying-out camp regime was toughened up on 28 November 1941, the SS-*Richter beim* RF-SS (Dr Wehser) sought to discover who was responsible for funding the therapy. The SS-FHA administration expressed some concerns about the cost of this facility in January 1942 and although declaring their willingness to bear the costs for men of the *Waffen*-SS, they were unwilling to do so for the *Polizei* and other branches of the SS. However, agreeing to pay for theatre visits, trips to the swimming baths, the SS-FHA also provided finance for an additional six riding horses on 20 February 1942. That same month, the head of the SS permitted expelled felons to enter this institution and he abolished the officer-only rule. In late January the *Amt* III granted permission for inmates to take long walks, reiterated the ban on receiving of food and permitted the courts to impose drying-out camp sentences.[104]

Equestrian activities were evidently poplar in this institution. In late November 1942 the SS leader authorised drying-out camp inmates to ride horses in the woods adjoining the concentration camp.[105]

Name: Rudolf Röder.
Last Rank: SS-*Hauptsturmführer.*
Born: 30.10.1902 in Munich.
NSDAP-Nr.: 1.200.757 (joined 1.8.1932).
SS-Nr.: 60.390 (joined 30.6.1932).
Promotions:

0.0.19__	*Gefreiter der Reserve.*
30.1.1935	SS-*Untersturmführer der Allgemeine*-SS.
19.9.1936	SS-*Obersturmführer der Allgemeine*-SS.
11.9.1938	SS-*Hauptsturmführer der Allgemeine*-SS.
0.0.1941	SS-*Obersturmführer* (*Sonderführer der Waffen*-SS).
7.11.1941	SS-*Schütze.*
0.0.1943	SS-*Oberscharführer der Reserve.*
1.11.1944	SS-*Obersturmführer der Reserve.*

Prewar Assignments:
Freikorps Epp and the *Bayerisches Schützenkorps* 2.5.1919–19.8.1932.
SS-*Standarte* 1 (Munich) from 1.1935.
Wartime Assignments:
Warsaw Governor HQ in 1940.
Waffen-SS 18.3.1942
HSSPF *Ost Amt* IVa on 7.10.1942.
Decorations & Awards:
0.0.19__ *Orden Auszeichnung Für Schlesien Eisen Adler* 2. *Klasse*.
0.0.19__ SS-*Ehrenwinkel für alte Kämpfer*.
0.0.19__ *Totenkopfring der* SS.

Notes: Attending *Volksschule* for eight classes, Röder studied at *Handelschule* for three years, was then employed as a salesman and worked as a state employee at the labour office. Then engaged with the office of the chairman of the II. Medical clinic in 1932, Röder mustered with the SA from 1932. The SS noted that Röder had a leg injury that required the aid of a crutch to walk. Marrying his fiancée Elisabeth J., (b. 13.12.1902 in Munich), they had no issue from this union up to the point when records ceased in May 1945. Röder carried out his compulsory military training for eight weeks with the *Schützen*-Rgt. 41. Drafted into state service in 1940, Röder was posted to the Polish capital and here instigated a prank that resulted in his punishment and transfer to the *Entwöhnungsaufenhalt*. Wearing his SS uniform, Röder entered a bar on 25 May 1940 and began drinking with a police officer and some Nazi party officials. Becoming inebriated, he hit upon the idea to telephone both Dr Fischer, who he disliked, and a local hospital. When his calls were answered, Röder made loud rude noises and quickly replaced the receiver. An investigation revealing that he was the instigator of this prank, the local court initiated proceedings against him on 2 September 1940. Arraigned before the court martial of the SS- *und Polizei-Gericht* VI, Krakau, the tribunal judged the unruly Röder guilty for indiscipline, commanded his demotion and expelled him from the SS. In addition to this sentence, the *Reichsführer* imposed a five years' alcohol ban on Röder on 7 November 1941 and he received orders to spend on year in the *Entwöhnungsaufenhalt*. While awaiting confirmation of the sentence in 1941, Röder was appointed a *Sonderführer der Waffen*-SS (Special Officer) with the rank of *Ostuf*.

Released from the drying-out camp in the spring of 1942, Röder deployed with the HSSPF *Ost* headquarters in October the same year and here, he obtained accommodation for SS men and their families and supervised Polish workers repairing or building dwellings. He had replaced the *Rechnungsführer* (accountant officer) in this department by 5 August 1943, but his superiors considered Röder 'circumspect' in his duties and complained that he was occasionally inattentive to his commander's orders. 'He has a soldierly appearance and good leadership skills and has a good relationship with the SS staff and was a good comrade. As expected of a long serving member of the Nazi party, Röder was judged politically reliable' in fitness report composed on 7 August. Maintaining his drinking ban, Röder's return to officer rank was then recommended and he had been promoted and granted a partial rehabilitation by 21 August. Undergoing a medical examination before *Stubaf.* Dr Hermann Sirk of the SS-*Standort* Krakau on 14 October, the HSSPF *Ost* was informed that Röder experienced mobility problems with his left leg, it had been observed that his bending and stretching was restricted and he had flat feet. Despite his clear unsuitability for front probation, the *Reichsführer* rejected Röder's promotion to officer rank on 1 March 1944 and ordered his deployment on the Galicia-Polish border. It is not clear if whether order was carried out, but promoted to officer rank in November the same year, Röder was not re-admitted into the SS. Writing on 3 November, the SS-FHA recommended Röder was transferred to Italy to fight partisans, but the final decision in this matter was left to Himmler to decide.[106]

1.11 Disciplinary Case Studies

Name: Heinz Gloger.
Last Rank: SS-*Hauptsturmführer.*
Born: 27.12.1910 in Berlin.
Died: 2.8.1944 in Warsaw.
SS-Nr.: 58.113 (joined 2.1933).
Promotions:
21.6.1941 SS-*Untersturmführer der Reserve.*
0.0.19__ SS-*Obersturmführer der Reserve.*
20.4.1944 SS-*Hauptsturmführer der Reserve.*
Wartime Assignments:
Waffen-SS from 1940.
3. / SS-FLAK *Abt.* 5 in 6.1941.
4. / SS-FLAK *Abt.* 5 from 1.1.1942.
Decorations & Awards:
0.0.19__ 1939 *Eisernes Kreuz I. Klasse.*
0.0.19__ 1939 *Eisernes Kreuz II. Klasse.*
0.0.19__ *Totenkopfring der* SS.

Notes: A member of the SS since February 1933, Gloger was a battery commander in the SS-FLAK *Abteilung* 5 when the 5th SS-*Panzer*-Division *Wiking* field court initiated a court investigation against Gloger to determine why a junior NCO of the light anti-aircraft troop in his battery had mistakenly shot down a JU-52 aircraft on 20 April 1943 (the plane was mortally hit and the wounded crew were forced to make an emergency landing). When questioned about the incident, Gloger claimed the German aircraft approached from the same direction and at a height that had been used for two days previously by a Soviet fighter plane, (dropping bombs on his troops resulting in two deaths and five wounded). Further, Gloger claimed that the aircraft had failed to fire a recognition flare, ignored three warning shots and approached his FLAK gun position from a ten degree angle, against a dark background, which in his opinion, had made it impossible for the gun crew to identify the aircraft. The court investigator observed that during the incident, Gloger had loitered with the nearby 8.8 cm gun battery during this event and due to a shortage of equipment, no telephone wire communication existed between the batteries. 'For his unfortunate mistake, made while in command of his battery' the *Wiking Gerichtsherr* punished the remiss Gloger with a four weeks' *Stubenarrest* for his dereliction of duty on 19 June 1943, (case Nr. St. L. I 167/1943). The *HA* SS-*Gericht* later recommended amending the sentence to negligent damage to military equipment and judged the punishment appropriate. The *Reichsführer* confirmed Gloger's sentence in March 1944 and despite this penalty, he remaining in command of the FLAK battery until killed in action in Warsaw in August 1944. His *Totenkopfring der* SS was returned to Germany on 30 December.[107]

Name: Eduard Johannes **Limion.**
Last Rank: Waffen-*Untersturmführer.*
Born: 11.5.1918 in Dorpot/Estonia.
Prewar Assignments:
Estonian Army 1.7.1936–8.9.1940.
Red Army 8.9.1940–17.7.1941.
Kriminalpolizei in 1942.
Wartime Assignments:
Waffen-SS from 1.7.1943.
Promotions:
7.8.1944 *Waffen-Untersturmführer.*

Notes: Attending *Volksschule* for six classes, Limion obtained his *Abitur* from *Höhere Schule* and marrying his fiancée on 29 March 1941, they had one child together. A professional officer in the pre-war Estonian Army, Limion then served with the Red Army until July 1941 and then worked the German-controlled *Kriminalpolizei* during 1942. Transferring to the *Waffen*-SS on 1 July 1943, Limion deployed with Estonian forces on the frontline near Nevel in November 1943 when he drank a bottle of spirits with two visiting Estonian war correspondents at his front-line post. During the course of their revelry, Limion ordered the artillery bombardment of a coastal peninsula where he believed a Red Army bunker was emplaced. Personally directing the fire, many shots missed the target, but a little over 30 rounds hit a church roof, setting it ablaze. That same night Limion and another then NCO undertook a search a house and coming across a German policeman, a member of *Kampfgruppe* Jeckeln, they proceeded to abuse and threatened him with their weapons and fired a number of rounds into the floor at his feet.

'For his senseless waste of ammunition,' the court instigated a court investigation and this recommended the feckless Limion's arraignment before the courts martial for the unauthorised artillery bombardment and his assault of the German police official (case Nr. St. L. I 1/44). Judged guilty of drunkenness the court punished Limion with six weeks' sharp room arrest, which the *Gerichtsherr* confirmed, but the *HA* SS-*Gericht* recommended the tariff was increased to eight months *Gefängnis* for disobedience and a further eighteen months *Gefängnis* for the abuse of the German policeman. The *Gerichtsherr* refused to confirm this decision, arguing that he had no desire to lose a capable artillery officer, he also expressed his fears that imposing this punishment would result in Limion deserting to Sweden. At the end of 1944 the *HA* SS-*Gericht* demanded Limion was placed in handcuffs and sent to prison for six months. However, presenting the case report to the *Reichsführer* for a sentencing confirmation in February 1945, the head of the SS commanded Limion serve six weeks' arrest in lieu of the jail sentence and spend the remainder of the punishment as probation with his division.[108]

Name: Quinus de Veer.
Last Rank: SS-*Sturmbannführer.*
Born: 5.1.1903 in Groesbeek/Holland.
Died: 29.4.1945 in Sperenberg.
Promotions:

3.11.1941	SS-*Hauptsturmführer der Waffen*-SS.
30.1.1945	SS-*Sturmbannführer der Waffen*-SS.

Wartime Assignments:
Waffen-SS from 3.11.1941.
SS-*Freiwilligen*-Legion *Niederlande* in 1941.
SS-*Artillerie-Ausbildung- und Ersatz*-Rgt. from 21.3.1943
7. / SS-*Artillerie*-Rgt. 5 from 28.3.1943.
II. / SS-*Panzer-Artillerie*-Rgt. 54 from 20.1.1944.
Attended a training course at the *Artillerieschule* Großborn 31.5.–18.7.1944.
II. / SS-*Panzer-Artillerie*-Rgt. 54 in 2.1945.
Decorations & Awards:

0.0.1944	1939 *Eisernes Kreuz I. Klasse.*
0.0.1943	1939 *Eisernes Kreuz II. Klasse.*
0.0.1942	*Kriegsverdienstkreuz II. Klasse ohne Schwertern.*
0.0.1942	*Medaille 'Winterschlacht im Osten* 1941/42'.
0.0.19__	*Infanterie-Sturmabzeichen in Bronze.*
0.0.19__	*Verwundetenabzeichen*, 1939 *in Schwarz.*

Notes: De Veer had been a professional soldier in the Dutch Army, prior to joining the *Waffen*-SS in November 1941 and obtained the rank of *Hauptmann*. As was customary, de Veer was accepted into the ranks of the *Waffen*-SS with his former military rank in November 1941 and mustered with the *Niederlande*. Transferring to the SS-*Artillerie*-Rgt. 5 in March 1943, De Veer found himself arraigned before the courts martial of the

5th SS-*Grenadier*-Division *Wiking* field court on 4 December 1942. Judged guilty of drunkenness, the tribunal sentenced de Veer to serve a term of ten months' *Gefängnis* for contravening paragraph §183 RStGB. Confirming the sentence on 21 February 1943, the *Reichsführer* reduced de Veer's punishment to three weeks' sharp *Stubenarrest* and the *HA* SS-*Gericht* concurred with the decision on 5 March. Held in detention during the investigation of the offence for this length of time, de Veer then found himself placed on probation and died in action near Sperenberg in April 1945 while leading and artillery battalion.[109]

Name: Enn Sirvet.
Last Rank: *Waffen-Hauptsturmführer.*
Born: 24.10.1916 in Reval/Estonia.
SS-Nr.: (joined 7.5.1943).
Promotions:
7.5.1943 *Waffen-Obersturmführer.*
30.1.1944 *Waffen-Hauptsturmführer.*
Wartime Assignments:
39. *Schutzmannschaftbataillon* summer of 1941
Schutzmannschaft (*Kompanieführer*) on 21.9.1941.
Waffen-SS from 3.6.1943.
SS-*Freiwilligen*-Legion *Estland* from 7.6.1943.
SS-FLAK *Ersatz-Bataillon* (Munich) 17.7.-15.9.1943.
FLAK *Abt.* / 3. SS-*Freiwilligen*-Brigade (Est.) from 15.9.1943.
6. / *Waffen-Grenadier*-Rgt. *der* SS 46 in 1.1944.
I. / *Waffen-Grenadier*-Rgt. *der* SS 46 in 1944.
I. / *Waffen-Grenadier*-Rgt. *der* SS 45 in 3.1945.
Decorations & Awards:
0.0.19__ *Infanterie-Sturmabzeichen in Bronze.*
0.0.19__ *Medaille 'Winterschlacht im Osten* 1941/42'.

Notes: Attending *Volksschule* for six classes, Sirvet obtained his *Abitur* from *Höhere Schule* after five classes and then found employment in the textile industry. Marrying his fiancée on 17 December 1939, they had one child up to the point when records ceased in May 1945. Transferring to the *Waffen*-SS in June 1943, Sirvet served as battery commander in the Estonian brigade's FLAK battalion when he refused to obey an order and apologise for his behaviour on 31 October 1943, *Brigadef.* Franz Augsberger ordered the brigade field court to initiate a court investigation against Sirvet (case Nr. St. L. 55/1943) and as a consequence of *Hstuf.* Hans-Helmet Bredehöft's findings, the disobedient artillery officer received a punishment of three weeks' intensified *Stubenarrest* on 23 December the same year. As his actions had caused little harm to the combat effectiveness of the brigade, Sirvet served his penalty in his quarters.[110]

Name: Jan Hendrik Wessel.
Last Rank: SS-*Obersturmführer.*
Born: 11.6.1921 in Berlin.
Died: 18.12.1944 in Elbing.
Wartime Assignments:
Waffen-SS from 15.7.1941.
SS-*Infantrie-Ersatz-Bataillon Westland* in 1.1943.
8. *Kriegs-Reserve-Führer-Anwärter-Lehrgang* SS-*Junkerschule* Bad Tölz 1.2.–31.7.1943.
Zugführer 6. / SS-*Panzergrenadier*-Rgt. 48 in 2.1944.
III. SS-*Panzerkorps* on 23.3.1944.
SS-*Panzer-Grenadier-Ausbildung- und Ersatz-Bataillon* 11 (Graz) spring of 1944.
6. / SS-*Panzer-Grenadier*-Rgt. 48 on 21.7.1944.
Ordnance Officer 1. / SS-*Panzergrenadier*-Rgt. 49 *de Ruyter* in 12.1944.
Promotions:
1.9.1943 SS-*Untersturmführer der Waffen*-SS.
1.12.1943 SS-*Obersturmführer der Waffen*-SS.
Decorations & Awards:
2.11.1944 1939 *Eisernes Kreuz I. Klasse.*
7.2.1944 1939 *Eisernes Kreuz II. Klasse.*
0.0.19__ *Verwundetenabzeichen*, 1939 *in Schwarz.*

Notes: Attending *Volksschule* for six classes, Wessel obtained his *Abitur* from *Höhere Schule* and volunteered for military service with the *Waffen*-SS in July 1941. They noted Wessel spoke Dutch, English and French. Attending and passing a cadet training course at Bad Tölz, Wessel's course commander noted that he was proven in battle and recommended him for position of section leader only. In 1943, Wessel was then accused of plundering and found himself arraigned before the courts martial on 1 December 1943. As a consequence of its findings, Wessel was punished with one week of *Stubenarrest*. The *Reichsführer* and the *HA* SS-*Gericht* confirmed this sentence on 10 March 1944 and he served his punishment with the reserve battalion at Graz. Wessel died at the Elbing *Reserve-Lazarett* on 18 December 1944.[111]

2

Strafvollzugslager der SS- *und Polizei* Origin, Structure and Activities

The 17 October 1939 edict permitted the SS-*Richter* of the *HA* SS-*Gericht* to discipline their miscreants with jail sentences as prescribed in the RStGB and MStGB. These penalties included terms of *Gefängnis*, or *Zuchthaus* and those committing offences that warranted their removal from society faced incarceration in a concentration camp as prisoners:

Gefängnis: A prison sentence of between six weeks' and fifteen years' duration with the loss of civil and honour rights. This penalty was usually imposed on offenders who had committed less serious crimes, or had committed a wrongdoing against military discipline. Punishable wrong doings included committing an act of disobedience, drunkenness on duty, behaving insubordinately or judged lazy. Those punished with a term of twelve months', or greater *Gefängnis* were usually suspended temporarily from the SS. *Gefängnis* convicts normally served only a portion of their sentences and then either returned to their original unit on parole, or undertook a period of field probation.

Zuchthaus: A hard labour punishment of between six weeks' and fifteen years' duration with the loss of civil and honour rights. Usually imposed on those who had committed serious criminal offences, such as murder, manslaughter, transgressions against paragraph §175 RStGB, rape and acts of theft. Those sentenced to a term of *Zuchthaus* was usually declared unworthy to bear arms and then dismissed from the SS and Nazi party. *Zuchthaus* inmates awaiting confirmation of a capital punishment remained in the SS-*Straflager* Dachau until their sentence was confirmed. The punishment of those whose sentence of death had been postponed indefinitely had their sentence converted to a term of *Zuchthaus*, permitting their eventual probation with the *Bewärhungsabteilung*, or the *Sonderkommando Dirlewanger*.[1]

The *Reichsführer* retained the right to amend all prison sentences and impose lesser punishments with or without front probation. Released from their sentences, a decision was then taken by the *Amt* III and the SS-*Richter beim* RF-SS to either recommend a discharge, or retain these disgraced soldiers within the *Waffen*-SS.

Prior to the introduction of the SS judiciary on 17 October 1939, it was the practice of the SS-VT and *Polizei* to expel their malfeasant elements from their organisations and permit their trial and punishment before the civil courts. During the negotiations to establish his jurisdiction in 1938, the *Reichsführer* and his advocates had neglected to seek financial provision from the *Reichsjustizministerium* to establish their own SS ran prison institution. Content to hand his convicts into the care of the civilian and military prison system, the SS leader was convinced that dismissing these troublesome elements from his fighting force would preserve their elite image in the eyes of the nation.

2.1 Wartime Imprisonment Provisions of the SS- *und Polizei-Gerichtsbarkeit*

In the absence of a permanent penal institution in which to detain court punished *Waffen*-SS offenders, the *HA* SS-*Gericht* arranged with the *Reichsjustizministerium* the detention of court martialled criminals inside the civil judiciary controlled *Oberlandgericht Gefängnis* (upper regional court prison). Their number included the condemned and those sentenced to terms of *Zuchthaus*, or *Gefängnis* of greater than twelve months' duration. Expellees and those judged unworthy to bear arms and troops denied their civil rights were among those sent to civil jails. Qualified wrongdoers found themselves placed in the custody of the KL Esterwegen. In addition to this arrangement with the *Reichsjustizministerium*, the military authorities agreed to detain *Gefängnis Waffen*-SS offenders inside their military penal institutions.[2]

Alongside these arrangements, Himmler continued to remand those who had contravened the disciplinary regulations in the *Erziehungssturm*. Usually those he judged redeemable, these felons remained in Sachsenhausen until judged suitable for front probation. It was left to the field courts of the LSSAH, *Verfügungstruppe*, *Polizeidivision* and *Totenkopfdivision* to negotiate their own individual arrangements with the *Reichsjustizministerium* and secure cell space in their *Oberlandgericht Gefängnis* for this category of inmate.[3]

Following the successful conclusion of the 1940 summer campaign the *Totenkopfdivision* field court ordered their *Gefängnis* convicts to serve their penalties in the Dax *Oberlandesgericht Gefängnis*. On arrival, these miscreants were informed of their *Ehrenstrafe* punishment (expulsion or release) and completing their sentences, they then either transferred to a reserve battalion for a formal discharge from military service, was returned directly to the *Totenkopfdivision*, or assigned to another unit. Arriving at their new posting, their new company leader usually announced the former convict's recent misfortunes to his new comrades and this policy of naming and shaming continued to be practised throughout the war as a method of dissuading troops from committing acts of indiscipline. Later, the Dax convicts transferred to the Freiberg in Breisgau *Oberlandesgericht Gefängnis* and remained incarcerated until their punishment had been fully served.[4]

2.2 *Festungshaft*

Within the pantheon of imprisonment punishments available to the German military authorities there existed *Festungshaft* (fortress detention). This form of imprisonment took place under the watch of military jailers in forbidding military fortress. In its pre-war discussions with the German High Command in November 1939, the RSHA arranged for this form of detention for its offenders to be undertaken inside the *Wehrmacht Festungshaftanstalt* at Germersheim.[5]

Writing to the OKW *Rechtsabteilung* on 11 March 1940, the *Chef HA* SS-*Gericht* proposed that SS-VT troops sentenced to a term of court-judged *Festungshaft* serve their punishment under the guard of *Heer* troops in *Wehrmacht Festungshaftanstalt*. The OKW *Rechtsabteilung* (legal department) accepted this proposition in May 1940 and this category of SS-VT convict then transferred from civil institutions to the Ingolstadt *Wehrmacht Festungshaftanstalt*.

However, warning the *HA* SS-*Gericht* that only a limited number of cells existed in Ingolstadt to detain convicts on 30 September 1940, the military then supplied additional space for SS-VT inmates in Germersheim and notified this fortress of this decision with a command to prepare the necessary cells for their new charges. The *HA* SS-*Gericht* cancelled the imprisonment of its fortress convicts in Ingolstadt on 1 November 1940.[6]

Becoming increasingly concerned that his convicts were mistreated in military custody, the *Reichsführer* expressed his disfavour with the policy of imprisoning SS-VT felons in military fortresses in May 1942 and commanded this arrangement discontinued on 10 August the same year. Demanding that the transfer of SS and *Polizei* offenders from Germersheim to SS custody, Himmler then ordered the *Chef HA* SS-*Gericht* to establish a *Waffen*-SS *Festungshaftanstalt* where this category of inmate would be able to undertake some form of labour during their incarceration.[7]

General Breithaupt wrote to the SS leader on 11 September 1942 to request the indefinite postponement of the construction of this institution on the grounds of the critical war situation and the low numbers of men punished in this fashion (in the first half of 1943 only four convicts had been incarcerated in Germersheim).[8]

Stepping into the debate, the *HA* SS-*Gericht Amt* III recommended that those punished with *Festungshaft* become the direct responsibility of their office and served their sentence in barrack cells. Proposing that those punished with between three and four months' fortress detention be detained in the cell block at Munich-Freimann, the *Amt* III argued that their cells already held suspects awaiting trial at the SS- *und Polizei-Gericht* I, Munich. Also known as the *Gerichtgefängnis* Munich, this institution also had the use of cells located in the barracks roof. Searched on arrival, forbidden possessions such as tobacco and alcohol was removed from each fortress convict and retained by the staff until their release. Permitted to wear their uniform, without weapons, the inmates found themselves held under constant guard and incarcerated in a single room with a lock between 10.00 p.m. and 5.00 a.m. in summer and 9.00 p.m. to 6.00 a.m. in winter. Those completing four months of their punishment was then permitted to share a common room and receive visitors. Completing three months of their sentence, the fortress convict was then only locked in his room on the grounds of security, or to maintain good order. Expected to labour for ten hours a day, the inmates' working day began at 8.00 a.m. and his one or two hours free time was spent playing sports (officers reported for work without a guard). Privileges included receiving post and packages, the purchasing of books and newspapers, a monthly visit from a relative and the commandant permitted leave in special circumstances. Rule breakers risked locked door detention in their room for one day, the removal of privileges and the loss of association time for up to two weeks (the imposition of disciplinary punishments against fortress convicts was forbidden). Selecting the guards for this institution from the SS garrison, for much of the war this punishment process remained under the constant review of the SS-*Richter beim* RF-SS.[9]

Name: Eduard Leendert **Voorwinden.**
Last Rank: SS-*Sturmbannführer.*
Born: 7.7.1899 in Rotterdam/Holland.
Died: 13.12.1947 in Westerbork.
RAD Service: 7.12.1940–1.3.1941.
Wartime Assignments:
Waffen-SS from 7.8.1941.
Freiwilligen-Legion *Niederlande* in 1941.
SS-*Panzer-Grenadier-Ausbildung- und Ersatz-Bataillon* 11 (Graz) on 23.5.1943.
III. SS-*Panzerkorps* (*Stogas*) in 1943.
I. / *Waffen-Panzer-Grenadier*-Rgt. *der* SS *de Ruyter* until 21.12.1943.
SS-*Panzer-Grenadier-Ausbildung- und Ersatz-Bataillon* 11 in 1944.
SS-*Unterführerschule* Arnhem 15.8.–5.12.1944
Seconded to the RuSHA in Berlin on 5.12.1944.
Promotions:
0.0.19__ *Hauptmann.*
7.8.1941 SS-*Hauptsturmführer der Waffen*-SS.
9.11.1944 SS-*Sturmbannführer der Waffen*-SS.
Decorations & Awards:
00.0.19__ 1939 *Eisernes Kreuz II. Klasse.*
00.0.19__ *Infanterie-Sturmabzeichen in Bronze.*
00.0.19__ *Medaille Winterschlacht im Osten* 1941/42.

Notes: His father, Arie Hendrik Voorwinden, worked as a diplomat. Voorwinden attended *Volksschule* for six classes, *Höhere Schule* for three classes and studied jurisprudence at university between 1927 and 1930. Receiving his degree in 1927, he mustered with the Dutch Army from 1 April 1915 to 15 July 1940. Marrying his fiancée Anna. L., (b. 24.12.1899) on 26 January 1925, the couple had three children up to the point when records ceased in May 1945 and lived in Leiden. Following the defeat of his nation, Voorwinden presented himself for military service in the *Waffen*-SS with officer rank in August 1941. A court investigation was initiated against Voorwinden in May 1943 to examine his 'revolting behaviour' and this recommended his arraignment before the courts martial of the SS- *und Polizei-Gericht* VII, Vienna. Judged guilty of the charges on 13 January 1943, Voorwinden was punished with a term of three months' *Festungshaft* and permitted a period of probation. Surviving the collapse of German resistance in May 1945, Vorwinden died in Holland during December 1947.[10]

2.3 *Strafvollzugslager der* SS- *und Polizei Dachau*

In pre-war discussions with the *Reichsjustizministerium*, the military successfully negotiated for permission to establish prison institutions which was separate from the civil penal system. As a consequence of this decision the German High Command ordered the establishment of three military prisons at Germersheim, Glatz and Torgau on 3 November 1939 and each jail brought into being a *Straflager* (punishment camp) in which to detain those military convicts serving indeterminate terms of *Gefängnis*. Subordinate to each punishment camp were the *Straflagerabteilung* (punishment camp battalion). The prison commandants received instructions to handle the military convicts with great firmness in an effort to impose a lasting deterrent effect on these delinquents, especially those who had considered deserting in battle. The *Straflager* inmates wore the uniform of his military service, less all insignia, rank and shoulder straps, and were permitted to send a letter once every six weeks. With consideration for the amount of daylight, the convicts performed heavy manual labour tasks for ten to fourteen hours a day and worked four hours on Sundays and celebratory days. Each day the inmates undertook military drill without weapons and exercise periods were performed at the beginning and end of work duties (this time was extended during periods when suitable work was unavailable). Reading books and magazines, notice boards and other privileges was forbidden and all electric lights were extinguished at the end of duty time. The *Straflager* staff received orders to use exceptionally strong measures against those inmates caught offending against these regulations, but the use of side arms was forbidden. Convicts received no military pay and ate 70 per cent less food than that given to serving soldiers (daily 650 grams of bread).[11]

Eventually, the *Straflager* become the gateway through which the even the incorrigible military offender, even those held indefinitely in the concentration camps, could be selected for frontline probation. When the time came for the *HA* SS-*Gericht* to construct and operate its own penal institutions, the SS Judges used the punishment camp template to design their own penal regime.[12]

The SS judiciary had been predicated on the basis that the civil and military judiciaries had no understanding for the unique needs of his men, but in 1938, the head of the SS had failed to realise that Adolf Hitler's territorial ambitions would extend the conflict and had not considered that the rapid expansion of his armed forces would result in an exponential growth of his convict population. Plagued by similar levels of disciplinary problems which existed in the military in early 1940, the head of the SS had also become concerned that his existing imprisonment arrangements threatened the institutionalisation of SS and *Polizei* felons. Fearing that fraternising with incorrigible criminals risked fatally undermining their belief in the Nazi world vision, rendering them useless for continued military service in the *Waffen*-SS, Himmler's fears were realised when he received news that military jailers had mistreated his convicts and he was also perturbed to discover that meaningful work had been denied to his convicts. Finally declaring that the existing detention arrangements had proved insufficient for his needs, the SS leader then sought to end these imprisonment arrangements.[13]

The German armed forces stood on the cusp of the invasion of France and the Low Countries in early 1940 when the Nazi leadership demanded that their military convicts serve a portion of their prison sentences at the front as probationers. This announcement included the felons of the *Waffen*-SS and in response, Himmler instructed the *HA* SS-*Gericht* to implement the September 1939 clemency and field probation edict.[14] Published on 18 April 1940, the long titled 'Exercising of Clemency Rights in Punishment Cases, which are the Responsibility of the Courts of the SS and *Polizei*' authorised Himmler and his subordinates to offer front probation to all categories of offender punished with a prison sentence of greater than six months' duration.[15]

With the front probation concept about to play a central part within the court punishment process, the SS leader concluded that the prevailing conditions existing in civil and military institutions would prevent his malefactor's rehabilitation and render them useless for future deployment at the front as probationers. Resolved to end his accommodation with the civil and military authorities in the spring of 1940, the *Reichsführer* then placed the responsibility for detaining his *Zuchthaus* convicts solely in the hands of the *HA* SS-*Gericht* and arranging the removal of inmates from the control of the civil judiciary, General Scharfe was tasked with establishing a prison institution in a secure, but isolated location.[16]

For next couple of years, Himmler's *Gefängnis* category inmates would continue to serve their sentences in civil jails, as no facilities existed for their detention.[17]

Disappointment with the existing imprisonment arrangements, the commander of the *Totenkopfdivision*, *Gruf.* Theodore Eicke, demonstrated his discontentment by formulating his own unique front probation programme in November 1939. Refusing to hand his miscreants into the care of the civil judiciary, Eicke suspended his field court imposed *Gefängnis* and disciplinary arrest penalties and commanded the guilty to join a newly created parole unit, the *Sonderkommando* (special commando) and they undertook dangerous labouring and pioneer tasks. Eicke's experiment ended in the late summer of 1940 when the *Reichsführer* concluded that his probation process offered the parolees little chance of meaningful rehabilitation.[18]

Deciding that the KL Dachau was a suitable location for the new prison institution, Heinrich Himmler commanded the camp command to provide accommodation for a prison which would be termed the *Strafvollzugslager der Waffen*-SS *und Polizei* Dachau.

In its favour, this site provided secrecy and was located conveniently to both the *HA* SS-*Gericht* and the SS-*Kaserne* Munich-Freimann.[19]

The decision to establish a prison inside the environs of the KL Dachau placed this institution at very heart of the Nazi terror state. On the direct orders of the *Reichsführer*, in his capacity as Munich Police President, the KL Dachau had been established on the site of a disused munitions factory ten miles north-west of the city in late March 1933. Designed to isolate political opponents of the Nazi party in Bavaria, the KL Dachau rose to become the prototypal camp to which all others would emulate. No words can adequately describe the horrors of Dachau; designed to cowl its inmates, its omnipotent guards earned for themselves a well-deserved reputation for sadistic abuse and exercised fear of death and torture to subjugate its inmates. By the autumn of 1933 the sadistic SS guards were routinely murdering prisoners and explaining their deaths as 'shot while attempting to escape'.[20]

A month after its opening the camp authorities ordered the conversion of a factory toilet block into a five-individual cell *Kommandantur-Arrest* (headquarters detention) which was also known as the *Lager Arrest* (camp arrest). Here, the SS camp guards detained prisoners sentenced to terms of intensified arrest and isolated prominent inmates from the rest of the camp. The original camp and camp arrest were demolished in 1934 and its bricks used to build a troops barracks with accommodation and a new protective custody camp. At this time a new 22 single cell camp arrest were erected in the camp and due to its squat design, the prisoners referred to this building as the 'bunker' (dungeon). By early 1937 Dachau had once again undergone a radical re-modelling in August 1938 and the camp, now consisting of 32 wooden barracks, was encircled by a neutral zone, a several-yards-high electrified barbed wire fence, intertwined with a medieval style barbed-wire *cheval de fries* and a water-filled canal with high concrete walls. Seven guard towers were positioned around the wire fence and held four carbine armed guards, armed with two machine guns and a powerful search light.[21]

Demolishing the Dachau camp arrest in April 1938, a road was built in its place and the former prisoner and author Paul-Martin Neurath recalled that this led to greenhouses in the southern end of the camp. Dismantling these buildings, the prisoners constructed a new, much larger one-storey 137 cell camp arrest in their place, (parallel to the south side of the *Wirtschaftsgebäude* (housekeeping building, where the canteen and wash rooms were located)). All the windows in the building had stout iron bars attached to the outside and the building contained administrative and utility rooms.[22]

A short road/yard, ending at a brick wall topped with barbed wire, divided the camp arrest from the *Wirtschaftsgebäude* and a double metal gate at the western end of the road divided the prison from the rest of the *Schutzhaftlager*. The camp arrest main entrance was located midway down the yard and this led directly to the reception, interrogation and investigation rooms. Leading east and westwards from the centre of the building were two wings and running the length of the white-painted walled stone parquet floored corridor were heavy wooden doors that secured the cells. Each door had a small hatch with metal bars, a peephole and a metal locking device. The cell number was painted above the door on the wooden frame. Each chamber measured 2.20 metre wide by 2.90 metres deep and 3.10 metres high and contained a radiator, sink, toilet, ventilation duct and two to four bunks. A three-pane window, covered with two horizontal bars and six vertical bars, offered views of a grass space upon which the prominent prisoners exercised.[23] Separated from the rest of the building with a metal bar gate and secured with a metal lock, the SS reserved the far end of the western wing for priests.[24]

Hidden from prying eyes, the camp arrest guards could torture and execute inmates with impunity. The officer responsible for this state of affairs was a former labourer named *Ostuf.* Johann Kantschuster. Supervising the camp arrest between 1933 and 1939, Kantschutser and his underlings quickly earned for themselves a well-deserved reputation for drunkenness and sadism. Believed to have participated in the Röhm executions in late June 1934, the equally barbaric *Hscha.* Joseph Seuss succeeded Kantschuster in 1940. Assigned to the KL Dachau since 1933, for his crimes the Allies hanged Seuss in 1946.[25]

Official documents from this time reveal that in addition to its official name; *Strafvollzugslager der* SS *und Polizei* Dachau, the *HA* SS-*Gericht* and other departments referred to the prison as the SS-*Straflager* Dachau, the *HA* SS-*Gericht* 3K and *Abteilung Zuchthaus* (department prison).[26]

Entrusting responsibility for the new institution to *Stubaf.* Bruno Kegel of SS-*Rechtamt* III in Munich, he delegated the day-to-day running of the prison to the capable *Hscha.* Wolfgang Walther. Appointed to head the *Amt* III prison office on 1 June 1940, Walther remained in this post until 29 April 1945.[27]

Commanding General Scharfe to select prison staff from long-serving, proven troops of the SS-VT, the SS leader voiced his conviction that these 'ideological sound troops' would set a positive example to the inmates. Scharfe then handed Dr Reinecke responsibility for advertising and selecting prison staff from within the ranks of the *Beurkundungsführer* (certification officer) and those recruited for this task remained troops of the SS-VT and their career path followed that of the judges. Expected to work unsupervised, the primary task of the certification officers, who described themselves as *Gerichtsoffiziere*, was to re-educate the inmates and ensure that those who had 'blotted their copybooks' returned to the front as useful soldiers.[28]

Searching for an officer to run the prison, *Stubaf.* Kegel selected a dour-faced Austrian named *Ustuf.* Erich Albert, a member of the SS since July 1931, for the newly-created post of *Leiter* (leader) on 1 May 1940. Reporting to Dachau that same day, Albert established his jail inside the east wing of the camp arrest and arranged for a metal bar gate to be erected in the corridor which isolated his 55 cells from the rest of the building. The prison was accessed via the camp arrest administration office and reception room. To reach their cells the convicts passed the sound-proofed torture room. Requiring guards for this institution, the *Totenkopfstandarte Oberbayern* seconded a handful of junior non-commissioned officers and men to serve in what would be known as the *Straflager Wachzug* (guard section).[29]

In addition to these arrangements the KL Dachau commandant supplied a small office for *Ustuf.* Albert's use and provided him with his own phone extension (telephone

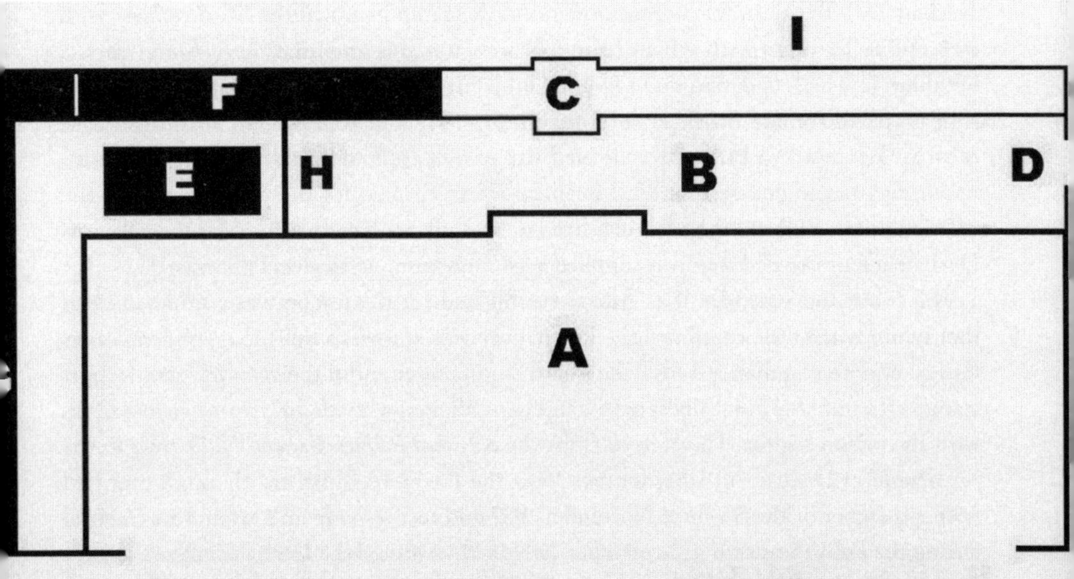
I
F
C
E
H
B
D
A

Dachau 293). Besides these accommodations, the camp provided the SS-*Straflager* with a reception barracks with which to induct new inmates and an *Arrestgebäude* (prison building) in which to detain undisciplined inmates. From his office, Albert and his senior staff prepared inmate fitness reports for the *Amt* III and secured their administrative records. Later, a WVHA officer joined the prison staff to handle its administrative requirements and ensure that local business concerns paid for the convicts labour. The married prison staff and their families lived in SS-built accommodation near the village of Dachau and unmarried staff was supplied accommodation in the local barracks .[30]

The command structure that Albert established for the prison was a microcosm of that in use within the camp system. His deputy was known as the 1. *Lagerführer* (camp leader) and he commanded over the guard commander and the *Rapportführern* (report leaders). To fulfil his task, Albert led a handful of SS men who would become synonymous with the prison regime. Transferred from the SS- *und Polizei-Gericht* IV, Danzig to the SS-*Straflager* Dachau on 1 September 1940 the Bavarian, Edmund Baumgärtner had been a member of the SS since November 1932 and recovered from a wound he received during the Polish invasion in September 1939 he then joined the Dachau staff as the Nr. 1 *Lagerführer*. Two report leaders arrived in Dachau in 1940: Joining the *Waffen*-SS in 1938, the Sudeten lander, Otto Langer arrived in July 1940 and Franz Sturmann, a member of the Austrian SS since August 1932, reported for duty in Dachau in April or June of 1941. Sturmann would rise to occupy many senior posts in the prison service.[31]

Prison Headquarters: Leiter

From its inception and until at least early 1943 the functions of a commandant in the SS-*Straflager* appear to have been undertaken directly by the *Amtschef des Amt* III (no evidence has arisen to suggest that an SS-*Richter* joined the prison staff to perform this role). On site, the prison leader had sole responsibility for the institution and all guards and inmates were subordinate to his command. Prior to considering an inmate's fitness for front probation, the leader supplied the *Amt* III and the sentencing court with a fitness report, which commented on a felon's capability for front probation and included observations on the inmate's general attitude, his willingness to work, the fulfilment of their quota and recorded punishments received during his incarceration. A convict remained in prison until these reports had been evaluated and a judgment had been made about his future deployment. A fitness report was also manufactured for those inmates requiring a transfer to another penal institution, including concentration camps.

Ostuf. Erich Albert (1.5.1940–20.7.1941).
Hstuf. Edmund Baumgärtner (20.7.1941–6.1943).
Hstuf. Erich Albert (6.1943–29.4.1945).[32]

Stellvertreter Lagerführer

The *Stellvertreter Lagerführer* (deputy camp leader) was responsible for maintaining discipline and order in both the *Abteilung* 'Z' and 'G'. In 1943 this post was combined with that of *Führer des Aussenstelle* Allach *der Straflager* SS *und Polizei* Dachau (leader of the branch office).[33]

Hstuf. Edmund Baumgärtner (1.9.1940–20.7.1941).
Ostuf. Franz Sturmann (early 1941–5.1943).
Ostuf. Gottfried Biedermann (5.–9.1943).

Adjutant

The adjutant, or aide-de-camp, expedited on behalf of the leader and worked from Barrack 201 in the Allach branch prison.

Ostuf. Josef Schwaiger (8.11.1944–4.1945).

Kompanieführer

The *Kompanieführer* (company leader) led the *Wachzug*, (guard section), later enlarged to a *Wachkompanie* (guard company) and this unit was tasked with supervising and preventing the escape of the inmates. The company leader also presided over the activities of the various report leaders.

Oscha. Rudolf Hieß (until summer of 1943).

Rapportführer

The *Rapportführer* held non-commissioned officer rank and was also known as the *Zugführer* (section leader). A paramilitary SS title in common use within the camp system, the report leader conducted daily and evening camp roll calls, supervised work details, he maintained discipline in the *Abteilung* 'Z' and 'G' and trained junior personnel.

Lagerarzt

The *Lagerartze* (camp physician) held responsibility for maintaining sanitary conditions in the prison and supervised the health of the prison staff and inmates in the *Lager Lazarett* (camp hospital). Located within the eighteen barracks camp clinic, inmates were also admitted for treatment in the SS-*Lazarett* (SS Hospital) which stood in the SS-Übungslager Dachau. Supplying medical reports for those selected for parole and for those inmates judged suffering from psychological problems, these inmates faced a transfer to the Gießen, or Stettin SS-*Sanitäts-Ersatz-Bataillon* to undergo specialised psychiatric treatment and evaluation. Those the camp physician deemed unfit for hard labour were selected for transfer to the KL *Revier* (clinic).

Name: Dr Med. Cassio Castelpietra.
Last Rank: SS-*Sturmbannführer.*
Born: 19.8.1898 in Lofer, *Kreis* Pinzgau.

NSDAP-Nr.: 1.208.035 (joined 1.6.1932).
SS-Nr.: 311.421 (joined 20.12.1936).
HJ Service: 5.1935–19.12.1936
Prewar Assignments:
Kaiserschützen.Rgt. 1 (Alpine Front) 19.5.1915–31.12.1918.
Freikorps Oberland 5.1921-6.1921.
Gauverband der Pongauer *Heimatvereinigungen* in 1926.
Wartime Assignments:
Waffen-SS from 3.2.1940.
Sanitäts Staffel I. / SS-*Standarte* 34 (Munich) in 1940.
Ergänzungs Amt der Waffen-SS until 15.10.1940.
SS-*Lazarett* Prague until 1.3.1941.
SS-*Standortkommandantur* Munich-Dachau from 1.3.1941.
Sanitäts Amt Berlin on 6.10.1941,
Ersatztransport für die 6. SS-*Gebirgsjäger*-Division *Nord* on 7.10.1941.
Bataillonsärztin des SS-*Aufklärungsabteilung Nord* until 16.7.1942.
8th SS-*Kavallerie*-Division (Debica) 16.7.1942–10.12.1943.
Truppenarzt des SS-*Truppenübungsplatz* Seelager from 10.12.1943.
Sanitäts-Ersatz-Abteilung der Waffen-SS Stettin on 1.1.1944.
SS-*Lazarett* Prague until 20.2.1944.
Straflager der Waffen-SS *und Polizei* Dachau 20.2.1944-29.4.1945.
Promotions:
1.3.1940 SS-*Untersturmführer der Reserve*.
20.4.1940 SS-*Hauptsturmführer der Reserve*.
30.1.1943 SS-*Sturmbannführer der Reserve*.
Decorations & Awards:
0.0.19__ *Medaille 'Winterschlacht im Osten* 1941/42'.

Notes: Obtaining his *Abitur* from *Höhere Schule*, Castelpietra then studied medicine at university. Passing his final exams in 1925, Dr Castelpietra then worked as a private practicioner. Marrying his fiancee Ilenore Froch, (b. 24.6.1906) on 5 May 1929, the couple had five children up to the point when records ceased in May 1945 and lived in Hafling über Rosenheim/Oberbayern. Drafted into the *Waffen*-SS in February 1940, Dr Castelpietra became a military physican with reserve officer rank on 1 March the same year and a recommendation for his promotion was submitted on 11 November 1942:

> An exemplary–, hospital–, family carer and battalion doctor. Approbation in 1925. Flawless execution of his duties in the above mentioned positions. A battalion doctor within the *Nachschubführer* of the SS–*Kavallerie*-Division. He is a quiet, sincere, old Nazi and possesses an immaculate and honest character. Something of a loner with a decent, soldierly and SS suitable attitude in service. Off duty less firm, but always dutiful and responsible.

The promotion was supported by his superiors in Berlin. Posted to the SS-*Straflager* Dachau in February 1944, Dr Castelpietra visited home until 3 March. Taking responsibility for the welfare and care of both the *Straflager* Dachau and *Aussenstelle* Allach inmates, he was appointed the camp physician for the SS-*Straflager* on 30 May 1944. The physicians former convict clerk, Johann Ott, recalled that he remained in this post until 28 April 1945. Surrendering to the US Army, they had placed Dr Castelpietra in the Kornwestheim prisoner of war camp near Ludwigsberg by 5 August 1945. His court process completed in 1948, Dr Castelpietra once again took up private practice and became involved with the folk music and costumiery (Blackbird singing). The chairman of the *Trachtenverein* St Johann *im* Pongau between 1963 and 1964, Dr Castelpietra served as the *Gauobmänner* of the Pongauer *Heimatvereinigungen* between 1966 and 1968 (*Volkstumsforscher* with the *Bauernkapelle* Bischofshofen).[34]

SS-Sanitätsdienstgrade

The SS-*Sanitätsdienstgrade* (SS medical orderly), or SDG, was usually a non-commissioned officer who assisted the medical staff with their duties. A combination of convict and non-convict medical orderlies were utilised in Dr Castelpietra's clinic. Liberating Dachau in April 1945, the US Army discovered a large number of prison inmates hiding on the hospital wards.

Hscha. Alfred Poltz, a 25- year-old Bavarian in 1945. Dr Castelpietra's assistant, Poltz was last seen in Dachau on 26 April. 'I am going to a farmer's family that I know about 500 yards from here. I intend to continue my studies at the Munich University' were his last words to Ott.

Rttf. Jackstieß; a 28- year-old in 1945 and limped on right leg. The chief clerk at the hospital, it was Jackstieß who reportedly burned all prison documents on or around 24 April 1945. Last seen by Ott in the Dachau hospital on the day the US troop's arrival, the former convict then informed his American interrogators that Jackstieß remained working in the Dachau hospital for a short time after the camps liberation.

Uscha. Berberich; a 45-years-old in 1945. Berberich had worked at the *Zweiglager* Hammerweg until 1 April 1945. Ott, describing him having an ugly appearance and a round fat face, last saw Berberich at the Dachau hospital on the day of the US occupation and was told that he worked there for a short time after the liberation.

Oscha. Brand; a 38-year-old Prussian in 1945. By profession a pharmacist, Ott last saw Brand in the Dachau hospital on 29 April 1945.

Rttf. Friedrich; a 36-year-old ethnic German. By profession a pharmacist, Ott last saw him in the KL Dachau clinic on 27 April 1945.

Rttf. Nitsche; a Bavarian, he had an artificial right leg and was last seen by Ott at the Heilbronn Prisoner of war camp in July 1945.[35]

Verwaltungsführer

The *Verwaltungsführer* (administrative officer) had responsibility for maintaining the prison's records and ensuring that inmate labour was made available for business enterprises.

Name: Karl Martin.
Last Rank: SS-*Untersturmführer.*
Born: 21.11.1920 in Feistritz, Drau/Villach.
NSDAP-Nr.: 6.381.461 (joined 15.5.1938).
SS-Nr.: 496.364 (joined 1.10.1938).
HJ Service: 1.1.1935-30.9.1938.
Wartime Assignments:
III. / SS-*Standarte Der Führer* from 1.10.1938.
SS-*Kaserne* Graz late 1942/early 1943.
5. *Kriegs-Reserve-Führer-Anwärter-Lehrgang* SS-*Junkerschule* Bad Tölz 1.5.–31.8.1943.
SS-*Kaserne* Klagenfurt in 1944.
SS-*Straflager* Dachau, *Aussenstelle* Allach 15.1.1941–28.4.1945.
Promotions:

0.0.1940	SS-*Rottenführer der Waffen*-SS (*Aktiv*).
1.12.1941	SS-*Unterscharführer der Waffen*-SS (*Aktiv*).
1.7.1944	SS-*Hauptscharführer der Waffen*-SS (*Aktiv*).
30.1.1944	SS-*Standartenoberjunker.*
9.11.1944	SS-*Untersturmführer der Waffen*-SS (*Aktiv*).

Decorations & Awards:

0.0.19__	SS-*Ehrenwinkel für alte Kämpfer.*
0.0.19__	SA-*Sportsabzeichen in Bronze.*
0.0.19_	*Die Medaille zur Erinnerung an den* 1. Oktober 1938 (Sudetenland).
0.0.19__	*Die Medaille zur Erinnerung an den* 13. März 1938 (Austria).
28.7.1940	1939 *Eisernes Kreuz II. Klasse.*
28.7.1940	*Verwundetenabzeichen,* 1939 *in Schwarz.*

Notes: Attending *Volksschule* for eight classes between 1927 and 1931, Martin studied at a *Bürgerschule* until 1935 and then attended *Fachschule* for two classes. Leaving full-time education, Martin then worked as a salesman and mustered with the *Hitlerjugend* from 1935. Attending a youth gathering at Wolfsburg from 18 to 24 December 1936, his political activities led the Klagenfurt public prosecutor to indict him in accordance with paragraph § 5 OStGB on 11 February 1937. Judged guilty, Martin was sentenced to a short prison punishment. Joining the Klagenfurt Nazi party in May 1938, Martin found that he had no job opportunities in Austria and decided to cross the border illegally into Bavaria. Accepted into the SS-VT in October 1938, Martin participated in the 1939 march into Czechoslovakia, the invasion of Poland in September 1939 and the spring 1940 Western campaigns until wounded on 13 May 1940. Recovering from his injuries at the Graz-West barrack, from here, Martin applied to the RuSHA for permission to marry his fiancée Elfriede L., (b. 19.1.1921 in Remschenik). Receiving the required permission, the couple married on 5 May 1943 and had three children up to the point when records ceased in May 1945. Appointed an officer candidate on 10 January 1944, Martin passed the final examination at a reserve officer training course and received a promotion to officer rank in November 1944. He remained in Klagenfurt until his transfer as a WVHA administrative officer to the SS-*Straflager* Dachau, *Aussenstelle* Allach in January 1941. Speaking in the summer of 1945, the former inmate Johann Ott recollected that he had identified Martin to the 17th CIC Detachment in the Heilbronn PWTE.[36]

Interrogated by his captors in 1945, a former convict recollected that *Ustuf.* Rieth was the *Gerichtsoffiziere des Straflager der* SS *und Polizei* and described him having greying hair and a slender built.[37]

Born in Pforzeim on 14.4.1890, *Ustuf.* Artur Rieth joined the Nazi Party on 1.5.1937 (NSDAP-Nr.: 5.611.759) and the *Allgemeine*-SS in 1933 (SS-Nr.: 233.111). Joining the SS-TV on 31.8.1939, he served in the KL Dachau in 1939 and led the KL Dachau *Abteilung* VI (instruction) in December 1943. Rieth spent most of the war assigned to the KL Dachau. His office held responsibility for the training of prisoners for specialised tasks from December 1943. Faking an illness, Rieth hid in the Dachau SS-*Lazarett* in April 1945.[38]

Published in response to the publication of the edict 'Regulation on the Execution of Prison Sentences for an offence committed during the War' from 11 June 1940, a *Reichsjustizministerium* supplementary edict for the sentencing of offenders was circulated on 20 September 1940 which commanded that any act committed during the war would be assumed to have taken place after 1 September 1939 at 5.45 a.m.[39]

Induction

Opening in the spring of 1940, for most of the remaining year the SS-*Straflager* Dachau only accepted court-sentenced *Zuchthaus* felons. Considered to be the most serious miscreants in the penal system, these offenders hailed from the field units, the security services, the uniform and the plains clothes branches of the *Ordnungspolizei*. Later, the prison would accept malefactors from the *Feuerwehr*, the *Luftschutzpolizei* and the *Deutsche Rot Kreuz*. Convicts sent to the SS-*Straflager* to serve their prison sentence arrived singly under armed escort, or in small groups from their previous unit, office or place of detention. Travelling by car or train, the felons were kept separate from other travellers and their feeding was left to the discretion of their escorts. The offender's personal papers and court documents normally accompanied him on his journey to prison.[40]

Those punished to a term of *Zuchthaus* for committing offences such as undermining the war effort, or militarily unworthiness, continued to serve their penalties in the Emslandlager and they remained here until *HA* SS-*Gericht* penal institutions were able to accept them in early 1942.[41]

Bending to enter the camp through the small *Jourhaus* gate, upon which was written in wrought iron the ironic legend 'Work Frees', the newly-arrived convict then reported to the reception barracks. Here, his personal possessions, medals and uniforms were confiscated and a former earth-brown *Landespolizei* uniform, without insignia was issued in its place. Handed a brown *kratchen*, a peak-less beret, and plain greatcoat, the convict also accepted a two piece white fatigue uniform which he wore during work details.[42]

The inmate's eligibility for military service was suspended from their moment of arrival and it was usual practice to notify his family of their incarceration. The pay and the benefits of *Zuchthaus* felons were usually withheld and the family notified of this decision. With the *Reichsführer*'s approbation, the pay and benefits were continued if their removal had the potential to cause the family undue distress (those serving *Gefängnis* sentences continued to receive their pay and benefits). In exceptional circumstances, an inmate could apply and be granted leave on compassionate grounds, or to marry their fiancées. When released from detention, the inmate's pay and benefits were resumed and his family informed of this change.[43]

Disciplinary Punishments

To enforce discipline, the staff resorted to the imposition of the *Strafexerzieren* (punishment drill) for up to an hour at a time. Presented with further evidence of indiscipline against prison rules, or the inmate demonstrating a failure to carry out an appointed task could result in the deprivation of food, or the imposition of a period of intensified arrest, which was carried out in the *Arrestgebäude*. A single man cell, the offender lay in darkness for eleven hours straight and one hour per day was provided to permit the punished to exercise and clean their cell. All inmate penalties were announced during parades and the details posted on the prison notice board. Continued disobedience normally resulted in the inmate's transfer to a concentration camp as a prisoner. A draconian measure, there is evidence that those convicts punished in this fashion did survive the experience.[44]

The names of those attempting, or successfully escaping from the prison were reported to the SS- *und Polizei-Gericht* I, Munich and the would-be, or actual escapee was then indicted on suspicion of committing an absence without leave offence or for committing an act of desertion. The court usually imposed a capital punishment for these offences. On one occasion, a *Gefängnis* and *Zuchthaus* felon colluded together to escape from the prison. Successfully escaping their guards, the pair evaded capture, stole a car and drove to the city of Innsbruck with the intention of making their way to Italy. Here, during the blackout, they stole fuel for the car and prowled the city streets searching for valuables to steal. The desperate escapees finally resorted to robbing a woman of her valuables in the street, but this rash act alerted the local *Polizei* to their presence and a manhunt successfully apprehend them. Returning to Dachau, both escapees then found themselves arraigned before the Munich tribunal. Judging the pair guilty of desertion, the theft of the car, petrol and robbery, the court sentenced both to death and their execution by firing squad was carried out as a deterrent to other would be escapers.[45]

In February 1943 the *Reichsführer* commanded that military unworthy convicts caught attempting to escape would no longer be court prosecuted for desertion, but would face trial for the less crime of taking an unauthorised leave. Concurring with the *HA* SS-*Gericht*, Himmler announced his belief that the judicial punishment for attempted unauthorized leave was a suitable penalty for would-be escapees.[46]

Capital Punishment

The SS-*Straflager* Dachau held under lock and key those offenders awaiting confirmation of a court-imposed capital punishment and it was the responsibility of *Stubaf.* Meder's office at the *Amt* III to supply the prison with the order to undertake an execution. Speaking to his captors in 1945, the former medical clerk Johann Ott claimed that each day *Hstuf.* Erich Albert handed him a signed mimeographed list of transfers upon which was written the names of all new convict arrivals, those departing from the *Straflager* and the condemned that had been selected for execution. Recalling that the condemned names were denoted with a 'T', Ott claimed that executions took place three, or four times a week and the number of condemned varied between five and fifteen men. Delivering the list to the office of *Ostuf.* Schwaiger in the branch prison at Allach, Ott would then accept Albert, or *Hscha.* Seipel's telephone call on the night prior to the execution date and recalled that they always communicated same message; 'the doctor in charge and one SDG are to appear at the place of execution at 6.45 a.m. Rope and chloride of lime is to be brought along.' In the presence of the trial judge, witnesses and the garrison doctor all executions were undertaken by the prison guards at the Herbertshausen rifle range. Returning to the clinic, Ott assured his interrogator that the attending medical orderly always described to him how the victims had died.[47]

Once the guards had performed their onerous task, the firing squad commander then gave the *coup de grace* and the attending physician confirmed that the death had taken place. The attending judge then transmitted the date and time of death via telegram to the SS-*Richter beim* RF-SS and the bodies were interred in the cemetery at Leitenberg. Talking in 1967, a former prison officer, Rudolf Heiß, recalled witnessing only one execution and this took place in Dachau and involved a Viennese SS man named Rudolf Danzer for attempting twice to desert. Further, Heiß claimed that this was the only execution that he witnessed throughout the entire war.[48]

Speaking in 1947, the former *HA* SS-*Gericht* officer, Karl Lang, recollected that 56 Austrian nationals of the *Luftschutzpolizei*, who had collected contributions for their circle which was engaged in illegal work against the Nazi system, were convicted of high treason by the *Oberste* SS- *und Polizei-Gericht* in 1943 and of their number, six were sentenced to death and 50 punished with terms of *Zuchthaus*. Lang voiced his conviction that the capital judgments were fully carried out.[49]

In the latter war years this officer was responsible for reporting executions directly to the SS-*Richter beim* RF-SS:

Name: Franz Zeber.
Last Rank: SS-*Obersturmführer.*
Born: 13.2.1914 in Sachsenberg, *Kreis* Spittal/Kärnton.
NSDAP-Nr.: 8.801.052 (joined 1.7.1941).
SS-Nr.: 473.361 (joined 20.4.1938).
Promotions:
30.1.1944 SS-*Untersturmführer der Reserve.*
30.1.1945 SS-*Obersturmführer der Reserve.*
Prewar Assignments:
SS-VT from 20.4.1938.
Wartime Assignments:
3. / SS-VT FLAK *Kompanie* in 9.1939.
3. / SS-*Verplegung-Ersatz-Abteilung* until 1.3.1940.
SS-*Reserve-Abteilung Für Verwaltungsaufgaben* from 18.10.1941.
Waffen-SS *Hauptamt* SS-*Gericht* on 16.4. 1944,
SS- *und Polizei-Gericht* I, Munich 16.4.1944 (*Beurkundungsführer* training).
SS- *und Polizei-Gericht* XIX, Belgrade from 4.2.1944.
Hauptamt SS-*Gericht Amt* III in 1945?
Decorations & Awards:
0.0.19__ 1939 *Eisernes Kreuz II. Klasse.*
0.0.19__ *Kriegsverdienstkreuz II. Klasse mit Schwertern.*
0.0.19__ *Verwundetenabzeichen*, 1939 *in Silber.*
0.0.19__ *Die Medaille zur Erinnerung an den* 1. Oktober 1938 (Sudetenland).

Notes: Attending *Volksschule* for three classes, Zeber then found employment in the logging industry and joined the SS-VT in April 1938. He appears to have remained unmarried until May 1945. Participating in the Sudetenland march, Zeber took part in the invasion of Poland and seriously wounded during this campaign, doctors amputated his right arm above the elbow. Receiving a prosthesis in Germany, Zeber's rehabilitation was then undertaken by the orthopaedic clinic of the Munich SS-*Reserve-Lazarett*. Judged possessing a physical capability of 11/z on 1 March 1940, Zeber was accepted into the *HA* SS-*Gericht* in April 1944 and undertook his *Beurkundungsführer* training at the Munich tribunal. He applied to the Welfare Commando in the RuSHA *Abt*. I for a disabled soldier's identify card in the late summer of 1944. Supplied to him in September the same year, (disabled category III), at this time, Zeber had deployed with the Munich tribunal and he represented this office at a number of executions that took place at Hebertshausen. Writing on 27 January 1945, the *HA* SS-*Gericht Amt* III adjutant, *Stubaf.* Langbehn, requested they handled the re-enlistment of Zeber in a unit of the *Waffen*-SS, but his request was denied on 14 February 1945.[50]

Daily Life

The SS-*Straflager* Dachau had been conceived to offer the most incorrigible felons of Himmler's fighting troops a hard labour punishment regime and the prisons daily routine ensured that the inmates had very little time for reflection, or any opportunity for mischief-making. Absolute obedience and silence was demanded in the prison at all times and each convict was expected to fulfil his work norm and partake in daily exercises. The inmates' day began at 5.00 a.m. in the summer and at 6.00 a.m. in winter. Washed and dressed, the felons sat for breakfast, which consisted of a cup of coffee, a slice of bread, about fifteen grams of margarine and when available a little preserve. Breakfast consumed, the convicts then undertook the cleaning of their cells and uniforms in preparation for the first of two dreaded daily inspections. At an appointed time the report leader examined the cells and felons' lockers in an effort to discover infractions against the regulations. These included writing material, money, possession of banned material, a dirty uniform, an improperly made bed or a dirty cell. Recording the names of the disobedient for future punishment, the report leader then commanded the inmates to assemble outside the prison block at around 7.00 a.m. and marched the felons to the Dachau parade ground for their first of three periods of exercise and drill. The report leader issued all instructions using a series of blasts on a whistle. Different whistle blows indicated a change of exercise and failure to properly execute the mix of calisthenics and marching would result in a repeat of the exercise regime. The first exercise period had usually completed by 9.00 a.m. and the convicts were then permitted a ten minutes rest.[51]

Mounting his bicycle, the report leader then led the inmates out of the camp to the gravel pit, located some five kilometres distance. Marching at the pace of 90 steps per minute, the report leader occasionally commanded his charges to run some of the route. Remaining in the prison were those assigned to the camp kitchen, those detained in the *Arresträumen* and inmates reporting sick. Reaching the gravel pit at around 9.40 a.m., a variety of labouring tools and wheel barrows was distributed to the felons and in complete silence they dug gravel from depressions that were often many yards deep and filled with water when it rained. When deep enough, the convicts dug terraces into the pit sides and evacuated gravel, sand or quartz upwards. Reaching the top, the quarried gravel was shovelled into wheelbarrows and tipped into prisoner-drawn wagons. The German Excavation and Quarrying Company Ltd was a large SS-owned concern and the convicts work rate/norm for this business had been calculated by the Organisation Todt. When gravel digging was unavailable the report leader would attempt to find other labouring/quarrying tasks or organise further drill.[52]

The first period of work ended at midday and the names of those felons who had failed to complete their work norm was recorded for future punishment. Marched back to the prison for their hour-long lunch, the inmate's fare normally consisting of a quart of water stew, what the inmates described as *Eintopfgericht*. The ingredients varied, but this meal usually consisted of potatoes, peas, or beans with another vegetable and less occasionally meat or fish. Following lunch, the convicts gathered again on the parade ground at around 1.30 p.m. for their second spell of calisthenics and drill, or were directed to the prison building to clean or repair the institution's environs. The exercise period completed, the report leader once again led the felons back to the gravel pit to undertake a further two hours of quarrying. Returning to the prison for their 6.00 p.m. evening meal, this consisted of a sweet tea, bread and either a herring, cheese or sausage. This course was followed with a pudding such as prunes with rice or porridge. Food was the inmates constant worry and it is known that their families were permitted to send them food parcels on special holidays (cigarettes were banned, but much sought after).[53]

Concluding their evening meal, the felons spent the rest of the evening cleaning their cells and uniforms in preparation for the much-feared evening inspection. The search for dirty cells, uniforms and banned contraband began at 8.00 p.m. and this was an opportunity for the report leader to impose punishment drill on those who had not fulfilled their 'norm', or had committed prison rule infractions. Speaking on this subject, a former convict recalled that finding anything amiss, the report leader would fly into an artificial rage, overturn carefully made beds, empty lockers and throw bucket, after bucket of water into the brown tiled cells. Once the occupants and their belongings were thoroughly soaked, the report leader left them in peace to clean up the mess and visited the neighbouring cell to inspect it in a similar fashion. Typically, the irascible report leader would re-visit a cleaned up cell to conduct another inspection and engage in this charade again. The evening inspection usually ended at midnight, permitting the inmates around five hours sleep. Ground down by this regime, it is without irony, that the convicts knew the prison as the *Knochenmühle* (bone mill).[54]

At times in winter when the ground became too hard for quarrying, the felons then replaced shovelling for military drill and exercise on the parade ground, even if covered in snow. Inmates injured during these exercises were placed on medical report and then assigned to light duties, such as preparing meals in the *Wirtschaftsgebäude*.[55]

The inmates of the military *Feldstraflager* worked only four hours on a weekend and this rule was probably extended to the SS-*Straflager* Dachau. There is some evidence that the prison staff reduced the convict's workday on Sundays to enable them to clean personal equipment and uniforms and carry out essential building maintenance (these reduced duties permitted the guards to spend time with their families). Later, a handful of felons reported to the *HA* SS-*Gericht* HQ in Munich and Prien am Chiemsee to perform administrative work, work as mechanics in the car pool and courier internal mail.[56]

Abteilung Gefängnis

Originally designed to imprison *Zuchthaus* inmates, Dachau quickly became the focus of the *Reichsführer* plan to detain long-sentenced *Gefängnis* category offenders. His desire to implement a policy of a mixed jail/probation sentencing programme for his felons resulted in the SS leader deciding at the end of 1940 to remove this category of felon from the custody of the civil and military authorities and detain them inside Dachau. Himmler had become convinced of the need for this measure when made aware of the sentencing concerns of the chief of the SS-*Verfügungstruppe* field court in late 1940. Growing increasingly perturbed at the rise in the numbers of young soldiers that he had punished with terms of *Gefängnis*, *Stubaf.* Wetzling, with the approval of his *Gerichtsherr*, spoke with the SS-*Richter beim* RF-SS, Eberhard Hinderfeld and Dr Hans Braußе on this issue at the SS-*Rechtamt* on 4 November 1940 and in an effort to avoid sending his miscreants to prison, Wetzling suggested that they was employed in factories. Agreeing with the judge's assessment, the Organisation Todt was then contacted to establish whether they would accept these felons into their organisation as labourers. Discussing this issue with *Ministerialrat*, Franz Xaver Dorsch, in December 1940, the SS-*Richter beim* RF-SS sought his opinion on the feasibility of the proposal and asked whether convicts would be permitted to work in France, he wished to know if their deployment with the Org. Todt would be considered a form of probation and questioned whether the time spent labouring would contribute to the felon's military service. Though expressing interest in the idea, the Org. Todt required that the *HA* SS-*Gericht* supply them with a written order before accepting the first transport of convicts. Ultimately, Wetzling's proposal was rejected and no convicts were sent to the Org. Todt. As a consequence of the failure of these talks, the leader of the SS then commanded the expansion of the SS-*Straflager* Dachau to be undertaken at the end of 1940 to enable the institution to accommodate troops punished with terms of *Gefängnis* exceeding three months' duration.[57]

Selecting a piece of land situated east of the *Wirtschaftsgebäude* on which to construct the extension, camp prisoners built this new building along a north-south axis of the camp arrest. The officer in charge of the Dachau construction office at this time was *Ostuf.* Karl Weitzel and he almost certainly designed and oversaw the construction of the new wing. Congratulated for his efforts in the construction of the new wing, The new wing on the bunker for the SS prison must have expanded the prison capacity by at least another fifty new cells, depending obviously on their size and layout. The task of building the new annexe had been completed by mid-February 1941 and was accepting its first inmates in early March the same year.[58]

In the spring of 1941 the prison was detaining three categories of convicts:

- *Abteilung Zuchthaus*; convicts punished with hard labour sentences,
- *Abteilung Gefängnis*; convicts punished with short prison sentences,
- *Abteilung Verurteilte mit Straflagerverwahrung*; those awaiting trial or sentencing.[59]

Commanding the SS-*Hauptämter* chiefs and divisional *Gerichtsherrn* to begin sending their court punished *Gefängnis* offenders, those with sentences of greater than three months, to the *Abteilung* 'G' of the SS-*Straflager* Dachau on 14 June 1941, at this time, Himmler forbad his generals from sending their malefactors directly to front probation units as this decision had become the sole responsibility of the *Amt* III. The head of the SS commanded the transfer of rehabilitated probationers from the SS-*Pionier-Reserve-Bataillon* in Dresden to the SS-Division *Reich* on 29 July 1941 and those failing to have rehabilitated themselves were ordered to the SS-*Straflager* Dachau.[60]

Gefängnis offenders punished with less than three month sentences and stationed outside of Germany's borders continued to serve their sentences in civil institutions, in

Standortarrestanstalten, the divisional *Strafvollstreckungszug*, SS-*Hauptämter*, barracks cells and other types of suitable arrest rooms. Post-war, this former Dachau *Gefängnis* inmate recalled his first impressions of the new prison wing:

> [...] When I arrived in Dachau there was heavy snow. That must have been in January. It was about nine in the morning and we were still in Munich at the railway station. I was accompanied by an *Uscha.* who had been granted leave. Under escort, he and I drank a glass of beer together. Then he took me to Dachau to deliver me there. Arriving in the reception barracks, I can still recall the food, it seems that as a newcomer I received potatoes with gravy for lunch. There was plenty... Oh man, here they had finally given me enough to eat! But no, ten days later I could have eaten twice the amount. On the first day I was taken into the cell block.
>
> On the second day I was brought into the barrack of the *Abteilung* 'G'. In the cell block were the *Zuchthaus* people, also some convicts and those who had been sentenced to death for desertion. In the *Abteilung* 'G' was also those who had received *Gefängnis* sentences. The next day I began my duties. We had to make do as soldiers serving with the spade. As soldiers, we were still under oath. I did not know at the time that I had been expelled out of the SS. I only learned this recently. About the prison camp, so much to me has remained in my memory because it was a very eventful and difficult time for me. One cannot say what the worst was. This has also changed with time. In my opinion today, the worst of it was the mainly pointless jobs to undertake. To undertake absolutely meaningless work that consumes humans. But that is still better than to not be busy at all. [It is worse] to be able to think ahead for months, years or just days without nothing to do. That is what I have myself come to believe.[61]

1941–43: The Years of Victory

In 1941 the *HA* SS-*Gericht* had almost established its hegemony over the front probation process and within a month of its opening, the *Abteilung* 'Z' and 'G' held 150 and 250 inmates respectively. Other sources report that both institution held a total of 320 inmates, [62] and 182 convicts are known to have been detained in the prison on 25 June 1942 (106 *Gefängnis* and 29 *Zuchthaus* category inmates).[63]

Given Himmler's interest in the development of the prison there remains a possibility that visiting the KL Dachau with the Dutch collaborator Anton Mussert on 20 January 1941, that he may have used this opportunity to inspect the *Straflager* before sampling food at the *Wirtschaftsgebäude*.[64]

Who were these early entrants to the *Abteilung* 'G'? Born in Hagen/Westphalia on 14 January 1922, SS-*Mann* Wilhelm Müller mustered with the 2. / SS-*Pionier-Bataillon* 2 in the summer of 1940 when he found himself accused of committing an unauthorised leave offence and carrying out three cases of comrade embezzlement. Arraigned before the courts martial of the SS- *und Polizei-Gericht* V, Dresden on 8 July 1940, the tribunal judged Müller guilty of the charges and sentenced him to a term of six years' *Gefängnis* (case Nr. St. L. 93/1940). His sentence confirmed, Müller then reported to the

SS-*Straflager* Dachau to serve his penalty. Permitted fourteen days' home leave during 1943, Müller then returned to the front to undertake his period of probation. Seeing active service in a *Bewährungsabteilung*, Müller was later wounded by a grenade splinter in his right shoulder and recovered from his wounds in the Prague SS-*Lazarett*. From here, Müller obtained permission to undertake a short home leave and at its conclusion, he then returned to the *Bewährungsabteilung* and perished fighting with the SS-Rgt. *Kalthofen* in the Danzig Kessel during March 1945.[65]

The construction of the *Abteilung* 'G' was of great interest to General Paul Scharfe and shortly after its opening he visited the prison to conduct an official review. The inspection was photographed by *Stubaf.* Friedrich Franz Bauer and his images capture the general, the camp commandant, *Ostubaf.* Alex Piorkowski, and a coterie of camp staff, *Polizei* and court officers walking in the yard between the camp arrest and gathering in the *Wirtschaftsgebäude*. Arriving at his destination, *Ostuf.* Albert, greeted General Scharfe with the Nazi salute and then invited him to appraise his great-coated staff. Around 100 inmates then received the order to parade in the courtyard and under the watchful eye of the sallow-faced Albert, they stood to attention along the southern wall of the *Wirtschaftsgebäude* while the grim-faced general to review their gaunt, great-coated-clad convict ranks. The general's inspection completed, the inmates then marched to the camp parade to perform military drill with spades. Here, under the keen eyes of their visitors, Albert and his staff put their charges through their paces. General Scharfe completed his tour of the institution with an inspection of the camp's pristine kitchens. Here, the inmates had prepared a lunch which the visitors ate in the building. During the visit, *Ostubaf.* Piorkowski appeared happy, but accused of corruption shortly after the general's inspection, he was removed from his command and the SS leader dismissed him ignominiously from the SS.[66]

In July 1941 *Ostuf.* Erich Albert and Otto Langer accompanied a portion of the *Abteilung-Gefängnis* to a newly built, larger prison near the city of Danzig. In their wake *Ostuf.* Baumgärtner was selected to replace Albert as the prison leader in August 1941.[67]

> Among those held in the prison at this time was an eighteen-year-old felon named Stulner (b. 28.3.1924). Arraigned before the courts martial of the SS- *und Polizei-Gericht* IV, Danzig in 1941 (case Nr. St. L. I 494/1941), the tribunal judged Stuhler guilty of the charges and sentenced to a term of five years' *Zuchthaus*.

Another inmate, a non-commissioned officer of the *Polizei-Bataillon* 306, Fritz S. was assigned to its second company when he found himself indicted for insubordination and libel. Surviving the war, Fritz S. explained the circumstances surrounding his arrest and indictment:

> [...] At this time I was not in action and was sentenced to five months KL Dachau early 1941. A skirmish with shooting took place in the spring of 1941 in which I led the third section. It was wet and the men were frozen in the cold weather. The company

> commander was Waltz, but the manoeuvre was actually under the command of *Leutnant* S. I called on S. to stop shooting because of bad weather, but he did not respond. Then telling him that he should lick my ass, S. then forwarded this message to the battalion headquarters. The *Gerichtsoffiziere* was Plantius. I was imprisoned in the castle and then convicted by the higher SS and *Polizei* Court in Krakow to five months in a *Straflager.* I was then locked up again at the castle until the *Reichsführer*-SS upheld the sentence. After that I was taken to Dachau. Overall, I spent eight months in prison and I served the full penalty sentence. After my release, I had to return to active duty with my losses and transferred to the *Polizei-Ersatz-Bataillon* 121.

Questioned in 1963, Fritz S. made no secret of his disgust at the poor conditions that existed in Dachau:

> [...] My conviction took place as a consequence of errosion of fighting ability. The food was lousy in the KZ. Here, I had lost so much weight, that when I returned back to my unit, my comrades could no longer recognized me. In addition, we undertook punishment drill throughout the day. I can still remember a case where a prisoner, a comrade serving time for theft, was sentenced to death for stealing two potatoes and before our eyes was shot within 24 hours.

The following year, Josef Kotzab found himself standing on trial before the SS- *und Polizei-Gericht* VI, Prague and judged guilty of the charges, the tribunal imposed a term of *Zuchthaus* on him, which was amended to a period of *Gefängnis* on 19 September 1944. Serving his sentence in the SS-*Straflager*, Kotzab later applied and was accepted for front probation in the SS-*Sonderbrigade Dirlewanger.*[68]

Among those detained in the prison during 1941 was a felon who had formally been a concentration camp guard: Born in Trostberg bei Trauenstein on 13 August 1913, by trade Simon Kiern worked as a saddle maker and was married with two children. Deployed with the I. / *Infanterie*-Rgt. 19 between October 1932 and March 1936, Kiern was promoted to the rank of *Gefreiter* on 1 October 1934. Leaving military service, he then accepted a post at the Passing branch office of the Munich telegraph from 15 March 1936. Mustering with the *Allgemeine*-SS from 1937, Kiern was admitted into the communications branch of the SS-VT just prior to the outbreak. A signals instructor until 1939, Kiern then joined a unit in Bohemia and received orders to report to the KL Dachau in 1941. Here, *Hscha.* Kiern became a *Blockführer* in the camp in July 1941 and a clerk in the camp administration in early November the same year. Assigned to the camp censor until early December 1941, Kiern was denounced at this time for stealing ten cigarettes from a letter and his act of theft resulted in his remand detention for six weeks. Subsequently arraigned before the courts martial of the SS- *und Polizei-Gericht* I, Munich and judged guilty of theft, Kiern was placed on remand detention in the SS-*Straflager* Dachau to await confirmation of his sentence. Transferred to Danzig-Matzkau in mid-1943, Kiern served a portion of his sentence and accepted front probation on 12 February 1945. Surrendering to the US Army on 30 April 1945, the military authorities brought Kiern to trial on 15 November 1945 for the mistreatment of prisoners and the participation in three executions of prisoners. Judged guilty of the charges, Kiern was sentenced to death on 13 December 1945 and hanged for his crimes at the US military prison Landberg on 28 May 1946.[69]

It was the task of the prison staff to oversee the removal of convicts from their institution and from its inception and until the end of June 1942, the prison leader and *HA* SS-*Gericht* approved the release of 47 inmates.[70]

Telexing the prison authorities in the summer of 1942, the SS- *und Polizei-Gericht* VII, Vienna requested a fitness report for the inmate Franz Stiebes who they noted was due for release on 5 July 1942. Contacting the SS-*Straflager* Dachau on 1 October 1942, the chief judge of the SS- *und Polizei-Gericht* X, Den Haag, *Stubaf.* Härtel, revealed that he had yet to decide whether the convict *Oberleutnant d. Pol.* Heinz Nellen would serve his prison sentence in Dachau or Matzkau (St. L. II 279/41). Incarcerated in Matzkau, Nellen would accept front probation in early 1943.[71]

The war ground on and Himmler's judiciary began accepting responsibility for a greater number of uniformed services and the SS-*Straflager* Dachau began inducting convicts who did not share the ideals of the pre-war SS: Born in Osnabrück on 25 May 1901, Friedrich Deters was by profession a glass cutter, had been a member of a *Freikorps*. He married his fiancée Anna F. in 1925 and the couple had three children and lived in Westerberg. Reporting to the recruitment office in July 1940, the judged Deters partially disabled and rejected him for military service. Assessed fit only for deployment with the' training reserve II', Deters then volunteered for service in the *Luftschutzkorps*. Denounced for making defeatist comments, Deters was arrested by the *Gestapo* on 13 August 1942 and detained in the Osnabrück *Gefängnis* to await trial. The Osnabrück *Amtsgericht* indicted Deters for committing an act that threatened to erode the nation's fighting ability on 9 March 1943 (case Nr. 15 GS 297/42).

Judging that the *HA* SS-*Gericht* was the competent authority to punish Deters, he then found himself arraigned before the courts martial of the SS- *und Polizei-Gericht* II Düsseldorf on 6 May the same year. The presiding judge's summation expressed his view that Deters was a communist who had exercised his subversive activities for at least two years and judged that the defendant had defamed the leadership and undermined his comrade's belief in victory (the court record noted that *Frau* Deters had reported her husband for making disparaging remarks about Hitler and expressing negative opinions about the war). Judged guilty of the charges, the Düsseldorf tribunal imposed a term of eight years *Gefängnis* on Deters and he reported to the SS-*Straflager* Dachau on 23 July 1943. His last letter, written to his wife from the prison on 2 January 1945, reveals that he had accepted front probation with the SS-*Sonderbrigade Dirlewanger*. A little later, Deters transferred to a concentration camp to await his transfer to the front. Writing to Deter's wife on 6 March 1945, the brigade reported that her husband had died from a bullet in the heart while training at the battle school at the *Aussenstelle* Lieberrose and had been buried with full military honours. Recognising that her husband was a victim of Nazi terror, the city of Osnabrück awarded Deters widow the status of victim on 3 February 1948 and she was granted an honorary pension of 100 *Reichsmark* per month. Later, this compensation was stopped on the grounds that Deters had been court-martialled and punished by a legal military tribunal.[72]

In January 1942 the *HA* SS-*Gericht* commanded *Ostuf.* Baumgärtner to undertake preparations for the transfer of all *Gefängnis* convicts in Dachau to the newly opened prison at Danzig–Matzkau. Writing after the war, Otto Langer confirmed that this order had been carried out at this time and recalled that those SS and *Polizei Gefängnis* felons detained in civil and *Wehrmacht* penal institutions were also commanded to Matzkau.[73]

This transfer did not go without incident. Discovering that the opening of Matzkau had been delayed, this decision resulted in 150 *Gefängnis* inmates diverting to the Daimler-Benz aircraft engine factory in Genshagen near Berlin in March 1942. Here, for two, or three weeks these convicts laboured to pull up tree stumps and clear land for a new work camp. When Matzkau's commandant finally announced his willingness to accept *Gefängnis* convicts, the SS and *Polizei* inmates in Berlin were then loaded into three locked cattle trucks and travelled to Danzig, passing through the cities of Stettin and Bromberg. Arriving at their destination, the felons were put to work constructing accommodation and building an electric wire fence around the newly constructed *Häftlingslager*.[74]

> Emptied of its *Gefängnis* inmates, the SS-*Straflager* then reverted to its original purpose, to accommodate *Zuchthaus* convicts. On 4 June 1942 the prison accepted the following inmates from other institutions: Adolf Bender, Leo Blanke, Wolfgang Keonig and Otto Koester. It is worth noting that these convicts were all aged 22 years-old or younger.[75]

The *Amt* III insisted that their prisons maintained records and submitted regular reports to their office which stated the number of inmates under their care. It is evident from surviving material that the prison experienced some difficulty supplying these documents. During the first week of August 1942 the *Amt* III wrote to both prison institutions to command their commanders to immediately submit their reports for the months June/July 1942.[76]

Operating for over two years, it was still possible for inmates to escape from Dachau. Writing to the *Kriminalpolizei* on 20 August 1942 the *HA* SS-*Gericht* informed them that Karl Leitersbach had appeared before the SS- *und Polizei-Gericht* I, Munich for escaping from the SS-*Straflager* Dachau and had been punished with a capital sentence. Born in Unterleinach/Würzburg on 21 March 1919, the former Würzburger *Kriminalpolizei*, Karl Leitersbach was serving an eleven year *Zuchthaus* sentence when he attempted his escape. At this time other felons made good their escape from the jail via the normal channels. The *HA* SS-*Gericht* paroled an inmate named Willem van Londen on 1 October 1942. Later, that same month the SS- *und Polizei-Gericht* XVII, Kiev ordered *Schütze* Egon Seinsche, who was recovering in a Bobruisk hospital, to report to the SS-*Straflager* Dachau. The prison received orders to release the 22 year-old inmate SS-*Kanonier* Karl Lupski on 15

November 1942. Assigned to the 5. / SS-*Totenkopf-Artillerie*-Rgt., Lupski left Dachau to undertake front probation.[77]

The eligibility for front probation for both *Zuchthaus* and *Gefängnis* inmates was expanded during 1942 and 1943 and those judged suitable for the SS-*Sondereinheiten* were selected on the recommendation of *Ostuf.* Baumgärtner, who provided the *Amt* III with fitness reports for those considered suitable for active service on the most dangerous sectors of the front line.[78]

Writing to the *Straflager* on 15 December 1942, the SS- *und Polizei-Gericht* IV, Danzig confirmed that the 24 year-old convict Stulpner had been sentenced to a term of five year *Zuchthaus* in the SS-*Straflager* for committing an unspecified offence (case Nr. St. L. 494/1941).[79]

In anticipation of an expansion of the prison, the staff rota was increased and internal transfers were enacted: *Ostuf.* Josef Schwaiger joined the prison staff to assist the *Leiter* with his administrative tasks on 6 January 1943 and *Hstuf.* Baumgärtner left Dachau in late February the same year to replace *Ostuf.* Dieterle as the Nr. 1 *Lagerführer* in Danzig–Matzkau. *Hstuf.* Erich Albert returned to Dachau to replace *Hstuf.* Baumgärtner as *Leiter* and *Ostuf.* Gottfried Biedermann joined Baumgärtner in Matzkau in September 1943.[80]

The *HA* SS-*Gericht* and WVHA secured contracts with the company BMW in late 1942 to deploy their convicts in their aircraft engine factory near Allach, (close to Dachau). Initially, 106 inmates marched daily from Dachau to the Allach factory, but with the *Reichsführer* demanding that greater numbers of convicts were engaged in such work, the *Chef* WVHA, *Ostubaf.* Günther Burmeister, issued orders on 10 February 1943 for the creation of a sub-camp in Allach. Proposing that this *Stammlager*, later known as the *Aussenstelle*, was constructed along the southern outside edge of the Karlsfeld *Arbeitslager*, Burmeister demanded the prison included sleeping accommodation for the *Gefängnis* inmates and staff alike. The completed institution at Allach also contained a clinic and a canteen in which the inmates prepared their own meals. The detailed arrangements for this new prison were agreed between Burmeister, *Hstuf.* Helmut Gießelmann and the WVHA. When built, Allach contained many of the administrative posts that had formally been located in the KL Dachau.[81]

This offender languished in the SS-*Straflager* in 1943: Born in Danzig in 1919, Alfons Zündler had mustered with a pre-war Danzig militia and served with the 1. *Landespolizei*-Rgt. in September 1939 (later absorbed into the *Polizeidivision*). Wounded on the Eastern Front in 1941, Zündler recovered and was posted to Amsterdam in Holland in 1942. Here, he was appointed the watch commander of the *Umschlagplatz* Plantage Middenlaan, a building where Dutch Jews were collected prior to deportation and death in the east. When aOp 3 mei 1943 werd hij gearresteerd nadat de SD een Joodse familie had opgepakt die kort daarvoor uit de Schouwburg gevlucht was.When a prisoner he had helped escape was apprehended by the security forces, he revealed Zündler's part in their escape and he and three of his comrades was arrested on 3 May 1943. Arraigned before the courts martial of the SS- *und Polizei-Gericht* X, Den Haag for coercing young Jewish girls into having sexual intercourse in return for promises of freedom and for helping Jews escape in return for material benefit, the tribunal judged Zündler guilty of committing race offences and punished him with a capital sentence, which was commuted to ten years *Zuchthaus* during the confirmation stage of the legal process. Accepting front probation, Zündler spent some time with the *Bewährungsabteilung* and fought with the 36th *Waffen-Grenadier*-Division *der* SS in February 1945. Surviving the war, Zündler appeared before the *Spuchkammer* Munich III. Judged 'unburdened' on 21 April 1948, Zündler was released and died in Munich on 17 January 1996. It is now claimed that Zündler helped Jews escape detention and certain death.[82]

This felon found himself incarcerated in Dachau in 1943: Born in Legnica, Poland, on 6 November 1909, Erich Lachmann had an undistinguished and unpleasant career. Training at Trawniki, a training camp for non-German death camps guards in September 1941, Lachmann then joined the staff of the *Vernichtungslager* Sobibor in June 1942. Returning to Trawniki, Lachmann's commander submitted an unfavourable fitness report for him at the end of 1942 which persuaded him to desert from the SS. On the run with his girlfriend, the authorities arrested Lachmann in 1943 and arraigned him before the courts martial of the SS- *und Polizei-Gericht* XVII, Lublin. Judged guilty of desertion, the court punished him with six years *Zuchthaus*. Accepting front probation in early 1945, Lachmann fought with the 36th *Waffen*-Grenadier-Division *der* SS until the collapse.[83]

Committing a particularly unpleasant criminal offence, this policeman earned his passage to the SS-*Straflager*: Born on 25 may 1912, *Kriminalkommissar* Arnold Himmel found himself arraigned before the courts martial of the SS- *und Polizei-Gericht* XV, Breslau on 15 March 1943 for engaging in sexual intercourse with the wife of a soldier serving at the front and attempting to abort his lover's child. During the trial, the tribunal heard how Himmel had attempted to abort his mistress's child using a china white tablet and alcohol, but when this attempted failed, he abandoned his service post without permission on 14 October 1942 to take his paramour to a Dr Kaulich in Berlin. Refusing to perform the abortion, the physician then reported the couple to the authorities and Himmel returned to his post on 16 October 1942 to await his fate. Judged guilty of the charges and punished with a 33 months term of *Zuchthaus*, the *Gerichtsherr*, *Gruf.* Dr Kaltenbrunner then recommended Himmel's front probation on the basis that the incident had occurred when his subordinate had feared a reprimand and was upset. Confirming his sentence on 15 June 1943, the *Reichsführer* commanded Himmel's incarceration in the SS-*Straflager* Dachau for a year before any consideration would be given to offering him front probation. Remaining in Dachau for eight months, the *Leiter* judged Himmel indifferent to his fate, but recommended his parole. Spending fifteen months in the *Bewährungsabteilung*, Himmel was then considered for service in the Skorzeny commando troops in the spring of 1944.[84]

This policeman found himself incarcerated in the SS-*Straflager* Dachau for an unknown offence in the spring of 1943: Born in Dresden on 20 September 1903, *Polizeiinspektor* Edgar Kühnel was employed with the *Polizeipräsident* Posen when he faced a court-martial before the SS- *und Polizei-Gericht* XIII, Posen on 20 May 1943 (St. L. I 84/43). From his field headquarters, the SS leader confirmed the judgment against Kühnel and ordered his detention in the SS-*Straflager* Dachau.[85]

The opening of the prison at Allach had not gone unobserved in some quarters and in the summer of 1943 the SS-*Straflager* Dachau was commanded to relinquish many of their cells in the original camp arrest. Writing to the *Amt* III during the first week of August 1943, the SS-*Richter beim* RF-SS ordered the *Leiter* to temporarily allocate 53 of his cells to the head of the *Stapoleitstelle* Munich, *Stubaf.* Dr Oswald Schäfer, who required the space to accommodate 90 of his prisoners. This order provoked *Ostubaf.* Burmeister to immediately complain that the prison, the camp arrest and the punishment cells in the camp barracks were all overcrowded with convicts and he revealed that the *Straflager Leiter* had for three months permitted the camp commandant to have use of twelve of his cells to detain camp prisoners. Protesting that cooperating with this order would leave the prison with only 30, or 40 cells, Burmeister declared this an insufficient number with which to detain *Zuchthaus* inmates, who due to their sentences could not be secured in wooden barracks. Offering all but 30 of the prison cells for Dr Schäfer's use, Burmeister's counter-offer was refused and SS-*Richter beim* RF-SS demanded that all but fifteen of the prison cells were handed to the RSHA for the detention of 20 prisoners. In the event of trouble, the *Reichsführer* authorised the *Leiter* to place three or more convicts together in one cell and shackle their hands and feet.[86]

From its inception, the SS-*Straflager* Dachau had experienced periods of overcrowding and as the war progressed this problem became ever more acute. The opening of the Allach prison in early 1943 had done little to alleviate the problem and overcrowding in the jail had become critical. The August 1943 order exacerbated an already chronic situation and to ease the situation, the prison staff are thought to have permitted inmates, and those awaiting trial, to sleep in the crawl space of the prison roof. In addition to these troubles, the KL Dachau staff came under close scrutiny from the RKPA and SS- *und Polizei-Gericht* z.b.V. investigators in second half of 1943. These corruption specialists remained in the camp until April 1945 and detained their suspects and interviewed them inside the SS-*Straflager*.[87]

Aside from overcrowding, it is possible that the regular outbreaks of tuberculosis, meningitis and intestinal problems plaguing the camp also affected the convicts. When diagnosed with such an illness, the affected inmate then transferred from the clinic to the garrison hospital for specialist treatment. For a short period, the chronically ill, and those requiring long a long period of rest and recuperation were ordered to the Danzig–Matzkau hospital.[88]

In addition to *Waffen*-SS and *Polizei* offenders, the prison also detained non-German miscreants:

Name: Georg van Kempen.
Last Rank: SS-*Obersturmführer*.
Born: 21.5.1910 in Sloten/Holland.
Prewar Assignments:
Dutch Army 1.9.1933–10.1940.
Wartime Assignments:
Waffen-SS from 1.11.1941.
SS-*Freiwilligen*-Legion *Niederlande* in 9.1941.
Promotions:

4.10.1933	Officer Cadet.
1.1.1935	*Leutnant der Reserve.*
1.11.1941	SS-*Obersturmführer der Waffen*-SS.

Notes: His father was a lawyer and his mother a medical doctor. Attending *Volksschule* for six classes and then *Gymnasium*, van Kempen obtained his *Abitur* in July 1928 and then studied jurisprudence at the University of Amsterdam for one semester. His studies interrupted on economic grounds, van Kempen served in the Dutch Army from September 1933 and spent some time in administrative positions in the Dutch Government. Punished with a four-day term of arrest for committing an unknown offence during his military service, in the wake of the German occupation of his country, van Kempen volunteered for military service with the *Waffen*-SS in 1941. Swearing his oath of loyalty on 12 May 1942, van Kempen remained unmarried by May 1945. Accused of military embezzlement while assigned to the *Niederlande*, the court's investigation recommended van Kempen's indictment and he found himself arraigned before the courts martial of the 2. SS-*Infantrie*-Brigade (mot) at Gorskaja, Russia on 1 January 1943. The court chairman, *Hstuf.* Erich v.Locquenghien, was assisted in his deliberations by *Hstuf.* Dethier and *Legion-Ustuf.* Reijer Klijn of the fourth company. Judged guilty of stealing alcohol, cigarettes and other foodstuffs from the troops for private gain, the court punished van Kempen with a term of ten years' *Zuchthaus* and stripped him of his honour. While waiting for confirmation of the sentence, van Kempen was assigned to the reserve battalion in Graz. Confirming his sentence on 19 May 1943, the *Reichsführer* ordered van Kempen's detention in the SS-*Straflager* Dachau and demanded he served a minimum of two years of his sentence before consideration was granted for his front probation. Writing to the *HA* SS-*Gericht* on 24 January 1943, the III. Germanic SS-*Panzerkorps* confirmed that van Kempen had been judged suitable for accepting front probation.[89]

If the prison *Leiter* had thought that August 1943 had been a challenging time, the remaining months this year would prove more so. In the second week of September 1943 the SS-*Straflager* Dachau accepted 175 Croatian ethnic-German's of the 7th SS-*Freiwilligen-Gebirgs*-Division *Prinz Eugen* who had refused to become mule handlers when their command of the German language had been judged too poor to remain as soldiers. Placed in *Zuchthaus* detention to await their trial for insubordination and mutiny, the *Reichsführer* was informed of the Croats grievances and then commanded *Ostubaf.* Dr Hans Braußе to arrange their release and wholesale transfer to the troop training ground at Kurmark on 2 October 1943. Here, the ethnic-German Croatians underwent a re-education and re-training programme and the training staff then judged their suitability for continuing to fight as soldiers.[90]

In addition to the Croat mutineers, that same month the *Straflager* accepted responsibility for 825 Bosnian Muslim's from the 13th SS-*Freiwilligen-Gebirgs*-Division *Handschar*. Expelled from this formation in the wake of a mutiny in the 13. SS-*Pionier-Abteilung* at in Le Puy in France, these disloyal troops entrained for the KL Dachau on 27 September 1943. Reaching their destination two days later, the suspected mutineers were almost certainly incarcerated in the *Aussenstelle* Allach. A short time after their arrival, the Muslim SS men received orders to transfer to the KL Oranienburg. On arrival the former *Handschar* troops were offered a stark choice of joining the Organisation Todt as labourers or becoming camp prisoners. After three days without food, all but 265 of their number volunteered for the labour force and the unhappy remnants were sent to the KL Neuengamme.[91]

This former Dachau camp guard found himself incarcerated in his former service post:

Name: Albert Breh.
Last Rank: SS-*Obersturmführer.*
Born: 22.4.1912 in Kempton.
NSDAP-Nr.: 864.871 (joined 2.1931).
(Joined 15.2.1932).
SS-Nr.: 33.882 (joined 1.3.1932).
Prewar Assignments:
1. / I. / 29. SS-*Standarte* (Kempton) in 1932.
Wartime Assignments:
KL Dachau 1933-29.1.1942.
Promotions:

1.5.1933	*Unterscharführer der Allgemeine*-SS.
1.12.1933	SS-*Scharführer der Allgemeine*-SS.
20.4.1934	SS-*Oberscharführer der Allgemeine*-SS.
1.4.1935	SS-*Hauptscharführer der Allgemeine*-SS.
1.6.1935	SS-*Untersturmführer der Allgemeine*-SS.
13.9.1936	SS-*Obersturmführer der Allgemeine*-SS.
10.6.1939	SS-*Untersturmführer der Waffen*-SS.
5.12.1941	SS-*Obersturmführer der Waffen*-SS.

Decorations & Awards:

0.0.19__	SA-*Sportsabzeichen in Bronze.*
0.0.19__	*Totenkopfring* der SS.
0.0.19__	*Ehrendegen des Reichsführer*-SS.

Notes: Attending *Volksschule* for four classes and *Höhere Schule* (U-II), Breh left full time education and found employed as a clerk/salesman. Mustering with the auxiliary *Polizei* at the KL Dachau in 1933, Breh joined the Dachau SS-*Wachtruppe* and took charge of the camp canteen in June 1935. Undertaking a service journey to Graz between 25 and 31 March 1937, Breh applied and received permission in 1939 to undertake military service. Possibly injured with the troops, Breh then returned to the KL Dachau and again took command of the canteen. Breh found himself investigated and convicted of causing an accident, causing physical harm and disobeying standing orders on 9 July 1941 (case Nr. St. L. I 372/1941). However, this case was aside while another process was conducted against Breh on 29 January 1942 (case Nr. St. L. I 48/1941). Arraigned before the courts martial of the *Totenkopfdivision* field court for committing military insubordination on 29 January 1942, the court chairman, *Stubaf.* Dr Barth, judged Breh guilty of the charges and punished him with two months *Gefängnis*. Confirming the sentence, Himmler amended his punishment to a three weeks intensified arrest. A court's investigation establishing that Breh had committed fraud, he then faced a third trial (case Nr. St. L. 20/43). Accused of smuggling 918 bottles of alcohol across the Dutch border without paying import duty, the court discovered that finding a seller in Holland who was prepared to sell his stock of alcohol for two million *Reichsmark*, Breh had been unable to raise the amount required and decided to appropriate half a million *Reichsmark* from the canteens funds to make the purchase. Then without seeking permission, Breh travelled to Holland to secure the deal and brought the alcohol through the Saarbrücken customs post without paying import tax. Selling the alcohol at profit, without any benefit to the canteen, Breh's embezzlement was revealed during an audit of the canteens books and uncovering his arrangement with a local hotel to supply canned meat, alcohol and cigarettes, the investigator revealed that Breh defrauding these goods from the SS and in great secrecy, he hid his ill-gotten gains in a secret bank account.

'A harm to the people' who had 'grossly abused the social work of General Eicke' stated the tribunal judge and punishing him with a 200,000 *Reichsmark* fine, he imposed a term of ten years' *Zuchthaus* and ordered his expulsion from the SS and the deprivation of his civil rights (it was recommended that Breh serve half the punishment). The *Gerichtsherr*, General Eicke, regretted that he could not impose the death penalty, but remained unconvinced that the court had proved malicious intent on Breh's behalf. In Eicke's opinion, Breh was lucky to have made so much money, rather than having done so as a consequence of his criminal genius. Bemoaning that the canteen had passed from his control to the WVHA, Eicke observed that at the time of his embezzlement, Breh was not as closely supervised as he had been under his command. A fourth trial was then initiated against Breh to determine his guilt for smuggling and defrauding the customs of revenue (case Nr. St. L. I 6/1942 is mention in his personal file on 6.7.1943). Writing on 19 September 1942, the SS-*Straflager* Dachau reported that Breh had been detained in single cell detention for a year and had been denied an appeal against his sentence. His wife Inge and a *Herr* Hermann Dames attempted during 1944 to intercede on his behalf and Breh applied in writing for permission to join the SS-*Sonderregiment Dirlewanger*. These appeals were all rejected on 6 August 1944 and although Breh was a *Zuchthaus* inmate, the *Reichsführer* ordered his transfer to Danzig–Matzkau on 26 October 1943. Banned from holding any position of trust in this prison, Breh's disablement precluded any manual labour or any physical work and it was left to the Matzkau commandant to determine what tasks he was capable of undertaking. Writing to the SS- *und Polizei-Gericht* III, Berlin in 1944, the SS-*Richter beim* RF-SS supplied the tribunal with the court's evidence along with statements from the customs service, who had prosecuted Breh for failing to pay import duty. It is not certain whether Breh accepted front probation in the 36th *Waffen-Grenadier*-Division *der* SS in 1945 or ended the conflict in the SS-*Straflager* Dachau.[92]

A particularly nasty specimen of criminality earned his place in the prison in the autumn of 1943:

Name: Carl Juels.
Last Rank: SS-*Obersturmführer*.
Born: 22.5.1911 in Hamburg.
NSDAP-Nr.: 3.278.405 (joined 1.5.1933).
SS-Nr.: 116.355 (joined 6.8.1934).
Prewar Assignments:
SS-TV until 31.10.1938.
Wartime Assignments:
1. / SS-*Infantrie*-Rgt. 9 in 1939.
III. / SS-*Infantrie*-Rgt. 9 in 11.1939.
Officer candidate training course SS-*Junkerschule* Bad Tölz 11.1940–31.1.1941.
Stab Befehlshaber Waffen-SS *Nord* in 1.1941.
SS-*Gebirgsjäger-Ersatz-Bataillon* 6 *Nord* from 23.3.1942.
7th SS-*Freiwilligen-Gebirgs*-Division *Prinz Eugen* in 1942.
SS-*Gebirgsjäger*-Rgt. from 13.7.1943.
SS-*Gebirgsjäger Ausbildung- und Ersatz-Abteilung* 7 from 24.9.1943.
Promotions:

9.1939	SS-*Rottenführer der Reserve*.
20.4.1941	SS-*Untersturmführer der Reserve*.
30.1.1943	SS-*Obersturmführer der Reserve*.

Decorations & Awards

0.0.19__	SS-*Zivilabzeichen* (Nr. 124.897).
0.0.19__	SA-*Sportsabzeichen in Bronze*.
0.0.19__	*Deutsches Reichssportabzeichen in Bronze*.
0.0.19__	*Die Medaille zur Erinnerung an den* 13. März 1938 (Austria).
22.11.1941	1939 *Eisernes Kreuz II. Klasse*.

Notes: Attending *Volksschule* and *Höhere Schule*, Juels left full time education and found employment as a salaried salesman. Marrying his fiancée Irmgard K., (b. 4.10.1912) on 23 April 1938, the couple had two children up to the point when records ceased in May 1945. Discovering the dead body of a German soldier near the village of Košutica, Bosnia, on 13 July 1943, the incensed Juels ordered his company to attack the village. During their murderous assault, his men killed 69 Muslims, including women and children and stole their victim's possessions. When news of the atrocity reached the ears of his commanders it was feared that some of the dead were related to members of men fighting in the *Handschar* and this concern resulted in the divisional tribunal initiating a court's investigation to examine the affair. The investigator recommended his trial on 26 July 1943 and Juels was indicted for harming service duty in two cases and suspicion of murder.

Arraigned before the courts martial of the *Prinz Eugen* on 3 September 1943, the tribunal judged Juels guilty of committing manslaughter and military embezzlement and punished with a term of eight years' *Zuchthaus*, expulsion from the SS, declared him unworthy to bear arms and denied him his civil rights for five years (the month spent in remand was not subtracted from his sentence). Following the trial proceedings, Juels transferred to a reserve battalion to await confirmation of his sentence. His *Gerichtsherr*, *Gruf.* Phleps, expressed his conviction that Juels had obeyed Hitler's orders and supported his actions, but when the matter was presented to the *Reichsführer* for his confirmation, he expressed fury with Juels actions and voiced his concerns that his behaviour would negative effect the recruitment of Muslim fighters for the *Handschar*. Via the clemency path, the field court attempted to mitigate his sentence to *Gefängnis*, but confirming the sentence on 12 November 1943, Himmler disagreed with Phleps judgment and given his crimes, the SS leader almost certainly confirmed Juels' *Zuchthaus* sentence at a later date and he remained in the SS-*Straflager* Dachau until front probation was authorised.[93]

This junior communications officer found himself detained in Dachau in late 1943:

Name: Ludwig Bahrke.
Last Rank: SS-*Untersturmführer*.
Born: 12.8.1922 in Berlin.
Wartime Assignments:
III. / SS-*Artillerie*-Rgt. 2 in 10.1941
III. / SS-*Artillerie*-Rgt. 1 in 12.1941.
Nachrichten-Lehrgang SS-*Nachrichtenschule* Metz in 1943.
Bewährungsabteilung in 1.1944.
SS-*Nachrichtenschule* Nuremberg in 1944.
Artillerie-Abteilung / SS-*Sturmbrigade Dirlewanger* (Slovakia) from 1.12.1944.

Promotions:

12.1941 SS-*Rottenführer der Reserve.*
0.0.1943 SS-*Untersturmführer der Reserve.*
17.12.1943 SS-*Mann.*

Decorations:

20.10.1941 1939 *Eisernes Kreuz* II. *Klasse.*

Notes: Unmarried prior to May 1945. Attending the communications course II in Metz, Bahrke was accused of stealing a camera and photography equipment to the value of a 1,000 *Reichsmark* from the school commander *Stubaf.* Fuchs. Confronted to answer this accusation, Bahrke swore the accusation was untrue, but finding the stolen camera's guarantee number written in his notebook and lacking an explanation for this entry, Bahrke found himself arraigned before the courts martial of the SS- *und Polizei-Gericht* XIV, Metz on 17 December 1943 (case Nr. St. L. I 357/1943). The court chairman, *Hstuf.* Neuberger, was assisted in his deliberations by *Stubaf.* Schreiber and *Ustuf.* Müller. *Hstuf.* Dr Mers prosecuted the case and the *Beurkundungsführer* was *Revier Obermachts der Schupo* d.R. Gekler. Hearing the evidence, the court judged Bahrke guilty of the charge of comrade theft and punished him with four years' *Zuchthaus*, ordered his expulsion from the SS, denied him his civil and honour rights and declared him unworthy to bear arms. The sentence was confirmed by the *Gerichtsherr*, the HSSPF *Rhein-Westmark Gruf.* Jürgen Stroop, and Bahrke reported to the SS-*Straflager* Dachau to serve his sentence. Having only served two months of his sentence, the errant Bahrke was then evaluated for front probation and found himself released from his sentence on 31 January 1944. Undertaking a period of probation and further communications training, Bahrke received orders to report to a newly established artillery battalion at the SS-*Truppenübungsplatz* Böhmen-Mähren on 1 December and joined the SS-*Sonderbrigade* during its retreated through Slovakia. His artillery unit was overrun during the 1945 Red Army spring offensive in the Forst Forrest, but surviving the battle, Bahrke remained alive into the early 2000s.[94]

The prison required that each convict was photographed upon entry to the prison. Writing to the SS-*Straflager* on 27 August 1943, the SS- *und Polizei-Gericht* XIX, Belgrade requested that the prison office sent them a copy of the 27 year-old Jakob Brenner's image and supplied a fitness report. At this time, Brenner was serving a term of *Zuchthaus*.[95]

1944–45: The Years of Defeat

At the beginning of 1944 this prison had the use of very few cells in the east wing of the Dachau camp arrest and much of its administrative activities had transferred to Allach. At this time, the *Reichsführer* commanded the detention of offenders in the camp arrest where KL guards stood guard. Incredibly, the SS leader ordered two former judges of the SS- *und Polizei-Gericht* VI, Krakau, *Stubaf.* Kurt Sachs and *Hstuf.* Willy Oshues, to be detained on remand in individual cells of the camp arrest during July 1944 and here, they remained until their trial before the *Oberstes* SS- *und Polizei-Gericht*. Condemned to two and a half years' *Zuchthaus* for committing injury to the service, Osthues and Sachs were released from Dachau in January 1945 with orders to report to the 36th *Waffen-Grenadier-*Division *der* SS.[96]

The growth of the convict population required the recruitment of trained prison staff. Newly recruited *Beurkundungsunterführer*, *Uscha*. Herbert Fritzsch, Puchtler and Volkhausen, were assigned to this SS-*Straflager* on 25 January 1944 and *Oscha*. Diermeier joined the staff from the Krakau tribunal on 3 October 1944. A senior *Beurkundungsunterführer*, *Hscha*. Seipel, reported for duty in Dachau on 28 February 1945.[97]

Following his commission of a particularly savage crime, this officer arrived in Dachau in January/February 1944: Born in Kieselbach on 26 July 1923, Karl-Ernst Gebauer left the SS- *Nachrichtenabteilung* 4 in January 1944 for a posting with the SS-*Panzer-Nachrichtenabteilung* 11. Shortly after his arrival, a judge of the 11th SS-*Panzer-Grenadier-*Division *Nordland* field court initiated an investigation against him and ordered his arraignment before the courts martial on suspicion of raping a seventeen year-old Croatian girl at pistol point (case Nr. St. L. 89/1943). Judging Gebauer guilty of the offence, the court punished him with ten years' *Zuchthaus* and ordered his expulsion from the SS. Later, receiving favourable prison reports, which noted his good conduct and sentiments of remorsefulness, Gebauer was granted parole and then transferred to the *Bewährungsabteilung* to prepare for front probation in June 1944.[98]

As 1944 ground inexorably over the precipice of defeat, the prison would continue to accept other convicted criminals:

Name: Josef Brendel.
Last Rank: SS-*Oberscharführer*.
Born: 16.10.1909 in Mannheim-Plankstadt.
NSDAP-Nr.: (joined 1937).
SS-Nr.: 227.307 (joined 1.2.1934).
Promotions:

24.12.1939	SS-*Rottenführer der Reserve*.
24.3.1940	SS-*Unterscharführer der Reserve*.
19.2.1941	SS-*Scharführer der Reserve*.
1.4.1942	SS-*Oberscharführer der Reserve*.

Notes: By profession a master builder, Brendal became a concentration camp guard in the pre-war years and had been assigned to the Hinzert camp clinic since 1939. Here, he earned a reputation for displaying a particularly sadistic attitude towards prisoners. Facing a court's investigation in the late summer/early autumn of 1943 on suspicion of smuggling a package to a prisoner, the investigator subsequently recommended Brendel's arraignment before the courts martial of the SS- *und Polizei-Gericht* XIV, Metz (case Nr. St. L. I 26/1943). Judged guilty of harming the well-being of the people in contravention of paragraph § 4 RStGB on 25 October 1943, the court punished Brendel with ten years' *Zuchthaus*, expelled him from the SS, declared him unworthy to bear arms and denied him his civil and honour rights for ten years. Held in Trier jail while he waited for confirmation of his sentence, Brendel's punishment was up-held by the *HA* SS-*Gericht* on 12 January 1944 and by the *Gerichtsherr*, the HSSPF *Rhein-Westmark* on 21 January the same year. His sentence confirmed, Brendel then reported to the SS-*Straflager* Dachau to serve his punishment. His worthiness to bear arms reinstated in 1944, Brendel accepted front probation with the SS-*Sonderbrigade Dirlewanger*. Surviving the war, Brendel faced trial and conviction before the *Landgericht* Trier on 20 December 1961.[99]

This thoroughly unsuitable junior officer was cashiered in 1942 and earned his passage to the prison:

Name: Heinz-Paul Sieling.
Last Rank: SS-*Obersturmführer*.
Born: 2.15.1914 in Berlin.
Died: 15.9.1944 in Warsaw.
SS-Nr.: 256.271 (joined 1935).
Wartime Assignments:
7. / SS *Totenkopf-Infantrie* Rgt. 3 in 11.1939.
3. / SS-*Totenkopf-Infantrie* Rgt. 8 in 4.1942.
Bewährungsabteilung in 1944.
SS-*Sonderregiment Dirlewanger* in 1944
Promotions:

11.1939	SS-*Untersturmführer der Waffen*-SS.
0.0.1942	SS-*Obersturmführer der Waffen*-SS.

Notes: A member of the *Allgemeine*-SS, Sieling had obtained officer rank in the SS-VT by November 1939. Assigned to a *Totenkopf* regiment in April 1942, at this time, Sieling came under suspicion for misusing service fuel on numerous occasions, taking unauthorised leaves, abusing his service rank to obtain vehicles, failing to record journeys in log books and avoiding the sending and receiving letters via the official postal service. In addition, Sieling was accused of consuming wine that had been set aside for his men and stealing 93 *Reichsmark* from the other ranks' canteen to replace the money he had stolen from the officers' mess (case Nr. St. L. II 209/1942). Also accused of mistreating a non-commissioned officer near Gruschewski-Kut on the road to Nikopol, the investigator revealed that reporting to the unit doctor to lance his boils, Losskan then approached Sieling unsuccessfully for permission to rest from his duties. Arraigned before the courts martial of the SS- *und Polizei-Gericht* I Munich, the tribunal judged the irascible Sieling guilty of the charges and punished him with a term of four years' *Zuchthaus*. Confirming his sentence on 6 January 1944, the *Reichsführer* commanded his assessment for possible front probation after serving six months of his sentence. Remaining in the SS-*Straflager* Dachau for 22 weeks, the prison leader observed that Sieling was overbearing, arrogant and his behaviour in gaol had proven unsatisfactory. Although unwilling to recommend his probation, the *Leiter's* advice was ignored and Sieling found himself released from his sentence for service in the *Bewährungsabteilung*. Spending 42 months with this probation unit, Sieling was then briefly considered for service with the Skorzeny commando troops in the spring of 1944. Taking into account the prison leader's poor opinion of him, the SS leader commanded Sieling's transfer to the SS-*Sonderregiment Dirlewanger* and he died in action in September 1944 while fighting the Home Army in Warsaw.[100]

The year 1944 witnessed a rapid growth in the prison population. Writing in February 1944, general Breithaupt reported that the inmate population of the SS-*Straflager* Dachau had reached 2,400 felons of all types and some two-thirds of this number were held in the *Aussenstelle* Allach and had been put to work for the BMW plant.[101]

Writing to the SS- *und Polizei-Gericht* XXXI, Verona on 28 March, the *HA* SS-*Gericht* informed them that a Dachau convict named v.Maestre had been released from his sentence on 26 March 1944. Citing political reasons for the decision to suspend his death sentence, the prison received orders to release *Feldwebel der Polizei* Scilla, of the *Polizei Freiwilligen-Bataillon Italia*.[102]

In an effort to alleviate the overcrowding in the prison and to supply labour for the dispersing aircraft engine factories, the SS-*Straflager* Dachau transferred a handful of *Gefängnis* inmates to the newly constructed *Zweiglager Hammerweg* in Mosbach/Baden during the spring of 1944. On arrival, these convicts laboured to construct an underground factory and converted their new accommodation from a work camp to a prison.[103]

In addition to incarcerating convicts, this prison continued to operate as ante-chamber for condemned inmates.

Following two trials for desertion, this convict was executed in March 1944: Born in Graudenz on 5 September 1917, Bruno M., and his family moved to Dortmund in 1922. Leaving school, he undertook an apprenticeship with the intention of becoming a carpenter. Joining the *Hitlerjugend* in 1933, Bruno M. was accepted into the SS-VT in 1937 and marrying his fiancée, the couple had one child. Fighting with the SS-*Verfügungstruppe/Reich* during the Polish, Western and Balkan campaigns, Bruno M. fought on the Eastern Front from June 1941 to March 1942. Attending an officer training course in France from late 1942 to January 1943, he then returned to the Eastern Front with the rank of *Uscha*. Becoming separated from his unit in the spring of 1943, Bruno M. then spent a month driving around the rear echelon before finally reporting back to his unit. Shortly after his return to his unit, he deserted again and committed several thefts while attempting to reach home. Apprehended, Bruno M. faced a trial before a court for desertion, absence without leave, gross misconduct and theft. Judged guilty of the charges, the court punished him with a term of eight years' *Gefängnis*. Under armed escort, Bruno M. boarded a train that would take him to prison, but during the journey he escaped from his escort. Leaping from the train when it slowed, Bruno M. escaped his guards, stole a motorbike and with two women passengers aboard, he drove around until caught three days after his escape.

Brought to trial before the SS- *und Polizei-Gericht* XXIV, Stettin on charges of committing an unauthorised leave offence, theft and other offences, Bruno M. excuse his behaviour with a claim that he suffered from weak nerves and had experienced an overwhelming desire to see his family again. Examined by a physiatrist, apart from an active interest in women, he concluded that Bruno M. did not suffer from any form of mental illness. Punished with a capital punishment, Bruno M. waited for the confirmation of the sentence in the SS-*Straflager* Dachau. In the meantime, his father submitted a request for clemency and in his letter, he informed the *HA* SS-*Gericht* that his son was the last living of five sons. 'An incorrigible criminal' stated the *Amt* III when submitting his case file to the *Reichsführer* for confirmation, but the case worker asked whether his sentence could be amended in favour of imprisonment sentence on the grounds of his last son status. Himmler refused him a pardon on 21 March 1944 and the execution order was communicated immediately to the SS- *und Polizei-Gericht* I, Munich. Bruno M. found himself executed by firing squad at the Herbertshausen firing range on 23 March 1944.[104]

Among those held in this prison were some with a very nefarious history: Born on 3 June 1909, *Oscha.* Anton Endres had worked as a gardener prior to joining the *Waffen*-SS on 7 September 1939. Married with three children, Endres deployed in the KL Dachau as an SDG. He found himself injured in a vehicle accident in November 1939 which put him out of commission for many months. When recovered, he joined the KL Inspectorate who assigned him to the troop doctor between December 1940 and June 1941. Then deployed in the KL Dachau until May 1942, here, Endres abused and caused the deaths of prisoners. Transferred to the KL Lublin between May 1942 and June 1943, Endres then fund himself seconded to the KL Auschwitz for a short time (where he became familiar with the function of the gas chambers). Returning to Dachau by mid-1943, Endres then deployed as an SDG in the *Aussenstelle* Augsburg and found himself denounced for permitting prisoners to leave the camp without authorisation. Taken under arrest and incarcerated in remand in the SS-*Straflager* Dachau, Endres was then detained in Weimar from November 1943 to September 1944. Arraigned before the courts martial of the SS- *und Polizei-Gericht* XXII, Kassel for dereliction of duty, the tribunal punished Endres with a term of imprisonment and an expulsion from the SS on 20 May 1944. Returned to the SS-*Straflager* Dachau, Endres remained here until his release in April 1945 and the Allies indicted him for war-crimes on 13 December 1945. Judged guilty of murder, Endres execution took place on 28 May 1946.[105]

No matter how far away the sentencing court stood, if the offender received a term of *Zuchthaus*, then he then found himself incarcerated in the SS-*Straflager* Dachau. Danach wurde er als Häftling in das Straflager der SS und Polizei in Dachau eingewiesen, wo er bis zum 30. April 1945 inhaftiert war.Danach wurde er von US-Army weiterhin interniert. Writing to the *Gefängenenhaus* Lublin on 21 July 1944, the SS- *und Polizei-Gericht* XVIII, Lublin informed them that *Meister der Schutzpolizei* Johannes Häse, who had been convicted of cowardice, was to be immediately transferred into the care of this prison.[106]

Returning to the SS-*Straflager* Dachau in disgrace from Danzig-Matzkau in late July 1944, *Hstuf.* Biedermann accepted a disciplinary punishment for committing an unauthorised absence offence on 20 July 1944. He remained in this prison for a short time until his transfer to the 12th SS-*Panzer*-Division *Hitlerjugend* field court. Wounded at the front, Biedermann had returned to the prison service by December 1944.[107]

Convicted of multiple counts of cowardice and assaults on subordinates, this SS man began his hard labour sentence in April 1944:

Name: Ernst Schumacher.
Last Rank: SS-*Obersturmführer.*
Born: 7.8.1908 in Hattingen/Ruhr.
Died: in Mitterndorf/Österreich.
NSDAP-Nr.: 832.002 (joined 1.1.1932).
SS-Nr.: 276.527 (joined 9.4.1936).
Prewar Assignments:
Hilfpolizei in 1933.
Unterführer-Lehrgang SA-*Hilfswerklägern* under the *Chef des Ausbildungswesens* in 1933.
SS-*Hauptamt* in 1936.
Salaried position in the SS-*Hauptamt* (personnel office) in 1936.
Adjutant/*Personalreferent* II. / 46. SS-*Standart*e (Dresden) 1.1937–1.7.1939.
Personalreferent Adjutant 100. SS-*Standarte* from 1.7.1939.
Deployed in Reichenberg.
Wartime Assignments:
Wehrmacht from 22.5.1940.
Waffen-SS from 6.6.1940 (mustered on 12.7.1940).
1. / SS-*Infantrie-Ersatz-Bataillon Der Führer* from 28.7.1940.
Gruppenführer-Lehrgang Waffen-SS-*Unterführerschule* Radolfzell 1.11.1940–30.1.1941.
2. / SS-*Artillerie-Ersatz*-Rgt. until 9.2.1941.
StuG Zug / SS-*Artillerie-Ersatz*-Rgt. 1 until 24.2.1941.
2. / SS-*Artillerie-Ersatz*-Rgt. from 24.2.1941.
7. / SS-*Grenadier*-Rgt. *Westland* from 1.4.1941.
7. *Kriegs-Reserve-Führeranwärter-Lehrgangs* SS-*Junkerschule* Bad Tölz 4.6.–5.9.1942.
3. / SS-*Gebirgsjäger*-Rgt. 1 autumn of 1942.
Zugführer 13. / SS-*Gebirgsjäger*-Rgt. 2 in 5.1943.

Zugführer 15. / SS-*Gebirgsjäger*-Rgt. 2 in 5.1943.
Officer of the 100. SS-*Standarte* on 10.3.1944.
Front probation in 1945.

Promotions:

20.5.1936	SS-*Hauptscharführer der Allgemeine*-SS.
10.2.1937	SS-*Untersturmführer der Allgemeine*-SS.
10.9.1939	SS-*Obersturmführer der Allgemeine*-SS.
6.6.1940	SS-*Schütze.*
1.5.1941	SS-*Sturmmann der Reserve.*
12.1941	SS-*Scharführer der Reserve.*
1.6.1941	SS-*Unterscharführer der Reserve.*
21.12.1942	SS-*Untersturmführer der Reserve.*

Decorations & Awards:

0.0.19__	SA-*Sportsabzeichen in Bronze.*
5.10.1941	1939 *Eisernes Kreuz II. Klasse.*
0.0.19__	1939 *Eisernes Kreuz I. Klasse.*
20.4.1942	*Infanterie-Sturmabzeichen in Bronze.*
0.0.1942	*Medaille 'Winterschlacht im Osten* 1941/42'.

Notes: The son of a businessman, Schumacher attended *Volksschule* for four classes, obtained his *Abitar* from *Gymnasium*, (O-I) and studied at the University of Bern and Poppelsdorf near Bonn (*Geodäsie*) from the autumn of 1929. Failing to complete his studies on the grounds of financial difficulties, Schumacher mustered with the SA from December 1931 to 1 May 1936 and undertook one months' military training with the *Schwarzen Reichwehr* in 1929, 1930 and 1933. Achieving NCO rank, his brother Dr Friedrich Schumacher became a *Waffen*-SS officer. Applying to the RuSHA for permission to marry in 1939, this union never took place. Fighting along the Galician border, Schumacher participated in the advance on Tarnopol between 22 and 28 June 1941 and fought along the Mius position between 1 December and 1 May 1942. Qualifying as a company, group and deputy section leader in September 1942, Schumacher took command of a mountain warfare company in the autumn of 1942 and almost immediately experienced great difficulty imposing his authority on his company, which was composed of Banat ethnic-Germans (50 per cent of the men under his command was aged over 35 and some over 40-years-old). The SS-*Hilfrichter*, *Oscha.* Dr Strauß of the field court initiated an investigation against Schumacher in May 1943 to examine claims that he had committed acts of cowardice and had mishandled his subordinates (St. L. 132/43). Submitting his investigative report on 16 June 1943, Dr Strauß acknowledged that Schumacher had obtained good fitness reports from his superiors, but the judge expressed his conviction that Schumacher had morphed into a sadist and a brutal man and criticised his performance:

> It has been revealed that he, as a full-time SS officer, had encountered difficulties in his career. In individual evaluations he had been criticised for his nervousness and inability

> to achieve a good collaboration with subordinate service officers. However, the service reports are not uniform, sometimes even contradictory. However, according to the witness SS-*Usha. Lorenz,* he would at times question the whereabouts of the accused and question whether he was in fact a full-time SS officer. For the accused, this personal critique and friction was the consequence of personal differences that resulted in a personal war between the two men.

Ordered to train the Banats as Prussians, Schumacher, overwhelmed with nerves, failed in his task. Making derogatory statements to his assembled men in late 1942, his utterings were denounced to his superiors in an anonymous letter and a second court investigation was initiated against Schumacher on 16 June 1943. On 23 June, both Dr Strauß and the chief judge, *Stubaf.* Wetzling, confirmed that Schumacher would face trial:

> Concerning: Arrangement of a criminal investigation against Schumacher 3. / SS-*Gebirgsjäger*-Rgt. 1.
>
> This court opened an investigation against SS-*Ustuf. der Reserve* Ernst Schumacher for the continual abuse and degrading treatment of his ethnic-German subordinates. The leading investigator was SS-*Ustuf. Gündisch,* who had been employed as a *Gerichtsoffizier.* The investigation has now been taken over by the undersigned, SS-*Stubaf.* Wetzling.
>
> SS-*Ustuf.* Schumacher is accused of repeatedly beating members of his unit and others and to have enforced a term of imprisonment by *Ausbinden* in accordance to the old Hungarian method. He is still suspected of the degrading treatment of his subordinates, who are mostly Banat ethnic-German's and to them he had assigned defamatory and disgraceful words. During the procedure, the investigation was extended on the suspicion of injury to service out of fear, especially cowardice before the enemy.

Arraigned before the courts-martial of the field court of the *Prinz Eugen* on 27 August 1943, Schumacher faced a cacophony of offences:

> 1. Four cases of the abuse of subordinates by slaps and blows,
> 2. The degrading treatment of subordinates, for two days he had left on a tree as the punishment *Ausbinden,*
> 3. The continued degrading treatment of the ethnic-German company-members by insults such as 'idiots' and 'Banat bastards' and he had demanded the withdrawal of their membership from the people's community. In the *Ausbinden* order he had expressed his opinion that all the Bananter should be throw in a big hole and then 'shit on before sending them to the *Luftwaffe,*'
> 4. For revealing cowardice before the enemy in two battles on 23.1.1943 and 27.2.1943,
> 5. For desertion; a dereliction of duty in accordance to § 62 MStGB by having caused by inadequate securing a rest area on 26.5.1943 and blaming the subsequent losses on the bandit attack.

During his trial, Schumacher alleged that his dereliction of duty had occurred from a fear for personal danger in the attack on 26 May 1943. During the proceedings, he found himself accused of issuing an order to *Jäger* Raikov with improper phrases and then slapping the soldier when he failed to carry out the command immediately (a holder of the *E.K. 2. Klasse*, Raikov was promoted shortly thereafter to *Strm.* and complained to *Ostuf.* Megerle about his treatment). Finding *Jäger* Kunz hanging around in the kitchen during a scheduled period for cleaning horses in March 1943, Schumacher ordered Kunz several times to carry out his assigned duties, but growing tired of Kunz's procrastination, he commanded him to perform press-ups as a method of achieving instant obedience in the future. Failing to execute the commands quickly enough, Schumacher then beat *Jäger* Kunz three times with a branch on the buttocks. On the same day, *Jäger* Wagner accused Schumacher of hitting him on his back with a stick for failing to clean a saddle adequately. During the trial, Schumacher's advocate, *Ustuf.* Caveal, a future SS-*Richter*, argued that the defendant had hit his men with a cane on 26 May 1943 in the belief that he had received prior permission to do so in an emergency.

Schumacher's advocate argued that his actions on 26 May could not be construed as a criminal act as he was aware that assaulting his subordinates was permitted to avoid panic in accordance with the special requirements of §124 MStGB, (he had learned this during an officers meeting with his commander *Stubaf.* Vollmer on 2.12.1943). Although the court refused to accept that he had concluded from this meeting that it was acceptable to punish miscreants with the caning as an educational measure, as an alternative of a prison sentence, the court rejected Schumacher's guilt for the abuse committed on 26 May 1943.

Schumacher's company rested on 11 and 12 March 1943 and at this time, he punished *Jäger* Birk with a five days' arrest for his 'crude, aggravated treatment of a horse' and imposed this punishment in the form of the former Austro-Hungarian Army punishment of *Ausbinden* (outside binding). For two days, Birk's back and hands were bound to a tree trunk and then facing the assembled company, Schumacher warned his troops that he had applied this type of punishment as an improvised imprisonment deterrent. News of Birk's disgraceful treatment sparked outrage across the division and worse still, photographs of Birk were taken secretly and used as propaganda against the German leadership of the Division in the Banat. The punishment of *Ausbinden* consisted of handcuffing miscreant soldiers hand to the ankle above ground for up to 48 hours duration to prevent them sitting or lying down. Variants of this punishment included the *Kurtz Schliesen*, or *Lang Schliesen*, which varied the length of chain used to bind the prisoner. Banning the imposition of *Ausbinden* at the previously mentioned officers' meeting, *Stubaf.* Vollmar described its use as an alternative to a detention punishment unworthy for German soldiers and unsuitable for the SS. At this time Vollmar explained to his officers that other means of education existed (here, Schumacher was overheard to complain that the caning should be introduced).

Reviewing the sentence in September 1943, Dr Strauß took into account the considerable loss of respect for the German leadership by the ethnic-German men and their families back home, when it became known that Schumacher had introduced the *Ausbinden* punishment. Recommending his detention for six months as minimum punishment, Dr Strauß similarly considered a four months prison sentence suitable for his degrading handling of subordinates by abusing their folklore. Rejecting Schumacher's argument that educational problems in the division mitigated his behavior, Dr Strauß took into account the mitigating factors, but expressed his certainty that Schumacher had reasonable grounds to apply arrest penalties, the judge argued that his imposition of the *Ausbinden* had been undertaken as part of his tendency to express harshness to his subordinates. Rejecting Schumacher's argument that he had imposed the *Ausbinden* from ignorance, Dr Strauß assessed that he had failed to prove himself a leader of his company (convinced of his unsuitability as an officer, Dr Strauß wondered how he had been promoted to officer rank).

Dr Strauß then accused Schumacher of displaying cowardice before the enemy. During the battle of Miholske on 26 January 1943, the first deployment of his unit, Schumacher was tasked with advancing his company ahead of the battalion. Reaching the target of their march, (two heights), Schumacher then committed two of his sections to the action and the third section remained in reserve to provide security for the battalion supply section. Enemy heavy fire suddenly broke over *Ostuf.* Megerle's section as they advanced uphill and without cover they found themselves exposed to the enemy over an 80 meters wide front on the forward slope in a narrow pass. For a while Schumacher maintained a 30 meters gap between him and the leading sections, but when the heights came under enemy fire, he and his command post then sought cover to observe the terrain and refused to offer *Ustuf.* Megerle any support (Schumacher's panicked messages suggested a catastrophe, when in fact only the loss of one heavy machine gun and six dead and eight wounded was reported). Reporting to the battalion headquarters, Schumacher presented a 'helpless and distraught impression.'

His second act of cowardice occurred on 27 February 1943. On this day, Schumacher's third company received orders to occupy ridge 1316 near Solmuni. Finding their route complicated by high snow and wind damage in the forest, the leading section, commanded by *Ustuf.* Megerle, continued in their attempt to cross this difficult terrain until they suddenly came under automatic weapon fire from height 1.341. Megerle observed some civilians occupying the height and radioed Schumacher for him to supply fresh orders:

> Schumacher: 'Kurt, what's wrong?'
> Megerle: 'Up there are a few civilians.'
> Schumacher: 'What do you mean, what do we do?'
> Megerle: 'We are attacking! I am certain that if each *Zugführer* takes a group, we can throw them off the thing.'
> Schumacher: 'You take the responsibility?'
> Megerle: 'I'm not a company commander!'

Though positioned 80 meters from the height, Schumacher made no attempt to break the enemy resistance and in single file, his troops retreated back along the trail. Later, demanding an explanation for his behavior, Schumacher informed Vollmer that the deep snow and the high wind had made it impossible for his troops to advance and complained that his men had run at the onset of enemy resistance. Declaring Schumacher a pessimist, Vollmer then reproached him for his intolerable behavior and informed him that height 1.341 had been reached on the same day, using a new approach, without encountering any enemy resistance, (as the enemy had not subjected the withdrawing unit to devastating fire, his superiors and the court concluded that this was a sure sign that the height was not occupied by an organized enemy group). Schumacher's allegations of his troop's cowardice soon reached the ears of his section leaders and far from happy with his assessment of the situation, they refuted his allegations and judged him a coward (the judge noted that Schumacher's men had compared him to *Unteroffizier* Himmelstoss in Remarque's—*All Quiet on the Western Front*).

His position with this company now untenable and clearly unsuited to act as a company leader, Schumacher found himself dismissed from his post in May 1943 and transferred to the 15. / SS-*Gebirgsjäger-Rgt* 2 to await the results of a court' investigation. Following a two days march, Schumacher's section received orders to secure height 1473 near Vojnik in Montenegro on 26 May 1943. Believing that the position was free of partisans, Schumacher ordered group Haberkorn to take the height while he followed with the other two groups. While occupied with pitching their tents, the partisans took advantage of Schumacher's failure to post guards to attack his section with hand grenades from a woodland, located some ten to fifteen meters away from his position. Panic among the SS troops then ensued and Schumacher and his men fled downhill, abandoning their backpacks and part of their weapons. Hitting his non-commissioned officers and men with his cane, Schumacher managed to halt the retreat of his terrified men and gathered them together some 100 meters from height 1473. Meanwhile, group leader Haberkorn and five, or eight men had organized themselves atop the height, resisted the attack and returned fire with a light machine gun. After five minutes resistance these troops were able to repel the attack. Elsewhere, the group leader Prunkel attempted to rally some men. 'Look where the section leader is, so we must go down' his men exclaimed and refusing to join the fight they then also ran away from the battle. After a thorough examination of all the evidence, the trial judge, Wetzling, agreed to Schumacher's indictment and observed that his ability to lead the troops, perplexity and confusion was mixed with his fear of personal danger.

Judging Schumacher guilty of subordination abuse in the cases involving Reikov, Kunst, Wagner and Birk, the court rejected any suggestion that an 'extreme hardship and most urgent threat' existed of their punishment, but accepted that in the case of the *Jäger* Pollinger there had existed 'the most urgent threat' when Schumacher had hit him during a forced night march from the enemy. Indicting Schumacher for three cases of cowardice and concluded that he had brought about his dereliction of duty from a fear of personal danger within the meaning of §§ 84, 85 MStGB (the court was convinced that Schumacher understood the real situation at Miholsko and believed that he had lied about the circumstances at height 1316 on 27.2.1943). Judging Schumacher guilty of committing his dereliction of duty from fear, the tribunal acquitted him of dereliction of duty on height 1473 as the losses in weapons was insufficient to reduce his company's fighting ability.

Accepting that he had, on many occasions, insulted his men unfairly and on more than one occasion used profanities against them, the court adjudicated that this contravened paragraph § 122 MStGB and deciding his guilt in this issue, the judge's verdict took into consideration the *Reichsführer* edict concerning the treatment of ethnic-German and Germanic volunteers from 6 December 1942. Concluding that his behavior commanded the strictest punishment for mistreating ethnic-Germans, the judge accepted that within the division leadership corps there existed an historical failure of legal education concerning the abuse of subordinates and recognized that beating the men had been necessary. Dr Strauß observed that this order revealed how difficult the task of education was for the troop officers in this division, but rejected Schumacher's defense that he had announced these insults only to close comrades (the court judged that such insults were a degrading treatment of ethnic-German subordinates).

On the issue of sentencing, the court took into consideration Schumacher's personality and the effect this had on the individual facts and the overall situation in the division according to its guidelines. Judged guilty of the charges, the court imposed a term of three years' *Zuchthaus* for the third case of blatant cowardice before the enemy and imposed a total term of five years' *Zuchthaus* on Schumacher and commanded his expulsion from the SS. The loss of military worthiness and the loss of civil rights was imposed for a period of five years and he was denied his medals and decorations. In view of the amount of actual punishment, the time Schumacher spent on remand was not subtracted from the sentence and the *Reichsführer* provisionally confirmed his sentence on 10 December the same year and finally confirmed the judgement on 22 March and ordered Schumacher's deprivation of liberty between the announcement and confirmation of the judgment to be credited against the sentence. Demanding the enforcement of the punishment, the SS leader commanded him to serve this in the *Straflager der* SS *und Polizei* (from 4.1944). His case file became the responsibility of the Nuremberg tribunal on 18 November and later, Schumacher found himself released from imprisonment to undertake front probation. Schumacher died at Mitterndorf in Austria.[108]

A handful SS-*Straflager* Dachau inmates with no desire to remain in the prison, or patience to wait for front probation successfully escaped in the summer of 1944. Reporting the absconding of Anton Krug from Dachau on 27 July 1944, the *Kripoleitstelle* Munich requested the following day that all border posts keep a look out for the following escapees: Franz Bordeufel, Hermann Rietz and Otto Günther. As embarrassing as these escapes were for the prison authorities, the *Polizei* reported that the convict Josef Weinacht had escaped from a prison work detail on 28 August. The Munich *Kriminalpolizei* circulated a description of Weinacht to all border posts and warned that he spoke both German and Hungarian.[109]

The following day *Ostuf.* Julius Mülthaler, a 47-year-old ethnic-German officer of the 8. / SS-*Artillerie-Ausbildung- und Ersatz*-Rgt. in Prague found himself indicted for committing fraud and faced trial before the SS- *und Polizei-Gericht* VIII. Commanded to serve a term of six years' *Zuchthaus* and expelled from the SS, the larcenous Mülthaler's civil and honour rights were denied to him for five years and he found himself incarcerated in the SS-*Straflager* Dachau.[110]

One Dachau inmate, who accepted front probation had an interesting view of his recruitment and those undertaking this work: Recorded in secrecy while held as an Allied prisoner of war on 1 August 1944, former SS-*Mann* Langer, who had been captured at Caen on 27 June 1944, was overheard telling his cell mate, Kursteiner, that he had served time in the SS-*Straflager* Dachau. Denounced for listening to an English transmitter, Langer was placed in remand detention on 8 November 1943 and his trial took place on 15 December the same year. Judged guilty as a people pest, the tribunal punished Langer with a term of four years and two months' *Zuchthaus*, expelled him from the SS, declared him militarily unworthy and denied him his civil rights for four years. Sent to the *Straflager* Dachau to await confirmation of his sentence, Langer's sentence was then amended to fourteen months' *Gefängnis* after three months detention, which the SS leader had yet to confirm. Three months later, Langer found himself released from jail and accepted probation with the *Bewährungsabteilung*. 'The *Reichsführer's* right hand, he was the man who signed death warrants' asserted Langer when discussing the SS-*Richter beim* RF-SS and complained to his cell-mate that Horst Bender had been the man who submitted all prison and death sentences to Himmler and signed the orders on his advice. In Langer's opinion, this 'swine' visited Dachau every two or three weeks and the inmates were paraded for selection, for what he described as 'suicide jobs.' During this conversation Langer would also assert erroneously that 70 per cent of the men who took part in the operation to free Benito Mussolini were recruited from the prison.[111]

In the autumn of 1944 the prison was still receiving convicts' files that lacked photographs of the offenders. Writing to the *HA* SS-*Gericht* on 8 September 1944, the prison requested that they sent them an image for the convict *Revier der Polizei* Zahard.[112]

Despite endemic overcrowding in the SS-*Straflager* Dachau and *Aussenstelle* Allach, the prison had no choice, given the deteriorating war situation, but to accept convicts from prisons that lay in the path of the Allied forces: A former Dutch SS veteran recollected that the orderly of the commander of the SS-*Wachbataillon Nordwest*, *Hstuf.* Friedrich Ziegler, received orders in September 1944 to take command of two railway box cars in Scheveningen which contained convicts who were destined for the SS-*Straflager* Dachau. A guard company of Ukrainians was provided as escorts, but instinctively distrusting them, Ziegler selected twelve Dutch men from his battalion to accompany him on his journey to Bavaria. Reaching Munich, the Dutch and Ukrainian guards were replaced by local troops and Ziegler accompanied them by rail to Holland. The convicts remained aboard the train and continued their journey to Dachau.[113]

This offender narrowly escaped a long detention in the prison in the autumn of 1944:

Name: Otto Raab.
Last Rank: SS-*Obersturmführer.*
Born: 22.2.1916 in Fürth/Bavaria.
Died: 16.3.1945 near Stuhlweissenburg.
SS-Nr.: 314.094 (joined 20.11.1935).
HJ Service: 1.11.1932–20.11.1935.
RAD Service: 3.4.–1.10.1937.
Prewar Assignments:
16. / V. / SS-*Totenkopfstandarte Brandenburg* 20.11.1935–30.6.1937.
18. / V. / SS-*Totenkopfstandarte Brandenburg* 1.7.1937–30.4.1938.
KL Sachsenhausen 1.5.–10.11.1938.
Wartime Assignments:
Heer from 20.11.1940.
III. / 67. *Infantrie*-Rgt. (signaler) 1.5.–25.6.1940.
Waffen-SS from 1.1.1942.
Rundfunk-Lehrgang Heer Schule Glatz 16.2.–20.5.1942.
1. *Technisch-Führer* (N) *Lehrgang Waffen*-SS *Nachrichtenschule* 20.7.–15.11.1943.
SS-*Nachrichten-Ausbildung- und Ersatz-Bataillon* (Nuremberg) spring of 1944.
SS-*Panzer-Grenadier*-Rgt. 6 *Theodor Eicke* (acting communications officer) early 1945.
Promotions:

0.0.1940	*Unteroffizier.*
0.0.1942	SS-*Rottenführer der Reserve.*
0.0.1943	SS-*Oberscharführer der Reserve.*
30.1.1944	SS-*Untersturmführer der Reserve.*
21.6.1944	SS-*Obersturmführer der Reserve.*

Decorations & Awards:

0.0.19__	SS-*Ehrenwinkel für alte Kämpfer.*
0.0.19__	S.A-*Sportsabzeichen in Bronze.*
0.0.19__	*Deutsches Reichssportabzeichen in Bronze.*
13.6.1940	1939 *Eisernes Kreuz II. Klasse.*

Notes: The son of a shop keeper. Attending *Volksschule* for five classes, Raab studied at *Oberrealschule* for four classes and attended a trade for one year. Employed as a radio technician with the radio-Raab in Fürth, Raab participated in the Polish campaign between 1 and 18 September 1939 and in French campaign between 10 May and 25 June 1940. Marrying his fiancée Ethel F., (b. 23.3.1923 in Friedrichsthal) on 31 May 1941, they had two children together up to the point when records ceased in May 1945. Hospitalized with stomach problems in mid-1941, this illness precluded Raab's participation in the USSR campaign. Believing his prospects for promotion were better in the *Waffen*-SS, Raab transferred to them in January 1942. A technical specialist, Raab had received a high ratings in an evaluation report on 22 August and this document offered special mention of his organisational talents. Following the submission of a factual report, Raab found himself taken into custody on 8 May 1944 and placed on remand for suspicion of committing multiple counts of forgery. Other charges included his involvement in several crimes against the war economic regulations, disloyal behavior and embezzlement. Arraigned before the courts martial of the SS- *und Polizei-Gericht* XXV, Nuremberg on 20 August, Raab was jugded guilty and was punished with a capital sentence. Finding himself incarcerated in the SS-*Straflager* on 3 October the *Reichsführer* confirmed his sentence and amending it to a term of *Gefängnis*, he permitted Raab to accept front probation. Commanded to the *Totenkopfdivision*, Raab was reported missing as his regiment withdrew from Stuhlweißenburg in Hungary on 16 March 1945.[114]

A small group of fifteen SS-*Straflager* Dachau convicts were commanded to undertake front probation with the SS-*Sonderregiment Dirlewanger* in November 1944. Arriving at this command, these *Knochenmanner* (bone men) then mustered with the newly created ninth and tenth companies of the Rgt. 2. A new comrade, the former political camp prisoner, Peter Wiesen, recalled that these jail birds were referred to as the 'Black Rats' and one of their number was SS-*Mann* Ernst Otto Moser who had served a prison sentence for stealing from the KL Dachau canteen. These former Dachau inmates and camp prisoners were then assigned to the 9. / II. / SS-Rgt. 2 and the former *Oberleutnant* Erich Langlotz was placed in command. Prior to joining *Dirlewanger*, the grey-haired Langlotz, a former accountant and soldier, had served a term of nine months *Gefängnis*. Post-war, a former camp prisoner recollected that Langlotz had been chosen as the company leader in November 1944 by a show of hands, the probationers preferring a former SS inmate occupying a position of responsibility than one of their own political prisoners; In the event of any failure, this person would face *Oberf.* Dirlewanger's retribution.[115]

Leaving the prison service for the front in the second week of November 1944, the long-serving prison administrator, *Hstuf.* Franz Sturmann transferred to a reserve unit to undergo an assessment of his capabilities. Later, qualifying as a company leader, Sturmann led a company of the 32th SS-*Freiwilligen-Grenadier*-Division until his capture by the Red Army at the end of April 1945. In a strange twist of fate, Sturmann escaped his captors and ended the war in Dachau, surrendering to the US Army in April 1945.[116]

Fritz Sturmann's loss to the prison service had absolutely no effect on its daily routine: His appeal for clemency rejected on 3 December 1944, the 26 year-old former SS officer, Sascha Bibrich, who had been judged guilty of contravening paragraph §175 RStGB, was brought under guard to the Dachau-Herbertshausen firing range on 16 December 1944 and executed by a firing squad at 8.22 a.m. *Ostuf.* Franz Zeber of the SS- *und Polizei-Gericht* I Munich witnessed the entire process.[117]

Last Months and Dissolution

The military situation for the German Army on all fronts had reached a critical juncture by the spring of 1945 and within weeks, the Allied armies would envelope the Nazi party's last levies and defeat and occupy Germany. Though their world was collapsing around them, the prison staff continued to carry out their primary function, the incarceration and re-education of court punished offenders.

Writing to the prison on 28 February 1945, the SS- *und Polizei-Gericht* XXIV, Stettin requested a fitness report for Paul Goetze (case Nr. St. L. I 189/1943). *Rttf.* Weilenmeier contacted this prison on 3 March 1945 to inform them that the convict Krüger would soon arrive in the prison (travelling via Gennep). Writing to the Vienna tribunal on 29 March 1945, *Ostuf.* Schwaiger reported that the convict Emil Senvas had arrived safely in the prison following his trial and sentencing before the Stettin tribunal, (case Nr. St. L. II 48/1945).[118]

In the dying weeks of the war the prison found itself having to accommodate the flotsam of inmates that had been forced to abandon the satellite prisons: Closing the Förrenbach prison near Heppurg in the spring of 1945, its inmates and staff then transferred in their entirety to the Allach branch prison. Here, a few of their number were selected for front probation and the remainder laboured for the BMW factory. On 7 February 1945, the *HA* SS-*Gericht* once again expanded the prison muster and commanded the transfer of *Uscha.* Stanko and 25 newly promoted *Beurkundungsunterführer* to SS-*Straflager* Dachau to assist the senior staff with the prisons administration. Joining this group was *Rttf.* Göttfert, who transferred from the SS- *und Polizei-Gericht* III, Berlin remand centre to Dachau.[119]

In the spring of 1945 the allied armies had crossed the River Rhine, were advancing into Bavaria and threatened to occupy the city of Munich, the birthplace of the Nazi movement. Realising that the prison was now directly threatened with attack, senior SS leaders then discussed the fate of the convicts languishing in the SS-*Straflager* Dachau and Allach. The UK Government's highly secret enemy monitoring station at Bletchley Park intercepted a message from *Ogruf.* F. W. Krüger, the GOC V. SS-*Freiwilligen-Gebirgskorps*, (Prague) to *Gruf.* F. Steiner, the commander of the 11th SS-*Panzerarmee* at Neustrelitz on 16 March 1945, which suggested a new course of action:

> (i) It is necessary to accelerate the full powers for the plenipotentiary officer (of the RFSS) as promised by telephone. The agreement of the military districts is necessary, otherwise this task will be impossible.
>
> (ii) I propose that the overcrowded armed forces punishment camps and the prison camp of the SS and *Polizei* should to the greatest possible degree be dissolved. Sentences of death should be carried out, and all other personnel collected into punishment or disciplinary battalions.[120]

Talking after the war, the former *Kriminal Sekretär* Heinrich Nett recalled that the convict population in Dachau and Allach had swollen to around 3,000 inmates by late

April 1945 and of these, some 400 to 600 felons had been prosecuted and sentenced by the special commissions examining corruption in the concentration camps. Nett recollected that two or three days prior to the liberation of Dachau, the entire SS-*Straflager* inmate population was paroled without regard to their offences, uniformed, equipped and armed for battle and then given orders to guard the camp and defend the locality.[121]

Prior to the decision being taken to release this convict population, the KL Dachau took delivery of 130 prominent prisoners on 24 April 1945 and the camp arrest commander, *Ustuf.* Edgar Stiller, received orders to watch over them. Placing some of these prisoners in the clinic barracks 8c, *Uscha.* Ludwig Rottmaier received orders to see to their needs.[122]

A little after their arrival, the first group of the prominent prisoners boarded three trucks and omnibuses in preparation for a journey to Innsbruck. A decision was then taken at this point to release a small number of convicts from the SS-*Straflager* and task them with guarding the convoy. One of the 40 guards selected to watch over the prisoners was *Ostuf.* Friedrich Engelke of the WVHA, who had found himself detained in the prison to await his trial for corruption (his brother was an SS-*Richter*). The prominent prisoner's column left Dachau on 17 April 1945 and journeyed south to the *Arbeiterziehungslager* 'Reichenau' near Innsbruck. From here, they travelled to Niederdorf near Hochpusterfal on 28 April and rested in a local guest house. Fearing that their SS guards planned to execute the prisoners, Army troops relieved Stiller's men of their duties and the redundant SS troops then proceeded to drink themselves insensible until abandoning their posts and weapons on 30 April 1945. On this date, Stiller began walking northwards towards the border. Captured on the road to Glockner by US Army forces on 12 May 1945, Stiller found himself detained at the prisoner of war camp at Bruck *an der* Grossglocknerstraße and was moved to a camp at Orthofen/Post Egmating in Bavaria on 25 May 1945. Surviving the war, Engelke became a prisoner of the US Army and transported to Italy, he found himself released after a short detention.[123]

Born in Greughausen/Unterwesterwald in 1923, Herbert H. was by profession an aircraft mechanic who had worked in Kassel from 1 September 1937. A member of the *Hitlerjugend* from 1933 to 1941, he volunteered for military service with the *Luftwaffe* in November that same year. Drafted forcibly into the *Waffen*-SS on 1 October 1944, Herbert. H. could not reconcile himself to this unhappy turn of events and failed in his attempt to desert some fourteen days prior to marching to the front to the *Totenkopfdivision.* At the front, Herbert H. grew convinced that he and his comrades were simply cannon fodder. 'Such a government with unfair methods of fighting can never win a war' exclaimed Herbert H. during an argument with a superior on 25 October and his outburst was reported to his superiors. Finding himself arraigned before the *Totenkopfdivision* field court in Modlin, the tribunal judged Herbert H. guilty of political unreliability, undermining the war effort and abetting the enemy on 14 December and imposed a capital punishment on him. His execution scheduled to be carried out at 29 December at 1.00 a.m., a decision was then taken to postpone this decision and Herbert H. was detained in the SS-*Straflager* Dachau on 30 December. On 28 April, he and other inmates were then suddenly commanded to re-attach SS runes to their uniforms. Re-armed, the paroled convicts then marched from Dachau with orders to defend Munich against the American advance. At the earliest opportunity, Herbert H. and his comrades deserted from this column and hid until able to surrender to the US Army. Hiding with farmers in Gröbenried near Dachau until 30 April 1945, Herbert H. worked as a farm labourer until 12 September and then arrived back home in Kassel on 18 September 1945.[124]

Other former convicts chose at this time to hide in the *Straflager* clinic amongst the medical staff and sick inmates. Captured shortly after the battle for the KL Dachau, Roland Lihotzky, a 33 year-old from the Sudetenland, informed his American interrogators that he had been a medical student in Prague during 1939 and joined the *Gestapo* in June the same year. Claiming to have been taken into detention while an investigation was undertaken against him for the theft of soup and coffee on 17 June 1940, Lihotzky found himself arraigned before the courts martial of the SS- *und Polizei-Gericht* III, Berlin in January 1942 and judged guilty of the charges, the tribunal sentenced him to serve a term of five year and three months' *Gefängnis*. Entering Dachau on 5 November 1942, Lihotzky became a prison medical orderly in April 1943. The former inmate, Johann Ott accused Lihotzky of involvement in the euthanasia of sick convicts and claimed that he and other clinic staff were released from their sentences and issued Red Cross identification and armbands on 25 April 1945. Lihotzky hid in the Dachau clinic until the camps liberation by US forces on 30 April 1945.[125]

Post-war, Heinrich Nett recalled that only a few of the released SS-*Straflage*r convicts were actually killed in action. Some, like the notorious former *Hstuf.* Hermann Hackmann posed as a political prisoner and were released by the American authorities. At the conclusion of the short battle for the KL Dachau, the surrendering former convicts risked lynching at the hands of vengeance-seeking prisoners. The vast majority of SS and *Polizei* convicts that had been released in April 1945 survived the liberation to face many years in internment. Here, they awaited interrogation and faced many years of imprisonment until their denazification.[126]

His offence is unclear, but this *Gestapo* official was executed in Dachau as the US Army stood poised to take the Bavarian capital: Born in Heersbruck on 12 April 1896, SS-*Sturmbannführer* Alfred Kurt Franz Bauer, a Great War veteran and career policeman, joined the Nazi party on March 1933 and the *Allgemeine*-SS in October 1938. A department leader at the III *des Stapoleitstelle* Munich, Bauer was promoted to the rank of *Stubaf.* on 20 April 1940. Executed for committing a capital crime in March 1945 just two days prior to the US Army entered Munich, another source claims that he had been shot in the KL Dachau for disobeying orders and attempting to desert.[127]

This remand inmate, held in the Dachau camp arrest, did not live to see the camp's liberation:

Name: Dr Med. Sigmund Rascher.
Last Rank: SS-*Hauptsturmführer.*
Born: 12.2.1909 in Munich.
Died: 26.4.1945 in Dachau.
NSDAP-Nr.: 3.092.414 (joined 1.5.1933).
SS-Nr.: 347.142 (joined 1.10.1939).
Prewar Assignments:
Personal Stab RFSS *Ahnenerbe* in 10.1939.
Wartime Assignments:
Luftwaffe FLAK-*Artillerieschule* Schonau in 5.1939.
Luftgausanitätsabteling 7.10.1942.
Leiter der Abteilung 'R' (*Ahnenerbe*) 9.3.1943.
Waffen-SS from 1.9.1943.
Persönlicher Stab Reichsführer-SS from 1.9.1943.
Promotions:

12.1938	*Leutnant/Ass.Arzt der Reserve.*
29.8.1943	*Hauptmann/Stabsarzt der Reserve.*
1.10.1939	SS-*Untersturmführer der Allgemeine*-SS.
20.4.1941	SS-*Obersturmführer der Allgemeine*-SS.
9.11.1942	SS-*Hauptsturmführer der Allgemeine*-SS.
23.8.1943	SS-*Hauptsturmführer der Reserve.*
14.2.1945	SS-*Mann.*

Decorations & Awards:

0.0.19__	SA-*Sportsabzeichen in Bronze.*
0.0.19__	*Die Medaille zur Erinnerung an den* 1. Oktober 1938 (Sudetenland).
0.0.19__	*Die Medaille zur Erinnerung an den* 13. März 1938 (Austria).
20.4.1941	*Kriegsverdienstkreuz II. Klasse mit Schwertern.*
30.1.1944	*Kriegsverdienstkreuz I. Klasse mit Schwertern.*

Notes: His father, a medical doctor, moved the family to Stuttgart in 1918 and later to Konstanz (his mother may have been English and his parents' marriage ended in divorce). Attending *Volksschule*, Rascher obtained his *Abitur* from the Zeppelin-*Oberrealschule* in Konstanz and then studied medicine at the university of Freiberg i. Br. Working alongside his father in Basel, Rascher completed his studies in Munich during 1934. Passing the *Vorphysicum*, he obtained his doctorate on 27 December 1937. Supported by a stipend from the *Deutsche Forschungsgemeinschaft am Pathologischen Institute der Universität* Munich, he studied cancer diagnostics under Prof. Dr Trumpp in the Bavarian capital from 1936 to 1938 (*Volonassistant der Chiurgischen Uni-Klinik*) and became a guest physician at the

Chiurgischen Abteilung der München-Schwabinger Krankenhaus in Munich during 1939. In 1933 Dr Rascher accepted a post at the *Kassenwart Zelle* in Herdern (Freiburg Br.) and mustered with the SA between 1936 and 1939. Accepted into the *Allgemeine*-SS in October 1939, they noted that Dr Rascher spoke a little English and French and could converse in Italian.

Holidaying in Spain, Portugal and other European countries, Dr Rascher attended a military training course with the *Luftwaffe* between May and December 1938, achieved officer rank and prior to the outbreak of war, he attended a further three other training courses. Drafted into the *Luftwaffe* in May 1939, Dr Rascher obtaind the K.v.K 1. *Klasse* as a reward for his efforts with Rommel's *Afrika Korps*. Applying to the RuSHA to marry his fiancée Karoline 'Nini' Diehl *nee'* Wiedemann, (b. 21.9.1903), their approbation was only given when the doctor reported that this 39 year-old widow was pregnant with his child. The marriage took place on 16 July 1941 and the family lived in Munich. The *Reichsführer* took a keen interest in the Rascher family, especially when he discovered that despite her advanced age, *Frau* Rascher had borne three children.

With Himmler's permission, the *Luftwaffe* commanded Dr Rascher to the KL Dachau on February 1942 to undertake horrifying hypothermia and prolonged exposure to cold temperature experiments for themselves and the *Institut für Wehrwissenschaftliche Amtes* 'A'. Authorised to select condemned inmates for experiments that led to certain death in April 1942, Dr Rascher visited the *Reichsführer* in October 1942 to request his transfer to the *Waffen*-SS. Impressed with his undertakings, Himmler wrote to *Generalfeldmarschall* Milch on 13 November 1942 to request Dr Rascher's transfer to his force and promised to share his research findings with the air service. The doctor's application to transfer to the *Waffen*-SS was submitted and accepted in August 1943 and he was discharged from the *Luftwaffe* on 1 September 1943. A promotions application was submitted for Dr Rascher on 21 September 1943.[128]

Dr Rascher's fall from grace resulted from a criminal investigation, conducted by the *Kriminalpolizei*: Investigating a child-snatching incident in Munich in the late winter of 1943, *Hstuf.* Erich Schnitzler of the RF-SS *Amt* grew to suspect that the Rascher's were involved in a conspiracy to pass off seven children as their own. Reporting his suspicions to the *Kriminalpolizei*, the allegations were then passed to *Kriminalpolizei Kommissar* Hans Schmid who initiated an investigation and reported the matter to the Munich chief of the criminal police, *Regierungs-und Kriminaldirektor* Greiner. Aware of Dr Rascher's close relationship to the SS leader, Greiner expressed his reluctance to deal with this issue and advised Schmid to seek the HSSPF *Süd* permission, in his capacity as *Polizeipräsident* Munich, to continue his investigation. When made aware of the issue, the HSSPF acceded to Schmid's request and a court's investigation was initiated in early 1944. Quickly, the policeman discovered that *Frau* Rascher had faked her pregnancies to marry Dr Rascher and to further her husband's career, she had adopted children legally and illegally from mothers and hospitals and Dr Rascher had manufactured fake birth certificates and illegally registered the children as their own, (compounding the problems facing the Rascher's, Himmler was godfather to some of the children and Rascher's wife had erroneously accepted the *Gelb Ehrenkreuz der Deutschen Mutter*). As a consequence of the allegations, Schmid and *Kriminal Obersekär* Küsterer visited the KL Dachau to question Dr Rascher and discovered many staff and prisoners willing to speak against him and his methods. Told that Dr Rascher worked directly for the SS leader to develop blood clotting agents from dehydrated food concentrates, the investigators were informed that the doctor had presented the results as his own work when in fact they had been produced by a Jewish prisoner and former Viennese chemist named Felix (a far from unusual camp occurrence). On the strength of these results, Himmler had commanded the *Ahnenerbe* to hand Dr Rascher 10,000 *Reichsmark* for start-up expenses related to mass production, but the doctor is thought to have pocketed the cash and only accounted for the money when made aware of the investigation against him.[129]

'A dangerous and incredible person' was the camp commandant's opinion of Dr Rascher and aside from committing embezzlement, a senior SS physician alleged that he had murdered his prisoner assistant and reported misleading results to the *Reichsführer*. Here, in Dachau, the investigators was warned that anyone attempting to interfere in then surfaced, talking to Hans Schmid, the camp staff reported their suspicions that Dr Rascher and two prisoners had undertaken so-called business trips for personal use and on their return were found with large sums of cash which they handed to the doctor. Convinced that Dr Rascher had a case to answer, the HSSPF *Süd*, *Ogruf.* v.Eberstein, ordered his detention at the Munich-Freimann barracks at the end of March 1944 and he is thought to have been later detained in the KL Buchenwald. Suspected of committing four charges of kidnapping children, *Frau* Rascher found herself taken under arrest to the *Polizeigefängnis* (police prison) at the *Polizeipräsidium* Munich. In detention, both proved uncooperative and attempted unsuccessfully to implicate the WVHA chief, *Stubaf.* Rose and *Blutorden* holder SS-*Schwester* Pia Bauer in their nefarious schemes. When the investigators findings were submitted to the SS leader at his field command post, he scolded v.Eberstein, accusing him of attempting to gain publicity from the case. Although annoyed by the revelations, Himmler was persuaded of Dr Rascher's guilt and fearing the publicity that would be generated by his deceptions, he commanded the HSSPF to ensure that Dr Rascher was detained in the KL Dachau camp arrest. Brought here in April 1945, the doctor found himself locked inside cell Nr. 73. Following an assault on a prison guard, his wife was incarcerated in the KL Ravensbrück and was later reported for attempting to escape. Observing that a courts process had been initiated against Dr Rascher, his promotions recommendation was halted on 16 May 1944.

Given that the disgraced Dr Rascher had worked directly for the *Reichsführer*, it was decided that a prosecution before the SS- *und Polizei-Gericht* I, Munich would be unwise and the SS-*Richter beim* RF-SS received instructions to investigate the case with a view to its presentation before the *Oberste* SS- *und Polizei-Gericht*. Speaking on this subject after the war, v.Eberstein recollected that the case proceeded slowly and the trial was delayed as a direct consequence of Horst Bender's office requesting additional information. The case file was eventually returned to the criminal police in April 1945 with no recommendations and no trial was undertaken. Himmler finally handed Dr Rascher a disciplinary punishment in early 1945:

> The *Reichsführer*-SS 14.2.1945
> Disciplinary Punishment Order
> To SS-*Hstuf.* Dr Sigmund Rascher, SS Nr. 347.142.
> SS-FHA–*Amtsgruppe* D
>
> I order your degradation under Nr. 2 and 3 of the SS-DBO to the rank of SS-*Mann* and exclude you from the SS.
>
> 1.) You have endorsed and supported the four children foisted upon your wife in the years 1939/1944.
> 2.) With a protected prisoner of the KL Dachau you have had undertaken private and private-business in 1943/1944 and unreliably permitted freedoms to these prisoners.
> 3.) In connection with this commerce you have embezzled from the protected prisoner Fachelegg a total of 15.000 *Reichsmark*.
>
> By your actions you have violated in the heaviest way against your duties as a SS officer and by your own self-design have placed yourself outside the ranks of the SS.
>
> Himmler.

Interviewed after the war the former camp arrest overseer, a man named Wauer, alleged that the *Reichsführer* had personally ordered Dr Rascher's execution on the day the prominent prisoners were evacuated from Dachau. When questioned about this, v.Eberstein expressed his certainty that the execution order originated from Himmler's field headquarters at Aigen. Concerned that he would be implicated with this order, v.Eberstein would claim that Dr Rascher had been captured by the US Army, or had successfully passed himself off as a prisoner. The fate of *Frau* Nini Rascher to this day remains uncertain. According to one source, she was hung in the KL Ravensbrück just prior to the end of the collapse of German resistance.[130]

Questioned about Dr Rascher's fate, the former Dachau guard, *Uscha.* Franz Xaver Lechner, claimed that *Oscha.* Theodor Bongartz had shot the doctor three times in his cell on 26 April 1945.[131]

Emptied of its convicts and their carefully accumulated files destroyed, the majority of the redundant SS-*Straflager* personnel decided to flee the camp and escape retribution. One unconfirmed statement purports that a single prison officer remained in Dachau to lead an inmate probation unit. Questioned by the *Landpolizei* Oberbayern in June 1947, Rudolf Heiß's parents claimed that their son led a *Bewährungskompanie* in the camp at the end of the war. Investigating this statement, the local police were unable to confirm this information using official documents.[132]

Questioned in 1962, a former guard recalled leaving Dachau with a prisoner transport in April 1945 and then surrendered to the US Army in Grossholzhausen on 30 April 1945. The former inmate, Johann Ott, recollected that *Hstuf.* Albert remained at his post until 27 April 1945 and then precipitately left Dachau to attempt to join his family in Garmisch-Partenkirchen. In fact, successfully extricating themselves from Dachau, Albert and Schwaiger both avoided US troops and made their way to Salzburg to link up with the surviving remnants of the *HA* SS-*Gericht* and their families. Here, Albert found himself arrested by the CIC and in a surprising twist of fate, he then found himself detained in the former KL Dachau for the better part of 1946.[133]

Returning to the SS-*Straflager* at the end of 1944, *Hstuf.* Gottfried Biedermann took command of the SS-*Zweiglager* Hammerweg in the town of Mosbach. Evacuating this prison in April 1945, Biedermann accompanied its inmates to Allach and later the same month, he fled from here and surrendered to US forces at Zell am See near Salzburg on 8 May 1945.[134]

The former prison staff were not alone in their effort to escape retribution. The vast majority of the permanent camp guard had abandoned their posts by the time the American troops began their attack on the camp on the morning of 29 April 1945. Some SS troops continued to resist from the guard towers, but during the afternoon of the same day, US soldiers witnessed the raising of white flags by anxious SS guards. Command of the camp had been entrusted to a relatively junior officer named *Ustuf.* Heinrich Wicker and surrendering the garrison to troops of the US 42nd division on 30 April 1945, he died in mysterious circumstances while escorting the egregious Allied troops around Dachau.[135]

Following the cessation of hostilities, the abandoned SS-*Straflager* Dachau and camp arrest were taken over by the US administration for use as a prison to hold former SS men facing trial before the Nuremberg tribunal for war crimes. Known as the war crimes enclosure Nr. 1, the former concentration camp detained also detained former high ranking SS-*Richter* of the *HA* SS-*Gericht*. The war crimes enclosure Nr. 1 held trials for 489 former SS men from November to 31 December 1945 and a total of 40 defendants were court-martialled by the Dachau military court for their alleged participation in the Malmedy massacre on 13 December 1945. Of these, 36 were judged guilty and 23 were executed at the end of May 1946. A Dachau military tribunal decided the culpability of 74 former officers and men of the LSSAH between 16 May and 16 July 1946: Amongst them were Sepp Dietrich, Fritz Krämer, Hermann Prieß and Joachim Peiper. Handing down 43 death sentences on 16 July 1946, the tribunal later commuted these judgements to life imprisonment sentences.[136]

The US authorities brought to trial some 1,700 alleged war criminals in 489 separate tribunals between November 1945 and August 1948. Those convicted before this military tribunal then faced execution, or served commuted sentences in the Landsberg prison. Trials were also held in Dachau against the former staff of the KL Mauthausen between March and April 1946, for the KL Flossenbürg between 12 June 1946 and 19 January 1947, for former guards of the KL Buchenwald from April to August 1947, the KL Mühldorf process on 13 May 1947 and the KL Dora-Nordhausen trial between July and August 1947. Closed in 1948, the Dachau wooden camp barracks were handed to a refugee agency to provide shelter for German refugees, those displaced by the new border agreements with Czechoslovakia. The *Gefängnis* extension to the former SS-*Straflager* was demolished in the late 1940s, or early 1950s and its entrance sealed.[137]

Post-War Investigation

Dachau liberated, the US intelligence services begun questioning a handful of former SS-*Straflager* guards and inmates to determine their knowledge of events that took place in the camp arrest during April 1945. During their questioning, one former inmate implicated the former prison *Leiter* and doctor in the abuse and murder of convicts:

Name: Johann Ott.
Last Rank: SS-*Untersturmführer*.
Born: 14.4.1895 in Vogldorf/Sudetenland.
NSDAP-Nr.: 6.632.895 (joined 1938).
SS-Nr.: (joined 1.11.1943).
Prewar Assignments:
Schützen-Rgt. 8 from 15.3.1915.
Schützen-Rgt. 6 11.8.1916–19.11.1918.
Czech Army Infantry Rgt. 35 27.10.–7.11.1921.
Wartime Assignments:
Wehrmacht 26.10.1942–15.3.1943.
Waffen-SS / SS-RuSHA from 5.11.1943.
Lehrgang OCS Fürth in 1943.
Hauptfürsorge- und Versorgungsamt-SS (Berlin) in 1943.
Dienststelle der Fürsorge-SS-*Führer Main* (Nuremberg) in 1943.
Dienststelle der Fürsorge-SS-*Führer Main*, *Aussenstelle* Karlsbad in 1943.
Promotions:
1.8.1940 SS-*Untersturmführer der Reserve*.
Decorations & Awards:
1914-1918 *Ehrenkreuz für Frontkämpfer*.
1914-1918 *Ungarische Weltkriegs-Erinnerungsmedaille*.
1914-1918 *Tiroler Landesdenkmünze*.
1914-1918 *Signum Laudis mit der Krone u. Schrs*.

Notes: One of seven siblings, his parents had both died by 1925. Attending *Volksschule*, Ott then studied jurisprudence at Prague University and here, became a member of the Catholic student organisation *Cavellverband*. Undertaking teacher training at the *Lehramt*, Ott was appointed a civil servant and was employed as an elementary teacher at a school in Scheft near Karlsbad in 1915. Promoted to officer rank, Ott saw front service between 2 February 1917 and 19 November 1918. At the conclusion of the Great War he returned to Scheft, now a part of the Czech Republic, to work as a teacher and head teacher until October 1942. A member of the SDP, NSDAP and NSLB until May 1945, Ott mustered with the SA from December 1938 to April 1939. Ott obtained officer reserve rank with the Czech Army in 1921 and married his fiancée *Frau* Frida Bedriska nee' Riha, (b. 29.6.1901 in Drahonitz). They had two children together and lived in Vogldorf *Kreis* Neudeck and Silberback *Kreis* Graslitz. As a consequence of his political leanings, Ott found himself punished with a military degradation in 1924. Drafted into the *Wehrmacht* in October 1942, he was discharged on the grounds of ill-health on 15 March 1943. The death of Ott's son, Max, while fighting with the LSSAH at Kharkov on 19 February 1943, compelled Ott to volunteer for military service with the *Waffen*-SS in November 1943.

Prior to joining the *Wehrmacht*, Ott was employed as a headmaster and was entrusted with the issuance of vouchers for food special allocations. When drafted into the military, his wife volunteered to undertake this activity. On leave during March 1944, Ott visited the municipal office, which was located in his house, and appropriated two blocks of vouchers (each block contained 50 numbered vouchers and copies). On his own behalf, Ott then submitted various eligibility certificates for special allocations from mid-March to 9 June 1944 and claimed to have distributed this food to deserving Sudetenlanders. His embezzlement discovered during an audit of the Karlsbad grocery stores. The auditor found only sixteen different coupons for seven kilogrammes of butter, 1,800 grams of meat and six eggs. The court would later assume that Ott had submitted many more vouchers, but these were destroyed when returned to the food office (he was also accused of occasionally giving comrades and acquaintances small quantities of food). Finding himself arrested by the criminal police for stealing food vouchers on 17 June 1944, Ott's wife was questioned but released without charge.

In addition to this accusation, Ott found himself accused of engaging in a sexual relationship with a fifteen year-old girl, Maria S., a compulsory year girl assigned to his household. When questioned, the girl admitting having consensual sex with Ott on at least three occasions between July 1941 and June 1942, but claimed having no affection for the accused. Given the seriousness of the charges, it is no surprise that the avaricious Ott was arraigned before the courts martial of the SS- *und Polizei-Gericht* VIII, Prague on 31 August 1944 (case Nr. St. L. 385/44). Judged guilty of war economic crimes, theft, for forgery, fornication and abuse of a dependency relationship, he was punished with six years' *Zuchthaus* and the *Gerichtsherr* confirmed the sentence on 6 September. Dr Reinecke of the *HA* SS-*Gericht* confirmed the penalty on 17 September and the *Reichsführer* agreed with their decision on 30 November. Although acknowledging that his crimes were 'pretty bad,' his case officer, Dr Wehser declared his suspicion about the case on 9 October and recommended a relative mild punishment of one year's *Gefängnis*. The SS leader supported his recommendation and upheld the sentence on the grounds of the war situation and amended the judgment to a year's *Gefängnis* and ordered his incarceration in the SS-*Straflager* Dachau. On 30 November the SS leader demanded that Ott spend six months in the *Straflager* before permitting him probation with the SS-*Sonderbrigade Dirlewanger* (a case review was commended for a year later).

Speaking to the American investigators in 1945, Ott claimed that the SS leader amended his sentence to six years' *Gefängnis* and he was incarcerated in Allach from 11 January 1945. Appealing to the *Reichsführer* for clemency on 25 December, *Frau* Ott's four-page appeal was acknowledged by the case officer (Killing) on 12 January 1945 and he assured her that receiving good fitness reports, her husband would then qualify for probation after six months imprisonment. Working as a medical clerk at the *Straflager Revier* from 12 March to 30 April 1945, here, Ott took care of the filing system. Surviving the liberation of Dachau, Ott was taken into custody and his captors noted that he had an operation scar on the right and left side of his neck. Interned at Dachau as a witness for the trials, Ott was then detained at the Fürtstenfeldbruck, Ulm and lastly inside the Heilbronn PWE. Delivered to SAIC from Heilbronn on 17 August 1945, Ott, in an effort to ingratiate himself with his captors, alleged to have witnessed numerous instances of illegal behaviour committed by medical staff and claimed erroneously that he had been indicted for undermining the war effort and handed a capital punishment. At this time, the interrogating intelligence officer noted that his source was highly intelligent and very willing to give information and declaring Ott a cooperative and trustworthy witness. As a consequence, he cleared him of complicity in crimes committed at Dachau.[138]

Of particular interest to the American investigators was Ott's sensational claim that convicts judged unfit for service in the camp were then selected for what he described as the 'Special Section' in the eighteen barracks camp clinic and assured his interrogators that none of those sent here recovered from their illnesses. Using powers conferred on him by an *Amt* III edict from 22 September 1942, ('the execution of sentences of persons convicted by SS and *Polizei* courts'), Ott alleged that *Hstuf.* Albert ordered the transfer of 500 convicts to what Ott described as the 'Special Section of the Camp Clinic' between 12 March and 29 April 1945 and in the presence of Ott, or his adjutant, *Hscha.* Seipel, Albert telephoned Dr Castelpietra once a week to order a list drafted with the names of inmates judged unfit for service in the camp. Ott then alleged that between 50 and 70 inmates were selected per week and convicts and prison medical staff assigned to the *Lagerrevier* would daily visit the camp barrack, the daily sick call and the SS clinic to perform this task and arranged transfers. The criteria used by the inmate physicians to judge these patients fitness was an examination for extreme undernourishment, a decision as to whether they was able to perform any duties and a selection of the physically and mentally sick, those whose treatment required a long period of time. Ott also claimed that the physicians selected inmates with minor illnesses and those they disliked for personal reasons.

Recollecting that the inmate doctors then passed this list of names to Lihotzky, Ott then consolidated the names into a handwritten list and this register was approved at a weekly medical meeting attended by *Stubaf.* Dr Castelpietra, Lihotzky, Ott, *Hscha.* Seipel and *Hscha.* Poltz. Recalling that the number of names was never enough for 'Seipel, Ott claimed that additional names were added to the list the following day as a consequence of Seipel's interjections. 'The way these lists of unfit persons are drawn up is a crime. Amongst them are even wounded soldiers. Whoever wrote and signed such an order will have to take responsibility' Ott exclaimed and recalled Poltz often protesting to Dr Castelpietra and Lihotzky. Once the list was agreed, a slip was then typed for each inmate which included the inmate's name, birth date and his diagnosis. Signing the slips, Dr Castelpietra then handed them to *Hstuf.* Albert, whose office immediately ordered the named inmates to transfer to the special section. The chief physician of this ward was Dr Arco and although Ott was unable to describe what medical treatment was available in this clinic, he expressed his certainty that none of the patients transferred to this barracks survived the experience. When an inmate of the special section died, Ott was informed of this event by telephone.[139]

During his questioning, Johann Ott then described the treatment of the so-called *Kachexie Fälle* (cachexia cases) inmates who was starved beyond further medical help. He recalled that in only a few exceptions during his tenure did any cachexia cases recover their health and transfer back to the camp hospital and SS-*Straflager*. Regardless whether they were in the special section, the SS-*Straflager* hospital or in camp barrack, Ott alleged that all cachexia cases transferred into the dispensary of the SS-*Straflager Revier* and in the presence of himself, the half-dead inmates were placed on a table and given four, or more injections and had two or more pints of blood removed, (Ott asserted that the experimental injections were injected into two, or more patients daily and none survived their treatment). Dying within two hours, Ott claimed that the inmate medics and SDG working in the hospital usually placed bets on the length of the patient's death struggle.[140]

Turning his attention to another matter, Ott revealed to his interrogators that on, or about 20 April 1945, in his presence, Dr Castelpietra ordered *Rttf.* Friedrich to procure identification from the International Red Cross for his medical personnel. Obtaining these documents, Dr Castelpietra then ordered Ott to add to them his name and rank and those of Berberich, Brand, Friedrich, Hansen, Dr Honig, Lihotzky, Jacksteiss, Nitsche, Poltz, Rupp and five other members of the guard to the certificates. Examining his identity document, Dr Castelpietra then reproached Ott for including his SS rank to his and the others papers. Attempting unsuccessfully to procure new certificates to correct this almost deliberate mistake, Ott was unable to recollect who signed the certificates, but claimed that everyone receiving one retained the documents about their persons. Although Erich Albert and other guards were questioned in captivity about their wartime activities, my research has so far failed to reveal any specific post-war trials to apportion blame for the abuses inside the prison as reported by Johann Ott. It would appear from this lack of action that the authorities had concluded that his allegations had no basis in truth.[141]

2.4 *Strafvollzugslager der SS- und Polizei Dachau, Aussenstelle Allach*

Chronic overcrowding became a facet of the SS-*Straflager* regime and this intractable problem, and the *Reichsführer*'s demand that *Gefängnis* inmates undertook war-winning labour resulted in protracted discussions between the *HA* SS-*Gericht* and the WVHA in early 1943 to establish new branch prisons. These talks culminated in an agreement to construct a branch prison in Ludwigsfelde for the *Strafvollzugslager der* SS *und Polizei* Danzig-Matzkau and a branch jail for the SS-*Straflager* Dachau in Allach.[142]

Discussing the command to establish a *Zweiglager* (branch camp) for *Gefängnis* convicts between 5 and 10 February 1943, the interested parties considered constructing the prison camp near Allach, where factories were involved in the war effort. Presenting this proposal to the head of the SS, his approbation was received on 15 February and with all the various SS agencies in agreement, a decision was then taken to construct the camp for *Gefängnis* inmates near the Allach BMW concern. The actual building work was undertaken by KL Dachau prisoners on a patch of land, adjacent to the south entrance of the of the former Karlsfeld Organisation Todt *Arbeitslager* fence (located between Dachauerstraße and Karlsfelderstraße). The *Amt* III, the SS leader's advocate, *Hstuf.* Gießelmann, and the WVHA then agreed that the *HA* SS-*Gericht* would accept responsibility for the prison, the WVHA was responsible for the inmates' employment and the convicts would sleep and eat in a separate institution from the prisoners. Construction was underway when Himmler ordered *Zuchthaus* inmates in Dachau to be immediately deployed to high quality work in an 'SS suitable' factory in the camp and only if absolutely necessary would he permit these felons to displace camp prisoners and deploy outside of the camp.[143]

Confirming that the Dachau inmates were employed in essential war work in early March 1943, the *HA* SS-*Gericht* noted that the construction of the '*Arbeitslager* Allach' had been completed on 19 March 1943 and in official documents the institution was referred to as the *Strafvollzugslager der* SS *und Polizei*, *Zweiglager* Allach-Karlsfeld, or more commonly as the SS-*Aussenstelle* Allach (Branch Office).[144]

Placed in charge of this new prison was the *Straflager* deputy leader, *Ostuf.* Biedermann in the capacity of the Führer der Aussenstelle Allach des Straflagers Dachau. He was later superseded by *Hstuf.* Franz Sturmann. Questioned after the war, the former Matzkau commandant, Dr Beelitz, recalled that Bäumgartner was in sole command of Allach prior to his transfer to Danzig in June 1943.[145]

The former Cologne court official and *HA* SS-*Gericht Beurkundungsführer*, *Ostuf.* Theodor Janssen, joined the Allach prison staff in April 1944.[146]

The newly constructed prison at Allach, consisting of eleven wooden barracks on concrete bases, it included a parade ground, was enclosed by electrified barbed wire fence and was watched over by wooden guard towers. The daily regime and punishments for indiscipline was identical to those in use in the other prisons. By April 1945 this prison was detaining the vast majority of the 1,600 convicts incarcerated in the SS-*Straflager* Dachau.[147]

As intended, the Allach convicts were employed at the BMW 801 aircraft engine factory and according to one source, some 400 of them worked at the Präzifix screw factory.[148]

It is reported that 300 convicts were detained in Allach in 1943 and another source intimated that 564 felons were employed as labourers in factories at this time. Later, Himmler's felons took on more specialised work, operating lathes and other specialised machines in their own workshop.[149]

Writing in August 1947, former *Ustuf.* Karl Lang recollected that approximately 1,200 inmates were employed in the *Flugzeugwerke* BMW–*Werk* II Allach: 'These prisoners had already been condemned by the SS jurisdiction and formerly belonged to the organisations already mentioned. The food of these people was of a very low quality and bad. I heard from the camp physician, that about 70 per cent of these prisoners was malnourished.' Caught stealing twenty army breads, Lang claimed that the fourteen convicts of this work detail were sentenced to death and the judgement was carried out as a deterrent to other would be thieves.[150]

Allach's existence was predicated on its ability to find work that aided the war effort. However, this labour was not given freely. Writing to BMW on 11 December 1944, the Allach 'work deployment officer', *Hscha.* Dick, reported that between 57 and 1,127 convicts had worked for their concern from 3 November and 30 November 1944 and the prison was therefore owed 269,649.25 *Reichsmark.*[151]

Writing in February 1944, the *Chef HA* SS-*Gericht* observed that the joint inmate population of the SS-*Straflager* Dachau and SS-*Aussenstelle* Allach numbered 2,400 inmates of all types and of these, two thirds, or 1,600, was detained in Allach and worked at the BMW plant. The Dachau archive estimates that the Allach inmate population had risen to around 1,200 convicts by April 1945.[152]

The long-time prison service report leader, *Ustuf.* Otto Langer transferred to Allach from the *Zweiglager* Ludwigsburg in August 1944 and here, he remained until the prisons dissolution in April 1945.[153]

Contacting all border posts on 21 October 1944, the *Kriminalpolizei* in Munich warned that an Allach inmate, named Friedrich Koch had escaped from his work detail and demanded that when caught, he was returned immediately to Dachau.[154]

The war situation had seriously deteriorated by the spring of 1945 when a decision was taken to transfer the entire *Gefängnis* inmate population of the *Strafvollzugslager der* SS *und Polizei* Förrenbach to Allach. On their arrival these felons were put to work for the BMW concern.[155]

Obeying the orders of the *Chef* RSHA, *Ogruf.* Dr Kaltenbrunner, the Allach-Karlsfeld leadership ordered the evacuation of the camp in late April 1945. Gathering the prisoners together for a last roll call, the camp staff handed out three days rations at midnight on 26 April 1945 and those judged fit to walk were then marched out of the camp at 9.00 a.m. These first steps of ths death march put the prisoners on course for a torturous week-long death march south to Waakirchen, where the survivors were finally liberated by the US Army on 2 May 1945.[156]

What of the *Straflager* inmates? Without consideration for their offences, each and every convict held in Allach was paroled two, or three days before the camp's liberation and issued combat uniforms, equipment and weapons. They then received orders to march out into the Bavarian countryside and defend the locality.[157]

Talking in 1970, the former prison administrator, *Ustuf.* Langer, confirmed that all of the Allach inmates were released from their sentences towards the end of the war and were then armed and equipped for battle. He, himself did not remain in Allach for this final

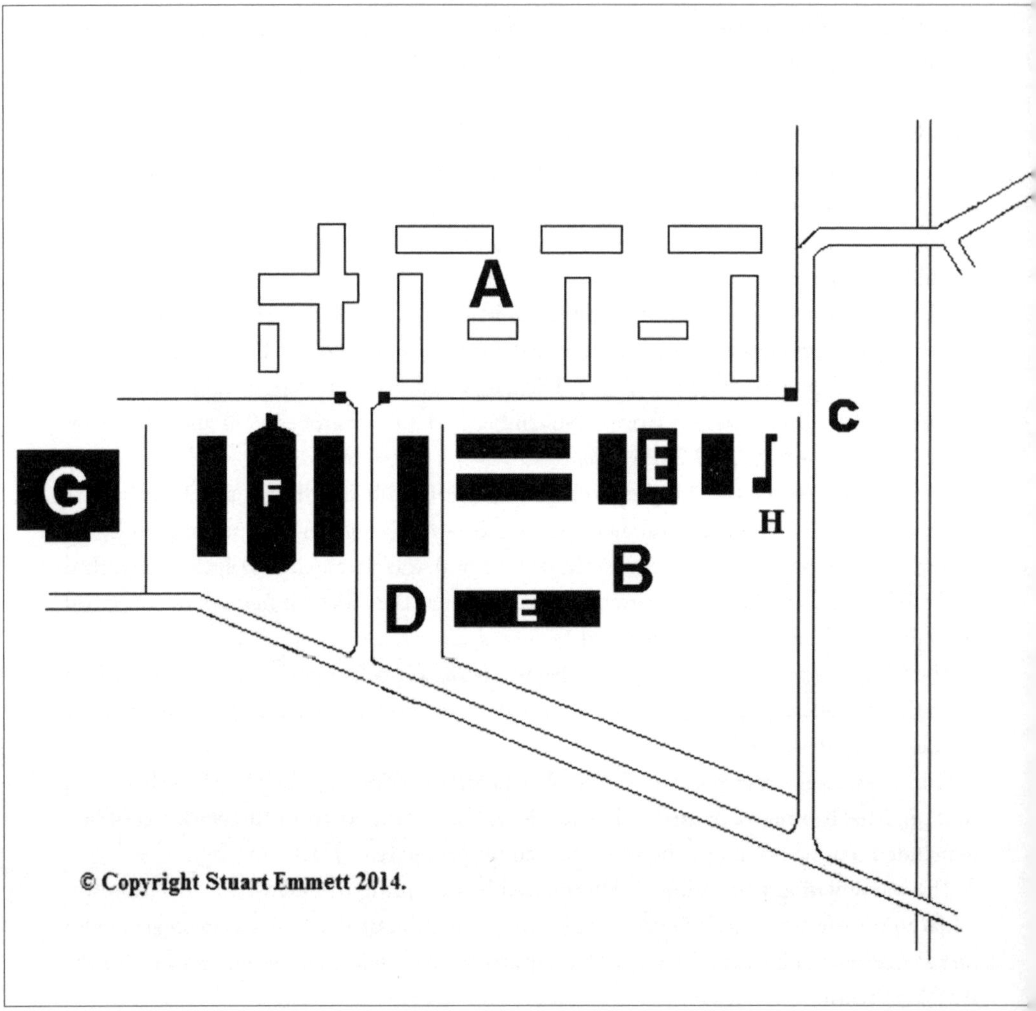

battle, joining a combat unit in April 1945, Langer fled southwards when the German's unconditionally surrendered on 8 May 1945 and was later captured by American forces near Kufstein in the Tyrol.[158] The camp prisoners of the Allach labour camp were liberated by US forces on the morning of 30 April 1945.[159]

In the wake of the collapse of Nazi Germany, the barracks of the former camp at Karlsfeld and Allach were put to use, housing refugees and displaced persons. The entire site was demolished in the 1950s and an extensive building project was undertaken to construct a housing estate. Interestingly, the estate's roads are named after types of rocks and today nothing remains of the labour camp or the prison. A camp memorial is located at Ludwigfelde, Granatstraße 8.

2.5 *Strafvollzugslager der* SS- *und Polizei* Dachau, *Zweiglager Hammerweg*

Establishing a business relationship with the Daimler Benz concern in the spring of 1943, the *HA* SS-*Gericht* happily agreed to supply convict's to work for the company at the newly-constructed underground factories in Baden during 1944. In 1974 the Baden-Württemburg interior ministry acknowledged the existence of the *Barrackenlager* Hammerweg in the town of Mosbach/Oldenwaldkreis during the Second World War and revealing that it was a prison camp for of members of the SS, *Polizei* and *Wehrmacht*, the ministry was unaware what type of prison Hammerweg had been, but expressed their belief that its inmates were very tightly controlled and they had no contact with the outside world, or with the camp prisoners working underground.[160]

Established on the site of the disused women's national labour service camp on Hammerweg Street, a few hundred yards north-west of the Turnhalle *Realgymnasium* in the Baden town of Mosbach, on 20 December 1944 the *HA* SS-*Gericht* announced that this branch prison camp had been built as a direct replacement for the branch prison at Ludwigsfelde (all mail for this prison arrived via Mobach/Baden, *Postlleitzahl* 17a. post box 49). At first subordinate to the *Strafvollzugslager der* SS *und Polizei* Danzig-Matzkau, the Hammerweg had been placed under the command of the SS-*Straflager* Dachau by December 1944 and detained *Gefängnis* category convicts. Remedial work on the camp was undertaken by slave labour and provisionally setting the prison, the first convicts arrived at the end of August and the beginning of September and was accommodated in tents and the fifteen wooden barracks accommodated around 320 convicts. The inmates were employed at the Daimler Benz aircraft engine factory, which had been built in an abandoned gypsum mine in the Schloß Neuburg, Obrigheim.[161]

Here, slave workers toiled in atrocious and life threatening conditions to construct the top secret V-2 rocket engines and under the yoke of their harsh taskmasters it is no surprise that many debilitated prisoners died of mistreatment, exhaustion and accidents. The tunnels proved dangerous for the 'Hammerweg' convicts too; one source reveals that a convict working in the tunnel was killed by falling rocks.[162]

Kommandant

Ustuf. Otto Langer (until 12.1944).
Hstuf. Gottfried Biedermann (12.1944-1.4.1945).

Lagerführer

Ustuf. Otto Langer (until 12.1944).
Hscha. Knecht (until 8.12.1944).
Hscha. Josef Graf (from 8.12.1944)

SS-Vertragsarzt

Dr Bergemann (10.1.1945).[163]

Prison staff

Ustuf. Max Dolles (10.1944).
Oscha. Lohberg
Uscha. Berberich (until 1.4.1945).
Uscha. Gustav Layer (until 8.12.1944).
Uscha. Thomas.

In addition to the main prison, the commandant organised two smaller prisons, the first in the Oberschefflenz *Grundschule* (vocational secondary school) and another elsewhere in Mosbach. One former *Straflager* inmate recalled that an *Hscha.* Hansen—a Bavarian with a false right leg—led the Hammerweg guard section and ending the war at Dachau, Hansen was last seen in the Kornwestheim Prisoner of War Cage near Ludwigsburg on 5 August 1945.[164]

In addition to the risk of death, or injury in the Obrigheim tunnels, the Hammerweg felons also ran the risk of death, or injury from Allied air attacks: On 8 December 1944, an air raid took place on Mosbach which killed staff and prisoners. SS-*Oscha.* Gustav Layer was killed at home by shrapnel and buried in the town cemetery. This prisoner died during the same attack: Born in Waldau/Kreis Boleslawiec on 7 April 1905, Alfred Bruno Rudolph was by profession anWohnort: Wiener Straße 65, Kreuzberg (Wohnort der Witwe nach 1945)Der Bürokaufmann Bruno Rudolph heiratet 1927 in Görlitz Charlotte Rühnle. office administrator. Marrying his fiancée Charlotte R. in Görlitz during 1927, Rudolph suffered long bouts of unemployment during the depression and was employed as a clerk in the *Milchwirtschaftsverband Schlesien* in 1935. Drafted into the Breslau *Schutzpolizei* in 1939, Rudolf was assigned to the administrative departments of various police units and was aAnfang November 1940 wird er stellvertretender Leiter der Buchhaltung in der von Himmler geschaffenen Dienststelle zur „Erfassung und Lenkung des fremdvölkischen Arbeitseinsatzes in Ostoberschlesien" in Sosnowitz.AAppointed the deputy chief accountant in the office for the *Erfassung und Lenkung des fremdvölkischen Arbeitseinsatzes in Ostoberschlesien* in Sosnowiec in early November 1940.

Rudolf found himself arraigned before the courts martial of the SS- *und Polizei-Gericht* XV, Breslau in late February 1942 on charges of military disobedience in the field in contravention of paragraph § 92 MStGB (St. L. I 42/1942). Judging him guilty of the charges, the court punished Rudolf with a whole sentence of 25 months' *Gefängnis*, which was set aside until after the war. Detained in the *Emslandager* II at Aschendorfermoor in early June 1942, Anfang Juni 1942 kommt Rudolph in das Lager II Aschendorfermoor, im Februar 1943 nach Börgermoor und danach in weitere Lager.Rudolph was then incarcerated in the KL Börgermoor from February 1943 and then languished in other camps. Several appeals for clemency and front probation, including one from his wife on 13 September 1943, were rejected and *Hstuf.* Adolf Meder dismissed another clemency appeal on 2 October the same year (Gns. L 3/1943). Am 2. März 1944 wird er in das KZ Mauthausen und Ende Oktober 1944 in das SS-Straflager Mosbach überstellt, wo Tausende Häftlinge Flugzeugmotoren für Daimler-Benz fertigen müssen.Transferred to the dreaded KL Mauthausen on 2 March 1944, Rudolf earned his release and was then incarcerated in the *Zweiglager* Hammerweg at the end of October 1944. Bruno Rudolph kommt bei einem Bombenangriff am 8. Dezember 1944 ums Leben.Rudolph died during an Allied air attack on Mosbach at 2.15 p.m. on 8 December 1944.[165]

Rudolph's death was not the only casualty suffered at the hands of the so-called 'Terror Fliers.' Crailsheim, a small town between Nuremberg and Heilbronn found itself attacked by around six Allied aircraft on 1 November 1944 and the local police observed that the Maulach railway station and the *Luftwaffe* base near Crailsheim were attacked on Sunday, 5 November 1944 between 2.00 and 2.30 p.m. (one plane was hit by FLAK fire, crashed and the pilot handed over to the *Luftwaffe*). Then attacking a transport train at Maulach, the Allied aircraft strafed some railway trucks, setting them alight and hit cars containing Croatian convicts making their way to Hammerweg. Receiving a head wound, Ivan Stumiek died and was buried in Crailsheim. Six other wounded convicts were taken by ambulance to the Crailsheim *Luftwaffe* hospital. During the twenty minute allied attack, the town Cathedral was also hit and two other people injured.[166]

In the wake of Operation *Plunder* US and British forces began advancing across the River Rhine on a broad front from 23 March 1945 and French and US troops had made significant progress along the Neckar valley by the first week of April 1945. As a result of this deteriorating situation, the SS arranged rail transport for some prisoners to the KL Dachau on 28 March 1945, but with insufficient transport available, a decision was taken for *Ustuf.* Heinrich Wicker to force-march a prisoner group to Dachau. An estimated 900 mainly sick or debilitated abandoned camp prisoners were liberated by the US Army when they overrun the Neckarlez complex.[167]

Prior to the evacuation of the Neckar camps, the *Zweiglager* Hammerweg received orders to close and its inmates had left Mosbach by rail for the Nuremberg SS-*Standort* by 31 March. Here, the convicts underwent a selection between 15 and 20 April 1945 and suitable candidates were offered front probation. Those selected to defend the city of Nuremberg were then armed, equipped and formed into an ad hoc combat unit.[168]

One of those selected for front probation at this time was an inmate named Günther Londner. Assigned to the 4. Matzkau *Strafkompanie* in June 1943, later, he found himself held in Hammerweg and has been missing since his arrival at the Nuremberg SS-*Kaserne* in April 1945. Writing to his family on 28 June 1943, Londner made light heart of his predicament:

> Matzkau 28 June 1943.
> Dear Parents!
>
> Warm thanks for the last letter I received. Also from Alfred.
>
> I am still fascinated by those two beautiful hours, which will forever remain with me the most beautiful of my *Straflager* time. Mum, I can imagine what stimuli Gotenhafen and Zoppot offered you. I wish I could visit sometime. I am very sorry to hear that Aunt

Sofie is now dead. Now live none of the three of my loves anymore. About Alfred's letter, I again was inwardly very pleased. He's a splendid boy. His mistress can be really proud of him. I will also thank him for his loyal words. Yesterday I waited in vain for aunt Rosenkranz's parcel. This was due about four weeks after your letter to me. Now I hope that, if not next Sunday, but at the very latest it will arrive in fourteen days, that is on 11.7. Hopefully it brings some skin and shoe cream, skin oil, and one or two combs. I am also in very necessary need of a toothbrush. Otherwise everything is the same.

Thank you therefore very much for all the love today and the greetings from home, kisses from your Günther.

P. S., Alfred can still sometimes send me a few lines.[169]

During this time, another inmate would be reported missing and his family would never hear from him again: Born in Amsterdam on 7 October 1912, Hendrik Joacobus Bouwmeester's family reported him missing in the August 1945 edition of the *De Waarheid*. The last letter they received from Bouwmeester was posted from Hammerweg in March 1945.[170]

The Mosbach town council informed me that the Nikolaus Kistner-Gymnasium was constructed on the location of the former prison camp at Hammerweg and their assertion is backed by the recollections of a young woman who worked here in the spring of 1945. Twenty year-old *Frau* Hildegard Radolko was conscripted at that time to help in what she described as the *Straflager Katzenhorn* near Mosbach (located on the Hammerweg). *Frau* Radolko‘s kitchen was feeding convicts and local *Volkssturm* on 31 March 1945 when she observed an anti-tank gun team emplacing their weapon near the camp entrance. At 9.00 a.m. that same day, Hildegard noted that the convicts were marching out of the *Straflager* in some haste and enquiring of their fate, their guards explained that they were going to Dachau. Emptied of its inmates by 11.00 a.m., the local *Volkssturm* took over the abandoned prison. The precipitous evacuation was well timed, later that same day the US forces had taken Hassbachtal and was in the process of attacking Neckarburken, a village a few miles north-east of Mosbach.[171]

Those *Gefängnis* inmates deemed unsuitable for front probation continued their journey from Nuremberg to Förrenbach and the remainder journeyed to Allach with *Hscha*. Alfred Mueller.[172]

Nazi Germany's collapse assured and the borders of Europe re-drawn, the wooden barracks of the *Hammerweglager* found themselves providing accommodation for a thousand Donauschwaben refugees who had been forcibly ejected from their homes in the east.

3

Strafvollzugslager der SS *und Polizei* Danzig-Matzkau

Riding high on their recent victories in the West, the military forces of Nazi Germany stood prepared in the spring of 1941 to embark on their next venture; the invasion of the USSR, but at this time it had become apparent to the *HA* SS-*Gericht* leadership that the *Abteilung-Gefängnis* cells in the SS-*Straflager* Dachau were insufficient to cope with the increasing numbers of offenders requiring this form of detention. Compounding this situation, SS and *Polizei* courts were required to punish offenders with mixed jail/front probation sentences from 12 November 1941 and the prison lacked insufficient space to offer the necessary level of physical and military training required for those inmates accepting parole. Concluding the first cruel winter's fighting on the Eastern front, the Dachau leader reported that his lock ups were filled to capacity and overcrowding had resulted in the multiple-occupancy of cells which had been originally designed for one inmate. So great was the pressure to find space for *Gefängnis* category convicts, that he had resorted to commandeering single cells in the Dachau concentration camp for short periods, but this solution resulted in an upsurge of disciplinary problems and hindered his ability to evaluate inmates for rehabilitation. In an effort to alleviate the pressure on the prison, the *HA* SS-*Gericht* continued to permit *Gefängnis* inmates serving sentences of less than three months to undertake their penalty in barracks and SS-*Hauptämter* cells. In addition to these measures, orders were also issued to establish new detention centres in Berlin and Prague and a small prison for this purpose was built in the grounds of the SS-FHA HQ. However, these measures did little to diminish the problem of overcrowding in the SS-*Straflager* Dachau and as a consequence of this situation and a desire to see the institution revert back to its original task of detaining *Zuchthaus* inmates, the *HA* SS-*Gericht* concluded that a new, much larger prison was required for their needs and the construction of a new facility received the SS leaders approbation on 21 January 1941. General Paul Scharfe, himself a native of the Free State of Danzig, often visited the place of his birth for holidays and it was here that he found the solution to the inmate overcrowding problem.

3.1 Conception

The Drei Schweinsköpfe, or the three pig's heads, which was also known as the Danzig Mountains, dominate the southern approaches to the port city of Danzig. Running between its hills, the Ernstthal valley road connected the village of Matzkau with the city (route 222, Starogardzka). Commanding scenic views of the Vistula estuary and the city of Danzig, the Drei Schweinsköpfe and Ernstthal had formed part of the Gulgowski family estate until at least 1923 and the hills consisted of convoluted pastureland, woods, a stream and a scattering of dilapidated stables in 1939. At this time the farmer, Paul Bözel lived and worked in the Ernstthal and renting land to tenant farmers, he also leased property to Gerhard Hausen, the owner of a small workshop. Stating his desire to take advantage of the views offered by the site to construct a hotel complex and tourist venture, a private developer purchased a large plot of hilly, uncultivated boggy land along the northern side of Ernstthal in May 1939, but failing to realise his project, he sold the property to a representative of the Free State and the site was handed to the SS in June 1939 to enable the construction of barracks for the newly formed SS-*Infantrie*-Rgt. *Heimwehr Danzig*. Created ostensibly to defend the city against an imagined threat of Polish aggression with Danzig volunteers, this military formation was buttressed with members of the SS-TV in 1939 and provided the Free State with an armed force for a future assault on Poland.[1]

The decision taken to build a military garrison at the Ernstthal, the SS-*Neubauleitung* Matzkau established its office at Danzig, Hindenburgerallee 50 to coordinate its construction. Contracting the building contractor L. Rohmer and Dehlert of Danzig and other companies to undertake the necessary works, the builders proceeding quickly into the dale to clear the land. Laying an unpaved road among wheat fields from the valley floor to a newly constructed parade ground at the top of the hill, the contractors also paved the Ernstthal track creating an all-weather road to the village of Matzkau which the SS knew as the *Lagerstraße* (Camp Street). Planted trees at the sides of the roads, in two months the civilian labourers raised 25 wooden barracks in a small semicircle around the parade ground atop a hillock. Concrete paths linked the barracks and a water tower dominated the hill. Once completed, the camp was placed under the direct command of the HSSPF *Danzig-Westpreußen*, but wishing to disguise its true purpose from the League of Nations officials and the Polish army, the SS referred to the new barracks as the 'gymnasium.'[2]

Proud of its construction, the *Danziger Vorposten* printed a glowing progress report in October 1939:

> This major construction project was implemented quickly and is a masterpiece of Danzig Company's construction. Until this summer, the attitude of Poland over Danzig was always threatening and aggressive and therefore the SS-*Heimwehr Danzig* had been established in the city and it was necessary to establish barracks for their many troops. In the last few weeks the Danzig construction companies have built the extensive complex of buildings that you see on our image, although other major tasks have yet to be carried

> out, such as the Käfemark-Rothebude's construction of large swimming pool. The Danzig construction companies have delivered with this building plan, the impressive proof of their efficiency and commitment, but we must also not forget the workers, who have over a twelve hour long working day often constructed in bad weather and thus have delivered this exemplary performance on the inner front, which is the greatest contribution to the defense of the homeland.[3]

Despite this glowing testimonial, the construction of the barracks had not been completed in time for the return of the *Heimwehr Danzig* from Berlin and as a consequence of this situation, their troops were accommodated in the former Prussian barracks at the Wiebenwall, Samtagsse and Langfur and at a variety of state owned and private premises. Elements of the *Heimwehr Danzig* took up residence in Matzkau in July 1939 once a few dozen wooden barracks with electric lighting, heating and running water had been constructed and some much needed basic drainage had been dug.[4]

Marching from Matzkau to participate in the Polish campaign in September 1939, the *Heimwehr Danzig* never returned to the garrison at the conclusion of the surprise offensive. In their absence, the 36. SS-*Standarte* utilised Matzkau's facilities throughout the summer of 1940.[5]

For reasons that remain obscure, a decision was taken in late 1939 to improve the facilities at Matzkau and to undertake this new phase of building work, *Oscha*. Hans Rach escorted the first 21 prisoners, of an eventual workforce of 1,500 Polish slave labourers from the Stutthof *Arbeitslager* to the *kaserne* on 20 September 1939 (amongst their number was Alfa Liczmanski, the leader of the Danzig boy scouts movement). For next couple of months these unwilling labourers worked in egregious conditions to repair existing buildings, construct new barracks and established a new infrastructure for the camp. Cultivating farmland, the prisoners built a barbed wire fence along the perimeter of the site, fitted heating to some of the barracks, enlarged the washing facilities, assembled an electronic speaker system and dug additional drainage ditches to alleviate persistent flooding of the site. Forbidden from sleeping in the barracks, the SS forced the prisoners of the *Aussenkommando* Matzkau (branch commando) to sleep on open ground with damp straw for bedding. Unsurprisingly these insanitary conditions provided a breeding ground for body louse and caused the death of some prisoners from typhus. The prisoners ration consisted of 100 grams of bread, beet jam and a cup of black coffee for breakfast and lunch and the evening meal consisted of a little under one litre of watery soup. Such was their debilitation by winter's time that the camp authorities permitted the prisoners families to send them food parcels and they arranged for the Poles to sleep in the half-constructed buildings. A small group of Polish-Jewish forced labourers from Danzig are thought to have arrived in Matzkau during November 1939. One prisoner, a Catholic priest, escaped from Matzkau in December the same year. Formally subordinate to the KL Stutthof in April 1940, *Aussenkommando* Matzkau prisoners remained on site until August the same year and laboured on neighbouring farms until ordered to return to the KL Stutthof.[6]

Their task completed, the Polish prisoners left behind them a *kaserne* consisting of 45 wooden buildings, each with built-in central heating, a small camp clinic, a storehouse, an armoury, firing range and gymnasium. Over half of the electrified buildings was designated for troop accommodation and the remainder set aside for administrative purposes. The also site included a kitchen and mess hall capable of seating 3,000 people at one sitting. It is thought that the swimming pool was completed during this building phase.[7]

In the midst of this building programme, Matzkau accommodated the recruits of the SS-*Totenkopf-Infantrie*-Rgt. 9 on 11 November 1939. Reporting infestations of body lice, the trainees also complained of inclement weather and reported the water-logging of at least two barracks. On top of these woes, a fire broke out, destroying officer's accommodation and it proved necessary to demolish another building to prevent the destruction of the *Wirtschaftsgebäude*. The SS trainees gratefully left Matzkau for the city of Brünn on 24 April 1940.[8]

The focus of the war had moved westward in preparation for the invasion of France and the Low Countries in early spring of 1940 when the SS-FHA decided that it had no further use for Matzkau and handed control of the site to the SiPo-*und* SD in October 1940. The secret service then placed the camp at the disposal of the *Einwanderungszentralstelle*, or EWZ who designated Matzkau a temporary settlement camp for newly arriving ethnic-German emigrants from the Baltic States. Once their loyalty and racial suitability had been established, the settlers were allocated homes and businesses stolen from Poles. Forced from their homes in Danzig-Westpreußen and the Warthengau, the EWZ commanded these dispossessed Poles to live in the overcrowded region of occupied Poland, which the Germans called the *Generalgouvernement*. The victimisation of the Polish Jews in 1940 would prove a significant step on the road to the Nazi regime's extermination of Europe's Jews.

This so-called 'resettlement operation' was overseen by *Hstuf.* Henry Bösche of the VoMi from his headquarters in Zoppot and his office accepted the first ethnic-German settlers from the USSR and Baltic States in October 1940. These people then entered an observation camp to undergo screening by the SS specialists, who judged their racial suitability and loyalty to the state. A typical EWZ temporary settlement camp was organised and ran by a small mixed SS/civilian staff who ensured that the settler's medical, food and work needs were met. Guards and administration staff was selected from settlers and these men wore an armband with an emblem, or the camp name printed upon it. The VoMi is known to have sent Latvian settlers to Matzkau in February/March 1941 and at its peak the *Kaserne* housed 2,963 emigrants. At that time Matzkau was under the command of *Lagerführer* John and he possessed the powers of a small town mayor. The final group of ethnic-Germans transferred from Matzkau to the Konradstein bei Preußisch camp near Stargard in January 1941.[9]

The numbers of ethnic-Germans arriving in Matzkau increased month on month from October 1940 and the NS-*Frauenschaft* Danzig-Land received notification of the imminent arrival of the first Lithuanian settlers to Matzkau in November 1940 and the first batch of travellers arrived the following month. Under no illusions that they faced a difficult task, the NS-*Frauenschaft* district leader ironed out the details of this assignment with the *Lagerführer* and 541 settlers, people of both sexes, all ages and children, arrived in Matzkau on 8 February 1941 (the older men prepared the barracks for habitation). The NS-*Frauenschaft* volunteers worked in the camp kitchen from 4.00 a.m. to 9.00 p.m. daily and the settlers' food consumption was carefully calculated to ensure that their intake satisfied them between meals. Those settlers assigned to work in the city were served their breakfast at 4.30 a.m. and the remainder at 7.00 a.m. Around 2,500 litres of food was served for lunch at midday and the volunteers dished up supper at 6.00 p.m. Baby food, children's meals for up to two years old and meals for special dietary requirements was also provided, but this complicated food regime caused extra work for the catering manager. To relieve the monotony of camp life the NS-*Frauenschaft* volunteers conducted what they described as 'happy afternoons' for the children. They also held home economics lectures for the woman and organised cultural events in the evenings (singing etc.). Accepting that life in Matzkau was far from easy for all its volunteers, the NS-*Frauenschaft* revealed that the steaming cauldrons in the kitchen had made life uncomfortable during the hot summer months.[10]

Flush with success following the successful campaign in the west, the Nazi regime then planned a further expansion of the armed forces for the proposed invasion of the Soviet Union in 1941. As we read at the beginning of this chapter, the *HA* SS-*Gericht* at by this time undertaken a search to find a suitable site on which to construct a new prison for *Gefängnis* category inmates. Becoming aware that Matzkau lay empty in early 1941 General Scharfe grasped immediately the significance of the site. Observing that the SS-*Kaserne* offered ample space for the construction of a Häftlingslager (prison camp), the general noted that convicts would also be able to conduct military exercises on the surrounding land. Expressing his interest in the garrison, the SD formally handed Matzkau to the *HA* SS-*Gericht* chief on 21 January 1941 and with the SS leader approbation orders were issued immediately to provide funding for the construction of the *Häftlingslager*. The *Hauptamt Haushalt-und Bauten Amt* II in Berlin approved a building plan in March 1941 and armed with orders to draft architect plans for the new prison, a *Bauleitungleiter* (building manager) possessing the rank of *Oscha.*, reported to the site on 20 June with instructions to undertake the construction of the *Häftlingslager* north of the existing parade ground and ensure that an electric barbed wire fence and watch towers were built to secure the site. At this time it was proposed to expand the *kaserne* westwards along the *Lagerstraße*. With the various interested parties agreeing to a completion date of 1 September 1941, the prison's opening was scheduled for the following month. Unfortunately, Himmler's lack of foresight concerning the erecting of a *Waffen*-SS prison resulted in significant difficulties sourcing the materials to complete the task and the arrival of the *Bauleitungleiter* in Matzkau during the summer of 1941 would mark the beginning of a nine month herculean task to redesign the waterlogged site.[11]

The *HA* SS-*Gericht* considered it expeditious to have experienced prison staff on site during the construction phase and as a consequence of this decision and in expectation of an autumn opening, they issued an order, transferring a small group of experienced prison staff to Danzig:

The *Reichsführer*-SS *HA* SS-*Gericht Amt* II dated 12.8.1941.

Until the final personnel are selected it is with immediate effect that SS-*Stubaf.* Kegel, the department chief of the *HA* SS-*Gericht Amt* III, will be utilized as the commandant of the prison camp of the SS and *Polizei* Danzig-Matzkau. The commandant of the prison camp Danzig-Matzkau is granted the disciplinary authority of an independent *Sturmbannes* leader over the permanent staff, the guard unit and the prisoners.

It is with effect from 20 July 1941 that SS-*Ostuf.* Albert is appointed the *Lagerführer* and transferred to the prison camp of the SS and *Polizei* Danzig-Matzkau from the penal camp of the SS and *Polizei* Dachau. The *Lagerführer* is the permanent deputy of the camp commandant and has the punitive service powers of a *Sturmes* leader.

With effect from 20 July 1941 the following are to transfer to the SS and *Polizei* prison camp Danzig-Matzkau:

a) From the *HA* SS-*Gericht*:
The administrator for the SS and *Polizei* punishment camp Danzig-Matzkau, SS-*Oscha.* Schwabe as leader of the administration for the SS and *Polizei* punishment camp Danzig-Matzkau,
   2.) SS-*Scha.* Josef Graf,
   3.) SS-*Strm.* Willi Pagels.

b) From the *Straflager der* SS *und Polizei* Dachau:
   4.) SS-*Oscha.* Erich Laimgruber,
   5.) SS-*Oscha.* Kilian Kranzmayr,
   6.) SS-*Scha.* Otto Langer,
   7.) SS-*Scha.* Anton Sorg,
   8.) SS-*Scha.* Karl Münch,
   9.) SS-*Uscha.* Edmund Mansbach,
   10.) SS-*Rttf.* Willi Kunz,
   11.) SS-*Strm.* Melchior Hofmann,
   12.) SS-*Strm.* Hans Heuser,

c) From the SS and *Polizei* Court IV, Danzig:
   13.) SS-*Uscha.* August Henning.

Signed Sharfe.

Both *Ostuf.* Erich Albert and his newly appointed Austrian deputy *Hscha.* Erich Laimgruber, an SS man since November 1931, had left Dachau for Matzkau by the end of July 1941 with orders to report progress of the build directly to the SS-*Richter beim* RF-SS in Berlin, to *Stubaf.* Bruno Kegel in Munich and to *Ostuf.* Kurt Lehmann at the SS- *und Polizei-Gericht* IV. Throughout the jail's existence, the Danzig tribunal exercised a supervisory role over the institution and on occasion provided staff, acted as an intermediary for messages and assisted in the preparation of inmate probation reports. In the wake his arrival, Albert set about establishing a command which would quickly grow to approximately 60 staff, which included himself, the commandant, the garrison physician, the head of finance, a heating engineer with three subordinates and a senior fireman (almost certainly seconded from the Danzig *Feuerschutzpolizei*). In addition, the *Hauptamt Ordnungspolizei* supplied a *Polize-Kompanie*, consisting of one officer, nine non-commissioned officers and 80 men, to guard the perimeter of the site until an electric fence had been constructed. A permanent *Waffen*-SS *Wachzug* (guard section) was not established for the prison until January 1942.[12]

Turning once again to the *Arbeitslager* Stutthof to supply forced labour for the construction work, the first Polish prisoners arrived at the barracks on 28 July 1941. Accommodated in the unheated gymnasium, this was the only building equipped with iron bars on the windows.[13]

General Scharfe retained a keen interest in the Matzkau project during its construction phase and visiting his holiday home at the coastal town of Gotenhafen near Danzig between 10 July and 11 August 1941, the *Bauleitungleiter* intimated in a letter that the *HA* SS-*Gericht* chief interrupted his holiday to visit Matzkau on 16 July.[14]

Once ensconced in Matzkau, the *Bauleitungleiter* engaged the architect *Herrn* Pfail to draw up new architectural plans on 19 July and then invited local companies to tender bids for the construction work. These works included street paving, road kerbs, a new camp entrance, wire mesh fencing, an electric fence, iron window bars, concrete posts and wooden watch towers. Requiring the delivery of irons bars for 28 July and fencing for 1 September, the *Bauleitung* quickly experienced difficulties meeting these dispatch dates and in an attempt to overcome the shortage of barbed wire, he requested that the *Hauptamt Haushalt-und Bauten* (Main Office for Budget and Buildings) interceded with the military authorities to supply his requirements. At this time a calculation of how much wood was required for construction and fuel had not been done and later, General Scharfe would demand an increase in the number of watchtowers from six to seven and this decision exacerbated the shortage of lumber.[15]

Writing to the *Hauptamt Haushalt-und Bauten* in August 1941, the *Bauleitungleiter* submitted the estimated costs for the following works:

1. Street paving, kerbs and a new entrance: 37,500 *Reichsmark.*
2. Wire mesh fence: 7,300 *Reichsmark.*
3. Outside window bars: 840 *Reichsmark.*
4. Concrete posts: 29,200 *Reichsmark.*
5. Watch Towers: 1,060 *Reichsmark.*

These costs did not include material that had yet to be delivered to the site and at this time the *Bauleitungleiter* requested credit capital. Unwilling to release the construction funds until they had examined his costings, the *Hauptabteilung* IIB I completed this task and then expressed their consternation at the problems obtaining construction materials and berated the *Bauleitungleiter* for his lack of progress. Estimating the cost of the project at an estimated 89,500 *Reichsmark* in August 1941, the *Bauleitungleiter* also requested a contingency of 6,000 *Reichsmark*. Agreeing to his cost estimates on 16 September, the *Hauptamt Haushalt-und Bauten Amt* II added a contingency of 1,000 *Reichsmark*, raising the total cost of the build to a total of 90,500 *Reichsmark*. With the approbation of the *Hauptamt Haushalt-und Bauten Amt* II, the barracks administrative officer (*Oscha.* Schwabe) released these funds to the *Bauleitungleiter* he finally received permission at this time to proceed with constructing the new prison.[16]

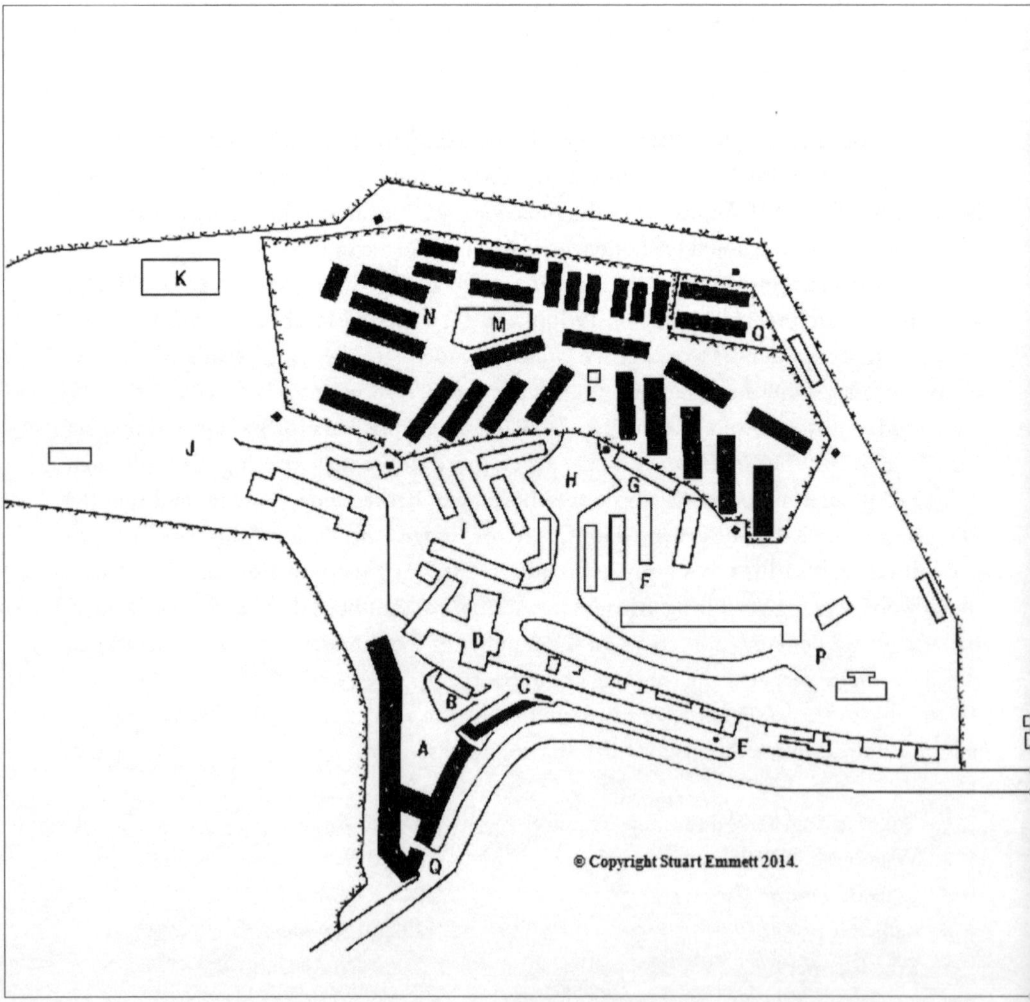

Ordered to assist the *Bauleitung* with his task, this 'old fighter' joined the Matzkau staff in August 1941:

Name: Franz Josef **Ott.**
Last Rank: SS-*Obersturmführer*.
Born: 26.12.1908 in Würzburg.
NSDAP-Nr.: 504.190 (joined 1.4.1931).
SS-Nr.: 9.252 (joined 25.6.1931).
Prewar Assignments:
1. / III. / SA-*Standarte* 3 in 1932.
1. / I. / 56. SS-*Standarte Franken* (Bamberg) in 1933.
Officer with the *Abschnitt* IX (Nuremberg) HQ 4.3.–20.4.1936.
I. / 73. SS-*Standarte* (Ansbach) in 1936.
II. / 73. SS-*Standarte* on 1.6.1936.
Dienststelle Vierjahresplan (Wöllershof near Neustadt) in 1936.
I. / 4. SS-*Standarte* (Altona) on 1.10.1937.
Wartime Assignments:
SS-VT from 1.10.1939.
Verflegungsamt 300 15.9.1940–26.1.1941.
2. / *Polizei* SS-*Sänitatsabteilung* until 7.4.1941.
Kassenleiter der Versuch Dienstellen der Waffen-SS, *Hauptabteilung* V9 from 9.4.1941.
Kassenleider for the Danzig-Matzkau *Verflegungsamt* on 26.8.1941.
SS-*Polizeidivision* on 4.8.1942.
20. *Kreigs-Lehrgang* SS-*Führerschule des Verwaltungsdienstes* (Dachau) 5.8.-31.10.1942.
4th SS-*Polizei-Panzergrenadier-Division Amt* V on 1.11.1942.
III. / SS-*Polizei* Rgt. 2 (administrative officer) on 15.4.1943.
Verwaltungsführer SS-*Panzer-Grenadier* Rgt. 8 in 1943.
WVHA from 20.2.1944
HSSPF *Ostland-und Russland Nord* HQ (Riga) from 3.10.1944.
VI. SS-*Freiwilligenkorps* / SS-*Bau-Bataillon Zvaigzne* 15.1.–23.5.1945.
Promotions:

1.10.1939	SS-*Oberscharführer der Reserve*.
31.10.1942	SS-*Untersturmführer der Reserve*.
20.4.1943	SS-*Obersturmführer der Allgemeine*-SS.
9.11.1943	SS-*Obersturmführer der Reserve* (R.D.A. 24.9.1943).

Decorations & Awards:

0.0.19__	SA-*Sportsabzeichen in Bronze*.
0.0.19__	*Abzeichen des* SA. *Treffens* Braunschweig 1931.
0.0.19__	*Deutsches Reichssportabzeichen in Bronze*.
0.0.19__	*Ehrendegen des Reichsführer*-SS.
0.0.19__	*Totenkopfring der* SS.
0.0.19__	SS-*Ehrenwinkel für alte Kämpfer*.

Notes: Ott knew his father, but his parents never married. Leaving full time education, Ott found employment in the hotel trade and worked as a cook with a Dutch shipping company in Amsterdam from September 1923 to April 1924. Employed in various Dutch hotels until September 1929, Ott worked aboard ships travelling between Java and Sumatra in the Dutch East Indies until January 1931. Returning home, he experienced difficulty obtaining work and was unemployed until October 1934. Becoming a salaried administrative SS officer in June 1931, they noted that he spoke Dutch and had fathered a child out of wedlock in November 1934. Denounced in the summer of 1936 for the unauthorised use of an SS vehicle, Ott was transferred to another unit as a consequence of his actions. 'An untrustworthy SS officer' who had 'no excuse for his unworthy, unwise behaviour' announced Ott's commander and considering him unsuitable as an SS administrator, he was transferred to the *Stab Reichsführer*-SS. Receiving another strong reprimand for absenting himself from an official SS meeting on 27 August 1937, Ott was then transferred to another unit. Marrying his fiancée Gertrud J., (b. 2.11.1908 in Tanna/Silesia), on 6 November 1937, they had four children together up to the point when records ceased in May 1945 and lived in Weissenburg in Bavaria and then in Blankenstein in Saale.

Appointed to Matzkau in August 1941, *Brigadef.* August Frank reprimanded Ott on 25 August for ignoring the cigarette smoking ban in the administration building on 17 July 1941. The SS granted Ott just over a 1,000 *Reichsmark* on 10 May 1943 to assist him with child and housing costs. 'He is a willing collaborator, but offers little to the tasks before him. His character is impermeable; he is quiet, he is matter of fact, but a correct and good SS man' wrote Ott's commanding officer from Salonika in 13 October 1943 and would later complain that his subordinate had an idiosyncratic character. An extremely strange occurrence happened in December 1943 which cast further doubts on Ott's character. In his own words, *Stubaf.* Heinrich Schuster explains the unusual incident:

> On 23 December 1943 at about eleven o'clock before mid-day and I was in the section IIa/b office when SS-*Ostuf.* Ott came to my service room. When I asked for the reason for his visit he told me that he had overheard the personnel of the section *IIa/b* in the service office discussing between themselves that he would be arrested. Since division had not commanded him to come to the office of the section *IIa/b* I then enquired of the *Abteilung* III (court) whether there was something held against Ott?
>
> As Ott was acting strangely disturbed, (but not drunk) I then asked him why he had visited the divisional building and he then explained that accompanying an SA-*Brigadef.* Herdwig to the divisional offices, (whom he had met in the course of his journey from Salonika), he had then been seated in the service rooms of the section *IIa/b* for over an hour. He then asked whether he could he pay a fine instead of being arrested. When I discovered that the division had nothing against Ott I ordered him to return to his unit. Ott then asked me how he should do this and was so distraught was he that I had to repeat my request four times. I then questioned the office personnel of the section *g IIa/b*, the men who had been working while Ott had been seated there.

The conversation occurred in the presence of *Ostubaf.* Dr Richard Sprenger, the divisional doctor. Concluding his interview with Ott, Schuster reached the view that the administrator had suffered a breakdown and called the divisional doctor to intervene. No further action appears to have been taken in this matter, but Ott found himself subsequently transferred to another divisional unit. It was evident from this incident and two further fitness reports prepared by the SS-*Panzergrenadier*-Rgt. 8 commander in Larissa that Ott had experienced problems with this command. The first report, composed on 5 February 1944, observed that Ott was 'proven and self-controlled' and observed that his attendance of the WVHA officer's course had only been partly successful. The following observations were expressed concerning Ott's personality:

> He works very slowly and is long winded, he is willing and ambitious and industrious and in his own way is very hard working, he has no work organisation, no outside interests, he gives no clear military instructions, his thinking is complicated and he sees difficulties where none exist. His foot dragging causes a mountain of work backlog and he is only just legible. The man gives the impression of feeling responsible for this backlog and appears to be ailing under the pressure of it. Amongst the men he is a total loner, he has a genuine taciturn character, he holds himself back and has amongst his comrades little friends. Ott has no marked sense of honour, but always endeavours to do the best he can.

A second report, compiled on 6 February 1944, confirms that Ott was experiencing problems in Greece:

> Technically skilled, he approaches his work in a relaxed manner, but leaves a backlog of work. He has no business sense and his abilities have narrow boundaries and are impracticable. He has little self-awareness, a slow mind, he is a typical loner, has little military manner and has no one close in comrade circles. Despite his ease amongst comrades, he has found no close comrade whom he can call a friend.

Ott's attitude to the troops was described as 'clumsy' and his commander judged him unhappy in his situation, noted that he possessed no talent for training, was non-committal and disliked, or unpopular among the other officers. Remaining with the *Polizeidivision* until February 1944, Ott had undergone a medical examination after complaining of a persistent cough and the physician concluded that he had contracted tuberculosis. It was the physician's recommendation that Ott limited himself to five cigarettes a day and recovered in a sanatorium. The following day, Ott transferred to the WVHA in Berlin and in the wake of his departure the divisional administrator of the *Polizei* observed that both he and *Stubaf.* Tschentscher agreed that Ott had experienced a hard time in the regiment. On one occasion Tschentscher recalled Ott admitting that he had not always done his best and confessed to often devoting too much time to minor issues. From his performance, Tschentscher concluded that Ott was 'unimpressive and unsuitable for divisional administrative work'. Then assigned to the HSSPF *Ostland-und Russland Nord*

HQ in Riga in March 1944, Ott was transferred to the SS Economic office under *Staf.* Eduard Bahl and worked in barracks twelve of the SS Collection Office Danzig. This thirteen wooden barracks camp had been built on parkland close to the Oliviaer Tor and supplied food and material for SS forces fighting in the Baltic States and Northern Russia. The appearance of the Red Army in Prussia resulted in the termination of this post and Ott found himself re-assigned to the VI. SS-*Freiwilligen-Armeekorps* in the Kurland pocket on 15 January 1945. Seconded to the *Zvaigzne* battalion, this unit performed labour tasks for the German 16th Army until their surrender to the Red Army on 12 May 1945. These Latvian's had been detained in the Valdai Hills prisoner of war camps by 23 May 1945.[17]

Since its inception, Matzkau had suffered from poor drainage and this situation was little improved in 1941. The job of improving the camps existing sewage system and drainage was undertaken by a specialist engineer and the new sewers he designed was constructed at depths of three metres:

Name: Dr Ing. Rudolf Götze.
Last Rank: SS-*Hauptsturmführer.*
Born: 13.3.1908 in Berlin.
SS-Nr.: 150.593 (joined 1.9.1941).
Wartime Assignments:
SS-*Bauwesen* from 1.9.1941.
WVHA *Amt* II in 1941.
WVHA *Amt* C from 1.12.1943.
SS-*Wirtschaft* HSSPF *Russland-Süd* (Rowno) 1.12.1943–25.12.1944.
Bauinspektor der Waffen SS *Böhmen-Mähren* (Prague) in 1944.
Bauinspektor der Waffen-SS *Reich-Ost* (Posen) from 15.2.1944.
SS-*Wirtschaft* HSSPF *Serbien* (Belgrade) from 1.8.1944–26.10.1944.
WVHA *Amt* Cv. from 26.10.1944.
Led the 12. SS-*Baubrigade* in 1944.
Promotions:
1.9.1941 SS-*Hauptsturmführer der Reserve.*
Decorations & Awards:
0.0.19__ SA-*Sportsabzeichen in Bronze.*
0.0.19__ *Kriegsverdienstkreuz II. Klasse mit Schwertern.*

Notes: A civil engineer by profession, Dr Götze held a doctorate in this field and drafted into the SS-*Bauwesen* in September 1941, Dr Götze was promoted directly to the rank of *Hstuf.* Marrying his fiancée Hildegard S., (b. 12.3.1913 in Berlin), on 13 March 1938, they had one child together up to the point when records ceased in May 1945. Dr Götze designed a new sewage and draining system in Danzig-Matzkau and when this task had been completed, he then transferred to the WVHA to undertake special duties in

December 1943. Remaining with the WVHA until the collapse, during the last months, Dr Götze led a labour brigade within the KL Sachsenhausen until the collapse.[18]

The Munich jurist, *Stubaf.* Dr Leo Ernst, a pre-war member of the SS.-*Gericht* and respected senior SS-*Richter* of the *HA* SS-*Gericht*, took on the post of chief judge of the SS and *Polizei* Court IV, Danzig in September 1941 and in addition to these duties he become the Matzkau commandant.

Aside from the construction of the *Häftlingslager*, the *Bauleitungleiter* also designed and oversaw the construction of a *Kraftfahrstaffel* (garage) in the south-western edge of the *Kaserne*. Consisting of a workshop, 100 individual, two door covered and uncovered parking spaces, this garage enjoyed the use of its own entrance, which led directly to the *Lagerstraße*. Requesting the use of the car pool for vehicles of the *Polizeidivision* on 19 February 1942, the *Bauleitungleiter* responded favourably to the SS-FHA appeal six days later, but warned them that the commandant's approval was required before final permission could be granted and cautioned them that their vehicles would only be permitted to park in Matzkau for a short period. At this time the *Bauleitungleiter* reported that bad weather and a lack of materials had resulted in insufficient electric lighting and heating. He also complained that the spring thaw made concreting the garage flooring impossible and cautioned the SS-FHA against storing the *Polizeidivision* vehicles for a long period, unless they was able to provide him with additional building materials with which to complete the works.[19]

In late 1941 and early 1942 some 200 convicts arrived in Matzkau from Dachau to assist with the completion of the prison compound's electric enclosure. This fence isolated the *Häftlingslager* from the *Stabsgebäude*, the warehouses, workshops and guard accommodation. In addition to this task, the convicts refurbished the offices and accommodation, repaired the kitchen, attached iron bars to the buildings windows, dug drainage ditches and assisted with the construction of the *Arrestgebäude*.

One of their number, *Schütze* Alexander Jeske, had been sentenced for an act of military disobedience and arrived in Matzkau on 10 September 1941. He would accept military service with the SS-*Fallschirmjägerabteilung* in 1943.[20]

On 8 September 1941 the *Bauleitungleiter* revealed that the Gubener Zementformen- und MachinenFabrik Wolf & Co. had won the contract to build two iron moulds, which were required to make concrete posts with a hook and nib attached (to hold the barbed wire and porcelain conductors). Sub-contracting the construction of the iron moulds to Max Brennmahl of the Stettiner Kunssteinwerke GmbH on 15 September, this company estimated that the moulds would cost 85 *Reichsmark* each and planned to deliver them in December 1941. This company also constructed an iron mould for the formation of curved posts and at this time they requested drawings of a corner section to enable them to design a mould for this part of the fence. The cost of these moulds was estimated at 80 *Reichsmark* each which did not include packaging (a total weight of 160 kg).[21]

With Ott's assistance the *Bauleitungleiter* continued his search for iron with which to construct window bars. Agreeing to purchase the iron moulds for the concrete posts on 19 September, Ott complained that their price had risen from 80 to 165 *Reichsmark* each and the previous estimates for the amounts of iron and steel had tripled. Both the *Bauleitungleiter* and Ott were unable to estimate how much metal they required to complete the task and at this time asked their superiors for help to source iron. Estimating that 3,000 metres of concrete was required for the fence posts on 25 September, Ott cynically judged that a private company pouring the concrete into the moulds would cost the SS an estimated 1.25 *Reichsmark* per metre, or 3,000 *Reichsmark* in total, but using forced labour from Stutthof, Ott calculated that the cost would reduce to 25 *pfennigs* per metre, a saving of 3,000 *Reichsmark*. In addition, he observed that using slave labour gave them more control over the supply of posts and the work could continue through the winter months. At this time, the Matzkau cash leader had no idea how much metal would be required, but assured the *Hauptamt Haushalt-und Bauten* that he would report the amount when the figure was known.[22]

Purchasing iron for the window bars remained a constant problem and at the end of September 1941 many of the buildings, including the storage rooms and work station windows still lacked this defence measure. At this time the *Bauleitungleiter* approached *Brigadef.* Christoph Diehm to obtain storage space in Danzig for his building materials and informed his superiors that he had located a company to supply porcelain conductors for a total cost of 750 *Reichsmark*, but given there was a long wait for delivery, he warned that the proposed opening date for September 1941 would be unobtainable. The building costs had reached a total of 840,000 *Reichsmark* by September 1941, which did not include the cost of the iron bars for the windows (an extra 1,600 *Reichsmark* in costs).[23]

Falling ill from sleeping in the unheated gymnasium in September 1941, (temperatures had reached -7° C) one sick Polish prisoner required medical treatment in Danzig and used this visit to the physicians' surgery to make good his escape. As a consequence of his daring, the remaining prisoners were relocated to barracks 6, 7 and 9, which were heated and had steel bars on the windows. They languished here until the prison works had been completed.[24]

Inspecting the site, in October 1941, *Ostubaf.* Dr Ernst requested further changes to the designs. He now requested a new main fence built around the convicts' accommodation, he demanded the provision of extra agricultural and petitioned for the construction of a football field, which would include a viewing stand for spectators and railings along the north-western boundary for the staff and inmates. To improve visibility, Dr Ernst ordered the weather-proofed watch towers be spaced in positions that eliminated blind-spots and asked for an additional seventh watchtower to be built near the guard's number five barracks accommodation and main gate. Lastly, he requested that a 375 metre rifle range, surrounded by an un-electrified fence, be constructed. While waiting for his villa to be completed, Dr Ernst informed his superiors that he would live on the local court premises at Danzig, Rennerhilfegasse 11.[25]

The *Bauleitungleiters* earlier optimism had evaporated by October 1941, but he could report arranging concrete deliveries and storage for the mixture for 1 August and had concluded his the negotiations with a company to handle the deep excavations and met with the company that would provide the electrified fencing on 14 August. However, in October 1941 the *Bauleitungleiter* expressed his concern that the architect's drawings had failed to taken into account Dr Ernst's new demands and again complained that he was experiencing problems obtaining building materials. This situation had been alleviated a little when the SS-*Abteilung Bauwirtschaft* (department for construction) supplied him 168 tons of cement and 23.50 cubic metres of wood, but this department reported experiencing problems transporting the wood to the site. At this time the *Bauleitungleiter* had calculated that he required 9.5 tons of iron for the six vertical bars and two horizontal bars for each large window and two vertical bars and one horizontal bar for the smaller ones and although enough iron lay on site to begin this work. Fearing further shortages, he had contacted the WVHA to request that they supplied him with a minimum of 18.8 tons of iron and delivered a two-metre-high security fence (when his appeals fell on death ears, the *Bauleitungleiter* resorted to contacting numerous private wholesalers in Danzig to fulfil the five tons shortfall). In addition to these problems the *Bauleitungleiter* informed his superiors that had been unable to source the estimated 65,000 bricks for the new buildings and had resorted to writing to General Scharfe and the HSSPF *Weichsel* to intercede on his behalf with the *Ogruf.* Albert M. Forster for permission to use the bricks earmarked for the Adolf Hitler School in Jenkau. It appears from a later correspondence that the HSSPF interceded on his behalf to overcome the shortage of bricks.[26]

The SS-*Richter beim* RF-SS inspected Matzkau on 21 November 1941 with the intention of supplying the SS leader with a report on his findings. Interestingly, the head of the SS visited the *Arbeitslager* Stutthof on 23 November the same year and one wonders if he found the time to visit Matzkau.[27]

In addition to the building of the *Häftlingslager*, plans were also drawn for officers' accommodation on 27 November 1941. These noted that the commandant and doctor's villas had been built from scratch and included a spacious gardens. Other staff accommodation was constructed from existing buildings in the villages of Matzkau and Borge and the *Bauleitungleiter* received responsibility for decorating the officers' homes (at this time plans for the *Arrestgebäude* had not been drawn). Requesting further details about the positioning and design of the prison watchtowers, the *Bauleitungleiter* submitted these new designs to the *HA* SS-*Gericht* in December 1941. The four-legged wooden constructions were anchored to concrete foundations, the covered viewing platforms stood open to the elements and was accessed via a ladder attached to one side. These changes further delayed construction and speaking with the architect *Herrn* Pfail on 24 January 1942, the *Bauleitungleiter* realised that he had failed to order an adequate amount of wood with which to construct the additional prison watchtower. Writing to his superiors in November 1941, the *Bauleitungleiter* complained that the drawings for the rabbit hutches had yet to arrive from the KL Neuengamme and the officers' homes had not been completed.[28]

Work on the prison had advanced considerably by February 1942. Corresponding with the *Bauleitungleiter* at this time to approve changes to the prison watchtowers, the chief of the *Allgemeine*-SS works department urged their correct construction, even if this added extra costs to the build budget and recommended that additional materials were sourced from the *Hauptabteilung* o V/3, (general construction) and department II/Ro 5 *Rohstoffstelle* (raw materials). At this time the construction team had begun to consider a new design for the officers' villas and on first view all had been judged excellent. Each home had a kitchen and dining room to permit the officers to relax in each other's company after their duties. Submitting his designs and costs for the *Arrestgebäude* by February 1942, the *Bauleitungleiter* estimated that the proposed building schedule had doubled when he took into consideration the additional heating and ventilation work. That same month, the SS-*Richter beim* RF-SS observed that the original accommodation had been upgraded and cleaned, the hospital facilities were improved and new beds had been ordered. In addition, he could report that a new concrete road and a sewer system had been built in and around the prison, the prison security fence had been improved and an additional watchtower built. He also noted that an electric fence had been added to the *Kaserne*.[29]

3.2 Command Structure and Teething Problems

Though scheduled to open in September 1941, this deadline had ultimately proved impossible to maintain and after nine months' construction, the *Strafvollzugslager der* SS *and Polizei* Danzig-Matzkau opened officially in March 1942. His work completed, the *Bauleiting der Waffen*-SS, now possessing officer rank, left Matzkau to take up his appointment as the SS-*Aufbauführer des* SS-*Oberabschnitt Weichsel*. Questioned about the staff strength, a former guard recalled that it stood at about 80-men strong in 1941 and towards the end of the war the unit numbered around 220 men. Capable of imprisoning 800 to 1,000 inmates, the new institution would incarcerate between 2,000 and 3,000 convicts by early 1945. Here, this former custodian explained how the inmates were disposed:

> [...] The greater part of the inmates were divided into work commandos, this included a 1,000 prisoners for the Schichau shipyard and smaller work commandos for commercial businesses, agriculture and very small groups of three or five men for agricultural businesses in Danzig. The work commandos were accompanied physically from the camp to their workstations by guard members and came back to the camp in the evenings. [...][30]

Commandant

The SS-*Standort* Danzig-Matzkau was led by the commandant, normally an SS-*Richter*, who was directly subordinate to the *HA* SS-*Gericht Amt* III. Responsible for the entire garrison, an adjutant and 23 non-commissioned officers of the garrison office, supervised by a senior non-commissioned officer, was assigned to his staff and the commandant approved staff promotions and disciplined the staff and felons. Evidently a remote figure in the inmates' lives, speaking in the early 1960s, a former inmate who had been detained in Matzkau between February and May 1944, was unable to recall the commandant's name until prompted. He then erroneously claimed that Edmund Baumgärtner occupied this post between early 1944 and March 1945.[31]

Stubaf. Bruno Kegel (provisional commandant 12.8.1941).
Ostubaf. Dr Leo Ernst (9.1941–21.2.1944).
Hstuf. Gottfried Baumgärtner (21.2.–20.7.1944).
Hstuf. Dr Fritz Beelitz (provisional commandant 20.7.1944–18.8.1944).
Hstuf. Dr Fritz Beelitz (18.8.–17.3.1945).

The prison's mail was delivered via the post office box 5 and was available by telephone using Danzig 24.719. In charge of the commandant's office was the *Kommandanturschreiber und Büroleiter, Uscha.* Hans Kötterl (headquarters clerk and office leader).[32] Replaced by *Uscha.* Albert Müller in the summer of 1943, he was superseded by *Strm.* Heinz Becker in the summer 1944 (a salesman and native of Weimar).[33]

Nr. 1 Lagerführer

An important figure in the day-to-day life of the *Häftlingslager* was the *Lagerführer*. A *Beurkundungsführer*, he and his deputy reported directly to the commandant and were responsible for maintaining inmate discipline, securing the *Arrestgebäude* and deputising for the commandant in his absence. Here, a former post holder explained his duties:

> [...] The Nr. 1. *Lagerführer* had to write fitness reports for the inmates, he took care of the sports and teaching activities, the drill and food as well as the labor of the inmates. My activities as the 2. *Lagerführer* also extended to monitoring the service expiration; moreover, I had to give military instruction to inmates, to enable all of them to return to the troops again.[34]

Supervising the *Häftlingslager*, the Nr. 1. *Lagerführer* furnished the SS and *Polizei* courts and the *HA* SS-*Gericht* with inmate's fitness reports.

Ostuf. Erich Albert (20.7.1941–1.3.1943).
Ostuf. Walter Dieterle (1.3.1943–29.3.1943).
Ustuf. Erich Laimgruber (provisional *Lagerführer* 29.3.–6.1943)
Ostuf. Edmund Baumgärtner (6.1943–21.2.1944).
Ostuf. Gottfried Biedermann (21.2.1944–8.1944).
Ostuf. Rudolf Heiß (8.1944–12.3.1945).

Nr. 2 Lagerführer

Ustuf. Erich Laimgruber (20.7.1941–15.3.1944).
Ostuf. Rudolf Heiß (15.3.1944–9.1944).

Nr. 3 Lagerführer

Ostuf. Rudolf Heiß (?–15.3.1944).

Wachkompanieführer

Responsibility for guarding the garrison and *Häftlingslager* lay in the hands of the *Wachzuges der* Danzig-Matzkau (guard section). Established by *Oscha.* Edmund Mansbach on 1 May 1941, a former guard recalled post-war that the section expanded into a company sized-unit in 1943. *Ostuf.* Fritz Ringel replaced Mansbach as its commander and in his own words he recalled his duties:

> [...] This unit was composed of convalescents who were not yet fully operational for combat. I myself was not fully operational due to an injury in the Poland campaign. Therefore, I worked in court service until 1942. The object of the *Wachkompanie* in the Danzig-Matzkau camp was to only undertake supervisory duties. This guard duty involved watching over the barracks, guarding the camp and accompanying the *Begleitkommando* to the outside workstations. In addition to the security duties, field and drill service were carried out to maintain the operational capability of the soldiers. For the soldiers the drill service was purely a formal duty.[...][35]

The Matzkau guard company consisted of six non-commissioned officers and 92 SS guards divided into three *Wachmannschaft* (Guard Sections). While one guard section rested the other two guarded the internal and external parts of the prison in two, twelve hour shifts. Armed with rifles and side arms the guard's task was to prevent escapes and kept a close watch on inmates working outside the prison. Questioned about this topic in the post-war period, Edmund Baumgärtner stated that two guard companies existed in 1943/44, the first led by *Ostuf.* Ringel and the second by *Ostuf.* Heiß who submitted regular reports to the SS-FHA. The guards slept in barracks which was located in the *Stabsgebäude*.[36]

Führer des Wachzuges / Kompanieführer der 1. Wachkompanie

Oscha. Edmund Mansbach (1.5.1941–1.1943).
Ostuf. Fritz Ringel, (1.1943–late 1943/early 1944).
Ostuf. Gottfried Biedermann (9.1943–21.2.1944).
?
Ostuf. Fritz Ringel (21.7.–1.12.1944).

Spieß der Wachkompanie

Oscha. Karl Vogt (in civilian life a forester, he lived Kaarten/Mosel).

Wachkompanie 1. Schreiber

Uscha. Josef Lerchner (b. St Anna in Österreich).
Uscha. Albert Müller (—).

Kompanieführer der 2. Wachkompanie

Ostuf. Rudolf Heiß (?–15.3.1944).

Wachkompanie 2. Schreiber

Uscha. Albert Müller (22.9.1941).
Uscha. Hans Kötterl.[37]

The member of staff entrusted with the welfare of the guards worked in the *Truppenpersonalstelle* (troop's personnel office). With intimate knowledge of all the members of the troops, he reported directly to the commandant and from the autumn of 1944 he was engaged as the personnel case worker for all the military personnel.[38] *Uscha.* Erich Lage fulfilled this post until the summer 1944 and *Uscha.* Albert Müller until 22 February 1945.[39]

Häftlingslager

The SS and *Polizei* inmates of the *Häftlingslager* were divided into four, later five *Strafkompanie* (punishment companies) and each was the responsibility of report leader, who was also referred to as the *Strafkompanieführer* (punishment company leader) or *Blockführer* (block leader). A room in each barracks was set aside for an inmate *Scribe* whose task was to complete forms and letters for the report leader. Emulating the command structure existing in the concentration camps, a convict *Barrackenältesten* (barracks senior) was subordinate to each report leader and below him existed a *Stellvertreter Barrackenältesten* (deputy barracks elder).[40]

Verwaltungsführer

Three *Stabsgebäude* barrack, which had formed part of the original camp, was set aside for the *Amtsgeschäfte* (administrative offices). Led by the *Verwaltungsführer* (administrative officer), he was directly assigned to this post by the WVHA in Berlin and he ensured that daily contact was maintained with the local *Oberabschnitt*, he managed detailed records, arranged the payment of staff and obtained invoices related to the running cost of the prison. Maintaining the camp buildings, he carried out property planning and the construction of new buildings, organised the supply of clothing, supplies and food and also ensured that the prison garage and vehicles were properly maintained. The administrator facilitated the exploitation of the inmate's labour potential and to carry out this task, he organised prison workshops, agricultural projects, work schedules, decided on the composition of labour gangs and calculated the invoices for non-SS companies employing inmates in accordance with WVHA guidelines. An enormous amount of paperwork was generated daily by the prison and correspondence concerning inmates usually required copies sent simultaneously to the *Amt* III, other main offices, the offender's former post, the SS-*Richter beim* RF-SS, the WVHA and if applicable, to his original *Allgemeine*-SS unit. Edmund Baumgärtner recalled that between 300 and 400 inmates were deployed in the administrative offices.

If there existed a political dimension to his sentence and imprisonment, the RSHA was kept informed of a convict's progress and later in the war they established an *Erkennungsdienste* (rogues gallery) in the prison administration to maintain files and images of inmates.

A limited amount of specialised work was provided for the inmates in 1942, but over time, the economic heart of the prison was gathered together into what became known as the SS-*Hauptwirtschaftlager* Danzig-Matzkau. This economic area consisted of small workshops, a lumber and ammunition box factory. Usually under the command of the senior NCO (*Hscha.* Langer until 1.3.1943), the *Hauptwirtschaftlager* received its orders directly from the administrative officer.[41]

Name: Stefan Golda.
Last Rank: SS-*Obersturmführer.*
Born: 22.12.1917 in Konin/Warthengau.
SS-Nr.: 378.432 (joined 1.4.1939).
Prewar Assignments:
9. / LSSAH in 4.1939.
Wartime Assignments:
LSSAH *Ersatz-Bataillon* (Berlin) in 10.1940.
Litzmannstadt SD 26.2.1941–1.9.1941.
1. / VI. / LSSAH 1.9.1941–13.3.1942.
SS-WVHA from 3.1942
5. / *Ersatz-Bataillon der* SS-*Verwaltungsdienst* in 1942.
SS-WVHA *Rechnungslehrgang* 15.4–15.5.1942.
19. *Kreigslehrgang SS-Führerschule des Verwaltungsdienstes* (Dachau) 8.8.-15.12.1942.
1. *Zugführerlehrgang für Sonderdienst* SS-*Junkerschule* Braunschweig 6.1.–19.2.1943.
Strafvollzugslager der SS *und Polizei* Danzig-Matzkau on 19.2.1943.
Promotions:

1.6.1940	SS-*Sturmann der Waffen*-SS (*Aktiv*).
20.4.1941	SS-*Rottenführer der Waffen*-SS (*Aktiv*) (R.D.A. 1.4.1941).
0.0.1942	SS-*Oberscharführer der Waffen*-SS *der Reserve.*
18.2.1944	SS-*Untersturmführer der Reserve.*
9.11.1944	SS-*Obersturmführer der Reserve.*

Decorations & Awards:

0.00.19__	*Verwundetenabzeichen in Schwarz.*
0.00.19__	*Deutsches Reichssportabzeichen in Bronze.*

Notes: Born in the Polish city of Posen, Golda was one of four children of an ethnic-German family living in Łódź. Concluding a three year apprenticeship at a German speaking school, Golda was employed as a cloth dyeing specialist in Litzmannstadt (Łódź). Avoiding military service in the Polish Army, Golda left Poland on 5 March 1939 and reported for military service in Berlin. Golda's application to join the *Allgemeine*-SS was submitted on 10 March 1939 and once accepted, he joined the LSSAH for military training (they noted he spoke fluent Polish). Participating in the invasion of Poland during September and October 1939, Golda fought with the LSSAH during the May 1940 invasion of Holland and remained with this regiment until his wounding on 26 May 1940. Released from hospital in October 1940, Golda attended two WVHA financial training courses in Dachau in 1942 and at their conclusion was judged suitable as an accounts officer for the administrative service. His chief instructor reported the following observations:

> He has an orderly appearance, is physically fit for service, his character is impeccable, energetic, conscientious, clear thinking and fairly good. He is an able specialist, his leadership very good and he has no reported disciplinary problems.

Judged suitable as an SS officer candidate in the administrative service, Golda then attended a section leader training course for special service and passed his final test on 31 January 1944. His chief instructor offered the following observations about his performance:

> It is possible to promote him to officer in part to his fresh, lively, ambitious, industrious, succinct and thoroughly hard work, his good intentions and willingness to learn. He is suitable as a *Zugführer*, but requires further training before he become a *Gruppenführer*.

Promoted an officer of the WVHA in February 1944, Golda found himself assigned to Danzig-Matzkau as its administrative leader in the same month. Marrying his fiancée Erika A., (b. 30.12.1922 in Angersburg/Königsberg) on 26 April 1943, the couple lived in the city of her birth and they had one child up to the point when records ceased in May 1945. His promotion recommended on 26 April 1944, here, *Hstuf.* Baumgärtner recorded the following observations about Golda:

> SS-*Ustuf.* Golda's belief strongly improves, he is a suitable SS man and his character is also suitable. Every day he himself is always impeccable. Golda came here on 1 March 1943, as leader of the local administration. In this service position he has been infallible in his work and deals with it satisfactorily. He is honest and makes an effort to circumspectly administer for the troop members and the prisoners in his care. He is understanding and gives his all to the work of the service position and is an example to all. He is suitable for the position and I support his promotion to SS-*Ostuf. der Reserve* on 9 November 1944.

Writing on 26 April 1944, Golda requested his personal papers were sent to the prison. Writing again on 7 September 1944, he reported that he was living in the prison staff accommodation. It is not clear if Golda was reassigned to Förrenbach in March 1945, but given the high regard he was held by his comrades, this transfer appears probable.[42]

Lagerartze

The responsibility for maintaining the health of the staff, inmates and local SS and *Polizei* lay in the hands of the *Lagerartze* (camp physician). Also known as the garrison physician for the SS and *Polizei* for Danzig and Gotenhafen, this officer held responsibility for maintaining sanitary conditions in the prison, he performed minor operations, bandaged wounds, prepared medical certificates for felons, he ensured that convicts were fit for punishment and combated outbreaks of disease in the prison. One of his more onerous tasks was the selection homosexuals for castration. Commanding over all other doctors, dentists, pharmacists and medical staff, the camp physician permitted inmates to work as medical orderlies in the garrison hospital. His hospital was located in the south-eastern corner of the *Stabsgebäude* and two barracks were set aside for a clinic inside the *Häftlingslager*.[43]

Almost from its inception, Matzkau accepted convicts with psychological problems. Those inmates judged to be suffering from mental illness were transferred to the *neurologisch-psychiatrische Beobachtungsstation der Waffen*-SS at Gießen and Würzberg and here received specialised psychiatric treatment and evaluation.

Telexing to the prison on 2 December 1942, the SS- *und Polizei-Gericht* VII, Vienna informed them that *Schütze* Hans Kopplow had been undergoing an examination at the Gießen psychiatric department of the SS-*Lazarett* since 7 November 1942. Writing to the SS- *und Polizei-Gericht* XXV, Nuremberg on 29 June 1944, the Belgrade tribunal informed them that *Gren.* Philip Manz had been sent to Gießen for examination. Manz had previously served with the SS-*Polizei-Infantrie*-Rgt. 2 and had been court martialled for taking an unauthorised leave.[44]

Arriving in the prison during the summer of 1941, this SS doctor established the Matzkau clinic, but would leave the camp under a cloud:

Name: Dr Frank Ludwig Müller.
Last Rank: SS-*Obersturmführer*.
Born: 27.12.1911 in Chemnitz/Saxony.
NSDAP-Nr.: 4.306.864 (joined 1.5.1937).
SS-Nr.: 277.223 (joined 30.10.1936).
Prewar Assignments:
2. SS-*Motorstandarte* (*Oberabschnitt Elbe*) in 1936.
SS-*Sanitätsstaffel* of the III. / 84. SS-*Standarte* (Chemnitz) in 1.1938.
I. / 78. SS-*Standarte* (Wiesbaden) in 2.1938.
Wehrmacht Heer Sanitäts-Lehrgang 20–24.11.1939.
Wartime Assignments:
III. / 84. SS-*Standarte* (Chemnitz) in 2.1940.
Waffen-SS from 15.4.1941.

SS-*Sanitätsabteilung* Dachau from 15.4.1941.
KL Dachau medical staff 6.6.–28.7.1941.
Strafvollzugslager der SS *und Polizei* 29.7.1941–2.3.1943.
SS-*Panzergrenadier-Ersatz-Bataillon* I *Totenkopf* 2.3.1943–8.1944.
V. SS-*Freiwilligen-Gebirgskorps* in 8.1944.
SS-*Panzergrenadier-Ersatz-Bataillon Totenkopf* in 2.1945.

Promotions:

31.1.1936	SS-*Bewerber*
10.1936	SS-*Mann.*
20.4.1938	SS-*Sturmann der Allgemeine*-SS.
10.9.1939	SS-*Unterscharführer der Allgemeine*-SS.
0.0.1941	SS-*Hauptscharführer der Reserve.*
9.11.1941	SS-*Untersturmführer der Reserve* (R.D.A. 1.10.1941).
9.11.1942	SS-*Obersturmführer der Reserve.*

Decorations & Awards:

0.0.1943 *Kriegsverdienstkreuz II. Klasse mit Schwertern.*

Notes: Attending *Volksschul*e, Müller obtained his *Abitur* from *Höhere Schule* and then studied medicine at university for twelve semesters. Qualifying as a doctor in 1937, the SS noted that Dr Müller's brother suffered from schizophrenia and lived in a mental hospital in Döbeln in Saxony. Employed with the T; Bremen-Aumund district hospital at Osterholz on 1 March 1940, the appointment ended after fourteen months when Dr Müller was drafted into the *Waffen*-SS in the spring of 1941. Appointed the garrison physician at Matzkau in July 1941, here, Dr Müller performed a cranial operation on an inmate named Kandler in the summer of 1942. He replaced *Ostuf.* Dr Siegfried Bottge as physician for a reserve battalion in March 1943. Speaking to this author in June 2014, the former *Ustuf.* Kurt Grawe recalled visiting Matzkau with an SS Judge in late 1941 to investigate an inmate's claim that the camp physician had ordered sick inmates to stand in the cold and poured water over them. Postwar, Dr Beelitz recollected arriving in Matzkau during the summer of 1943 and would recall being told that the former camp doctor had been dismissed as a consequence of dissatisfaction with supervision in the prison. I am certain that both these recollections refer to Dr Müller's tenure and explain his sudden transfer. From Warsaw, his commanding officer related his opinions of this military physician:

> He has an open, quiet nature and is a candid character; he works independently as a doctor for ten training and reserve units. He is untiring in his work and has a conscientious sense of duty toward the soldiers; he has good teaching abilities with the medical orderly trainees and as an older SS man he is at one with SS values. Lastly he has the perfect composure of an SS officer.

A report dated 10 December 1943 noted that Dr Müller was 'impeccable,' a 'valuable member of the battalion' and observed that he 'investigates the needs of the recruits and cares for those discharged from the military hospital safely and in silence, he has a well-balanced character and is suitable as a troop doctor.'[45]

Name: Dr Karl-Heinz Flothmann.
Last Rank: SS-*Sturmbannführer.*
Born: 3.7.1909 in Kupferdreh/Essen.
NSDAP-Nr.: 4.776.869 (joined 1.5.1937).
SS-Nr.: 367.749 (joined 25.4.1940).
Prewar Assignments:
1. SA-*Marine-Standarte* (Hamburg) 12.5.1934-25.4.1940.
Wartime Assignments:
Waffen-SS from 4.1940.
9. / SS-*Totenkopf-Infantrie*-Rgt. 6 (Prag-Rusin) in 4.1940.
5. / SS-*Totenkopf-Infantrie* Rgt. 14 in 1940.
SS-*Totenkopf-Infantrie*-Rgt. (Prague-Rusin) 1.7.1940-1.8.1940.
KL Mauthausen in late 1940.
Waffen-SS *Sanitätsabteilung* Gießen from 30.1.1941.
Ersatz-Bataillon SS-*Verwaltungsdienste* Dachau from 25.6.1941.
Kommandostab RF-SS (Russia) from 26.6.1941.
SS-*Kavallerie*-Brigade *Nachschubabteilung* (Debica) on 25.8.1942.
Sanitäts-Ersatz-Bataillon der Waffen-SS (Stettin) 15.2.1943–2.3.1943.
Strafvollzugslager der SS *und Polizei* 2.3.1943–2.1945.
Promotions:
25.4.1940 SS-*Oberscharführer der Allgemeine*-SS.
1.8.1940 SS-*Untersturmführer der Reserve.*
30.1.1941 SS-*Obersturmführer der Reserve.*
9.11.1942 SS-*Hauptsturmführer der Reserve.*
30.1.1945 SS-*Sturmbannführer der Reserve.*
Decorations & Awards:
0.00.19__ SA-*Sportsabzeichen in Bronze.*
0.00.19__ *Kriegsverdienstkreuz II. Klasse mit Schwertern.*

Notes: Attending *Volksschule* for four classes, Flothmann received his *Abitur* from *Höhere Schule* and then studied medicine at the University of Marburg and Rostock for eleven semesters between 1928 and 1933 (first exam 1933, doctorate in 1935 and App. in 1935). While studying for his final exams, Flothmann married his fiancée H. B., (b. 1.10.1907 in Velbert) on 16 July 1930 and he accepted a post as a child psychologist for orphans and children with behavioural, or delinquency problems under Dr Heinrich Lottig at the *Landesjügendamt* Hamburg from May 1934. Passing his final medical exams in Bremen during 1935, Dr Flothmann specialised in psychiatry at the Kaiser Wilhelm hospital in Duisburg and was appointed the deputy physician at the Thüringia state mental hospital on 1 January 1939. That same year, he begun working for the *Ämt für Volksgesundheit Zugelassen* under *Ogruf.* Dr Leonardo Conti. This secretive organisation co-ordinated medical practices in Germany and was heavily implicated in the euthanasia programme which murdered the mentally ill and physically disabled in Germany. Re-assigned to Gießen in January 1941, here, Dr Flothmann specialised in troop psychiatry and began an affair with a local woman which later resulted in her falling pregnant. As a consequence of his infidelities the civil court in Hamburg granted his wife a divorce on 24 August 1942, (backdated to 3.7.1942) and the RuSHA granted him permission to marry his seven months pregnant fiancé on 5 September. Re-marrying five days later, Dr Flothmann had two children from his marriages and another child out of wed-lock up to the point when records ceased in May 1945.

In Debica, Dr Flothmann's assistant was Walter Röder (b. Mulheim/Main). Selected to replace Dr Müller at Danzig-Matzkau in March 1943, here, Dr Flothmann and his family lived at the Villa Lindenhof in Borgfeld, a spacious home with a large garden. Aside from his official duties, Dr Flothmann also ran a private medical practice for local people and had access to a private car for these purposes. In Matzkau, he is known to have interviewed homosexual inmates and prepared psychological reports for those under consideration for castration. Talking in 1967, Rudolf Heiß recalled Dr Flothmann attending the executions undertaken in the prison and his surviving family recollect that the doctor and his family abandoned their home in Borgfeld in late February 1945 and had the presence of mind to take his medical files of castrations to Gießen. Captured by US Army forces on 8 May 1945, they handed Dr Flothmann to the Red Army and he spent eleven years in soviet captivity before returning to Germany in January 1956 (he arrived on the last transport). Dr Flothmann then settled with his family in Hesse, north of Frankfurt.[46]

Name: Dr Viktor Schode.
Last Rank: SS-*Untersturmführer.*
Born: 23.1.1915 in Puneveschys/Lithuania.
Wartime Assignments:
SS- *Sanitätsabteilung* Dachau in 1941.
Waffen-SS *Sanitätsabteilung* Gießen until 1.11.1944.
Strafvollzugslager der SS *und Polizei* Danzig-Matzkau from 1.11.1944.
Strafvollzugslager der SS *und Polizei* Förrenbach from 22.-24.1.1945.
Promotions:
21.3.1941SS-*Untersturmführer der Reserve.*

Notes: An ethnic-German Catholic from Puneveschys, (modern day Panevėžys in Lithuania), Dr Schode joined the *Waffen*-SS as a war recruit on 19 March 1941. His home town was occupied by German forces a couple of months later and Puneveschys became part of the *Gebietskommissariate* in the *Reichskommissariat Ostland.* Married with no children, Dr Schode spoke both Russian and English and worked in Matzkau and Förrenbach as a psychiatric specialist.[47]

Lager-Zahnarzte

The dental health needs of the prison staff, inmates and the local SS and *Polizei* were handled by the *Lager-Zahnarzte* (camp dentist). His *Zahnärztliche Ordination* (dental clinic) was located in the south-eastern corner of the *Stabsgebäude*.[48]

Name: Dr Med. *Zahn.* Johannes 'Hans' **Eggert.**
Last Rank: SS-*Hauptsturmführer.*
Born: 28.12.1909 in Eisenach/Thüngaria.
NSDAP-Nr.: 1.187.869 (joined 1.5.1932).
SS-Nr.: 141.836 (joined 30.5.1933).
Prewar Assignments:
4. / I. / 14. SS-*Standarte* (Gotha) from 2.1934.
1. / III. / 14. SS-*Standarte.*
2. / III. / 67. SS-*Standarte* (Erfurt).
1. *Reserve Sturm* / 67. SS-*Standarte* by 3.2.1936.
Wartime Assignments:
Waffen-SS from 10.4.1940.
LSSAH until 5.6.1940.
Waffen-SS *Sanitäts Inspektor* in 1940.
SS-*Sanitätssturm* XXVII (Weimar) in 3.1941.
Waffen-SS *Sanitätsabteilung* Gießen from 30.1.1942.
Strafvollzugslager der SS *und Polizei* Danzig-Matzkau 30.1.1942–1.1945.
Promotions:

30.1.1942	SS-*Untersturmführer der Reserve.*
30.4.1943	SS-*Obersturmführer der Reserve.*
30.1.1945	SS-*Hauptsturmführer der Reserve.*

Decorations & Awards:

0.0.19__	SS-*Zivilabzeichen* (Nr. 99.998).
30.1.1945	*Kriegsverdienstkreuz II. Klasse mit Schwertern.*
0.0.19__	SS-*Ehrenwinkel für alte Kämpfer.*

Notes: Attending *Volksschule* for three classes, he obtaining his *Abitur* from *Realgymnasium* in 1930 and then studied medicine and dentistry at university for eleven semesters. Passing his first state examination in 1939, Eggert was awarded his doctorate in 1940 and marrying his fiancée in 1 June 1941, they had one child to the point where records ceased in May 1945. A member of the *Stahlhelm*, Dr Eggert was accepted into the Erfurt *Allgemeine*-SS in February 1934. Drafted into the *Waffen*-SS in the spring of 1940, Dr Eggert was discharged from active service the same year to work in private practice. Taking command of the

Danzig-Matzkau dentistry clinic in January 1942, the *Oberabschnitt Weichel* adjutant ordered Dr Eggert's secondment from the *Oberabschnitt Fuld-Werra* on 1 June 1944 and his salary was paid to a bank in Rudelstadt, lower Silesia. At this time it was observed that Dr Eggert had received permission to bring his family to Matzkau and they remained there until the prisons evacuation in early March 1945. 'SS-*Hstuf.* Dr Eckert was a very correct human being, it is never known me anything derogatory about him' recalled Edmund Baumgärtner when questioned about Dr Eggert. Questioned about Dr Eggert, Baumgärtner expressed his belief that it was impossible for the dentist to have murdered Stutthof camp prisoners by injection at his clinic, as accused in the post-war testimony of former Matzkau inmates.[49]

Standort Adjutant and Gerichtsoffizier

The garrison adjutant assisted commandant with his administrative tasks and when required, he handled disciplinary investigations in the role of (*Gerichtsoffizier. Ostuf.* Heimo Wurm held this post from 3 November 1942 to 15 February 1944 and his post was then amalgamated with that of investigator for the Danzig tribunal.

'Juristischen Abteilung'

This post, what a former Matzkau guard described as the 'legal department' or 'justice department', was established by the SS-*Richter*, *Hstuf.* Dr Beelitz in the summer of 1943 to ensure the balanced implementation of the jurisdiction for criminal cases committed by Matzkau's inmates.[50]

This post had been amalgamated with that of garrison adjutant and *Gerichtsoffizier* in February 1944. Replaced by *Ustuf.* Horst Sack in July 1944, later, that same year, *Ustuf.* Alfred Vollmer replaced Sack. The office clerk was *Uscha.* Manhard Barthelmi until his transfer to the troops in 1944.[51]

3.3 Opening and Daily Routine

The construction work finally completed, Danzig-Matzkau had become unrecognisable from its first incarnation. A combination of concrete walls, deep ditches and wire fencing now surrounded the garrison and every consideration had been given to prevent inmates using roofs to jump the fence (the height of the fence depended on the elevation of the nearest building). Entering the garrison through two wooden, barbed wire gates, the credentials of the visitor or convict were checked at the two windowed concrete guard room and a wooden guard post stood in the centre of the road. Divided into two distinct zones, the garrison consisted of the *Stabsgebäude* (staff buildings) and the *Häftlingslager* (prison compound). Surrounded by barbed wire fencing, the *Stabsgebäude* contained the command buildings, administrative offices, the garage, guard's accommodation and medical and the dentistry clinic. This zone also included the *Wirtschaftsgebäude*, the gravel pit in which the firing range was located and the *Schreibstube* (writing room) stood directly south of the *Häftlingslager* compound, looking onto the parade ground.[52]

Dr Ernst, a keen equestrian, had overseen the construction of a small stables in Matzkau and a riding arena had been erected in which horses exercised. The officers' club and commandant's home, were also located inside the *Stabsgebäude* environs.[53]

Atop the hill stood the *Häftlingslager*. Surrounded by a ditch, the site was enclosed by a double electrified barbed wire fence and a medieval style *cheval de frise*. Each concrete fence post held nine porcelain conductors and fourteen or fifteen barbed wire strands linked each post. Inside the fence had been built twelve barracks for convict accommodation and two for a clinic (the number of accommodation barracks was almost certainly increased at a later date). Each building was linked by concrete paths and stairs and the uneven topography and the risk of flooding had persuaded the builders to construct the barracks atop concrete bases and small hillocks. The two barracked *Arresträumen* was constructed in the north-eastern corner of the *Häftlingslager* and isolated from the remaining inmates with an electrified wire fence. One barracks detained disciplinary offenders and the other inmates awaiting the enforcement of their capital punishment.[54]

Questioned about his command tenure in Matzkau in the 1960s, Edmund Baumgärtner discussed the prisons governance:

> [...] With regard to the organization of the *Lager* Danzig-Matzkau I want to specify, as already mentioned, that the prisoners were housed in fifteen barracks. Located outside the camp was the office building and three barracks in which the individual administrative departments were housed. Inside the camp, there was the so-called 'reception' barrack. Now, when prisoners were sent to the camp—they came mostly in trucks—they went first to the 'reception.' In the 'reception' barrack the convicts were re-clothed and given uniforms of the *Landpolizei* without insignia. They were each then assigned to a barracks where they had to report to the *Stubenältesten.* Regarding the command structure and the current conditions I would like to specify that as far as Danzig-Matzkau camp is concerned, I was the commandant of the camp. I commanded the two guard companies with their commanders and the *Lagerführer.* When I arrived in Danzig-Matzkau the camp commandant Ernst was still there.[55]

Post-war, Dr Beelitz, explained the function of this new penal SS institution:

> [...] The Danzig Matzkau camp was a prison camp of the SS and *Polizei* jurisdiction and served to accommodate those that were subordinate to the SS and *Polizei* judiciary and had been condemned to prison terms before the SS and *Polizei* courts. In particular, the focus was against members of the *Waffen*-SS and the *Polizei.* Also, the auxiliary troops of the *Polizei,* or those that were subordinate to the *Polizei* were also brought in to Matzkau to serve prison sentences. In addition to this camp, there was just one other for those serving *Gefängnis* sentences, which was located at Allach in Bavaria. The prisoners, after their conviction by a SS and *Polizei* courts in the Reich, or in occupied areas served their detention in Danzig and were put to work, for example, on the Schichauwert. After having served their punishment they were transferred to a probation unit in accordance to the decision of their service office.[56]

The surviving Matzkau buildings have flat roofs, but it is clear from original drawings and surviving images that most, if not all the barracks was constructed with an A-frame sloping roofs. A handful of the original administrative buildings were two storey constructions. The only notable addition to the SS-*Kaserne* during the war was a small graveyard; the graves were marked with German sounding names. [57]

The *HA* SS-*Gericht* commanded the transfer of all *Gefängnis* convicts, including those detained in Dachau, to Danzig-Matzkau on 17 January 1942 and each prison received orders to arrange their own transports. The first of the Dachau convicts and those from other detention sites declared their willingness to depart for Danzig on 1 March 1942, but when news reached them that the prisons opening had been delayed, the felons were diverted to Ludwigsfelde near Berlin to prepare the ground for a new labour camp. Remaining here for around three weeks, they made their way to Danzig once the prison announced its official opening. One of those arriving at this time was SS-*Mann* Karl Hölblinger, a former KL Auschwitz guard. Hölblinger was accompanied by offenders who had been sentenced before the SS- *und Polizei-Gericht* IV, Danzig and were waiting the result of an appeal.[58]

With the agreement of the OKW the *HA* SS-*Gericht* organised the transfer of felons serving sentences longer than three months duration inside military prisons in the west to Matzkau. As a consequence of this order 347 convicts undertook the journey to Danzig. Offenders serving detention sentences of less than three months in duration remained in military institutions, or served their time in the *Strafvollstreckungszug*.[59]

The vast majority of these *Waffen*-SS felons reported to Matzkau from the military prisons located in occupied cities in Russia and the Ukraine:

Wehrmachtgefängnis Wilna: Located near Dünaburg, (Daugavpils), this institution served the *Heersgruppe Nord* and the *Wehrmacht Befehlshaber Ostland* and was abandoned in July 1944.

Wehrmachtgefängnis Borrissow: Located in Belorussia, this institution served *Heersgruppe Mitte* and the *Wehrmacht Befehlshaber Ostland.* This prison was abandoned in June 1944.

Wehrmachtgefängnis Dubno: Located in the Ukraine, this institution served *Heersgruppe Süd* and the *Wehrmacht Befehlshaber Ukraine.* A branch prison existed in the Ukrainian capital of Kiev. Abandoned in late September 1943, the Kiev branch prison was closed a few weeks later.[60]

Felons from Dubno were escorted to the military goal at Glatz in lower Silesia and those held in Borrissow, Dünaburg and Vilna were taken under guard to the military goal at Graudenz. From these two prisons, the inmates made their way to Matzkau, guarded by troops supplied by the SS-*Infantrie-Ersatz-Bataillon Ost*, the *Kommandostab* RF-SS and troops on leave from Graudenz. It is no longer possible to establish how many convicts were affected by this movement order, but it was certainly many hundreds.[61]

Despite the opening of Matzkau, military jails are known to have continued accepting SS and *Polizei* convicts. Writing to the SS-*Richter beim* RF-SS in September 1944, the commandant of the military jail at Torgau informed him that 50 of their felons had recently arrived at his prison and he demanded to know he should be done with them! The *HA* SS-*Gericht* accepted responsibility for the group in October 1944 which consisted of two inmates punished with death sentences, two serving terms of *Zuchthaus* and 24 non-German offenders. Arrangements were then made to transfer the group to Dachau.[62]

The construction phase of the prison at Matzkau almost complete and the opening date looming closer, Dr Ernst faced further tribulations. Lacking sufficient *Waffen*-SS guards, security at the prison had until this point in time been maintained by a company of *Ordnungspolizei*, but the *Reichsführer* had demanded that these policemen were replaced with a permanent guard section composed of *Waffen*-SS troops. As a consequence of the SS leaders wishes, the SS-*Infantrie-Ersatz-Bataillon Westland* received orders to transfer a company of men to Matzkau on 26 May 1941, but proving unable, or unwilling to comply with the order, the intransigence of the SS-FHA forced the *HA* SS-*Gericht* to arranged for the *Polizei-Kompanie* to remain at Matzkau until June 1942. In the face of the SS-FHA's unwillingness to supply the necessary guards, Günther Burmeister then attempted to extend the policemen's tour of duty for another two months on 26 June 1942, but the *Chef Hauptamt Ordnungspolizei* rejected his overtures on the grounds of 'extraordinary personnel difficulties for his service in its work in the east and homeland' and flatly refused to extend their tour of duty past 30/31 August 1942. If it proved absolutely necessary, then the general grudgingly offered to extend their tour for a further four days, but would not prolong their return to his command for one day extra.[63]

Expecting the imminent arrival of around 800 felons, Dr Ernst telephoned the SS-FHA on 19 June 1942 to demand they immediately transferred 100 personnel to his command. For his efforts, the commandant received only a promise to bring the matter to the attention of the SS leader. Out of options, Burmeister was tasked with contacting the SS-*Richter beim* RF-SS on 5 August 1942 to inform him that in expectation of the inmate population to rising quickly to 1,300 detainees, he had taken the decision to delay the further transfer of convicts from Dachau to Matzkau and asked him to intercede on this matter with Himmler.[64]

Against the backdrop of the war, this concern was a rather trivial matter for the head of the SS, but it took Himmler's personal intervention to solve the problem. On 25 August 1942, Himmler commanded the immediate transfer of 94 troops from the *Westland* battalion to Matzkau. Among their number was a small number of Belgium and Dutch volunteers, a mix of new trainees and those recovering from wounds. An agreement reached over this matter, the *Hauptamt Ordnungspolizei* and the SS-FHA agreed to a handover date of 30 August 1942 and as the deadline for the withdrawal of the policemen drew closer, Himmler commanded the transfer of seven SS soldiers from the SS-*Panzerjäger-Ersatz-Bataillon* 2 at Hilversum in Holland to the newly formed SS-*Wachzug* Matzkau. Prior to receiving his order, these troops had been earmarked to join the SS-*Panzerjäger-Abteilung* 4, which transferred in its entirety to the *Totenkopfdivision* on 1 June 1942.[65]

One of those destined to join the guard section at this time was a privileged young Dutchman, who would end the war with a rather chequered reputation:

Name: Jan Robertson.
Last Rank: SS-*Untersturmführer.*
Born: 10.6.1922 in Rotterdam.
Died: 23.8.1995.
Wartime Assignments:
Waffen-SS from 1.4.1941.
SS-*Truppenübungsplatz* Sennheim 4.-5.1941.
1. / SS-*Feldersatzbataillon Westland.*
SS-*Infanterie-Ersatz-Bataillon Westland* (Klagenfurt) until 8.1941.
SS-*Feldausbildung Westland* 8.1941-24.11.1941.
SS-*Infantrie-Ersatz-Bataillon Westland* in 1942.
Strafvollzugslager der SS *und Polizei* Danzig-Matzkau 8.1942–6.1943.
11. SS-*Kriegsjunkerlehrgangs* SS-*Junkerschule* Bad Tölz 6.9.1943–11.3.1944.
34th SS-*Freiwilligen-Grenadier*-Division *Landstorm Nederland* from 24.2.1944.
Led the 1. / *Grenadier*-Rgt. 1 *Landstorm Nederland* from 6.5.1944.
II. / SS-*Freiwilligen-Grenadier*-Rgt. 83 from 2.9.1944.
Promotions:
10.3.1944 SS-*Standartenoberjunker.*
21.6.1944 SS-*Untersturmführer der Reserve.*
Decorations & Awards:
0.0.19__ S.A-*Sportsabzeichen in Bronze.*
0.0.19__ *Verwundetenabzeichen*, 1939 *in Schwarz.*
0.0.19__ *Medaille* '*Winterschlacht im Osten* 1941/42'.

Notes: His father was a bank manager with the Dutch Bank in Amsterdam and a member of the NSB. Against his parents' wishes, Robertson volunteered for military service with the *Waffen*-SS as a wartime recruit on 1 April 1941. Hospitalised on the 11 May the same year, he later recalled that his illness prevented him from taking the oath of allegiance to Hitler (at this time his blood group was tattooed under his left upper arm and he removed this in a prisoner of war camp in 1945). Transferring to the Eastern Front in August 1941, here, Robertson served as a runner until his wounding. Robertson spent a year in Russian and German military hospitals and once recovered, he was posted to the reserve battalion *Westland* in 1942. From here, he and 93 men transferred to the Matzkau *Wachzug* in August that same year. Remaining in this post until October 1942, Robertson was granted study leave in Munich until April 1943. Obtaining his diploma for the HBS, he then returned to Matzkau and worked in the quartermaster's barracks until June 1943. 'Has a great work character, sporty, thoroughly trained, agile, workmanlike attitude' was the opinion of his course instructor when Robertson completed the officer training course B at Bad Tölz between June 1943 and March 1944.

As a consequence of his two older brothers' deaths, Robertson senior, supported by *Generalsekretär* Rost van Tonningen, applied successfully to the HSSPF *Nordwest* to have his only surviving son sent home. Completing his officer training course the HSSPF, the SS-FHA proposed the transfer of Robertson to the *Landstorm Nederland* in February 1944. Posted to the *Grenadier* Rgt. 1 in s'Hertogenbosch in May 1944, this formation later became the SS-Volunteer Grenadier Rgt. 83 and Robertson served as a section leader in its thirteenth company when his unit transferred to the Frederik-Hendrik barracks in Vught (armed with captured Red Army artillery). With this formation, he fought allied forces in Belgium until forced to retreat on 2 November. Robertson's company then regrouped in Vaassen, near Apeldoorn and remained here until February 1945. Then deploying on the so-called Waal-front in the villages of Tiel and Echteld, here, Robertson and other members of his unit are believed to have used explosives to break into a bank safe in the Rotterdamse bank in Tiel on 7 March 1945. Taking two days to remove all the cash and valuables, it appears that the SS authorities did not seek his or his men's prosecution for committing this serious offence.

Surrendering to the British/Canadian army at Veenendaal on 11 May 1945, Robertson was detained in the prisoner of war camp at Harskamp, near Ede and was questioned by the special political police about the Tiel bank robbery. Providing them with enough information about the bank robbery to enable the police to recovery much of the stolen property, Robertson was then transferred to a prisoner of war camp near Vuren on 3 September 1945. Bought to trial for his membership of the outlawed NSB, membership of the *Waffen*-SS and his participation in a bank robbery, Robertson was judged guilty of the charges and punished with a fifteen-year term of imprisonment. Escaping from the camp at Vuren on 8 January 1947, Robertson fled across the border to Germany. The authorities issued an arrest warrant for Robertson and the police judged correctly that he had escaped to München where his fiancée lived. Remaining free, Robertson became a German national, changed his name and married his fiancée in Munich on 26 August 1950. He and his family returned to Holland on 28 December 1960 and lived in Tiel from 30 July 1993 until his death in August 1995.[66]

It remained the practice until the mid-war years to select Germanic men for guard duties with the Matzkau guard company. Born in Deventer, Holland on 3 December 1914, Pieter Albertus Gerhardus Willems had attended *Volksschule* for six classes, *Realschule* for three classes and then worked as a food goods salesman. Leaving Holland for Germany on the grounds of political reasons, Willems obtained employment in a factory and worked as a salesman. Remaining politically active, Willems acted as the *Ortsgruppenleiter der* NSB Holland for the *Ortsgruppe* Osnabrück between January 1940 and March 1941 (NSB 97.312) and volunteered for the *Waffen*-SS on 12 March 1941. Posted to the SS-*Panzer-Grenadier-Ausbildung- und Ersatz-Bataillon* 5, Willems fought on the Eastern Front between 22 June 1941 and 14 July 1942. Surviving the winter campaign, *Strm.* Willems was then assigned to the Matzkau *Wachzug*. From here, Willems applied to marry his fiancée Susanna B., (b. 24.3.1921, Halfweg) on 2 July 1943 and both *Ostuf.* Ringel and *Hstuf.* Dr

Flothmann signed his RuSHA application. Surviving the collapse, Willems settled in Waldstetten, Schwäbisch near Gmünd.[67]

The prison opened officially in March 1942 and begun accepting a small number of *Gefängnis* court-punished miscreants. The prison was warned by telex message prior to the convict's arrival and the felon arrived under escort by truck or via the Guterherberge railway station. The inmate induction process was identical to that in use within the SS-*Straflager* Dachau. Arriving in Matzkau, the convict reported to the so-called reception barracks and their uniforms, insignia and medals were removed from their possession for storage in the garrison office. Their personal details recorded, each inmate was informed of the prison's rules and regulations and their personal possessions were searched for forbidden items such as pens and pencils, which were confiscated. Receiving their prison garb, consisting of an earth-brown former *Landespolizei* and *Gendarmerie* tunic and trousers without insignia, this uniform was styled similarly to the M25 tunic and trousers (the so-called *Sarasaniröcke*).[68]

Completing the induction process, the new inmate was allocated to a barracks and a *Strafkompanie* (Punishment Company). In 1941 each barracks held 150 and 180 felons and each room contained two single, later two bunk beds. Each convict stored his uniform and shaving kit in a locker and overcrowding led to three men split between two beds. The number of bunk beds per room had increased by four by 1943 and at this time each barracks slept between 300 to 400 inmates.[69]

Awoken by the SS guards whistles at 5.00 a.m. in summer and at 6.00 a.m. in winter, the Matzkau inmates completed their ablutions quickly before gathering in their companies on the *Häftlingslager* parade ground for the first of four roll calls at 5.30 a.m. / 6.30 a.m. The count completed in fifteen minutes, the felons then returned to their barracks to clean themselves in washing basins that tended to between six and eight convicts at a time. Two showers in each barracks supplied warm water to eight inmates. A former convict recollected that the mornings were best for washing, but expected to complete their ablutions in eight minutes flat, former inmates recalled that the paucity of washing facilities resulted in around 50 inmates forced to clean themselves with sand. Over the next 20 minutes the felons washed, made their beds and tidied their lockers and rooms. Once this task completed, the five companies marched in silence to the *Wirtschaftsgebäude* for breakfast (the 5. *Strafkompanie* always reported last). Former inmates contend that the food was inadequate and complained of its inadequacy. Breakfast usually consisted of black *Ersatz* coffee and a 200 gram slice of bread and completed by 6.00 a.m. in summer and 6.30 a.m. in winter, the inmates then marched to the *Häftlingslager* parade ground to undertake 30 minutes military drill and calisthenics. 'Torture marching' is how one former inmate described this undertaking and claimed that at a minimum of two one-hour periods were devoted to drill and exercise each day. Convicts assigned to outside work parties engaged in only an hour's exercise and drill per day and avoided exercise altogether when the weather was inclement. Those allocated no work details spent much of the day drilling and exercising, which took place again at midday and the evening, at night and in all weather and temperatures (-22° C in winter, +30° C in summer). 'Until there was blood' complained one former inmate when asked to describe the physical training and stated that there existed inside Matzkau the strongest discipline and order and the guards exercised enormous power.[70]

Breakfast consistedThe inmate's work period began at 7.00 a.m. and each convict laboured for between eight and ten hours a day (the length depending entirely on the weather and amount of sunlight). The drill period ended, the inmates then divided into those selected for the *Arbeitskommando* (work commandos) and those assigned to *Üblichendienst* (usual service). Those selected for work details inside the *Häftlingslager* included:

- *Turmreinigungskommando*: Two or three inmates cleaned the watchtowers.
- *Putzer*: Cleaners for various garrison officers, they wore an armband and were permitted to leave the *Häftlingslager*. Their work tasks depended on the vagaries of the officer.
- *Schreiber*: Clerks assigned to the *Häftlingsschreibstube* and other posts outside the Häftlingslager. Eight to twelve convicts worked in the *Schreibstube* and wore an armband. The guards did not supervise these felons closely.
- *Kartstoffelschälkommando*: Fifteen to twenty inmates worked in the kitchen daily. Usually unsupervised, they peeled potatoes and punishments were harsh for those caught stealing.
- *Reinigungsdienst*: Ten to twelve felons per day kept the *Häftlinglager* clean. They picked up cigarette butts and removed trash from the *Stabsgebäude* and administrative buildings.
- *Sanitätsdienst im Lager*: Two or three inmates were appointed to the prisoners' medical clinic and deployed inside the *Häftlinglager*, they offered some medical treatments and undertook record keeping. Two, or three convicts were assigned to the hospital in the *Stabsgebäude*.

In addition to these duties, an estimated 150 to 200 felons was put to work in various labouring tasks inside the *Häftlingslager*. For the first two years of his sentence one former inmate did not pass the electrified fence and spent a small part of the day working in the sewers. From here, the inmates transported the extracted human excrement to the fields to be used as fertiliser. Those with no appointed tasks remained in the Häftlingslager to undergo drill and exercises on either of the two parade grounds until lunchtime. Exercises consisted of military drill, knee bends and arm pumps and any other activity that kept the convicts active and built up muscle tone. Those preparing for front service at the front, or with the *Bewärhungsabteilung* undertook many hours of military exercise and drill and were permitted access to the sports field. Former inmates confirm that the convicts cleaned their uniforms, polished boots, or underwent instruction between 10.00 a.m. and midday. Instruction consisted of a question and answering session and the inmates were questioned about important Nazi party events. Forbidden from sitting on their beds in daylight hours, the harshest punishments were handed to those caught sleeping in a bed in daytime.[71]

Lunch was served to the inmates in the The SS convicts working outside the prison halted work at eleven o'clock and marched or drove back to the prison for lunch, those working in the prison stopped work or drill at twelve o'clock. Lunch was served in the *Wirtschaftsgebäude* at around midday and consisted of a litre of *Kraut* and *Tellersuppe*, which contained no meat, no bread or potatoes. Completing this meal at around 1.00 p.m., the felons then assembled on the parade ground to endure another period of military drill before continuing with their work duties. Those without work tasks continued drilling and exercising for many hours longer.[72]

The evening meal was eaten at the *Wirtschaftsgebäude* between 5.00 p.m. and 6.00 p.m. and consisted of a 200 gram slice of bread, black *Ersatz* coffee and a salted herring, or a small piece of *Blutwurst*. Returning to their barracks at 7.00 p.m., the convicts spent the next hour cleaning the toilets, their lockers, rooms and uniforms in preparation for the report leader's evening inspection. In theory, each inmate was permitted two hours rest per day, but fear of failing this inspection prevented all but the most recalcitrant inmates from lounging around their barrack. Dirty rooms, slacking, or rule breaking would result in punishment and a bad fitness report. The lTheoretically the SS and police convict's day ended when the barrack ights extinguished at 9.00 p.m., the barracks were locked and this was the moment that the *Rapportführer* began their evening inspection and punished miscreants with night exercises. The report leaders continued to harass the inmates until 10.00 p.m. or 11.00 p.m.[73]

Matzkau convicts are not thought to have worked on Saturday afternoons, or Sundays. This time was set aside for cleaning and repairing the prison buildings and permitted the guard's quality time with their families. As a means of punishment, only the inmates of the 5. *Strafkompanie* appear to have undertook any meaningful work at weekends. No church services existed for the inmates on Sundays; excluding a handful of non-German field units, religious services were banned in the SS.[74]

The 6.00 a.m. exercise period concluded, a small number of felons were then assigned to various commandos that conducted their duties outside of the fences of the *Häftlingslager* and the garrison. Guarded the closest, any fraternisation with civilians risked two weeks arrest and bread and water punishment. A number of inmates was employed at the *Wurstfabrik*, *Schichauwerft*, *Schachthof* and *Holzkommando* and between 200 and 400 specialist convicts found themselves put to work in at the Schickau-Werft in Danzig (among them welders, fitters and electricians). Between 20 and 25 inmates tended the gardens and 60 convicts landscaped the officers' accommodation. Convicts possessing the requisite skills found themselves assigned to the administrative building, the around two hundred inmates worked inside the prison, some were employed in the *Wirtschaftsgebäude* and the store rooms. A few inmates supplied coal to the barracks and attended to the prison rabbits. Kept in special cages, these animals were bred for food and their fur was used in the manufacturing of winter uniforms.[75]

Those possessing the appropriate mechanical training were put to use in the garrison garage and drove trucks into Danzig. Only the most trusted 20 to 40 convicts exited the walls and wire fences of the garrison to work on the prison farmland in the farmland commando.[76]

It was a source of concern for the SS leader that Matzkau convicts undertook work that aided the war effort. To this end, the WVHA sought work for 50 convicts in the SS-*Hauptwirtschaftlager* in March 1942 and later that same year this workforce was expanded to around 150 men. In addition, a lock smithy, a blacksmith and a basket weaving workshop was created in the *Hauptwirtschaftlager*. Here, the repair of uniforms was undertaken and eventually a paint shop and a cobbler business was established. The WVHA created the 'Sperber' lumber company during August and September 1942 and although expected to employ 600 to 800 inmates, the company employed a paltry 150 inmates by mid October 1942. Equipped with old tools and using second hand machinery that continually broke down, the workshop managed to secure only a handful of contracts and proved uneconomical.[77]

An SS-owned cement factory, a clay works, sewing factory and a brickworks employed convicts and Matzkau inmates was assigned labouring tasks on local construction projects. Others found themselves placed at the disposal of the *Wehrmachtsverpflegsamt* (military catering office) who found employment for them at the *Heimatkraftfahrpark* (home automotive park). The SS-*Hauptwirtschaftslager* Danzig-Langfuhr provided a handful of convicts with hard labour tasks and inmates are known to have exerted themselves at the Danzig airfield. Some 50 convicts worked alongside Soviet prisoners of war in the freezers of the 'Hardtke' abattoir in Danzig for three months during 1942 and others packed meat for the cold storage company 'Mazat' (a few inmates transported meat to the *Wehrmacht*). An outside commando worked for the 'Scheffler' cabinet maker for five months and manufactured furniture for the *Wehrmacht*.[78]

In later years, Matzkau convicts repaired bomb damage to the indoor market at the Dominican square in Danzig and provided labour for an enamelware factory in Langfuhr. One of the convicts lasting contributions to the city was their contribution to the construction of the concrete bunkers and imposing air raid shelter on present day Olejarna Street in 1942. Located near the city's port, this seven-storey structure has a bomb proof roof made of reinforced concrete and covers an area of 1,000 square metres, forming part of a chain of FLAK towers and bomb shelters that protected the cities docks. These defences provided invaluable support for the defenders of the city in March 1945 and repelled the Red Army besiegers long enough for the remaining Matzkauer staff to flee Danzig.[79]

Other inmates shovelled coal in the Danzig docks for the 'Stillert' company. Talking post-war, a former French prisoner recalled that around 150 convicts worked under guard as stevedores on the Danzig quayside. Wearing uniforms without insignia, he observed that they laboured very hard and were forbidden from fraternizing with the prisoners of war. In his opinion, the convicts were treated more strictly than he and his comrades and he voiced his certainty that the convicts would be shot if found shirking their work. In spite of this assertion, the Frenchman recalled speaking to the SS convicts and recalled them voicing their certainty of final victory.[80]

'Expert workers' existed in the prison and in September 1944 the *HA* SS-*Gericht* excused 200 inmates, some with long sentences, from accepting front probation on the grounds of their work specialisation. Some of their number had been incarcerated for contraventions of paragraph § 175 RStGB.[81]

The sending and receiving of mail was an important part of the convict's life. This was an opportunity to reassure family of their well-being and obtain extra rations: Born in Reckendorf on 14 April 1924, Georg Müller's parents were farmers. Leaving *Volksschule*, Müller worked as a farm labourer for the *Brauerei* Schmidt in Reckendorf and volunteered for the *Waffen*-SS in the autumn of 1942. Posted to the 4. / SS-*Panzergrenadier-Ersatz-Bataillon Totenkopf* I in Warsaw in October the same year, Müller and 239 of his comrades received orders to transfer to the SS-*Truppenübungsplatz* Ayrs on 3 January 1943. The following day they reported to the 2. / *Reichsführer*-SS *Begleit-Bataillon*. Training with the SS-*Sturmbrigade* 'RF-SS' in the *Truppenübungsplatz* Rennes in France in February 1943, this formation moved to Italy in June the same year and at this time *Strm.* Müller marched with its second company. Deployed on the island of Corsica between April and 4 October 1943, Müller mustered with the *Verbindungsstab der Deutschen Wehrmacht beim Duce* between November 1943 and March 1944 and during this time he guarded the deposed Italian leader at Gargnano am Gardasee. Assigned to the 6. / II. / SS-*Panzergrenadier*-Rgt. 35 from 19 March to 5 May 1944, Müller participated in Operation *Margarethe* near Debrecen in Hungary, but his battalion was disbanded on 23 May and its manpower used to create a new *Begleit-Bataillon* 'RF-SS' and provided replacements for the *Totenkopfdivision*. That same month, Müller and 25 comrades were assigned to the 10. / SS-*Panzergrenadier*-Rgt. 35, but the SS-*Panzer-Sanitätsabteilung* 16 treated Müller for malaria in September 1944.

Writing to his family on 6 October 1944, Müller revealed that he had been arraigned before the courts martial of the 'RF-SS' field court at that time for an unauthorised leave offence. Judged guilty, he was punished with a six months' term of *Gefängnis* and incarcerated in Matzkau in October 1944. Assigned to the 4. *Strafkompanie*, Müller wrote home and expressed his expectation to leave prison for front probation by January 1945. Writing to his parents and sister 30 November 1944, Müller complained that he had not heard from them for eight weeks and confessed that 'a small stupidity,' which 'had not been malicious' had brought him to Matzkau three weeks earlier. Hoping that the time would pass quickly, he assured his family that the food was adequate, but complained that the meals wanted for fat and consisted mostly of a watery soup. At this time he revealed that he undertaken plenty of exercise and for a week had worked in an outside work commando. Permitted to receive and send a letter each month, Müller informed his family that the prison permitted the receipt of a five kilogram package for the Christmas holiday. Looking forward to receiving his package, Müller warned that sending cigarettes were forbidden, but sweets and food was permitted. Preferring they sent food and fats, he asked that they sent the package, or two packages for the same weight, quickly by insured post.

Concerned that he had not heard from his family, or received his Christmas package, Müller wrote to his parents on 3 December 1944 and complained that he had no cigarettes and asked them to send him a jar of sweet honey and a comb. This was the last letter his family received after 1 January 1945 and all probability, Müller had accepted front probation with the II. / SS-Rgt. *Kalthofen*. According to Mr Kuchelmeister, an Augsburg *Justizinspektor*, who had been released from Soviet detention in November 1945, Müller survived the collapse in May 1945 and found himself a prisoner in the Nr. 292 Narwa Prisoner of War Camp in April 1946. Here, Müller and his compatriots were bombarded with Soviet propaganda and were put to work rebuilding the city. After receiving this news, his family had no further communication from Müller and have assumed that he died in Soviet captivity.[82]

Writing to his family in the spring of 1944, this Matzkau convict of the 1. *Strafkompanie* reported his safe arrival in the prison and looking forward to his release, he expressed concern that he had yet to hear from them:

> Thorwald Bleisch
> Danzig, on 4.3.44
>
> My dear ones!
>
> Well I have arrived here in Danzig-Matzkau. When I arrived here, the duration of my remaining sentence was also announced. This is on 25.4. (1944). Thank god, that the sun will then again shine. I will undertake my front probation with my own troops. That is also fine. Here, we may only receive one as well as write one letter every four weeks. Packages are prohibited. So do not now worry, if sometimes there is no post. In eight weeks it's all over. If all goes well I will visit on leave in early May.
>
> Greet cordially all who ask of me and your Thorwald greets you warmly.
>
> Greetings to all.

Writing again two weeks later, Bleisch had in the meantime received a much appreciated care package from his family, but had suspicions that its contents had been pilfered:

> Thorwald Bleisch
> Danzig, on 26.3.44
>
> My dear ones!
>
> So as far as I can, now I am once again able to write. How are you still? Hopefully well, of myself I can only tell you the best. Time goes by pretty quickly here. On Thursday, it is already four weeks that I am here in Matzkau. Hopefully everything will go well and in twenty-nine days I will then be dismissed to the troops. So I hope and to date I have not yet experienced any unpleasantness. If everyone pulls himself together, anything goes. Then everything isn't so bad. However, there are also some [convicts] who can go outside and work.

By the way, I was handed the package I received and a few days ago with the sewing kit. I have received the following: one roll of wool, one skein of yarn, two threads, some needles and two pieces of soap. Was that all? I hardly think that the package was completely kaput. Thank you for the packet.

In the whole time of my stay I have so far received only one letter from you and this was forwarded to me from Krakow. Have you written again?

So, now both fingers are crossed that I will be released on 25.4., (44) and then I'll receive five or six weeks leave.

It greets you sincerely your Thorwald

Greetings to all.[83]

Disciplinary Punishments

A constant refrain of former Matzkau staff in the post-war period was the demand for the strictest discipline from the convicts. To maintain good order, the commandant utilised a variety of disciplinary punishments and he and his subordinates placed obstreperous elements on report for bad behaviour, or rule breaking. Badly behaved inmates risked punishment drill, which consisted of military drill and calisthenics for an hour's duration at a time in all weather conditions, the loss of food and the withdrawal of privileges. All punishments were recorded in the convict's personnel file.[84]

The *Lagerführer* had responsibility for imposing punishment drills on the parade ground inside the *Häftlingslager*. The punishment of those inmates deployed outside the fence lay in the hands of the guard commander. One former guard recalled that punishment drills were undertaken outside of the Häftlingslager, on the main parade ground:

> [...] I can only recall that this (punishment drill) corresponded to the formal exercise drill, however, it was carried out in an intensified form. I have never been able to observe that this drill had resulted in any injury of the prisoners. Concerning the stricter form of exercise duty, I understand this was composed of excessive running, crawling and the like.[85]

Persistent offenders and those caught stealing risked up to fourteen days' arrest in the ***Punishments:*** *While the guards rewarded hard work with cigarettes they were permitted to punished offenders with extra drill, loss of food or the withdrawal of privileges. Beatings were forbidden on the grounds that they prevented Persistent offenders were placed on report for offences such as possession of banned items such as a knife or pencil or were caught stealing and could face a short detention in the Arrestgebäude.* Here, in absolute silence for 23 hours a day they shared a darkened cell with three other inmates. Released from their torment for one hour each day, they used this time to clean themselves and their cell and eat the daily meal, which consisted of 200 grams of bread and a pot of coffee. Miscreants penalised with a third period of sharp arrest were automatically transferred to a concentration camp as a deterrent to the other inmates.[86]

Frustrated that the punishment drill often failed to enforce discipline, the *Lagerführer* gathered his ubiquitous persistent rule breakers, malfeasants and hardened criminals into the 5. *Strafkompanie* from February 1943. These convicts lived on reduced rations, received extra duties, undertook hard labour and were banned from sending letters to family and friends. It is thought that the convicts of the 5. *Strafkompanie* undertook the soul-destroying practice of shovelling of gravel piles from one place to another. Once this task was completed, they then shovelled the pile back to its old spot and so forth for many hours. Another penalty thought to have been reserved for these convicts was the unenviable job of breaking in new boots. The inmate accomplished this by running around in circles for hours on end. Bloody blisters on the feet and crippling pain in the legs were a consequence of this punishment and hospitalisation resulted for some inmates.[87]

Despite these privations and punishments, the convicts of the 5. *Strafkompanie* appear to have fought back against this tough regime. Writing in 1943 the SS and *Polizei* Court IV observed that these felons shirked their duties, were slothful and arriving late for parade, they would often refuse to stand to attention.[88]

The beating of inmates was officially forbidden on the grounds that this punishment prevented rehabilitation, but it is clear from the testimony of guards and inmates that arbitrary beatings by guards with a cane was a regular occurrence in Matzkau. In addition, former convicts alleged that the punishment of *Prügelstrafe*—a beating with a stick while the offender lay across a trestle—or block also occurred in Matzkau. Talking in 2014, Kurt Grawe, a former *Beurkundungsunterführer* of the Danzig tribunal, recalled that a labor brigade of Matzkau inmates had been sent into Danzig to help clear damage in the aftermath an air raid in the summer of 1942 when one of their number, a 22-year-old convict named Sauter, took the opportunity afforded by this deployment to steal a bag of prunes. Denounced by a fellow inmate, Sauter faced trial before the SS- *und Polizei-Gericht* IV, Danzig for looting and was punished with a death sentence. Confirming the judgment, the *Reichsführer* amended the judgement to life imprisonment. In addition, Grawe recalled that Sauter also received 25 strokes of the cane.[89]

From his appointment to the post of Nr. 1 *Lagerführer* in February 1943, *Ostuf.* Dieterle had, without the commandant's permission, implemented the use of the cane against undisciplined inmates. Punishing the undisciplined with up to 25 strokes on the bottom with a cane or tree branch, this practice was halted when the beatings were reported to higher authorities.[90]

Capital Punishments

The provisions of the *Reichsführer*'s jurisdiction permitted the trial of those inmates discovered planning, or successfully attempting an escape from prison. Reporting these cases to the SS and *Polizei* Court IV, Danzig as desertion, or unauthorised leave offences, those successfully decamping from the prisons environs were punished with a death penalty in absentia and this sentence was carried out when the escapee was re-captured.[91]

Talking in March 1967, a former guard recalled that the SS guards had orders to shoot would be escapers:

> […] There was a command announced to all inmates at a briefing that against those attempting to escape in, or outside the camp, after three warnings the guard post was permitted to make use of their firearms. However, deaths in such a cases are also not known to me. […]

Unaware of any case in which the Danzig court had pronounced the death penalty against a would-be escapee, this former guard affirmed that an arrest punishment was excluded in these cases as the camp commandant did not possess the authorisation to impose the death sentence against would-be escapees. The camp commandant was only permitted to assess arrest penalties of up to six weeks' duration.[92]

'The barracks for the death sentenced candidates and *Arrestgebäude* was divided from the convict section by an additional fence and they were secured by an electric fence' recalled a former inmate when asked about this secretive corner of the prison.[93] Asked what he knew about executions in Matzkau in 1962, this former guard related the following:

> […] An estimated twenty men were executed by rifle fire during my time in camp Matzkau from September 1941 until its dissolution in 1945. These had not been carried out by hanging. The executions took place within the camp in a sand pit near the troop firing range.
>
> The names of delinquents I can no longer remember. A part of the execution orders were accessible to me in my role as the headquarters clerk. So I know for sure that these execution orders had been sent from a field unit to the SS and *Polizei* Court Danzig. This court determined the execution date. I then dutifully addressed this execution order to the commandant as a secret case file (in any case this is how I still remember) and in the form of a daily order to the guard company for enforcement. This daily order was of course signed by the commandant and it stipulated that the execution must be carried out by members of the guard company. The leader of the *Wachzug*/ *Wachkompanie* had then to determine which of his men would enforce the execution.
>
> The camp commandant, the *Lagerführer*, the guard company leader and the troop physician were all present at the execution respectively. The *Wachkompanieführer* gave the command. The camp physician, Dr Flothmann, to my knowledge from Rheydt, then confirmed the deaths. With care the body was placed in a coffin and then driven in a car to a Danzig cemetery.[94]

Denying his participating in any executions, this same guard admitted to witnessing five events:

> […] During the first execution, all inmates had to attend as spectators. In the later cases, only those inmates who had not been assigned work details took part as spectators. Here, I would like to emphasize that the execution was carried out by rifle fire. Everything was done correctly. I wish to express that no torture or ill-treatment occurred. In the cases mentioned earlier, each time before the execution the commandant read out loud

> and clear the judgment, on whose orders the execution was to be enforced and why this had occurred. [...] The delinquents spent only one night in our camp, which they had to spend in a dedicated arrest cell. Their desire for special meals was accepted and they were permitted to smoke without restriction.[95]

The 'delinquents' mentioned above were convicts who had been brought from the troops to stand trial before the SS- *und Polizei-Gericht* IV, Danzig. The condemned were brought into to Matzkau on the evening prior to their execution. Several witnesses confirmed these recollections and talking in 1967, Dr Beelitz revealed that inmates assembled before the condemned at the firing range to watch the proceedings as an educational measure.[96]

Questioned in August 1968, Fritz Ringel denied any knowledge of unlawful killings occurring in Matzkau, but he related his part in the execution of court-judged death sentences against two Dutch SS soldiers in 1942 or 1943:

> [...] I received at that time from the commandant of the prison camp, Dr Ernst, the order, to ensure the isolation and security of the execution site. Executions were carried out at the firing range, which was in the camp area. To ensure isolation and security I posted a soldier of the *Wachkompanie.* This was only, as I have already mentioned, to ensure isolation and security during the execution. The commandant, SS-*Ostubaf.* Dr Ernst then determined the firing squad. As far as I know, the firing squad was composed of a subordinate commander and eight or ten soldiers. I can no longer recall which military unit of the prison camp, or which [individual] men composed this firing squad. Present during the execution was myself, the field court, the commandant, the *Lagerführer* and the firing squad. Who and how many people composed the field court, I can no longer recall. The court judge was left to carry out the judgement announcement. In the judgment it was stated that the two Dutch SS soldiers (names not known) had been sentenced to death for desertion and undermining the war effort. After reading of the death sentence the firing squad then carried out the execution. I do not know of any other shootings.[97]

It is reported widely that the SS- *und Polizei-Gericht* Danzig initiated a trial against *Strm.* Albert Wagner of the Stutthof SS-*Wachbataillon* for attempted desertion, rape and fraud in 1942. Judged guilty of the charges, the tribunal punished Wagner with a capital punishment and it is reported that this sentence was carried out in Matzkau.[98]

Zabito go za "dezercję, gwałt i oszustwa" - opisuje Jan Daniluk. - Pierwsi skazani, a było to 347 osób, przybyli tu w styczniu 1942 r. Do końca tego roku było ich jFearing the negative effect that the imposition of the death sentences would have on the recruitment of ethnic-Germans, the SS leader commanded his courts to replace capital sentences with terms of *Gefängnis* for ethnic-Germans born in friendly countries on 11 September 1942. In future, the tribunals were to occasionally punish these miscreants with a war length term of *Zuchthaus*. In addition, Matzkau received orders to detain this category of inmate in

Auszug aus der Lagerordnung

des Strafvollzugslagers der ϟϟ und Polizei, Danzig-Matzkau.

1. Jeder Lagerinsasse darf alle 4 bis 6 Wochen, je nach Art seiner Strafe, einen Brief in Quartformat (14,5×21 cm) von 4 Seiten mit je 15 Zeilen empfangen und einen gleichen Brief schreiben. Sämtliche ein- und ausgehende Post wird zensiert.
2. Der Empfang von Paketen und Rauchwaren ist verboten. Hiervon ausgenommen sind zum täglichen Gebrauch bestimmte Toilettengegenstände. Eingehende Lebensmittelpakete werden den Betreffenden nicht ausgehändigt, sondern dem Häftlingsrevier zur Verfügung gestellt. Bekleidungsstücke u. dgl. werden zu den Effekten gelegt.
3. Geldüberweisungen werden erst bei Entlassung ausgefolgt.
4. Besuche sind nur nächsten Angehörigen in dringenden Fällen gestattet. Erlaubnis hierzu muß rechtzeitig schriftlich beim Lagerführer eingeholt werden.
5. Auskunft über Urteil und Strafmaß erteilt das ϟϟ- und Polizeigericht, welches den Lagerinsassen verurteilt hat.

Der Kommandant.

Wehrkreisdruckerei XX 2987 20 000 8/44

intensified detention, but if this form of incarceration complicated the imprisonment situation then the commandant was authorised to set-aside this punishment. The leader of the SS ordered all Germanic volunteers, legionnaires and ethnic-Germans facing trial for desertion to be punished with a term of *Gefängnis* from 10 October 1942.[99]

Recalling in 1969, a former inmate revealed that the bodies of executed convicts were interred at the cemetery, located towards the Ohra side of the prison, around 500 metres from the *Häftlingslager*.[100]

3.4 The First Years

Within a fortnight of its opening, the *Reichsführer* was demanding to know exactly how many staff was deployed in Matzkau, how many convicts were held in detention and wanted details of the inmate's daily regime. As a result of his demands, the *HA* SS-*Gericht* established that between its opening and December 1942 the inmate prison population of Matzkau inmate population had climbed from 347 to 1,858 men (by the spring 1943 around a 1,000 inmates were incarcerated here). Of this number some 600 offenders were judged suitable for probation, or completing their sentence they return to the troops or service office.[101]

Talking in 1966, the former inmate Alfred Hubrig reported arriving in Matzkau during February 1943 to serve his eight month prison sentence. He estimated that the prison held 1,500 convicts at this time and the Matzkau commandant estimated that 2,400 inmates were incarcerated behind his barbed wire fence on 21 June 1944.[102]

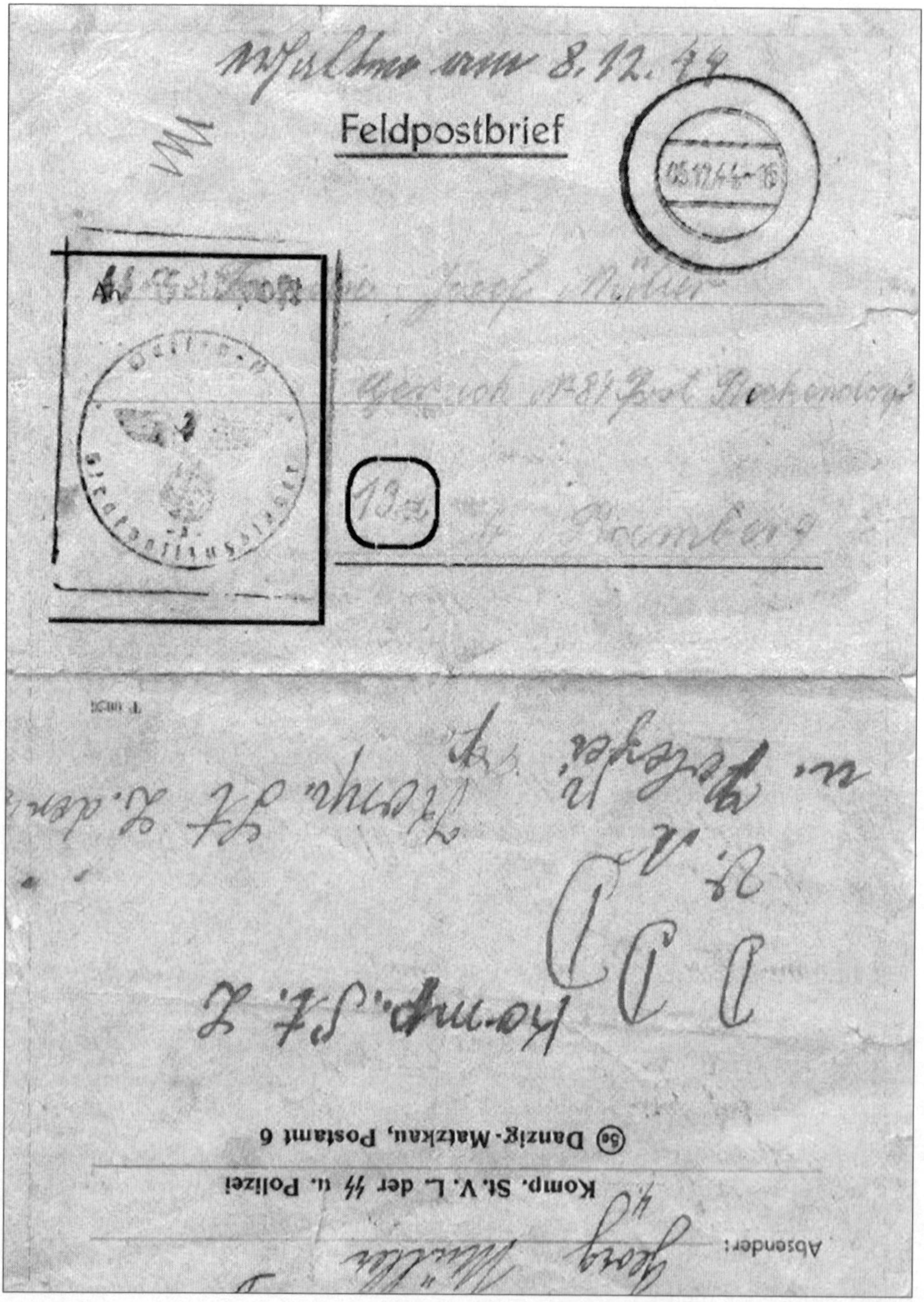
Feldpostbrief
Absender:
Komp. St. V. L. der SS u. Polizei
Danzig-Matzkau, Postamt 6

Intimately concerned with the policy arrangements that affected the day-to-day running of Matzkau, the *Amtshef des Amt* III, *Ostubaf.* Burmeister was returning from a judges' gathering in Zoppot on 30 April 1942 when he took the opportunity of this trip to inspect the prison. Revisiting Matzkau in June the same year, Burmeister concluded his survey and then submitted a detailed report about his discoveries to the *Reichsführer*. Estimating that the prison admitted and released an estimated 500 men a month, Burmeister judged that the length of sentence for each inmate averaged between six and nine months' duration and he had discovered that an overwhelming number of the court-punished *Gefängnis* convicts belonged to the SS or *Polizei* and was ethnic-German and *Germanic* volunteers aged between 20 and 25. By Burmeister's estimation, these felons had been educated below the modern high school standard and he estimated that five per cent of them had been incarcerated for committing crimes such as theft, disobedience and drunkenness on duty. Completing their sentence, he fully expected the vast majority of felons to re-join their prior unit, or the *Bewährungsabteilung*.[103]

As a consequence of his visits to Matzkau, Burmeister recommended that only in exceptional cases would certain categories of convicts, such as persistent criminals and homosexuals, serve their sentences in civil prisons in future. Agreeing with his assessment, on 25 July 1942 the head of the SS commanded this category of inmate to in future serve their sentence in his penal system and only if necessary be sent to a concentration camp (the final decision in these matters was left to the *Amt* III to decide).[104]

Aside from determining how many convicts languished in Matzkau, Burmeister was also tasked in 1942 with discovering how many *Gefängnissen* and *Zuchthäusern* felons languished in civil institutions including the Emsland. Noting that as a direct consequence of Matzkau's late opening, the transfer of *Gefängnis* inmates from civil jails to the prison had not been carried out in accordance to his 8 April 1942 command, Burmeister demanded that the complete transfer of the *Dachau Abteilung-Gefängnis* to Matzkau now be urgently carried out. Contained within this report, are Burmeister's concerns about how the handling of those convicts suffering from serious physical, or mental infirmity that required a special medical treatment in an appropriate hospital. As a consequence of these worries, Burmeister announced his plan to arrange a new medical arrangement for sick convicts, which permitted their detention in an SS-ran prison hospital (non-member convicts of the SS or *Polizei* remained in civil institutions). As Matzkau would become the repository for the vast majority of convicts, Burmeister planned to tackle the thorny issue of how to determine which *Zuchthaus* offenders were capable of re-education and work in the SS-*Straflagers Dachau* or should remain imprisoned in civil institutions.

Turning his attention to those incorrigible criminals and homosexuals held in civil jails for incarceration in concentration camps, Burmeister explained that he had taken this measure to enable their recovery back into the SS, *Polizei* and the national community. Henceforth, Burmeister expressed his plan to order all court condemned convicts to serve their sentence in a suitable SS prison and on a case by case basis he would decide which permanently unfit would be sent to civil jails. This included those inmates judged permanently unfit for camp duty as a result of physical, or mental disability, pulmonary tuberculosis, other infectious disease units and invalids or those of advanced age. At this time, Burmeister also called for *Zuchthaus* and *Gefängnis* offenders in civil prisons, those sentenced with a deprivation of their civil rights and other certain categories of offences, be transferred to a concentration camp.[105]

Amongst those languishing in Matzkau at this time was *Rttf.* Hans Beuthner of the 5./ SS-*Totenkopf-Infantrie*-Rgt. 3. He appeared before the field court of the *Totenkopfdivision* on 24 April 1942 charged with committing military theft. Judged guilty of the offence, the court punished Beuthner with eighteen months *Gefängnis*, ordered his expulsion out of the SS and commanded his detention inside Matzkau.[106]

Within a year of its opening the prison had also begun to accept convicts whose sentences had been amended to a term of *Gefängnis* and their number included those convicted of capital and paragraph § 175 offences. Although these offenders had little chance of rehabilitation until the latter months of the conflict, Himmler commanded these miscreants to serve their punishment in Matzkau and be put to work within the German war industry.[107]There would be a mixture of different cassifiactions of convict in Danzig-Matzkau, some were serving *gefängnis* sentences and were expected to be sent back to their units or to the *Bewärhungsabteilung*, there were also those serving *zuchthaus* sentences who had little chance of rehabilitation, but in time could be eligible for the *Bewärhungsabteilung*, and lastly group there were convicts *zuchthaus* sentences who were not suitable for front line service and had little or no chance of release, but could be found useful employment in the prison. [8]

A keen equestrian, *Stubaf.* Dr Ernst received permission on 13 May 1942 to visit Hamburg. Travelling via Berlin, he planned to attend an event with *Gruf.* Querner at the SS-*Remontanstalt des* SS-*Hauptamt*.[108]

From its inception, the *Reichsführer* had voiced his desire that the Matzkau inmates performed meaningful work, labouring tasks which aided the war effort. As a consequence of his wishes, a small number of convicts undertook work details outside of the prison, but any meaningful form of exertion was unavailable for the vast majority of the prisons inmates. In mid-1942 the head of the SS and the *HA* SS-*Gericht* began to receive reports that Matzkau's inmates assigned to projects outside of the prison had been caught smuggling stolen food, letters, alcohol and cigarettes into the prison. Demanding an explanation for this lapse in supervision, Dr Ernst contended that this lax supervision situation had arisen as a direct consequence of the insufficient guard-to-inmate's ratio of one to ten. On these grounds, Dr Ernst then complained that his guards had been unable to prevent inmates from fraternising with civilians and far more seriously, he then reported that the guard deficit had resulted in other disciplinary offences which included accepting cigarettes and alcohol from their civilian co-workers. Dr Ernst then expressed his belief that few convicts had taken advantage of the security lapse to persuade sympathetic people to send illicit letters and post them to their families. Incredibly, Dr Ernst then revealed that felons had obtained civilian clothing and money during these liaisons to facilitate their escape from prison. These complaints are supported by another source; deploying a group of convicts to repair roads and dig trenches for a gas pipe between Danzig and Zoppot in the spring of 1943, some locals took pity on the felon's plight and distributed food to them. On another occasion, an inmate from Hamburg is alleged to have leaped from a trench when the guards were distracted and broke into a woman's home to steal food. His nefarious attempt discovered, the convict fled the house and slunk back to the work gang to await his punishment. The house owner reported the attempted theft to the *Polizei* and informing the prison of the incident, the would be burglar then found himself confined to the *Arrestgebäude* to suffer a term of arrest.[109]

Dr Ernst could not have been ignorant of the response that his complaints would elicit from the *Reichsführer* and sure enough, he became incensed when made aware of the commandant's complaints about guard numbers and ordered the WVHA *Amt* C to prepare space in the KL Sachsenhausen in preparation for the immediate closure of Matzkau. Here, he demanded the inmates be closely supervised and engaged in meaningful war work. Proposing that Matzkau reverted back to an SS-*Kaserne*, the head of the SS suggested that a motorised battalion utilised its facilities, or the garrison converted into a school for non-commissioned officers. Following a short period of reflection, the *Reichsführer* rescinded the closure order, but commanded the *HA* SS-*Gericht* and WVHA to jointly undertake a search for purposeful convict employment and arrange better security arrangements for the Matzkau felons (the guard company was doubled in size). In the meantime, all inmate labour was withdrawn from military businesses in Danzig and the convicts involved in these escapades found themselves transferred to the *Arbeitsabteilung* in Belorussia.[110]

Telexing the *HA* SS-*Gericht Amt* II in Munich on 2 June 1942, *Ostuf.* Albert reported that Dr Ernst would be absent from the prison from 6 June to visit the town of Schwabe. Despite Himmler's recent anger about the lack of supervision in the prison, Dr Ernst applied for permission to undertake another fourteen days leave on 28 June. This trip included two days travel time.[111]

The Matzkau garrison did not isolate itself from the world around them. The garrison's facilities were readily available to those members of the *Waffen*-SS and *Polizei* that were stationed in the surrounding district and aside from having their medical needs seen to, the veteran Kurt Grawe, recalled visiting Matzkau on official court business in the summer of 1942 when he decided to use this opportunity to have a haircut at the garrison barber shop. Seated next to a *Hauptmann der Schutzpolizei*, the two struck up a conversation while waiting to be served and the police officer introduced himself as Hans Woellke, the Olympic gold medal shot-put winner from the 1936 Berlin games. During their talk, Woellke expressed his regret that the 1940 games had been cancelled and expressed his certainty that he would have won again. At the time, Grawe was under the impression that *Hauptmann* Woellke was a member of the camp administration staff.[112]

On 17 July 1942 the SS- *und Polizei-Gericht* XIV, Metz contacted the prison to confirm that the *Polizei* inmate, Wilhelm Schaefter, had arrived the previous day (case Nr. St. L. II 137/1941). The Posen tribunal ordered the release of the convicts Rudolf Coesfeld (b. 3.8.1920) and Willi Kunert (b. 12.11.1912) on 20 June 1942.[113]

At this time it was noted that following his conviction for receiving stolen goods, *Polizei-Wachtmeister* Arthur Wildemann, (b. 28.9.1916) had arrived in Matzkau to serve his sentence on 5 August 1942.[114]

An incident occurring in the summer of 1942 brought further unwelcome attention upon the Matzkau garrison. The wedding of *Oscha.* Edmund Mansbach and his fiancée Lucia. T. Carczynski at a Catholic church in Neustadt was witnessed by the *Kreis* Neustadt, *Landrat* Lorenz, Dr Ernst and three non-commissioned officers from his prison staff. Following this happy event the attending SS men were denounced to the RSHA for wearing service uniforms in church. A serious act of disobedience, Himmler had expressly forbad the wearing of SS uniforms in religious ceremonies and those disobeying this order risked prosecution for disobedience for contravening paragraph § 92 MStGB. Informed of the accusation, the *HA* SS-*Gericht* ordered *Oscha.* Manzbach, *Oscha.* Anton Sorg and *Hscha.* Otto Langer to remain under house arrest in Matzkau until the RSHA had concluded their investigation. When questioned about these events, Dr Ernst revealed that arriving late to the ceremony he had been under the impression that the actual wedding ceremony had actually been conducted in the priest's priory, not inside the church itself. The RSHA accepted his explanation and no further disciplinary action appears to have been taken over this event.[115]

On 18 August the *Reichsführer* took action to answer some of Burmeister's earlier concerns about the imprisonment of SS and *Polizei* in civil goals. Commanding that those brought for trial before the SS jurisdiction should always be detained in SS jails, Himmler accepted personal responsibility for answering all questions about individuals, especially cases involving wounded invalids. The RSHA then received orders to accept concentration camp applications from the *HA* SS-*Gericht* without the SS leaders prior examination. Lastly, Himmler ordered the *Amt* III to accept responsibility for all sentencing and releases by clemency decisions for these inmates and demanded that both the *Amt* III and RSHA report to him the results of their co-operation.[116]

From its inception the *Reichsführer* had expressed concerns about Matzkau's operations and returning to this subject again in 1942, Himmler observed that the institution was failing to offer its inmates much in the way of meaningful work and noted that overcrowding in the prison had become commonplace. Unhappy with this state of affairs, the SS leader then demanded that the *HA* SS-*Gericht* and other agencies found employment for the Matzkau miscreants in German industrial concerns. As part of his demand, the *Reichsführer* proposed sending parolees to the HSSPF HQ in Russia and despite a rather lukewarm response on the part of the *Chef* SS-FHA for this idea, Himmler used the opportunity of a visit with the HSSPF *Rußland Mitte* in Mogilew on 6 August 1942 to put the proposal to *Ogruf.* Erich v.dem Bach. 'In the interests of the people and nation' the general agreed to accept responsibility for the parolees of the *Arbeitsabteiling der Waffen*-SS and put them to work on confiscated farms in his region on 12 August, but warned the SS leader that he had few guards available to watch over them.

Concerned that this order was incompatible with the SS leaders demand that the felons were kept fit in expectation for their eventual return to combat duties, on 24 August the *HA* SS-*Gericht* reiterated their demand that both prisons battle trained those inmates that they expected to return to the front. In the wake of the decision to send a handful of *Arbeitsabteilung* probationers to the HSSPF *Rußland Mitte*, parolees who had previously been court punished with *Zuchthaus* sentences by the Minsk tribunal, v.dem Bach reported that a few were sent to a collective farm in his command region (*FPNr* 41.786). Writing to the *Reichsführer* on 26 August, the general reported that five of these 'probationer-farmers' used the opportunity of their deployment to desert to the partisans! The *Russland-Mitte* supplies officer, *Staf.* Georg Martin, would later reveal that the parolees had escaped from the SS-*Waldlager Arrestgebäude* and as a consequence of their flight, he requested the deployment of additional guards and submitted the escapee's names to the RKPA in Berlin. Writing in October 1942, General v.dem Bach observed ruefully that the farm scheme would only work if supplementary guards were provided. Acknowledging that this defeated the object of the plan, the *Arbeitsabteilung* parolees were returned to their original accommodation and a guard unit was established to watch over them. Reviewing the entire sorry enterprise, Himmler decided to cancel the project, but reiterated his demand that the prison inmate population was reduced and meaningful work was found for the convicts. Ordering the *HA* SS-*Gericht* and WVHA to again work together to solve this problem, a search was then undertaken to find activities in which inmates could be deployed as 'capable workers' and machinery was sought with which the Matzkau inmates could use towards the war effort.117

In addition to these concerns, in August 1942 the *Reichsführer* commanded that the Matzkau commandant establish a sub-unit for Scandinavian volunteers serving in the *Germanic* and *Waffen*-SS legions who had been punished with a term of *Gefängnis*. Dr Ernst was warned to house these offenders separately from the German and ethnic-German inmates.[118] Once this segregated unit had been arranged, Himmler commanded Norwegian SS men, punished with a term of *Gefängnis* in their home country, to be sent to Matzkau to serve their punishment.

One of these Scandinavian volunteers was a disgraced junior officer: Born in Norway on 24 September 1914, *Ustuf.* Harald Svenke, was assigned to the SS-*Freiwilligen*-Legion *Norwegen* when a courts' investigation was conducted against him to establish the grounds for a trial. Arraigned before the courts martial of an unidentified SS and *Polizei* court, Svenke was judged guilty of the charges and was punished with a two year *Gefängnis* sentence. Serving this sentence in Matzkau during 1942, his file does not record the nature of his crime, but it may have been conducted in connection with doubts that he had actually served as an officer with the pre-war Norwegian Army (he had claimed to be an officer candidate). Certainly, at the time of his arrest, the SS-FHA sought confirmation that

Svenke had formally held officer rank. Released from prison, Svenke was then assigned to the 1. / SS-*Panzer-Aufklärungsabteilung* 11/*Panzer-Gruppe* Saalbach in January 1944. A legal process was initiated by Norwegian authorities in the post-war era against Harald Svenke from Bergen.[119]

At this time, Himmler also commanded that Scandinavian volunteers serving *Zuchthaus* sentences to no longer undertake their punishment in civil jails, but be incarcerated in the SS-*Straflager* Dachau. Post-war, the former chief judge of the *Nordland* field court, Ullrich Dümichen, recollected that he received an order in 1944 to no longer send Scandinavian offenders to Matzkau and was instructed to handle these cases leniently. It certainly does appear that by mid-1943 every effort was made to keep Scandinavian offenders out of prisons. The veteran and author Wilhelm Tiecke, confirms that Germanic troops of the 11th SS-*Panzergrenadier*-Division *Nordland* were punished with one years' *Gefängnis* for committing serious crimes such as desertion. Offences, which if committed in other units, would usually have resulted in the imposition of a capital sentence.[120]

In the wake of the failure to turn convicts into farmers, the SS leader continued to express concern that the Matzkau inmates lacked any meaningful work and as a consequence of this demand, the *Reichsführer* called for a 1,000 Matzkau's inmates to deploy at the Großraming power station near Linz on 10 August 1942. *Stubaf.* Burmeister then discussed this proposal with the *Chef* WVHA *Amt* D and the *Gauleiter* for Oberdonau and concluding the meeting, *Brigadef.* Richard Glücks then visited Großraming. Later, Glücks reported that the site lacked any barrack space for convicts and proposed that the transfer of inmates was delayed until he had spoken with the *Gauleiter* of Oberdonau and discovered a solution to the problem. Writing to his subordinates on 4 November, Himmler once again urged them to continue working on the Großraming plan. *Bauleitung Direktor* Nietsch at *Ennskraftwerke* Großraming then become aware of Himmler's plan and Dr Ernst undertook a service trip to Linz to talk with the *Gauleiter* A. Eigruber and *Regierungsdirektor* Schmöller. During their meeting, Dr Ernst proposed the construction of a branch prison at Großraming with barrack space for 1,000 inmates and demanded barbed wire fencing, five watch towers, a kitchen, hospital, a watch room, communal rooms, a clothing storeroom and furniture. Demanding that a building office was placed at his disposal, Dr Ernst insisted that the finished prison remained physically separated from the slave workers camp and called for the convicts and prisoners to be kept apart at all times. At this time the WVHA demanded that the construction company reimburse them for the convict labour at the same rate of pay as civilian workers and only when these terms were agreed would the Matzkau convicts transfer to Großraming in one single transport on 1 March 1943. The demand for equal pay priced the Matzkau inmates out of the project and the construction company expressed their preference to use slave labour from the KL Mauthausen. The Großraming proposal was stillborn when the stricken German 6th Army found itself surrounded at Stalingrad. This news added greater impetus to the SS leader's demand that prison inmates was engaged in the war effort. Considering the problem further, Himmler next hit upon the idea to send 2,000 Matzkau labourers to the SS-*Truppenübungsplatz* at Debica and Beneschau. Meeting with *Brigadef.* Dr Kammler on 9 December, General Scharfe used this opportunity to discuss this mass deployment. As a consequence of their talk, the SS-*Richter beim* RF-SS wrote to *Stubaf.* Burmeister on 11 December to order him to arrange the deployment of these felons to both camps.[121]

The transfer of inmates to Debica was imminent when *Hstuf.* Reinhold Pfaff, of the 8th SS-*Kavallerie*-Division telephoned his field court on 3 September to discuss the transfer of five offenders to Matzkau. Gathered together, these convicts was then placed under the command of the *Gerichtsoffizier* of the SS-*Kavallerie*-Rgt. 3 in preparation for their journey and incarceration in Matzkau. Pfaff would not survive the collapse. This reconnaissance officer died in Burg on 30 May 1945.

Contacting the prison on 11 September 1942, the *HA* SS-*Gericht* informed them that a date for the 8. *Kriegs-Reserve-Führeranwärter-Lehrgang* had yet to be determined. Evidently at least one non-commissioned officer in Matzkau was seeking promotion to officer rank.[122]

Concluding their negotiations with the RSHA in 1942, the *HA* SS-*Gericht* arranged the subordination of their legal investigations under their scrutiny and General Scharfe gave permission for an RSHA officer from the *Polizei* recognition department to establish a 'rogues gallery' office in the Matzkau administrative office. Here, the RSHA officer managed a library of inmate photographs.[123]

Joining the Matzkau staff in a senior position on 1 November 1942, *Ostuf.* Walter Dieterle, a former communications specialist from Loßburg bei Freudenstadt in Baden-Württemberg, took over the post of Nr. 1 *Lagerführer* from Erich Albert in March 1943. Two after Dieterle's arrival the former Munich dancer, *Ostuf.* Heimo Wurm arrived in Matzkau and became the commandant's new adjutant. Wurm a *Blutorden* holder and a former *Luftwaffe* observer was 70 per cent disabled and walked with a pronounced limp.

On 5 November 1942 the *HA* SS-*Gericht* announced that any prison inmate failing to demonstrate an improvement in their character during their imprisonment, or judged to have rebelled against the prison regime, would face a transfer to a concentration camp as a prisoner. Visiting Matzkau in November 1942, the SS-*Richter beim* RF-SS confirmed Dr Ernst to his post and then returned to the *Reichsführer*'s field command headquarters to inform him that the unexpected increase in inmate numbers was a direct consequence of the expediential expansion of the *Waffen*-SS.[124]

The prison accepted this former *Polizei* officer for incarceration in late 1942:

Name: Dr Otto Heinen.
Last Rank: SS-*Schütze.*
Born: 28.7.1909 in Munich.
SS-Nr.: 141.994 (joined 10.9.1933).

Prewar Assignments:
Trained with the FLAK Rgt. 12 (Berlin) 8.5.1939–5.8.1939.
1. / 8. SS-*Nachtrichten-Sturme* in 1939.
Wartime Assignments:
Waffen-SS from 1940.
KL Dachau *Sanitätslager* 20.4.1940–23.8.1941.
SS-*Sanitäts-Ersatz-Abteilung* Dachau from 23.8.1941.
Ministerium für die besetzten Ostgebiete 23.8.1941–30.11.1941.
SS-*Totenkopfdivision* from 31.7.1943.
Promotions:

0.0.1939	*Unteroffizer der Reserve.*
6.10.1939	SS-*Untersturmführer der Reserve.*
20.4.1940	SS-*Obersturmführer der Reserve.*
14.7.1942	SS-*Schütze.*

Decorations & Awards:

0.0.19__	SA-*Sportsabzeichen in Bronze.*

Notes: Attending *Volksschule* for four classes, Heinen obtained his *Abitur* from *Höhere Schule* and studied pharmacy for seventeen semesters. Qualifying as an *apotheke* in 1937, Dr Heinen lived in France and Switzerland for six months. Marrying his fiancée Maria P., (b. 14.4.1907 in Warsaw) on 4 September 1934, they had no children up to the point when records ceased in May 1945. Drafted into the *Waffen*-SS, Dr Heinen became a *Waffen*-SS physician in the spring of 1940. For offending a *Wehrmacht* officer, Dr Heinen was punished with fourteen days' *Stubenarrest* between 11 and 23 August 1941 and then faced a courts' investigation for suspicion of committing an act of military disobedience while assigned to the Ministry for the Occupied Eastern Territories. He entered remand custody on 31 January 1942. Remaining incarcerated until arraigned before the courts martial for trial, here, the court judged Dr Heinen guilty of the offences and punished him with a term of six months' *Gefängnis* and ordered his demotion on 14 July 1942. The *Reichsführer* confirmed the sentence on 6 October 1942 and added a further three months to the undisciplined Dr Heinen's tariff on 19 November 1942. Danzig-Matzkau was informed of his imminent arrival on 25 November 1942 and Dr Heinen arrived on 30 November. Serving eight of his nine months of his sentence, Dr Heinen was released from his sentence on 31 July 1943 and then posted to the front for field probation.[125]

The Matzkau radio room buzzed with telegram messages at the end of 1942: The prison was notified that the offender *Rttf.* Wesseller would be transferred to Matzkau to serve his prison sentence on 2 November and writing to SS- *und Polizei-Gericht* I, Munich on 9 November, the Matzkau commandant informed the tribunal that nineteen year-old Josef Farnschinger had been judged fit for front line service.[126]

Foremost in Dr Ernst's mind during Christmas 1942 was Himmler's order to send 2,000 convicts to the SS-*Truppenübungsplatz* at Debica and Beneschau. The prison office telegrammed the *HA* SS-*Gericht* on 3 December 1942, to notify them that the commandants home leave had been approved for 8 December and once completed, he planned to travel by train to Debica on 14 January 1943 to meet with the training camp commandant to discuss the transfer proposal (he suggested constructing a new prison in the training camp using inmate's as labourers).[127]

In Dr Ernst's absence the prison continued to receive instructions from SS courts: Messaging the prison on 9 December 1942, the Posen tribunal ordered the release of the convict Ludwig Wallner who had originally been sentenced to a prison term by the 8th SS-*Kavallerie*-Division field court.[128]

The *Chef HA* SS-*Gericht* approved Christmas leave for the entire prison officer corps on 13 December and command of Matzkau during the season's holiday was entrusted to *Hscha.* Otto Langer.

One particularly violent inmate was granted permission to spend two days in a friend's home for Christmas:

Name: Willi Prager.
Last Rank: SS-*Oberscharführer*.
Born: 9.9.1901 in Kauschwitz *bei* Plauen.
NSDAP-Nr.: 1.068.038 (joined 12.3.1932).
SS-Nr.: 47.262 (joined 1932).
Prewar Assignments:
Oberabschnitt Spree 1932-2.1942.
Wartime Assignments:
Waffen-SS from 14.9.1940.
Batteriechef / SS-*Gebirgs-Artillerie*-Rgt. *Nord* in 1941.
Bewährungsabteilung from 1.3.1942.
Promotions:

0.0.1940	SS-*Obersturmführer der Waffen*-SS.
18.2.1944	SS-*Mann*.
0.0.1944	SS-*Unterscharführer der Reserve*.
21.6.1944	SS-*Oberscharführer der Reserve*.

Decorations & Awards:

00.0.19__	1939 *Eisernes Kreuz II. Klasse*.

Notes: Born into a farming family, Prager fought with the *Freikorps* in 1919 and then undertook a twelve year career in the German Army. Over the next four years, Prager trained recruits and taught Jiu-Jitsu and military drill at the *Heerssportsschule* Wünsdorf for five months. Achieving NCO rank, Prager fought communists in 1932 and received an injury that required three stitches to his head. Marrying his fiancée on 5 November 1927, they had two children together, but this marriage ended in divorce on 25 August 1939 (on numerous occasions his ex-wife took him to court for the non-payment of child maintenance). Prager accepted a strong warning in the pre-war years for committing an unknown offence. Transferring to the *Waffen*-SS in September 1940, Prager married his 33 year-old, bank clerk fiancée on 27 March 1941. Drinking alcohol with the *Nord* commandant, *Stubaf.* Constantin Heldmann, in Finland in early December 1941, a violent argument broke out between the two officers and Prager smashed a glass of schnapps against his superiors head. Refusing to apologise for his behaviour, Prager was suspended from his duties and posted to Berlin to await the result of a courts' investigation by the SS- *und Polizei-Gericht* I, Munich (case Nr. St. L. I 102/42). Thoroughly disgruntled by this turn of events, Prager began drinking heavily at his Berlin-Dahlem home and terrorised his pregnant wife to the extent that she contacted various SS agencies to ask their protection from his brutality.

SS investigators then undertook enquires and informed the NS *Frauenschaft* of *Frau* Prager's plight. Passing the affair to *Oberf.* Tondock of the *HA* SS-*Gericht*, he received instructions to intercede in the affair. Contacting the family, Tondock's unwelcome interjection incensed Prager and he beat his wife severely. Bravely, she again contacted the SS to complain about his behaviour on 18 February 1942 and Prager was warned that if he continued to assault his wife then he would be detained in a concentration camp. Ignoring this threat, Prager once again assaulted his wife and a doctor had to be called to deal with her injuries. Exasperated with the irascible Prager, Horst Bender sought a detention order and his subordinate, *Ostuf.* Dr Marx, placed his wife in a *Lebensborn* e.V. home for her own safety.

When informed of the situation, Himmler commanded Prager's detention in a single cell inside the KL Sachsenhausen on 27 April and an arrest order was handed to Himmler's *Polizei* adjutant two days later with orders to pass on to the appropriate departments. The SS- *und Polizei-Gericht* I, Munich *Gerichtsherr* signed Prager's detention order on 7 May and that same day, Dr Marx contacted the *Schutzhafdezernat* to inform them of his location. The *Gestapo* arrested Prager at his home at 10.00 p.m. and taking him directly to the KL Sachsenhausen, he retained his uniform and was locked into an *Abteilung* Z single cell for eight weeks. The courts martial of the Munich tribunal convened without Prager in attendance on 28 July and judged him guilty of assaulting *Stubaf.* Heldmann in contravention of paragraph §29 MStGB. Punishing Prager with a term of four weeks' *Gefängnis* in Matzkau, the SS-*Richter beim* RF-SS then initiated a new investigation into his behaviour and *Ostuf.* Bleyl of the SS- *und Polizei-Gericht* III, Berlin undertook a new court's investigation (case Nr. St. L. II 189/1942). As a consequence of this process a one month's term of *Gefängnis* room arrest was imposed on Prager for contravening paragraph § 17 MStGB and his expulsion from the SS was ordered.

Fearing for her safety, *Frau* Prager telephoned Dr Wehser daily for news of her husband. Assuring her on 20 April that all had been done to prevent her 'pig headed' husband from returning home, *Frau* Prager revealed her decision to seek a divorce and asked that her husband be prevented from returning to the family home. In ignorance of his wife's decision, Prager applied to the KL Sachsenhausen commandant to send and receive letters from his family. His request passed to Horst Bender, he advised against any further contact (the letters were placed in his case file to be used as court evidence). Unaware of his detention, Prager's first wife, living in Berlin, contacted the SS to discover why her court-ordered children's maintenance payments had fallen into arrears. It took the personal intervention of the head of the SS on 4 September to ensure the continued payment of her maintenance.

Recommending Prager's probation in the spring of 1942, Dr Marx suggested Prager was transferred to either the *Bewährungsabteilung* or the *Arbeitsabteilung*. Leaving the KL Sachsenhausen on 31 March, Prager transferred to Matzkau to await the court's judgment. Announcing their judgement on 23 June, the Danzig tribunal commanded Prager to serve his intensified room arrest in the Matzkau *Arrestgebäude* for six weeks. Released from here on 26 September, the *Oberabschnitt Weichel* investigator in Zoppot, *Ostubaf.* Hellmuth Goerz, wrote to an officer on Himmler's personal staff, *Stubaf.* Paul Baumert, on the same day to complain about his friend's treatment. De-crying his condition, Goerz claimed that Prager was a 'wreck' who had no idea why he had been detained. Goerz then appealed directly to Himmler for his friend's clemency on 21 November and requested permission to entertain Prager at his family home for Christmas. Agreeing to his proposal, the *Chef HA* SS-*Gericht* granted Prager one days' leave on 24 December and commanded that he return to the prison the following day. The detained arrangements were agreed with the Matzkau *Lagerführer* and Goerz was responsible for collecting and delivering Prager from the prison.

Volunteering for probation on 22 January, this decision enabled the commandant to prepare his parole recommendation, Prager's request was granted on the understanding that he did not visit his estranged wife's home. Warned that he faced a transfer to the *Bewährungsabteilung*, Prager's wife was informed of this decision in December 1942 and *Schütze* Prager received notification of his impending divorce in February 1942. Reporting for parole on 1 March 1942, Prager fought with either the 20, 21, or 22 section *Bewährungszug* on the Eastern Front from 9 April 1943. Wounded by a shell splinter in the upper arm during an attack on an enemy bunker on 19 July 1943, the Berlin Nazi party *Gaugericht* regional court decided on 15 June to set aside Prager's case until he had completed his military service. A rehabilitation report dated 27 July, observed that this parolee had partaken in three reconnaissance patrols, received good fitness reports, had been mentioned by name in a divisional daily order on 23 July and received a combat day for 1 December 1943. Receiving this news, Burmeister ordered Prager's demotion to the rank of SS-*Mann*, ordered his expulsion from the SS and then set in motion a process for his rehabilitation on 18 February.

While awaiting a decision in his case, Prager continued to fight on the Eastern Front as section leader and deputy company leader with non-commissioned rank between 15 January and 1 October 1944. During this time, Prager led an additional three reconnaissance patrols, but suspected of contracting tuberculosis, he found himself hospitalised on 3 April. The *HA* SS-*Gericht* finally recommended Prager's promotion to the rank of *Uscha.* on 5 May 1944 and the *Reichsführer* communicated positive opinions about Prager's behaviour on 12 May. With the agreement of the *Oberabschnitt Spree*, the tribunal recommended his rehabilitation on 16 May and supported the decision to transfer him from the *Bewährungsabteilung* to the *Allgemeine*-SS with the following caveats: If promoted, Prager was to remain at the front for a year and only with Himmler's approbation could be considered for promotion to officer rank. A decision to finally reprieve Prager was postponed until the end of the war and converting his expulsion order to a service release on 20 June, Himmler acknowledged that he was no longer a member of the SS, but commanded his continued military service with the *Waffen*-SS until the end of the war. On the condition that his health permitted this transfer, Horst Bender ordered Prager's return to the front on 6 July.[129]

In January 1943 the *HA* SS-*Gericht* contacted the Matzkau garrison adjutant, *Ustuf.* Heimo Wurm, to request that he immediately submitted to them a completed personnel questionnaire. Their personnel office planned to use this information to create Wurm's new pay book.[130]

> The New Year brought no relief for the prisons workload: The Den Haag tribunal requested a medical and fitness report for the 21 year-old Dutchman *Schütze* Hendrik Kranz. Released from detention on 3 February 1943, Kranz was then commanded to the *Freiwilligen*-Legion *Niederlande* to undertake a period of front probation.[131]

The surviving soldiers of the German 6th Army trekked ignobly into Red Army prisoner of war camps on 2 February 1943, forcing the Nazi regime to declare a total war policy. In line with this new Nazi policy, the *Reichsführer* sought to buttress the front line with more of his felons. On 24 February 1943 the SS-*Richter beim* RF-SS agreed with a *HA* SS-*Gericht* decision to spare inmates attempting to flee the prison from the death penalty.[132]

Heinrich Himmler reiterated his demand to deploy Matzkau inmates in vital war work at Debica and Beneschau on 29 January 1943 and when questioned on this topic, Dr Ernst confirmed that Matzkau would be detaining 2,000 inmates by 1 March 1943. However, subtracting the discharged, those accepting probation and other considerations, the commandant judged that only 500-700 convicts would actually be available for labouring at these two training grounds. Apologising for his inability to be more precise, Dr Ernst informed the SS leader that he required the *Amt* III to state how long exactly each convict in his care had left to run on his sentence. As a result of Dr Ernst's information, the *Reichsführer* commanded 500 Matzkau inmates to journey to Debica and Beneschau in February 1943 and here undertake the construction of a small prison (at this time a camp leader was proposed for each prison). The same month, the first 50 of a proposed 3,000 to 5,000 felons had left Matzkau for Beneschau by March 1943 and at this time,

Dr Ernst voiced his conviction that 1,000 inmates would be available for new projects in Debica. In expectation of this mass transfer the training ground commandant received orders to prepare for their arrival. The *Reichsführer* desire to empty Matzkau appeared to have been met and he then decided not only to detain convicted felons in the new Debica prison, but also those parolees preparing for their transfer to the *Arbeitsabteilung* and delinquent soldiers from training units. Although the instigator of this scheme, the SS leader suddenly complained of his dissatisfaction with the proposal. Indicative of his oft indecisive decision-making process, Himmler decided that enough local labour was on hand to undertake labouring tasks in Beneschau and Debica on 1 January 1943 and decried the whole project 'a waste of men' on 3 February 1943. Re-considering the use of convicts as labourers, the SS leader once again tasked the WVHA with finding the SS and *Polizei* felons semi-skilled vital war work which included secure accommodation and the approval of the *HA* SS-*Gericht*. In expectation that this order would finally result in quality work for its inmates, the *Reichsführer* commanded the *HA* SS-*Gericht* to prepare to hand control of the SS-*Kaserne* to the SS-FHA and again recommended it was found some other purpose.[133]

Demanding Matzkau's quick closure, the *Reichsführer* commanded the entire inmate population to relocate to the KL Sachsenhausen on 12 February 1943. Here, Himmler claimed that 'SS suitable high class factory work' existed for the felons and if necessary, he demanded that the convicts erected a new prison outside of the camp environs. The SS leader's impatience also extended to the SS-*Straflager* Dachau, where he demanded the *Zuchthaus* inmates be employed in high quality suitable factory work in the camp (if necessary, he permitted their deployment outside of the camp and the displacement of camp prisoners). A week later, the leader of the SS reiterated his demand that the entire Matzkau inmate population evacuated the prison and transfer to the yet to be built *Aussenlager* Allach where they would build BMW aircraft engines. Writing on 11 February 1943 *Oberf.* Dr Reinecke agreed with this plan and four days later the SS leader demanded that he be kept abreast of any developments effecting the transfer of Matzkau inmates. Entrusting the construction of the Allach camp to *Ostubaf.* Maurer of the WVHA, the *HA* SS-*Gericht Amt* III understood that there was no prospect of its quick construction and so recommended deploying Matzkau inmates at the Daimler-Benz-*Werke* at Berlin–Tegel, where suitable accommodation already existed.

The guard arrangements for the new prisons at Allach and Ludwigsfelde near Berlin were agreed in discussions between *Brigadef.* Glucks, Maurer and an unidentified Matzkau officer on 19 February and during their talk, it was revealed that an officer of the SS-FHA had inspected Matzkau a couple of weeks earlier and decided that the site was wholly unsuitable for military use! Dr Ernst, Dr Hans Brauße and *Hstuf.* Walther of the *Amt* III then received news of Matzkau's reprieve and the plan to send convicts to Berlin found favour with Himmler. The *Reichsführer* then rejected *Ogruf.* Pohl's suggestion to send the entire inmate population of Matzkau to the KL Sachsenhausen on 1 March 1943 and talks between the *Amt* III and the WVHA culminated in plans to construct a new shell basket and ammunition box workshop inside Matzkau. In the event of this plan proving unfeasible, the WVHA recommended establishing a new branch prison inside the KL Buchenwald, or another camp, where the SS and *Polizei* convicts could be put to work in the war industry.[134]

Writing to Günther Burmeister on 5 February 1943, the SS-*Richter beim* RF-SS urged him to renew his efforts to relieve the pressure on the prison population. Estimating that 600 Matzkau inmates were suitable for front probation—a figure Dr Reinecke confirmed on 27 April 1943—Himmler demanded that the 'unreliable elements' judged unsuitable for continued service in the *Waffen*-SS be sent to the front in a whole unit and fight in the most dangerous and difficult of circumstances (their eventual fate depended on their transgressions and sentences). The inmates discussed in this letter were almost certainly deployed with the *Arbeitsabteilung* at Bobruisk.[135]

In addition to this measure, Dr Ernst found himself tasked with selecting 100 convicts for service in the newly forming SS-*Fallschirmjägerabteilung* in the first weeks of February 1943. The criteria for selection the non-commissioned officers and men was as follows: Each volunteer had to stand between 160–185cm tall, be no older than 30 years-old, not suffer from air sickness and not stutter. Those the commandant finally selected for this duty averaged an age of 22 and it was noted that 22 of their number had committed acts of theft and looting. The remainder had committed offences of a military indiscipline nature—mostly guard duty—late from leave offences. Eighteen of this sample were former *Polizei* and the remaining men from the SS.

Despite the felon's willingness to undertake this dangerous activity, not all of those selected by Dr Ernst were eventually selected for this dangerous form of front line service. known to have been selected were: On the advice of the RSHA, the *Reichsführer* de-selected 40 would-be paratroopers and commanded them to the Hradischko SS-*Pionierschule* in the SS-*Truppenübungsplatz Böhmen-Mähren* to undertake training in the detection and neutralisation of enemy minefields (31 passed the course). As a consequence of this high failure rate, Dr Ernst had to explain the criteria he had used to determine their selection. The commandant then explained that based on his personal experience, he had selected the felons on their general behaviour, he had noted whether they had followed prison rules and were willing to accept probation.[136]

At this time Dr Ernst also selected 250 convicts for probation in the *Bewährungsabteilung*. Their place in the prison was quickly replaced with new offenders, one of whom was an officer prosecuted for drunkenness and negligent manslaughter:

Name: Fritz Uhrig.
Last Rank: SS-*Untersturmführer*.
Born: 5.3.1912 in Frankfurt am Main.
Died: 15.1.1945 in Kozlowo.
NSDAP-Nr.: 2.463.012 (joined 1.5.1933).
SS-Nr.: 64.385 (joined 1.3.1933).

Prewar Assignments:
33. SS-*Standarte* (Darmstadt) 1.3.1933–1.11.1934.
2. SS-*Standarte* (Frankfurt a. M.) until 1.1.1936.
SS-*Sänitatsstaffel* II. /2 until 1.4.1936.
SS-*Sänitatsstaffel Oberstaffel* 2 until 1.3.1938
Apotheker of the *Oberabschnitt* (Königsberg) HQ until 1.3.1938.
Stab Oberabschnitt Nordost (physician) until 1.5.1939.

Wartime Assignments:
Stab Oberabschnitt West until 5.2.1941.
Salaried adjutant/personnel *Referenten* for the *Abschnitt* XXXXV (Straßburg) until 31.3.1941.
Oberabsschnitt Südwest SS-*Sänitatsstaffel* until 5.1945.
Waffen-SS from 22.11.1939.
SS-*Sanitätsabteilung* Berlin from 22.11.1939.
SS-*Infantrie-Ersatz-Bataillon Deutschland* 29.11.1939–24.1.1940.
Feld-Lazarett / *Freiwilligen*-Legion *Niederlande* and SS-*Lazarett* Kiev 6.11.1941–9.11.1941.
1. SS-*Infantrie-Brigade* (mot) *Feld-Lazarett* from 9.11.1941.
SS-*Sanitätsabteilung* / 8th SS-*Kavallerie*-Division (Debica) on 1.7.1942.
Stab SS-*Kavallerie*-Rgt. 2 in 8.1943.
8. *Batt.* / SS-*Nebelwerfer-Ausbildung- und Ersatz-Bataillon* (Lübbinchen) 8.1944.

Promotions:

7.5.1941	SS-*Hauptscharführer der Reserve.*
1.9.1941	SS-*Untersturmführer der Reserve.*
3.1.1943	SS-*Oberscharführer der Reserve.*
1.9.1944	SS-*Standartenoberjunker der Reserve.*
1.9.1944	SS-*Untersturmführer der Reserve* (R.D.A. 1.9.1941).

Decorations & Awards:

0.0.19__	SS-*Zivilabzeichen* (Nr. 150.427).
0.0.19__	SA-*Sportsabzeichen in Bronze.*
1.10.1943	1939 *Eisernes Kreuz I. Klasse.*
25.8.1943	1939 *Eisernes Kreuz II. Klasse.*
0.0.19__	*Deutsches Reichssportabzeichen in Bronze.*
0.0.19__	SS-*Ehrenwinkel für alte Kämpfer.*

Notes: Attending *Volksschule*, Uhrig obtained his *Abitur* from *Höhere Schule* in 1930, (*Oberprima*) and then studied pharmacy at the University of Frankfurt am Main for four semesters between 1934 and 1935. Passing his final examinations on 17 October 1936, Uhrig was employed as an *Apotheker* for the *Chem. Fabr.* E. Merk in Darmstadt from 1 November 1937 (working in Königsberg, he then became *Leitung der Filiale* in Straßburg). Joining the Reichbach/*Gau* Hesse Nazi party in May 1933, Uhrig married his fiancée Lott Beyer, (b. 23.7.1914 Frankfurt am M.) on 4 June 1938. It appears that the marriage remained childless. Drafted into the SS-VT in November 1939, Uhrig served in its medical branch.

Reported for driving his car in a drunken state and crashing the vehicle in Kiev on 11 July 1942, Uhrig injured two SS officers and caused the death of an NCO. As a consequence of his actions, his *Gerichtsherr*, *Brigadef.* Bittrich, tasked *Hstuf.* Aumund of the SS- *und Polizei-Gericht* XVIII, Kiev with carrying out a court's investigation on 12 July 1942 (St. L. 139/42). Writing on 19 August 1942, *Hstuf.* Aumund recommended Uhrig's six months' imprisonment for committing offences against paragraph § 92 MStGB, § 230 RStGB and § 73 RStGB. *Brigadef.* Bittrich agreed with the court's recommendation on 22 August and the *Reichsführer* confirmed the judgement on 30 August. Setting aside the sentence in favour of a part *Gefängnis*, part probation punishment and the *Chef HA* SS-*Gericht* commanded his demotion for his disobedience, committing negligent manslaughter and transgressions of the National Road Accident statutes. His punishment agreed, the unruly Uhrig was incarcerated in Danzig-Matzkau between 15 March and 15 June 1943. Released from goal and proving himself at the front, Uhrig's rehabilitation was obtained via a clemency path on 15 August 1944 and on this date, General Breithaupt discharged him from the rest of the prison sentence and returned him to him his officer rank. The *Oberstaatsanwalt bei dem Landgericht* Frankfurt am Main, *Stubaf.* Floret, was then tasked with providing an order of expiation of the punishment remark in the punishment register.

The erasure of his punishment had been carried out by early September 1944 and the rehabilitation process had gotten underway. Submitting good conduct reports for Uhrig, the rocket training battalion observed that he had a good practical and theoretical knowledge of a battery officer and was a proven section leader in infantry training and battle. Considering him for promotion on 20 August 1944, this reserve battalion commander expressed a favourable impression of Uhrig:

> SS-*Oscha.* Uhrig is an energetic personality with decent character. He possesses a clear command language and knows how to enforce it at any time. His knowledge and services especially as a battery officer and training officer in a training battery are to be regarded as quite good. Before the enemy Uhrig has proven to be effective. He has good manners and is predisposed to comradeship.

His whole personality at the front persuaded Uhrig's commander to recommend his promotion to officer rank and he judged his subordinate suitable as a reserve battery officer. The promotion recommendation signed by his battalion commander, conferring the promotion on Uhrig in early September 1944, his battalion commander recommended him for further use as a chemist on 30 October 1944. Fritz Uhrig did not survive the war; he was killed in action at Kozlowo, north of Warsaw in mid-January 1945.[137]

An ULTRA intercept from 1 March 1943 revealed that Dr Ernst had expressed his satisfaction with the punishment of convict F. and on the grounds that this inmate regretted his transgressions and he had been judged fit for front service, Dr Ernst now requested that the recipient of this message, inform him by telegram whether F. had received a part-punishment sentence to enable his release from Matzkau on 2 March 1943.[138]

Writing on 25 February 1943, the WVHA confirmed that a disused labour camp with barracks and enclosed with a barbed wire fence had been located close to the Daimler Benz factory in Ludwigsfelde and had been judged suitable for use as a branch prison for Matzkau to incarcerate between 1,200 and 1,400 convicts. *Ostubaf.* Günther Burmeister, *Hstuf.* Helmut Gißelmann, (representing Himmler) and *Ostubaf.* Maurer of the WVHA then arranged the detailed construction arrangements for what would become known as the SS-*Zweiglager* Ludwigsfelde. The decision finally taken to open this branch-camp, Günther Burmeister personally selected *Ostuf.* Albert as its *Lagerleiter* (camp leader) and a *Wachzug* was established from a Matzkau cadre. The first 100 convicts left Danzig for Ludwigsfelde on 1 March 1943 and was put to work in a closed workshop, separate from civilian workers. Naturally, few, if any convicts had any aircraft engine building skills and as a consequence of their deficiencies, Himmler ordered civil workers to undertake their training. 'If women could be trained to work the machines in two to three weeks then his SS convicts could also learn quickly' was the SS leader's response when informed of the felon's skill shortage. Satisfied that the inmates of Ludwigsfelde and Allach would be employed in high quality factory work and their labour exploited for the war effort, Himmler warned his subordinates that the convicts would not be permitted to work a day longer than necessary. Matzkau's capacity problem had finally been alleviated and the *Reichsführer* order to close the Matzkau was finally rescinded on 11 March 1943.[139]

An ordinance, published on 15 April 1943, commanded all responsible departments to transfer convicts to the prison along with their personal papers and identification cards. When the inmates became available for probation, it was ordered that their personal papers accompanied them to their place of probation in a timely fashion.[140]

The Berliner jurist, Dr Fritz-Ernst Beelitz, arrived in Matzkau from the *Amt* III on 24 May 1943 with orders to liaise between the local court and the prison. The scandal surrounding the brutal activities of the Nr. 1 *Lagerführer* had exposed a lack of supervision in the institution and here, in his own words, Dr Beelitz explained how he was to play his part in improving this state of affairs:

> [...] In the summer of 1943 I was assigned to the SS- *und Polizei-Gericht* Danzig and my office was located in the *Strafvollzugslager* Danzig Matzkau. On a given occasion I was re-assigned in the capacity as an investigative officer. The agreed reason for my appointment was the dissatisfaction with the implementation of the supervisory authority of the penal system in Matzkau. Before my time, the camp doctor had already been replaced because of this. The main office was keen to strengthen the influence of the SS- *und Polizei-Gericht* Danzig within the *Strafvollzugslager der* SS *und Polizei* Danzig-Matzkau.
>
> The camp commandant in Matzkau had to decide in each case whether the members of his guard unit, or the prisoners would receive a disciplinary, or a war court's

> prosecution. My appearance was to guarantee, and I emphasize this explicitly, that it was to guarantee that he (the commandant) had not resorted too far in disciplinary fines and penalties. Now in principle I mean to express that, on the basis of my legal education I was to strictly separate all occurrences, namely one to a disciplinary path and another to a judicial. My task was to investigate reported criminal history, i.e. to hear the offender and the witnesses. Observing whether they had strayed outside the responsibility of the local *Gerichtsoffizier*. Each task ended with me sending a summary report to the SS- *und Polizei-Gericht* Danzig. The cases with which I had to deal were only new offences such as theft outside the camp, trying to escape, so incidents that were newly incurred. As far as I was concerned, if members of the guard force, or other SS members had transgressed against the existing laws outside the camp, then I was then employed as an investigator.
>
> During my service in the camp Matzkau I had on one single occasion helped out as a judge in Danzig. It was here, as far as I can remember, that a canteen manager had committed a theft in a Danzig *Polizei* unit. When I arrived the commandant was SS-*Hstuf.* Dr Ernst. To my knowledge he was removed in early 1944 and was sent to the front. His successor was then the former leader of the Allach camp, SS-*Hstuf.* Baumgärtner.[141]

In addition to this post, which the former guard *Uscha.* Albert Müller described as the 'Leader of the Legal department', Dr Beelitz also ensured the correct implementation of capital punishments in accordance with the SS and *Polizei* jurisdiction. In Britain, Bletchley Park intercepted a message from Matzkau on 23 November 1943 that identified Dr Beelitz as the commandant's adjutant on 7 October the same year.

On 21 July 1943, the SS leader commanded the *HA* SS-*Gericht* and its courts to no longer punish women non-members of the SS and *Polizei* with *Zuchthaus* sentences. These offenders were now commanded to serve their punishment inside a concentration camp and be put to work in a factory for the war effort.[142]

Turning to the subject of convicts expelled from the SS or *Polizei*, but judged fit for battle, the SS leader commanded these felons to be recommended for the *Bewährungsabteilung* or the *Polizei Sondereinheit* on 21 June 1943 and those judged unfit for combat, or disabled in some other way, were ordered to work in factories. With battle training suspended for those deployed in factories, the question of how to maintain the fitness of inmates expecting front probation was left to the *HA* SS-*Gericht* to detirmine.[143]

In the summer of 1943, the training of potential probationers became a major concern to the *HA* SS-*Gericht* and they struggled to balance the need to arrange battle training for those transferring to the probation units and the need to comply with Himmler's June 1943 work order. This conflict of interest between work and probation was never fully satisfied and although the inmates continued to participate in a rigorous exercise regime, this would prove an inadequate substitution for combat training. As a consequence of this situation, those probationers sent to the *Bewährungsabteilung* in Dublowitz then required more battle training. However, this situation did not concern the SS leader. In his opinion, their deployment in the German war industry equated with frontline service.[144]

Writing to the SS-*Richter beim* RF-SS in August 1943, *Ogruf.* Frank voice his concern that harm was caused to the children of inmates who father's had been convicted by the Prague tribunal and was then imprisoned in Berlin, Dachau or Matzkau. Proposing that a new prison was constructed in Brünn, Frank's suggestion found its way to *Ostubaf.* Horst Bender and he forwarded the matter to the *HA* SS-*Gericht.* 'There is no compelling military necessity to purchase the plot of land that is required for his idea' wrote General Breithaupt in response to this proposal on 20 August, and reporting no intention of interfering in this matter, he did however, prepare a report on this subject for the SS leader and expressed his intention to discuss the issue with him at the earliest opportunity. Bringing Frank's suggestion to Himmler's attention, he exhibited no interest in building a prison in Brünn, but did express his concern by the issue. Writing to the SS-*Richter beim* RF-SS on 13 November, Breithaupt declared that he had no further intention of raising this proposal with the *Reichsführer* again and left the issue to the SS leader and *Ogruf.* Frank to discuss.[145]

Born in Den Haag, Leo Brockmann was languishing in the *Strafvollzugslager der* SS *und Polizei* Danzig-Matzkau on 26 August 1943 when his father applied for his clemency. Receiving a reply to his entreaties, the *Amt* III informed Brockmann senior that a confirmation in this matter was still pending. Sentenced to serve a term of *Gefängnis* by the Viennese tribunal, 24 year-old *Rttf.* Bruno Zimmermann entered the electrified fence of the Matzkau *Häftlingslager* on 1 September 1943.[146]
Answering questions about the murder of Matzkau inmates in 1963, the former KL Stutthof guard, Otto Haupt, revealed that Stutthof prisoners, former SS and *Polizei*, were detained in Matzkau from as early as the autumn of 1943:

> [...] In this camp stood approximately 50 prisoners of the KL Stutthof who had been sent outside the wire to work. These prisoners of KL Stutthof lived in Danzig-Matzkau, but were segregated from the other felons in their own prison compound (*Arrestgebäude*) and detained in a specially secured barrack under the watchful eyes of the Matzkau guard troop. I only visited these prisoners when they were hospitalised, I then looked after them as they had formally belonged to the KL Stutthof. [...]

Claiming never to have cared for Matzkau inmates, Haupt revealed that he only ever visited the barracks of the Stutthof prisoners and firmly rejected the suggestion that Matzkau convicts had visited the KL Stutthof for medical treatment.[147]

This professional *Polizei* officer arrived in Matzkau to serve his prison sentence in late 1943:

Name: Wolfgang Plaul.
Last Rank: SS-*Hauptsturmführer*.
Born: 13.4.1900 in Grimma, Antonstadt/Sachen.
NSDAP-Nr.: 18.213 (joined 3.3.1925).
SS-Nr.: 59.933 (joined 28.10.1932).

Prewar Assignments:
Pionier-Bataillon 22 (Riesa).
Feld-Rekruit-Depot Nr. 3 (Remilly be Sedan) in 1918.
Landesjägerkorps Menke 6.2.1919–29.4.1919.
15. SA-*Sturm* (I. / 179. SA-*Standarte*) 1925–25.7.1932.
2. *Sturme* of the 48. SS-*Standarte* (Leipzig) 28.10.1932–1933.
3. / III. / 2. SS-*Standarte* (Frankfurt am M.) in 1933.
Offizier-Lehrgang Hosterwitz/Dresden *Polizeiführerschule* from 1.4.1934–30.6.1935.
Officer of the *Stamm Mitte* of the 12. SS-*Standarte* (Hannover) from 12.9.1937.
Officer of the *Stamm Sudost* / 104. SS-*Standarte* (Troppau) from 1.1.1939.
Wartime Assignments:
Officer of the *Stamm Nordsee* of the 28. SS-*Standarte* (Hamburg) from 1.10.1940.
2. / II. / *Hilfspolizei-Bataillon* in 1941.
Led the II. / *Hilfspolizei-Bataillon* in 10.1941.
SS-*Panzergrenadier-Ausbildung- und Ersatz-Bataillon* 1 (Spreehagen) on 12.4.1944
SS-*Sonder* Rgt. *Dirlewanger* from the spring 1944.
36th *Waffen-Grenadier*-Division *der* SS from 19.2.1945.
Promotions:

20.9.1935	*Leutnant der Schutzpolizei.*
0.0.1936	*Hauptmann der Schutzpolizei.*
12.9.1937	SS-*Hauptsturmführer der Allgemeine*-SS.
12.4.1944	SS-*Hauptsturmführer der Reserve.*

Decorations & Awards:

1914-18	*Ehrenkreuz Für Kreigsteilnehmer.*
0.0.1944	*Kriegsverdienstkreuz II. Klasse mit Schwertern.*
0.0. 19__	*Dienstauszeichnung der* NSDAP *in Bronze.*
0.0. 19__	*Dienstauszeichnung der* NSDAP *in Silber.*
0.0. 19__	*Dienstauszeichnung der* NSDAP *in Gelb.*
0.0.19__	*Ehrendegen des Reichsführer*-SS.
0.0.1938	*Die Medaille zur Erinnerung an den* 1. Oktober 1938 (Sudetenland).

Notes: Attending *Volksschule*, Plaul obtained his *Abitur* from *Höhere Schule* and then studied farming at the University of Leipzig. Plaul fought at the front with the Pioneer Battalion at Riesa during the Great War (*Fahnjünker-Gefreiter*) and participated in the ill-fated Kapp–Lüttwitz Putsch in Berlin in the spring of 1920. Plaul married his fiancée Veronika K., (b. 7.11.1915 in Berlin) on 14 July 1923 and they had four children together. The couple later divorced. Leading the Grimma Nazi party between 1 January 1923 and 22 June 1932, Plaul mustered with the SA in 1925 and gained admittance to the *Polizei* in Hannover on 11 September 1933 (36. *Polizei Revier*). Posted to the *Polizeipräsidium* Dresden (*Abt.* I) between 6 January 1936 and 28 March 1936, Plaul went on to serve with the Hannover police. Plaul left the SS on 30 May 1934 as a consequence of the ban on state officials holding membership of political parties, but was re-admitted with his original membership number on 12 September 1937. Deployed with the Troppau *Polizei* from 1 January 1939 to 1 December 1940, Plaul was then assigned to the Hamburg, St Pauli *Polize*i on 1 October. Posted to the Banat in occupied Serbia on 10 October 1941, here, Plaul formed a company of auxiliary police from ethnic-German volunteers and then took command of the second company of Major Josten's battalion. Replacing him as battalion commander when Josten was then appointed commander of the I. / 5. *Polizei*-Rgt. 5, Plaul conducted the training of his unit over four classes from mid-October 1941 to the end of January 1942 and was engaged in the battle against the partisans in Croatia and Serbia between 15-26 July 1942.

A court's investigation as conducted against Plaul to examine three allegations of him misusing his service position (he had loaned monies to officers in the unit, pocketed the interest and overcharged for the purchase of company uniforms). Arraigned before the courts martial of the SS- *und Polizei-Gericht* XIX, Belgrade between 14 and 16 January 1943, (case Nr. St. L I 97/42), the court was convinced that Plaul had misused unit funds, misused service funds in three instances, violated SS officers regulations from 16 January 1943 and stolen money from the staff canteen during the 1941 summer festival. The court president, *Stubaf.* Wetzling judged the edacious Plaul guilty of committing the offences and punished him with a term of two years *Gefängnis*, imposed six weeks' *Stubenarrest* and ordered his expulsion from the SS.

Observing that *Major* Josten bore some blame for his activities, Wetzling then accused his wife of selling material at profit and hoarding goods. The trial judge then sent a report of their activities to the RSHA for further investigation. His sentence confirmed, Plaul was incarcerated in Danzig-Matzkau on 5 November 1943. However, he did not remain here for long: Himmler confirmed and reduced his original sentence to eleven months' *Gefängnis* and in view of the time already spent in detention between the sentence and confirmation period, the SS leader qualified Plaul for probation and ordered him to the SS-*Sonderregiment Dirlewanger* with his former rank in 25 January 1944. Released from Matzkau on 12 April, Plaul reported to a training battalion before making his way to Belorussia.

Rising quickly to become one of Dirlewanger's trusted lieutenants, *Hstuf.* Plaul returned to Matzkau on 9 June 1944 to collect and escort a former officer to the SS-*Sonderregiment Dirlewanger*: Born in Weidenau/Sudetenland on 1 November 1908, Josef Grohmann, an SS man, (SS Nr. 207.848), had participated in the invasion of the Sudetenland in 1938 and then reported for duty at the SS-*Hauptamt*. Brought for trial in 1943, Grohmann found himself punished with a term of seven months' *Gefängnis* on 7 February 1944 for committing a weapons offence, drunkenness on duty and submitting a false report. Sent to Matzkau, the *Reichsführer* confirmed Grohmann's sentence on 17 April 1944 and demoted him to the rank of SS-*Mann* on 3 June. Later reinstated to his former rank, Grohmann took command of the fourth Russian Company and ended the war fighting with the 36th *Waffen-Grenadier*-Division *der* SS on the Niesse Front.[148]

Concerned at the deployment of non-German guards in Matzkau, *Oberf.* Dr Reinecke announced that it would be best practice when prison guards were only selected from German's and older men. Acknowledging that the majority of the prison population was either ethnic-German, or non-German in origin and admitting that a language problem existed between the staff and inmates, Dr Reinecke expressed his hope in November 1943 that the SS-FHA would stop assigning non-German staff to Matzkau. Supporting Dr Reinecke's proposal on 17 November, the *Reichsführer* commanded the prison guards were selected from older, German SS men in future and only guards speaking German would supervise German inmates. This order was communicated to the Matzkau *Wachkompanie*, but finding suitable troops that could be spared for prison service remained a thorny issue. As a consequence of this problem, the SS-*Richter beim* RF-SS recommended that wounded veterans was selected as prison guards and judging by the large number of disabled men deployed in the *Waffen*-SS prison service, this proposal was implemented.[149]

Born on 4 October 1919, the *Gerichtsherr* for the SS- *und Polizei-Gericht* XVIII, Nikolajew agreed that the inmate Werner Beidal had been judged suitable for front probation on 6 December 1943 and ordered his release from Matzkau on 10 December.[150]

The *HA* SS-*Gericht* estimated that around 2,400 convicts had been partitioned between Matzkau and the branch prison at Ludwigsfelde at the end of 1943.[151]

One of those convicts incarcerated in Matzkau at this time was a deserter from a *Waffen*-SS training unit in Nuremberg. Richard P. was assigned to the *Arbeitsdienstlager* Poppenhausen/Rhön in 1943 when he came under pressure to join the *Waffen*-SS. Fearing his refusal would be interpreted as an insult to the *Führer*, or a sign of resistance, he along with seventeen other staff marched to Nuremberg for induction. On arrival, Richard P. feigned illness to avoid taking the oath of allegiance and then attempted to desert from his training unit. Captured, by a *Feldgendarme* patrol within the city limits, they gave him a black eye for his troubles and returned him to the SS-*Kaserne*. Arraigned before the courts martial of the SS- *und Polizei-Gericht* XXV, Nuremberg for desertion, the tribunal judged Richard P. guilty of the charge and punished him with five years' *Gefängnis* on 30 October 1943. Richard P. was still detained in Matzkau on 15 February 1945. Surviving this experience and the conflict, Richard P. was employed as a businessman in post-war Kassel.[152]

This officer barely escaped imprisonment in Matzkau during December 1943, but did not survive the war. Born in Neuss/Rhine on 27 April 1912, *Ustuf.* Anton Mennen was assigned to the SS-*Infantrie-Ersatz-Bataillon* 11 in Klagenfurt during 1943 when he began playing table top tennis and drinking alcohol with *Ustuf.* Bittner in the officers' mess. During the course of the evening, Mennon drank 22 glasses of cognac and up to two bottles of champagne. Refused the home address of a kitchen maid, Mennen barged his way into the kitchen, smashed crockery and punched *Rttf.* Dengel in the mouth. Arraigning Mennen before the courts martial of the SS- *und Polizei-Gericht* VII, Vienna, the tribunal heard the presented evidence presented to them and judged Mennen guilty of the charges on 25 December 1943 and punished him with a term of one year's *Gefängnis* and a demotion to non-commissioned officer rank. Confirming the sentence, the *Reichsf*ührer set aside his prison sentence, degraded Mennon to the rank of *Strm.* and ordered him to apologise to the ethnic-German *Rttf.* Dengel for the assault. Undertaking his act of contrition in the presence of his commander on 11 February, Mennon then transferred to an unidentified panzer grenadier division and died in action at Iville on the Normandy Front on 23 August 1944.[153]

3.5 1943 Brutality Scandal

Surviving the threat of closure, the prison then found itself at the centre of a brutality scandal in mid-1943 which resulted in the commandant's dismissal and the transfer of many senior prison officers to the front. It is evident from surviving documents that the day-to-day running of the *Häftlingslager* had been left in the capable hands of *Hstuf.* Erich Albert and Dr Ernst had rarely interfered with his command. Requiring a replacement for Albert, Dr Ernst selected *Ostuf.* Walter Dieterle for the post of Nr. 1 *Lagerführer* on 1 March 1943. A relatively junior officer, Dieterle had served under Dr Ernst since November 1942, but the commandant thought highly of his subordinate and continued entrust the day to day running of the jail to Dieterle as he had done to Albert. This trust soon proved misplaced and the subsequent court record describes what occurred next:

> [...] Immediately after taking over the *Häftlingslager* in February 1943 the accused, SS-*Ostuf.* Dieterle, discussed at a report leaders' meeting and repeated elsewhere how the SS and *Polizei* prison camp commandant had abandoned the use of the cane, but he had expressed the need to introduce a new professional and disciplinary measure in the *Häftlingslager* and explained this need to the leaders of individual companies. Here, Laimgruber and others unequivocally expressed the view that the cane was necessary and should be re-introduced without further delay. The accused SS-*Ostuf.* Dieterle then several times spoke to the commandant of the prison camp, SS-*Ostubaf.* Dr Ernst, about reintroducing the cane, but Dr Ernst rejected the defendant Dieterle's request outright and stated that he, himself could not introduce caning as the *Reichsführer*-SS and the *HA* SS-*Gericht* would never give their approval. During a *Rapportführer* meeting the accused Dieterle explained that the maladjusted convicts were now to be gathered into a separate company.

Taking up his new post, *Ostuf.* Dieterle appointed *Oscha.* Fritz Pölking to the post of *Rapportführer* for the newly established 5. *Strafkompanie*. To improve inmate discipline, the new *Lagerführer* introduced a punitive regime which consisted of punishment press-ups, but shortly after its introduction, Pölking spoke with Dieterle to report that he was experiencing difficulties maintaining discipline and complained that elements of his company were arriving deliberately late to parades and often refusing to stand attention, they shirked work details and had gotten into the habit of greeting each other with a *Heil Moskau*! Fearing the further erosion of discipline, Dieterle, without seeking the permission of Dr Ernst, then ordered the implementation a beating by cane against persistent offenders of the 5. *Strafkompanie*. To protect himself and his guards from convict complaints, he demanded Pölking recorded the inmate's name, his offence and penalty in a punishment book. Composed of loose half sized pages bound into a hard cardboard book cover, Pölking presented this record to Dieterle for his signature on the day of the sentencing.

Fully aware that the use of the cane was contrary to standing orders, Pölking then sought the advice of *Uscha.* Anton Kerschreiter and Karl Rath and both recommended he ensured that the punishment book entries were witnessed by the *Barrackenältesten*, his deputy Ittrich, who took care of the book and the barrack scribe, a convict named Günther. The first beatings were conducted before the assembled 5. *Strafkompanie* and the miscreants received between five to ten strokes each. Punishing Wilhelm Tessner for shirking work duty and attacking a convict company leader named Herzberg, Günther wrote 'punishment; whole arse is beaten' on the punishment card. The punishments completed, Dieterle counter-signed all twelve entries from 6 to 8 April 1943, but significantly, he failed to record the caning punishments in the inmate's punishment card, which was kept in the administration office with the convict's personal file (entering these punishments in this file, Dr Ernst would have undoubtedly discovered that Dieterle had disobeyed his orders).

Replacing Pölking when he was admitted into hospital for an operation between 10 April and 20 July 1943, *Rttf.* Schulz was informed of the unofficial punishment regime and suspecting that something was amiss, he decided to speak with Pölking and seek clarity on its use. During their conversation, Schulz was assured that Dieterle handed the completed punishment pages to *Hscha.* Anton Sorg and he passed it to the commandant. Unconvinced by this explanation, Schulz then approached Dieterle to clarify the issue and he repeated Pölking's explanation. Satisfied that the legality of the punishment had been guaranteed, Schulz continued imposing the penalty. However, the convicts of the 5. *Strafkompanie* had become extremely unhappy with their treatment and taking advantage of Dieterle's absence between 31 May and 6 June 1943, the company scribe, Günther, wrote a letter of complaint to the *Oberabschnitt Weichel* to expose the illegal use of the cane. In his letter, Günther described how on one occasion Pölking had beaten a convict so badly that his birch had broken and the badly injured inmate had become bedridden. He also alleged that without seeking his superior's approval, Pölking had ordered the detention of convicts in the *Arrestgebäude* for between three and six days.

Receiving this complaint, the *Oberabschnitt Weichel* forwarded its contents to the Danzig tribunal with orders to initiate a court's investigation into the allegations. Making his way to Matzkau, the SS-*Richter Hstuf.* Erich Dauer reported first to Dr Ernst and explain the reason for his visit. Shocked by the allegations, both judges immediately set about interviewing convicts and staff involved in the affair. Confronting Dieterle, he initially denied knowledge of the beatings, but grudgingly admitted the existence of the punishment book. Ordered to produce this potentially damning evidence, Dieterle retrieved the book and handed it to Dauer. At this point, the judges observed that the entries numbered nine to twelve were missing (Pölking later informed *Uscha.* Rath that these missing entries had been removed from the book when the four inmates had complained about their beatings). Although it was apparent that Dieterle had countersigned each punishment, the young officer continued to assert that he had not been aware of the beatings and attempting to place responsibility for the punishments on Pölking's shoulders alone. Realising that his superior did not accept his explanation, he then sought to convince the judges that that the punishment book entries represented extra drill. Rejecting his excuses, Dr Ernst suspended Dieterle and Pölking from active duty and *Hstuf.* Edmund Baumgärtner took over as the Nr. 1 *Lagerführer*.

Returning from a week of leave on 31 August 1943, Dieterle discovered that he and Pölking would face trial for imposing the beatings (case Nr. St. L. II 155/1943). Both were arraigned before the courts martial of the SS- *und Polizei-Gericht* IV, Danzig on 17 September 1943 and the chairman, *Stubaf.* Dr Herbert Kuß, was supported in his deliberations by *Hstuf.* Schlüter and *Ostuf.* Wirth. The prosecution was conducted by *Ostuf.* Dietrich Voß and the *Beurkundungsführer* was *Hstuf.* Hugo Sahlender. The trial witnesses included *Ustuf.* Laimgruber, *Hscha.* Sorg, *Uscha.* Kerschreiter, *Uscha.* Rath and *Rttf.* Schulz. The convicts Günther, Ittrich, Heinz Quendt, Fritz Schwenk, Wilhelm Tessner and Kleinöder also provided the court with statements. During the court proceedings Dieterle continued to deny any knowledge of the beatings, but when questioned, Pölking did not hesitate to implicate the young officer in the offences. Expressing sympathy for Pölking, the trial judge agreed that he had experienced difficulties commanding the 'shirkers,' the worst criminal cases and those avoiding front service of the 5. *Strafkompanie* and then expressed his certainty that the NCO had acted under orders at the time of the beatings. 'An outstanding character at work, he is upright, true and responsible and his world view is good. His service performance is good and he took his function as *Strafkompanieführer* seriously' announced Dr Kuß on 17 September and judging Pölking guilty of mishandling convicts and military disobedience, he ordered him to serve a six weeks' arrest penalty.

Despite an exemplary disciplinary record, the court judged *Ostuf.* Dieterle guilty of military disobedience and handed him a term of three months' *Gefängnis* for committing perjury, two months' *Gefängnis* for ordering the beating of Heinz Glaser, Otte Wedddinger, Quendt, Schwank and Tessner in April 1943 and a further two months' *Gefängnis* for other offences (a total sentence of nine months' *Gefängnis*). Commanding his demotion to the rank of *Oscha,* Dieterle now faced the real prospect of becoming a Matzkau inmate. The trial completed, he remained free until his sentence had been confirmed by the SS leader. Unwelcome in Matzkau, Dieterle transferred to the SS-FHA and they re-deployed him to the communications branch of the *Waffen*-SS. Confirming Dieterle's sentence on 6 January, the *Reichsführer* amended the judgment to four months' *Gefängnis*, confirmed his demotion and granted him a period of front probation. At this time, Himmler amended Pölking's sentence to two weeks' arrest.[154]

This was not the end of the affair and further heads would roll. Prior to this incident, the commandant had warned his superiors about the deployment of unsuitable staff in Matzkau and complained that rehabilitation was hampered by overcrowding. Grumbling that the prison suffered from a lack of weapons and qualified training instructors, Dr Ernst had also warned his superiors that there existed in the prison the constant threat of inmate institutionalisation. Expressing his fears that the prison's deficiencies threatened the development of a camp mentality, Dr Ernst had recommended the wider application of probation for inmates to enable them to regain their honour in battle. Despite his forewarnings, the commandant would not be spared punishment. Called to Berlin shortly after Dieterle's sentence confirmation, Dr Ernst met with the SS-*Richter beim* RF-SS who blamed him personally for the prison's ills, criticised him for his neglectful supervision and warned him that his tenure as commandant would soon end. The transfers did not end here, the commandant's adjutant, *Ostuf.* Wurm, had received orders to report to the *HA* SS-*Gericht* in Munich seven days earlier and the SS-PHA ordered *Ustuf.* Erich Laimgruber to join the troops on 8 March 1944.[155]

On this date, the *Reichsführer* then turned his invective on the *Chef HA* SS-*Gericht*:

> The deplorable state of affairs in camp Danzig-Matzkau displeases and distresses me personally. Please take a service journey to the local HSSPF and talk to him seriously about the how this re-education centre has become a playground for sadists. Also I'd like to speak about your own responsibilities, now and again I want you to specially take a service journey direct to our detention institution and with your own eyes look it over. In the fifth year of war you must halt your activities as *Sportsgauführer* and devote yourself fully to the duties of the *HA* SS-*Gericht* chief.

Himmler's stinging rebuke provoked General Breithaupt to lay the blame the prison's ills entirely at the feet of Dr Ernst and in addition to expressing his conviction that the institution's ills were a consequence of the commandant's supervisory deficiencies, the general also criticized the ignorant mentality of the ethnic-German guards, who in his opinion lacked the high standards expected of SS men.[156]

3.6 *Schloß* Hornburg Proposal

Writing during the first week of February 1944, the *Chef HA* SS-*Gericht* reported that the *Straflager* Dachau was full to capacity with 500 inmates and the re-education for these convicts was proving impossible in these conditions. It is clear, that at this time, both Dachau and Matzkau were struggling again to meet the requirements of the jurisdictions-part—sentencing-part front probation process, but worse news was to come. The *Waffen*-SS detention centre at Berlin-Lankwitz destroyed in an allied air raid on the night of the 24/25 August 1943 the WVHA forbad the construction of any new barracks -style prison in Berlin and as a consequence of this decision, General Breithaupt then undertook a search for a new site on which to establish a prison. Coming across the Schloßgutes Hornburg, a castle, located some 20 km south-east of M*ü*lhausen, the general then sought funds to purchase the land and ordered Günther Burmeister to journey to travel to Elsaß and look over the site. In the company of the SS- *und Polizei Bau Inspektor Reich West, Ostubaf.* Rudlieb Görcke, Burmeister examined the castle and returned to Munich to report that with 65-rooms, the Schloßgutes Hornburg had good security potential and was located near many SS units refitting in France for the expected Allied invasion (nearby was the cigarette factory 'Burrus' whose family had fled to Lyon).

Explaining that the site had stables, barns, around 200 acres of suitable land on which to cultivate vegetables, Burmeister noted that 270 acres of woodland existed around the castle. A guest house with accommodation for visitors stood in its grounds and he estimated that 200 to 300 inmates could be employed on the land and supply its produce to the Sennheim troop training ground and other service offices in the region (he also proposed that around 100 inmates laboured inside Sennheim). 'Advantageous' is how Breithaupt described the castle and expressed his belief that a barracks -style camp and work station could be constructed in its grounds. Enthusing further, the general imagined retaining the Schloßgutes Hornburg for the *HA* SS-*Gericht* after the war. With the support of Breithaupt, Burmeister contacted the SS-*Richter beim* RF-SS on 1 February 1944, to request that he interceded with the SS leader to arrange to the purchase of the castle. Political grounds eventually precluded the purchase of this site and Himmler rejected the proposal at the end of February 1944. Despite this decision, the SS-*Hauptamt* proceeded with their plans to the purchase the site and the *HA* SS-*Gericht* prisons continued to run at full capacity until new institutions had been constructed in the Neckar valley and in Bavaria.[157]

3.7 First Half of 1944

Matzkau had been in operation for around twenty months by January 1944 and at this time its barracks were filled to capacity, the staff was experiencing problems supplying food and the inmates were plagued with illnesses and indiscipline. Still in command of the prison on 4 February 1944, Dr Ernst's deputy was Edmund Baumgärtner and under the judge's leadership were eight officers, eight senior non-commissioned officers and 65 other ranks.[158]

In late 1943 a decision was taken to transfer senior prison officers to the front:

> *HA* SS-*Gericht* IIIb to the SS-*Richter beim* RF-SS dated 20 January 1944.
>
> Subject: Officers of the *Strafvollzugslager der* SS *und Polizei* Danzig-Matzkau and the *Straflager* Dachau.
> Reference: Letter from the SS-*Richters beim* RF-SS from 8 December 1943 and an oral consultation from 19 January 1944.

According to the aforementioned letter the officers of the of the *Strafvollzugslager der* SS *und Polizei* Danzig-Matzkau and the *Straflager der* SS *und Polizei* Dachau are to be released to the troops: SS-*Hstuf.* Albert, SS-*Hstuf.* Baumgartner, SS-*Ostuf.* Sturmann, SS-*Ustuf.* Baumeister and SS-*Ustuf.* Laimgruber.

This coincides with the transfer to the troops of the commandant of the *Strafvollzugslager der SS und Polizei,* SS-*Ostubaf.* Dr Ernst, on 1 February 1944.

SS-*Hstuf.* Albert, as the leader of a *Straflager der* SS *und Polizei,* SS-*Hstuf. Baumgärtner* as the leader of the *Straflager der* SS *und Polizei* Dachau and SS-*Ostuf.* Sturmann as the leader of the *Straflager der* SS *und Polizei* Dachau, *Aussenstelle* Allach, are in use as leadership prison officers and we would ask that all at once you would cancel their release to the troops.

Adequate substitution for them is not available, especially since the incorporation into the responsibilities of a correctional officer requires special experience. I therefore ask that SS-*Hstuf. Albert* and Baumgärtner and the SS-*Ostuf. Sturmann* are retained for the punishment camp.

For this I would like to cite the following: The construction of an SS and *Polizei* own run prison during the war was conducted with considerable difficulties, which are even now not yet completely overcome. Therefore, to enable them to fulfill their educational tasks the prominent leaders of each camp are needed for special requirements that arranging a substitute for them is difficult to devise.

In addition, the negotiations at this time on the establishment of another SS and *Polizei Straflager* in Alsace-Lorraine is underway. Once the establishment of this camp is completed, we will also need again to make available suitable officers, however, I can reveal that the release of SS-*Ostubaf.* Dr Ernst and the SS-*Ustuf.* Baumeister and Laimgruber to the troops has already significantly diminished my current inventory.

I beg to bring about a decision by the *Reichsführer*-SS in this sense.

Burmeister.

At the time this letter was composed, Dr Ernst could be found in Matzkau and Sturmann had been appointed the leader of the branch prison at Ludwigsfelde. *Stubaf.* Burmeister's spirited argument to retain Albert, Baumgärtner and Sturmann in the prison service was presented to the SS leader for his opinion and the results of his interjection were revealed in the spring of 1944:

The *SS-Richter beim* RF-SS to the *HA* SS-*Gericht* dated 26 April 1944

Re.: Officers of the *Strafvollzugslager der* SS *und Polizei* Danzig-Matzkau and the *Straflager* Dachau.
Reference: Your letter dated 20 January 1944—IIIb 353 and 361.

In the above matter I have spoken with the *Reichsführer*-SS. The *Reichsführer*-SS agrees that *Hstuf.* Baumgärtner, Albert and Sturmann are to remain in the SS and *Polizei* jurisdiction and in the services that they hold presently within the penal system. A release for the troops has thus been cancelled for these three officers.

Dismissing Dr Ernst from his post as commandant in late February 1944, the disgraced SS-*Richter* handed command of the garrison directly to the Nr. 1 *Lagerführer Hstuf.* Edmund Baumgärtner and Dr Beelitz was appointed his deputy commandant (*Ostuf.* Biedermann replaced Baumgärtner). 'The commandant of the prison camp was *Ostubaf.* Dr Ernst. About two months after my transfer, he was demoted because of bad leadership and sent to the troops' recalled Fritz Ringel when asked to describe Dr Ernst's ignoble end. In addition to these command changes, the *Amt* III had ordered the transfer of three newly trained certification non-commissioned officers to the prison by 1 February 1944.[160]

Post war, Edmund Baumgärtner was also asked to recall Dr Ernst's ousting and explain his new responsibilities:

> [...] Ernst transferred command of the camp directly to me. Further I can recall that SS-*Hstuf.* Dr Beelitz was there when I arrived at the camp. Dr Beelitz exercised the function of a *Gerichtsoffizier* and in this post he did not report to me. The *Lagerführer* was responsible for the discipline in the camp and he ordered the relevant disciplinary penalties. The *Lagerführer* was not obliged to report on the imposition of a disciplinary penalties. Only when a punishment was required against the members of the guards was I notified. My deputy was Dr Beelitz and the *Lagerführer* of the SS and *Polizei* Danzig-Matzkau prison camp was SS-*Ostuf.* Gottfried Biedermann, a native of Düsseldorf, who was born about 1909 or 1910. The deputy *Lagerführer* was Erich Laimgruber from Austria (Innsbruck) and born around 1908. I presume that Laimgruber had fallen in the war. The commander of the first *Wachkompanie* was Fritz Ringel who was also native of Innsbruck. Ringel is the nephew of the famous general, the former mountaineer Ringel, who died in a plane crash during the war. *Ostuf.* Ringel was born in 1911 or the 1912. Under Ringel were about seventy male members of the guard. The commander of the second *Wachkompanie* was SS-*Ostuf.* N. Heiß. Heiß was a few years younger than all other SS-officers of the camp Matzkau. I think he was a nineteen or twenty years old. Heiß came from Bavaria. The administration office was occupied by SS-*Ustuf.* Golda, who was born in Litzmannstadt.[...]

Calling to mind that the Matzkau officers assisted him to guard the site and ensure the maintenance of order and discipline, Baumgärtner then remembered that Matzkau had originally been built for the *Heimwehr Danzig* prior to the Polish campaign and then turned his attention to the inmate population:

> [...] There were at the time of me taking office about 400 to 500 prisoners—of which, assuming that they did not all intend to escape, were put to use in outdoor work in the fields, or out to an establishment located near the estate. The rest were put to work within the camp. The remainder of the command usually drilled every day. [...]

Contained within Gottfried Biedermann's 1944 promotion recommendation are a few facts about the prison that contradict Baumgärtner's post-war impressions. At that time this report observed that the Häftlingslager held 2,400 convicts and 250 staff were assigned to the garrison. Adamant that no political prisoners had been incarcerated in Matzkau during his command tenure, when pressed, Baumgärtner conceded that those detained for the offence of undermining the war effort could be placed in this category. Recounting that the prison held felons who had been sentenced legally for offences such as plundering, defilement, murder, theft, Baumgärtner then recalled that among the inmates were high ranking officers and at any time, some 500 convicts were detained inside the prison, serving short sentences, usually of six months' duration. 'I ruled the *Häftlingslager* with the strongest discipline and order. This was the only leadership style that was possible with such serious criminals' stated Baumgärtner unambiguously when asked to describe his command style and confirming that punishment exercises were imposed against recalcitrant inmates, he assured his interrogator that no arbitrary acts of murder had occurred in Matzkau. When asked about his superiors, he recalled reporting to both *Stubaf.* Hermann Meder and Wolfgang Walter at the *Amt* III (*Strafvollzugs*).[161]

Some Matzkau inmates became seriously ill during their incarceration: Born in Hattenhof/ Fulda on 11 December 1920, *Hscha.* Josef Malkmus was punished with a term of *Gefängnis* and then detained in Matzkau during 1944 (case Nr. St. L. I. 32/44). Recovered from diphtheria, Malkmus served his sentence, returned to his former rank and then reported to the SS-*Nachrichten-Ersatz-Bataillon* in Nuremberg on 28 August 1944.[162]

Ordering *Rottwachmeister d. Gend.* Peter Koller's discharge on 14 January 1944, the SS- *und Polizei-Gericht* XXVIII, Agram revealed that Koller had been assigned to the *Gendarme* post in Krapina in Croatia prior to committing his disciplinary offences.[163]

Writing on 14 March 1944, General Berger of the SS-*Hauptamt* forwarded a copy of Oskar Dirlewanger's probation proposal to the *Reichsführer*. Its contents would directly threaten Matzkau's existence:

> In view of the difficult reinforcement situation, it is my wish that SS-*Ostubaf.* Dirlewanger, or a special representative experienced in anti-partisan warfare nominated by him in agreement with SS-*Ogruf. Berger*, should select from the inmates of the SS and *Polizei* punishment camps and other prisons those *Waffen*-SS men of suitable character and because of the nature of their offence be employed in the Dirlewanger unit. In view of the urgency and importance of anti-partisan warfare, the regulations should be interpreted liberally. By showing courage, the selected men would have the opportunity to rehabilitate themselves. This order will take precedence over all general and special instructions regarding the serving of sentences. In pending, or future cases of investigation against *Waffen*-SS men, investigating officers will check on whether a man's character and nature of the offence is such that they can be made available to SS-*Ostubaf.* Dirlewanger and, if the answer is in the affirmative, they be made available

to him. Summaries of evidence will be held by SS-*Ostubaf. Dirlewanger* until the end of the probationary period.

Until this time only *Zuchthaus* inmates, or those felons who had committed very serious offences, had found themselves subordinated to Dirlewanger's command and only with Himmler's approval. Unwilling to permit the prison to become a reserve unit for Dirlewanger, the *HA* SS-*Gericht* skilfully argued against the proposal and insisting that the inmates were not 'merchandise' to be passed around, the *HA* SS-*Gericht* maintained that each convict remain subject to the legal process until serving their prison sentence and then transferring to the *Bewährungsabteilung* or *Arbeitsabteilung*. Expressing fears that Dirlewanger's proposal would subvert the entire SS legal process, the leader of the SS sided with his SS-*Richter* and refused to enact this proposal, or permit any member of the *Waffen*-SS, even those accused of a simple crime, from transferring to the SS-*Sonderregiment Dirlewanger* without undergoing any form of legal process. However, though supporting the *HA* SS-*Gericht* position, the *Reichsführer* conceded that Dirlewanger's force required re-enforcement and agreed that the regiment would in future receive suitable SS probationers from the prisons and he gave the courts permission to command offenders to report directly to Dirlewanger for front probation. With the *HA* SS-*Gericht* in agreement, the SS leader clarified the criminal types that would be selected for each probation unit on 6 June 1944:

- SS-*Fallschirmjägerabteilung* 500 for *Gefängnis* offenders,
- *Sonderverbände* z.b.V. *Friedenthal* for convicts willing to perform dangerous missions,
- *Sonderregiment* Dirlewanger for convicts judged unsuitable for parachute training and serious *Zuchthaus* cases,
- *Bewährungsabteilung- und Arbeitsabteilung der Waffen*-SS for all other cases.[164]

The worsening war situation, serious reverses on the battlefield and a need to reinforce Dirlewanger's regiment would lead to a radical departure from this agreement and by the autumn of 1944 the SS-*Sonderregiment* was inducting the vast majority of parolees, many of whom had served prison sentences in Matzkau.

Contacting Matzkau on 22 April, the Belgrade tribunal requested that they sent them a fitness report for the convict Stephan Moravck.[165]

Considering Danzig-Matzkau a part of its economic empire, a copy of *Ogruf.* Oswald Pohl's circular to all concentration camps for the WVHA was sent to the prison in mid-1944 and requested that all inmates' valuables and belongings after death were handed to his main office. All cash collected was deposited in SS numbered accounts and usable goods repaired and then sent to Germany.[166]The SS-*und Polizeigerichte* XIX, Belgrade contacted the prison on April 22nd 1944 to request a fitness report on Stephan Moravck, (born August 10th 1925). [8]

Telexing this prison on 3 May 1944, the SS- *und Polizei-Gericht* XIV, On May 3rd 1944 the SS-*und Polizeigerichte* XIV, Metz requested the prison send Otto Klink, (born, May 27th 1916) to the *Sondereinheit.* [10] Metz requested the release of the inmate Otto Klink to the *Sondereinheit.* That same month the prison contacted the SS- *und Polizei-Gericht* XX, Galatz on 20 May to report that the Matzkau convict, Heinz Galick had been judged suitable for inside and outside work details. Noting that his overall behaviour had proved satisfactory, the tribunal warned that Galick often behaved arrogantly towards other inmates and had an immature personality. Having received no punishments during his prison sentence, the court concluded that Galick was now suitable for front line service.[167]

The Red Army's devastating summer offensive on the Eastern Front had successfully pushed the German armies to the Polish border by 22 June 1944 and destroyed the equivalent of 20 to 30 German divisions. In Belorussia, a handful of former Matzkau inmates fighting with the SS-*Sonderregiment* had successfully extricated themselves from encirclement and capture at Minsk. The Red Army's offensive succeeded in bringing their forces to the River Vistula, a little more than one day's drive from the city of Danzig.

Prior to this catastrophe for the German Army, an appeal was announced on, or around 5 June 1944, for convicts to volunteer to undertake missions with a high chance of death or injury. Henceforth, *Waffen*-SS felons and those incarcerated in other penal institutions would be offered the opportunity to volunteer for commando type service in the SS-*Sonderverbände* z.b.V. *Friedenthal* near Berlin. As a consequence of this appeal, a handful of Matzkau volunteered for specialist commando training in the German capital.[168] Any SS convict wishing to volunteer for dangerous front line duties could make this known to the prison *Kommandant*. His details were taken and the request forwarded to the *Hauptamt* SS *Gericht*, *Amt* III for a response. After examining the SS convict's prison and service records the *Amt* III would decide if to grant the request.

As the Allied forces prepared to burst out from the Normandy bridgehead, the prison was beset with another disciplinary scandal.

3.8 20 July Plot

General Briethaupt had perhaps hoped that designating a certification officer to the post of commandant would lead to an improvement in discipline and security, but if this was his intention, then his expectation would be dashed in the summer of 1944. Taking control of the prison at a critical period of the war, Baumgärtner's short tenure was marked with controversy and resulted in his and other officers' transfer to the front. Tasked with obtaining cement for the prison, Baumgärtner arranged for the Feitsch and Münchau companies in Stargard to supply his needs. While negotiating with these companies, he undertook an affair with *Frau* Wilms, the daughter of a company director and under the pretext of meeting local companies, he used service vehicles to visit his mistress in Stargard and invited her for trysts in his accommodation. Planning another liaison with *Frau* Wilms on 19 July, Baumgärtner instructed his driver *Strm.* Paul Kuschel, a hotel owner, to take a motorcycle from the Matzkau car pool and drive him to his business in Stargard. Soon after setting off on their journey the motorcycle developed a puncture and Baumgärtner had to phone the garage to arrange for a *Kubelwagen* to collect him and he continued his journey to Stargard. Returning to his accommodation by 4.00 a.m. the following morning, (20 July), Baumgärtner, *Hscha.* Heinrich Müller and Kuschel gathered together in the officers' club and proceeded to drink half a bottle of Korn together. A little later, *Oscha.* Kunze joined the merry group and the impromptu party then consumed a whole bottle of Sekt. Coming upon the drinkers at 10.30 a.m., *Hstuf.* Biedermann drank with them until the gathering broke up at around 1.00 p.m. At this time, Baumgärtner decided he would return to Stargard, but as Kuschel was too inebriated to drive, Biedermann, a keen motorcyclist, offered to take his place. Leaving the prison astride a motorcycle, both officers neglected to appoint a deputy commander, or inform the prison office of their absence. Passing through Gross-Golmkau the motorcycle developed a puncture and the attending Matzkau mechanic did not repair the punctured tyre until 4.00 p.m. This delay angered Baumgärtner, but both officers continued their journey to Stargard and here, they registered at the 'Hotel Kuchsel.' Later that same evening the commandant met *Frau* Wilms and it was around 11.00 p.m. that same night that both officers become aware of the attempt on Adolf Hitler's life. Despite the serious implications of this event, both Baumgärtner and Biedermann agreed to return to Matzkau the next day.

In the commandant's absence the HSSPF *Weichel* in Danzig issued warnings to all SS units and service offices under his command that an army coup was in progress and placed them all on high alert. When the Matzkau office failed to acknowledge this message, the HSSPF feared that the inmates had been armed and stood prepared to assist the plotters (which speaks volumes about his perception of the felons) and ordered his subordinates to try and contact the prison by telephone. It was not until later that same night that Fritz Ringel finally answered the apparatus and reported that both the camp commandant and *Lagerführer* were absent from the garrison. Pressed to explain their absence, Ringel was unable to reveal their location. In response to this state of affairs, the HSSPF ordered *Hstuf.* Dr Beelitz to take immediate command of the institution and demanded that the missing officers report to him when they eventually surfaced.

Arriving back in Matzkau early on the morning of 21 July, both Baumgärtner and Biedermann received the order to and presented themselves before *Gruf.* Katzmann in Danzig to explain their absence. As a consequence of their egregious dereliction of duty, the HSSPF back-dated both officers suspension from their posts from 6.30 a.m. on 21 July and placing them under his direct command, he ordered both to put themselves under arrest in their own quarters. Reporting sick on 21 July, Baumgärtner remained in his service accommodation until 8 September.

The HSSPF *Weichsel* then instructed the SS-*Richter*, *Hstuf.* Dietrich Voß of the SS-*und Polizei-Gericht* IV, Danzig to undertake an investigation into the officers' dereliction of duty. Presenting his report, Voß recommended Baumgärtner was punished with a disciplinary sanction and as a consequence of this proposal, the *Disziplinaramt* punished the former commandant with fourteen days' intensified arrest for dereliction of duty (the time spent in home detention was deducted from the punishment). Also recommending that Baumgärtner applied for a front line posting when he reported fit for duty, his request was communicated to the SS-FHA on 18 August and the former commandant then joined a reserve mountain training unit near Gradisca in north-eastern Italy. As a consequence of his dereliction of duty, Biedermann found himself posted to the SS-*Straflager* Dachau in August 1944. Accepting a strong warning for negligence while acting under the direct orders of a superior, Biedermann, and *Ostuf.* Ringel, were assigned to a field court in the late summer of 1944 to undertake a short period of front line probation. In their wake, *Hstuf.* Dr Beelitz found himself appointed the permanent commandant and *Ustuf.* Rudolf Hieß accepted the responsibilities of Nr. 1 *Lagerführer* respectively. Both officers held these posts until the closure of Matzkau in the early spring of 1945.[169]

3.9 Second Half of 1944

'When he was removed from his post in the late summer of 1944, I was entrusted with responsibility for the service office on the instigation of the HSSPF Katzmann' is how Dr Beelitz recalled the circumstances of Baumgärtner's downfall. Another scandal behind the prison institution, the Berlin jurist was entrusted with leadership of the Matzkau headquarters on 21 July 1944.[170]

Speaking after the war, Dr Beelitz recalled that the SS-*Standort* Matzkau was composed of the service office, the headquarters staff, the *Lagerführer* of the *Häftlingslager* and the guard company troop leader. He recalled the prison detaining an average of around 1,000 to 1,500 inmates who lived in barracks and the guard contingent numbered around 100 men.[171]

In his post for only a few weeks, Dr Beelitz fell from his horse and severely injured his ankle. Handing command of the *Standort* to the garrison administrative officer, (probably the *Lagerführer*), the commandant recovered in his service accommodation. On 1 September 1944 the *HA* SS-*Gericht* appointed a newly recruited SS-*Richter*, *Uscha.* Dr Hans-Georg Mayer, to the prison with orders to liaise between this institution and the local court.[172]

These two disgraced officers arrived in Matzkau during the summer of 1944:

Name: Albert Knobelspieß.
Last Rank: SS-*Hauptsturmführer.*
Born: 2.11.1918 in Elbingen/Württemburg.
SS-Nr.: 326.75 (joined 12.11.1937).
Wartime Assignments:
Waffen-SS from 1939.
SS-*Totenkopf-Infantrie*-Rgt. 9 between 9.11.–11.12.1940.
SS-*Totenkopf-Wachbataillon Prag* until 15.3.1941.

SS-*Infantrie-Ersatz-Bataillon Westland* from 15.3.1941.
Led the *Wiking* StuG *Kompanie* on 13.6.1942.
SS-*Infantrie-Ersatz-Bataillon Westland* on 1.2.1943.
2. / SS-StuG-*Abteilung* 11 on 15.2.1943.
SS-*Panzer-Grenadier-Ausbildung- und Ersatz Bataillon* 11 on 21.2.1944.
3. / SS-*Panzerjäger-Abteilung* 16 in mid-1944.
Led the 16. SS-*Panzer-Abteilung* 2.1945-19.3.1945.

Promotions:

9.11.1940	SS-*Untersturmführer der Reserve.*
30.1.1942	SS-*Obersturmführer der Reserve.*
9.11.1943	SS-*Hauptsturmführer der Reserve.*

Decorations & Awards:

0.0.19__	*Deutsches Reichssportabzeichen in Bronze.*

Notes: Attending *Volksschule* for four classes, Knobelspieß then studied at *Höhere Schule*, (U-II *Mittel*) and *Handelschule* for two classes. By profession a salesman, Knobelspieß was drafted into the *Waffen*-SS in 1939. Having caused death by dangerous driving, an act of disobedience, Knobelspieß found himself arraigned before the courts martial. Judged guilty of the charges, the court punished him with six months' *Gefängnis* on 12 July 1944 and ordered him to the Danzig-Matzkau to serve his sentence. This punishment was later suspended and the errant Knobelspieß accepted six months' front probation with an anti-tank battalion. Promoted to his last rank in 1943, Knobelspieß led a tank battalion until his wounding on 19 March 1945.[173]

Name: Max Jumpertz.
Last Rank: SS-*Obersturmführer.*
Born: 8.12.1912 in Jülich/Rhineland.
NSDAP-Nr.: 2.121.512 (joined 1.5.1933).
SS-Nr.: 192.030 (joined 10.6.1933).
RAD: 3.5.–30.10.1934.

Prewar Assignments:

2. / IV. / 58. SS-*Standarte* from 10.6.1933.
Trained with the11, 22 and 7 FLAK-Regiments 1.11.1935–30.9.1936.
Polizei Offizieränwarter-Lehrgang Köpenick in the spring of 1938.
Stammabteilung Ost / 75 Bezirk 21.3.–10.12.1938.
Gleiwitz *Polizeipräsidium Verkehrskommando* from 28.11.1938.
Stammabteilung Südost/ Bezirk 23 from 14.12.1938.
Sturm 8 / 23. SS-*Standarte* (Beuthen) from 10.12.1938–1.4.1942.

Wartime Assignments:

Polizei-Bataillon 82 at Karwin/Olsagebiet on 18.11.1940.
Waffen-SS from 1.4.1942.

1. / *Polizei* SS-FLAK-Bataillon until 24.8.1942.
SS-FLAK-*Ersatz-Battalion* from 24.8.1942.
FLAK-*Abteilung* / SS-*Totenkopfdivision* on 28.8.1942.
Stabbatteriechef / SS-FLAK-*Abteilung* 3 in 1.1943.
SS-FLAK *Ausbildung- und Ersatz*-Rgt. (Munich) in 9.1944.

Promotions:

10.6.1933	SS-*Anwärter*.
0.0.19__	*Wachtmeister der Reserve*.
21.3.1938	*Leutnant der Schutzpolizei*.
21.3.1938	SS-*Untersturmführer der Allgemeine*-SS.
10.9.1939	*Oberleutnant der Schutzpolizei*.
1.4.1942	SS-*Untersturmführer der Reserve*.
10.9.1939	SS-*Obersturmführer der Allgemeine*-SS.
1.4.1942	SS-*Obersturmführer der Waffen*-SS (*Aktiv*).

Decorations & Awards:

0.0.19__	SS-*Zivilabzeichen* (Nr. 152.265).
0.0.19__	SA-*Sportsabzeichen in Bronze*.
3.3.1942	1939 *Eisernes Kreuz II. Klasse*.
0.0.19__	*Verwundetenabzeichen*, 1939 *in Schwarz*.
0.0.19__	*Deutsches Reichssportabzeichen in Bronze*.

Notes: His father was a locomotive driver. Attending *Volksschule* for five classes, Jumpertz obtained his *Abitur* from *Höhere Schule* (OI). A professional gymnast, the SS noted that he enjoyed light athletics and swimming. Joining the *Polizei* on 12 October 1936, the *Inspekteur der Stammabteilung Südost* wrote to Jumpertz's commander in Breslau on 24 January 1939, to report that he had refused the award the SS-*Ehrendegen* to his subordinate on the grounds that his application contained untruths. Assigned to *Major* Walter Kegel's *Polizei-Bataillon* on 18 November 1940, this security formation was deployed in the central sector of the Eastern Front in 1941. Released for active service with the *Waffen*-SS in April 1942, Jumpertz was in command of the headquarters battery of a FLAK battalion in January 1943 when he faced investigation for committing an unauthorised leave offence in the early summer of that same year. Placed on remand to await trial, Jumpertz transferred to the command of a reserve FLAK unit on 1 June 1943. Standing trial before the SS- *und Polizei-Gericht* I, Munich, the tribunal judged Jumpertz guilty of the offence and punished him with a term of two years' *Gefängnis*. The *Reichsführer* confirmed this sentence on 30 April 1944 and ordered Jumpertz to serve a minimum of ten months' *Gefängnis* and spend the remaining fourteen months on front probation. Sent to Danzig-Matzkau to serve his punishment, Jumpertz found himself assigned to a reserve unit in Munich during September 1944.[174]

Returning to Matzkau a few weeks after his injury, Dr Beelitz received news that the garrison physician was battling to contain a serious outbreak of tuberculosis, diphtheria and dysentery amongst the inmates in the prison and its environs. Exacerbating the situation, by the late summer of 1944 the prison had become a collection point for felons suffering from tuberculosis. The situation became so acute that on 15 June, the *Reichsführer* announced that all convicts suffering from this disease would henceforth be admitted to the KL Dachau *Lazarett*. Seeking clarification about this order on 15 June, the *Amt* III asked whether *Zuchthaus* inmates suffering from tuberculosis were also included in this command.[175]

Writing in the summer of 1944, Dr Reinecke expressed concern that troops receiving prison terms for serious crimes were returning to their units too quickly for their comrades to grasp the seriousness of committing an offence. As a consequence of his concerns, the SS leader's opinion was sought about the divergence between higher and lower execution time penalties in the jurisdiction. Replying to this message on 27 July, the SS-*Richter beim* RF-SS agreed that the troops had begun to notice that courts sentencing did not reflect the actual time spent in jail, but revealed to Dr Reinecke that the head of the SS was unwilling to change the process from a fear that the deterrent effect of court announced long sentences would be lost on impressionable troops.[176]

The prison staff found time in late 1944 to organise a party in the prison at which an unidentified senior member of staff, performed a 'skit,' a comical after dinner speech, before the audience of SS men and five of their wives. A copy of this comedy sketch survives and it was delivered as though the speaker was a radio announcer:

> The MAFFAG, or Matzkauer telephone and radio AG, [are the friendly Matzkauer prisoners listening?]. It is only over the shortwave and worldwide pirate stations that the following shocking message has been received by the current residents of the Matzkauer settlement. With partly a great pride, not least amongst the circles of all explorers of mankind and earth history, it has been surprisingly announced that the ingenious horse learner, geologist and geographer Professor Dr Fritz Beelitz, currently the commander of prison camp Danzig-Matzkau, and his cautious wizard, SS-*Uscha.* Kurt Korngiebel, to whom the supervision of the extensive excavation had been entrusted, have cumbersomely researched for many months, under the greatest of difficulties and suffering and then succeeded in discovering a pre-age settlement within Danzig.
>
> Here they discovered well-preserved partial remains and the presumption is to confirm that people have lived in this area during prehistoric times. Amazingly, it seems that the mountain hunter Matzkauer, who are now so long gone, has in the distant past been found to correspond to the current camp. This includes the following sensational excavations. Every life must have been interrupted at one blow by the suddenly encroaching ice so that without further ado we can, from the previously buried found remains, see the former way of life and activity of the inhabitants. Thus, a rider on a mammoth was excavated, who undoubtedly corresponds to the chief of this camp. The one foot hangs limply down. A break can be properly identified in the ankle. In his right hand is a long stone club that serves to enable him to walk forward around his newly acquired locale. He is surrounded by numerous employees that are equipped with stone surveying device and stone tablets.

The residential camp for the guards appears to have been located at a further distance. This surprised the ice team, but amongst this great mess, the leader was accompanied by a sub-chief. The couch is torn apart and their equipment and stone weapons are scattered before their hovel. A large part of the population is well-ordered and participated in the output of the camp. There are at least 1,200 people [convicts]. Before the column, atop a horse stands a typical louse scourge. His rider has buried his hands in his coat pockets. Around his neck he wears a wonderfully crafted necklace of polished pebbles, whose effect is enhanced by the opened coat collar.

But in addition to this formation are the remains of a man. This sub-chief seem to have lost his life as the result of a sudden cardiac weakness. At his side, he has like all guards a simple stone ax, signed with the letter D [Dieterle?]. This creature's resting place was probably located at the south end of the camp. There is another sub-chief and around him lie the bodies of different men who have strikingly large holes in the heads. The acting second camp leader has asked why these people have holes in the head.

With great excitment another excavation site has revealed the dwelling of the medicine man. He possesses a gigantic body shape. But the sudden natural disaster had obviously not shaken him in the least. Around his mouth plays a dangerously seductive smile that even thousands of years could not efface [Dr Flothmann]. Next to him on a stone plate are scattered familiar medical instruments, on which are not yet fully deciphered characters. Is it perhaps the archetype of a frequently played operetta at the present time? Even back then was the popular form of 'poor Jonathan known?'

In the next few weeks, this mystery is solved. In the adjacent rooms there are scattered about the man a stone chisel and wood drills for which the meaning is not yet clear. Here, it is fully understood that the representatives of the opposite sex have liked what they saw and must have visited him. Also remains of female workers have been found. Should he in this state have already acceded to the Geneva Convention? So far, five women were recovered at this point [...] a drain on better days and had not noticed this administrative burden. (He had the typical feature of lung typhoid and found in his crumbled hands was a message which contained frankness about the settlements food. Eagerly, further evaluation of the material is still being worked on. Finally, it is reported that the commonly listed gait of the people of that time was a stooping posture. Therefore, he will in future be found in the Brockhaus Encyclopedia under the name *Hüfmensch* or *homo matzkauiensis*.

In another reference, there has been found in the great storage house some stone tablets with mysterious characters. Next to this was a slender fir ice age youth who was reading a sign of his high dignity while wearing mammoth teeth on his shoulders [Golda?]. After painstaking efforts in deciphering the strange characters it was noted that this ice age youth was a man of the higher administrative type, who highly meticulously calculated the food portions of the camp inmates at the time, with some portions dissolving in bristles and in an ineffective fizzle.[177]

In addition to mentioning Dr Beelitz's injury and Dr Flothmann's philandering, this skit includes the name of this disgraced junior officer who appears to have been dealing with the camp drains in early 1944:

Name: Kurt Korngiebel.
Last Rank: SS-*Obersturmführer.*
Born: 12.3.1907 in Bochum.
Died: 8.1944.
SS-Nr.: 163.487 (joined 1933)
Wartime Assignments:
5. SS-*Totenkopf-Infantrie*-Rgt. 12.1939-11.1942.
SS-*Feld Ersatz-Bataillon* 3 in 6.1941.
6. / SS-*Freiwilligen*-Legion *Neiderlande* 11.1942-6.1943.
Bewährungsabteilung from the spring 1944.
SS-*Fallschirmjägerabteilung* 500 in the spring of 1944.
III. SS-*Panzerkorps* until 8.1944.
Promotions:

6.1939	SS-*Sturmann der Reserve.*
21.6.1941	SS-*Untersturmführer der Reserve.*
0.0.1943	SS-*Obersturmführer der Reserve.*
0.0.1944	SS-*Oberscharführer der Reserve.*

Notes: Korngiebel mustered with an SS infantry regiment until November 1942. Arraigned before the courts martial in June 1943 for committing an unknown offence. Judged guilty, Korngiebel then found himself incarcerated in Danzig-Matzkau from June 1943. Here, he became Dr Beelitz's convict orderly. Possessing the rank of *Oscha.*, Korngiebel joined the SS-*Fallschirmjägerabteilung* in the spring of 1944. Participating in the air attack on Drvar on 26 May 1944, Korngiebel survived this difficult battle and his rehabilitation was granted in August the same year. He continued to fight on the Eastern Front until his death that same month.[178]

Rebuilding their strength in Pomerania in late August 1944, the *Waffen-Grenadier-*Brigade *der* SS *Charlemange* (*franzönische* Nr. 1) took the opportunity at this time to 'weed out' from its ranks those troops judged unfit for further military service. At this time the brigade commanded 184 malefactors and those judged no longer welcome in the *Waffen*-SS to appear before the SS- *und Polizei-Gericht* Danzig. Here, depending on the nature of their offence, the undisciplined were punished with various penalties including short terms of *Gefängnis* which they would serve in Matzkau or in the KL Stutthof. Contacting the Matzkau commandant from camp Saalesch in the *Truppenübungsplatz* Westpreußen.Die Masse der Angehörigen waren straffällig gewordene Militärangehörige der Waffen SS und Polizei.Westpreußen on 10 October 1944, the *Gerichtsoffizier* of the

SS-*Grenadier*-Rgt. 2 advised Dr Beelitz that 25 French felons, judged guilty of a variety of crimes including theft, desertion, absence without leave and defeatism, were on their way to his prison.[179]

Events elsewhere led to a mass exodus of Matzkau inmates to the frontline in the autumn of 1944. Taking advantage of the German retreat before the Red Army, the Home Army launched a daring operation in the Polish capital on 1 August 1944 with the intention of capturing the city before the Red Army's arrival. Though initially successful, the Home Army failed to dislodge all the German units in the city and quickly lost the initiative. Responsibility for defeating the Polish forces in Warsaw was then entrusted to the *Reichsführer* and among the units he ordered to re-take the city was the SS-*Sonderregiment Dirlewanger*. Deploying in Warsaw, the former felons daringly took the battle to the Home Army, but in the process, they besmirched the honour of the German Army when they terrorised and engaged in the mass murder of the civilian population. To enable his regiment to participate in this battle, Dirlewanger requested immediate reinforcement and responding to his need, the SS leader entrusted *Brigadef.* Ernst Rode to contact the *HA* SS-*Gericht*, SS-FHA, WVHA and the Matzkau commandant in early August 1944 to arrange the dispatch of a large number of convicts to Dirlewanger:

> As a consequence of the conversation between SS-*Ostubaf. Grothmann* and SS-*Hstuf.* Beelitz, the *Reichsführer*-SS has ordered a calculation of 1, 500 prisoners from the Danzig-Matzkau prison camp to be made available into a *March* battalion for the Rgt. *Dirlewanger*. Ensuring good catering for the *March* battalion, they are to march-off immediately with clothing, hand weapons and munitions. The implementation of the marchers has to take place within three days. The marchers target; the command post of Corps Group *von dem Bach,* Warsaw. Front probation deployment will takes place to suppress the uprising in Warsaw.
>
> The WVHA in direct consultation with SS-FHA, is asked to make the necessary arrangements to ensure the required terms of investiture. I ask to be informed of their arrival.
>
> Signed. Rode, SS-*Brigadef. und Generalmajor der Waffen*-SS.[180]

In addition to commanding 1,500 SS and *Polizei* Matzkau to join the SS-*Sonderregiment Dirlewanger* on 20 September, the *Bewährungsabteilung* in Dublowitz received orders in early September to despatch two companies, with a total of 500 probationers to the same destination. Led by two officers, these parole companies entrained for the city, but were intercepted before their destination and fought with the *Totenkopfdivision*. After many weeks' hard fighting the survivors of these companies were rehabilitated and continued to fight with the *Waffen*-SS.[181]

Post war, the *Landgericht* Munich II discovered that two former members of this draft had survived the battle: *Bauhilfsarbeiter* Viktor Zerfass and *Heilgymastiker* Josef Stoll. The latter left the Polish capital for Slovakia on 3 October 1944.[182]

Nineteen years-old *Funker* Horst-Rudi Becker had deployed with the headquarters company of the SS-*Nachrichten-Ausbildung- und Ersatz-Bataillon* at Eichstäatt prior to his imprisonment. Released from his prison sentence in the autumn of 1944, Becker transferred directly to the SS-*Sonderbrigade Dirlewanger* on 21 September.[183]

It is by no means clear whether the 1,500 convict draft left Matzkau for the SS-*Sonderregiment Dirlewanger* in one single group, or in small batches throughout the late autumn of 1944. The historian Hans-Peter Klausch contends that the vast majority of the parolees assigned to Dirlewanger during the battle for Warsaw had actually originated from *Wehrmacht* goals and concentration camps. In addition, he believes that the better part of the Matzkau parolees joined the newly forming SS-*Sonderbrigade Dirlewanger* at Krakau and Dublowitz once the battle for Warsaw had concluded.[184]

In the wake of Himmler's 20 September command, an *Amt* III case worker travelled to Matzkau to audit the prison. He reported the results of his population examination in the autumn of 1944:

> 30.9.44 HSSPF Danzig to the *Reichsführer*-SS Field Headquarters at *Hochwald* z. hd. *Staf.* Bender.
> Subject: Occupancy of the *Strafvollzugslager* Danzig-Matzkau.
> References: Telegram reply to *Staf. Bender* from 29.9.44.
>
> Overcrowded, Danzig-Matzkau presently consists of 2,213 prisoners and 255 personnel. Capacity is around 1,600 prisoners and the underutilization of all possibilities is 2,000. However, because of the demonstrated immediate increase of T.B. we must consider the seriously medically ill. After subtracting these, there are approximately 560 investigative prisoners detained here which includes the newly processed, there are 250 receiving treatment in the hospital clinic, 200 skilled employees are reserved for the shipyards and other tasks and the 500 monthly average addition is expected to increase by 150 as a result of the closure of Salaspils, Heidelager and Herzogenbusch.
>
> Signed. Dr Zolly, presently at *St. -. v. L.* Danzig-Matzkau.

Noted on the bottom of this telegram in Horst Bender's own hand are the following observation:

> SS-*Ostubaf.* Burmeister has received no explanation from *Gruf.* Katzmann about the assignment to the camp of troops that are not his concern. The *Reichsführer*-SS has been informed and his decision, is sought urgently to retain the camp for the prisoners.[185]

We note that despite the immediate transfer of 1,500 inmates from Matzkau to Dirlewanger, the prison population had doubled since Dr Beelitz had taken command of the institution in July 1944.

Telexing the SS leader in mid-September 1944, the HSSPF *Weichsel* informed him that the SS-*Truppenübungsplatz* Westpreußen near Bütow/Konitz was fully occupied with troops for the 15th *Waffen-Grenadier*-Division *der* SS (1. Latvian) and he now sought permission to accommodate the 20. SS-*Ausbildung- und Ersatz*-Brigade in Matzkau for a period of reorganisation. Promising to return control of the prison to the *HA* SS-*Gericht* once the brigade was reconstituted, the HSSPF *Weichsel* anticipated approval for this measure and notifying the city defence commissar of the brigades re-deployment, the general ordered this formation to deploy near Danzig. Bringing this telegram to Himmler's attention, he immediately denied its entry to Matzkau and the HSSPF *Weichsel* was informed that the prison institution was filled to capacity and experiencing a serious outbreak of tuberculosis.[186]

A few Estonians did enter the prison at this time, but these were offenders awaiting trial before the SS- *und Polizei-Gericht* XVI, Riga branch court, which conducted court-martials inside Matzkau in September 1944.[187]

Name: Willi Baier.
Last Rank: SS-*Hauptsturmführer*.
Born: 6.3.1917 in Schweinfurt.
SS-Nr.: 264.414 (joined 11.9.1934).
HJ Service: 20.10.1933-9.11.1939.
Prewar Assignments:
SS-*Junkerschule* Braunschweig 20.4.–1.5.1937.
Military training with the SS-*Standarte Oberbayern* in 1937.
5. / SS-*Standarte Germania* in 12.1937.
Officer of the SS-PHA HQ in 1937.
Wartime Assignments:
SS-*Infantrie*-Rgt. *Germania* until 1.1944.
Led the 3. / SS-*Polizei-Gebirgsjäger*-Rgt. 18 in 5.1944.
SS-*Grenadier*-Rgt. *Kalthofen* in 2.1945.
Promotions:

4.1937	*Leutnant der Polizei*.
20.4.1937	SS-*Untersturmführer der Allgemeine*-SS.
0.0.19__	*Oberleutnant der Polizei*.
30.4.1939	SS-*Obersturmführer der Allgemeine*-SS.
0.0.19__	*Hauptmann der Polizei*.
30.1.1942	SS-*Hauptsturmführer der Waffen*-SS.

Decorations & Awards:

0.0.19__	SA-*Sportsabzeichen in Bronze*.
0.0.1944	1939 *Eisernes Kreuz II. Klasse*.
0.0.19__	*Ehrendegen des Reichsführer*-SS.
0.0. 19__	*Dienstauszeichnung der* NSDAP *in Gelb*.
0.0.19__	D.L.R.G *in Bronze*.

Notes: Attending *Volksschule* for four classes, Baier then studied at *Höhere Schule* for seven classes. Leaving full time education, Baier was employed as a professional policeman and was a member of the Nazi party. Mustering with the *Ordnungspolizei/Polizeiverbände* in Bavaria from 1 May 1937, Baier married his fiancée on 15 May 1941. Deployed with an SS and *Polizei* mountain regiment in Greece, Baier found himself arraigned before the courts martial of the SS- *und Polizei-Gericht* XXIX, Athens on charges of theft. Judging Baier guilty, the tribunal imposed a temporary sentence on him on 14 May 1944 (§ 47 Abs III KStVO) and this judgment was confirmed on 29 May 1944. The *Reichsführer* ordered his detention in Matzkau on 13 November and Baier remained in this institution until his selection for front probation with the *Kalthofen* in February 1945.[188]

In late September 1944 the Matzkau At this time Even at this late stage of the war At this timeIn th eatumnAt this time Even at this late stage of the war inmatesinmates were observed labouring in the port of Danzig. Here, they helped to construct FLAK towers and air-defence bunkers. In the post-war period a civilian labourer recollected his conversation with a convict:

> I had the opportunity to talk with one of the convicts from Danzig-Matzkau, who worked with me at a construction company. Udało mi się to, chociaż rozmowy z nimi były surowo zabronione - mówi.Talking to the convicts was forbidden, but I managed to ask one how he had ended up in his situation. He told me that he had refused to go to the front and fight and that condition's in the camp were very 'hard.' And in addition, I observed that the prisoners were treated very strictly.[189]

By late 1944 the health situation amongst the Matzkau inmates had deteriorated so seriously that the *Hygiene-Institutes der Waffen*-SS seconded a physician to the garrison to assist with the fight against a fresh outbreak of disease amongst the inmates:

Name: Dr Waldemar Ültzhöffer.
Last Rank: SS-*Sturmbannführer.*
Born: 17.11.1909 in Betzdorf a Sieg/Bonn.
SS-Nr.: 277.089 (joined 15.10.1936).
Prewar Assignments:
Officer of the 7. SS-*Sanitäts-Sturm* from 15.10.1936.
SS-VT Sä*nitatsabteilung* (Dachau) 15.10.1936–1.8.1937.
16. / IV. / SS-*Standarte Deutschland* 1.5.-31.7.1937.
Officer of the 107. SS-*Standarte* (Brünn) from 1.8.1937.
Truppenarzt III/ SS-*Standarte* Deutschland from 1.8.1937.
Truppenarzt Jüterbog *Abteilung* 1 SS-*Artillerie-Ersatz-Bataillon* from 12.6.1939.
Truppenarzt SS-VT-*Sanitäts-Staffel* (Greifenhagen) 12.6.1939-1.11.1941.
Personalabteilung SS-VT & *Truppenarzt* I. / SS-*Artillerie-Standarte* 25.8.1939.

Wartime Assignments:
Bataillonarzt SS-*Pionier-Abteilung Wiking* 1.1.41–30.1.1942.
Truppenarzt SS-*Junkerschule* Bad Tölz on 1.11.1941 (arrived 18.11.1941).
Seconded to the *Frauenklinik* Munich 1.5.-6.6.1942.
SS-Ä*rzt-Akademie* (Graz) on 15.12.1942.
7th SS-*Freiwilligen-Gebirgs*-Division *Prinz Eugen* until 21.6.1944.
Reichsarzt SS- *und Polizei* Berlin (*Hygiene-Institut der Waffen*-SS) 21.6.1944-8.5.1945.

Promotions:

10.1936	SS-*Untersturmführer der Allgemeine*-SS.
12.9.1937	SS-*Obersturmführer der Allgemeine*-SS.
25.8.1939	SS-*Hauptsturmführer der Waffen*-SS.
30.1.1942	SS-*Sturmbannführer der Waffen*-SS.

Decorations & Awards:

0.0.19__	SA-*Sportsabzeichen in Bronze.*
1.9.1940	1939 *Eisernes Kreuz II. Klasse.*
0.0.19__	*Totenkopfring der* SS.

Notes: Attending *Höhere Schule* for nine classes, Ültzhöffer obtained his *Abitur* and then studied medicine at university until qualifying to work as a physician. Mustering with the SA between 5 November 1933 and October 1936, Dr Ültzhöffer married his fiancée Lea F., (b. 20.8.1908 in Srobran/Yugoslavia) on 29 April 1935 and the couple lived in Munich. Assigned to the *Deutschland* in May 1938, here, he examined Gottfried Biedermann as this time as part of the future prison guards preparations to marry. Diagnosed with asthma in January 1941, Dr Ültzhöffer was appointed the troop physician for Bad Tölz in November the same year and here, he met the leader of the Hygiene Institute of the *Waffen*-SS, *Oberf.* Dr Joachim Mrugowsky on 15 December 1942. Joining Dr Mrugowsky's service office on 21 June 1944, this department funded and co-ordinated experiments on prisoners, provided safe drinking water for troops, it undertook vermin extermination, provided sanitation and tackled outbreaks of disease in camps and garrisons. Its most onerous task was supplying Zyklon B to death camps, the poison used by the SS to murder Jews, Soviet prisoners of war and Gypsies. Reporting to Danzig-Matzkau during the winter of 1944/45, Dr Ültzhöffer was tasked with assisting the garrison physician to combat the outbreak of communicable diseases in the garrison (he lived at Danzig, Hindenburgerstraßes 51). Assisting the prison medical staff to organise a transport of sick inmates to the *Strafvollzugslager der* SS *und Polizei* Förrenbach on 9 February 1945, Dr Mrugowsky contacted Matzkau on the same day to request Dr Ültzhöffer's immediate transfer back to his service post. This order was quickly carried out and Dr Ültzhöffer's remained with the Hygiene Institute until the end of the war.[190]

In addition to the mass transfer of felons to Dirlewanger, the Matzkau commandant also oversaw the selection of a large number of his guards, including long serving senior non-commissioned officers, for front service. On 17 October 1944 the SS-FHA

Amt II commanded 47 troops of the guard company, including twelve 'suitable' senior non-commissioned officers to transfer to the SS-*Panzergrenadier-Ausbildung- und Ersatz-Bataillon* 18 at Breslau. In addition, 24 men, including one junior NCO, received orders to report to the SS-*Panzergrenadier-Ausbildung- und Ersatz Bataillon* 2 at Prague-Rusin. It was planned that these men would set off for their new posts on 21 October and this mass transfer included sixteen non-commissioned officers and men from branch prisons. To replace these losses, Dr Beelitz commanded 27 troops who had been selected for the SS-*Panzergrenadier-Ausbildung- und Ersatz-Bataillon* 9 at Stralsrund and the SS-*Sanitäts-Ausbildung- und Ersatz-Bataillon* in Stettin to report back to Matzkau and it branch prison on 21 October 1944.[191]

Dr Beelitz authorised the transfer of fourteen non-commissioned officers and men to the SS-*Panzergrenadier-Ausbildung- und Ersatz-Bataillon* 9 on 27 October and also directed a further fourteen junior non-commissioned officers and men to the SS-*Kavallerie-Ausbildung- und Ersatz-Bataillon* at Beneschau (these included *Reiter* Alexander Glowatzke and *Reiter* Johann Isaak, who had been judged unsuitable for service as guards. They left their prisons on 24.10.1944). A further twelve non-commissioned officers and men were pronounced fit to join the IV. / SS-*Artillerie-Ausbildung- und Ersatz*-Rgt. at Olmütz. In addition to these losses, eleven troops set off on their journey for the SS-FLAK *Ausbildung- und Ersatz*-Rgt. at Munich-Freimann. Recently arrived from the *Zweiglager* Hammerweg on 20 October, *Strm.* Hermann Kusche received orders to join the SS-*Panzergrenadier-Ausbildung- und Ersatz-Bataillon* 2 and *Schtz.* Konrad Bartschitsch and Theo Wittkowski were commanded to report to the SS-*Artillerie-Ausbildung- und Ersatz* Rgt. in Prague (21 men transferred from Mosbach/Baden to Matzkau on 24.10.1944). Nineteen non-commissioned officers and men were ordered to report to the SS-*Panzergrenadier-Ausbildung- und Ersatz-Bataillon* 9 on 27 October and amongst their number was Dr Beelitz's former orderly *Uscha.* Manhard Barthelmi. In addition, six guards were selected for this training battalion on 27 October and the following day, a further seventeen men, including the veteran guard *Oscha.* Anton Kerschreiter, begun their journey to Stralsund on the Baltic coast.[192]

Hstuf. Dr Beelitz received orders to release *Uscha.* Dr Mayer from his post and arrange the judge's transfer to the SS- *und Polizei-Gericht* Salzburg. In an effort to streamline the front probation process, the *HA* SS-*Gericht* wrote to all courts on 17 December to command them to incarcerate *Zuchthaus* category offenders directly in prison following the pronouncement of their sentence to enable the gaol staff to quickly judge their demeanour. Appeals were submitted from the prison institution along with the prison staff report, which enabled the *HA* SS-*Gericht* to decide whether to offer them front probation or clemency.[193]

Despite the need to supply the SS-*Sonderbrigade Dirlewanger* with fresh probationers in late 1944, Matzkau inmates continued to leave this prison at this time to undergo a period of parole with the *Bewährungsabteilung*: Born on 21 November 1926, *Funker* Friedrich

Marchardt had previously been assigned to the SS-*Nachrichten-Ersatz-Bataillon* at Eichstäatt. Released from his sentence in Matzkau at the end of 1944, Marchardt then reported to the *Bewährungsabteilung* on 29 December.

Born in Gross Breeson/Uckermark on 29 October 1920, *Rttf.* Arthur Fritz remained in Matzkau until his transfer to the *Bewährungsabteilung* in late 1944 and has been missing in action since 20 December the same year.[194]

3.10 Denouement Punishments: While the guards rewarded hard work with cigarettes they were permitted to punished offenders with extra drill, loss of food or the withdrawal of privileges. Beatings were forbidden on the grounds that they prevented

The New Year revealed that the prison's former commandant, Dr Leo Ernst, had fallen in battle while fighting with the *Totenkopfdivision* to relieve trapped Axis forces in Budapest on 3 January. This news coincided with the realisation that the Red Army had breached the German front line along the Vistula-Narew line on 12 January 1945 and fourteen days later their armoured spearheads had forced the German forces beyond the River Vistula and surrounded the city of Königsberg. From the Matzkau environs, the staff and inmates could clearly hear the unmistakable sound of the Soviet artillery bombarding the harried German frontline forces. To rectify this critical situation, the *Reichsführer* accepted command of *Heeresgruppe* W*eichsel* on 23 January 1945 and received orders to establish a stable front between the Vistula and Oder Rivers. Ensconcing himself in his new field headquarters in Deutsch Kroner on 24 January 1945, Himmler set about gathering fresh troops for a counter offensive, but unfortunately for him, the Red Army had by this time advanced on a rough line Elbing–Thorn–Poson–Breslau, mauling the German 2nd *Armee* and leaving Danzig unprotected (a German front north of the fortress Posen no longer existed). Hurridly transporting the III. SS-*Panzerkorps* to the SS-*Truppenübungsplatz* Westpreußen to prepare for a counter offensive, this armoured force and other troops were re-equipped in time to participate in Operation *Sonnenwende* on 15 February. Intending to close the breach in the front line, the German assault smashed into the over-stretched Red Army flank, but despite early successes, the Soviet forces absorbed this onslaught and struck back fiercely on the 18 February. Buckling under the counter-move and facing imminent destruction, the German forces retreated to the Baltic coast ports and Altdamm on the River Oder. As a consequence of the Red Army's sudden riposte, East Prussia found itself isolated from Pomerania and ripping a 30 mile gap in the German front line, the Baltic Sea ports, including the city of Danzig, were suddenly exposed to a direct assault by Soviet forces.[195]

As these momentous events swirled around them, the Matzkau headquarters continued to receive and obey instructions from SS courts: Born on 7 July 1922, Franz Reichardt, a former member of the SD, found himself incarcerated in Matzkau in early 1945. Telexing the prison on 11 January 1945, the *HA* SS-*Gericht* ordered the prison to release Reichardt when part of his sentence had been served and then commanded him to report to the *Auffanglager des Befehlshaber der Sicherheitspolizei und des* SD *Serbien* in Graz. This message clearly states that Reichardt was not to be transferred to the *Bewährungsabteilung*.[196]

All land links to East Prussia were effectively cut off from Germany when the Matzkau commandant received orders from the *HA* SS-*Gericht* on 20 January 1945 to initiate the selection and transfer of suitable felons for immediate front probation. It was planned to send those judged unsuitable for front probation to penal institutions in Bavaria.[197]

Telexing the HSSPF *Weichel* on the morning of 25 January, Himmler's adjutant, *Ostubaf.* Werner Grothmann, commanded the establishment of a front probation battalion from Matzkau convicts and the local HSSPF received orders to supply these parolees with all available armament.[198]

As a consequence of this order, the HSSPF *Weichel*, Dr Beelitz and the commander of the III. Germanic SS-*Panzerkorps* collaborated together to establish a three battalion SS-*Grenadier*-Rgt. from a cadre of Matzkau probationers, from military stragglers and staff/training troops from the SS-*Truppenübungsplatz* Westpreußen.Die Masse der Angehörigen waren straffällig gewordene Militärangehörige der Waffen SS und Polizei. Westpreußen (at Sophienwalde, near Bruß). The III. Germanic SS-*Panzerkorps* provided the regimental leadership and a support weapons company (mortars and machine guns). In addition to planning a FLAK and *Aufklärungkompanie* for the new regiment, *Stubaf.* Hans-Heinrich Kalthofen was selected to lead this new formation. An experienced combat officer, Kalthofen had previously served as a guard in the KL Sachsenhausen and had fought in the Balkans with the 13th SS-*Freiwilligen-Gebirgs*-Division *Handschar*.[199]

Identifying prospective probationers for the *Kalthofen*, the HSSPF *Weichel* then approached the *HA* SS-*Gericht Amt* III in the first week of February 1945 to request that their office clarified the rehabilitation situation for those waiting for provisional probation orders. The matter was considered so serious that Burmeister contacted the HSSPF *Weichel*, Dr Beelitz and the Danzig tribunal on 10 February to report that he had handed temporary authorisation powers to the HSSPF to enable him to announce rehabilitation decisions in these cases. Granting the SS general permission to select parolees of the *Bewährungstruppe* for front parole with the troops, Günther Burmeister warned all concerned in this process that the final decisions in all cases remained his offices responsibility. As part of this process Dr Beelitz received orders to supply a rehabilitation report for each inmate and the local court supplied the rehabilitation applications. This included the provisional rehabilitation report which contained a photograph and observations about the probationer's personality, the seriousness of his criminal/disciplinary act, the length of the punishment, his type of imprisonment, probation deployment and an explanation for why the felon was considered suitable for probation. Any acts of extraordinary bravery, or serious wounds were mentioned in this document and a rehabilitation application could not be considered unless the probationer had served in a probation unit for between three to six months. When compiled, these reports were then submitted to the *Amt* III to enable them to issue a final clemency decision. All those in Danzig involved in this procedure received a warning that the rehabilitation decisions concerning SS and *Polizei* officers remained the responsibility of the SS-*Richter beim* RF-SS and obtaining these decisions could be arranged by telex or radio.[200]

Dr Beelitz subsequently identified 500 suitable candidates for front probation with the *Kalthofen* between 25 January and 12 February 1945 and their number included those serving prison sentences for committing acts contrary to paragraph § 175. These parolees had left Matzkau for the SS-*Truppenübungsplatz* Westpreußen.Die Masse der Angehörigen waren straffällig gewordene Militärangehörige der Waffen SS und Polizei. Westpreußen by 12 February and on arrival were inducted into *Stubaf.* Paul Schneeberger's first Battalion. The new regiment hurriedly put together, Kalthofen then deployed his force some 500 metres north of Marienburg, a town located some two kilometres south of the town of Halbstadt, along the line Nogatdamm–Wesufer.[201]

The following Matzkau inmates did not survived the transfer to Kalthofen's command: Born in Groß Breeson/Uckermark on 29 October 1922, *Rttf.* Arther Fritz found himself assigned to the *Kalthofen* in January 1945 and has been missing in action since March 1945. Born in Ahrenfeld/Hamm on 14 August 1925, *Schütze* Hesse has been missing from Matzkau since February 1945.[202]

Amongst those assigned to the *Kalthofen* were officers who had formally served jail sentences, or were imprisoned in Matzkau:

Name: Bjørn Elith **Binnerup.**
Last Rank: SS-*Obersturmführer*.
Born: 6.1.1910 in Kopenhagen.
Prewar Assignments:
Danish Army 16.6.1930–1.4.1933.
Danish Army 29.2.-1.11.1936.
Danish Army 1.5.1939–31.7.1940.
Wartime Assignments:
Waffen-SS from 15.5.1941.
Sonderlehrgang SS-*Junkerschule* Bad Tölz 17.6.-17 .7.1940.
SS-*Infantrie-Ersatz-Bataillon Westland* from 13.6.1941
SS-Division *Wiking* from 31.1.1942.
2. / SS-*Artillerie*-Rgt. 5 in 11.1942.
6. / SS-*Artillerie*-Rgt. 5 in 1.1944.
SS-*Artillerie-Ausbildung- und Ersatz*-Rgt. (Prague) from 10.8.1944.
SS-Rgt. *Kalthofen* in 2.1945.
Promotions:

0.0.1939	*Hauptmann der Reserve*.
15.5.1941	SS-*Untersturmführer der Waffen*-SS.
9.11.1942	SS-*Obersturmführer der Waffen*-SS.

Decorations & Awards:
18.8.1942 1939 *Eisernes Kreuz II. Klasse.*
13.10.1943 1939 *Eisernes Kreuz II. Klasse.*

Notes: Binnerup obtained officer rank with the Danish Army and married his fiancé Inger-Sophie N. in 1932. The couple had three children together until the collapse and lived in Copenhagen. As a response to the invasion of the USSR, Binnerup volunteered for military service in the *Waffen*-SS in May 1941. His family was awarded him a little over 300 *Reichsmark* for the death of his child on 18 November 1942 (he lived for nine days). Binnerup successfully extricated his artillery unit from the mountainous Caucasus region in 1942 and escaped the Red Army winter offensive. In January 1944 the *Wiking* field court conducted a court investigation against Binnerup on suspicion of two instances of miss-handling a subordinate, drunkenness and military disobedience. Arraigned before the *Wiking* courts martial, the court judged Binnerup guilty of the charges and punished him with a two years, seven months *Gefängnis* and declared him unworthy to bear arms on 2 April 1944. Serving part of his sentence in Matzkau, he then transferred to a reserve artillery unit in August 1944 and remained with this unit until his transfer to the III. SS-*Panzerkorps* and the *Kalthofen* in early 1945.[203]

Name: Friedrich-Wilhelm Meier.
Last Rank: SS-*Mann.*
Born: 27.6.1912 in Berlin.
Died: Mar.1945 in Danzig.
NSDAP-Nr.: 278.440, (joined 1.8.1930).
SS-Nr.: 13.847 (joined 1932).
Prewar Assignments:
Infantrie-Rgt. 9 at Potsdam 1.10.1929-15.11.1930.
LSSAH 17.5.1933–7.4.1934.
75. SS-*Standarte* (Berlin) 11.1935.
Wartime Assignments:
Waffen-SS from late 1939.
SS-*Kraftfahr-Ersatz-Bataillon* (Berlin-Lichterfelde) 6.1941–11.7.1941.
SS-*Truppenübungsplatz* Heidelager from 11.7.1941.
RKFDV HQ from 1.8.1942.
SS-Rgt. *Kalthofen* in 2.1945.
Promotions:
0.0.1934 SS-*Oberscharführer der* SS-VT.
3.11.1935 SS-*Untersturmführer der Allgemeine*-SS.
Decorations & Awards:
0.0.19__ *Totenkopfring der* SS.
0.0. 19__ *Dienstauszeichnung der* NSDAP *in Bronze.*

Notes: Attending *Volksschule* and *Höhere Schule*, (O-III), Meier left full time education and found employment as a bank clerk and then as a night watchman at the *Städtische Elektrizitätswerke Akt.-Ges.* (BEWAG). A rifleman with an infantry regiment between 1929 and 1930, Meier mustered with the LSSAH between the spring of 1933 and 1934 and during this deployment he was judged 30 per cent disabled. Marrying his fiancée on 17 November 1934, this marriage ended in divorce on 22 September 1936. Marrying again on 17 July 1937, one child emerged from these unions. Drafted into the *Waffen*-SS in late 1939, Meier deployed at Debica/Heidelager when he became embroiled in a widespread RKPA investigation into allegations of corruption amongst officers of the headquarters staff. Seventeen officers, including Meier, were investigated and one officer was later executed and another punished with front probation. A court's investigation was initiated against Meier just two days after his arrival in Debica on suspicion of committing a paragraph § 175 offence. Arraigned before the courts martial of the SS- *und Polizei-Gericht* VI, Krakau in Debica, the tribunal judged Meier guilty of the charge, condemned him to death and punished him with a five years and six months term of *Zuchthaus* for other criminal acts. Confirming the judgment on 6 May 1942, the *Reichsführer* set-aside the punishment and ordered Meier's re-trial. Incarcerated inside Danzig-Matzkau in February 1945, we must presume that the new court-martial punished Meier with a term of *Gefängnis*. From here, Meier received front probation with the *Kalthofen* and was killed in action during March 1945 while defending the approaches to Danzig.[204]

Name: Ernst Michael.
Last Rank: SS-*Untersturmführer*.
Born: 4.1.1919 in Spitzkummersdorf, *Kreis* Zittau/Sa.
NSDAP-Nr.: 6.961.713 (joined 1.9.1938).
SS-Nr.: 455.307 (v) (joined 1.4.1939).
RAD Service: 1.11.1938-31.3.1939.
HJ Service: 1.12.1933-31.10.1938.
Prewar Assignments:
SS-VT from 4.1939.
2. / SS-*Nachrichten-Bataillon* (Unna) in 1939.
Nachrichtenzug III. / SS-*Artillerie*-Rgt. in 6.1939.
Wartime Assignments:
SS-Division *Reich* in 1941.
14. *Kriegslehrgang bei der* SS-*Fuhrerschule* Dachau *des Verwaltungsdienstes* 15.8.–20.12.1941.
HWL *der Waffen*-SS Berlin (WVHA) 12.1941–14.2.1943.
II. / SS-*Panzergrenadier*-Rgt. 19 (France) from 14.2.1943
Ersatz-Bataillon Verwaltungsdienste Dachau from 7.4.1944.
SS-Rgt. *Kalthofen* in 2.1945.
Promotions:
30.1.1943 SS-*Untersturmführer der Waffen*-SS.

Decorations & Awards:

0.0.19__ SA-*Sportsabzeichen in Bronze.*

0.0.19__ *Kriegsverdienstkreuz II. Klasse mit Schwertern.*

Notes: His father, a shoemaker died during the Great War in July 1918. Attending eight classes at *Volksschule*, Michael was by profession a salesman. Michael volunteered for the *Waffen*-SS in April 1939 and undertook specialised communications training at Unna. Assigned as a radioman with an artillery regiment in June 1939, Michael participated in the attack on Poland, the invasion of the Low Countries and France in 1940. Deployed with the *Reich* for the assault against on Serbia in the spring of 1941, he fought in the USSR for seven weeks before leaving to attend a training course. An administrator with a panzer grenadier battalion in France in February 1943, Michael received a strong warning for an unknown offence on 20 December 1943, Michael married his fiancée Clare Kloy on 19 February 1944, but they had no issue up to the time when records ceased in May 1945.

His battalion commander issued orders for Michael to prepare an exercise area for his battalion on 11 March 1944, which would be located some distance from the regiments barrack. Completing this task, Michael then travelled to Tarascon, near St Remy in attempt to procure extra rations for the troops. Visiting a local tavern, Michael drank around six glasses of alcohol over the following two hours when he met with black marketers to purchase coffee and potatoes. Driving to Miramas, around three kilometres from his battalion, he attempted unsuccessfully to enter a brothel and then began drinking at a bar with an Army captain who promised the supply of further rations for his battalion. Later that night, at around 10.00 p.m. the two officers drove Michael's vehicle to the town of St Remy to buy cigarettes. Here, they visited another bar and drank cognacs until around 1.30 a.m.

Telephoning his office to report he was returning soon, Michael permitted his driver to sleep and took the wheel of the service car for the journey to Miramas. During the drive, Michael drove the car into a ditch, jammed it between a wall and a tree and damaged the suspension, chassis, right and left fenders and lights. In addition, the fuse box was damaged, the windshield shattered, the gearbox broken, the rear right and left front side of the car body was impaired. His companion suffered a cut to his head, but recovered sufficiently to walk with Michael to Miramas. Here, Michael organised a tow back to their accommodation and reporting to his battalion post at around 3.00 a.m., he immediately fell asleep on the adjutant's table. Later, he awoke and pushing three chairs pushed he went back to sleep. At 6.30 a.m. that same morning, Michael was awoken by a messenger who gave him a coded message from the Regiment headquarters. Michael failed to notify the battalion commander of its contents, or decode the message for the messenger to pass on the important warning. As a result of his negligence the Regimental commander did not receive this important message for at least another hour.

As a consequence of his negligence, the *Gerichts*-SS-*Führer* of the WVHA initiated a court's investigation against Michael in the spring of 1944 and recommended he faced trial for military disobedience, negligence, physical injury and shaming the SS on 9 May (case Nr. St. L II 208/1944). Placed on remand for eleven days from 11 May, he found himself arraigned before the courts martial of the SS- *und Polizei-Gericht* I, Munich on 23 August 1944 and the court chairman, *Stubaf.* Wolfgang Wetzling, was supported in his deliberations by: *Hstuf.* Gustav Bäuerle and *Ustuf.* Dimitri Amon (both from Bad Tölz). The *Beurkundungsführer* was *Oscha.* Ernst Kaninke, and *St.OJ.* Wilhelm Wirth from the SS Officer School of the Administrative Service in Dachau prosecuted the case. Unrepentant, Michael denied taking the wheel in a drunken condition and claimed that although he was an inexperienced driver, the accident was caused by exhaustion and mechanical failure (the gear shift lever was broken). Obstinately, Michael contended that the alleged 400 *Reichsmark* of damage was in fact worth only 45 *Reichsmark*, his claimed that his failure to de-code the message from Regimental headquarters was a consequence of his sound sleeping. Incredibly, he asserted that he was always difficult to awake, regardless if he had been drinking alcohol or not. The court did not accept his explanations and placed great emphasis on the evidence of a mechanic witness from the technical branch. In the opinion of *Ostuf.* Walter Leßmann, the vehicle was in perfect running order and the court discovered that Michael had regularly driven a vehicle in Russia and was a competent driver.

Convinced of Michael's drunkenness while driving his service vehicle, an act of disobedience in contravention of paragraph § 92 MSGB, the court rejected his falsehoods, judged him guilty of the charges on 22 May 1944 and imposed a term of four years' *Gefängnis* upon him and ordered his expulsion from the SS for disobedience, negligence, physical injury and undermining the war effort. The judgment confirmed by the *Gerichtsherr*, the *Reichsführer* upheld the sentence on 25 August 1944 and commanded Michael to serve a minimum of nine months' *Gefängnis* before permitted to accept probation with a *Sondereinheit* for the remainder of his punishment. Noting that Michael had been imprisoned for three months between the verdict and confirmation, this time was deducted from his overall sentence. Serving six months of his sentence, Michael was released from Matzkau for front probation with the *Kalthofen* at the end of February 1945 and participated in the fight to defend the city of Danzig against the Red Army in March 1945.[205]

Name: Jörgen Salskov.
Last Rank: SS-*Obersturmführer.*
Born: 17.11.1917 in Assens/Denmark.
Wartime Assignments:
Waffen-SS from 1940.
Freiwilligen-Legion *Danemark* 19.7.-17.11.1941.
4. *Kriegs-Res.-Führer-Anwärter-Lehrgang* SS-*Unterführerschule* Radolfzell 19.7.–17.11.1941.
SS-*Kradfahr-Ersatz-Abteilung* 17.11.-3.12.1941.
Kommandostab RF-SS 3.12.1941-3.12.1941.

Freikorps Danemark from 3.12.1941.
Seconded to the *Kommandostab* RF-SS 22.2.-9.7.1942.
SS-WVHA *Verwaltungsamt* z.b.V. from 29.5.1944.
Seconded to the SS-*Panzergrenadier*-Rgt. 24 *Danemark* from 5.1943.
14. *Krieglehrgang bei der SS-Führerschule Dachau des Verwaltungsdienstes.*
Verwaltungsführer II. / SS-*Panzergrenadier*-Rgt. 24 *Danemark* in 1944.
SS-Rgt. *Kalthofen* in 2.1945.

Promotions:

19.7.1941 SS-*Untersturmführer der Reserve.*
9.11.1943 SS-*Obersturmführer der Reserve.*

Notes: Salskov had served in the Danish Army in 1939. In the wake of his country's defeat, he volunteered to join the *Waffen*-SS. Salskov fought in the fortress Demyansk from 8 May 1942 and at Welikije Luki during December 1942. At that time his Legion was pulled out of the front to disband at the *Truppenübungsplatz* Grafenwöhr and the survivors formed the cadre of the newly established panzer grenadier regiment *Danemark.* This regiment then became part of the newly formed 11th SS-*Panzer-Grenadier*-Division *Nordland* and it was with this unit that Salskov became drunk and disorderly on 4 May 1943, resulting in his punishment of ten days' sharp arrest. The *Nordland* deployed in Croatia as part of the III. SS Germanic *Panzerkorps* at the end of August 1943 and spent much of the following September disarming the Italian troops in the country. Salskov was then appointed an administration officer for the regiment *Danemark* and his commanding officer was complimentary about his efforts for the men in November the same year. Unbeknown to him, Salskov had become involved in complex fraud involving stolen meat from divisional stores. A subsequent court's investigation recommended his trial and the purloining Salskov found himself arraigned before the courts martial of the field court of the *Nordland* (St. L. I 134/1944). The trial judge, *Hstuf.* Hackmeister was supported in his deliberations by *Stubaf.* Erich Hartmann of the SS-Div. *Nachschubtruppe* 11 and *Ostuf.* Otto Bothe, the Ordnance Officer for the *Nordland.* The case was prosecuted by Oscha. Dr Heinrich Ries and the *Beurkundungsunterführer* was *Uscha.* Drucker. Declaring Salskov guilty of attempted fraud and document falsification in May 1944, the tribunal sentenced him to a term of two years' *Gefängnis.* Serving his punishment in Matzkau, Salskov accepted front probation in February 1945 and joined the *Kalthofen* for the defence of Danzig.[206]

Name: Geert Ziegler.
Last Rank: SS-*Hauptsturmführer.*
Born: 9.6.1913 in Flensburg.
NSDAP-Nr.: 3.602.409 (joined 1.3.1935).
SS-Nr.: 265.734 (joined 1.8.1934).
HJ Service: 3.9.1936–1.2.1934.

Prewar Assignments:

LSSAH from 1.8.1934–1.4.1936.

Führer-Lehrgang SS-*Junkerschule* Braunschweig in 1936/37.

Stab SS-*Junkerschule* Braunschweig until 1.5.1937–12.4.1942.

Ordnungspolizei-Polizeiverbände Hamburg in 1937

SS-*Personalhauptamt* 1937-1.3.1942.

Wartime Assignments:

Seconded to the SS-*Infantrie-Ersatz-Bataillon Deutschland* from 1.3.1942.

LSSAH from 30.4.1942.

LSSAH *Ersatz-Bataillon* (Berlin) from 30.4.1942.

SS-*Wachbataillon* Berlin and LSSAH from 1.12.1942–7.2.1943.

SS-*Panzergrenadier-Ausbildung- und Ersatz-Bataillon* LSSAH 7.2.–10.6.1943.

VII. / LSSAH early 1943.

SS-*Kampfgruppe Schuldt* 12.4.–10.6.1943.

13th SS-*Freiwilligen-Gebirgs*-Division *Handschar* from 10.6.1943.

SS-*Panzergrenadier-Ausbildung- und Ersatz-Bataillon* 35 from 18.4.1944.

SS-Rgt. *Kalthofen* in 2.1945.

Promotions:

0.0.19__ *Oberleutnant der Schutzpolizei.*

0.0.19__ *Hauptmann der Schutzpolizei.*

20.4.1937 SS-*Untersturmführer der Allgemeine*-SS.

9.11.1938 SS-*Obersturmführer der Allgemeine*-SS.

30.1.1942 SS-*Hauptsturmführer der Reserve.*

Decorations & Awards:

0.0.19__ SA-*Sportsabzeichen in Bronze.*

0.0.19__ *Ehrendegen des Reichsführer*-SS.

0.0.19__ *Totenkopfring der* SS.

0.0.19__ *Goldenes Hitler-Jugend Ehrenzeichen.*

0.0.19__ *Deutsches Reichssportabzeichen in Bronze.*

0.0.19__ D.L.R.G. *in Bronze.*

Notes: Obtaining his *Abitur* from *Höhere Schule*, Ziegler was a policeman by profession. Mustering with the SA between 1 February and 1 July 1934, he spent six months in Denmark. Marrying his fiancée Elisabeth F., (b. 31.10.1913, Harlinge-Rode) on 4 December 1937, the couple had two children up to the point when records ceased in May 1945. Fighting on the Don Front in early 1943, Ziegler transferred to the *Handschar* in Bosnia in June 1943. For committing an unknown offence, Ziegler found himself arraigned before the *Handschar* courts martial who ascertained his guilt and punished him with a term of fifteen months' *Gefängnis*. Transferred to the SS-*Truppenübungsplatz* Westpreußen in April 1944 to await confirmation of his punishment, the SS-FHA disagreed with his sentence on 11 May 1944 and the *Reichsführer* ordered his re-trial before another court on 20 June. Judged guilty, Ziegler then found himself incarcerated in Matzkau to serve a term of *Gefängnis*. Accepting front probation, Geert Ziegler joined the *Kalthofen* in February 1945 and is thought to have perished in the battle for Danzig.[207]

The storms of war raging around them, the Matzkau headquarters then turned its attention to arranging the evacuation to Bavaria of those convicts judged unsuitable for front probation. *Ustuf.* Dr Viktor Schode, accompanied by *St.Obj.* Fehlauer, *Hscha.* Karl Münch and five non-commissioned officers, left Matzkau for Hersbruck on 22–24 January 1945 and the *Vorkommandoführer*, *Ostuf.* Rudolf Heiß and his squad consisting of *Stabsscharführer* Morr, Alfred Engelhardt, *Hscha.* Kilian Kranzmayr, nine other ranks, then received orders to lead another group of convicts to Hersbruck on 27 January. *Scha.* Gramer led one section composed of nine troops, *Rttf.* Stuhlsatz led another nine man section and *Scha.* Henning was selected to lead seven guards to Förrenbach (he was later substituted for another name). Each guard section was equipped with one LMG, one sub-machine gun on two bicycles and each rifleman received 60 rounds of ammunition.[208]

Speaking after the war, Rudolf Heiß recalled that the camp saw off about three or four company's worth of inmates to the front during the course of January 1945 and at this time the prison staff had arranged the evacuation of 80 per cent of the institution, amongst them convict patients. The wives and children of the headquarters staff and those troops incapable of fighting at the front had begun to set off for the Reich by mid-January and Heiß recalled celebrating his birthday in the officer *casino* on 26 January. The following day he received orders to escort a *Vorkommando* (advance commando) by rail to Hersbruck near Nuremberg (Förrenbach). With the knowledge that the Red Army would soon batter its way towards the city, Heiß then raced to his Danzig apartment and staying only long enough only to fill their hand luggage, he and his wife abandoned their possessions and fled the stricken city for Matzkau. Travelling by locomotive to Hersbruck with the last of the Matzkau convicts and the very last of the debilitated and medically unfit felons, the *Vorkommando Heiß* arrived in Förrenbach on 11 February 1945.[209]

Here, the convicts were divided into those capable of working at Förrenbach and into those judged incapable of working, or requiring a tough prison detention. These felons boarded a train and continued their journey to the SS-*Straflager* Dachau (Allach). At this time, *Hstuf.* Dr Flothmann, clutching his medical files, abandoned Matzkau for the Stettin SS-*Lazarett*. Among his reports were those detailing the castration of convicts who had been convicted for contravening paragraph § 175 RStGB.[210]

The convict's arrival in Förrenbach did not go entirely without problem. Contacting the Matzkau commandant from Bavaria on 9 February 1945, *Ostuf.* Ringel reported that a column of 44 sick inmates had arrived the previous day with two doctors, three sisters, five guards and medical material. With Dr Beelitz's permission, Ringel reported his intention to forward some of their number to the SS-*Straflager* Dachau, leaving only *Gefängnis* inmates in Förrenbach. At this time Ringel complained to Dr Beelitz that his prison lacked clothing, underwear, socks and leather belts for 500 inmates. Contacting the *HA* SS-*Gericht*, Ringel asked them to supply him with 600 pieces of crockery and cardboard case file binders.[211]

Among those transported to the Dachau at this time were offenders awaiting confirmation of capital sentences and one of their number did not survive the journey: Born in Nusserhof/Bozen on 27 December 1910, Josef Mayr-Nusser's peasant family were very religious. His father dying when Mayr was five years old, he and his eldest brother's musical studies at the *Gymnasium* were interrupted when the family experienced financial difficulties. Employed as a salaried salesman in Bozen, Mayr was active in the Catholic Church and became the director of the 'Catholic Action' in the diocese of Trentino in 1934. Mayr married his fiancée Hildegarde Straub, on 26 May 1942 and the couple had one child together. A secret member of the anti-Nazi *Andreas Hofer Bund*, Mayr opposed the vote to absorb the Südtirol into Germany. Forcibly drafted into the *Waffen*-SS, Mayr, along with 80 other ethnic-Germans, were transported in cattle waggons from Bozen station to Westpreußen.Die Masse der Angehörigen waren straffällig gewordene Militärangehörige der Waffen SS und Polizei.Westpreußen on 7 September 1944 and here, they undertook basic military training with the SS-*Grenadier-Ausbildung- und Ersatz-Bataillon* 35. Writing to his wife on 27 September 1944, SS-*Mann* Mayr-Nusser informed her that he planned to refuse to take the oath of allegiance on religious grounds. Ignoring his comrade's appeals to reverse this decision, Mayr stood before the assembled company on 4 October and carrying out his threat, his refusal led to his incarceration in Danzig-Matzkau on 14 November. Arraigned before the courts-martial of the SS- *und Polizei-Gericht* IV, Danzig on 5 December, the tribunal judged Mayr guilty of oath refusal and imposed capital punishment on him. Incarcerated in Matzkau, here, he was badly treated and starved. Evacuated from the prison in January 1945, Mayr and 40 other capital punishment inmates boarded a freight train to undertake their journey to the SS-*Straflager* Dachau. An escort, SS-*Mann* Fritz Habicher, recalled that the cattle trucks diverted to Erlangen's railway station as a consequence of Allied bomb damage and was forced to remain here for one day. Under great strain, mistreated, hungry and thirsty, Mayr's exhausted body succumbed to the stress and he passed away here on 24 February (the prison notified his wife that he died of Broncho-pneumonia). Mayr's remains were interred at St Joseph's church in Bolanzo in 1958 and the Church has taken steps to begin the process of beatification.[212]

Wishing to take advantage of the rail transport that had been made to transport the last felons from Matzkau, the SS leader had one last important task for Dr Beelitz to perform before he could leave the garrison. In the wake of the 20 July plot to assassinate Adolf Hitler, the arrest of the plotter's families and their detention in concentration camp was undertaken. ADie Ehefrau von Alexander Stauffenberg, Melitta, war zunächst auch inhaftiert worden, aber als Testfliegerin bei den Stukkas von der Haft verschont geblieben, weil ihr Fliegereinsatz kriegswichtig war.Thetwenty twenty strong *Sonderhäftlinge* (special prisoners group), which included Clemens *Graf* Schenk v.Stauffenberg, Mika Berthold Klaus *Graf* Schenk v.Stauffenberg, *Weiter waren inhaftiert sechs Familienmitglieder der Familie Goerdeler, darunter die Ehefrau Anneliese und die Töchter.Freiin* Anni v.Lerchenfels, six family members of the Goerdeler family, Ilselotte v.Hofacker with her two older children and Fey v.Hassell, found themselves incarcerated in the KL Stutthof on 29 November 1944 (the group included eleven women). With the Red Army poised to advance into Westprussia, a decision was taken to transport the *Sonderhäftlinge* to Bavaria.[213] LInsgesamt waren 20 Personen in Sippenhaft genommen worden, davon waren 11 Frauen.LL oaded aboard unheated cattle cars in Stutthof on 28 January 1945, *Hscha.* Kupfer watched over the group as they exited the camp at 2.00 p.m. and the cold and exhausted prisoners finally arrived in Danzig after a difficult three day journey at 5.00 a.m., in -20° C temperatures.[214]

Post-war, Gugi Stauffenberg recollected that their train had been forced to halt as they crossed the River Weichel, but escaping attack, they had been able to continue their journey to Danzig. Here, a decision was then taken to transport the group in Matzkau. Boarding two vehicles at the railway station, their SS guards drove southwards, passing columns of refugees, many stationary vehicles and exhausted men and animals waiting their turn for water. Here, one survivor describes their arrival in Matzkau at 8.45 a.m. on 27 January 1945:

> [...] On foot, up a hill we made our way upwards, where the accommodation barracks lay. The climb for all and especially the sick was very difficult. The exhausted found pity from the SS people and they helped us along. [...]

One survivor recalled that the guards, taking them for refugees, behaved with 'compassion' and helped the prisoners 'lug' their luggage to a convict barrack. Reaching their destination, the special group noted that the barracks 'swarmed' with convicts and left a very dirty impression on them.[215]

Here, two rooms were provided for the use of the completely exhausted group, one for the men and the other for the woman. Gugi Stauffenberg recollected that the bunk beds in her room were dirty and had only recently been evacuated by troops going to the front. Offered a meal of potato salad and *wurst*, the group was a little revived and quickly fell asleep. Later, that same evening, a Dr 'Eckert' visited the barracks to greet them as guests in the name of the commandant. Examining *Freiin* Anni v.Lerchenfels, the physician noted her cough and suspected that she had contracted tuberculosis. The entire group relocated to what was described as the *Kranzenzimmer* on 30 January and the men and women were divided into two rooms with good beds and sprung mattresses. According to Gugi Stauffenberg, this turn of events was greeted with 'great joy' and although their new accommodation was an improvement on the first barracks, *Weiter waren inhaftiert sechs Familienmitglieder der Familie Goerdeler, darunter die Ehefrau Anneliese und die Töchter.Freiin* Anni v.Lerchenfels died here of pneumonia on 6 February 1945 (Clemens v.Stauffenberg would also became deathly ill with typhus). Around this time a further fourteen special category prisoners joined the original group.[216]

Without warning the special prisoners were gathered together at 5.30 a.m. on 8 February and ordered aboard an ambulance at 12.30 a.m., they were then driven from Matzkau to the Danzig-Ohra station, where they waited for four days until the Allied air attacks subsided long enough for them to continue their journey by rail. Leaving Danzig on 11 February, the *Sonderhäftlinge* passed through Lauenburg–Stargard–Stettin–Berlin and they were finally delivered to the KL Buchenwald on 21 February 1945.[217]

His prison finally emptied of felons, special prisoners and the majority of his staff, Dr Beelitz then received orders on 12 February to establish a rifle unit from his remaining guards. These troops formed the 1. / I. / SS-*Grenadier*-Rgt. *Kalthofen*. Retaining a small number of soldiers with which to defend the garrison, Dr Beelitz and his remaining certification non-commissioned officers watched as the shattered units of the III. Germanic SS-*Panzerkorps* entered Matzkau to rest and re-build their shattered units. Among this force were units of the *Polizeidivision*. Establishing a company-sized unit of Greek infantrymen from their *Hiwis*, these troops were annihilated during the battle for Danzig.[218]

Dr Beelitz's anxious wait for orders to evacuate the prison came to an end on 18 March 1945. 'I received an order from Munich to leave and I set off in that direction. In southern Germany a new prison had been established for those of the SS and *Polizei* who had been sentenced to *Gefängnis* punishments' recalled Dr Beelitz when questioned about his wartime activities in the 1960's.[219] A convict's widow wrote to Dr Beelitz in September 1973 to ask for news of her missing husband and discover if he had been transferred to Hersbruck near Nuremberg at the end of February 1945. Suspecting that *Rottwachmeister der Luftschutzpolizei* Gustav Kögel had perished in Danzig, the former commandant explained that the Red Army had cut the land route west at that time and following the sinking of the MV *Wilhelm Gustloff* on 30 January 1945 no shipping was available for evacuations for a period of four weeks. Recalling that he receiving orders to evacuate Matzkau in the second week of March 1945, the day following the surrender of Kolberg to the Red Army, Dr Beelitz assured her that Gustav Kögel had almost certainly died defending Danzig.[220]

Wasting no time, Dr Beelitz and a small coterie of his staff made their way to the Danzig harbour on 18 March and waited on the quayside in winter weather with many thousands of refugees in the hope of obtaining a spot on a ship bound for the safety of Germany. Around him, thundered the city's defiant FLAK guns, built on towers that his convicts had built. These heavy calibre guns prevented the Red Army tank spearheads from overrunning the weak German defences. 'In Danzig itself the boarding of ships was conducted without pause, both day and night, while the Soviet air force constantly bombed the city', is how one witness described the conditions in the city at that time.[221]

Successful in his attempt to board a ship, Dr Beelitz and his men escaped the stricken city and safely disembarked at the port of Swinemünde (north of Stettin). Making their way south by rail to the *HA* SS-*Gericht* in Prien, here, Dr Beelitz received orders to take command of the prison camp at Förrenbach at Hersbruck near Nuremberg and replicate a Matzkau-type institution. Writing in 1973, Dr Beelitz confirmed his arrival in Hersbruck during the last days of March 1945.[222]

Speaking on this subject in 1967, Rudolf Heiß confirmed the arrival of Dr Beelitz and his staff in Hersbruck in March 1945. Curious about the circumstances of their evacuation from Danzig, he approached the commandant to ask how he had fared during the evacuation. 'Everything had gone smoothly there', replied Dr Beelitz curtly, but dissatisfied with this response, Heiß then spoke with a non-commissioned officer on the same subject. 'In Matzkau finally everything went haywire', was his response to the same question and refused to elaborate further on this the issue.[223]

Meanwhile, back in Danzig the armed and equipped elements of the SS-Rgt *Kalthofen* were placed under the command of *Generaloberst* Walter Weiß's 2nd *Armee* and then deployed with *Kampfgruppe Schmidt* on the Nogat front near Neuteich in Westpreußen (built around a cadre of the *Grenadier*-Rgt. 627). Deployed between Marienburg and Elbing in the Blumenstein bridgehead, the *Kalthofen* and *Grenadier*-Rgt. 62 attempted to relieve the Marienburg fortress on 6 February 1945, but the assault failed to dislodge the Red Army and *Ustuf.* Günther Brand lost his life during the attack. The mauled *Kalthofen* then found itself subordinated to the XXIII. *Korps* on 20 February. Taking up a blocking position at Dirschau, here, Schneeberger's battalion suffered heavy losses and a Red Army assault overran the troops of the former Matzkau *Wachkompanie*, capturing many of its men. The Soviet troops are thought to have been executed many of their number.[224]

This former convict did not survive the battle for Danzig: Born in Rodewisch/Vogtland on 3 July 1920, *Rttf.* Erich Wagner, (SS Nr. 364.163), had fought with the LSSAH in February 1941 and found himself detained in Matzkau during February 1945. Wagner was killed in action in the city of Danzig on 18 February.[225]

Detained in Matzkau on 6 December 1942, *Uscha.* Martin Hoffmann was arraigned before the courts martial of the SS- *und Polizei-Gericht* XI, Stuttgart and judged guilty of the charges, the tribunal then punished him with a term of *Gefängnis*. Hoffmann was reported missing in action after being assigned to a *Bewährungsabteilung* in 1945.[226]

The veteran Red Army troops of General Fedyuninskii's 2nd Shock Army began their final assault on the port city of Danzig on 24 February 1945. Under constant attack the survivors of the *Kalthofen* and the fought alongside the SS-Regiment Kaltofen bei Pelplin/Westpreußen neben 4.*Polizeidivision* SS-Polizei-Division AOK 2 grudgingly fell back towards the city until the surviving near Pelpin, elements of the regiment disengaged from the crumbling front and regrouped in Praust (a town located few miles south-east of Matzkau). Digging trenches, Kalthofen's troops then waited for the inevitable Soviet assault. When it came, the Red Army troops ejected the SS men forcibly from their positions and Kalthofen led his remaining troops to a new position between Neufahrwasser and Weichel where they fought desperately alongside Army troops. In the city, the last elements of the *Kalthofen* fought until Danzig's defences collapsed. Its survivors surrendered to the Red Army on 30 March.[227]

Towards the end of the battle for Danzig, German civilians seeking to escape the cities destruction, stopped briefly at Matzkau to rest and have their wounds and injuries treated at the *Standort-Lazarett*. Here, a handful of German troops dug trenches in the sandy soil and prepared to defend the approached to Danzig. In the wake of the battle, the former prison was occupied by forces of the Red Army and NKVD and prisoners of war and captives were gathered here. In a twist of irony, the surviving parolees of the *Kalthofen* that had become prisoners of the Red Army found themselves returned to Matzkau for incarceration and an uncertain fate. In an effort to identify SS men, the Soviet troops examined their prisoners' left arms for evidence of a blood group tattoo (an often pointless method as some categories of *Wehrmacht* troops underwent this life saving measure).[228]

The 1950 edition of *Unser Danzig* Nr. 1 confirms that the former SS prison detained civilian prisoners in the immediate aftermath of the battle for Danzig. One of these, the railway technician *Reichsbahn Obersekretär* William Vollrath, a Danzig resident, was held in Matzkau on 28 March 1945 and has been missing since that date. A local man named Mr Bogdan visited the former SS-*Kaserne* in 1946 and observed that the site was partially destroyed and locals had stolen doors, bricks, wood, brass and other fittings. Inside the former garrison, Mr Bogdan noted that there existed a cemetery where graves were marked with German-style crosses (*Eisernes Kreuz*). Confirming the existence of trenches dug outside the camp, Mr Bogdan recalled that German prisoners of war were tasked with disinterring the graves of dead soldiers and tidying up the environs.[229]

For a while the former prison detained German civilians waiting expulsion from Polish territory and when this task was complete, the Polish security services used the site to detain enemies of the communist regime. For much of the Cold War, Matzkau was occupied by various secret state organs and the Polish Army, who stored ammunition here.[230]

70 years after the end of the war little remains of the former prison camp Danzig-Matzkau. The officers' accommodation was expropriated by local farmers, most of the barracks have been demolished and the hillside is largely covered with trees and bushes. A few of the administrative building remain standing as does the *Lagerstraße* and the base of the garage petrol tank. The parade ground, where many thousands of felons had once endured many excruciating hours of military drill and the concrete buildings of the garage are still in evidence and many of the former garrison's outer ring of concrete posts and barbed wire fencing remain. Scavengers regularly scour the site for memorabilia and items such as medals, insignia and cutlery regularly come up for sale on auction sites. The village of Mazkowy is now known for its dairy product co-operative and a housing estate and private houses have been constructed on various parts of the site. Along the former garrison's southern boundary new businesses are developing and much of the remaining site will probably be demolished as part of a proposed building development.

3.11 *Strafvollzugslager der* SS-*und Polizei* Danzig-Matzkau, *Zweiglager 'Ludwigsfelde'*

Prior to the opening of Danzig-Matzkau in the spring of 1942, the *Reichsführer* had demanded that his convicts was engaged in meaningful war work. However, it soon became obvious that his expectation could not be realised in Danzig and as a consequence of this situation, Himmler commanded the *HA* SS-*Gericht* and WVHA to establish a new prison where worthwhile work was abundant. Negotiating a contract with the Daimler Benz concern, which had SS officers on its board of directors, the WVHA successfully arranged for *Gefängnis* convicts to aid in the construction of aircraft engines. Discussing the deployment of convicts in the Daimler Benz concern, the SS agreed that the felons would labour in a segregated workshop inside the compound. Identifying a disused labour camp in the Berlin suburb of Ludwigsfelde (*Kreis* Teltow) in which to establish a Matzkau branch prison, this institution would be known officially as the *Strafvollzugslager der* SS *und Polizei* Danzig-Matzkau, *Zweiglager* 'Ludwigsfelde' and was also referred to as the SS-*Strafkompanie* Genshagen. Located halfway along the west side of the Potsdamerstraße, (the L 79), between the Brandenburgerischestraße and the Berlin ring road, a Daimler Benz built housing estate existed opposite the camp and a prisoner of war camp had been constructed to its rear.[231]

With all parties in agreement, *Hstuf.* Erich Albert and *Uscha.* Otto Langer escorted the first 100 convicts to Ludwigsfelde from Matzkau on 1 March 1943 and the convicts' first task was to improve the wire fence and construct a few small watchtowers.[232]

To the north of the main gate were three of five large convict accommodation barracks, each with a sloping roof. Built on a concrete base, each barrack was constructed of brown-painted wood and had white window sashes. Behind these buildings, located further west, were four further barracks, two for convict accommodation and the remainder for washing/toilet facilities. A corridor ran the length of the inmate barracks and led to rooms on both sides that accommodated four convicts on two bunk beds. Each barrack contained a toilet and storeroom. Facing the main gate was the prison headquarters and behind this stood two buildings for the guards' washrooms and for a clinic. The commandant and guard accommodation stood west of the main gate, behind the administrative barracks, and the convicts were divided into least four *Strafkompanie*.[233]

Lagerleiter

Hstuf. Erich Albert (1.3.1943-1.2.1944)
Hstuf. Franz Sturmann (until 20.2.1944)

Wachzugführer

Ustuf. Otto Langer (1.3.1943-10.4.1944)
Ustuf. Otto Langer (10.4.-6.5.1944)
Sturmscharführer Fritz Bohn?

Verwaltungsführer

Ustuf. Otto Langer (6.5.1944-8.1944)

This source observed the conditions in Ludwigsfelde and it appears that *Hstuf.* Albert ran a tough penal regime:

> [...] Here too there was members of an SS punishment company working alongside foreign civilian workers and prisoner of war. The SS inmates from Danzig-Matzkau in Berlin-Marienfelde replaced German workers to enable their change and improvement through work. On the same parade ground the Russian and English prisoners of war were able to observe them. [...][234]

The Daimler Benz company director, *Herr* Werner Romstedt complained to the SS-*Hauptamt* chief, *Gruf.* Gottlob Berger, about the prison regime on 16 November 1943:

> Dear Gottlob,
>
> Yesterday evening I heard something that I urgently have to discuss with you; as you know there is an SS punishment company assigned for work in Genshagen; these people undergo very harsh treatment by their guards which is fine; however, a high ranked official in Genshagen reported to me recently, that their prison regime takes place in full view of the working foreigners and prisoners of war.
>
> Those men of the punishment company have to undertake what is known as 'squats with guns' and creep around the hallways and buildings. Meanwhile, the foreigners and prisoners of war lean against the fence and laughingly watch these actions. The punishment of Germans, especially SS men in front of such an audience is undesirable and unbelievable, it most likely originates from the over enthusiasm of some lower ranked commander. I think you are certainly interested in the subject, you will investigate it and if confirmation is obtained, you will stop this nonsense.[235]

Punished with a term of *Gefängnis* while training in the Sennheim troop training ground, a Swiss volunteer found himself imprisoned in Matzkau during May 1944. He, along with 200 other inmates transferred to Ludwigsfelde in August 1944 and not including his draft, he claimed that at this time the prison held 1,000 inmates, a figure confirmed by the *HA* SS-*Gericht* in February 1944.[236]

Contacting the SS- *und Polizei-Gericht* XX on 25 February 1944, Matzkau advised them that the inmate, Julius Rogers had given satisfactory service in and out of the Ludwigsfelde prison environs and had served more than six months of his prison sentence.[237]

Born on 27 July 1923, Gunther Goerke, a former radio operator of the 2. / 8. SS-*Nachrichtenabteilung*, found himself arraigned before the courts martial of the Posen tribunal on 20 December 1942. Convicted of an undisclosed crime, the tribunal punished him with a term of *Gefängnis*. Initially serving this sentence in Matzkau, he was later incarcerated in Ludwigsfelde. Accepting field probation on 4 July 1944, Goerke then underwent military service in the *Bewahrungsabteilung*.[238]

On 27 April 1944 the SS- *und Polizei-Gericht* XX, Galatz in Romania requested that Matzkau supplied them with a fitness report for the convict Herbert Loewe who was incarcerated in Ludwigsfelde.[239]

Hospitalised between 10 and 18 April 1944, *Ustuf.* Langer had returned to Ludwigsfelde by 6 May 1944 and transferred to the *Aussenstelle* Allach when Ludwigsfelde closed in August 1944.[240]

The Ludwigsfelde prison operated a small garage of vehicles. Writing to the *HA* SS-*Gericht* in July 1944, the Berlin court complained that the PKW 'Imka' licence plate Nr. SS301907 had not been despatched to their service office and as a consequence of this message, the court received instructions to take a vehicle from the Ludwigsfelde motor pool.[241]

Given its importance to the war effort, the Daimler-Benz factories in Ludwigsfelde and Genshagen inevitably became prime targets for the Allied air war. Ordering valuable war industries—those threatened by air attacks—to disperse essential parts of their factories to safe locations in December 1942, Albert Speer, the German armaments' minister, commanded production in these places to continue uninterrupted. As a consequence of this order the fighter staff, the body in charge of aircraft construction planning, undertook a search for suitable sites for aircraft engine production and finally decided that much of the production and assembly in Berlin should be spread among different underground factories. The sites chosen for new factories ranged from an ore mine in Luxembourg, Hochwalde near Frankfurt on Oder, Rote Erde and a specially constructed tunnel in the Obrigheim near the town of Neckarlz in Baden.[242]

The German armaments minister's fears about the effect of Allied air attacks on the German war industry were realised in March 1944. From that time the Daimler-Benz factories underwent a sustained bombing assault by Allied aircraft and a raid on Genshagen on 6 August resulted in the deaths of 150 factory workers. Another air assault shattered the Untertürkheim factory on 5 September and rendered much of the factory workspace unusable. As a result of these air attacks major components of the factory were dispersed to the new factory sites. Given the high level of destruction in and around Genshagen, the *HA* SS-*Gericht* unsurprisingly issued orders to evacuate this prison from the beginning of July and the process of transport until the last week of August 1944. Prior to abandoning the prison, some felons accepted front probation and the remaining inmates transferred to the *Aussenstelle* Allach. Remaining here for a few weeks, they were then transported to the *Zweiglager* Hammerweg in the Baden town of Mosbach between August and September 1944.[243]

This disgraced officer found himself incarcerated in Ludwigsfelde during June 1944:

Name: Helmut Bufe.
Last Rank: *Schütze.*
Born: 5.8.1915 in Görlitz/Schles.
Died: 9.1944.
SS-Nr.: 175.151 (joined 6.5.1935).
Wartime Assignments:
3. SS-*Pionier-Bataillon* 1.11.1943–16.6.1944.
SS-*Pionier-Ersatz-Bataillon* 1 (Dresden) from 16.6.1944.

Promotions:

9.11.1943	SS-*Untersturmführer der Allgemeine*-SS.
9.11.1943	SS-*Untersturmführer der Reserve.*

Decorations & Awards:

0.0.19__	SA-*Sportsabzeichen in Bronze.*
19.9.1941	1939 *Eisernes Kreuz I. Klasse.*
8.7.1941	1939 *Eisernes Kreuz II. Klasse.*
0.0.19__	*Infanterie-Sturmabzeichen in Bronze.*
0.0.19__	*Verwundetenabzeichen*, 1939 *in Schwarz.*
0.0.19__	*Medaille 'Winterschlacht im Osten* 1941/42'.
0.0.19__	*Deutsches Reichssportabzeichen in Bronze.*
0.0.19__	D.L.R.G. *in Bronze.*
0.0.19__	4 *Jähr Dienstauszeichnung der* SS.
0.0.19__	*Die Medaille zur Erinnerung an den* 1. Oktober 1938 (Sudetenland).
0.0.19__	*Spange zur Medaille zur Erinnerung an den* 1. Oktober 1938 (Sudetenland).

Notes: Attending *Volksschule* and then *Fachschule* for three classes, Bufe was later employed as a carpenter. Admitted into the SS-VT or SS-TV in May 1935, Bufe underwent specialised pioneer training at the outbreak of war and married his fiancée on 23 May 1942. Qualified to drive ten ton trucks and amphibious vehicles, Bufe fought with a pioneer battalion until a court's investigation was initiated against him for committing an act of rape on 19 April 1944. While awaiting his trial, Bufe was posted to a training battalion. Arraigned before the courts martial of the SS- *und Polizei-Gericht* V, Dresden, the tribunal judged Bufe guilty of committing an act of rape and punished him with a term of two years' *Gefängnis* and ordered his expulsion from the SS. While waiting for the *Reichsführer* to confirm his judgement, Bufe was held on remand in Ludwigsfelde. Killed in action during September 1944; Bufe's death at this time suggests that his sentence had been confirmed and he accepted front probation.[244]

The former prison did not remain empty for long. *Ostuf.* Kurt Ludewig and a coterie of female guards accompanied 850 women and children from the FKL Ravensbrück to Ludwigsfelde on 11 October 1944. The camp guards were provided by the 7. SS-*Totenkopf-Sturmbann* and the slave labourers worked in the 24. *Werkehalle* until the camp's evacuation in April 1945. A few Ludwigsfelde prisoners were liberated at the KL Sachsenhausen by Red Army forces on 22 April 1945, but others underwent a forced-march to Schwerin and Zechlin and American and Soviet forces liberated them here.[245]

Today nothing remains of the former *Zweiglager* Ludwigsfelde and the land on which it stood has been covered by housing and businesses. Where the convicts' accommodation once stood is the Kaufland shopping centre, and the prison entrance, located between Karl Liebknechtstraße and the Straße der Jugend, is where the Fontane Apotheke is presently located.

3.12 *Strafvollzugslager der* SS- *und Polizei* 'Förrenbach'

Conceived as a branch prison for the SS-*Straflager* Dachau, the penal institution at Förrenbach in Bavaria, became an independent jail for the detention of *Gefängnis* offenders in March 1945. The prison at Förrenbach was conceived as a direct consequence of Himmler's command for convicts to assist in the construction of engine components for aircraft engines for the BMW industrial complex and for the Daimler-Benz plant. The aircraft planning staff had long proposed the dispersal aircraft engine production away from places under threat from Allied air attacks and when the Daimler-Benz plant came under sustained and heavy allied air attacks throughout the summer of 1944, a decision was then taken to discontinue production at Ludwigsfelde and disperse aircraft production to underground factories. Closing Ludwigsfelde in the last week of August 1944, its inmates transferred first to the *Aussenstelle* Allach and then to the newly-constructed *Zweiglager* Hammerweg in September 1944.

A disused mine at the *Doggerstollen* site near the town of Hersbruck, a town north-west of Nuremberg, was selected for a new production centre for BMW and to undertake this work the SS supplied forced labour in May 1944. Digging and enlarging eight existing tunnels, the camp prisoners blasted and dug their way into the mountain and made halls measuring five meters high and up to seven meters wide. Planning to relocate the entire BMW 801 engine plant from Allach to the *Doggerstollen* in late 1944, the WVHA commandeered a vacant *Reicharbeitsdienstlager* in Hersbruck in July 1944 to accommodate the slave labour force and this camp became a concentration camp under the command of the KL Flossenbürg. The Hersbruck slave labour complex grew quickly and the SS soon sought additional accommodation to house the prisoners required to labour in the factory tunnels. Submitting plans in May 1944 to construct a new 24-barracks sub-camp for so-called 'friendly workers', it was planned to construct this place of imprisonment upon reclaimed land halfway along the road between Happurg and Förrenbach in the Oberpfalz region of Bavaria. Three Nuremberg construction companies; Hans Müller, Hannemann, Thosti and Höllein of Bamberg were engaged to clear the land, divert the river Happach and construct the camp. Only seventeen of the planned 24 brick and wooden barracks were actually constructed and the completed *Fremdarbeiterlager* Förrenbach was enclosed by a double row of barbed wire fencing, separated by a 50 metre gap for the guards to patrol. The company Hans Müller oversaw the construction of watchtowers and dug a two-metre-deep air raid ditch. A clinic was established for the workers and placed under the command of *Oberstabarzt* Dr Ehrlich and a kitchen and washing/toilet facilities and staff accommodation were built on the north side of the road, outside the perimeter of camp. Appointing *Hstuf.* Robert Gschwendter to the post of camp commandant in the autumn of 1944, a little after accepting its first inmates, the *Fremdarbeiterlager* converted into a concentration camp and a crematorium was built outside the southern corner of the site to dispose of all the dead from Hersbruck.[246]

The *Strafvollzugslager der* SS *und Polizei* Dachau, *Zweiglager* Förrenbach, was built near the town of Heppurg in late 1944 to replace the defunct branch prison at Ludwigsfelde. Here, it was envisaged that the *Gefängnis* felons would build components for the aircraft engine factory at the *Doggerstollen* BMW 801 engine plant. The decision to construct a new prison for *Gefängnis*-category inmates at Förrenbach taken in late 1944, the *Reichsführer* and the *HA* SS-*Gericht* commanded that the new institution detained miscreants judged unsuitable for front line service. The head of the WVHA *Sonderinspektion*, *Hstuf.* Alfred Sorge, ordered the construction of the prison in November 1944 and it was established along the south-eastern fence of the *Fremdarbeiterlager*, approximately a kilometre west of Förrenbach, along the Förrenbacher–Happurg Straße. The Haberstumpf family mill at Heppurg, Obere Mühlstraße 3 served as the first quarters for the prison administration and the convicts provided labor for the construction of the barracks .[247]

The completed prison consisted of ten barracks to house the staff and inmates. A double barbed wire fence separated the prison from the *Fremdarbeiterlager* and five barracks were set-aside for the 200-bed convict accommodation. Two barracks were set aside for a showers and toilet block, another for an office, one for the guard accommodation and another for a kitchen. All buildings were linked with concrete paths to a parade ground in the centre of the prison.[248]

Lagerleiter/Kommandant

Ostuf. Fritz Ringel (1.12.1944-3.1945)
Hstuf. Dr Fritz Beelitz (3.1945-2.4.1945)
Stellvertreter Kommandant
Ostuf. Fritz Ringel (3.1945-2.4.1945)

Nr. 1 Lagerführer

Ostuf. Rudolf Hieß (1.1945-2.4.1945)

Verwaltungsführer

Ostuf. Stefan Golda (3.1945-2.4.1945)

Lagerarzt

Dr Lippmann.

A few *Gefängnis* convicts appear to have laboured side-by-side with prisoners and civilian workers in the *Doggerstollen* and their daily regime was almost certainly similar to that existing in other SS and *Polizei* penal institutions. This new prison had certainly opened by 1 December 1944, and initially under the administrative control of the SS-*Straflager* Dachau, Förrenbach had begun to replace Matzkau in February 1945.[249] *Stubaf.* Dr Beelitz's arrival in Förrenbach in late March 1945 and his arrival heralded the jail's full independence from the SS-*Straflager* Dachau.[250]

Around 500 convicts arrived in Förrenbach from the defunct prison institution at Matzkau in January/February 1945 and on arrival were divided into those capable of working and those who required further detention. The latter re-boarded trains at Heppurg and were transported to the SS-*Straflager* Dachau to complete their sentences.[251]

An ULTRA intercept reported that the SS- *und Polizei-Gericht* XVI was conducting trials in Hersbrück/Nuremberg during February 1945. This was almost certainly a branch court that was tasked with court-martialling malefactors in Förrenbach.[252]

Telexing this prison on 27 March 1945, the SS- *und Polizei-Gericht* XXIII, Veldes requested fitness reports for the following inmates: *Meister Gendarme* Otto Kadner, who was due for release on 12 March, *Meister Gendarme* Johan Hacker, whose sentence ended on 18 February and finally Heinrich Kunstmann, who had completed his part-punishment on 14 March. Completing his sentence, Kunstmann was ordered to report to a HSSPF *Sonderabteilung*.[253]

The satellite camps around the *Doggerstellon*, including the KL Förrenbach, were evacuated between 8 and 13 April 1945 and many of the half-starved and exhausted inmates were transported by rail from Heppurg to Dachau satellite camps on 7 April 1945. Abandoning those too sick to travel, another group of 2,100 prisoners marched south to the KL Dachau on foot in five columns. Those too weak to continue the march was executed and those abandoned in Heppurg were liberated by American troops on 20 April 1945.[254]

It appears that just prior to the evacuation of the Heppurg camps, the *HA* SS-*Gericht* issued evacuation orders to Dr Beelitz at Förrenbach. From surviving documents we discover that *Ostuf.* Ringel remained here until 2 April 1944 and this date almost certainly represents the exact moment that the prison was abandoned and its inmates travelled by rail to the SS-*Straflager* Dachau (Allach). Here, those convicts with the requisite skills, continued producing components for BMW.[255]

In the immediate post-war period, Förrenbach's abandoned barracks held prisoners of war. A former prison officer, Fritz Baumeister, found himself detained in Förrenbach for almost a year from the spring of 1945. Here, he recovered from wounds received at the front. Then accepting civilian internees, Förrenbach barracks were later utilised as a displaced persons' camp. Dismantling Förrenbach, the former prison disappeared as part of plans for the construction of a dam in 1955. An artificial lake now covers the land where the prison once stood.[256]

3.13 Postwar Danzig-Matzkau Investigation

The war long over, a few former Matzkau inmates then sought recompense for their mistreatment in the prison and various public prosecutors undertook investigations to examine the veracity of their allegations that the former commandant had ordered summary executions and permitted the inhuman treatment of the convicts between 1955 and 1971. Approaching the authorities on 4 December 1958, the former Matzkau inmate, Anton Rademacher accused the former guard, *Oscha.* Runge and Dr Beelitz of ordering the summary execution of SS member Bruno Lembach on 15 February 1945.[257] Writing to Dr Beelitz on 3 March 1959, the *Landgericht* Berlin informed the former commandant of the murder indictment and he refuted Rademacher's allegations on 14 April the same year.[258]

Born in Bonn on 6 September 1925, Anton Rademacher had joined the *Waffen*-SS in October 1942 (*Ausbildungslager* Dachau) but found himself arraigned before the courts martial of the SS- *und Polizei-Gericht* I, Munich on 20 January 1943 for committing comrade theft. Judged guilty of the charge, the tribunal punished him with a term of six months' *Gefängnis* which he served in Matzkau. Transferring to the *Bewährungsabteilung* three months later, Rademacher served his probation on the Finnish Front. Claiming to have returned to Matzkau in September 1944, here, he met Bruno Lembach. Both then fought on the Russian Front until Lembach was killed in action and Rademacher was wounded in his upper left leg. This injury resulted in an amputation and his hospitalisation in Freiberg in Sachsen.[260]

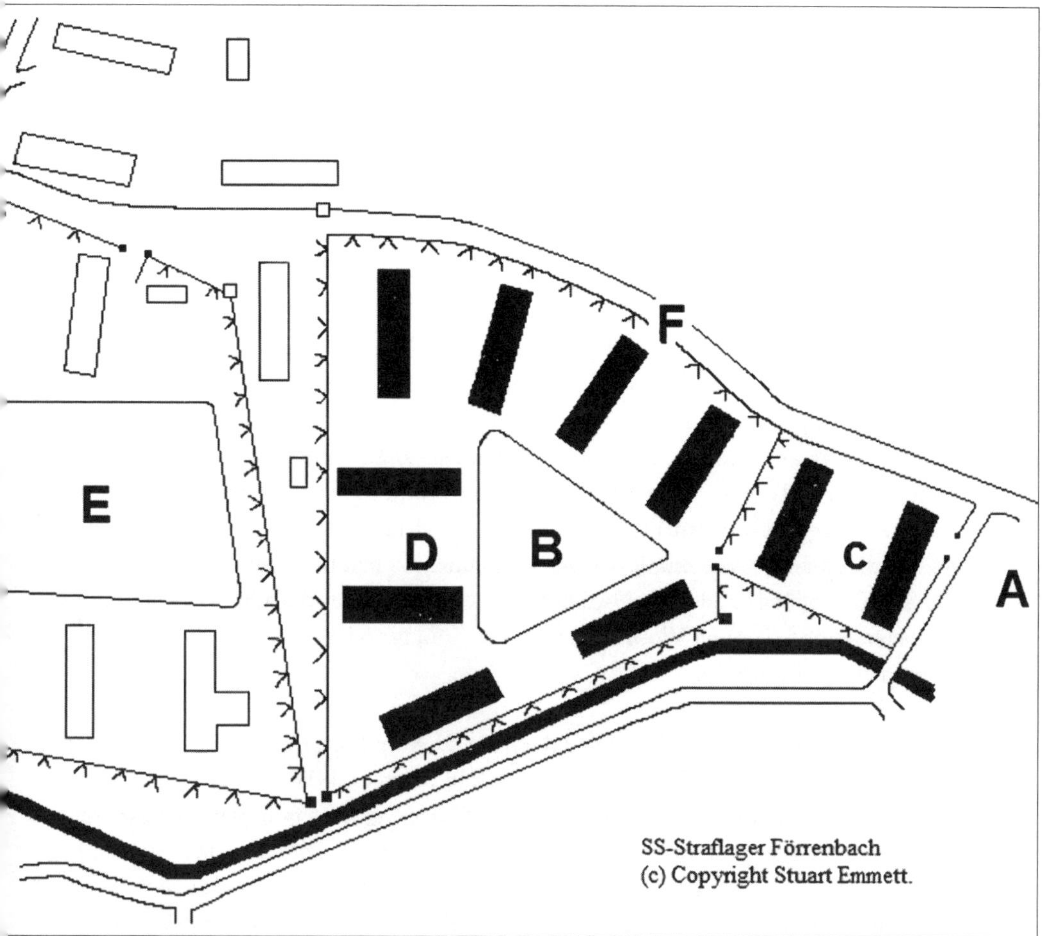

Released from hospital in the summer of 1945, Rademacher led a rootless life, undertaking various jobs in Düsseldorf from 1947. Struggling financially, he then concocted a scheme to receive compensation as a victim of Nazism. Submitting an application for compensation on 7 April 1956; he claimed to have been a political prisoner. Overreaching himself, Rademacher's erroneous accusation against Dr Beelitz resulted in the *Landgericht* Berlin initiating a court's investigation against him on 21 July 1959. Establishing that his claims against the former commandant were pure fabrication, Rademacher then faced trial before the *Landgericht* Mönchengladbach for committing perjury and obtaining money by false pretences on 2 October 1959. Judged guilty for these offences and dishonesty, the court punished him with a term of ten months' *Gefängnis* on 20 March 1961.[261]

Despite Rademacher's prosecution for perjury, the *Landgericht* Berlin prosecutor continued its investigation into his claims against Dr Beelitz. In 1959 the *Polizeipräsident*

Berlin *Abt.* I requested that *Staatsrat* Hermann Meder and Günther Burmeister was questioned as a possible witnesses to murder.[262]

In addition to the Dr Beelitz investigation, the Wiesbaden public prosecutor's investigative process against a former Matzkau guard named Elsner in July 1959 had led them to also question whether senior Matzkau staff had been involved in summary executions. Elsner was reportedly assigned to the prison between January and July 1942.[263]

The case against Dr Beelitz received given further impetus as the result of a former Matzkau inmate named Franz-Otto Hühn becoming embroiled in the *Landgericht* Tübingen's 1962 investigation against the former KL Stutthoff guard Otto Haupt. Questioned twice in 1962, Hühn alleged that former *Polizeirat* Josef Uhl had committed murder and Otto Haupt had inspected Matzkau between the autumns of 1943 and 1944 to seek out prisoners for execution by lethal injection. In addition to these claims, Hühn accused the Matzkau guard and native of Danzig, *Uscha.* Schulz, of killing a Dutch inmate in June/July 1944. To support his claims, Hühn identified both former *Uscha.* Hannes Krieger and Richard Vlothoerbäumer as a witnesses. Living in Herford during 1962, Vlothoerbäumer was employed as a mechanic and had been detained in Matzkau in the summer of 1942 and early 1943. When questioned about the allegations, Günther Burmeister poured scorn on Vlothoerbäumer's testimony and accused him of committing perjury in another court's process.[264]

Born in Meuhaus am Rennweg/Thüringen on 15 May 1911, Franz-Otto Hühn had attended the Meuhaus am Rennweg *Volksschule* in between 1917 and 1925 and studied for three years at *Berufsschule* (*Bautechnischer*). Volunteering for service with the Bavarian *Landpolizei* from the autumn of 1929, Hühn trained with the *Schutzpolizei* in Nuremberg-Fürth from 1 April 1930 and then found himself assigned to the *Polizeivorschule* in Eichstätt a. d. Altmühl from October 1930 to 31 March 1931. Posted to the *Polizei-Kavallerie-Schule* until 30 September 1932, he served with the Regensburg *Bereitschaftspolizei* from 1 October 1932 and again during the summer of 1934 (*Standort Landpolizei* Regensburg). In 1943 *Polizeiinspektor* Hühn found himself arraigned before the courts martial of the SS- *und Polizei-Gericht* III, Berlin on charges of undermining the war effort. Judged guilty of the charge, Hühn was taken under arrest from the *Gestapogefängnis* Berlin to the KL Stutthof and held in the reception barracks for between fourteen days and three weeks. Transferred to Matzkau in October 1943, Hühn remained here until he and 60 fellow inmates were transferred to the SS-*Truppenübungsplatz* Chlum in the autumn of 1944 to join the *Bewährungsabteilung* at Lublowie. Here, Hühn trained to lift enemy mines until January 1945 and was then sent to the Eastern Front. Becoming a Soviet prisoner of war on 20 April, Hühn would return home to Germany and attempted to kill himself with household gas, resulting in his admission to the psychiatric hospital.[265]

As a consequence of both Rademacher's and Hühn's allegations, the former Matzkau guard, *Uscha.* Albert Müller, was interviewed as a potential witness by the Düsseldorf police on 7 May 1962. Establishing his bona fide, Müller was questioned about the former commandant's responsibility for processing the offences committed by the military personnel. Stating confidently that only the SS courts were responsible for handling criminal cases, Müller affirmed that the camp commandant only dealt with disciplinary offences. Recalling that Matzkau's imprisoned inmates had been court-sentenced to serve their punishments in the prison, the former guard then stated that well-behaved inmates were released prematurely and then returned to their unit. Emphatically, Müller denied any knowledge of a single case in which a prisoner had been unlawfully killed inside Matzkau without trial.[266] He then responded to Hühn's allegation that summary courts took place in Matzkau:

> [...] I want to again to define explicitly, that these were judgments that had been conducted by the field courts, or the SS and *Polizei* Court Danzig, which were enforced only within the camp and only by members of the guard company. None of us had any influence on these events.

Müller elaborated further when asked if Hühn was correct to accuse Dr Beelitz of pronouncing a death sentences and selecting those participating in firing squads:

> [...] Dr Beelitz, in his capacity as *Leiter der Juristischen Abteilung*, was only responsible for the processing of detainee concerns (criminal records). These were files that had been sent from the field or SS court in question and once completed was then sent to us.

Expressing his unawareness of observing any executions being carried out when Dr Beelitz was camp commandant, Müller voiced his certainty that the judge had not ordered any shootings. 'Dr Beelitz was in all things correct and has, contrary to the allegations of Hühn, granted prisoners special privileges, in particular leave on parole.'[267]

'Such a thing was completely out of the question' stated Müller with assurance when asked if the shooting of a camp prisoners in the neck had been possible. Affirming that Laimgruber had been regarded a very strict officer, Müller denied knowing Hühn and offered an opinion of his allegations:

> [...] The incidents as described by him did not exist with us. That a prisoner had been trampled upon to death during drill service in the camp, is simply not possible, I would have probably heard about it if this had occurred. To my knowledge, no matter the cause no prisoners had died in the camp. The information relating to the clinic, where allegedly some have been 'injected' are completely untrue. I've never heard of such a case.[268]

Interestingly, Müller then revealed that the corpse of a dead inmate could not leave the camp unless a travel order was issued. As he had been responsible for issuing this order, he assured the investigator that it stood to reason that if issued, then he would be aware of the existence of any such orders. Confirming that Baumgärtner had a wife and school-age daughter that lived in the officer home in the camp, Müller affirmed that the commandants daughter rode her horse in the riding hall, but had no knowledge of her riding around in the camp, greeting the inmates and demanding they return her salute. Turning his attention to the KL Stutthof allegations, Müller claimed no knowledge of what occurred in the concentration camp and would only admit to knowing the place by name. Otto Haupt was unknown to Müller, but the former guard agreed that he may have been an *Uscha* and leader of the prisoner clinic in Stutthof—as Hühn had stated. Adamant that Haupt had no powers of control in Matzkau, Müller assured the investigator that he had no recollection of the guard *Oscha.* Willi Körfer, who later became an inmate.[269]

Turning his attention to Rademacher's allegations, Müller recollected reading his wanted advertisement in the *Rheinische Post* in 1959/60 and then meeting with the former convict. Here, in his own words, he related what occurred between them:

> [...] In the form of a classified advertisement, he asked for those who had been in the Danzig-Matzkau camp to reply. As a consequence of this advert I wrote to Rademacher and confirmed in writing that I had been in Matzkau. He then visited me in my apartment and suspected that I was a prisoner. During the course of our conversation, he realized that I was a member of the troops. A few days later he phoned to ask me visit him at his workplace, but a few days later he had not yet phoned to arrange this workplace visit. He worked as a telephone operator in the press house. So I went there and on this occasion he placed before me an 'affidavit' prepared by him that he wanted me to sign. This referred to the fact that he had been abused in the Matzkau camp. The exact contents of this statement I can no longer recall. On the other hand, Rademacher also wanted me to make a declaration, that I had done nothing in Matzkau for which I could be blamed for. I have signed neither. My guess was to the effect, that he wanted to capitalise from his stay in Danzig-Matzkau.[270]

Detained in the *Gefängnis* Tübingen, the *Sonderkommission Landkriminalamt* Baden-Württemberg accepted a statement from Otto Haupt in late 1963 which confirmed the existence of a separate barracks in Matzkau to detain inmates from the KL Stutthof. Here, these prisoner undertook outside work in an effort to earn their rehabilitation. Denying that he had murdered any of these camp prisoners by injection, Haupt claimed never to have met Dr Beelitz, or cared for any convicts in Matzkau or in the KL Stutthof. Haupt assured the investigator that he had only ever visiting the barracks of the KL prisoners in Matzkau.[271]

It was clear by now to the court that Rademacher's testimony was unreliable, but opening an investigative process against Otto Haupt in March 1964, the *Landgericht* Stuttgart public prosecutor decided to examine Hühn's allegations of murder in Matzkau. During these hearings and in his written submissions, Hühn once again accused all the defendants of having committed murders in Matzkau and reiterated his claim that Dr Beelitz had chaired summary camp courts martial, had on numerous occasions imposed wrongful death sentences on prisoners and arranged their executions without trial. Specifically, he also accused Dr Beelitz of ordering *Uscha.* König to shoot two Dutch prisoners without judgment in summer 1944 and watched as a convict stood in a water barrel for so long that he died of hypothermia. Accusing Baumgärtner of arbitrarily shooting two Dutch prisoners and shooting a French man in the neck, Hühn then denounced Schulz for shooting a French man in the sandpit and alleged that this NCO then received praise from Dr Beelitz. Lastly, Hühn again assured the investigators the inmates had been chased over fallen fellow convicts during 'punishment drills' and had trampled them to death.[272]

The 1966 Baden-Württemberg police investigation into the activities of Hope and others at the KL Stutthof *bei* Danzig had convinced them that punishable acts had occurred at Matzkau, but once again, their conviction was based almost entirely on Hühn's testimony. Speaking to investigators in August 1964, Hühn once again implicated Dr Beelitz and other members of his staff in summary executions, but the special commission was unable to elicit further statements from him.[273] As a consequence of Hühn's new claims, a fresh court's investigation was instigated against Dr Beelitz, Rudolf Heiß, Edmund Baumgärtner, Erich Laimgruber and *Uscha.* Schulz to examine their possible involvement in summary executions and torture in Matzkau. To aid their efforts, the *Zentrallstelle der Landesveraltung* was approached and asked to organise a search to identify the correct Baumgärtner and they achieved this in January 1966.[274]

Determined to discover further information about Matzkau, the investigators then questioned Günther Burmeister in August 1965 to ask him to explain the prison's status. The *Landgericht* Flensburg's 1967 court's process against Krizons enabled the court investigators to determine that the *Strafvollzugslager der* SS *und Polizei* Matzkau had never subordinate to the KL Stutthof.[275]

Seeking further clarification on the allegations, the investigative judge questioned Dr Günther Reinecke in April 1965. 'He had been active in the *Amt* III' he confirmed, but unable to recall the particulars of Dr Beelitz's career, Dr Reinecke elaborated further about the *Amt* III. 'That department dealt exclusively with imprisonment and the clemency concerns and therefore from this employment the commission of a crime was impossible' stated Dr Reinecke, and confirmed that Dr Beelitz had been commanded to the *HA* SS-*Gericht* as a qualified lawyer and then utilized as a case worker. Dr Reinecke refuted the accusation that Dr Beelitz had committed any wrong action during his employment in the *Amt* III and explained why he held this opinion:

> […] Similarly, it can be excluded that he would have to answer for the actions of other people, because in this service office there were no persons who had committed wrongdoings. If sentences were carried out, then it was only those which had been declared in accordance with the then existing laws and legal enforcement by the *Gerichtsherr*.[276]

Here, Dr Reinecke explains the purpose of the *Lager* Danzig-Matzkau:

> […] Basically, it must be stated that only those who had been convicted within the court system of the *Waffen*-SS and *Polizei* were sent to this prison. It had no connection or even

similarity to a concentration camp. Generally, the penal provisions which were available for the *Wehrmacht* jurisdiction also apply here. Special provisions were not available.

Unable to provide a detailed indication of the commandant's duties in Matzkau, Dr Reinecke recalled visiting the prison on one occasion, but could not recollect whether Dr Beelitz was the commandant at that time. Convinced that Dr Beelitz, like his predecessor, Dr Ernst, had kept fully within the statutory provisions, Dr Reinecke again assured the investigator that he was unaware of any contrary behavior on the part of the former commandant and could not imagine either the camp leader or the investigative officer having the opportunity to determine whether a judgment was final or not.[277]

Dr Reinecke was then asked to explain the relationship between the prison and concentration camp:

> […] Any connection to a concentration camp, in this case Stutthof, is completely erroneous. Maybe there is a possibility that there were economic ties, i.e., that there was a loose connection with respect to the catering and supply etc., but the connections to executions can be completely excluded within the organization of the prison. As there were legal requirements for each prisoner. The camp had to perform their duties properly and was also monitored. Accommodation and food and the service in this camp conformed to the given war legislation.

Considering the accusations, Dr Reinecke expressed his belief that arbitrary beatings could not have occurred in Matzkau, unless inmates had been selected for 'special training,' in which case, he could imagine injuries occurring to volunteers. Unable to recollect any individual cases to support this suggestion, he questioned whether mistreatment included the experience of those former convicts who volunteered for service in one-man submarines.[278]

Concluding his statement, Dr Reinecke asserted his belief that that court imposed death sentences had not been enforced against Matzkau felons. Certain that in most cases the offenders had been judged at their unit on the field and the execution enforced there, he also voiced his belief that these executions were undertaken in accordance with the statutory provisions then in force, namely the enforcement order for capital punishments was carried out in the rightful military form. Discussing this subject further, Dr Reinecke expressed his certainty that only in 'exceptional cases' was the death sentence carried out in the prison camps and these were usually undertaken at the SS-*Straflager* Dachau. Convinced that the camp leader was unable to order any executions and bound in principle to the rightful judgments of the courts, the former *Oberste* SS- *und Polizei-Gericht* chairman concluded his statement with the following observation:

> […] I am personally convinced that Dr Beelitz was not involved in any wrong action, because his supervisor would have learned of this. The person of the *Amt* III chief, presently *Oberlandesgerichtsrat* Dr Burmeister, vouched for the procedure in accordance to the strictest legal principles.[279]

Franz Hühn's allegations gradually permeated their way through the West German judiciary and by 1965, Dr Beelitz's employers had instigated an investigation to discover if he had advised them of his previous *Waffen*-SS service (as part of this process, a copy of Hühn's statement was sent to the *Herrn Senator für Finanz*). Writing to Dr Beelitz's employers on 11 August 1966, the *Landgericht* Munich II advised them that they had initiated a court's investigation against the former SS Judge and would examine allegations that he had ordered summary executions Danzig-Matzkau.[280]

Interviewed in the *Zuchthaus* Hamburg-Fuhlsbüttel on 13 July 1966, the former Matzkau inmate Alfred Hubrig had mustered with the LSSAH between 15 October 1942 and February 1943 and faced trial before the Berlin tribunal in January the same year for committing two cases of theft in 1942. Judged guilty of the charges, the tribunal punished Hubrig with a term of eight months' *Gefängnis* and he served this sentence in Matzkau. Finding himself detained in the *Zuchthaus* Hamburg-Fuhlsbüttel on 1 May 1966, from here, Hubrig denounced Dr Beelitz and his *Helfershelfern* for committing summary executions in Matzkau. Posted to the *Bewährungsabteilung* from the end of 1943 to early July 1944, Hubrig also claimed to have witnessed two summary shootings in Chlum.[281]

'I have no guilt in the sense of the accusations put before me' proclaimed Dr Beelitz when questioned about Hühn's allegations and denying that he had ordered arbitrary shootings in Matzkau, he assured his questioner that no members of the guard unit had killed inmates. Denying that he had ever signed a death sentence order, judged, or sat as a lay judge at a capital punishment trial, Dr Beelitz explained that the only executions that took place in Matzkau were those conducted as part of a courts process and convict spectators did not partake in the lawful executions at the shooting range (prior his appointment, he voiced his uncertainty as to whether felons had assisted the firing squad). In his summation, Dr Beelitz insisted he had never been asked about his former Nazi Party membership and his current employers were fully aware of his past.[282] Dr Beelitz's employers would contact the court in writing about his matter on 13 and 18 April 1959.[283]

The Austrian authorities questioned Edmund Baumgärtner on 28 May and 4 June 1968 and he too explained the impossibility of summary executions occurring in Danzig-Matzkau:

> [...] Basically, I would like to state emphatically that no executions had been carried out in the period in which I was commander of the Danzig-Matzkau camp. However, I am aware that death sentences were carried out in the various other prison camps. During my service time in Danzig-Matzkau, and this I would like to emphasize once again, to my knowledge, I did not enforce any death sentence.
>
> I am of the opinion that the men there would have reported if an unlawful death had been carried out. I can say with a clear conscience that such a report had never been submitted. Thus, such a judgment could not have been enforced without my knowledge. I think it is impossible that someone has carried out a death sentence without informing the camp commander. There still remains the remote possibility that my then deputy Dr Beelitz had sanctioned the carrying out of a death sentence. As I said, I also consider this

> possibility unlikely as Dr Beelitz would certainly have informed me of this. Excessive actions by the guards did not occur. Of this I am certain.[284]

Here, Baumgärtner responds to the accusation that his subordinates had murdered inmates with head shootings:

> [...] Of this occurring, I would certainly have learned something. The prisoner status was checked in the evening. Now, if a prisoners had been shot, or otherwise then there would always have been a requirement to provide a reason for their absence and then the reason for their absence would have had to be recorded. Heiß or Laimgruber would have had to worry about such an incident message because the word 'absent' would be entered. Had Heiß, Laimgruber, or any other member of the SS guards have shot a prisoner, then an investigation would have been carried out for sure. Dr Beelitz would have led this investigation. To my knowledge there has never been such an incident in the Danzig-Matzkau camp and an investigation was never undertaken for this reason.[285]

Confirming that the inmates underwent punishment drill until late in the night, Baumgärtner explained that this punitive measure was not arranged by the camp commandant, but by the *Lagerführer*. He did however, imagine it possible for some inmates to suffer injury during the punishment drill:

> [...] Prisoners who were not up to the rigors of such a punishment drill did collapse, but this did not correspond to the allegation that the other prisoners 'trampled' over the fallen for as long as it took until they were dead. As far as I am aware, no deaths have resulted from punishments. Also to my knowledge no one had died from the effects of punishment drill.

Turning his attention to Hühn's accusation that a convict was beaten on the block for failing to remove his cap in greeting to his daughter, Baumgärtner then explained:

> [...] It is true that my divorced wife Anna and my daughter Gudrun did visit me in Danzig-Matzkau. I cannot now for the moment remember when this visit took place and in this connection [to this visit] I think that it is incorrect that all prisoners had been ordered to greet my daughter by taking off their caps. It is true that during her stay in Danzig-Matzkau my daughter used a saddle horse (not a pony) but neither my wife nor my daughter entered the camp. Therefore, I dispute the accusation that I have condemned a prisoner to 25 strokes of the cane because he had not properly greeted my daughter. The disciplinary measure of 25 strokes of the cane has not been imposed. In our camp, a so-called 'block' did not exist. The 'block' was only used in the concentration camps.[286]

He then responded to the question of whether the inmate population had numbered 3,000 to 5,000 men:

> [...] There was no room in the Danzig-Matzkau *Häftlingslager* for such a large number of prisoners. The number of prisoners did not exceed 500. It is also untrue that aside from Germans there were Dutch, Flemings, Danes and French among the prisoners. As already emphasised several times, I would like to state once again that the prison only handled SS, or *Polizei* members, so no political prisoners in a general sense. It is perhaps possible that there were one or the other Dutch citizens from the Dutch Legion there, but I cannot remember myself to such a case.

Bäumgartner's memory was at fault, Matzkau had at various times detained a wide variety of non-German felons, including Dutchmen and Scandinavians. 'Pulled out of thin air' was his response to the accusation that that murders had taken place in the dentistry clinic and he recalled that *Hstuf.* Dr Eckert had been 'a very correct human being' and affirmed that he had never heard anything derogatory said about the dentist. Declaring that it was impossible for such incidents, as described by the witnesses, to have occurred at the dental clinic, Bäumgartner had no recollection of *Hscha.* Otto Haupt, but conceded that it possible that he had visited Matzkau. However, Bäumgartner remained adamant that Haupt could not have exercised the supervisory powers attributed to him without his knowledge.[287]

Denying emphatically that during his period of service there had occurred single case of summary executions in Matzkau as described by witnesses, Bäumgartner also rejected the implication that delinquents had been shot at the stake or hanged. When told that witnesses had seen these events occur, Bäumgartner explained why they were mistaken:

> [...] If such executions had been watched by all the prisoners of the camp, it would therefore have resulted in many more witnesses that could refute all of my justifications. I am sure that there are no such witnesses and there cannot be so, because—this you would again discover—that no such shootings had taken place there while I was commander of the Danzig-Matzkau camp.

Bäumgartner then responded to the allegation that he had ordered the summary execution of escaping convicts:

> [...] Of the incident I know nothing, I can only say in reflection that I myself have had shot no one and I have never given an order or command for a summery shooting. I also do not recall an escape from the Matzkau camp. I cannot explain from where this witness information has come from with which I totally disagree with.[288]

Bäumgartner now heard for the first time the allegation that *Uscha.* Schulze had shot a Dutch convict and had been congratulated by Dr Beelitz. Unable to recollect Schultz's full identity, he referred the investigators to Dr Beelitz for further information. Asked to describe his relationship with co-defendant, Bäumgartner, gave this surprising response:

> [...] Concerning the implication that I was good friends with Dr Beelitz and that together we had organized drinking evenings, I want to say that this is incorrect. The relationship between me and Dr Beelitz was always tense. We did not like each other. I suppose that he did not suit my Austrian type and I did not like his brash imperious demeanor. I do not deny that sometimes he came to spend his evenings in the officers' mess. And there, he has also consumed alcohol, but to conclude that I was a drinking friend of Dr Beelitz, would be absolutely wrong.

Concluding his statement, Bäumgartner once again emphatically denied that he had permitted any illegal actions to take place in Matzkau:

> [...] As long as I was the commandant of Matzkau I cared most for discipline and order, but I would not tolerate any assaults [on inmates]. Concerning executions, these never happened and I have also never made a request for the death penalty or otherwise been involved in summary executions. If I had gained knowledge, that is for whatever reason, that someone intended to shoot a prisoner without a trial, I would have prevented it with certainty. All disciplinary sanctions were imposed within the legal framework. In addition, I would not tolerate illegalities.[289]

Questioned at his home in March 1967, Rudolf Heiß explained that with one exception, no *Lagergericht* had been undertaken in the prison on the grounds that the inmates had already been convicted by individual SS and *Polizei* courts. Offending again, usually an act of comrade theft, Heiß revealed that the commandant held the authority to pronounce an arrest penalty and if this proved insufficient then the recidivists was brought before the Danzig tribunal for trial (the SS- *und Polizei-Gericht* IV, Danzig conducted the trial of convicts within the garrison fence). The exception to this situation was what Heiß described as 'special cases' and he recalled that during his time in the prison service he had become aware of a uniformed *Luftschutzmann* who had been denounced for quoting Götz and calling Himmler a bastard.[290] *Luftschutzmänner* were subject to the SS and *Polizei* jurisdiction when committing an offence in the line of duty and in uniform, so this air defence official then faced trial before an SS and *Polizei* court. Heiß then explained what occurred next:

> [...] In this case, Himmler had demanded the death penalty (at that time something like that was possible) and he reserved the confirmation of the judgment for himself. However, according to the MStGB the defendant could be convicted to only six to eight months' imprisonment for this offence and this [sentence] had already been imposed by another court.[291]

For this reason, this *Luftschutzmann* found himself detained in Matzkau, but, Himmler then reversed the judgment in the first instance and commanded his retrial in the prison in the summer of 1944. Heiß recalled that *Hstuf.* Dr Beelitz ordered him to attend this process as an officer lay judge and under the auspices of the Danzig tribunal, the SS-*Richter* announced the same punishment. Here, Heiß expressed his criticism of Himmler's decision:

> [...] I still remember exactly, that this judge an SS-*Hstuf.* (his name escapes me) complained about the methods of Heinrich Himmler and at the same time regretted that he himself now would fare as well as his predecessor, who had also not announced a death sentence.[292]

Heiß then contended that the trial judge was rewarded for his sentencing decision with a transfer to the front and emphatically denied that a summary court, as described by Hühn, had taken place in the camp. Aside from the above mentioned case, Heiß claimed never to have attended any other court hearings as a lay judge and had never participated in proceedings in which death sentences had been pronounced, not even when he had acted as what he described as the *Protokollführer* at the *Hauptamt der* SS *und Polizei* at Munich. Questioned once again about these matters in March 1967, Heiß was cautioned that he was suspected of participating as a lay judge at a *Lagergericht* in Danzig-Matzkau and contributing to the awarding of death sentences. Heiß again denied that the prison had organised summary trials inside the *Häftlingslager* and explained that while the commandant had the power to impose arrest punishments against undisciplined inmates and the SS members of the guard, those members of the staff, or inmates who were themselves guilty of criminal acts, then faced trial before the Danzig tribunal once the *Gerichtsoffizier* had filed a report and recommended this course of action. Again, Heiß denied knowledge of the execution of felons in Matzkau:

> [...] I would even go so far as to say that there have been no executions in this period. Although in my position as first 1. *Lagerführer* I was often inside the *Lager*, however, I am certain that an event such as an execution, would have been spoken about in comrade circles. I would have surely learned about executions in this way, as such events were discussed regularly at the dinner table in the *Lager Kasino*.[293]

Denying Hühn's allegation that the cane had been use by prison staff, Heiß attempted to convince the investigator that it had been strictly forbidden to mistreat inmates and he claimed having no recollection of a convict being forced to stand in a water trough as described by Hühn. Warming to his subject, Heiß explained that 'the *Strafvollzugslager* was not a concentration camp' and claimed that he had enjoyed a 'good relationship of trust with the inmates.' Turning his attention to Hühn's allegation that a Dutch convict had suffered 25 lashes as an alternative to serving four years of an eight year *Zuchthaus* sentence, Heiß recalled that only *Gefängnis* penalties were enforced in the *Lager* Matzkau and he expressed his certainty that the prison was completely excluded from other aspects of the clemency process, which were the responsibility of the responsible SS and *Polizei* courts and the *HA* SS-*Gericht* in Munich for important cases. Reconsidering the question,

Heiß again expressed his certainty that responsibility for these cases lay with *Staf.* Günther Burmeister.[294]

Discussing *Oscha.* Schulz's activities, Heiß explained that he had to 'sometimes calm him down,' especially during drill, as his subordinate would demanded a strict performance from the inmates as it often concerned Schulz that they was prepared for the front through punitive measures. However, Heiß expressed no knowledge of Schulz shooting and killing a Dutch SS man during his time in Matzkau (he initially denied that any Dutch were held in the prison, but later retracted this part of his statement).

Recollecting the name of the *Uscha.* König, Heiß claimed no knowledge of Dr Beelitz driving him to kill and could not recall König's fate. In summary, Heiß again declared never participating in any single act of killing and denied knowledge of the former inmate Reuer's allegation regarding the killing of Wallonien SS-member Van der Velden. Stating that he had no idea whether a death sentence existed against the man König, Heiß remained adamant that no executions of inmates occurred during his time in Matzkau and expressed his certainty that all death sentences were announced by the Danzig tribunal. Under the erroneous belief that capital punishments were never enforced in the prison, Heiß made the following disclosure:

> [...] If SS or *Polizei* officers were sentenced by the SS- *und Polizei-Gericht* IV in Danzig for any criminal offence and awarded a death sentence, these executions were reportedly carried out in KL Stutthof. This I know from the stories of the chief judge of the SS- *und Polizei-Gericht* IV, Danzig, SS-*Stubaf.* Pohl, who I met in the *Kasino*.[295]

Interviewed in mid-August 1968, former *Ostuf.* Fritz Ringel denied knowing Hühn personally or by name. Suffering epileptic seizures due to a brain contusion, Ringel conceded that his statement could contain inaccuracies, but in the belief that his testimony was correct, he confirmed that he had once commanded the *Wachkompanie*, but knowing nothing about unlawful acts of killing, he could only express his awareness of the execution of a field court judgment against two Dutch SS soldiers in 1942 or 1943. When questioned about the *Exerzierdienst* (drill) imposed on the inmates, Ringel offered the following explanation for its imposition:

> [...] I had control only over members of the SS and *Polizei.* The inmates were subordinated to the *Lagerführer* and he decided on the convicts *Exerzierdienst,* the work deployment and the inner service in the camp. Since the convict's camp was completely self-contained, I could not give any orders there, I was also not informed of the general conditions in the camp and how a day routine had been organised there.

Admitting responsibility for ordering drill for inmates deployed outside of the prison compound, on the parade ground, Ringel then explained its imposition; 'this corresponded to the formal drill, however, it was carried out in an intensified form. That this drill had led to any violence against the inmates, I have never been able to observe.' Confirming that a stricter form of drill took place in Matzkau, Ringel explained that this took the form of excessive running, crawling and the like. However, from hearsay only, Ringel conceded his awareness that a doctor and hospital had existed in the *Häftlingslager* and convicts received treatment there.[296]

The Austrian authorities contacted the *Landgericht* Munich II on 28 February and 6 November 1968 to ask if the court had discovered during its investigation any prosecutable evidence in the case of Bäumgartner. Concluding their enquires into this matter, the court revealed that they had found no evidence to substantiate the prosecution of the former commandants for criminally guilty behavior in their former capacity at the *Straflager* Matzkau.[297] However, this was not the end of the matter and in October 1968 the *Landgericht* Munich II reported actively searching for witnesses from the ranks of former inmates and guards at Matzkau.[298] In 1966 the *Bayerisches Landeskriminalamt* in Munich reported finding no concrete evidence supporting the accusation that Dr Beelitz had been complicit in murder at Matzkau.[299]

Approached by investigators as a possible witness on 29 April 1969, this former Matzkau inmate made further allegations against Dr Beelitz: Born in Vienna on 12 April 1921, Karl-Heinz Hirsch attended *Pflichschulen,* found employment as a porter in the student home *Academia* and prior to joining the SS-VT in 1938, he had waited at the 'Hotel Sacher.' Making his way to Berlin-Brandenburg on first transport in 1938, Hirsch reported to the SS-*Totenkopf-Infantrie*-Rgt. *Brandenburg* and participated in the 1939 Polish campaign with this unit as a company clerk. At this time, Hirsch falsified travel documents in an attempt to make contact with a girlfriend in Swinemünde. Three days later the *Wehrmachtstreife* picked him up at the Berlin-Anhalterbahnhof and he spent the next three months detained in the Berlin-Schmagendorf *Gefängnis*.

Then arraigned before the courts martial of the SS- *und Polizei-Gericht* III, Berlin, the tribunal judged Hirsch guilty of undermining the war effort and punished him with a term of five years' *Zuchthaus*. The RSHA then applied for a *Schutzhaft* and Hirsch found himself taken to the KL Sachsenhausen where he remained for two months in 1940 (*Erziehungssturm*). Sent to Matzkau in late 1941, one of the earliest entries, Hirsch recollected that placed in barracks 1, he did not leave the *Häftlingslager* for two years. Aside from working in the sewers for a short period, he recalled that most of his day was taken up with exercise in all weather conditions. Suffering two years of what he described as his 'hard life', Hirsch was hospitalised in 1942 and then judged no longer fit for use in the Üblichendienst (usual service). After a year's detention, the commandant judged Hirsch no longer a flight risk and permitted him to work outside the Häftlingslager. Appointed to the post of clerk in 1942, Hirsch wore an armband and a guard no longer watched his every move.[300]

Despite suffering from asthma, Hirsch was one of 2,000 probationers sent to the SS-*Sonderregiment* in the autumn of 1944. Sent to Warsaw and then Slovakia, Hirsch was later hospitalised in Slatemoravze *bei* Preßburg to have his tonsils removed. Sent to the Austrian capital to recover, Hirsch deserted again, but was quickly apprehended by a military police patrol in Munich. The SS- *und Polizei-Gericht* I, Munich then initiated his prosecution and judging Hirsch guilty of desertion, the tribunal imposed a prison sentence on Hirsch and he found himself incarcerated in the SS-*Straflager* Dachau and he remained here until the end of the conflict. Post war, Hirsch claimed that the time he spent in wartime jail prevented him from returning to normal civilian life. Turning to a life of crime, Hirsch spent six months in jail. At the time of making this statement, he had been jailed by the *Landgericht* Dornbirn on 24 February 1966 as a consequence of failing to pay his hotel bill in Dornbirn. Judged guilty, the court punished Hirsch with a fourteen days' arrest. Marrying in August 1966, Hirsch claimed his new wife had enabled him to return to a normal life.[301]

Appointed a clerk in the *Schreibstube*, here, Hirsch claimed that he had access to convicts' personnel files and his knowledge of the inmate's blue-bound disciplinary files formed the basis for his accusations against Baumgärtner and Dr Beelitz. These files contained all the inmates' punishments and a description of their crime and Hirsch alleged that a red 'T' was placed beside the names of those sentenced to capital punishment. Warming to his theme, Hirsch then claimed to have established from these documents that 4,000 inmates were detained in Matzkau by 1943 and by October 1944, the prison population had expanded by an additional 1,000 convicts (Baumgärtner would dispute this number). Claiming that 1,000 to 2,000 convicts transferred to the *Sonderkommando* or 'SK', Hirsch assured the investigator that these former inmates were involved in the secret shooting of Jews and lifted minefields. Fighting as *Sturmkommando* and *Sprengbrigaden*, Hirsch revealed that little was known of their fate, but he claimed that some had been sent to the *Fallschirmjägerabteilung* where they had a little chance of survival.[301]

Casting his mind back to his incarceration, Hirsch claimed that inmates were routinely struck and kicked by the Berliner *blockführer*, *Uscha.* Fritz Jankovski and he recalled that an inmate had his leg broken by a guard's rifle butt. Aware of rumours that a whipping block had been in use by prison staff, Hirsch had to concede that he not seen this instrument of torture and never witnessed anyone beaten in this fashion. He then attempted to convince the investigator that hanging tortures had been inflicted on inmates (hung by the arms). Asked to name guards, or prison command staff, Hirsch was unable to recall any, but stated with assurance that the guards had been sent to Matzkau for disciplinary reasons and were hard on convicts to earn their rehabilitation. Hirsch then claimed that the commandant's daughter rode her horse in the prison environs and named Jung as a potential witness.

During his time in Matzkau, Hirsch estimated that some 300 or 400 offenders had been executed in Matzkau; around four to five per week. Shot in the morning hours at the firing range, Hirsch stated that the condemned were escorted to the place of execution by two guards. An SS officer then announced the judgment and the sentence was carried out by guards with rifles. Recalling that an SS doctor was present and a pistol used for a *coup de grace*, pressed further, Hirsch recalled only two names of the 300 to 400 condemned that he had claimed were executed. Asked why he remembered that so few of the four or five men executed per week, Hirsch unsatisfactorily explained that reading, 'blue files' he had only counted the Red 'T's' against 70 to 80 names.[302]

Interviewing another former Matzkau convict on 20 September 1969, he too would allege that the Matzkau prison guards had brutalised their charges. Born in Vienna on 1 September 1915, Robert Jung left school and found employment as a cook, waiter and *Fleischhauer* before serving in the Austrian Army between 1934 and 1937. Joining the *Polizei*, Jung deployed at the *Kaserne* Berlin-Wrangel in 1938 and then mustered with the *Polizei-Hunderschaft* 86 (led by *Ustuf.* Anton Galla). During this deployment, Jung claimed to have been a *Sanitätsoberwachmeister* during the Polish campaign and witnessed the shootings of Jews and Poles. Stationed at Kattowitz, Tschenstockau, Hindenburg, Aussig and Auschwitz, Jung was accused of stealing camera equipment in Breslau during 1940 and found himself placed under six weeks' house arrest. A search revealed these stolen items in his office and Jung was then arraigned before the courts martial of the SS- *und Polizei-Gericht* XIV, Breslau.

Despite protesting his innocence, the court judged Jung guilty of comrade theft, ordered his expulsion from the *Polizei*, denied him his civil rights and declared him unworthy to bear arms. The sentence confirmed, Jung reported to the SS-*Straflager* Dachau to serve his penalty. Transferred to Matzkau in the autumn of 1941, he was allocated to barracks Nr. 3 and recalled that this building held 180 to 200 convicts and around 1,000 convicts were detained in the *Häftlingslager* at that time. His room, *Stube* II—which its inmates were expected to kept clean always—held ten to twelve convicts on double beds, with three men in double beds. His barracks had a washroom in which seven to eight inmates could wash at any given time and between the beds was a table. Deployed for three–four months in the *Lagerrevier* and the *Lagerlazarett*, Jung was unable to recollect the name of the supervising doctor, but recalled that he hailed from northern Germany and possessing the rank of a *Hstuf.* he was blond haired, 180 cm tall and used faultless High German. Returning to the SS-*Straflager* Dachau in the summer of 1943, Jung recollected that conditions there were no better than that found at Matzkau. Claiming to have then been sent to the KL Neuengamme as a political camp prisoner, Jung was 'liberated' by the British Army in May 1945 and then hospitalised at Bad Oldeslohe. Later, repatriated to Munich and then to Vienna, Jung returned to the *Polizei* service, but was discharged in 1951 when it became known he had served a prison sentence for theft. Jung was then employed as a chauffeur and later married.[303]

Speaking in 1969, Robert Jung contended that during his seventeen months' tenure in Matzkau he had witnessed many convicts reporting to the clinic with injuries caused by the guards. These ranged from feet injuries that had been caused by marching and wounds from torture. Claiming that convicts were raised by their arms for four hours at a time as a punishment, Jung was convinced that one particular inmate was hospitalised for ten weeks after this torture. Maintaining that he had personally witnessed six executions, Jung recalled that a deserter and traitor were tied to a stake with their hands behind their backs and a blindfold tied around their heads. Jung recalled correctly that the commandant was named Baumgärtner.[304]

The witness statements and police reports placed before him in 1971, *Herr* Weiß of the *Oberstaatsanwalt bei dem Landgericht* Munich II finally determined whether a decision should be made to indict Dr Fritz Ernst Beelitz, Rudolf Heiß, Edmund Baumgärtner and N. Schulz for unlawful murder (he accepted that Erich Laimgruber had died in 1944).[305]

In his summation, the state prosecutor observed that Jung had been unable to substantiate Hühn's allegation that several detainees had died as a result of punishment drill and considering Radermacher's allegations against Dr Beelitz, *Herr* Weiß rejected his evidence on the grounds of his prosecution for perjury. Although the witness Hirsch had testified that inmates were tortured, beaten and kicked by members of the guards, *Herr* Weiß recognised that he had been unable to specify whether detainees died as a result of this ill-treatment and had failed to identify a suspect.[306]

Herr Weiß refused to infer from Rudolf Heiß's statement about Schulz's strictness that this was evidence that he had committed murder. Observing that many convicts were employed in so-called outdoor commands and were therefore taken outside the camp to work in agriculture and in factories, *Herr* Weiß concluded that a constant connection to the outside world existed between the prison the community and rejected that murders had taken place in Matzkau as described by Hühn on the grounds that there was no obstruction to prevent the inmates from informing the population that murders were occurring in the camp. From all the witnesses heard, which included former felons and members of the guard contingent, *Herr* Weiß observed that none had supported Hühn's accusations and no other former Matzkau inmates who had regularly participated in 'drill' had reported witnessing convicts trampling to death those unable to walk (*Herr* Weiß was convinced that detainees commonly collapsed from exhaustion and accepted that those too sick and no longer able to walk were taken and stayed at the clinic). *Herr* Weiß then rejected that the caning incident involving Baumgärtner's daughter, as describes by Hühn, had occurred and accepted that it was forbidden for guards to mistreat prisoners. At this point, the state prosecutor observed that witnesses had described Hühn's accusations as 'untrue' or even 'lies' and when questioned, none had been unable to imagine how he had come to make such statements.[307]

Observing that several witnesses had confirmed that the execution of former SS and *Polizei* members had occurred in the camp, *Herr* Weiß expressed his certainty that no evidence existed to suggest that these executions had been carried out without prior court judgment and accepted Müller's assertion that Baumgärtner and Dr Beelitz were bound to the procedures of the SS jurisdiction. Finding no evidence that neither former commandant had enforced summary executions, or falsified death certificates in Matzkau, *Herr* Weiß observed the paucity of witnesses who were willing to confirm Hühn's allegations and noted that none, including former convicts who had no interest to help former members of the camp administration, had expressed any awareness that the illegal murder of individual convicts had taken place. The prosecutor observed that witnesses' expressed quite the opposite viewpoint and stated that both Dr Beelitz and Heiß had reportedly acted 'correctly' and were 'strict but orderly.' *Herr* Weiß also rejected Hühn's allegations of neck shootings, killings in a water barrel and ordered suicides.[310]

To determine his accuracy as a witness, *Herr* Weiß then had to consider the impact of the medical evidence which had been gathered by the State Health Department in Freiburg for Hühn. Diagnosing that he suffered from a severe psychoneurosis and psychosis, Hühn's physicians had concluded that his cross-psychopathic behavior had resulted in him seeking his own death which had resulted in repeated admissions to a psychiatric hospital. When interviewed, it was noted that Hühn had broken down in tears several times and became very excited. Therefore, it was the conclusion of his physician that his patient was unfit for cross examination, especially concerning the parts of the interrogation related to Nazi crimes. As a consequence of this decision, his doctors determined that Hühn was unable to support his own statements during cross-examination or face questioning about the inconsistences in his evidence.

Expressing no reservations about Hühn's credibility, Hühn's physician expressed his opinion that his police statements were unreliable. Agreeing that there existed evidence of psychopathic behavior in Hühn, *Herr* Weiß noted that Dr Beelitz's accuser had described himself as a 'physically and broken man' and on one occasion had declared that his interviewer was a DDR spy. In addition, Hühn announced that he had been 'persecuted like the Jews during the Nazi era'. Though observing that Hühn's statements were rich in detail, *Herr* Weiß believed that he possessed a fundamentally damaged credibility and doubting the veracity of Hühn as a witness and having no faith that his statements constituted court's evidence.

Concluding his assessment, the state prosecutor noted that documents from the defendants' *Spruchkammer* cases, and other agreements and documents from the Nazi period had failed to reveal any encumbrances on yet actionable offences and therefore, he concluded that there existed insufficient cause for public prosecution. Since the oncoming investigations had found no evidence for actionable offences and no further evidence was likely to become available, *Herr* Weiß took the decision to halt the courts process in accordance with paragraph §170, section 2 of the StOP (decision on an indictment) on 11 January 1971 and the accused were informed of his decision.[311]

3.14 SS-*Zweiglager Debica*

From its construction the SS-*Truppenübungsplatz* Debica in occupied Poland had a cell block within which delinquent troops were detained for short detention punishments. Its cells also held those awaiting trial at the SS- *und Polizei-Gericht* VI, Krakau. The court contacted the Debica headquarters when defendants were to report for trial.[312]

In the autumn of 1941 the Debica staff organized the '*Strafkolonne*' (punishment column) for those trainees who had been placed on probation for disciplinary offences. It is believed they were housed in the *Zwangsarbeitslager*.[313]

In the summer of 1942 the SS leaders concerns about the lack of meaningful work for the Danzig-Matzkau inmates resulted in a proposal to send 500 convicts to Debica where they would be put to work constructing a branch prison, an agricultural farm, guard barracks and convict accommodation. It was proposed that the prison leader would provide reports for those inmates who had earned probation. In November 1942 the first transport of 200 Matzkau inmates to Debica was arranged for 1 March 1943.[314]

Committing an act of comrade theft on his birthday in Debica on 11 October 1942, *Schütze* Franz Schmitt then faced investigation at the hands of the SS- *und Polizei-Gericht* VI, Krakau (case Nr. St. L. IV. 407/1942). Arrested at Kergyeliget, Hungary on 11 November 1942, Schmidt found himself held in detention until his trial.[315]

The Debica headquarters contacted the Krakau tribunal on 15 December 1942 to inform them that the command of their *Gefängnis* had been handed to *Ustuf.* Dr Großnigg.[316]

The Matzkau commandant, *Stubaf.* Dr Ernst, travelled by train to Debica on 14 January 1943 to meet with the troop training camp commander to discuss the construction of the new prison. That same day the Debica *Gefängnis* agreed to accept *Schutzmannschaft* convicts and the Debica *Gerichtsoffizier* requested interpreters were supplied for them.[317]

When constructed, the Debica/Heidelager prison almost certainly held parolees of the *Arbeitsabteilung der Waffen*-SS *Ersatz-Bataillon*. The inmates of the SS-*Zweiglager* Debica/Heidelager was evacuated to Danzig-Matzkau in September 1944 the.[318]

3.15 SS-*Aussenstelle Kolberg, Pomerania*

According to two sources the *Strafvollzugslager der* SS *und Polizei* Danzig-Matzkau *Aussenstelle* Kolberg was constructed near the coastal town of Kolberg, Pomerania (*Wehrkries* II). Here inmates worked on an agricultural projects.[319]

3.16 *Polizeigefängnis -und Arbeitserziehungslager Kurtenhof*

In the autumn of 1942 the SS leader ordered court convicted *Schutzmannschaft* to be detained separately from SS and *Polizei* convicts and as a consequence of this decision the *HA* SS-*Gericht* and SS-*Richter beim* RF-SS were tasked with undertaking negotiations with the RSHA for the construction of a segregated prison for this category of offender. Identifying the *Polizei-Gefängnis-und Arbeitserziehungslager* (police prison and work education camp) at Kurtenhof (Salaspils) as a possible location for the prison, the WVHA received orders in November 1942 to provide funds and building materials for the new institution.[320]

This forced labour camp was situated close to the Salaspils railway station, along the main road between Riga and Dünaburg some 20 km from Riga.[321]

The construction of the prison had been entrusted to the HSSPF *Ostland-und Rußland Nord* and a month after issuing his command the head of the SS was demanding to know what type of work would be available for the Salaspils convicts. Over the winter of 1942/43 the RSHA informed the *HA* SS-*Gericht* that the *Polizei-Gefängnis-und Arbeitserziehungslager* Kurtenhof operated under the command of the Sipo-*und* SD Latvia, it held Latvian political prisoners, Russians and the work shy. Pointedly, the RSHA did not recommend using the camp for this purpose and warned the *HA* SS-*Gericht* that if they continued with this plan, then they would require Estonian and Lithuanian interpreters. The decision was taken by Burmeister's *Amt* III on 21 January 1943 to proceed with the opening of a prison at Kurtenhof and explained that the *Polizeigefängnis -und Arbeitserziehungslager* would consist of two separate institutions; the first barrack held those serving long sentences and the second barrack detained those who had indeterminate sentences and could work during their punishment. The HSSPF *Ostland- und Rußland Nord* was made responsible for the administration of the new institution.[322]

Writing to the *HA* SS-*Gericht* on 18 February 1943, the SS-*Richter beim* RF-SS reminded them that it was a 'political necessity' that this new prison offered 'guaranteed impeccable standards of punishment.'[323]

On 29 March 1943 the *Amtschef des HA* SS-*Gericht Amt* III (Burmeister) supplied the RSHA with a draft proposal for a three parts punishment grading for *Schutzmannschaft* who had been punished by the SS and *Polizei* jurisdiction and would serve their sentences in Kurtenhof:

Group C, (light group) compares to grade I for the concentration camps.
Group B, (middle group) compares to grade II for the concentration camps.
Group A (Heavy group) compares to grade III for the concentration camps.[324]

The construction of the *Polizeigefängnis-und Arbeitserziehungslager* Kurtenhof was supervised by *Stubaf.* Dr Martin Lange and interpreters were selected from *Schutzmannschaft* personnel. Completed in June/July 1943, the Baltic States and the USSR convicts were guarded by men from a Latvian *Wachkompanie* and work was found for them in a lime quarry, a cement factory, a straw shoe making business and some were engaged in lumberjacking.[325]

From mid-1943 there were around 100 *Schutzmannschaft* inmates detained in Kurtendorf at any given time and only 87 offences committed by *Schutzmannschaften* had been registered during the first quarter of 1943.[326]

A deadly fate awaited the family members of eastern volunteers fighting alongside the German army who were caught aided the Red Army. In September 1943 the *Reichsführer* ordered eastern people found aiding the 'Bolsheviks' to be sent to a concentration camp for the duration of the war. This included the families of eastern volunteers fighting alongside the German army and those engaged in labour tasks at the front or in the occupied regions. The SS-*Richter beim* RF-SS forwarded a draft of this order to the RSHA and informed them that its implementation was the responsibility of the HSSPF. If these actions were carried out, the SS-*Richter beim* RF-SS asked that the RSHA was notified immediately. If judged impossible to carry out this order, then the HSSPF and RSHA were ordered to provide the SS leader with a detailed explanation of the circumstances and he would then act as the deciding power in the decision making process.[327]

On 17 November 1944 the *HA SS-Gericht Amt* IIIb reported that the entry conditions for the carrying out of court punishments against Baltic people in the *Arbeitsziehungslagers* Kurtendorf of the KL Stutthof would appear in the next *Anordnungsblatt* for 1943 (section 235).[328]

The Red Army threatening to overrun Salispils in the summer of 1944 a handful of *Schutzmannschaft* inmates were selected for front line service in the Bataillon z.b.V. and these parolees fought near Bolderaa and Riga.[329] Given the precarious situation in the Baltic States in late 1944, this prison was evacuated in September the same year and the remaining inmates were evacuated to Danzig-Matzkau, where they were segregated in their own barrack, separate from the other inmates.[330] According to one source a handful of the *Schutzmannschaft* convicts held in Matzkau were selected for front service in the SS-*Sonderbrigade Dirlewanger* at the end of the war.[331]

Former *Ustuf.* Kurt Grawe, a veteran of the 19th *Waffen-Grenadier*-Division *der* SS (Lett. Nr. 2) field court, surrendered to the Red Army in Latvia on 14 May 1945 and he and 100 comrades then found themselves held in segregated two barracks inside the Salaspils camp between September 1945 and March 1946.[332]

3.24 The Stutthof "*German*" camp3.17 SS-*Strafgefanggenenlager Vught*

Located within the KL Vught in Holland was a SS-*Strafgefanggenenlager* (prisoner punishment camp). This prison held convicts of the SS, *Polizei* and Dutch SS-*Frontarbeiter* volunteers. Evacuated in August 1944, the entire inmate population in Vught then transferred in their entirety to Danzig-Matzkau.[333]

4

SS-*Richter* and SS-*Beurkundungsführer*

Those tasked with running the SS *und Polizei* prison camps were selected from the ranks of the SS-*Richter* (judges) and the *Beurkundungsführer* (certification officers). Established in the city of Munich on 1 June 1939 as the central ministerial authority for the entire jurisdiction, the *HA* SS-*Gericht* was tasked with implementing the administration of justice for the *Waffen*-SS and *Polizei* units in special deployment.[1]

The first task facing this judiciary was the recruitment of qualified office staff. On 1 June 1939 almost, but not the entire staff of the prewar SS.-*Gericht* had transferred from the *Allgemeine*-SS to the *HA* SS-*Gericht*, but additional jurists were required and each of these prospective judges was required to have studied jurisprudence at university, possess his RechtswissenschaftenDas universitäre Studium der Rechtswissenschaften wird heute mit einer „Ersten juristischen Prüfung" abgeschlossen.*Referendarexamen* and if possible have completed his practical training and passed his *Assessorexamen* (a jurisprudence doctorate was welcome, but not essential). [2] In addition, the SS courts service required them to have been *Die Pflichtfachprüfung besteht je nach Bundesland aus 5 bis 7 Aufsichtsarbeiten, in allen drei Rechtsgebieten, Zivilrecht* , Öffentliches Recht *und Strafrecht des deutschen Rechts , die grundsätzlich zusammenhängend innerhalb von 2 Wochen direkt nacheinander geschrieben werden.Für Pflichtfachprüfung gibt es in allen Bundesländern zwei reguläre Versuche.*was welcome, but nemployed as a jurist in private practice, the state sector, or a legal administration. SS Judges were deployed in positions of command within the SS and *Polizei* prison camps and it was their task to ensure that the punishment of miscreants was carried out in accordance with the legal statutes, and to compose inmate fitness reports.

To assist the newly recruited judges with their task and perform the duties usually associated with court clerks and registrars, the *HA* SS-*Gericht* required certification non-commissioned officers and officers. Typically, these men had, in their civilian life, worked in accountant's offices, in office management, or possessed experience as clerks or salesmen. Maintaining the court's archive, preparing case files and handling the paperwork generated by the legal process, the certification officers assisted investigative judges in interviewing witnesses. The need for these specialists had long been anticipated for the proposed judiciary and applicants were sought during late 1937. Secret *Beurkundungsführer* candidate training courses were arranged in Munich from 2 November 1937 to 19 January

1938 and final examinations are known to have taken place in the Bavarian capital on the 18th and 27 February and 9 March 1939 and also took place in early 1942 and during January 1943.

Long-serving soldiers of the SS-VT were selected to attend a *Beurkundungsführer* candidate training course at the SS-*Junkerschule* Bad Tölz during the whole of March 1938 and again between 1 and 28 August the same year. Curiously, the vast majority of those selected for this training course were selected from the SS-*Standarte Deutschland* and other units stationed in Bavaria. Specialist training was also made available for prospective *Beurkundungsführer*. The *Amt* and *Landgericht* Berlin trained certification officer candidates from 31 March 1939 and the *public* prosecutor's office of the *Landgericht* and *Justizplatz* in Munich accepted candidates for three months practical training before the final certification officer examination was undertaken in Bad Tölz in November 1938.[3]

Those passing this examination the prospective *Beurkundungsführer* returned to their units to wait for the command to transfer to the *HA* SS-*Gericht* in August 1939, or at a later date. Attending the first *Beurkundungsführer* training course were at least five non-commissioned officers from the *Deutschland* who went on to become prison staff and occupy senior positions within the prison service.[4]

4.1 Prison Staff Biographies

The following biographies have been composed primarily from sources which include SSO files, German state court records and Bletchley intercepts. The *HA* SS-*Gericht* noted that 105 certification officers were assigned to the prison service on 15 February 1945.[5]

Name: Erich 'Rudolf/Adolf' **Albert**
Last Rank: SS-*Hauptsturmführer*.
Born: 9.6.1904 in Innsbruck.
NSDAP-Nr.: 614.074 (joined 10.11.1931).
SS-Nr.: 19.626 (joined 7.1931).
Prewar Assignments:
Freikorps Oberland 11.1926–10.1931.
2./I./37. SS-*Standarte* (Linz) on 7.1931.
Österreich Legion 11.7.1933.
SS-*Hilfwerk* Dachau 1.11.1933–1.1.1934.
Politische Bereitschaften 9.1934.
Zugführer II./SS-*Standarte Deutschland* in 1938.
K.K. II./*Deutschland* in 1938.
2./SS-*Standarte Der Führer* in 1938.
Beurkundungsführer training course SS-*Junkerschule* Bad Tölz in 3.1938.
SS-VT *Hauptamt* SS-*Gericht* 15.8.1939–29.4.1945.

Wartime Assignments:
SS- *und Polizei-Gericht* I, Munich in 9.1939.
Leiter des Straflager der SS *und Polizei* Dachau on 1.5.1940.
Nr. 1 *Lagerführer des Strafvollzugslager der SS und Polizei* Matzkau on 20.7.1941.
Führer des Zweiglager Ludwigsfelde on 1.3.1943.
Leiter des Straflager der SS *und Polizei* Dachau by 1.2.1944.

Promotions:

Nov.1938	SS-*Hauptscharführer der* SS-VT.
Nov.1938	SS-*Beurkundungsführeranwärter.*
15.8.1939	SS-*Untersturmführer der Waffen*-SS (*Aktiv*).
1.9.1940	SS-*Obersturmführer der Waffen*-SS (*Aktiv*).
30.1.1943	SS-*Hauptsturmführer der Waffen*-SS (*Aktiv*).

Decorations & Awards:

0.0.19__	*Ehrenwinkel für alte Kämpfer.*
0.0.19__	SS-*Zivilabzeichen* (12.326).
0.0.19__	SA-*Sportsabzeichen in Bronze.*
0.0.19__	*Deutsches Reichssportabzeichen in Bronze.*
0.0.19__	*Deutsches Reichssportabzeichen in Silber.*
0.0.19__	*Kriegsverdienstkreuz II. Klasse mit Schwertern.*
0.0.19__	*Die Medaille zur Erinnerung an den* 1. Oktober 1938 (Sudetenland).

Notes: His father, a labourer, died during the Great War. Attending *Volksschule* in Innsbruck between 1910 and 1915, Albert studied at *Realschule* for four classes and then at the College for Electrical and Mechanical Engineering for a further four years. As a child, Albert caught measles and injured and misaligned his left eye in 1933, which left him visually impaired. Qualifying as an electronics engineer, Albert found employment in his field and worked in Bavaria during the 1920s. Returning to Austria in 1931, Albert was employed in an Innsbruck factory until he fled across the border to Germany in the summer of 1934. Deprived of his citizenship, Albert joined the Schleißheim relief organisation at the SA-*Lager* Kloster-Lechfeld in July 1934 and was granted German citizenship in the wake of the party day in September the same year. Albert married his fiancée Irmi T., (b. 5.7.1912 in Grödig/Salzburg) on 19 September 1934 and had three children up to the point when records ceased in May 1945 and lived in Munich, Prittelbach *bei* Dachau and Salzburg. Albert participated in the invasion of the Sudetenland and Czechoslovakia with the automotive section of the SS-*Infanterie-Ersatz-Bataillon Der Führer* in 1938 and passing his final exam in Munich in November 1938, Albert was appointed a certification non-commissioned officer candidate and transferred to the *HA* SS-*Gericht* with officer rank on 15 August 1939.

Appointed the clerk at the Munich tribunal, Albert experienced an attack of angina in December 1939 that left him incapacitated for eight days. Despite his ill-health, he accepted leadership of the SS-*Straflager* Dachau in May 1940 and a former inmate named Johann Ott recollected that Albert was loud and harsh. Undergoing a medical examination to search for evidence of cardiovascular disease on 8 June the same year, Albert revealed during this consultation that he had experienced a similar attack in the spring of 1938 and on three or four occasions had encountered a feeling of constriction in the chest, a feeling which convinced him that his heart had briefly stopped. A serious angina attack in 1938 left him incapacitated for two or three days and he suffered a further two mild attacks. Examining Albert, the staff physician observed that he was in general good health, had some tooth fillings and normal reflexes, but in recent years he had developed a 'strong nervousness' and smoked between fifteen and twenty cigarettes a day. In response to his findings, the physician prescribed Albert a glycerin medication and recommended that he limited his nicotine consumption. Attending another medical examination three months' later, this diagnosis almost certainly precluded him from undertaking any further frontline duties with the troops.

Receiving orders to transfer to the SS-FHA in March 1944, the posting was finally rescinded on 11 April. Their family home in Munich destroyed during an Allied air attack in the summer of 1944, Albert's family moved to Anif *bei* Salzburg and his banking arrangements switched from Teltow to Salzburg on 1.4.1944. Remaining the leader of the *Straflager* Dachau until 27 April 1945, Albert abandoned his post as US troops stood poised to capture the camp. Fleeing eastwards, he was arrested after the cessation of hostilities in Salzburg by Harry B. Fleetwood of the 7th Army CIC at 13.00 p.m. on 19 May 1945 (on the grounds of the rank of *Hstuf.* in accordance with SHAEF directive, dated 15.4.1945). A search of his person produced his wallet with photographs, cash amounting to 176 *Reichsmark* and his pay book. Interned immediately, the American authorities initially confused Albert with another officer who was wanted for membership of the SS-*Jagdverbände* (Anton Albert). Under questioning, Albert revealed his role in the SS jurisdiction and claimed to have been employed as an investigative officer. The CIC produced reports for Albert on 19 and 27 May 1945 and again for the G2 on 27 July the same year and the 307th CIC detachment reported Albert's change of status on 12 August 1947 and revealed that he was detained with the 7th Army at that time. Not wanted by the United States, or other nations as a war criminal, Albert was cleared for internment in 1946. Released from the Dachau Hospital on 17 December the same year, Albert then found himself detained in the Dachau War Crimes Cage (prisoner of war enclosure 29) and remained here until at least 27 December the same year. A search of both the *Staatsarchiv* Munich and the Oberösterreichischen *Landesarchiv* has yet to reveal any evidence that Albert underwent a de-nazification process in either Bavaria or Austria.[6]

Name: Fritz Baumeister.
Last Rank: SS-*Obersturmführer.*
Born: 15.12.1913 in Erlangen.
NSDAP-Nr.: 4.262.071 (joined 1.3.1937).
SS-Nr.: 124.579 (joined 11.1933).

Prewar Assignments:
3. / II. / 3 SS-*Standarte* (Nuremberg) 11.1933.
Sturm 12. / 3 SS-*Standarte* on 6.5.1934.
SS-VT from 1.1.1935.
13. / SS-*Standarte* 1 (Munich) from 2.1.1935.
Nachrichtenzug / III. / SS-*Standarte Deutschland* in 8.1936.
SS-*Standarte Deutschland* (clerk) in 1938.
8. / SS-*Standarte Deutschland* 1.2.–25.10.1939.

Wartime Assignments:
SS-*Infanterie*-Rgt. *Deutschland* from 25.10.1939.
SS-*Totenkopf-Infantrie*-Rgt. 9 (Danzig) in 1939.
SS-VT *Hauptamt* SS-*Gericht* in 5.1940.
SS-Division *Wiking* field court 1940–22.9.1941.
Hauptamt SS-*Gericht Amt* III from 22.9.1941.
SS-*Straflager* Dachau from 22.9.1941.
SS-FHA *Amt* IIa from 15.3.1944.
SS-*Panzergrenadier-Ersatz-Bataillon* 18 (Breslau) from 16.3.1944.
Zugführer-Lehrgang Kienschlag SS-*Panzergrenadierschule* 26.3.–17.6.1944.
20th *Waffen-Grenadier*-Division *der* SS (Est. Nr. 1) 20.6.1944–19.2.1945.

Promotions:

1.11.1933	SS-*Anwärter*.
10.6.1934	SS-*Mann der Allgemeine*-SS.
20.4.1935	SS-*Mann der* SS-VT.
9.11.1935	SS-*Unterscharführer der* SS-VT.
Aug.1936	SS-*Sturmann der* SS-VT.
1.12.1937	SS-*Rottenführer der* SS-VT.
0.0.1938	SS-*Oberscharführer der* SS-VT.
9.11.1942	SS-*Untersturmführer der Reserve*.
1.5.1943	SS-*Untersturmführer der Waffen*-SS (*Aktiv*).
30.1.1945	SS-*Obersturmführer der Waffen*-SS (*Aktiv*).

Decorations & Awards:

0.0.19__	SA-*Sportsabzeichen in Bronze*.
0.0.19__	*Dienstauszeichnung der* SS *Stufe* 4.
0.0.19__	*Die Medaille zur Erinnerung an den 13. März* 1938 (Austria).
0.0.1939	*Kriegsverdienstkreuz II. Klasse mit Schwertern*.

Notes: His father, a joiner, died on the Flanders front on 1 September 1914. As a consequence of his loss, Baumeister's early years were marked by hardship, (his mother, a midwife, was often absent from home). Attending the Erlangen *Volkshauptschule* for eight classes between 1920 and 1928, Baumeister then undertook two years vocational training at the town technical works from 1932 until passing his final examinations on 31 December 1934. Three and a half years study behind him, Baumeister was then employed as a fully qualified gas and water technician. A member of the *Touristen-Verein, Die Naturallfründe* between 1928 and 1929 and again until dissolved in 1933, Baumeister found employment with the DAF in 1934. Accepted into the SS-VT in January 1935, he commenced his military training the following day. Falling from an ammunition limber and bruising his body during a field service exercise in 1935, Baumeister was accommodated at the SS-*Kaserne* Munich-Freimann from 9 November 1935. On 15 October 1936 *Ostuf.* Groß of the *Deutschland* first battalion voiced his concerns that discrepancies existed in Baumeister's ancestry:

> Against the numbers 38 and 39 in the attached family tree of the SS man Fritz Baumeister of the 13 / SS-*Standarte Deutschland* are written the names: Konrad Moses Fuss and Elisabetha Sarah Wasserman. There is no mention of these names in the purely evangelical Erlangen, I have also found it strange that we have been unable to find any record of their births in the archives of the Erlanger evangelical church. I would like to bring to your attention, that this entry perhaps may involve people of Jewish descent.

The matter concluded to the satisfaction of the RuSHA, Baumeister became a clerk in the *Deutschland* in 1938 and married his fiancée Emilie N., (b. 3.8.1920 in Munich) on 7 November 1939. The couple had one child and lived in Erlangen until 1934, in Munich from January 1935. Presipitously, Baumeister's wife and daughter were in the process of moving to his parents home at Erlangen on 22 April 1944 when their Munich home was totally destroyed by aftershocks on 31 July (hiding in an air-raid shelter, *Frau* Baumeister was buried alive and suffered serious head and spinal injuries that required medical treatment). From Danzig, Baumeister applied successfully to transfer to the *HA* SS-*Gericht* in early 1940 and reported for duty as an certification non-commisioned officer in the spring of 1940. His training in Munich complete, Baumeister was posted to the *Wiking* field court and remained in this post until transferred to the SS-*Straflager* Dachau in September 1941. Transferred to the SS-FHA in March 1944, Baumeister reported to a frontline division in June 1944 and became a battalion adjutant and then regimental ordnance officer. Fighting in Estonia and then Silesia, a Red Army artillery barrage near Lausitz on 19 February 1945 resulted in Baumeister's serious wounding (he received shrapnel injuries to his neck, a right chest injury, a fracture of the right hip, a bullet wound in right thigh, received two splinters below the left knee and wounds in his left buttock). Taken to the *Reserve-Lazarett* Fürstenwalde, he was then admitted to hospitals at Kirchhain in Lausitz and Schwandorf and ended the war in the *Reserve-Lazarett* Erlangen and the *Fürsorge und Vers. Kommando der Waffen*-SS Nuremberg was notified of his injuries.

Surrendering to US Army forces in Erlangen in May 1945, the same month Baumeister, as a prisoner of war, was interned in the Hersbruck civilian camp and recovered from his injuries in the Förrenbach clinic in November the same year. Taken to barracks 5 in the CIC Nuremberg-Langwasser in February 1946, Baumeister was declared a civilian internee on 8 June the same year. In late 1946 he supplied the court with eight character statements; three had been composed by former comrades and the remainder from people who knew him from his youth:

Haralt Erdmannsdorffer Nuremberg-Langwasser, dated 1.10.1946

As a consequence of my activities as a *Beurkundungsführer* in the SS and *Polizei* jurisdiction I have known *Herr* Fritz Baumeister, born 15.12.1913, since the year 1940.

A *Reichsführer*-SS command in the autumn of 1943 resulted in all *Beurkundungsführer*, who were formerly non-commissioned officers of the SS-VT, to be found a further use with the troops in the wake of their retirement from their professional career. In March 1944 I witnessed the seconding of former *Ustuf.* Fritz Baumeister from the *HA* SS-*Gericht* to a *Standartenoberjunker* training course to prepare for combat duty. Passing the course Baumeister was then assigned to a training company at the Kienschlag troop training ground. No political training took place here. Completing the course, Baumeister's transfer to the troops at the front line took place in July 1944. I have never found Baumeister adopting a spiteful attitude towards foreigners. I only know Baumeister as a good man and comrade.

An early member of the *HA* SS-*Gericht*, former *Hstuf.* Harald Hermanndorfer was assigned to the *Amt* III in late 1941 and early 1942. Baumeister's next referee had served alongside him in Dachau:

Otto Langer Nuremberg-Langwasser, dated 6.10.1946

Herr Fritz Baumeister is known to me personally as a consequence of my former membership of the *HA* SS-*Gericht* in Munich. Likewise, Baumeister was a member of the *HA* SS-*Gericht* during the period from 1 June 1940 to March 1944 and was in use there as a typist, *Beurkundungsführer* and after an examination in March 1942 as a *Beurkundungsunterführer*. His activities were of a purely office function and Baumeister, due to his subordination to the judicial staff, did not take an independent viewpoint in any decisions. It is not known to me that Baumeister has committed any violations against humanity.

Baumeister would reciprocate Langer's reference at his tribunal. Throughout the spring of 1947 Baumeister and his wife submitted defence statements and appeals for clemency to the Nuremberg-Langwasser camp *Spruchkammer*. Notably, Baumeiuster avoided all reference to his service in *Waffen*-SS prisons. Here, in his own words, Baumeister acknowledges the circumstances under which he had become involvement with the regime. I caution the reader to remember the circumstances under which he was making this statement:

My entry into the *Waffen*-SS was carried out in good faith, because it was an elite troop and I intended to later join the police, or the customs service. After the conclusion of the Nuremberg and other process, I concluded that we had been deceived, cheated and abused by Hitler and the other rotten leaders. From the criminal dark side, I have returned and in spite of my membership of the SS and party I declare that I had unknowingly given my support to these [criminal] activities. As a *Beurkundungsführer* within the SS-*Gericht* I did not exercise any command activities.

The SS jurisdiction itself extended only to members of the SS and *Polizei* and it operated in the same way as the military jurisdiction. I had nothing to do with the pursuit of wrongful thinking. I have never ever abandoned, or given up my original founded and reasoned political stance.

As supportive material I have attached various testimonies of Nazi opponents, with whom I still frequent and I continued to visit them during my membership in the SS although I was well aware that they were out-spoken opponents of the Nazis. Various testimonies about my membership of individual SS units, an affidavit from me concerning my total bomb damage and the wounding of my wife along with certified copies of medical report and a medical certificate about the operation which took place on my wife in August 1946. I also enclose a testimony about my own infirmity.

Politically, I am today of the opinion that the past twelve years was probably the biggest fraud to which the German people had fallen victim to. Therefore, I have come to the conclusion that it is necessary for a democratic form of government to be constructed and founded in Germany, in order that a similar evil cannot befall our people again. I have deleted permanently the teachings of National Socialism from my level thoughts. In the more distant future I imagine, that I will at first, after my possible release from prison, to prevent the slimmest financial support for my family which has come about by the bomb damage, the injury of my wife, the evacuation of my family, hospitalization and the operation on my wife, etc.

I can today still not decide my future political activities, because I do not know, how much political activity I am permitted after the process.

Professionally, I hope again to labor into my learnt profession and to contribute as such to build a new Germany. Moreover, I am prepared, to ask for special service to enable the orderly rebuilding of the state.

The public prosecuter applied to the tribunal to indict Baumeister on 20 May 1947 and sought to classify him in the group II of the 'responsible'. Here, Baumeister refuted the prosecutor's grounds for his indictment on 25 May 1947:

[…] I take the following position:

1. To the accusation under part B / five of the Act annexed list I refer to my written defense and declare once again that I was accepted automatically in the NSDAP as a member of the *Waffen*-SS on 1 May 1937. Any intervention on my part was not required at that time, I was asked as a matter of fait accompli.

2. According to section 14 annex list B I of the Act, the prosecution quoted that the exercises that I have undertaken for the SA-*Wehrsportabzeichen* in 1935 and was received from my company. These exercises were scheduled as a normal service, and it was incumbent for us to perform this duty. As a result of this one day's military exercise we were granted the SA-*Wehrsportabzeichen* automatically.
3. Referring to the prosecution in accordance with part A (group E) class II paragraph 2 + 1 I refer to my written defense and the accompanying documents.

Furthermore, my prior entry to the *Allgemeine*-SS had been influenced by my nineteen years youth and immaturity in political things. I had and could not have the slightest idea, of what it was, and because of my youth and political ignorance I became even more strengthened in favor of National Socialism after the seizure of power. A majority of the *Reichstag* deputies from other parties also voted for the Enabling Act and in my supportive view of the NSDAP they thereby fully recognized them and their policies. Also a short time after their arrest, the return of political prisoners led me to believe that justice had conquered. Furthermore, the large-scale propaganda of the Nazi Party was not without influence on me and I was repeatedly approached by the then newly recruited Nazis in the company where I was employed to become a party member. In particular, I found myself proposed for the entry into the SS especially because of my height.

At that time I myself deferred to my many elders and experienced comrades in political matters. They had pivoted from their former political direction and reversed their opinion of Nazism. Unable to resist I declared my entry to the *Allgemeine*-SS in November 1933. I have not sought any other material benefits through this entry and did not acquire any.

Then my entry into the *Waffen*-SS took place on 2 January 1935 specifically in Munich. Reporting to this troop I was decidedly hopeful, that in this way and as quickly as possible, that I would complete my military service with the intention of later stepping over to serve in the police or the customs service. I saw service in one of these organizations as my life goal. My promotions in the *Waffen*-SS had not been determined by my restless affirmation to the objectives of the NSDAP in political and militaristic ways. In fact, a few times during political instruction I spoke against it and asked uncomfortable questions about the subject, which led to me being deliberately overlooked in appointments. Not promoted, those with shorter service time than myself then overtook me. My promotion to SS officer was not based on my purely political and militant attitude, but rather on my special education as a *Beurkundungsführer.*

Only on the orders of the former *Reichsführer*-SS did I achieved the rank of *Ostuf.* He announced, that all *Ustuf.* with more than seven and a half years total service time must be promoted to *Ostuf.* According to this command, I would have already have been promoted to *Ostuf.* in 1943. However, this had not happened since I was generally regarded as the black sheep and it was known that I had never completely adopted the Nazi ideology and stood mostly in opposition to its ideals. Only after a reasonable wait at this rank was this promotion then realised without my having gained any benefits therefrom, because as a result of the residual non-collapse of the Reich I no longer received a paycheck.

Therein my conviction to Nazism consisted only in their provisioning and I actually believed that the NSDAP would bring everything for the German people including work and bread. Despite the upturn in the years of peace until 1939. I did not believe in warfare and thought it impossible. I saw in this upturn only a job-creation program and the production of military equality with other nations. After achieving this goal, I firmly believed that other work would be found for the German people.

I was not a particular supporter of the war and the related military objectives. I knew only the hardships and worries of my mother after the death of my father, who had fallen in the year 1914. However, my conviction was dealt a significant dent with the beginning of the crisis in 1939, especially as my former comrades assured me repeatedly that it would come to war, and otherwise had left me in no doubt about their political views. Had I stood here now as a convinced National Socialist, how the *Herr* Public Prosecutor has stated, then I would have denounced *Mssrs* Schuster, Martho, Deutinger and Ochs etc. and probably also others too who had revealed to me their anti-Nazi statements before 1939 which would have led to their sentencing and jailing? But as demonstrated, I refrained from such denunciations and done the opposite. Actually after that time [1939] I presented myself as an SS member as a matter of course and bringing upon myself the risk of exposure and suspicion, by working together with opponents of Nazism, you cannot possibly pretend that I was convinced National Socialist. Also throughout my membership in the SS I never visited a meeting of the NSDAP and I was only occasionally prompted. I have only participated in Nazi-cultural environments when this was recognized as a service for my unit. So during my entire working life in the *Waffen*-SS I have never participated in a Nazi Party Day. Incidentally, I would like to emphasize as particularly remarkable, that even the public prosecutor had to concede in his statement that apart from the formal responsibility, there is no evidence and are no known disadvantages known about me.

Furthermore, I also refer you to the comments in my rebuttal letter from 16 May 1947 and the related accompanying documents. As is clear from the date of the advocates' letter, this claim has obviously been adopted at a time, when my defense letter had not been submitted.

Furthermore, I must again expressly point out that the exemption law does not affected or classify my wife, I am totally bomb damaged and my wife suffers today the consequences of the airstrike burial and serious wounding. From the presentation in my defense letter and these applicants' replies, it follows that I have otherwise only marginally supported Nazism and am neither militarist nor shown any signs of activism. Furthermore, I have demonstrated that I was not a beneficiary of the past system

I ask, therefore, that I be integrated into the group III of the less responsible, and I particularly on evidence that I belong in that group of SS members who were acquitted at the Nuremberg judgment.

In conclusion, I assure my unconditional readiness again and to provide all my strength for the reconstruction of Germany.

Classifying Baumeister in the group II of 'less responsible' on 4 June 1947 the tribunal also imposed a one-off fine of 700 *Reichsmark* and ordered him to pay ten *Reichsmark* per working day in case of non-recovery. The amount in dispute was settled at 3,500 *Reichsmark* and Baumeister was ordered to pay the costs of the procedure. His parole and discharge from internment was commanded on 26 August 1947 and carrying one day's food he returned to his family. Employed with the Erlangen city works as a gas and water installer on a new construction at the *Ost* Water Works from 4 September 1947, he had paid 780 *Reichsmark* of his fines when the tribunal estimated that he owed two per cent of the disputed fine of 3, 500 *Reichsmark*. Burdened by his fines, Baumeister applied to the court for clemency on the grounds that prominent Nazis and major beneficiaries of the past regime had been re-classified. He also asked the tribunal to consider his almost two and a half years of detention, his 50 per cent disablement, his willingness to work for the Erlanger waterworks Ost in spite of the lower pay offered by other companies (he earned 39 *Reichsmark* a week) and his participation in the 30 April 1948 elections. The Bavarian State Ministry for Special Affairs agreed to permit his remaining probation to be undertaken in the group IV of 'followers' on 4 January 1949 and ordered Baumeister to bear the 3,500 *Reichsmark* costs of the new proceeding. The Munich appeal court overturned Baumeister's judgment in November 1950 and writing to the *Amtsgericht* Erlangen on 27 February 1957, the city council revealed that Baumeister had applied to the official welfare office for prisoner of war compensation.[7]

Name: Edmund Baumgärtner.
Last Rank: SS-*Hauptsturmführer*.
Born: 8.8.1909 in Deutsch-Feistritz *bei* Graz.
NSDAP-Nr.: 139.490 (joined 2.11.1932).
4.687.394 (joined 7.1937).
SS-Nr.: 139.490 (joined 12.1932).
Prewar Assignments:
3. / II. / 38. SS-*Standarte* (Leoben/Bruck) in 12.1932.
II. / SS-*Standarte Deutschland* in 9.1934.
4. / SS-*Standarte Der Fuhrer* in 1938.
Beurkundungsführer-Lehrgang SS-*Junkerschule* Bad Tölz in the spring of 1938.
SS-VT *Hauptamt* SS-*Gericht* from 15.8.1939.
Wartime Assignments:
Led the office for the SS- *und Polizei-Gericht* IV, Danzig in 11.1939.
SS-*Rechtamt* from 1.9.1940.
SS-*Straflager des* SS *Polizei* Dachau from 1.2.1941.
Nr. 1 *Lagerführer* of the SS-*Straflager des* SS *Polizei* Dachau in 1941.

Leiter des SS-*Straflager des* SS *Polizei* Dachau from 20.7.1941.
Nr. 1 *Lagerführer* of the *Strafvollzugslager der* SS *und Polizei* Danzig–Matzkau in 6.1943.
Kommandant des Strafvollzugslager der SS *und Polizei* Matzkau 21.2.1944–18.8.1944.
SS-FHA from 18.8.1944.
SS-*Gebirgsjäger-Ausbildung- und Ersatz-Bataillon* 7 (Graditzka) from 2.9.1944.
Mittenwald *Hoch-Gebirgsjägerschule* 17.11.–12.12.1944.
24. *Bataillon-Lehrgang* 12.1944.
SS-*Gebirgsjäger-Ausbildung- und Ersatz-Bataillon* from 7.1.1945.
10th SS-*Panzer*-Division *Hohenstaufen* in 4.1945.

Promotions:

11.1938	SS-*Beurkundungsführer Anwärter.*
15.8.1939	SS-*Untersturmführer der Waffen*-SS (*Aktiv*).
1.9.1940	SS-*Obersturmführer der Waffen*-SS (*Aktiv*).
20.4.1943	SS-*Hauptsturmführer der Waffen*-SS (*Aktiv*).

Decorations & Awards:

0.0.19__	SS-*Zivilabzeichen* (Nr. 164.318).
0.0.19__	SA *Sportsabzeichen in Bronze.*
0.0.19__	SS-*Ehrenwinkel für alte Kämpfer.*
0.0.19__	*Kriegsverdienstkreuz II. Klasse mit Schwertern.*
0.0.19__	*Die Medaille zur Erinnerung an den* 13. März 1938 (Austria).
0.0.19__	*Die Medaille zur Erinnerung an den* 1. Oktober 1938 (Sudetenland).

Notes: Attending the Deutsch-Feistritz *Volksschule* for six classes and the Graz *Mittel Schule* for four classes, Baumgärtner then studied at trade school for three years. Qualified, he was then employed as a clerk and salesman and served with the Austrian Army *Gebirgs*-Rgt. 10 in 1930 (he obtained the rank of *Alpenjäger* and received the *Sportsauszeichnung*). In his own words, Baumgärtner described his flight to Munich on 25 July 1934: 'Unprepared, I fled from Austria to Germany in August 1933 without possessing valid travel papers. In Munich I reported to the 'Braun Haus' and reported to the Österreich Legion in Lechfeld.' The Nazi party suggesting to him to join the *Hilfswerk Schleißheim* at the SA-*Lager* Kloster-Lechfeld, Baumgärtner accepted this advice and undertook military training. Carrying out the duties of a *Zugführer* with this unit between 20 August and 31 December 1933, Baumgärtner received his SS uniform during the winter of 1933/34. At this time he was accommodated at the SS-*Kaserne* Herzog Wilhelm and received military instruction from *Polizei* and LSSAH instructors from 1 March 1934. His unit was formally incorporated into the SS-VT at the conclusion of the September 1934 party day parade and Baumgärtner and other Austrians of this formation were granted full German citizenship at this time. His battalion transferred to the SS-*Kaserne* Munich-Freimann in the winter of 1935 and Baumgärtner married his pregnant fiancée Anni U., (b. 11.7.1915 in Kranixfeld) on 6 April 1935. At this time the couple lived apart, Baumgärtner living at the Ohestraße barracks and was appointed a *Zugführer* in 1938. Here, he elucidates further on his pre-war career: 'I was a member of the 2. SS-*Bataillon* that marched quickly into

Austria and to Vienna. Spending one month in Vienna I then returned to Munich. In expectation of the SS courts creation I was ordered to a training course for SS certification officers. I was at that time determined to follow a career in the SS, within the SS judiciary. The training course took seven or eight months to complete.'

Baumgärtner passed the final certification officers exam in November 1938 and as a certification non-commissioned officer he returned to the *Deutschland* and participated in the occupation of the Sudetenland and the *Anschluss* of Austria. Inducted into the *HA* SS-*Gericht* in August 1939, he then took charge of the Danzig tribunal office and lived on the court premises. Transferring to the *Straflager des* SS *Polizei* Dachau in the position of a *Zugführer* in 1 February 1941, Dr Beelitz would recall that Baumgärtner had been the leader of the *Aussenstelle* Allach prior to him reporting to Matzkau in the summer of 1943. Appointed Matzkau's Nr. 1 *Lagerführer* in June 1943, Baumgärtner was recommended for promotion on 23 February the same year:

> He has been in use as a *Lagerführer* at the *Straflagers der* SS *und Polizei* and with court supervision, Baumgärtner been active as the *Leiter der Straflagers der* SS-*und Polizei* Dachau since August 1941 and has t completed the work assigned to him there with the fullest satisfaction. Above all, his prudence and vigor was particularly prized during the establishment and expansion of the punishment camp. His understanding is excellent, he is capable of fending for himself and with decisive swiftness and happiness, he finds the correct decision to resolve and conclude emerging problems. His soldierly bearing is impeccable; he is a good comrade and has a proper understanding of the needs of his subordinates. His character and world-view it is strong. Baumgärtner's previous use at the front could not be undertaken because of his indispensability and his continued use in the service as *Leiter der Straflagers der* SS-*und Polizei* Dachau.

The report approved by *Gruf.* Breithaupt, the promotion was awarded in April 1943 and the *Reichsführer* supported his advancement on the proviso that he saw action at the front. Here, Baumgärtner describes why he had been appointed Matzkau's commandant:

> [...] For about a year, I was located in the *Strafvollzugslager der* SS *und Polizei* Danzig-Matzkau from the summer of 1943 to July 1944 and I then replaced *Stubaf.* N. Ernst. *Stubaf.* Ernst who had been displaced as a punishment for various incompetence's in the camp Matzkau, details of which I was not informed. [...]

Speaking to the Austrian authorities in June 1968, Baumgärtner confirmed that Dr Ernst had handed command of the prison garrison directly to him in early 1944 (21.2.1944) and claimed that no executions had been carried out in Danzig–Matzkau during his short tenure.

The SS-PHA commanded Baumgärtner's transfer to the SS-FHA on 7 March 1944, but a spirited defence by General Breithaupt resulted in this order being rescinded the same day. For committing a serious neglect of his duties on 20 July 1944, *Gruf.* Katzmann ordered Baumgärtner confined to his residence between 21 July and 8 September. Punished with fourteen days' intensified arrest for his negligence, less time detained at home, Baumgärtner then applied successfully for front line duties. Transferring to the mountain troops in August 1944, he then underwent officer training until Baumgärtner's instructors judged him unsuitable for use as a front line officer. He then returned to a reserve battalion. Elsewhere, his family moved to Graz in November 1944 and then to Deutsch-Feistritz in July 1945. Assigned to a panzer division for a short time, he became a prisoner of the British Army at Radkersburg in March 1945.

Released from internment, Baumgärtner returned to Austria and settled in Judenburg. Here, he volunteered for the Graz *Polizei* between 1948 and 1949, but when his former association with the SS was revealed to his superiors he was arrested and held in investigative detention for six months. Freed prior to his trial, the Graz public prosecutor initiated a court's process against Baumgärtner for committing high treason and he then faced trial before the *Volksgericht* in January 1950. Judged guilty, the court punished Baumgärtner with a year's *Zuchthaus*, but the remainder of this sentence was set aside in 1954. Remaining in Austria after his release, Baumgärtner then accepted a factory job. At the behest of the *Landgericht* Munich II, the Austrian authorities began searching for Baumgärtner from February 1968 and quickly discovered that he was once again an Austrian citizen and had settled in Leoben/Steiermark. From here, he was forced to defend himself against charges of murder in the late 1960s/early 1970s. Submitting a detailed statement to the *Bundesministerium für Innernes Abteilung* 18 on 28 May and 4 June 1968, Baumgärtner denied ordering summary executions of inmates in Danzig–Matzkau. Lacking evidence to substantiate the murder allegations, the court's investigation was halted in November 1971.[8]

Name: Dr jur. Friedrich 'Fritz' **Ernst Beelitz.**
Last Rank: SS-*Hauptsturmführer*.
Born: 22.3.1908 in Rixdorf.
Died: 11.6.2008 in Berlin.
NSDAP-Nr.: 4.578.637 (joined 1.5.1937).
SS-Nr.: 219.846 (joined 30.10.1933).
Prewar Assignments:
42. SS-*Standarte* (Berlin) in 10.1933.
5. / 3. SS-*Motorsturm* (Berlin).
3. SS-*Motorstandarte* in early 1936.
3. / 75. SS-*Standarte* (Berlin).
Übung at the end of 1938.
Postschutz in 1939.
Übung (8 weeks)15. *Res. Batt.* / *Art.* Rgt. 23 (Döberitz) 6.2.–6.5.1939.
Wartime Assignments:
Waffen-SS from 6.3.1940.
SS-*Unterführerschule* Radolfzell in 1940.

SS-*Totenkopf-Infantrie*-Rgt. 8 (mot) (Krakau) in 3.1940.
Waffen-SS *Hauptamt* SS-*Gericht, Amt* III in 12.1942.
Strafvollzugslager der SS *und Polizei* Danzig–Matzkau from 24.5.1943.
Kommandant des Strafvollzugslager der SS *und Polizei* Matzkau 18.8.1944–17.3.1945.
Kommandant des Strafvollzugslager der SS *und Polizei* Förrenbach 3.–4.1945.

Promotions:

30.10.1933	SS-*Unterscharführer der Allgemeine*-SS.
1.7.1940	SS-*Sturmmann der Reserve.*
1.9.1940	SS-*Unterscharführer der Reserve.*
21.2.1941	SS-*Oberscharführer der Reserve.*
21.6.1943	SS-*Untersturmführer der Reserve.*
9.11.1943	SS-*Obersturmführer der Reserve.*
20.4.1944	SS-*Hauptsturmführer der Reserve.*

Decorations & Awards:

0.0.19__	SS-*Zivilabzeichen.*
18.4.1936	SA *Sportsabzeichen in Bronze.*
0.0.19__	D.L.R.G. *in Bronze.*
10.6.1942	1939 *Eisernes Kreuz II. Klasse.*
10.3.1942	*Infanterie-Sturmabzeichen in Bronze.*
1.8.1942	*Medaille 'Winterschlacht im Osten* 1941/42.'
0.0.19__	SS-*Ehrenwinkel für alte Kämpfer.*

Notes: His father was a Great War veteran and *Justiz-Inspektor* at the *Amtsgericht* Berlin-Neukölln. One of two children, Beelitz attended *Volksschule* for three classes and the *Albrecht-Dürer-Oberrealschule* in Berlin-Neukölln for ten classes, but contracting an ear illness he was forced to repeat one year. Obtaining his *Abitur* on 12 September 1928, Beelitz matriculated on 17 October the same year and then undertook the study of jurisprudence at the Friedrich-Wilhelms University in Berlin from late 1928 until 19 March 1931. Beelitz continued his law studies at Göttingen University from mid-1931 and was a member of the Catholic *Wingolf* fraternity. Passing his *Referendarexamen* at the *Oberlandesgericht* Celle on 24 March 1933, Beelitz obtained his law doctorate from Göttingen University on 22 December 1933 (his 1934 dissertation is titled '*Die Urkundenzeichnung des Stellvertreters mit dem Namen des Vertretenen, insbesondere unter dem Gesichtspunkt des Handelns im fremden und unter falschem Namen*'). Engaged in *Gerichtsreferender* training at the *Kammergerichtsbezirk* between August 1933 and December 1936, Dr Beelitz then undertook *Referendar* training at the *Kammergericht* Berlin, the *Amtsgericht* Königswusterhausen and at the *Landgericht* Berlin for much of 1933. Undertaking practical training with the jurist and notary Dr Buth and Dr Martin in late 1933 and early 1934, he then trained at the *Oberlandesgericht* Berlin–Neukölln the following year. Swearing his oath for the civil service on 15 August 1935, Beelitz continued his training at the *Rheinischex Hypothekenbank* throughout that same year. Gaining court experience at the 8. *Zivilsenatx des Kammergerichts* Berlin until the late summer of 1936, Beelitz passed his *Assessorexamen* in Berlin before *Präsident* Dr

Spankus of the *Reichsjustizprüfungsamt* on 8 December 1936 (one of his examiners was Dr v.Dohnanyi, who would later be executed for his part in the 1944 assassination attempt on Adolf Hitler). He then accepted a post as a salaried legal caseworker at the *Abteilung Grundstücks- und Vermögensverwaltung der* NSV, *Reichsleitung der NSDAP im Hauptamt für Volkswohlfahrt*, Berlin (NSV) from 2 March to December 1937. Appointed a candidate in the Berlin city administration on 1 January 1938, Beelitz was then employed at the *Steueramt* in Berlin–Tiergarten. He received leave from his post to assist the *Polizei* with security and traffic arrangements for Admiral Hórthy's visit to Berlin on 22 August 1938 (*Absperrdienste*).

Appointed a *Magistrats-Rat* at the Berlin–*Verwaltungsbezirk* Neukölln in 1939, Dr Beelitz became a civil servant for life in November the same year and was then posted to the *Kammergerichts* Königswusterhaben. At this time, he was asked to list his membership of NS organisations and realising that his continued advancement depended on his involvement with National Socialism, Beelitz applied to join the *Allgemeine*-SS on the advice of his father. In early 1936, he volunteered his father's Adler six-seater for his SS-*Motor Standarte*. A member of the NS-*Rechtswahrerbund* from November 1933, Beelitz participated in a sport and training course at the *Rasse und Siedlungshauptamtes* SS in Templin between 4 and 10 November 1934, (under the leadership of *Ostuf.* v.Lettow) and attended the *Gemeinschaftslager* Hans Kerrl at Jüterbog between 24 February and 18 April 1936. Becoming a party candidate in May 1937, Beelitz later explained that he had become a convinced National Socialist while studying at Göttingen in 1931, but had been too busy to join the party prior to 1933. Applying to join the *Waffen*-SS in February 1940, here, he explains to post-war investigators his reasons for taking this decision:

> When the war began, I endeavoured again to enter the *Wehrmacht*. However, this endeavour failed and it was made clear to me by my responsible recruitment office, that as a member of the *Allgemeine*-SS, my draft papers had been submitted to them and I could therefore only join the *Waffen*-SS. This drafting occurred in February 1940 and I was assigned to a newly established SS unit in Poland. Likewise, I can only recall that my deployment a part of the SS-*Totenkopfverbände* was temporary and for around two or three months. This was the first part of my training. The name of my commander I can no longer remember. I was at that point in time that I was declared a specialist SS-*Mann*. Because of the frequent change of the regimental number, I am today not in a position to make a concrete statement about the unit. However, I recall being in Krakau and Lublin.

'I only trained fully for front service and was ordered to the Radolfzell leadership school at that time. Although in spite of receiving repeated letters of rejection, an SS officer is what I wished to become' was Beelitz's response to a question about his possible involvement with murder units. This statement contradicts what he wrote in his January 1943 RuSHA biography. Here, he claimed to have participated in what he described as *Säuberungskämpfe* (clean-up battles) in Poland just prior to the attack on the USSR. His surviving son is in no doubt that this was more than mere boasting and is convinced that his father had been involved in something nefarious in 1940. Inducted into the *Waffen*-SS on 6 March the same year, Beelitz received instruction in the use of artillery and his regiment relocated to Warsaw in December 1940. Appointed a *Zugführer* in the newly formed 13. *Infanterie-Gewehr-Kompanie* in early 1941, he remained with this formation until late 1942. Beelitz's regiment became part of the 1. SS-*Infantrie*-Brigade (mot) on 5 January 1941 and gathering in Debica between 5 and 23 July, his regiment then deployed behind *Heeresgruppe Süd* in the Ukraine on 25 July the same year. Here, his regiment initially fought partisans and provided men for firing squads that participated in the mass killing of Jewish civilians. Asked after the war if he'd taken part in these executions, Beelitz supplied an emphatic 'No' and stated that he had only fought Russian troops. Here, Beelitz explains the circumstances around his next posting:

> Roughly around Christmas 1942, I was on the grounds of my legal training and proven front deployment transferred to the *HA* SS-*Gericht* in Munich. Joining the *Abteilung Strafvollzug* in Munich in early 1943, this office was led by SS-*Ostubaf.* Burmeister, who to my knowledge is today active as an *Amts* or *Landesgerichtsrat* in Schleswig-Holstein. Also present there was *Staatsrat* in the *Bundeschuldenverwaltung* in Bad Homburg, SS-*Stubaf.* Meder, who I met at a gathering in 1957. In the same *Abteilung* and active under Meder was SS-*Stubaf.* Dr Walter, his activities today are unknown to me, but before the war he had been an *Oberstaatsanwalt* in Dresden or Leipzig. My task was to undertake the sentencing orders according to the StOP for the SS war jurisdiction. Furthermore, I created specialist legal reports for the cases assigned to me for the decision of the *Gerichtsherr.*

Becoming an SS-*Hilfrichter* of the *HA* SS-*Gericht* in December 1942, Beelitz attended a medical examination in Munich on 4 January 1943. 'As a *Magistratsrat*, SS-*Oscha.* Fritz-Ernst Beelitz has the financial basis for starting their own family and for his SS suitability I also have no concerns' wrote Dr Reinecke on 12 January the same year when his subordinate applied at that time for permission to marry his fiancée. Beelitz was in Munich when he received permission to marry his fiancée Gertrud V., (b. 29.1.1921 in Schöningen *Kreis* Helmstedt) on 18 February 1943. Re-submitting his application of marriage to the RuSHA in the summer of 1944, Beelitz planned a church marriage for February 1945, but the marriage did not take place. Transferred directly to Danzig–Matzkau in May 1943, here, he worked as an investigator, he represented the interests of the *HA* SS-*Gericht*, ensured the balanced application of capital punishments according to the jurisdiction and acted as an investigator for the local court. Fulfilling the role of garrison *Gerichtsoffizier* from February 1944, Beelitz occasionally prosecuted cases before the Danzig court.

On the express orders of *Gruf.* Katzmann, Beelitz took temporary command of Matzkau on 21 July 1944 and was appointed its commandant in August. Beelitz had taken to riding horses in Matzkau, but breaking his ankle while jumping from a horse on 21 October, he handed command of the prison to what he described as the administrative officer

(Nr. 1 *Lagerführer*) until he had recovered. The *Lagerführer* he remained in command of Matzkau until Beelitz had returned from sick leave. 'Horses try to kill you!' Beelitz would exclaim to his son and never rode horses again.

In the autumn of 1944 the *HA* SS-*Gericht* had undertaken the process of awarding Beelitz a promotion commensurate to his responsibilities at Matzkau. Writing to *Ostubaf.* Dr Klahre of the *Amt* Ic on 26 September, Beelitz could reported no changes to his marital status from when he had last communication on this issue (March 1940) and revealed that despite the assistance of the HSSPF *Welchsel*, he had been unable to find a wife in Danzig and remained unmarried. Mentioning that a Munich nurse had been willing to marry him, Beelitz explained that recent aerial attacks had prevented her travelling by rail out of the city. Writing to Beelitz on 18 September, Dr Klahre gave him until 1 October to supply a reason why the SS leader should grant his promotion (his options ranged from childless marriage, children born outside of wedlock of two or more years old or report an engagement to marry with the marriage date). Selecting the third option, General Breithaupt wrote to '*Stubaf.*' Beelitz on 6 November 1944 to inform him that he had proposed his promotion for 9 November. The promotion recommendation was then handed to the *Reichsführer* for his approbation: 'SS-*Stubaf.* Beelitz promotion is deleted until he is married; there are very many racially good girls in Danzig. Of the *Müncherin*, he must simply do without' was Himmler's reaction to his single status and denied him the promotion on the grounds of his continued church attendance. Wishing to extricate himself from this predicament, Beelitz used his injured ankle as an opportunity to take leave and visit Berlin on 30 November to obtain a certificate declaring his formal exit from the Lutheran Church from the *Amtsgericht* Neukölln for 31 December (the Danzig court received this document on 2.1.1945). Talking after the war, Beelitz explained that this document was not received in time for the January 1945 promotions list:

> My last service grade was SS-*Hstuf.* It was common practice that the service entry grade for this post was a *Major* or *Stubaf.* In early 1945 such a promotion was proposed, however it was refused because of my membership of the Lutheran Church.

Returning to the Berlin Lutheran Church in the postwar period, they re-issued Beelitz a new baptismal certificate in 1950.

To the sound of Red Army artillery, Beelitz finally received the order to abandon Matzkau in March 1945. Boarding one of the last ships to leave the stricken city, Beelitz disembarked in Swinemünde and made his way first to Munich and then to the *HA* SS-*Gericht* at Prien am Chiemsee. Here, he received orders to take command of the prison at Förrenbach and arriving in his new post in late March 1945, he oversaw the evacuation of this prison to the *Aussenstelle* Allach during the first and second week of April. Remaining in the prison service until the dissolution of the *HA* SS-*Gericht* on 29 April, Beelitz evaded allied patrols, rid himself of his uniform and hid at the house of an acquaintance in Hopfgarten/Wörgl in Austria. Elsewhere, his home town in Neukölln was occupied by Soviet forces until becoming part of the American sector. Escaping arrest by Allied forces, Beelitz does not appear to have been detained in a prisoner of war camp.[9]

Settling in Neubeuern *bei* Rosenheim in upper Bavaria from 3 May 1945, Beelitz changed his name to Dr Friedrich-Ernst Beelitz and making his existence known to a small group of family members he worked as a self-employed tax consultant in Neubeuern until 1952. Undertaking his de-Nazification process in 1947, the tribunal punished him with a 50 *Mark* fine for membership of the Nazi party. Speaking after the war, Beelitz recalled living in Rosenheim before the currency reforms took place in 1959. Under the auspices of the Lutheran Church, Beelitz married his fiancée Charlotte S., born N., (b. 24.9.1912) on 6 December 1952. He had known her briefly before the war and they had two children. Working in the office of city bursar, his wife was instrumental in his obtaining a civil service post in Berlin. Qualifying to re-join the civil service in the wake of the publication of the 131 law, Beelitz applied for civil service post in 1951, but his application omitted any mention of his membership of the *Allgemeine*-SS, or his previous service in the *HA* SS-*Gericht*. Initially employed as a salaried lecturer at the *Senatsverwaltung für Finanzen* on 3 July 1952, the *Senator für Inneres* arranged his appointment as a *Beisitzer der Dienststrafkammer bei dem Verwaltungsgericht* Berlin on 27 November 1953.

Appointed a civil servant for life with the rank of *Regierungsrat* on 29 June 1954, Beelitz was promoted *Oberregierungsrat* on 5 July 1954 and was later active as a *Referatsleiter in Landesausgleichsamt beim Senator für Finanzen*. In this post, he participated in a discussion with Dr Shepherd on 4 November 1968 concerning the evaluation of the German ethnicity of victims of persecution, especially of those from the areas where an independent Jewish minority had passed. From 1959 to early 1971, the Munich II prosecutor investigated a former convict's claims that Beelitz and others had committed illegal murders in Matzkau and mistreated inmates. Submitting his rebuttal on 5 July 1967, Beelitz denied the accusations. As a consequence of this investigation, Beelitz was denied further promotion for fifteen years and this prohibition was lifted in 1971 when the court prosecutor recommended a halt to the proceedings. Beelitz was never arrested in connection with these processes and no criminal charges were preferred against him. His surviving son recollected that the investigation was mentioned rarely at home, but when raised, his parents considered it an outrageous harassment and a persecution of the innocent. Rising to the rank of *Senatsrat*, aged 65, Beelitz retired from full time employment in 1973 and passed away shortly after his 100th birthday in 2008.[10]

Name: Gottfried Biedermann.
Last Rank: SS-*Hauptsturmführer*.
Born: 26.10.1907 in Villach/Carinthia.
NSDAP-Nr.: 13.073 (joined 1.5.1933),
1.616.385 (joined 1934).
SS-Nr.: 139.471 (joined 27.4.1933).
Prewar Assignments:
SS-VT 31.12.1934.
7. / II. / SS-*Standarte Deutschland* in 1.1935.

3. / I. / SS-*Standarte Der Führer* in 12.3.1938

Führer-Anwärter-Lehrgang 1.11.1935–30.3.1936.

Beurkundungsführer-Lehrgang SS-*Junkerschule* Bad Tölz on 31.3.1938.

3. / II. / *Der Führer* from 30.7.1938.

Wartime Assignments:

SS-VT *Hauptamt* SS-*Gericht* from 17.4.1940.

SS-*Straflager der* SS *und Polizei* Dachau from 1.1.1941.

Reichsluftschutzbund in 1943.

Nr. 1 *Lagerführer* SS-*Straflager der* SS *und Polizei* Dachau from 4.1943.

Strafvollzugslager der SS *und Polizei* Danzig–Matzkau from 21.7.1943.

Nr. 1. *Lagerführer* Danzig–Matzkau 21.2.–28.8.1944.

SS-*Straflager der* SS *und Polizei* Dachau from 28.8.1944.

12th SS-*Panzer*-Division *Hitlerjugend* field court 8.1944.

Leiter SS-*Zweiglager Hammerweg* 12.1944-2.4.1945.

SS-*Straflager der* SS *und Polizei* Dachau, *Aussenstelle* Allach 2.4.-27.4.1945.

Promotions:

27.4.1933	SS-*Bewerber*
1.5.1933	SS-*Anwärter der Allgemeine*-SS.
1.1.1934	SS-*Mann der Allgemeine*-SS.
1.8.1934	SS-*Rottenführer der* SS-VT.
1.2.1935	SS-*Unterscharführer der* SS-VT.
1.10.1936	SS-*Scharführer der* SS-VT.
1.8.1937	SS-*Oberscharführer der* SS-VT.
Nov.1938	SS-*Beurkundungsführer-Anwärter*.
1.7.1940	SS-*Hauptscharführer der* SS-VT.
1.1.1941	SS-*Untersturmführer der Waffen*-SS, (*Aktiv*).
9.11.1941	SS-*Obersturmführer der Waffen*-SS, (*Aktiv*).
21.6.1944	SS-*Hauptsturmführer der Waffen*-SS, (*Aktiv*).

Decorations & Awards:

0.0.19__	SS-*Zivilabzeichen* (Nr. 125.775).
0.0.19__	SA-*Sportsabzeichen in Bronze*.
0.0.19__	SS-*Ehrenwinkel für alte Kämpfer*.
0.0.19__	*Deutsches Reichssportabzeichen in Bronze*.
0.0.1938	*Die Medaille zur Erinnerung an den* 1. Oktober 1938 (Sudetenland).
0.0.1939	*Die Medaille zur Erinnerung an den* 13. März 1938 (Austria).
28.7.1941	SS-*Dienstauszeichnung* 4. *Stufe*.
0.0.1942	SS-*Dienstauszeichnung* 3. *Stufe* (8 *Jähr*).
0.0.1942	*Kriegsverdienstkreuz II. Klasse mit Schwertern*.
0.0.19__	*Kriegsverdienstkreuz I. Klasse mit Schwertern*.
0.0.1944	V*erwundetenabzeichen*, 1939 *in Schwarz*.

Notes: One of three children born to a middle class Villach family that relocated to Vienna in 1929, Biedermann attended the Villach *Volksschule* for five classes between 1913 and 1919, the Villach *Bürgerschule* for three classes between 1919 and 1922 and then studied business practice at the Vienna *Forbildungsschule* until 1923. Passing his business examination in Villach in 1923, Biedermann possibly changed courses after two months' study. A member of the Villacher *Postsport* from 1921 to 1933, he played football and ice hockey and participated in sporting events in Italy and Yugoslavia between 1928 and 1930 and in Switzerland during 1930. Employed at his father's leather factory as an apprentice merchant on a salary of 2,000 and 3,000 *Reichsmark per annum* from 1 January 1931 to June 1933, Biedermann fled Austria for Munich in June–July 1934 and was from that time until December the same year employed as an accountant in the cash office under an *Hstuf.* Hörhamer at the Österreich Hilfswerk (SA-*Lager* Kloster-Lechfeld). Transferring to the SS-*Hilfswerk* Dachau on 1 October 1934, Biedermann was admitted into the SS-VT in December 1934 and became a *Gruppenführer* with NCO rank (earning 1,200 *Reichsmark per annum*). Granted German citizenship on 1 January 1935, Biedermann became an accountant with the horse drawn SS-*Standarte Deutschland.* Motorcycle racing was popular in this regiment and it appears that Biedermann was a keen competitor who participated in at least one major racing competition at the Bergrennen race track. Participating in the *Anschluss* of Austria, his unit transferred to the SS-*Kaserne* Wien-Schönbrunn in March 1938 and his regiment become known as the *Der Führer* on that same time. Participating in the occupation of the Sudetenland on 1 October 1938, Biedermann returned to Vienna after this short deployment and then answered a call for certification officers. Passing the final certification officers exam in November 1938, he was appointed an SS-*Beurkundungsunterführer*/ *Offizier-Anwärter* and returned to his motorised regiment.

His battalion prepared for the occupation of Czechoslovakia on 14 and 15 March 1939 and was then deployed for a few weeks on the Westwall in the Waldkirch region during September the same year (earning 2,000 *Reichsmark per annum* in 1939). Satisfying stringent RuSHA tests, Biedermann married his fiancée Lieselotte W., (b. 18.11.1910) on 22 September 1939 and they had four children up to the point when records ceased in May 1945. They settled in Munich and Danzig. His regiment deployed at the *Truppenübungsplatz* Brdy-wald during October 1939 to prepare for the 1940 invasion of Western Europe. Transferring to the *HA* SS-*Gericht* as a certification officer in April 1940 (earning 2,900 *Reichsmark per annum*), postwar, Biedermann claimed to have been deployed as an administrator at the *HA* SS-*Gericht* under *Hstuf.* Richard Müller until September 1941, but official records do not confirm his recollections. Assigned to the *Amt* III under Müller in 1940, he joined *Ostuf.* Erich Albert's command at the SS-*Straflager* Dachau later that same year. Questioned in June 1947, Biedermann recalled entering what he described as the 'Police re-enforcements of the *Waffen*-SS' on 1 January 1941, but neglected to mention that he had been was appointed a National Socialist leadership officer during the war years. A promotion report was submitted for Biedermann in late 1940:

> He possesses a good to satisfactory capacity to promote SS values, he understands its meaning and is a convinced National Socialist, he is a good *Beurkundungsführer*, a willing and reliable worker who is able to complete in its entirety each request made to him. He has completed his *Beurkundungsführer* exam successfully and is a reliable, willing hard worker and deals with his tasks to my complete satisfaction. Biedermann completely deserves his promotion to *Ustuf.*

A recommendation for his further promotion was submitted on 26 September 1941 and this noted that Biedermann, possessed an orderly SS character, was restrained, knowledgeable and his capabilities were satisfactory. A recommendation for his further promotion on 27 November 1942 was refused. Accompanied by his family, Biedermann received orders to transfer to Danzig–Matzkau in July 1943 and was appointed the leader of the 1. *Wachkompanie*. Replacing Edmund Baumgärtner as Nr. 1. *Lagerführer* in February 1944, his superiors expressed their hope in June the same year that when promoted, he would transfer to the front to 'prove himself' (earning 4,800 *Reichsmark per annum* in 1944). Committing a disciplinary offence on 20 July 1944, Biedermann was punished with a simple reprimand and re-assigned to the SS-*Straflager* Dachau in August 1944. Speaking in 1967, Rudolf Heiß recollected that a short while after his removal from Matzkau, he replaced Biedermann as Nr. 1 *Lagerführer* in Matzkau in late July/August 1944 and the former prison compound commander transferred to the front. Leaving his wife and children in Danzig when re-assigned to Dachau, they were forced to abandon their possessions in the city during the spring of 1945 and flee to her parents in Essen. Post-war, Biedermann claimed to have then been seconded to the troops in the wake of his transfer from Matzkau and was wounded in action. Returning to prison service by December 1944, Biedermann avoided all mention of this during his denazification process, but an examination of his banking information reveals that his wages were paid to a bank in Mosbach/Baden and he had been appointed the *Zweiglager Hammerweg* commandant after his wounding. He held this post until the prison was closed and he escorted its inmates to the *Aussenstelle* Allach in April 1945.

Escaping from Dachau's environs before its liberation on 28 April 1945, Biedermann surrendered to US military forces near Zell am See on 8 May and was taken under arrest for his membership of the *Waffen*-SS and possession of the rank of *Hstuf.* in accordance with the automatic arrest category (security memorandum Nr. 1 section 1 dated 25.2.1946 HQ 3rd Army). Detained at the US Army's Prisoner of War Enclosure Nr. 409 Nuremberg–Langwasser, the II. / 26th Infantry Rgt. arrested Biedermann here at 9.00 a.m. on 8 June 1946. Hospitalised in Bruckberg on 25 June the same year, Biedermann recovered and was then placed into the care of the 1st Division's Civilian Internment Enclosure Nr. 409 at Nuremberg–Langwasser. Here, questioned on 6 November 1946, Biedermann camouflaged his association with the *Waffen*-SS prison service and claimed to have been subordinate to '*Hstuf.* Baumgärtner' as an administrator. Insisting that he had not involved himself in politics prior to 1933, Biedermann claimed never to have voted for the Nazi party. At the conclusion of the questioning, Captain J. Kallenbach recommended he was interned pending instructions from a higher headquarters for the disposition of his category.

The Bavarian State Ministry for Special Affairs sanctioned Biedermann's transfer to British custody on 29 March 1947 and he completed his denazification process on 22 August the same year, ('responsible'). Then released from internment to join his family in Essen, the *Hauptkammer* Essen classified Biedermann in the group III, 1 'less responsible' on 22 August 1947. Writing to the German denazification committee on 14 September 1947, Biedermann appealed against his classification when he was no longer receiving inpatient treatment in the city mental hospital. Writing to the German denazification committee—Review Committee on 13 April 1948, Biedermann's advocate, Schem u. Dr Greve applied for a quick scheduling of a date for an oral proceeding and his letter provided some interesting observations about Biedermann's life at this time:

> He is himself building a new freelance existence with the manufacture and sale of arts and crafts articles. He still suffers the consequences of his serious war wounds. Therefore, he intends to take up a much-needed long rest, but he can only undertake this journey when this process is completed. *Herr* Biedermann is a refugee from the east and has lost all of his assets, as well as all his household articles in Danzig.

On 16 July 1948, Biedermann's lawyers justifed their clients reasons for lodging an appeal and submitted character references:

> The person concerned has been a member of the SS-VT, in which he held the rank of *Hstuf.* at the end of the war. He became a member of this unit, when he left Austria for Germany in 1933 and service in this group was strongly suggested to him because he had no other way to make a living. The SS-VT was a unit that consisted of members who had signed up for a four years voluntary military service instead of serving in the army forcibly. This armed unit was organised so that it should be used in the event of mobilization by the army.
>
> This finding is in agreement with the Nuremberg judgment. In peace, the SS-VT was exclusively used for military service benefits, in particular for guard keeping and emergencies. He had nothing to do with the guarding of the concentration camps. You must not confuse this unit with the SS-*Totenkopfverbänden*, to which this task was conferred. Therefore, membership of the SS-VT cannot be considered only for itself as a form of activism. Until long into the war the person concerned only held the rank of an non-commissioned officer.
>
> His request to exit this service in 1939 after the completion of four years of service were always refused. From this service, the person concerned has not undertaken propaganda, or otherwise disseminated an activist ideology within the meaning of Nazism.
>
> In particular I point to the fact that he brusquely rejected the action taken against the Jews in November 1938 and a person could also exert considerable criticism of the Nazi regime in his presence, without fear that he would file a report. Although he was an

SS man one could be a particularly zealous activist in his presence. His classification in category III was therefore unjustified.

His advocate submitted to the court a total of nine written statement witnesses. One was composed by a former SS comrade:

Franz Xaver Kilger, Nuremberg-Langwasser, dated 15.2.1947.
As a member of the 7. / SS-Rgt. *Deutschland* and later the SS-Rgt. *Der Führer*, I have known *Herr* Gottfried Biedermann, born 26.10.1907, as an accountant for my company and later in the battalion respectively. He was in the same position within the administration.

I have known *Herr* Biedermann since my entry into the SS-VT in the year 1935. It is known to me, that he in no way wanted to pursue his service duty further than his four and a half years and therefore, he submitted a number of requests for his dismissal from the SS-VT in 1939, but each one was refused and Biedermann's release was referred to a later date.

Meanwhile, Biedermann participated in the mobilization at the beginning of the war and in reference to the state authority he obeyed orders accordingly and had to remain in the SS-VT and *Waffen*-SS respectively. Regarding the person of *Herr* Biedermann, I can only say, that I know him as a just and ordinary person who quietly and modestly fulfilled his duty and then after serving his military service he was once again able to return to his private profession.

Gottfried Biedermann's appeal was finally heard before the German denazification appeal committee Essen on 22 October 1948. The cancellation decision of 22 August 1947 was repealed and Biedermann found himself re-classified in category III and his court fees were fixed at 30 *Reichsmark*. Biedermann's advocate applied to initiate a review procedure on 24 May 1949 and at this time he also proposed that his client was classified in the category IV without seizing assets and the freezing of his accounts. Sitting on 18 July 1949, the *Hauptkammer* Essen published their sentencing review decision on the same day and classified Biedermann in the group IV without penalty, ('follower') and fixed the court fees at ten *Reichsmark*. On 2 August 1949 the court noted that he continued to work as an independent merchant. Questioned in 1968, Edmund Baumgärtner stated his belief that Biedermann lived in Düsseldorf.[11]

Name: Walter Dieterle.
Last Rank: SS-*Obersturmführer*.
Born: 18.5.1914 in Loßburg *bei* Freudenstadt/Baden-Württemberg.
NSDAP-Nr.: 2.277.288 (joined 10.4.1933).
SS-Nr.: 245.628 (joined 10.4.1933).
Prewar Assignments:
SS-*Fliegerssturm* L. /X (Böblingen) in 4.1933.
Württemberg *Politische Bereitschaft* 29–30.5.1933.

SS-VT from 29.11.1933.
SS-*Stabssturm* Stuttgart until 5.1.1935.
2. / SS-TV *Nachrichten-Bataillon* (Berlin-Aldershof) 6.1.1935–31.3.1939.
SS-TV *Nachrichten-Bataillon* (Unna) 1.4.1939–12.2.1940.
Rundfunk-Lehrgang Berlin–Lichtenberg on 6.1.1935.
SS-*Nachrichten Bataillon* (Ellwangen) in 1935.
Beurkundungsführer-Lehrgang SS-*Junkerschule* Bad Tölz in 11.1938.
5. / SS-*Nachrichten-Bataillon* (Ellwangen) 1.2.–31.3.1939.

Wartime Assignments:

SS-*Nachrichten-Bataillon* (Unna) in 10.1939.
II. / 14. SS-*Standarte* (Gotha) in 1939.
SS-VT *Hauptamt* SS-*Gericht* 6.1.1939.
Hauptamt SS-*Gericht* HQ 9.2.1940.
Assistant *Referent* with SS-*Rechtamt* from 14.2.1940.
SS- *und Polizei-Gericht* I, Munich in 1940 / *Oberste* SS- *und Polizei-Gericht*.
SS- *und Polizei-Gericht* III, Berlin in 1940.
SS- *und Polizei-Gericht* VII, Vienna in 1941.
Hauptamt SS-*Gericht* HQ 4.1.1941
SS- *und Polizei-Gericht* VI, Krakau from 1.1941.
SS- *und Polizei-Gericht* XIII, Posen from 30.5.1941.
Proposed transfer to the SS- *und Polizei-Gericht* XVIII, Kiev on 1.12.1941 cancelled.
SS-Division *Wiking* field court from 24.12.1941.
SS- *und Polizei-Gericht* II, Düsseldorf from 18.5.1942.
Beurkundungsführer training course SS-*Junkerschule* Braunschweig 1.9.–15.10.1942.
Strafvollzugslager der SS *und Polizei* Danzig–Matzkau from 1.11.1942–22.10.1943.
Nr. 1 *Lagerführer Strafvollzugslager der* SS *und Polizei* Danzig–Matzkau from 1.3.1943.
2. *Lehrgang* SS-*Nachrichten Ausbildung- und Ersatz-Bataillon* (Nuremberg) from 22.10.1943.
Offizier-Lehrgang SS-*Nachrichtenschule* (Metz) 25.11. 12.12.1943.
SS-*Korps Nachrichten-Bataillon* 103 from 24.12.1943–1.2.1944.
1. SS-*Nachrichten Ausbildung- und Ersatz-Bataillon* (Nuremberg) from 1.2.1944.
3. / 1. SS-*Nachrichten Ausbildung- und Ersatz-Bataillon* 21.2.1944–20.3.1944.
27th SS-*Freiwilligen-Panzer-Grenadier*-Division *Nederland* 20.3.1944–5.5.1945.

Promotions:

13.3.1936	SS-*Sturmann der* SS-VT.
1.9.1937	SS-*Rottenführer der* SS-VT.
15.2.1940	SS-*Oberscharführer der Waffen*-SS, (*Aktiv*).
1.9.1940	SS-*Hauptscharführer der Waffen*-SS, (*Aktiv*).
1.1.1941	SS-*Untersturmführer der Waffen*-SS, (*Aktiv*).
21.6.1942	SS-*Obersturmführer der Waffen*-SS, (*Aktiv*).
2.2.1944	SS-*Oberscharführer der Waffen*-SS, (*Aktiv*).

Decorations & Awards:

0.0.19__ SS-*Zivilabzeichen* (Nr. 123.638).
0.0.19__ SA-*Sportsabzeichen in Bronze.*
20.4.1937 *Deutsche Olympia-Ehrenzeichen* I. *Klasse.*
0.0.19__ SS-*Ehrenwinkel für alte Kämpfer.*
22.3.1939 *Die Medaille zur Erinnerung an den* 1. Oktober 1938 (Sudetenland).
2.3.1939 *Die Medaille zur Erinnerung an den* 13. März 1938 (Austria).
1.9.1941 *Kriegsverdienstkreuz II. Klasse mit Schwertern.*
0.0.19__ *Medaille* '*Winterschlacht im Osten* 1941/42'.

Notes: Leaving full time education, Dieterle attended a trade school and apprenticed at W. Dinkelaker, Bierbraueri in Böblingen. A salaried employee at this company in 1932, (earning 800 *Reichsmark per annum*), Dieterle was made redundant with the downturn in the economy and found employment with *Lufthansa* at Böblingen on 25 February 1933. Later, he worked for Zeppelin's at Friedrichshafen. Mustering with an SS flying unit from April 1933, Dieterle entered the SS-VT in November 1933 (his earnings rose from 180 *Reichsmark per annum* in 1934 to 600 *Reichsmark* by 1938 and 2,900 *Reichsmark* for 1944). Living in Böblingen during 1934, Dieterle received specialist communications training, he participated in the *Anschluss* of Austria on 12 March, the march into the Sudetenland on 15 March 1938 and took part in the surprise attack on Poland in September 1939. Transferred to the *HA* SS-*Gericht* as an SS-*Beurkundungsunterführer* in January 1939, Dieterle then undertook practical training for the jurisdiction in Berlin courts from 31 March 1939. Marrying his fiancée Else B., (b. 16.5.1914) on 27 May 1939 and they had one child up to the point when records ceased in May 1945 and lived in Berlin–Aldershof until 1947 and then in Langenau/Württemberg.

In his absence, the 2. / SS-*Nachrichten-Bataillon* initiated an investigation against Dieterle on 13 February the same year to examine his failure to report the loss of his rifle sight. On leave for the winter solstice celebration on 18 December 1939, his train was delayed at the Würzburg railway station and as a consequence of this situation, he and two comrades visited the station's waiting room. Later, noticing that his belt and rifle telescope had been stolen, Dieterle reported its loss to the *Stabsscharführer* and submitted a report to him the following day. Handing his rifle into the armoury on 2 February 1940, it was noted that his rifle telescope was missing and as a consequence of the *Stabsscharführer* denying that he received his loss statement, Dieterle was placed on report (later, his roommate confirmed that a report had been submitted). Becoming a certification officer on 16 March 1940, Dieterle's recommendation for a promotion to officer rank was submitted on 13 December the same year:

> Dieterle is a reliable and eager worker and worthy for this request, he has attended a course for *Beurkundungsführer* and passed the exam, clearing his work, he toils to my fullest satisfaction. On my part I warmly recommend his deserved promotion.

The promotion awarded in January 1941, the *Reichsführer* requested a copy of his photograph on 10 January the same year. The *HA* SS-*Gericht* briefly considered Dieterle for a post with the *Polizeidivision* in January 1941, but he reported to the *HA* SS-*Gericht* HQ on this day and over the following year was assigned to various courts. A promotions recommendation was submitted for Dieterle in the spring of 1942:

> Dieterle has been in use as a *Beurkundungsführer* in various SS courts since the introduction of the SS and *Polizei* jurisdiction and he attended and did well at the first *Beurkundungsführer* course at Bad Tölz. He possesses a good character and has a satisfactory SS suitability; in and out of service his leadership is impeccable. He complies with the demands of service and is a capable and good *Beurkundungsführer*.

The promotion awarded in June 1942, Dieterle was inoculated against Typhus on 27 June the same year and transferred to Danzig-Matzkau in November the same year. Undertaking fourteen days' home leave in January 1943, in his absence he was indicted for abusing inmates. Hospitalised on 13 February 1943, he again enjoyed home leave between 31 May and 6 June and again between 22 and 28 June 1943. Brought before the Danzig tribunal on 17 September 1943, the court judged Dieterle guilty of military disobedience and falsifying reports. Imposing a nine months' *Gefängnis* punishment on him, the court recommended he was offered front probation and demoted him to the rank to *Oscha*. Removed from his post on 29 September 1943, Dieterle received a strong warning from the *Chef HA* SS-*Gericht* on 8 October the same year for the misuse of a vehicle in the week starting from 25 September the same year. Transferring to a communications training battalion in October 1943, his instructor, writing on the 27th of the same month, observed that Dieterle had no disciplinary problems and granted him home leave between 19 and 23 November 1943. Failing the initial communications course, Dieterle attended another officer communications course at Metz until December 1943 and passing this course to his instructor's satisfaction, he was again hospitalised on 1 December 1943. At that time his communications training commander offered his opinion of Dieterle's service:

> He has been a communications officer in the third company since 29 September 1943. He endeavours with brisk interest to train recruits and has bridged the gaps in his technical knowledge with intensive self-training. When training his unit he displays a good intellect and possesses a flawless superior attitude. He has a great sense of duty and possesses an exemplary view of the service when training the recruits. Dieterle has a good soldierly appearance and looks acceptable. In his contact with superiors he is correct and polite; he makes a point of being polite, helpful and obliging towards his comrades. A sincere outstanding character who possesses an impeccable SS attitude, SS-*Ostuf.* Dieterle is a good SS officer.

Transferred to the front on 24 December 1943, Dieterle returned to Nuremberg in February 1944 and the *Reichsführer* finally confirmed his judgement on 2 February.

Amending his sentence to four months *Gefängnis*, Himmler upheld his demotion. Granted home leave between 17 and 21 February 1944, Dieterle returned to Nuremberg to find a letter waiting for him from the Danzig court. Sent on 19 February, this document confirmed his sentence, ordered his demotion to the rank of *Oscha.* Commanded to report to the front for twelve months' field probation from 24 February 1944, there is no mention of serving a prison sentence and Dieterle acknowledged his judgement the same day and remained in Nuremberg until joining a panzer grenadier division on the Narwa Front in March 1944. Remaining with this formation as a *Zugführer* until the end of the war, Dieterle saw action in Estonia, Latvia and fought in the Kurland pocket. Ending the war on the Oder Front near Stettin, he surrendered to British forces on 5 May 1945 and was interned in the Sandbostel *bei* Bremervörde internment camp until 5 January 1947.

For a short while after his release, Dieterle lived in the municipality Eutenhofen *Kreis* Riedenburg and then relocated to Böblingen near Stuttgart. The local *Spruchkammer* prosecutor handed responsibility for his denazification process to the Böbingen tribunal on 22 October 1947 and a mandatory review of Dieterle's court's judgement was initiated on 16 April the following year. Receiving notification for his application for a renewed *Spruchkammer* process in Böblingen on 20 April the same year, Dieterle then submitted five character references to this court on 26 April the same year. Responding to the courts demand for further information about his wartime career on 30 April 1948, Dieterle avoided any mention of his assignment in Matzkau or his court martial. Quite how these events failed to come to the court's attention is a mystery. From examining similar court verdicts, it is evident that the post war courts routinely requested and received copies of former officer's service files from Berlin and in this document, Dieterle's assignments are clearly presented. Announcing their judgment on 11 May 1948, the Böblingen tribunal imposed one year's probation, beginning from the legal force of the announcement, fixed the disputed costs to be borne by Dieterle at 3,600 *Reichsmark* and imposed a one-time contribution of 500 *Reichsmark* fine (one day's nonpayment incurred a twenty *Reichsmark* fine). At this time the court noted the following:

> [...] The person concerned now declares under oath that he never worked in a concentration camp. He also specifies under oath that at the time of his entrance into the *Waffen*-SS he was unaware of this organization's alleged criminal objectives and actions. Even war crimes, or crimes against the occupied territories, or the mistreatment of prisoners of war. He has thus rebutted the presumption that he belongs to the group of persons affected by the Nuremberg judgment. When tested, the chamber came to the following conclusion about the extent to which the person concerned is guilty in accordance with article 7-9:
>
> The person concerned, who completed his commercial apprenticeship at the local firm Dinkelacker and was released as a result of lack of work shortly after undertaking his training, had at a time when he was under the pressure of general unemployment then decided at the early age of nineteen years-old to become a professional soldier. The chamber acknowledges that the claimant did not know as a politically immature

young man at that time, to draw the correct consequences for his entry into the former SS-VT. The interested party has not persuaded the chamber of this view and aside from only purely economic considerations and prospects there is no doubt that he joined the SS and entered the former SS-VT for political reasons. As a volunteer of the SS-VT and later a member of the *Waffen*-SS the person concerned first appears responsible. However, we must consider the person concerns previous political naivety. Consideration must also be given, that the person concerned has never been in a concentration, or work camp, or has been involved in this type of activity, but only knew purely administrative duties until 1942.

A number of witness statements state, that the person concerned was neither officially nor internally politically active, revealed only a simple civil appearance, never denounced, attended or celebrated festivals, was observed with no luxuries and thus there is no reason to believe he has acquired any unlawful enrichments etc. He never advertised for the NSDAP and therefore always declared that he was only member of the party because he had to be to remain a soldier.

The witness Geiss has confirmed that the person concerned was friendly towards Polish nationals and portrayed him as a friendly person with a balanced character, who absolutely could not be described as a fanatic. The *Bürgomeister* referred to the person concerned as a decent young man with no political development and nothing detrimental is known about him at the labor office.

Given the very good overall attitude of the person concerned and taking into account the fact that he acted only as an administrative man and later only in infantry deployment for the SS, the chamber has classified the concerned in the group of lesser offenders in accordance with the meaning of Article 11 section I, paragraph 1 as in reference to his personality it appears that he is worthy of a more lenient judgment and can be expected during his probationary period to fulfil his duties as citizens of a peaceful democratic state.

The person concerned is thus a lesser offender within the meaning of Article 11 / I / 1 and the fixed atonement is considered sufficient and appropriate. The chamber has refrained from imposing special work on him.

The judgement came into force on 10 July 1948. Paying his 500 *Reichsmark* fine by 18 June 1948, Dieterle was employed as a labourer for Röderer Kauffirmas from 9 May 1949 and his probation period terminated on 9 June the same year. Writing to the Nordwürttemberg central court on 7 June 1949, the mayor's office reported that they had found no evidence that Dieterle had continued to support National Socialist methods during the period of his probation and voiced their satisfaction that he had complied with the conditions of his probation. Satisfied with this report, the central court confirmed his new judgement on 21 June 1949 and ordered Dieterle to pay the 36 *Reichsmark* costs of the process. The executing authority in Stuttgart for the central court ordered an end of the sentencing process on 10 July 1950.[12]

Name: Maximilian 'Max' **Dolles.**
Last Rank: SS-*Untersturmführer.*
Born: 22.10.1916 in Hirschau/Bavaria.
Died: 1986.
SS-Nr.: 282.923, (joined 1.4.1936).
RAD: 1.10.1936–31.3.1937.
Prewar Assignments:
11. / *Deutschland* (Munich) from 4.4.1936.
Wartime Assignments:
SS-*Infantrie-Ersatz-Bataillon Ost* (Breslau) in 4.1941.
Assigned to a post in Nuremberg 7–21.2.1942.
Waffen-SS *Hauptamt* SS-*Gericht* from 6.1942.
SS- *und Polizei-Gericht* XVII, Mogilew from 24.7.1942.
SS- *und Polizei-Gericht* XVII, Kiev, branch court Dniepropietrowsk on 25.5.1943.
SS- *und Polizei-Gericht* XVIII, Kiev, branch court Transnistrien in 1943.
Lehrgang in Munich 31.12.1943–30.1.1944.
SS- *und Polizei-Gericht* XXV, Nuremberg 4.2.1944–28.8.1944.
Strafvollzugslager der SS *und Polizei* Danzig–Matzkau from 28.8.1944.
Strafvollzugslager der SS *und Polizei* Matzkau, *Zweiglager* Hammerweg in 10.1944.
SS-*Straflager* Dachau in 4.1944.
Promotions:

0.0.1940	SS-*Unterscharführer der Reserve.*
0.0.19__	SS-*Hauptscharführer der Reserve.*
0.0.1944	SS-*Standartenoberjunker.*
30.1.1945	SS-*Untersturmführer der Reserve.*

Decorations & Awards:

0.0.19__	*Kriegsverdienstkreuz II. Klasse mit Schwertern.*
0.0.19__	*Verwundetenabzeichen*, 1939 *in Silber.*
0.0.19__	*Die Medaille zur Erinnerung an den* 1. Oktober 1938 (Sudetenland).
0.0.19__	*Spange Tschechei Die Medaille zur Erinnerung an den* 1. Oktober 1938.

Notes: His father had worked as a carpenter. Attending *Volksschule* for seven classes, Dolles studied carpentry for three years at *Fortbildungsschule* and was then employed as a carpenter from 29 September 1932. Training with the RAD 5/291 between October 1936 and March 1937, he married his pregnant fiancée Resi L., (b. 2.12.1922 in Würzburg) on 2 February 1942. This marriage ended in divorce and applying to marry his fiancée Grace F., (b. 1919) on 15 February 1945, the couple lived in Würzburg. Volunteering for military service in the SS-VT in Munich in 1936, Dolles participated in the 1939 Polish campaign and received a bullet wound in his upper arm on 1 September. Recovered in time to take part in the Western campaign, here, Dolles was wounded by a bullet in in upper right leg on 23 May 1940 and was hospitalised for five months. Released on 28 October 1940, Dolles transferred to a reserve battalion and undergoing a medical examination in Breslau on 4 February 1942, the physician judged him fit only for garrison duties. Transferred to the *HA* SS-*Gericht* as an SS-*Richter* in June 1943, Dolles reported to Danzig–Matzkau in August 1944. Around October 1944 he undertook officer training and received a three centimetre long head wound and light concussion during an Allied air attack on Mosbach on 8 December 1944. Promoted to officer rank in January 1945, as part of his marriage application Dolles was examined by the physician Dr Bergemann at the *Hammerweg Lagerrevier* on 10 January 1945. In *Hammerweg* on 13 January, at this time Dolles reported that his home was in Hirschau. When Hammerweg was evacuated in April 1945, Dolles transferred to the SS-*Straflager* Dachau and may have seen active service with a combat unit near Nuremberg.[13]

Name: Dr jur. Leo Ernst.
Last Rank: SS-*Hauptsturmführer der Waffen*-SS.
Born: 30.9.1907 in Ingolstadt/Bavaria.
Died: 3.1.1945 in Hungary.
NSDAP-Nr.: 3.208.415 (joined 1.5.1933).
SS-Nr.: 124.389 (joined 15.5.1933).
Prewar Assignments:
2. / II. / 1. SS-*Standarte* (Munich) 1.5.1933–1.1.1934.
Rechtsberater Stab 1. SS-*Motorsturm* in 4.1934.
1. SS-*Motorstaffel* from 4.1935.
RFSS SS.-*Gericht* from 9.1933.
SS-VT *Hauptamt* SS-*Gericht* (SS-*Rechtamt*) in 7.1939.
Wartime Assignments:
Divisionsrichter SS-*Totenkopfdivision* field court 17.10.1939–9.1941.
Chefrichter SS- *und Polizei-Gericht* XII, Hamburg 9.1940–9.1941.
Chefrichter SS- *und Polizei-Gericht* VIII, Prague 9.1941–22.9.1941.
Chefrichter SS- *und Polizei-Gericht* IV, Danzig 22.9.1941–15.8.1942.
Kommandant des Strafvollzugslager der SS-*und Polizei* Matzkau 22.9.1941–21.2.1944.
SS-FHA 21.2.1944.
Offizier-Lehrgang Kienschlag SS-*Panzergrenadierschule* 26.2. -12.3.1944.
Offizier-Lehrgang SS-*Unterführerschule* Lauenberg in 3.1944.
Frontleitstelle 'Vienna' in 5.1944.
3rd SS-*Panzer*-Division *Totenkopf* 4.5.1944–3.1.1945.
Led the 10. / III. / SS-*Panzergrenadier*-Rgt. 6 *Theodor Eicke* from 5.1944.
Led the III. / SS-*Panzergrenadier*-Rgt. 6 *Theodor Eicke* from 9.1944.
Promotions:

0.0.1935	SS-*Hauptscharführer der Allgemeine*-SS.
13.9.1936	SS-*Untersturmführer der Allgemeine*-SS.
12.9.1937	SS-*Obersturmführer der Allgemeine*-SS.
0.0.193	*Gefreiter der Reserve.*

11.9.1938	SS-*Hauptsturmführer der Allgemeine*-SS.
0.0.1939	*Feldwebel der Reserve.*
12.8.1939	SS-*Sturmbannführer der Allgemeine*-SS.
17.10.1939	SS-*Sturmbannführer der Waffen*-SS (*Aktiv*).
8.5.1943	SS-*Obersturmbannführer der Waffen*-SS (*Aktiv*) (R.D.A. 30.1.1943).
21.2.1944	SS-*Hauptsturmführer der Waffen*-SS (*Aktiv*).

Decorations & Awards:

0.0.19__	SS-*Zivilabzeichen* (Nr. 106.984).
0.0.19__	SA-*Sportsabzeichen in Bronze.*
0.0.19__	*Reiterssportsabzeichen in Bronze.*
0.0.19__	*Deutsches Reichssportabzeichen in Bronze.*
0.0.19__	*Ehrendegen des Reichsführer*-SS.
0.0.19__	1939 *Eisernes Kreuz I. Klasse.*

Notes: His paternal grandfather was an *Apotheke*, his father a retired *Oberst* and *General* Richard Hartmann his maternal grandfather. Attending the Ingolstadt *Volksschule* for three classes between 1912 and 1915, Ernst then studied at the Ingolsadt Humanistisches *Gymnasium* until 1925 and obtained his *Abitur* from the Munich Humanistisches Wilhelm *Gymnasium* in Easter 1926, (O-I). Studying jurisprudence at the University of Munich, Ernst passed his *Referendarexamen* in February 1930 and undertook his practical training at the *Amtsgericht* Munich and at *Herr* Ernst's legal chambers from May 1930 to March 1933 (his uncle). Studying in Fürth between November 1930 and January 1931, Ernst attended the Erlangen University for one semester and received his law doctorate on 4 August 1932. Passing his *Assessorexamen* in Munich on 26 July 1933, Dr Ernst then obtained a position as a lawyer with both the *Landgerichten* Munich I and II and later, was engaged at the *Oberlandgericht* Munich. A member of the *Bund Oberland* from early 1923 to its dissolution, Ernst participated in the abortive coup in Munich on 8 November 1923. The SS noted that he spoke schoolboy English and enjoyed bob sledging and mountain climbing. Living in Wesermünde in 1934, he attended to his compulsory military training with the 16. / *Gebirgs*-Rgt. 100 between August and September 1937, (training with *Hauptmann* Vielwerth's machine gun company, Ernst was recommended for officer rank on 6.10.1937), he trained again with the 2. / *Gebirgs*-Rgt. 100 (Brannenburg) between September and October 1938 and served with the 6. / *Gebirgs*-Rgt. 100 for four weeks in June 1939.

Ernst was granted leave from his law firm to work full time as a speaker at the SS.-*Gericht* on 15 May 1936 and the civil service released him from his post permanently on 12 October 1939. Referred to Dr Friedrich at the Nazi Party court in Munich on 21 November 1935 for his participation in a property scam involving an SS man named Max Reindl and a Jewish owned company, Ernst admitted completing Reindl's conveyance work and giving the company the appearance of Aryan ownership, when in fact the Jewish owners continued to own and run the business. Judged guilty for his part in the affair,

Ernst received a simple admonishment. Establishing himself as a valued member of the SS.-*Gericht*, a promotions recommendation was submitted for him on 22 June 1936:

> His performance is good and he prepares reports and investigations quickly. In this position Dr Ernst is dependable, hardworking and knowledgeable; he is very proven and has earned this promotion. He is a great (legal) authority compared those he is in charge of and assists to compose reports.

The promotions report supported by *Ogruf.* Scharfe, his promotion to officer rank was conferred on him in September the same year. A department leader in the SS-*Rechtamt* on 12 September 1937, Dr Ernst married his fiancée Herta P., (b. 14.2.1909 in Wessermünde) on 14 November 1936 and the couple settled in Munich and had four children. A promotion recommendation was submitted for Dr Ernst on 14 July 1938:

> An especially dependable and contentious worker, a thoroughly solid character, he has earned the total respect of his comrades with his model posture and wise and wholesome measure. He is capable in every respect and his promotion to SS-*Hstuf.* is approved.

As a consequence of this recommendation Dr Ernst received his promotion in September 1938 and he transferred to the *HA* SS-*Gericht* in July 1939. Another promotion report was submitted for him in 1939:

> As a department leader his work has been spot on, he has a conscientious capability and I have nothing to complain about. In his nature and behaviour he is modest and reserved and makes necessary decisions. Compared to his comrades he is very helpful and obeys commands. His judging view is undertaken as a justice officer for the SS special jurisdiction and he maintains his quota in the *Rechtamt.*

In October 1939 Ernst became an SS-*Richter* and was tasked with creating and leading the *Totenkopfdivision* field court. This division trained in the KL Dachau, but he worked initially from an office in Munich. Attaching his field court to the divisional supply train during the France campaign in May 1940, he and his staff assisted the *Gerichtsherr*, *Gruf.* Theodore Eicke to develop the *Verlorenen Haufen* front probation programme. Officially released from this post on 6 January 1941, Ernst had actually left in September 1940 and was replaced temporarily by Horst Bender. Commanded to the *Stab* HSSPF *Nordsee* in Hamburg to establish and lead a tribunal in early September 1940, a keen equestrian, Ernst took advantage of his new post to use the local SS riding school facilities. Refusing *Gruf.* Rudolf Querner's offer to remain on his staff in a full time position, Ernst was appointed the chief judge at the Prague tribunal during the first week of September 1941 and lived in the court's accommodation. Receiving orders on 22 September 1941 to report to the Danzig tribunal when Ulrich Dümichen replaced him in Prague, upon his arrival Ernst was ordered to take command of the yet to be built Danzig–Matzkau prison. This institution officially opened in March 1942, but this posting was not entirely to Ernst's satisfaction. Writing to his friend Leo Waldemar at the end of September 1942, he complained that the countryside around the prison was unsuitable for horse riding and even if it was, he had found no decent horses to ride. Corresponding with General Querner, Dr Ernst would express his misgivings about refusing his earlier offer to join his staff, but with General Scharfe's permission, he stated his hope to be able to join the general for a horse racing event in Hamburg. A promotion recommendation was submitted for him on 27 November 1942:

> He has been of use in various front and home courts, likewise as the *Lagerkommandant* of the *Strafvollzugslagers der* SS *und Polizei.* Dr Ernst is an old colleague of the *HA SS-Gericht.* He had created and led the court of the SS-*Totenkopfdivision.* Since the year 1941 he has accepted the leadership of the *Strafvollzugslagers der* SS *und Polizei* and the construction of this camp was entirely due to his wisdom. The performance of Dr Ernst is good and his character and SS attitude is suitably in order. He was with the *Totenkopf* during the Western campaign.

Ostuf. Daur relieved Dr Ernst as chief of the Danzig court on 22 September 1941, which enabled him to focus all his attention on his prison duties and he was officially released from this court in August 1942. 'An SS leader has to be firm and strict towards comrades who have made errors and they will be put to work during their punishment, SS officers committing a service offence must face a strong punishment compared to their comrades in the *Wehrmacht*' wrote Ernst to the SS-*Richter beim* RF-SS in February 1942 when asked to describe the task facing him. Following the court's investigation into allegations of brutality and abuse against Matzkau inmates in late 1943, Ernst was called to Berlin to account for his supervisory negligence. Returning to his service post, his tenure as commandant was soon to come to an end and a decision to transfer him to the troops was taken in January 1944. Commanded to the SS-FHA in February 1944, Dr Ernst handed command of the garrison directly to Edmund Baumgärtner and on the same day was demoted to the rank to *Hstuf.* A demotion was usual for those officers who were not qualified at their service rank to serve with the troops. Talking in 1967, Fritz Ringel recalled that Ernst was removed from his post and sent to the front as a punishment. Posted to Kienschlag in February and March 1944, here, his instructors commented on his fitness to become a frontline officer:

> Possessing a secure personality, SS-*Hstuf.* Ernst gives the impression of being quiet, but exhibits a ponderous tactical predisposition. Ernst is eager in his day to day service and makes an effort, but he still does not have a specialist's tactical grasp of this business. He is good enough for SS-*Hstuf.* and is a decent troop officer; it is granted that he can leave here for further service in the motorised troops.

Posted to the *Totenkopfdivision* in Romania in May 1944, a glowing fitness report was prepared for him on 9 June 1944:

> Possessing an open, honest character, he is an impeccable man. Absolutely dependable and true, he is eager to serve and conscientious, however, his poor characteristics are his inability to undertake long watches. He is intellectually above averagely, possesses a great sports physique and a tough stamina. He possesses enough service knowledge and is capable. Ernst is still endeavouring to further mould himself. He has a fresh, soldierly appearance, he behaves securely and self-consciously. He is very kind, polite and correct. Ernst is a good comrade, his manner is kind and strong, favourable and fair. His exceptional service behaviour is impeccable. He is a convinced National Socialist; his desire is free, convinced and forceful. Ernst up to now has only been in the front line for a short time and he has yet an occasion to prove himself in front of the enemy. Ernst fulfils his service position to my fullest satisfaction. Ernst is an admirable SS officer on the grounds of his personality, his good character qualities and capabilities.

Wounded during the retreat from Romania in July 1944, Ernst quickly recovered and returned to his command on 15 August. During September the same year his company fought near Modlin in Poland and was hit hard by the Soviet offensive. Interestingly, at this time his regiment absorbed parolees who had previously served prison sentences in Danzig–Matzkau. A fitness report was submitted for Ernst on 28 September 1944:

> He is knowledgeable and although a temporary deputy leader of the battalion, he still cannot be recommended for further advancement in this deployment. Since the last report there have been no changes.

Receiving 200 *Reichsmark* for the birth of his son on 28 November 1944, the *Totenkopfdivision* was at this time redeployed west of Budapest in Hungary where it was preparing to relieve the trapped Axis forces in the capital. Leading his battalion to Komarom in the Tatra-Almasfuzito region of Hungary, Ernst readied his troops for the first assault (Operation Konrad I) and his battalion advanced eastwards at 10.30 p.m. on 30–31 December 1944. The attack quickly shuddered to a halt in the face of determined opposition, forcing an end to the offensive. The troops and armour of the *Totenkopfdivision* were then committed to a second offensive and under the cover of *Luftwaffe* air attacks its mechanised forces struck the 4th Guards Army and the 31st Guards Rifle Corp flanks on 1 January 1945 (Operation Konrad II). A determined Red Army defence slowed the attack and the IV. SS-*Panzerkorps* had advanced as far as the towns of Biscke and Zsambek when a concentrated Red Army counter-attack inflicted such heavy casualties on the German forces that the German offensive was brought to a halt. Ernst did not survive the battle, killed in action on 3 January 1945 as his battalion fought for the Gereese hills, (Peliofoldszentkereszt), his remains are now lost, but his name is memorialised on a plaque in the Budaörs cemetery.[14]

Name: Synesius Hahn.
Born: 31.10.1914 in Antdorf/Bavaria.
Last rank: SS-*Obersturmführer*.

NSDAP Nr.: 1.926.084 (joined 1.5.1933).
SS Nr.: 75.629 (joined 10.3.1933).
Pre-War Assignments:
SS-VT SS-*Standarte Deutschland* on 2.1.1935.
War-Time Assignments:
Waffen-SS *Hauptamt* SS-*Gericht* late 1941.
SS- *und Polizei-Gericht* I, Munich 1941–1.3.1944.
1. SS-*Infantrie*-Brigade (mot) field court 21.5.1941–3.4.1942.
SS- *und Polizei-Gericht* I, Munich 3.4.1942–25.1.1943.
SS- *und Polizei-Gericht* II, Düsseldorf from 25.1.1943.
SS- *und Polizei-Gericht* VII, Vienna until 25.8.1943.
SS-*Sturmbrigade* 'RF-SS' field court from 25.8.1943.
Strafvollzugslager der SS *und Polizei* Danzig-Matzkau in 1944.
SS-FHA *Amt* IIa from 1.3.1944.
16th SS-*Panzergrenadier*-Division 'RF-SS' 1.3.1944.
SS-*Straflager* Dachau in 1.1945.
Promotions:

0.0.1940	SS-*Oberscharführer der Reserve.*
0.0.19__	SS-*Hauptscharführer der Reserve.*
9.11.1942	SS-*Untersturmführer der Reserve.*
1.5.1943	SS-*Untersturmführer der Waffen*-SS (*Aktiv*).
21.6.1944	SS-*Obersturmführer der Reserve.*

Decorations & Awards:

0.0.19__	SA-*Sportsabzeichen in Bronze.*
0.0.19__	1939 *Eisernes Kreuz II. Klasse.*
0.0.19__	*Medaille 'Winterschlacht im Osten* 1941/42'.

Notes: Attending *Volksschule* for eight classes, Hahn studied at a trade School for three classes and qualified to work as a cobbler. Mustering with the *Deutschland* in the SS-*Kaserne* Munich-Freimann, (same battalion as Rudolf Heiß), he married his fiancée Helene S., (25.4.1917 in Munich) on 22.12.1939 and they had one child up to the point when records ceased in May 1945. Recruited in to the *HA* SS-*Gericht* as an SS-*Beurkundungsunterführer*, Hahn passed the requisite tests to qualify as a certification officer in November 1942 and deployed with numerous courts, Hahn received orders by 28 February 1945 to leave the *HA SS-Gericht* and report to the SS-*Straflager* Dachau. Transferred to the troops in March 1944, he was then sent to the front. Hahn survived the collapse in May 1945 and spent many years detained in the Hammelburg internment camp, (Nr. 10767). He submitted a reference to the court for Rudolf Heiß in 1947 and appeared before the *Spruchkammer* Hammelburg for his own process in 1948. Released from internment, Hahn settled in Starnberg.[15]

Name: Rudolf 'Rudi' **Heiß.**
Last Rank: SS-*Obersturmführer.*
Born: 26.1.1919 in Inzell/Bavaria.
SS-Nr.: 287.989 (joined 1.10.1936).
HJ Service: 1.6.1933–1.4.1936.
RAD Service: 1.4.1936–30.9.1936
Prewar Assignments:
SS-VT from 1.10.1936.
9. / SS-*Standarte Deutschland* 1.10.1936–12.5.1940.
Wartime Assignments:
SS-*Infanterie-Ersatz-Bataillon Deutschland* (Prague-Rusin) from 9.1940.
Waffen-SS *Hauptamt* SS-*Gericht* 1.12.1940–29.4.1945.
Kompanieführer Straflager der SS *und Polizei* Dachau 14.2.1941–6.1943.
Nr. 3 *Lagerführer Strafvollzugslager der* SS-*und Polizei* Danzig–Matzkau in 6.1943.
Nr. 2 *Lagerführer Strafvollzugslager der* SS-*und Polizei* Danzig–Matzkau on 15.3.1944.
Nr. 1 *Lagerführer Strafvollzugslager der* SS-*und Polizei* Danzig–Matzkau in 8.1944.
Strafvollzugslager der SS-*und Polizei* Förrenbach from 27.1.1945.
SS-*Straflager* Dachau, *Aussenstelle* Allach in 4.1945.
Promotions:

20.4.1935	HJ-*Kameradschaftsführer.*
1.10.1936	SS-*Anwärter.*
0.0.1938	SS-*Rottenführer der* SS-VT.
1.7.1942	SS-*Hauptscharführer der Reserve.*
30.1.1944	SS-*Untersturmführer der Reserve.*
0.0.19__	SS-*Untersturmführer der Waffen*-SS, (*Aktiv*).
30.1.1945	SS-*Obersturmführer der Waffen*-SS, (*Aktiv*).

Decorations & Awards:

0.0.19__	*Hitler Jugend Gau Sieger.*
0.0.19__	SS-*Zivilabzeichen.*
0.0.19__	4 *Jähr Dienstzeichen.*
2.3.1939	*Die Medaille zur Erinnerung an den* 13. März 1938 (Österreich).
0.0.19__	1939 *Eisernes Kreuz II. Klasse.*
0.0.19__	*Kriegsverdienstkreuz II. Klasse mit Schwertern.*
0.0.1945	*Verwundetenabzeichen*, 1939 *in Schwarz.*

Notes: His father, *Gendarmeriekommissär* Pius Heiß, was a police officer in Altomünster, Furstenfeldbrück and finally in Plannegg from April 1925 to May 1932. The family settled in Gauting, *Kreis* Starnberg and Heiß attended the Plannegg Catholic *Volksschule* for eight classes between 1925 and 1933. Under the direction of a Catholic theologian he then studied at the Hansa Heime higher trade school in Munich for two years from 1 April 1933 and then completed a one year course at the Bürck & Eichenseer Commercial private school in Munich until April 1935 (*Mittleren Reife*). Intending to find a position as a salaried salesman, Heiß failed to find employment in this field. Postwar, Heiß claimed that his memberhsip of the *Hitlerjugend* on 1 June 1933 was accomplished in the wake of pressure from the trade school administrators. Leaving the *Hitlerjugend* in 1936, here, he explains in his own words about his time with this paramilitary youth organisation:

> [...] During my childhood I was brought up in a Catholic-ecclesiastical sense, which arose from the fact that I belonged to a Catholic youth organisation in 1931–1933. My entry into the *Hitlerjugend* was not undertaken for political reasons, but all the same I was accepted without further questioning. A 'political training' did not take place during my membership of the *Hitlerjugend*. In its service only walks, games, sports and singing were scheduled. I stood in the 14, 15 and 16 life age during my membership in the *Hitlerjugend*. I had little interest in the service and used the occasion of my entry into the RAD as an available opportunity to withdraw from the *Hitlerjugend*. I attended party celebrations and school celebrations with this closed association, when as a member of the *Hitlerjugend* attendance was mandatory. I attended no further party meetings since my resignation from the *Hitlerjugend* (1.4.1936).

'It did not happen because the *Landespolizei*, from which the *Polizei* recruited the youth, was disbanded and in their place, the SS-*Verfügungstruppe* emerged' stated Heiß in 1967 when asked why he had not joined the police in 1936. Satisfying his labour conscription in the Ainaü RAD camp from 1 April to September 1936, (3./300 Geisenfeld), *Arbeitsmann* Heiß then attended the *Reichsberufswettkampf*, an annual *Deutsche Arbeitsfront* spring trade competition that filtered out the future elite of Germany's workforce. At this event, awards were handed to winners of the national and regional competitions. Recipients received a badge, or watch bearing the national Eagle holding the DAF cog wheel with a *Hitlerjugend* diamond in the middle. On the grounds of his young age, Heiß failed in his attempt to undertake his bi-annual compulsory military training with the *Gebirgs*-Rgt. 100:

> [...] There were no political reasons that led me to satisfy my military service in the *Waffen*-SS. Although I admit that as a seventeen year-old young man I was lured by the uniform. In the main, my father and myself were keen that after my education I served out my two years' compulsory military service as soon as possible, and then immediately I would be able to exercise my chosen profession (export and import merchant).

Judged physically strong at an RAD camp, Heiß was targeted by a visiting recruitment commission from the *Deutschland* and they convinced him to undertake his military service with the SS-VT for only two years. Swearing the oath of allegiance in Munich on 9 September 1936, to his surprise, Heiß had to sign for four years' service and then joined the 9. / *Deutschland* at the SS-*Kaserne* Munich-Freimann on 1 October the same year. Participating in the 1938 *Anschluss* of Austria and the Sudetenland march, he then fought during the Polish, French and Dutch campaigns (front service 1.9.1939 to 12.5.1940).

Severely wounded in the upper arm in France on 10 May 1940, Heiß recovered in a Braunschweig clinic for many months and was judged unfit for front service. Appointed a SS-*Beurkundungsunterführer* of the *HA* SS-*Gericht* in December 1940, here in Munich, he completed his specialised training and then worked as a clerk in the *Amt* III. Heiß front experience resulted in his selection to join the *Straflager der* SS *und Polizei* Dachau in February 1941 and he remained in this position until the summer of 1943. While assigned to this post, Heiß undertook a medical examination by an SS physician in Dachau on 16 October 1942. He then applied to marry his fiancée Friedl P., (b. 15.5.1920 in Munich) and both Edmund Baumgärtner and Franz Sturmann supported his application. Receiving permission to proceed with the marriage, Heiß married his fiancée on 20 January 1943, the couple lived with her parents from this time until his transfer to Matzkau in the summer of 1943 and then rented a Danzig apartment. Speaking in 1967, Heiß recalled that Baumgärtner, his former supervisor in Dachau, had asked for his presence in Matzkau specifically and recollected that *Stubaf.* Dr Pohl was the *Chefrichter* of the Danzig tribunal. Here, he recalls his duties:

> [...] I oversaw and maintained the daily service plan. The convicted SS and *Polizei* members, depending on whether they had learned a craft, worked either in the Schichau or the Danzig shipyard. The rest were employed in the camp and undertook drill and attended classes.

During Biedermann's and Laimgruber's tenure as Nr. 1 and Nr. 2 *Lagerführer* respectfully, Heiß claimed he was the prisons third *Lagerführer*, but another places him as the *Kompanieführer* of the 2. *Wachkompanie* in 1943/44. The senior *Lagerführer* until his transfer from Matzkau in late January 1944, Heiß suffered from oxalated stones in his kidneys. Celebrating his birthday in the camp club on 26 January, he suffered a very dangerous renal colic attack and only a calcium injection relieved his 'raging pain' and the commandant then relieved him of his duties. The following day, Heiß collected his wife and a few possessions from their Danzig home and returning to Matzkau, he led a *Vorkommando* by train the same day to Hersbruck. Ending the war in the SS-*Straflager* Dachau, *Aussenstelle* Allach, the Upper-Bavarian *Landpolizei* questioned his parents in June 1947 and using official documents, they were unable to confirm that their son led a *Bewährungskompanie* in Dachau at the end of the war. Escaping the Dachau environs, Heiß lived with Emil Märtins and his wife in a small village near Kassel in the autumn of 1945, but arrested by the American authorities on the grounds of his membership of the *Allgemeine*-SS and *Waffen*-SS on 3 October 1945, he found himself detained in the Hammelburg PWE. Here, the camp authorities noted that Heiß was an invalid in accordance to classification II, had suffered a head injury and experienced gastrointestinal and renal diseases. A civilian internee from 2 July 1946, while detained in Dachau Heiß worked freely as a labourer between 6 October and 10 November 1945. Although disabled, his injuries did not preclude him from working as a driver in the Dachau motor pool. Detaining Heiß in the Bad Aibling PWE, he worked intermittingly between January and June 1946.

Returning to Dachau on 2 July 1946, here, Heiß suffered a fractured skull and spine as the result of his involvement in a serious car accident and was left with restricted upper arm movement. Recovered sufficiently to work as a volunteer driver between 11 July and 18 December, Heiß laboured as an agricultural driver from 19 December 1946 and was arrested by the MID 267 CIE at Dachau for posessing the rank of *Ostuf.* Interned in Camp Nr. 9 on 20 December 1946, Heiß worked voluntarily with the Bondland agricultural force between 24 March and 13 April 1947 and was received back into the Catholic Church on 17 April. On the grounds that he had been coerced by his trade school into joining the *Hitlerjugend*, was too young to have appreciated the dangers of joining the SS-VT and had been missrepesented by recruiters about the length of service he would have to undertake, Heiß applied to the authorities for a youth amnesty on 1 April 1947:

> It was not due to me that it proved impossible to retire from the *Waffen*-SS after two years, it was down to the fact that I had to resign myself to the command issued to me at the oath swearing and I was forced in writing to commit myself to another four years' service. I was aware as a soldier, that if I did not follow this instruction, then I would have been subjected to a war court martial punishment. Nevertheless, I have done everything, what as a soldier I could have done to avoid a lasting commitment with the *Waffen*-SS. With every contrary soldierly principle, I long refused to attend an officer course, and moreover I refused an order to attend a course in August 1938.
>
> This resulted in the most unpleasant consequences and later, through insight into my personal file, if you require convincing, I found that my refusal to register earned me the comment 'politically unreliable.' Further consequences were special and punishment service, exclusion from leave, blocked promotions and ongoing harassment on the part of my superiors, (only after four years' service was I promoted to SS-*Uscha.* on 9.11.1940). As a result of the war, I was forced to remain in the *Waffen*-SS. Again, I had only one thought and that was under no circumstances would I bind myself to them tighter, I would find a way to free myself and enable myself to finally exercise my chosen civilian occupation after the war. That this was my earnest desire, arising from my hard refusal to participate in a *Beurkundungsführer* training course and from the violent clashes I had with the course leader.
>
> I imagine this was a result of my education in the ecclesiastical sense. When I was asked to join the *Waffen*-SS, I connected this with the many perks, not the consequences. Only in 1942 was I forced to take this step, namely it was explained to me that it was impossible to obtain the approval of the RuSHA for my marriage, I would not obtain approval if I did not leave the church. An exit I had to undertake if I ever wished to marry my wife. For political reasons, this exit from the church was not made. With the exception of the *Waffen*-SS and the *Hitlerjugend*, I have belonged to no other organisations and successfully avoided my entry into the NSDAP. During my affiliation with the *Waffen*-SS I was not politically active. Finally, it should be noted that until the capitulation I had no knowledge of the criminal character of the SS, of the tasks of the SD and the *Gestapo* and the conditions in the camps.

Stating that he had no time or day for committing reprehensible or brutal behaviour, Heiß asked the court to conclude from the many character statements submitted, that he had proved his case in the sense required by law. Asking for his classification in the group of less incriminated, Heiß also demanded that the court applied the youth amnesty in his case. T support his claim, both the Grünewald police and the mayor of Gauting submitted character statements which reported that no known offences were recorded against him. Baumeister and another former wartime colleagues submitted character references on his behalf:

> Hahn, Synesius, born 31.10.1914 in Antdorf-Obb.
> I hereby confirm that Rudolf Heiß, born 26 January 1919 in Inzell, was in the same battalion and the same regiment of the SS-TV as myself from 1 October 1936 to 1 February 1941. A member of the *Waffen*-SS, as I was myself, he was as a non-commissioned officer and officer member of the *HA* SS-*Gericht* from 1 February 1941 to 8 May 1945. Rudolf Heiß had nothing to do with concentration camp inmates and prisoners of war.

On 28 January 1947, Heiß father confirmed that his 'Catholic son Rudi' was an unwilling SS man and explained how his son was a victim of circumstances:

> [...] Contrary to his and my will, he was duty bound to four years of service with the SS and as a result of the outbreak of war, with a further four years of service and could no longer leave the SS. He refused repeated invitations to attend an SS officer training course until 1938 and after five years of service he was promoted to *Uscha.* Commanded to an officer's course in the summer of 1943, he sought to cancel this by every means, which is why I made representations to his training leader, *Hstuf.* Geike, in Munich, but despite my son's reluctance he had to join another officer course on the orders of his superiors in late 1943. By this way, he was promoted to the rank of *Ustuf.* in January 1944. He was neither politically active during his *Hitlerjugend* or SS service and he never involved himself in propagandistic activity, or undertook propaganda of any kind. Never a member of the Nazi party, he only fulfilled his rank and duties and had never participated in a crime, or other criminal act actively, or passively and had no interest in politics at all.

Questioned by 1st Lt. John S. Hilliard at the headquarters of the 1st Infantry Division CIE Nr. 9 on 11 April 1947, he recommended Heiß's detention until his case could be turned over to the German courts for a denazification trial (at this time, Heiß claimed to be a student). His case was the handed to the Hammelburg camp *Spruchkammer* for them to determine his culpability. Volunteering as a transport worker between 15 January and 15 March 1947, he then worked on a farm from 24 March to 13 April and laboured on the Abbruch farm between 19 April and 11 October the same year and again from 13 October 1947. On 16 October 1947, Heiß wrote to the Hammelburg court prosecutor to express his dissatisfaction with the way his case had been handled and complain that he was one of 300 young people in the camp that were waiting for the remaining legalities to be concluded. Blaming the authorities for this situation, Heiß griped that the legal department had told him to undertake further rehabilitation. Asking that his work with American vehicles be taken into consideration, he mentioned that his family was experiencing financial hardship.

Announcing their judgment on 4 December 1947, the *Hammelburg Spruchkammer* V placed Heiß in the group III 'less incriminated' and imposed the usual employment caveats on his probationary period of two years. Fined 500 *Reichsmark*, the court noted that he owed eight *Reichsmark* in delinquency fees and subtracting the 300 special labor days from his sentence, he was ordered to bear the cost of the proceedings (2,850 *Reichsmark*). On 18 December 1947 the Hammelburg camp public prosecutor decided against lodging an appeal against this sentence and with the consent of the military government, he ordered Heiß's release. Discharged the same day, Heiß paid 500 *Reichsmark* of his court fine on 6 February 1948 and complying with his 300 days court-ordered special labour, he was then employed as a labourer with Josef Bauer, wood and coal merchant of Grünewald near Munich, and the Eierwiese from 2 February 1948, (he working here voluntarily from 27.1.1948). Reporting sick between 28 March and 1 July 1948, Heiß recovered and continued his special work as an auxiliary worker at the Blatt Gutsav optical factory in Munich (the employment office was aware of his disablement). Petitioning the public prosecutor to mitigate his sentence on 9 June and again on 4 August 1948, Rudolf Heiß complained that his family's situation had worsened since the currency reforms. Submitting his written appeal to the court on 26 August 1948, he reiterated his earlier mitigation, and with some bitterness, he bemoaned his personal situation:

> On the grounds of my impeccable attitude and human behavior I cannot be accused of any political activity or any other charges. For this reason, as I understand it to this day, my 1947 punishment was harsh and up to this point all the sanctions are equally hard and high for an 'adolescent' born after 1 January 1919. However, my current experience has showed me—unfortunately—that only the high and highest party officials, all our former superiors, who preached and persuaded us boys to follow Nazi teachings and Hitler's theory, are today acting as collaborators and, us still immature, political children—are today menial workers and special work is given to those, who were the actual carriers of the bacillus of Hitler's nefarious madness ideas. As burdened young people, we have been preferably released by the camp *Spruchkammer* (spring 1948), which is in great contrast to the main culprits, who (rightly) should have their turn later and with tougher sanctions. Who is now talking about law and justice?
>
> Since 1 February 1948 I have worked as a menial worker. My professional future remains for me continually spoilt and insufficient, (I am now in the 29th year of life), the nine year involuntary service, the two-and-a-half years' internment and a further one-and-a-half to two years' special employment respectively, are in turn not particularly useful for my next round and do nothing to alleviate the misery and suffering in the

family. With my wife I run a joint household with my parents in law who are both elderly, supporting needing parents. My father is paralysed in both arms. I am also a refugee from Danzig and belong to the wounded category II.

I ask the local *Spruchkammer* politely and urgently to change my atonement in the clemency way and the early advocacy of my request.Respectfully yours!

Sending the court a copy of his announcement on 17 October 1948, Heiß asked for the resumption of his trial and asked that the court took into consideration the loss of his possessions in Danzig and his voluntary work. Hearing his case on 18 October 1949 the Nuremberg *Hauptkammer* classifyed him a 'follower' and ordered Heiß to bear the costs of the process, 2,830 *Marks* (at this time he claimed to be a student). Writing on 29 September 1949, the Bavarian State Ministry for Special Affairs acknowledged that his two year probationary period would end on 15 October that same year. On the same day, the Hammelburg public prosecutor submitted an application for a re-examination of his case and a final decison in Heiß's process was obtained once the opinions of the Bavarian State Ministry for Special Affairs, the Nuremberg *Hauptkammer*, and the Minister for Political Liberation had been sought. On 12 January 1948 the Hammelburg court confirmed that Heiß had been placed in the group III of offenders with two years' probation and punished with a 500 *Reichsmark* atonement fine, with an order to pay almost 97 *Reichsmark* costs and undertake 300 days special work. Writing in the autumn of 1948, the Hammelburg tribunal reported that Heiß had atoned through his thirteen months' probation, confirmed that his special work had been completed and approved his clemency.

Writing to the Nuremberg *Hauptkammer* on 12 October 1949, the public prosecutor requested that Heiß be reclassified, without new atonement, in the group IV of the followers. The costs of the procure was again set to 2,830 *Reichsmark* and this process was concluded on 18 October the same year (the Bad Kissingen financial office calculated that Heiß owed almost 6,000 *Reichsmark* in fines and court costs). Rudolf Heiß applied for financial compensation from the Welfare Office for the War Damaged in the mid-1950s. Writing to this office at a later date, the court confirmed that Heiß had been interned on 3 October 1945, he had not been formally dismissed from the *Waffen*-SS until 2 July 1946 and was held on automatic arrest until 19.12.1947.

His marriage to Friedl ending in divorce, Heiß married a secretary named *Frau* Irmgaard Maria W. and the couple settled in Neugilching, *Kreis* Starnberg. Employed as a salaried salesman and then as a treasurer for Atlas in Grünwald *bei* Munich in 1967, the former Matzkau guard, Albert Müller, recalled Heiß working in a meat canning factory as an administrative leader in Munich-Grünwald and he met with him once in the Bavarian capital during 1959 (he called to mind Heiß driving in his car every day). In connection with allegations of complicity in the murder of convicts in Matzkau, the *Landgericht* Munich handed the Heiß *Spruchkammer* case file to the state prosecuter on 22 June 1966. In connection with this accusation, Heiß submitted himself for questioning in Munich on the 14 March 1967 and 5 August 1969 and discussed his service history and wartime prison service.[16]

Name: Theodor Janssen.
Last Rank: SS-*Obersturmführer*.
Born: 16.6.1904 in Duisburg/Westphalia.
NSDAP-Nr.: 6.212.477 (joined 1.5.1937).
SS-Nr.: 474.399 (v) (joined 24.4.1940).
Wartime Assignments:
Waffen-SS from 4.1940.
1. SS-*Totenkopf-Kavallerie*-Rgt. 1940.
Waffen-SS *Hauptamt* SS-*Gericht* 1940.
SS- *und Polizei-Gericht* VI, Krakau, branch court Warsaw until 3.12.1940.
SS- *und Polizei-Gericht* XIV, Metz from 3.12.1940.
SS- *und Polizei-Gericht* VI, Krakau until 6.11.1941.
SS- *und Polizei-Gericht* II, Düsseldorf on 6.11.1941–4.1942.
SS- *und Polizei-Gericht* XIV, Metz from 4.1942.
SS-*Straflager* Dachau on 25.11.1942.
SS- *und Polizei-Gericht* XIV, Metz in 1.1943,
9th SS-*Panzer*-Division *Hohenstaufen* field court 1.3.–22.10.1943.
SS-*Straflager* Dachau in 2.1944.
9th SS-*Panzer*-Division *Hohenstaufen* field court in 11.1944.
Promotions:

0.0.1940	SS-*Oberscharführer der Reserve.*
0.0.1941	SS-*Hauptscharführer der Reserve.*
9.11.1943	SS-*Untersturmführer der Reserve.*
9.11.1944	SS-*Obersturmführer der Reserve.*

Decorations & Awards:

0.0.19__	SA-*Sportsabzeichen in Bronze.*
0.0.19__	SS-*Ehrenwinkel für alte Kämpfer.*
0.0.19__	*Deutsches Reichssportabzeichen in Silber.*
0.0.19__	*Deutsche Olympia-Ehrenzeichen* I. *Klasse.*
12.7.1941	*Kriegsverdienstkreuz II. Klasse o. Schwertern.*
0.0.1945	*Kriegsverdienstkreuz I. Klasse mit Schwertern.*

Notes: Attending *Volksschule* for eight classes, Janssen was a keen athlete, who competed in weight lifting and bowl competitions. Undertaking three years' training as a justice inspector candidate between 1 April 1925 and 1 April 1938, Janssen attended a police school and was then employed at the *Amtsgericht* Oberhausen in the Rhineland. Marrying his fiancée Anna B., (b. 26.1.1904 in Duisburg) on 1 April 1931, they had one set of twins up to the point when records ceased in May 1945 and lived in Duisburg. A SS-*Beurkundungsführer* of the *HA* SS-*Gericht* in 1940, Janssen deployed in numerous courts before reporting to the SS-*Straflager* Dachau. From here, Janssen wrote to Danzig–Matzkau in late November 1942 and left this post for a field court in the spring of 1943.

Returning to Dachau by February 1944, he became the acting leader of the *Aussenstelle* Allach during April the same year and reported living in the prison. The command ordering him from the SS-*Straflager* to Danzig–Matzkau on 28 August was cancelled by 3 October. Janssen had returned to the *Hohenstaufen* field court by November and remained with this service office until May 1945.[17]

Name: Heinrich Köning.
Last Rank: SS-*Unterscharführer.*
Born: 19.5.1911 in Münster.
Died: 23.3.1944.
NSDAP-Nr.: 2.480.563 (joined 1.5.1933).
Wartime Assignments:
SS-*Totenkopf-Infantrie*-Rgt. 3 on 11.3.1941.
Strafvollzugslager der SS-*und Polizei* Danzig–Matzkau in 3.1944.
Promotions:

Mar.1941	SS-*Rottenführer der Reserve.*
0.0.19__	SS-*Unterscharführer der Reserve.*

Notes: He applied to the RuSHA to marry his fiancée from an infantry regiment in March 1941. His family recalled that Köning was assigned to the Danzig–Matzkau staff in the spring of 1944 and has been reported missing since that time.[18]

Name: Artur Kretzschmar.
Last Rank: SS-*Obersturmführer.*
Born: 25.3.1913 in Thale/H.
NSDAP-Nr.: 2.001/818, (joined 1.4.1933).
SS-Nr.: 132.854, (spring 1933).
RAD service: 1.4.–30.9.1935.
Wartime Assignments:
SS-TV from 9.1939.
Waffen-SS *Hauptamt* SS-*Gericht* in late 1941.
SS- *und Polizei-Gericht* X, Den Haag until 14.4.1942.
Strafvollzugslager der SS-*und Polizei* Danzig–Matzkau from 14.4.1942.
Promotions:

0.0.1942	SS-*Unterscharführer der Reserve.*
0.0.19__	SS-*Oberscharführer der Reserve.*
9.11.1942	SS-*Hauptscharführer der Reserve.*
21.6.1943	SS-*Untersturmführer der Reserve.*
9.11.1844	SS-*Obersturmführer der Reserve.*

Decorations & Awards:
0.0.19__ SS-*Zivilabzeichen* (Nr. 160.874).
0.0.19__ SA-*Sportsabzeichen in Bronze.*
0.0.19__ D.L.R.G. *in Silber.*
0.0.19__ *Kriegsverdienstkreuz II. Klasse mit Schwertern.*
0.0.19__ *Deutsches Reichssportabzeichen in Bronze.*

Notes: Attending four classes of *Volksschule*, Kretzschmar studied at *Mittelschule* for one year and then learned chemical masonry at a technical high school for five classes. Once qualified, Kretzschmar found employment at the Magdeburg railway Construction Company. Mustering with the NSFK from January to August 1933, he married his Quedlinburg fiancée on 13 August 1938. The couple lived in Magdeburg and had two children up to the point when records ceased in May 1945. Almost certainly drafted into the SS-TV in September 1939, Kretzschmar was assigned to the *HA* SS-*Gericht* as a SS-*Beurkundungsunterführer* in late 1941 and joined the Matzkau staff in April 1942.[19]

Name: Erich Laimgruber.
Last Rank: SS-*Untersturmführer.*
Born: 8.4.1908 in Innsbruck.
Died: 28.7.1944 in Pepelari, Zepce/Croatia.
NSDAP-Nr.: 687.042 (joined 10.11.1931).
SS-Nr.: 23.032 (joined 11.11.1931).
Prewar Assignments:
Freikorp Oberland 10.1927–11.1931.
2./ I. / 37. SS-*Standarte* (Linz) from 11.1931.
5./ II. / SS-Standarte *Deutschland* from 1.1.1935.
I./ SS-*Standarte Deutschland* from 20.3.1938.
I./ SS-*Standarte Der Führer* (Vienna) from 28.3.1938.
1./ I. /SS-*Standarte Der Führer* (Prague) 15.7.1939.
Wartime Assignments:
Waffen-SS *Hauptamt* SS-*Gericht* 20.11.1940–8.3.1944.
SS-*Straflager* Dachau 20.11.1940–20.7.1941
Strafvollzugslager der SS-*und Polizei* Danzig–Matzkau 20.7.1941–8.3.1944.
2. *Lagerführer des Strafvollzugslager der* SS-*und Polizei* Danzig–Matzkau from 22.7.1941.
Beurkundungsführer training course in early 1942.
SS-FHA from 8.3.1944.
SS-*Gebirgsjäger-Ausbildung- und Ersatz-Bataillon* 6 (Hallein/Salzburg) 15.3.–20.4.1944.
7th SS-*Gebirgsjäger*-Division *Prinz Eugen* 20.3.–7.1944.
7. SS-*Gebirgs-Aufklärungsabteilung* 31.5.-28.7.1944.
Promotions:
1.1.1935 SS-*Unterscharführer der* SS-VT.
20.4.1936 SS-*Scharführer der* SS-VT.

1.10.1937 SS-*Oberscharführer der* SS-VT.
1.9.1941 SS-*Hauptscharführer der Waffen*-SS (*Aktiv*).
20.4.1942 SS-*Untersturmführer der Waffen*-SS (*Aktiv*) (R.D.A. 1.4.1942).

Decorations & Awards:

0.0.19__ SS-*Zivilabzeichen* (Nr. 12.330).
0.0.19__ SA-*Sportsabzeichen in Bronze.*
0.0.19__ *Deutsches Reichssportabzeichen in Bronze.*
0.0.19__ SS-*Ehrenwinkel für alte Kämpfer.*
12.5.1944 *Totenkopfring der* SS.
0.0.1938 *Die Medaille zur Erinnerung an den* 1. Oktober 1938 (Sudetenland).
0.0.1938 *Die Medaille zur Erinnerung an den* 13. März 1938 (Austria).

Notes: Attending *Volksschule*, *Unterrealschule* and then studying business practice at a trade academy, Laimgruber left full-time education to undertake an apprenticeship. Qualifying, he found employment as a clerk. The SS noted that he spoke and wrote Italian. Living in Innsbruck during June 1933, Laimgruber fled Austria for Bavaria on 1 October 1933 and joined the SS-*Sturmbann* z.b.V. in Dachau. Laimgruber marched with the *Der Führer* during the *Anschluss* of Austria and the takeover of the Sudetenland. Spending three months in Prague, Laimgruber applied to the RuSHA on 4 July 1939 for permission to marry his fiancée Herla H., (b. 1.1.1920 in Villach). At this time he was living at the SS-*Kaserne* Faßangarten in Vienna. Permission given a short while later, the couple married on 9 August 1939, had two children and lived in Vienna. Laimgruber fought with the *Der Führer* along the Grebbe line, in Flanders and along the Weland line in May and June 1940. Transferring to the *HA* SS-*Gericht Amt* III in November the same year as an SS-*Beurkundungsunterführer*, Laimgruber was immediately assigned to the SS-*Straflager* Dachau as a *Rapportführer* and accompanied *Ostuf.* Albert to Matzkau on 20 July 1941. Here, Laimgruber became the Nr. 2. *Lagerführer* on 22 July the same year and was recommended for promotion to officer rank on 1 April 1942:

> This promotion is supported on the grounds of his personal qualities, his knowledge and outstanding achievements in difficult conditions, Laimgruber is a long valuable, tireless worker. His behaviour in and out of service is very flawless and his attitude is suitable for the SS.

This report supported by General Scharfe, the promotion was awarded in April 1942. Advocating the use of the cane for the 5. *Strafkompanie,* Laimgruber found himself a witness at *Ostuf.* Dieterle's court martial in September 1943 and his support for this forbidden punishment almost certainly resulted in selection for front service in March 1944. On 16 June, his training course leader revealed that Laimgruber had been trained in the use of light infantry weapons and had been judged suitable as a company troop leader and motorcycle officer. The report elaborated further:

> He is of medium size, slender build, is interested in sport and mountain climbing and suitable for combat, he is honourable, open and possess a calm and modest manner with an agile spirit. He needs to gain some maturity, but capable of wise judgement, he possesses good manners and is a polite and obliging type in the company of his comrades. He possesses an honest, open nature and his modest appearance is nimble, calm and mature. He has a polite and courteous manner and is popular with his comrades. About his family circumstances nothing at fault is known. His appearance on and off-duty life is correct and perfect.
>
> Possessing a firm world vision, he exhibits an educational talent and is a free speaker, etc. His world view is consolidated. He is an old fighter and reveals an exemplary attitude through his world vision. His convincing lecture style stamps him out as a good educator. He is hard against himself and as well as possessing a responsible and exceptionally good sense of duty, he has an impeccable service attitude. His skill as an instructor is good, but is still uncertain. He has been identified for use as an officer and he fulfils his service position.

Laimgruber was then posted to the *Prinz Eugen* on 20 March 1944 and arriving on 31 May, Laimgruber led a section in the reconnaissance battalion until his death in action in July 1944. His widow and children posted a bereavement notice in the *Das Schwarze Korps* on 5 October the same year.[20]

Name: Otto-Leo Langer.
Last Rank: SS-*Untersturmführer*.
Born: 14.3.1917 in Krummau on der Moldau/Böhmerwald.
Died: 26.5.1996 in Dortmund.
Prewar Assignments:
Freikorps 25.8.–15.10.1938.
SS-VT 1.11.1938.
SS-*Standarte Deutschland* from 1.11.1938.
Wartime Assignments:
SS-*Infantrie-Ersatz-Bataillon Deutschland* from 7.1940.
Waffen-SS *Hauptamt* SS-*Gericht* 8.7.1940–5.1945.
SS-*Straflager* Dachau 15.10.1940–20.7.1941.
Strafvollzugslager der SS-*und Polizei* Danzig–Matzkau 20.7.1940–1.3.1943.
SS-Beurkundungsunterführer-Lehrgang in 1941.
Beurkundungsführer–Lehrgang in 3.1942.
Zweiglager Ludwigsfelde 1.3.1943–11.1944.
SS-*Straflager* Dachau, *Zweiglager* Hammerweg in 12.1944.
SS-*Straflager* Dachau, *Aussenstelle* Allach from 3.1945.
38th SS-*Panzergrenadier*-Division *Nibelungen* 3.1945–5.1945.

Promotions:

Aug.1939	SS-*Sturmann der Waffen*-SS, (*Aktiv*).
1.8.1940	SS-*Unterscharführer der Waffen*-SS (*Aktiv*).
30.1.1941	SS-*Scharführer der Waffen*-SS (*Aktiv*).
31.9.1941	SS-*Oberscharführer der Waffen*-SS (*Aktiv*).
20.4.1942	SS-*Hauptscharführer der Waffen*-SS (*Aktiv*).
9.11.1943	SS-*Untersturmführer der Waffen*-SS *(Aktiv)*.

Decorations & Awards:

0.0.19__	*Kriegsverdienstkreuz II. Klasse mit Schwertern.*
0.0.19__	*Verwundetenabzeichen*, 1939 *in Schwarz.*

Notes: Born in modern day Český Krumlov, an ethnic-German community in the Sudetenland, Langer was one of nine children born to a goldsmith. Attending the Krummau *Volksschule* and *Bürgerschule* between 1923 and 1931, Langer learned business practice at *Fachschule* and with no salary he apprenticed at the *Firma* Cuba in Niesewanz über Schlochau. i. P. His family struggling to make ends meet, Langer, who lived at home, had no choice but to seek work. Gaining an unsalaried position as a salesman with the Cuba company, he earned a paltry 49 *Reichsmark* until his dismissal on 1 September 1934. Unemployed from 1 September to December 1934, Langer received a subsidy of ten *Kronen,* which was the equivalent of a single *Reichsmark.* Working at a brewery until January 1935, Langer then found employment with a construction company and laboured to build roads between March and June 1935. Labouring at the Spiro paper factory in Südböhmen until his dismissal in December the same year, Langer accepted a caretaker and porter post with the Firma Julius Meinl A.G. between February 1936 and August 1937, but convinced that he would not find work in his chosen profession unless he left home, he travelled to Niederböhme and accepted a position as a salesman with H. Lazak in Brüx/Erzgebirge. Dismissed in July 1938, having only earning 240 *Reichsmark*, he remained unemployed until the Nazi *Anschluss* of the Sudetenland in October 1938. Travelling to Munich in 1938, he applied successfully to join the SS-VT and reported to the *Deutschland* to undertake basic infantry training. Neglecting to join the Nazi party, Langer contributed towards the NSV and NSF).

The RuSHA refused Langer's application in 1939 to marry his fiancée Gertrud J., (b. 7.9.1909 in Niesse/Silesia). Training with his regiment near Tarau in East Prussia during July and August 1939, the following month, he was seriously wounded in the right lower leg during the invasion of Poland on 23 September. Fourteen shell splinters left Langer with a pronounced limp and he recovered in the Hamburg-Barmbeck *Reserve-Lazarett* (I) between 1 October 1939 and 15 March 1940. Discharged, he reported to a reserve battalion in Munich in July 1940 and was judged fit only for garrison duties. Transferred to the *HA* SS-*Gericht* in the summer of 1940, Langer became a *Rapportführer* at the SS-*Straflager* Dachau in October the same year. His application for marriage approved, Langer married Hildegard Z., (b. 29.6.1918 in Brüx/Sudetenland) on 28 June 1941 and the couple had two children and lived in Brüx (his bride's brother, Rolf Zinert, was an SS officer in the Brüx *Allgemeine*-SS).

'After about two to three months the dissolution of the camp took place. Both the staff and the convicts then transferred to Danzig-Langwasser' wrote Langer in 1970 and this statement almost certainly refers to the closure of the *Abteilung Gefängnis* Dachau. Speaking in 1947, Langer recalled reporting to Matzkau in the summer of 1941 and living in the non-commissioned officer's accommodation. The former guard, Albert Müller, called to mind that Langer was appointed the commandant's adjutant and succeeded by Emil Märtins, he was then placed in charge of the *Hauptwirtschaftlager* and the garrison office until January 1943. Speaking in 1970, Langer explained the duties he undertook in Matzkau:

> [...] I would like to add that I only acted as a clerk until the very end. Only in a few cases, was I entrusted with the defence of Dutchmen in Danzig, who appeared for trial for committing minor offences. Legal training was not required in such cases.

Ordered to remain in his room in the summer of 1942, Langer faced investigation for attending the marriage of *Oscha.* Edmund Manzbach and his bride in his SS service uniform. When questioned about this event, Dr Ernst provided the investigators with a satisfactory explanation for the incident and it appears that no further disciplinary action was taken against Langer.

The inmate capacity exhausted in Danzig–Matzkau, a decision was taken in early 1943 to construct a branch prison in the Berlin suburb of Ludwigsfelde. As a consequence of this situation, Langer accompanied *Hstuf.* Albert and 100 convicts from Matzkau to the capital in March 1943 (earning 4,100 *Reichsmark* for 1943). His wounds failing to heal correctly, Langer underwent a leg operation in the spring of 1944 and recovered in hospital between 10 and 18 April. Returned to Ludwigsfelde by 6 May 1944, Langer remained in this post until November the same year. The SS awarded Langer a crisis loan of 194 *Reichsmark* on 12 August 1944 and he remained at the *Zweiglager* Hammerweg until December 1944. Posted to Allach, here, Langer took over leadership of the prison office until the Allied advance threatened to overrun the town. Answering the call to fight at the front in March 1945, Langer reported to a panzer grenadier division, but judged incapable of fighting as an infantryman, he mustered with the divisional supply unit until the collapse (he earned 1,500 *Reichsmark* in 1945).

Surrendering to the US Army and incarcerated in Kufstein' on 8 June 1946, Langer transferred to the Darmstadt internment camp and from here, wrote a complimentary character statement for his former comrade Fritz Baumeister in June 1946. Elsewhere, *Frau* Langer and her parents were arrested and forcibly removed from Czechoslovakian territory. Making their way to Frankfurt am Main, *Frau* Langer discovered that her mother and child were ill and the group left the transport at Arnstadt in Thüringen. Placing her youngest child and mother in the care of a local hospital, they died in October 1946. *Frau* Langer then undertook a search for her husband and found him in Darmstadt in February 1947. As a result of their reunion, she then moved in with his parents in Flörsheim bei Höchst am Main, found employment with Siemens and relocated to Frankfurt am Main on 2 July 1947 to work in a canteen. While imprisoned Langer worked as a menial worker for the Odenwälder Hartstein-Industrie A.G. in Darmstadt/Roßdorf and helping to rebuild roads in Hesse, he expressed an interest in working at their Roßdorf quarry once released. The Frankfurt employment office then arranged or Langer to toil for A. W. Winkel Sohn Baugeschäft of Frankfurt am Main and he helped rebuild a hospital. Langer submitted his mitigation letter to the Darmstadt camp *Spruchkammer* on 16 February 1947 in an attempt to limit his culpability and submitted the following character references:

Fritz Niclasson, *Deutsch Internierungslager* III/9, dated 6.8.1947.
After my compulsorily transfer from the *Wehrmacht* to the *Waffen*-SS in 1942 I arrived in the office of the *Strafvollzugslager der Waffen*-SS *und Polizei* Danzig–Matzkau in March 1943 with the acquired rank of *Scha. der Reserve* (*Unterfeldwebel*). There I met and got to know Otto Langer, who at that time was leading the office as a SS-*Beurkundungsunterführer* and later as an *Ustuf.* Likewise, I was in the *Zweiglager* Berlin–Ludwigsfelde with Langer in the period from October 1943 to April 1944. I found him to be a man who did not accept hardship and applied to his subordinates the fullest understanding, especially towards the inmates, who saw for themselves his human thinking and actions.

For example, far beyond his service powers he permitted the work suitable convicts, those under my command, to leave the camp on Sundays for long walks, although he knew, that on these occasions I led them to meet their families.

Langer himself constantly ran this risk and would himself to be held accountable for these acts of humanity. Likewise, Langer was generous in the granting and approval of special letters and other perks and let himself be guided in all things by his humane emotion. He was appreciated by the prisoners and was popular. It is not known to me that Langer has participated in any inhuman attacks, or is guilty of other offences under the Act.

Wolfgang Walther, *Deutsch Internierungslager* II-22, dated 24.3.1947.
On the grounds of my legal civil profession I was with the *HA* SS-*Gericht* in Munich from 1 April 1940 to 30 April 1945 and at Prien *am* Chiemsee from the end of July 1944. Lastly, as a reserve judge of the *Waffen*-SS I held the active rank of *Stubaf. der Reserve* in the *Waffen*-SS.

As I recall, it was in the summer of 1940 when the then *Strm.* of the *Waffen*-SS Otto Langer, was transferred to the *HA* SS-*Gericht* for use as a clerk because of an injury, which made him unsuitable for further troops' service on the front lines.

In the course of years until the beginning of 1945, Langer, after appropriate training and participation in relevant professional courses had initially become a SS-*Beurkundungsunterführer* and then a SS-*Beurkundungsführer* and at the end of the war he held the rank of *Ustuf. der Reserve* of the *Waffen*-SS. His activities as a SS-*Beurkundungsführer* were purely for office duties within the region of the military jurisdiction of the *Waffen*-SS *and Polizei* and corresponded approximately to that of a *Feldjustiz-Sekretärs* in the *Wehrmacht* judiciary.

Excluding the time he spent with the *HA* SS-*Gericht* staff, Langer was engaged in various prisons of the SS and the *Polizei* (not concentration camps) as a certification non-commissioned officer and later a SS-*Beurkundungsführer* during the period from summer 1940 to early 1945. In the prisons of the SS and *Polizei* was carried out jail sentences against criminal offenders of the SS and *Polizei*: As far as Langer's work there, he has to my knowledge always demonstrated a human understanding for delinquents who found themselves in this war-related predicament.

As I understand it, in the last weeks of the war—about April-May 1945—Langer accepted *Fronthilfe* around that time and was reinstated for further service at the front with the troops. In personal respect I can only offer the best testimony for Langer, he exhibits ambition and is a willing worker who possesses a straight and sincere character with a constant willingness to help others and in his manners, he is polite and courteous. Wolfgang Walther.

His former prison comrade, Fritz Baumeister returned Langer's complimentary character reference:

Fritz Baumeister, Nuremberg-Langwasser, dated 6.10.1946.
Herr Otto Langer is known to me personally on the grounds of my former membership of the *HA* SS-*Gericht* in Munich. During my time, Langer was likewise a member of the *HA* SS-*Gericht* during the period from July 1940 to March 1944. Langer was of use as a typist, *Beurkundungsunterführer* and later, as a SS-*Beurkundungsführer* after passing the examination in March 1942. His activities were confined to office duties and Langer, due to his subordination to the superior jurist personnel he did not have a position in which to make independent decisions. With Langer I do not have any concerns or know of any violations of public life.

The statements Langer submitted to the court also included these two, written by former convicts:

Erwin Ittrich, Nuremberg-Langwasser, dated 4.10.1946.
I became acquainted with *Herr* Otto Langer, a former *Ustuf.* of the *Waffen*-SS, as a consequence of the time I served my sentence in the *Strafvollzugslager der* SS *und Polizei* Danzig–Matzkau. Langer was active in the camp personnel department and was of use as a *Beurkundungsführer*. He was always a role model and behaved as a full and decent superior towards us prisoners. Through discussions and evident demonstration, he soon earned the confidence of all prisoners, and was popular with us as he was with the guards. With respect to inhumanity and cruelty I am not aware that Langer in any way has somehow been guilty.

Alfred Reinhold Darmstadt, dated July 1947.
I became acquainted with the former SS-*Ustuf. der Reserve* Otto Langer on the grounds of my stay as a remand prisoner in the *Zweiglager des Strafvollzugslagers der* SS *und*

> *Polizei* Berlin-Ludwigsfelde in the period from September 1943 to 30 January 1944, in accordance with an order from the SS- *und Polizei-Gericht* VIII, Prague. Langer led the *Zweiglager* office in his capacity as a SS-*Beurkundungsführer.* As far as I am aware he always cultivated a decency and extended a humanist way towards us prisoners and was therefore generally popular. He was in every way helpful in as far as his service position permitted and often had a great understanding for the needs of prisoners. Among others he often gave the prisoners the opportunity to speak to unexpected arriving family, those who had failed to use the prescribed official channels, which did not permit the right to speak without obtaining prior written permission.

In addition to these letters of support, Langer also submitted a medical assessment of his physical capabilities which revealed that he continued to suffer from the consequences of shrapnel that he received in 1939. His leg injury compromised his ability to walk and stand for long periods and in 1947 his physician noticed that a further thirteen splinters was removed from his buttocks, back and face. The Darmstadt public prosecutor applied to classify Langer in the group III of the activists in 1947 and he appeared before a public session of the Darmstadt *Spruchkammer* at 10.30 a.m. on 3 October 1947. Uniquely, the minutes of Langer's trial have survived and typically for a former prison guard, he obfuscated his involvement with the prison service. Explaining how he came to volunteer for the *Waffen*-SS and how his wounds precluded his further use as a soldier, Langer turned his attention to his recruitment in the *HA* SS-*Gericht*:

> [...] I transferred from the office of the SS-*Gerichtes* to Danzig–Matzkau as a non-commissioned officer in July 1941 and passing a training course for *Beurkundungsführer* I was then promoted to *Hscha.* on 20 April 1942 (Sergeant).
>
> My further promotion to the rank of *Oscha.* took place on 31 September 1941. The only inmates handled before this SS court, were those who had belonged to the SS, or the *Polizei* and had been found guilty of committing any criminal offences. My activity was purely office-orientated. I only had dealings with the prisoners, when it concerned *Beurkundungsführer* issues. In May 1943, I transferred to the *Zweiglager Berlin-Ludwigsfelde* where I remained until November 1944. In December 1944, I transferred to the *Aussenstelle* Allach/Munich, and here, remained the *Beurkundungsführer* and office leader until March 1945. My transfer to the supply unit of the 38th SS-Division *Nibelungen* took place in April 1945. My promotion to *Ustuf. der Reserve* (*Lieutenant*) had taken place on 9 November 1943.
>
> I have been married since 29 June 1941, I had two children, of whom one died on the evacuation transport. My father in law was killed by the Czechs on the way to work. My sister died at 24 years-old from the effects of ill-treatment by the Czechs and my brother fell in the east. My parents, 75 and 70, live in Florsheim and under these conditions I am the only one to support them. I was never politically active, I had no interests except athletics and football.

Chairman: Why did you volunteer for the *Waffen*-SS in 1938? You had the opportunity in Czechoslovakia to understand the objectives of the NSDAP. Did you did not know that the existing parties from the extreme right to the extreme left had fought against the secession of the Sudetenland?

Langer: I believe, the politicians turned more towards the Germans. I stood a distance from these things and never cared about politics. I do not weaken myself, when I state that the inclusion of members of all parties was welcomed.

Chairman: After all, it is right to mention the danger, whether this secession was carried out by force or by the way of reasoning. And Hitler did it by force and to the detriment of the German people. When you talked about the unemployment in the Czechoslovakia, I can tell you that this was not only a phenomenon in Czechoslovakia, but also a global economic crisis, which also affected Germany.

Langer: In the Böhmerwald the unemployment was particularly strong because the glass industry was paralysed.

Chairman: Not just the German people, but big business around the world had hoped for this crisis. The German government was not interested. Big business thought that the workers would again become docile as a result of this crisis that they had created. And this situation was for the German capital an exemplary success. The press around the world had taken a stand against the machinations of Hitler. The whole outside world has seen the crimes of the Third Reich. You as a foreigner, was much more likely to identify this situation than a citizen.

Langer: That depends on whether one cares at all about these things. The region of Czechoslovakia was established in 1919, so it was more of a slope to Austria's existence. Possibly it was a mistake that I had taken so little interest in politics.

Chairman: It should be a reminder to you, to have to worry about politics in the future, the need today is no less great than it was after the emergency, or again a Satan could emerge, and again there would be a lot to lose.

Langer: In the last few years I have learned a lot for the future. But I have seen inhumanity, and am now burden with debts, with which I now reproach myself.

Prosecutor: How were the prisoners treated in this camp?

Langer: It was frankly a camp, the people undertaking drill were prisoners, members of the *Polizei* and SS, who had been tried by courts martial for crimes. Offences and abuses etc. are unknown to me and were forbidden. I worked as a protocol officer. It had occurred that an *Obersturmführer* had slapped a prisoner and this resulted in his transfer to the front.

Chairman: When did you become aware of the criminal acts of the SS and what had occurred in the concentration camps?

Langer: Only after the capitulation, via the magazine that we received in the prison camp. Oranienburg and Dachau were known by me by name, however, I did not know what was going on. I was not aware.

End of the questioning.

The public prosecutor requests: that he is classified in the group III minor offender, with the imposition of two years' probation and a 500 *Reichsmark* atonement to be paid to the reparation fund. The opportunity to fulfil this obligation by performance, or credit at a rate of ten *Reichsmark* per day should be given to the person concerned.

Langer: I have heard the statement of the *Herrn* prosecutor and must put him right. I never cared about politics and so I ran into it blindly, today I have the desire through my work, to help in the reconstruction. Despite my severe wounding I work voluntarily in the work detail in the quarry Rossendorf and I want to keep at it in the future. Out of consideration for my family circumstances and the great distress of my family, I would ask the chamber to judge my case mildly, since I also possess nothing except the suit I wear.

Classified in group III of 'minor offenders' and the trial concluded, Langer was released from internment on 12 November 1947 and the court office then calculated that the costs of the first trial process stood at 4,000 *Reichsmark*. On 29 January 1948 the public prosecutor applied to classify Langer in group II of the activists with a probation period of two years and an expiation fine of 500 *Reichsmark*. Despite acknowledging that he was a refugee from the east, and a worker who supported his family who had already participated in the reconstruction, the court demanded that he undertook special work as part of his punishment, (via the employment exchange Frankfurt). At this time Langer noticed that the tribunal had imposed this punishment without the public prosecutor demanding its imposition and without specifying its start day. As a consequence of this oversight, Langer applied into writing to the Darmstadt *Spruchkammer* on 5 January 1948 to request a sentence review to determine whether the court was correct to impose this punishment. At this time, Langer had obtained a post in the office of an American company in Frankfurt and he feared that carrying out the 60 days special work would result in his dismissal and the financial ruin of his family.

The court suspended Langer's obligation to undertake special labour until a review had taken place and Langer handed the full power of attorney to a Frankfurt am Main jurist on

12 February 1948 with authority to undertake on his behalf all measures needed to win a clemency case. Writing to the Wiesbaden Minister for Political Liberation on 13 February 1948, Dr Diehl appealed for Langer's special labour to be set aside by the clemency path. To support his argument, Langer submitted a medical certificate which confirmed that he suffered from heart problems and was therefore unsuitable for heavy manual work. On 1 April 1948 the court agreed to set aside Langer's 60 days' special labour. Langer wrote to the tribunal on 3 April 1949 to report that he had recently been summoned to the Main-Taunus *Amtgericht* in Hochheim/Main to provide expert witness testimony.

Adopting his voluntarily labour as a quarry worker during his internment as his special labour and imposing a financial atonement of 40 *Reichsmark* to the restitution fund, in addition to the 50 *Reichsmark* he already owed, the Hessisches Minister for Political Liberation in Wiesbaden proposed to terminate Langer's probation period from 31 May 1949. Accepting this proposal on 28 May the same year, Langer, on the grounds of economic hardship, requested that he pay this fine in ten monthly installments. Sitting on 21 June 1949, the 5th chamber of the Frankfurt am Main court concluded Langer's denazification case on 21 June 1949 and placing him in the probation category IV, they imposed a 500 *Reichsmark* fine on him and Langer agreed to pay a 40 *Reichsmark* payment to the restitution fund (the court imposed two years' probation period concluded on 23.10.1949).

Writing to the court on 1 July 1949, Langer brought it to their attention that for a long time during his internment in Darmstadt he had laboured in the commando 86, the Hessiches road office Darmstadt, the quarry commando at the Odenwälder Hartenstein industry and at the Rossendorf quarry from 1 March to 30 October 1947. Therefore, he demanded that his rightful wages were used to reduce his fine to the state treasury. Complaining that he was burdened by loans taken out for his family during his internment, Langer also applied for relief on his court fine payments. Confirming that he owed nearly 160 *Reichsmark*, the public prosecutor of the appeal chamber agreed to accept monthly payments, starting from 1 January 1950, for the amount of eleven *Reichsmark* and ten *Reichsmark* thereafter. Surviving the collapse and adjusting to the realities of the postwar Germany, Langer lived in a suburb of Dortmund and worked as a salesman during the 1970's. He died in sheltered housing in the city of Dortmund in May 1996.[21]

Name: Edmund Franz **Mansbach**.
Last Rank: SS-*Untersturmführer*.
Born: 8.12.1919 in Langfuhr-Danzig.
Died: 18.12.1946 in Sevastopol/Crimea.
SS-Nr.: (joined 6.1939).
HJ Service: 1.5.1933-23.7.1939.
Prewar Assignments:
2./ SS-*Standarte Heimwehr Danzig* in 6.1939.
SS-VT from 23.7.1939.

Wartime Assignments:
2. / SS-*Totenkopf-Infantrie*-Rgt. 3 in 5.1940.
SS-*Totenkopf-Ersatz-Bataillon* 3.8.1940.
SS-*Wachbataillon Böhmen-Mähren* until 24.4.1941.
SS-VT *Hauptamt* SS-*Gericht* 24.4.1941–1.9.1943.
Strafvollzugslager der SS *und Polizei* Danzig–Matzkau 1.5.1941–1.9.1943.
SS-*Artillerie-Ausbildung- und Ersatz*-Rgt. (Munich) 22.11.1942–1.2.1943.
9. *Kriegs-Reserveführer-Anwärter-Lehrgang* SS-*Junkerschule* Bad Tölz 1.2.–23.7.1943.
13. *Fahnjünker Lehrgang* I *für Panzertruppen* (Groß Born) 15.4.–23.7.1943.
I. / SS-*Panzer-Ausbildung- und Ersatz*-Rgt. in 8.1943.
SS-*Panzer-Ausbildung- und Ersatz*-Rgt.1.9.–8.12.1943.
SS-*Korps-Panzer-Abteilung* 102 HQ in 9.1943
SS-*Panzer-Abteilung* 17 HQ 21.1.1944–1.3.1944.
SS-*Panzer-Ausbildung- und Ersatz*-Rgt. (Seelager) from 1.3.1944,
Panzerschießschule Putlos 15.5.–3.6.1944.
I. / SS-*Panzer-Ausbildung- und Ersatz*-Rgt. (Senne-Nordlager) on 10.10.1944.
SS-*Panzer-Ausbildung- und Ersatz*-Rgt. (Seelager) on 17.12.1944.
Unidentified SS-*Panzer*-Rgt. in 1.1945.

Promotions:

0.0.1941	SS-*Unterscharführer der Waffen*-SS (*Aktiv*).
1.9.1941	SS-*Oberscharführer der Waffen*-SS (*Aktiv*).
1.9.1943	SS-*Untersturmführer der Waffen*-SS (*Aktiv*).

Decorations & Awards:

0.0.19__	*Verwundetenabzeichen*, 1939 *in Schwarz*.

Notes: His father was a farmer. Attending *Volksschule* for four classes, Mansbach obtained his *Abitur* from *Höhere Schule* and volunteering for military service in the summer of 1939, he participated in the invasion of Poland in September 1939 and the 1940 invasion of France. Wounded in the upper left arm on 27 May, Mansbach was hospitalised for three months and when recovered, he transferred to a reserve battalion to regain his health. Once judged fit for duty, Mansbach mustered with a guard battalion in Prague. Transferring to the *HA* SS-*Gericht* in April 1941, he immediately joined the SS-*Straflager* Dachau staff and the following month was assigned to Matzkau as the *Wachzug* commander. A post held until July 1943. Applying successfully to marry his fiancée Lucie G., (b. 15.10.1920 in Danzig) on 10 January 1942, the couple married on 20 April 1942 and had one child up to the point when records ceased in May 1945 and lived in Neustadt/Westpreußen. Transferred to the SS-FHA in September 1943, Mansbach undertook four weeks' armoured warfare evaluation and completing the course, his instructor noted that he had done well, learned gunnery skills and was suitable for use as a company leader. Posted to the Putlos gunnery school in May and June 1944, here, Mansbach was taught advanced operation techniques with various weapons systems and night fighting tactics. Remaining with armoured units until the collapse, Mansbach was captured by Soviet forces and died in a prisoner of war camp near Sevastopol in December 1946.[22]

Name: Emil Gerhard Reinhold **Märtens**.
Last Rank: SS-*Untersturmführer*.
Born: 3.1.1920 in Neudorf, Neustettin/Pomerania.
SS-Nr.: 319.092 (joined 1.10.1937).
HJ Service: 3.9.1933–30.9.1937.
Prewar Assignments:
SS-TV 1.10.1937.
12. / SS-*Totenkopf Standarte Brandenburg* 1.10.1937–1.2.1940.
Wartime Assignments:
4. / SS-*Totenkopf-Infantrie*-Rgt. 1 from 2.1940.
6. *Kriegs-Res.-Führeranwärter-Lehrgangs* SS-*Junkerschule* Braunschweig 2.5.–15.9.1941.
Strafvollzugslager der SS-*und Polizei* Danzig–Matzkau 1.12.1941–3.1945.
Strafvollzugslager der SS-*und Polizei* Förrenbach in 3.1945.
Promotions:

11.9.1938	SS-*Sturmann der* SS-TV.
1.7.1939	SS-*Rottenführer der* SS-TV.
1.2.1940	SS-*Unterscharführer der Waffen*-SS (*Aktiv*).
1.6.1942	SS-*Oberscharführer der Waffen*-SS (*Aktiv*).
1.7.1943	SS-*Hauptscharführer der Waffen*-SS (*Aktiv*).
1.4.1944	*Oberjunker der Waffen*-SS
1.9.1944	SS-*Untersturmführer der Waffen*-SS (*Aktiv*).

Decorations & Awards:

0.0.1938	*Die Medaille zur Erinnerung an den* 1. Oktober 1938 (Sudetenland).
0.0.19__	1939 *Eisernes Kreuz* II. *Klasse*.
8.12.1941	*Infanterie-Sturmabzeichen in Bronze*.
8.12.1941	*Verwundetenabzeichen*, 1939 *in Silber*.

Notes: One of eight children, his father was a farmer. Attending the Neudorf *Volksschule* for six classes, Märtens claimed eight years schooling and left full time education to work on his father's farm. A member of the *Jungvolk* from 16 June 1933, Märtens marched with the *Hitlerjugend* from 3 September 1933. Applying successfully to join the *Allgemeine*-SS and SS-TV on 3 September 1937, Märtens then mustered with an SS-VT regiment in Oranienburg. Participating in the occupation of the Sudetenland during October 1938, Märtens was hospitalised for pleurisy in March/June 1939, but recovered in time to take part in the attack on Poland in the autumn of the same year. The Polish campaign concluded, Märtens regiment was billeted in the KL Dachau and amalgamated with other units to form the *Totenkopfdivision*. Participating in the 1940 invasion of France, he failed

Convicts assemble on the KL Dachau parade ground in early 1941. Atop the *Wirtschaftsgebäude* roof is written 'There is only one road to freedom; its milestones are; obedience, diligence, honesty, cleanliness, temperance, truth, sacrifice and the laws of one's country.' The two figures standing separately from the main group are prison staff. (© *Copyright Yad Vashem: 99_15*)

The convicts stand to attention before *Ogruf*. Paul Scharfe. In the background are the Dachau *Schutzhaftlager* barracks. (© *Copyright Yad Vashem: 99_16*)

Convicts parade with spades in the KL Dachau *Schutzhaftlager*. (*© Copyright Yad Vashem: 99_14*)

SS recruits wearing drill uniforms march in the SS-*Kaserne* Matzkau during 1939. North of the parade ground stands the water tower which is evidently under construction. (*© Copyright Sueddeutschzeitung-Photo_404861*)

The wooden hut office for the KL Dachau angora rabbit station. (© *Copyright Wisconsin Historical Society WHS-Image 45276*)

SS-Officers of the KL Dachau pet an angora rabbit. Bred for their meat and fur, rabbit hutches such as these were erected in Danzig-Matzkau. (© *Copyright Wisconsin Historical Society WHS-Image 45276*)

A more comprehensive view of the large number of rabbit hutches erected in Danzig-Matzkau. (© *Copyright Wisconsin Historical Society WHS-Image 45276*)

Looking westwards from the main entrance, the Matzkau motor room and *Kraftstaffel* are in the process of construction in 1941. To the right are located the administration buildings and *Wirtschaftsgebäude*. The small building in the foreground is the original site office with a telephone connection. (© *Copyright K. Grynder 2015*)

Looking westwards from the main entrance, a more distant view with additional detail. (© *Copyright K. Grynder 2015*)

This 1941 image focuses our attention northwards towards the Matzkau water tower, which is flanked by barracks. (© *Copyright K. Grynder 2015*)

Above left: The final Matzkau commandant, *Hstuf*. Dr Fritz Beelitz's, poses in his *Oscha*. uniform adorned with the Iron Cross and Infantry assault award. An SS-*Richter*, Dr Beelitz played a leading role in Matzkau's disciplinary affairs and was its final commandant. (*Author's collection*)

Above right: Dressed in riding clothes, *Hstuf*. Dr Fritz Beelitz poses atop his horse behind the Matzkau dining hall. (© *Thomas Beelitz archive*)

Pictured in 1943, Dr Fritz Beelitz waters his horse in the Matzkau stream. (© *Thomas Beelitz archive*)

Here, *Hstuf*. Dr Fritz Beelitz poses astride his horse before the stables. In the distance stands the Matzkau water tower. (© *Thomas Beelitz archive*)

Dr Beelitz relaxes in a Russian panje cart on the Eastern Front during the winter 1941/42. (© *Copyright Thomas Beelitz 2014*)

It is the winter of 1941/42 and Dr Beelitz is pictured standing with binoculars in his hands on the Eastern Front. (© *Copyright Thomas Beelitz 2014*)

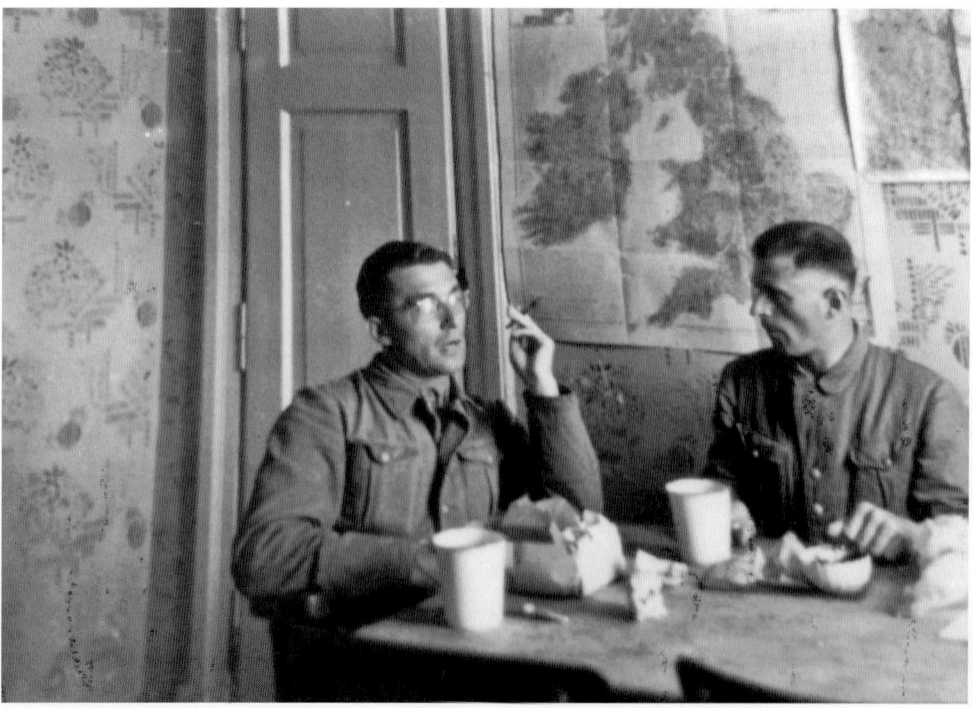

During a break in basic training, Dr Beelitz enjoys a cigar in his fatigues. A large map of Great Britain is pinned to the wall behind him. (© *Copyright Thomas Beelitz 2014*)

Photographed on the Eastern Front, Dr Beelitz stands guard over his artillery company's small arms. (*© Copyright Thomas Beelitz 2014*)

Posing for a photograph, *Rttf.* Dr Beelitz sports a moustache during the summer of 1942. The *Eisernes Kreuz 2. Klasse* is clearly visible through the slit in his camouflage smock. (*© Copyright Thomas Beelitz 2014*)

Seated, Dr Beelitz hand washes his clothing during basic training in 1940. (© *Copyright Thomas Beelitz 2014*)

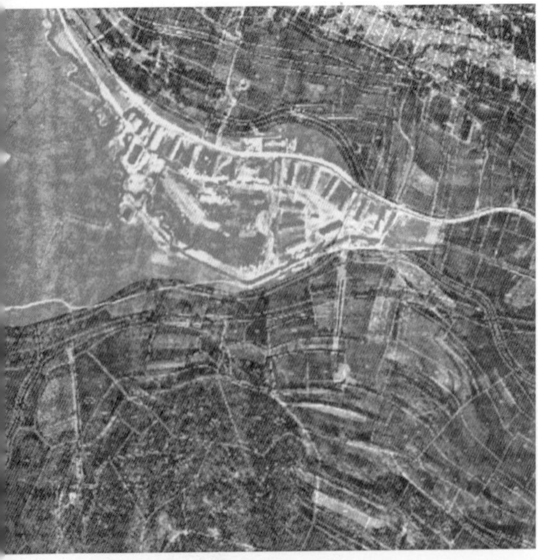

Above left: Strafvollzugslager Förrenbach. The prison buttressed against the eastern sector of the main camp. The shaded area is now covered by an artificial lake. (© Copyright *Bayerische Vermessungsverwaltung*)

Above right: In Oslo *Reichsführer*-SS Heinrich Himmler salutes members of the Norwegian SS. Throughout the war, Himmler remained deeply concerned that the work of the SS and *Polizei* jurisdiction did not impact negatively on the recruitment of Germanic volunteers. (© *Copyright Martin Månsson*)

Two SS Generals and a coterie of officers salute the graves of their fallen troops. (© *Copyright Berit Latza*)

Förrenbach wooden barrack in use to house refugees in the wake of the May 1945 collapse. (© *Copyright Thomas Wrensch*)

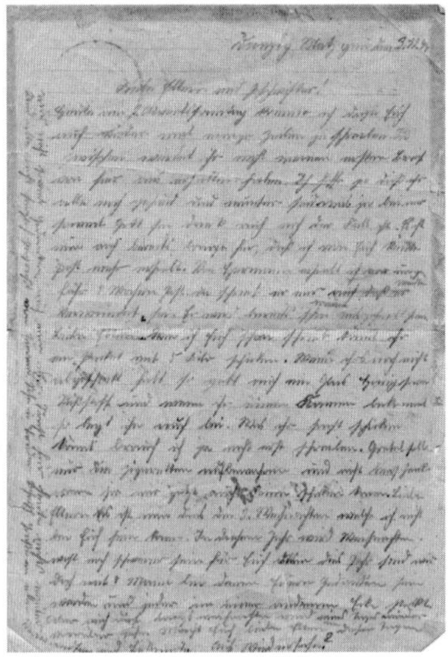

Above left: Strm. Georg Müller transferred from Matzkau to a front probation unit at the end of 1944 and did not survive Soviet captivity. (© *Copyright Franz Müller 2015*)

Above right: Pre-printed letters, such as this from Georg Müller to his family on 8.12.1944, were provided to enable inmates to write home to their families or friends. (© *Copyright Franz Müller 2013*)

Auszug aus der Lagerordnung

des Strafvollzugslagers der ϟϟ und Polizei, Danzig-Matzkau.

1. Jeder Lagerinsasse darf alle 4 bis 6 Wochen, je nach Art seiner Strafe, einen Brief in Quartformat (14,5×21 cm) von 4 Seiten mit je 15 Zeilen empfangen und einen gleichen Brief schreiben. Sämtliche ein- und ausgehende Post wird zensiert.
2. Der Empfang von Paketen und Rauchwaren ist verboten. Hiervon ausgenommen sind zum täglichen Gebrauch bestimmte Toilettengegenstände. Eingehende Lebensmittelpakete werden den Betreffenden nicht ausgehändigt, sondern dem Häftlingsrevier zur Verfügung gestellt. Bekleidungsstücke u. dgl. werden zu den Effekten gelegt.
3. Geldüberweisungen werden erst bei Entlassung ausgefolgt.
4. Besuche sind nur nächsten Angehörigen in dringenden Fällen gestattet. Erlaubnis hierzu muß rechtzeitig schriftlich beim Lagerführer eingeholt werden.
5. Auskunft über Urteil und Strafmaß erteilt das ϟϟ- und Polizeigericht, welches den Lagerinsassen verurteilt hat.

Wehrkreisdruckerei XX 2987 20000 8/44

Der Kommandant.

Each inmate received a copy of Matzkau's rules and regulations concerning the sending and receipt of mail:

1. Each inmate may every 4 to 6 weeks, depending on the type of his sentence, receive a letter, in quarter format (14.5 × 21cm) of 4 pages with 15 lines and write a same letter. All incoming and outgoing mail is censored.
2. The receiving of packets and tobacco products is prohibited. This does not include daily use items such as toiletry articles. Incoming food packages will not be delivered to the person concerned, but will made available in the prisoner area. Clothing etc. to be placed in his effects.
3. Money remittances are handed over only at discharge.
4. Visits are permitted only in urgent cases and only by next of kin. Permission to do so must be obtained in writing in time warden at the *Lagerführer*.
5. Information about judgments and punishments are provided by the SS and *Polizei* courts, which sentenced the camp inmates.

The Commandant.

Military district printing XX 2987 20 000 8/44 (© *Copyright Franz Müller 2015*)

The remains of the Matzkau main guard house. The architect's drawing reveals that the main gate was constructed of wood and barbed wire. (© *Copyright Mykiki Tyni*)

The remains of the *Kommandantheim*. (© *Copyright Mykiki Tyni*)

The guard's accommodation, this barrack stood behind the *Wirtschaftsgebäude*. (© *Copyright Mykki Tyni*)

The vehicle ramp led directly to the garrison *Kraftstaffel*. (© *Copyright Mykki Tyni*)

This building, located on the *Lagerstraße*, was constructed for junior officers and included a kitchen and parlour to permit them to entertain their comrades. (© *Copyright Mykki Tyni*)

The base of petrol pump is all that remains of the *Kraftstaffel* petrol station. (© *Copyright Mykki Tyni*)

The remains of the guard accommodation, this building had been constructed during the first phase of the building in 1939 and it stood to the west of the water tower. To the rear of the cameraman, the road leads to the parade ground and prison compound main entrance. (© *Copyright Mykki Tyni*)

Looking eastwards we are granted another view of the guards' accommodation. Built during the first phase of construction in 1939, the water tower stood behind the red painted building. The concrete fence in the foreground separated the *Stabsgebäude* from the *Wirtschaftsgebäude*. (© *Copyright Mykki Tyni*)

Above left: Erich 'Rudolf/Adolf' Albert (b. 1904). Erich Albert accepted leadership of the SS-*Straflager* Dachau in May 1940 and a former inmate named Johann Ott recollected that Albert was loud and harsh. Remaining the leader of the *Straflager* Dachau until 27 April 1945, Albert abandoned his post as US troops stood poised to capture the camp. Fleeing eastwards, he was arrested after the cessation of hostilities in Salzburg by Harry B. Fleetwood of the 7th Army CIC at 13.00 p.m. on 19 May 1945 (on the grounds of the rank of *Hstuf.* in accordance with SHAEF directive, dated 15.4.1945). A search of his person produced his wallet with photographs, cash amounting to 176 *Reichsmark* and his pay book. Not wanted by the United States, or other nations as a war criminal, Albert was cleared for internment in 1946. Released from the Dachau Hospital on 17 December the same year, Albert then found himself detained in the Dachau War Crimes Cage (prisoner of war enclosure 29) and remained here until at least 27 December the same year.

Above right: Maximilian 'Max' Dolles (1916-1986). Volunteering for military service in the SS-VT in Munich in 1936, Dolles participated in the 1939 Polish campaign and received a bullet wound in his upper arm. He was also later wound in France and hospitalised for five months. Released on 28 October 1940, Dolles transferred to a reserve battalion and undergoing a medical examination in Breslau on 4 February 1942, the physician judged him fit only for garrison duties. Transferred to the *HA* SS-*Gericht* as an SS-*Richter* in June 1943, Dolles reported to Danzig–Matzkau in August 1944. Around October 1944 he undertook officer training and received a three centimetre long head wound and light concussion during an Allied air attack on Mosbach on 8 December 1944. Promoted to officer rank in January 1945, Dolles transferred to the SS-*Straflager* Dachau and may have seen active service with a combat unit near Nuremberg.

Above left: Otto Andresen, (b. 1890). In 1942, Andresen became the subject of an RSHA investigation into allegations he had murdered a camp prisoner, a former SA man. The tribunal judged him guilty of murder and imposed a prison sentence. Confirming the judgement, the *Reichsführer* commanded Andresen's demotion and transfer to the *Reich Pionier-Bataillon*. 'It was not murder, but a political necessity' asserted Andresen from Dresden on 29 June 1942 and comparing his deed to the execution of the SA leadership in 1934. His training complete, Andresen left Dresden and deployed on the Eastern Front from October 1941. 'I have come to the judgement that the SS-*Mann* Andresen for me is an upright character, a dependable soldier and a true warrior' wrote *Hstuf.* Enseling when asked to comment on Andresen's performance. Andresen's eventual rehabilitation was in no small part credited to his exemplary behaviour at the front. Released from the *Verlorenen Haufen* in late 1942, Andresen regained his former rank and ended the war assigned to a pioneer labour battalion in the Kurland pocket.

Above right: Fritz Baumeister (b. 1913). Following training Baumeister was posted to the *Wiking* field court and remained in this post until transferred to the SS-*Straflager* Dachau in September 1941. Transferred to the SS-FHA in March 1944, Baumeister reported to a frontline division in June 1944 and became a battalion adjutant and then regimental ordnance officer. Fighting in Estonia and then Silesia, a Red Army artillery barrage near Lausitz on 19 February 1945 resulted in Baumeister being seriously wounded. He was then admitted to hospitals at Kirchhain in Lausitz and Schwandorf and ended the war in the *Reserve-Lazarett* Erlangen and the *Fürsorge und Vers. Kommando der Waffen*-SS Nuremberg was notified of his injuries. Surrendering to US Army forces in Erlangen in May 1945, the same month Baumeister, as a prisoner of war, was interned in the Hersbruck civilian camp and recovered from his injuries in the Förrenbach clinic in November the same year. After lengthy postwar investigation Baumeister was classifed in the group II of 'less responsible' on 4 June 1947.

Above left: Edmund Baumgärtner. (b. 1909). Baumgärtner had been the leader of the *Aussenstelle* Allach prior to Dr Bellitz reporting to Matzkau in the summer of 1943. Appointed Matzkau's Nr. 1 *Lagerführer* in June 1943, Baumgärtner was recommended for promotion on 23 February the same year. The promotion was awarded in April 1943 and the Reichsführer supported his advancement on the proviso that he saw action at the front. Postwar in the late 1960s/early 1970s he was forced to defend himself against charges of murder. Submitting a detailed statement to the *Bundesministerium für Innernes Abteilung* 18 on 28 May and 4 June 1968, Baumgärtner denied ordering summary executions of inmates in Danzig–Matzkau. Lacking evidence to substantiate the murder allegations, the court's investigation was halted in November 1971.

Above right: Gottfried Biedermann (b. 1907). Biedermann replaced Edmund Baumgärtner as Nr. 1. *Lagerführer* in February 1944. Committing a disciplinary offence on 20 July 1944, Biedermann was punished with a simple reprimand and re-assigned to the SS-*Straflager* Dachau in August 1944. He held this post until the prison was closed and he escorted its inmates to the *Aussenstelle* Allach in April 1945. He escaped from Dachau's environs before its liberation on 28 April 1945, but surrendered to US military forces near Zell am See on 8 May and was taken under arrest for his membership of the *Waffen*-SS and possession of the rank of *Hstuf.*

Walter Dieterle (b. 1908). Dieterle was found guilty of military disobedience and falsifying reports. Transferred to the front on 24 December 1943, Dieterle saw action in Estonia, Latvia and fought in the Kurland pocket. Ending the war on the Oder Front near Stettin, he surrendered to British forces on 5 May 1945 and was interned in the Sandbostel *bei* Bremervörde internment camp until 5 January 1947.

Dr Leo Ernst had been a camp commandant at Matzkau. In January 1945 is was learnt at the camp that he had fallen in battle while fighting with the *Totenkopfdivision* to relieve trapped Axis forces in Budapest on 3 January.

Above left: Ernst-Günther Heidelberg (b. 1908). Heidelberg was employed at the architect's office of the Warsaw governor in the spring of 1940. Criminal proceedings were later initated against him for military service disobedience and dereliction of duty on 13 July 1942, but assessing that the entire legal process against him was too complicated to continue, the *Reichsführer* commanded Heidelberg to the SS-*Sonderregiment* in March 1944. Reporting to Dirlewanger, Heidelberg took command of the fourth company.

Above right: Dr jur. Hans Heinsen (b. 1907). Deployed in France from 5 October 1942, first as commander of the *Ordnungspolizei* in the area of the military commander in Poitiers. In this post he is thought to have been involved in the deportation of Jews from France to concentration camps. Reported for taking an unauthorised leave and committing an act of military disobedience while assigned to Hellerau in late 1943, a court's investigation was also initiated against Dr Heinsen to examine allegations that he had engaged in an affair with a Frenchwoman. Heinsen was found guilty of the charges. Himmler commanded Dr Heinsen to the SS-*Sonderregiment* in Belorussia. Surviving the war, Dr Heinsen was employed in the West Berlin judiciary for 21 years.

Above left: Rudolf 'Rudi' Heiß (b. 1919). Postwar, Heiß claimed that his membership of the *Hitlerjugend* on 1 June 1933 was accomplished in the wake of pressure from the trade school administrators and that his subsequent military career leading to the SS was beyond his control and against his catholic principles. Notwithstanding this, potential conviction rumbled on to 1967 in a detailed account of his career.

Above right: Erich Laimgruber (1908-1944). Laimgruber fought with the *Der Führer* along the Grebbe line, in Flanders and along the Weland line in May and June 1940. Transferring to the *HA* SS-*Gericht Amt* III in November the same year as an SS-*Beurkundungsunterführer*, Laimgruber was immediately assigned to the SS-*Straflager* Dachau as a *Rapportführer* and accompanied *Ostuf.* Albert to Matzkau on 20 July 1941. Here, Laimgruber became the Nr. 2. *Lagerführer* on 22 July. Laimgruber was later posted to the *Prinz Eugen* on 20 March 1944 and arriving on 31 May, Laimgruber led a section in the reconnaissance battalion until his death in action in July 1944.

Above left: Otto-Leo Langer (1917–1996). Langer was a Sudeten German. Travelling to Munich in 1938, he applied successfully to join the SS-VT and reported to the *Deutschland* to undertake basic infantry training and on 23 September 1939 he was seriously wounded in the right lower leg following the invasion of Poland. Fourteen shell splinters left him with a pronounced limp and he recovered in the Hamburg-Barmbeck Reserve-Lazarett (I) between 1 October 1939 and 15 March 1940. Discharged, he reported to a reserve battalion in Munich in July 1940 and was judged fit only for garrison duties. Transferred to the HA SS-Gericht in the summer of 1940, Langer became a Rapportführer at the SS-Straflager Dachau in October the same year. His details are among the most comprehensive in the book. He long survived the war and died in social housing in Dortmund in May 1996.

Above right: Paul Friedrich Lindner (b. 1895). Appointed the vehicle officer of the II. / SS-*Infantrie*-Rgt. 4 in Assen from July 1939, a Zündapp motorcycle was placed at Lindner's disposal to carry out his tasks. On 18 November 1940 *Ostuf.* Gebhardt ordered all units to report their possession of motorcycles and this audit revealed that Lindner and other troops of this regiment had stolen many vehicles. The court judged Lindner guilty of an act of bribery and imposed a term of three and a half years *Gefängnis* on Lindner and ordered his expulsion from the SS and demotion to the rank of SS-*Mann* on 19 April 1941. While he awaited a confirmation of his sentence, Lindner mustered with a reserve battalion from 15 April and then joined the *Verlorenen Haufen.*

Dr jur. Hans-Georg Mayer (b. 1909). 'As a case worker in the SS courts my duties consisted of examining and judging cases and offences committed by SS and *Polizei* personnel' recollected Mayer when asked to explain his wartime duties to his American interrogator in August 1945. He was questioned about his knowledge of the persecution and extermination of Poles and Jews at Pabianice and **Łódź** and asked to discuss his time with the *Reichskomissariat* in Norway. Mayer was later extradited to the Polish authorities. Here, he faced trial before the **Łódź** regional court for crimes committed in Pabianice and **Łódź** and judged guilty of the offences, the court sentenced him to death on 29 September 1947. On the grounds of his membership of the SS and for preventing escapes from the Pabianice ghetto, this sentence was reduced to a term of five years prison on 14 April 1948. Released from jail, Mayer left Poland for the Federal Republic on 9 February 1951.

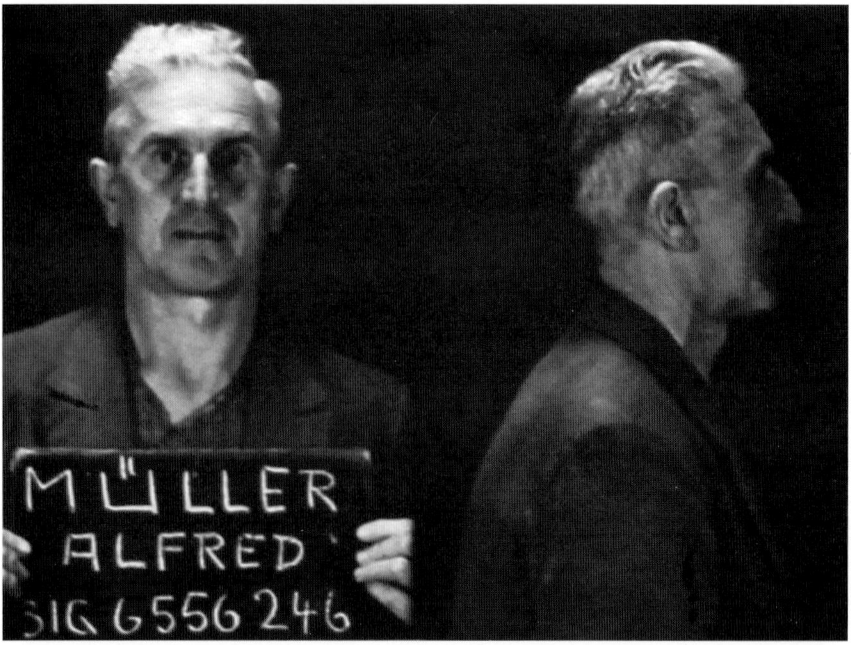

Alfred Mueller (b. 1893). Mueller joined the *Waffen*-SS 11 February 1940. Mustering with the KL Dachau guard unit until March 1941, Mueller then transferred to the *HA* SS-*Gericht* and was posted to the SS-*Straflager* Dachau, then Danzig–Matzkau and lastly to the *Zweigsstelle* Hammerweg. Returning to the SS-*Straflager* Dachau in April 1945, Mueller fled the camp environs prior to the US troop's arrival and hid in Königreich/Sachsen from 14 April. Arrested in Werda at 11.00 a.m. on 1 June 1945, Mueller was detained in a succession of prisoner of war camps including Treuen-Pössnick, Ohrdruf-Ziegenhain, Kornwestheim-Züffenhausen and Dachau until he ended up in British Army hands and they interned him in the camp Nr. 5 at Staumühle.

Above left: Dr Frank Ludwig Müller (b. 1912). Dr Müller was drafted into the *Waffen*-SS in the spring of 1941 and appointed the garrison physician at Matzkau in July 1941. Speaking to the author in June 2014, the former *Ustuf.* Kurt Grawe recalled visiting Matzkau with an SS Judge in late 1941 to investigate an inmate's claim that the camp physician had ordered sick inmates to stand in the cold and poured water over them. Post-war, Dr Beelitz recollected arriving in Matzkau during the summer of 1943 and would recollect being told that the former camp doctor had been dismissed as a consequence of dissatisfaction with supervision in the prison. Notwithstanding this a, report dated 10 December 1943 noted that Dr Müller was 'impeccable,' a 'valuable member of the battalion' and observed that he 'investigates the needs of the recruits and cares for those discharged from the military hospital safely and in silence, he has a well-balanced character and is suitable as a troop doctor.'

Above right: Wolfgang Plaul (b. 1900). After numerous misdemeanour Plaul was ordered to the SS-Rgt. *Dirlewanger* with his former rank in 25 January 1944. Rising quickly to become one of Dirlewanger's trusted lieutenants.

Above left: Jan Robertson (1922-1995). Robertson was posted to the *Grenadier* Rgt. 1, *Landstorm Nederland* in s'Hertogenbosch in May 1944, this formation later became the SS-Volunteer Grenadier Rgt. 83 and Robertson fought allied forces in Belgium until forced to retreat on 2 November. Robertson and other members of his unit are believed to have used explosives to break into a bank safe in the Rotterdamse bank in Tiel on 7 March 1945. Taking two days to remove all the cash and valuables, it appears that the SS authorities did not seek his or his men's prosecution for committing this serious offence. Surrendering to the British/Canadian army at Veenendaal on 11 May 1945, Robertson was detained in the prisoner of war camp at Harskamp and questioned by the special political police about the Tiel bank robbery. Robertson was judged guilty of the charges and punished with a fifteen-year term of imprisonment. Escaping from the camp at Vuren on 8 January 1947, Robertson fled across the border to Germany and became a German national. He and his family returned to Holland in 1960.

Above right: Paul Otto Radomski (b. 1902). Radomski was a sadistic camp commandant with a predilection for committing acts of sadism and became notorious for whipping, torturing and killing prisoners. After his downfall he was eventually transferred to a SS-*Sonderkommando* in Riga and took charge of a unit of forced Jewish labour who exhumed victims of the *Einsatzgruppe* from mass graves, cremated the corpses and crushed their remains to dust. Radomski is thought to have ended the war assigned to a reserve battalion and perished before the collapse. In 2005 the Hamburg public prosecutor revealed to the Ukrainian authorities that Radomski had died in March 1945 near Székesfehérvár in Hungary.

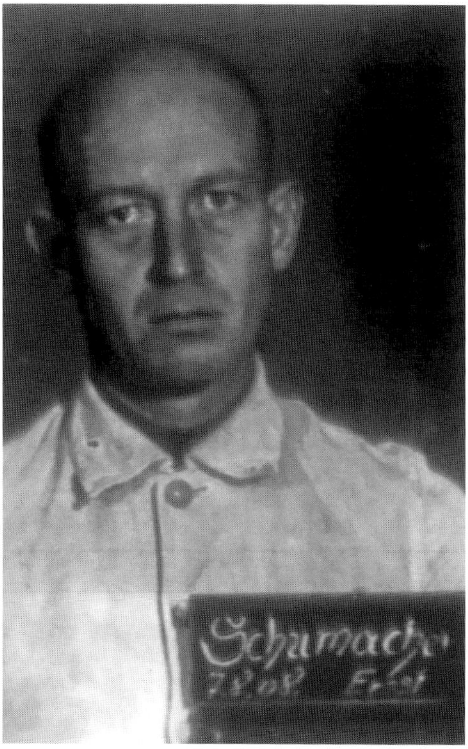

Above left: The only surviving image of a convict photographed inside the SS-*Straflager* Dachau. Here, the disgraced officer, Ernst Schumacher, holds a board containing his personal details. (© *Copyright NARA*)

Above right: Ernst Schumacher (b. 1908). The account of Schumacher is one of the most detailed in the book. His problems began when he mistreated Banats, ethnic Germans, who were under his training command. He was accused of repeatedly beating members of his unit and others and to have enforced a term of imprisonment by *Ausbinden* in accordance to the old Hungarian method which involved handcuffing miscreant soldiers hand to the ankle above ground for up to 48 hours duration to prevent them sitting or lying down.

Schumacher eventually found himself released from imprisonment to undertake front probation. He died at Mitterndorf in Austria.

Jörgen Salskov (b. 1917). In November 1943 Salskov had become involved in complex fraud involving stolen meat from divisional stores. A subsequent court's investigation recommended his trial and the purloining Salskov found himself arraigned before the courts martial of the field court of the *Nordland*. Declaring Salskov guilty of attempted fraud and document falsification in May 1944, the tribunal sentenced him to a term of two years' *Gefängnis*. Serving his punishment in Matzkau, Salskov accepted front probation in February 1945 and joined the *Kalthofen* for the defence of Danzig.

Josef Schwaiger (b. 1910). Schwaiger had responsibility for reporting disciplinary problems and accounting for weapons, ammunition and equipment. He took part in the attacks on Holland and France in the spring of 1940 and in the assault on the Soviet Union from 22 June 1941. Wounded on 20 February 1942, Schwaiger recovered at the Viennese SS-*Lazarett* between 27 February and 24 April the same year. He deployed at the SS-*Straflager* Dachau in January 1943 and became an SS-*Beurkundungsunterführer* of the *HA* SS-*Gericht* the same month. A *Rapportführer* in Dachau, Schwaiger later occupied the post of 2. *Lagerführer*. A promotion recommendation was submitted for him on 15 January 1944. Postwar his name was placed on the 5th wanted list, Crowcass, central registry of war criminals and security suspects. Schwaiger probably hid near Salzburg after the collapse.

Above left: Franz Sturmann, a member of the Austrian SS since August 1932, reported for duty in Dachau in April or June of 1941. Sturmann would rise to occupy many senior posts in the prison service. Leaving the prison service for the front in the second week of November 1944, Hstuf. Franz Sturmann transferred to a reserve unit to undergo an assessment of his capabilities. Later, qualifying as a company leader, Sturmann led a company of the 32th SS-Freiwilligen-Grenadier-Division until his capture by the Red Army at the end of April 1945. In a strange twist of fate, Sturmann escaped his captors and ended the war in Dachau, surrendering to the US Army in April 1945.

Above right: Rudolf Vincent Weiß lost is nerve as the US Army stood poised to attack the *Fortress* Metz and fled his post by car at 3.00 a.m. on 1 September 1944. Later that same day, he reported to the Saarbrücken *Gauleiter*, SA-*Staf.* Jansen, and claimed that he had abandoned the city when becoming aware that US troops threatened to advance into the city. His actions reported to the head of the SS, Himmler commanded the *Obersten* SS- *und Polizei-Gericht* to initiate an investigating against Weiß on suspicion of desertion ... Weiß was killed in action at Lieberose near the city of Cottbus on 22 February 1945.[258]

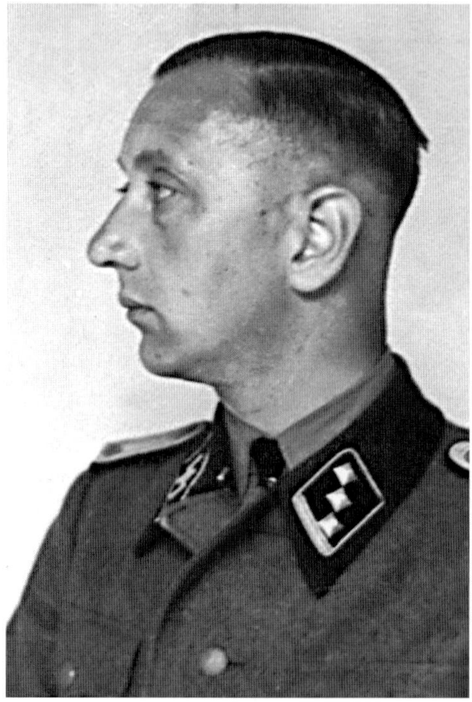

Wilhelm Sparwasser (b. 1905). Drafted into the SS-TV in September 1939, Sparwasser transferred to the *HA* SS-*Gericht* in December 1940 and became an SS-*Beurkundungsunterführer* on 1 January 1944. He had received orders to leave the Stuttgart tribunal for the *Strafvollzugslager der* SS *und Polizei* Danzig–Matzkau by October 1944 and then deployed with the staff company.

Alfred Hermann Vollmer (b. 1915). Vollmer transferred to the *HA* SS-*Gericht* in early 1942. Qualifying as an SS-*Beurkundungsunterführer*, he received orders in May 1943 to report to Danzig–Matzkau and had become *Hstuf*. Dr Fritz Beelitz's adjutant in Matzkau by 24 October 1944.

Kurt Weiße (b. 1909). Weiße's fondness for beating his men culminated in an assault that resulted in the death of a young soldier.

to pass an officer training course in 1941 and returned to his regiment (other candidates in his class were promoted to officer rank on 30.1.1942).

Taking part in the opening stages of the attack on Northern Russia in the summer of 1941, Märtens was wounded twice in early September 1941. An eye was removed while he convalesced at the VI *Reserve-Lazarett* in Stettin and his physician declared him unfit for front service on 3 October 1943. Once recovered, Märtens received orders in December 1941 to report to Danzig–Matzkau. Applying successfully for permission to marry his fiancée Gerda O., (b. 25.1.1926 in Gross Klingbeck near Elbing) in November 1943, his bride, a member of the BDM, was employed in the work office of the *Luftwaffe* airfield at Elbing. Marrying on 8 May 1944, the former Matzkau guard, Rudolf Müller, recalled that his bride called him Peter. The commandant's adjutant in September 1944, Dr Beelitz affirmed that Märtens became a *Kompanieführer*. Recalling that Märtens transferred to Förrenbach in early March 1945, Heiß believed that Märtens had received the *E.K.* 1. *Klasse* and after the collapse and revealed that he lived with Märtens and his wife in a small village near Kassel in the autumn of 1945 (Rudolf Müller suggested he settled in Hesse).[23]

Name: Dr jur. Hans-Georg Mayer.
Last Rank: SS-*Sturmbannführer*.
Born: 11.10.1909 in Erlangen.
NSDAP-Nr.: 3.069.636 (joined 1.5.1933).
SS-Nr.: 367. 767 (joined 1.8.1940).
Prewar Assignments:
SA-*Sturmbann* 1. /21 on 13.4.1933.
Rechtsreferent SA-*Sturmbann* 1. /21 on 1.5.1933.
Rechtsberater 15. SA-*Standarte* on 6.1.1934.
Gaugericht Munich from 1.5.1936–1.9.1938.
Kreisgericht Berchtesgaden 1.10.1938–15.10.1939.
Press *referent Stab* SA-*Jägerstandarte Dietrich Eckert* (Rosenheim) in 1939.
Gebirgsjäger-Rgt. 100 (military training) 3.1.–3.3.1938.
Gebirgsjäger-Rgt. 100 (military training) 1.8.–15.10.1938.
Wartime Assignments:
Polizei 10.1939–7.1942.
Regierungsrat der Ordnungspolizei at the *Polizeipräsidium* Litzmannstadt 1.4.–1.5.1940.
Led the Pabianice *Ordnungspolizei* until 21.9.1941.
Stab Abschnitt XXXXIII, (Litzmannstadt) until 1.1.1943.
Stab Befehlshaber der Ordnungspolizei (Oslo/Norway) from 15.7.1941 (*FPNr.* 40.206).
Reichskommissar für die Besetzten Norwegischen Gebiete in 7.1942.
Dienststellenleiter des Reichskommissariat Christiansand 10.1942–3.1943.
Officer of the *Stab Oberabschnitt Nord* from 1.1.1943.
Waffen-SS from 4.1943.

Waffen-SS *Hauptamt* SS-*Gericht* 7.6.1944–27.4.1945.
Officer of the *Stab Oberabschnitt Süd* 31.6.1944.
Strafvollzugslager der SS-*und Polizei* Danzig–Matzkau 1.9.1944–14.12.1944.
SS- *und Polizei-Gericht* XXIII, Veldes, branch court Salzburg on 14.12.1944.
Officer of the *Stammabteilung Süd, Bezirk* 34 (Munich) on 15.11.1944.
Chefrichter SS- *und Polizei-Gericht* XXXV, Salzburg from 12.1944.

Promotions:

1.6.1933	SA-*Scharführer.*
15.10.1938	*Gefreiter der Reserve.*
1.8.1940	SS-*Sturmbannführer der Allgemeine*-SS.
7.7.1944	SS-*Unterscharführer der Reserve.*

Decorations & Awards:

0.0.19__	SA-*Sportsabzeichen in Bronze.*
0.0.19__	*Deutsches Reichssportabzeichen in Bronze.*

Notes: Attending *Volksschule* for four classes, Mayer received his *Abitur* from the Erlangen *Höhere Schule* after nine classes in March 1929 and then studied jurisprudence and political science at the Erlangen University until passing his *Referendarexamen* in 1933. Mayer obtained his law doctorate in the same year and then undertook his practical training at the *Oberlandesgericht* Munich. Passing his *Assessorexamen* in 1936, Dr Mayer then accepted the post of administrative civil servant in the Bavarian Interior Ministry and was promoted to the rank of *Regierungsrat*. Becoming engaged to his fiancée Dr Liselotte H., (b. 10.7.1911 in Munich) on 24 December 1936, she had studied medicine at Erlangen University between 1930 and 1937 and during the war she worked for the VoMi in occupied Poland. Marrying on 10 July 1937, the couple had three children up to the point when records ceased in May 1945 and settled in Marktschellenberg bei Berchtesgaden auf der Götschen.

Joining the *Polizei* in the autumn of 1939, Mayer was assigned to Pabianice in 1941 and had responsibility for the local Jewish ghetto. Answering Himmler's order for policeman to join his organisation, Mayer applied successfully to join the *Allgemeine*-SS on 18 June 1940. Commanded into active service on 15 June 1941, he was employed with the Nordag I.G. Farben to ensure that essential war materials were taken from Norway for the German war effort. Drafted into the *Waffen*-SS in the spring of 1943, Mayer saw active service in Finland and then deployed in Norway. The *Chef* RSHA ordered his transfer from the *Gestapo* office in Prague to the service office in Münster on 30 April 1944. Appointed an SS-*Hilfrichter* of the *HA* SS-*Gericht* with the rank of *Uscha.* in June 1944, the following month Mayer deployed with the *HA* SS-*Gericht* in Prien am Chiemsee.

'As a case worker in the SS courts my duties consisted of examining and judging cases and offences committed by SS and *Polizei* personnel' recollected Mayer when asked to explain his wartime duties to his American interrogator in August 1945. It appears from this short passage that he had been assigned to the *Amt* III. Appointed to the *Strafvollzugslager der* SS *und Polizei* Danzig–Matzkau as the liaison officer between this institution and the local court from September to December 1944, Mayer then led the Salzburg tribunal. Claiming to have been assigned to an SS training and reserve unit in Austria during the last days of the war, Mayer hid at his home at the war's end until the American authorities arrested him in Schellenberg on 18 August 1945. Taken to the 3rd US Army intelligence centre on the 24 August, here, he was questioned about his knowledge of the persecution and extermination of Poles and Jews at Pabianice and Łódź and asked to discuss his time with the *Reichskomissariat* in Norway. Following this talk, his investigator, Major Edmund L. King submitted his thoughts to paper:

> Mayer is cooperative to the extent that he readily replies to all questions. Whether he merely knows about the crimes committed in Poland or is actually involved will have to be further investigated. The fact that he did not surrender to our authorities is incriminating in itself.

Gaining access to Mayer on 27 August 1945, the United Press journalist, Robert Musel, then published the interview in various newspapers under the sensational banner 'Nazis Planned to Kill All Jews':

> Dr Hans Georg Mayer, former ghetto commander who tried to ward off capture with a slab of firewood calmly told American authorities how the Nazis had planned to exterminate all of Europe's Jews. Mayer told interrogating officers yesterday that the plan took root at a Berlin conference in 1940 which was attended by Adolf Hitler, Heinrich Himmler, Joseph Goebbels, Reinhardt Heydrich, and Ernst Kaltenbrunner. Mayer, who held the rank of SS major, said the Nazi leaders' plan was very simple. All Jews unfit for heavy work would be gassed to death, and all Jews able to work would be given such hard work they would eventually weaken to a state where they, too would be gassed. The condemned category was called the *arbeit sunfaehig* (unable to work). Mayer was not at the meeting, he was not big enough for that but, as his record showed, he enthusiastically supported the plan and did everything that he could to make it run smoothly. He was reluctant to discuss his own activities but admitted he had been appointed police commissioner of Balbianice, a town of 60,000 in Poland, which held a ghetto of 8,000 Jews. These Jews lived under the most terrible conditions, and Mayer said they were all liquidated while he was away on temporary duty in Norway. He said be later heard that 4,000 had been gassed while the others disappeared through 'other methods'. Mayer was arrogant throughout the interview until he learned that he faced probable transfer to Balbianice for trial by the Russians or Poles. Then he turned pale and he gasped: 'For God's sake, please reconsider'.

This highly speculative story is not supported by surviving documentary material, or matches the known movements of those Mayer alleged had attended the meeting. Interrogated once again by the US Army intelligence service, Mayer was then extradited to the Polish authorities. Here, he faced trial before the Łódź regional court for crimes committed in Pabianice and Łódź and judged guilty of the offences, the court sentenced him to death on 29 September

1947. On the grounds of his membership of the SS and for preventing escapes from the Pabianice ghetto, this sentence was reduced to a term of five years prison on 14 April 1948. Released from jail, Mayer left Poland for the Federal Republic on 9 February 1951.[24]

Name: Alfred Mueller.
Last Rank: SS-*Hauptscharführer.*
Born: 11.2.1893 in Werda/Vogtland.
Wartime Assignments:
Waffen-SS from 11.2.1940.
II. / SS-*Totenkopf Sturmbann* (KL Dachau) 11.2.1940–3.1941.
Waffen-SS *HA* SS-*Gericht* spring of 1941-29.4.1945.
SS-*Straflager* Dachau spring of 1941-29.4.1945.
Promotions:

7.1940	SS-*Rottenführer der Reserve.*
6.1941	SS-*Unterscharführer der Reserve.*
0.0.1941	SS-*Scharführer der Reserve.*
0.0.1942	SS-*Oberscharführer der Reserve.*
6.1944	SS-*Hauptscharführer der Reserve.*

Notes: A knitting factory worker by profession in Kottengrün/Vogtland between 1 January 1939 and 11 February 1940, (near Werda), Mueller joined the *Waffen*-SS that same day. Mustering with the KL Dachau guard unit until March 1941, Mueller then transferred to the *HA* SS-*Gericht* and was posted to the SS-*Straflager* Dachau, then Danzig–Matzkau and lastly to the *Zweigsstelle* Hammerweg. Returning to the SS-*Straflager* Dachau in April 1945, Mueller fled the camp environs prior to the US troop's arrival and hid in Königreich/Sachsen from 14 April. Arrested in Werda at 11.00 a.m. on 1 June 1945, Mueller was detained in a succession of prisoner of war camps including Treuen-Pössnick, Ohrdruf-Ziegenhain, Kornwestheim-Züffenhausen and Dachau until he ended up in British Army hands and they interned him in the camp Nr. 5 at Staumühle.[25]

Name: Fritz Pölking.
Last Rank: SS-*Oberscharführer.*
Born: 27.5.1916 in Wülfing/Südlohe/*Kreis* Oldenburg.
NSDAP-Nr.: 5.274.438 (joined 1.5.1937).
SS-Nr.: 286.856 (joined 24.4.1935).
HJ Service: 28.8.1933–9.11.1934.
Prewar Assignments:
SS-VT 24.5.1935.
3. / III. / SS-*Standarte Germania* in 8.1938,
9. / III. / SS-*Standarte Germania* in 1938.

Wartime Assignments:
2. / III. / SS-*Standarte Germania* 1939–1940.
SS-*Infantrie-Ersatz-Bataillon Germania* in late 1940.
Waffen-SS *Hauptamt* SS-*Gericht* early 1941.
SS- *und Polizei-Gericht* XII, Hamburg in early 1941–1.12.1941.
SS- *und Polizei-Gericht* XIV, Metz 1.12.1941–13.7.1942.
Strafvollzugslager der SS-*und Polizei* Danzig–Matzkau 13.7.1942–25.1.1945.
SS-*Straflager* Dachau 25.1.–27.4.1945.
Promotions:
0.0.19__ SS-*Rottenführer der Waffen*-SS.
30.1.1942 SS-*Oberscharführer der Waffen*-SS.
Decorations & Awards:
0.0.19__ 1939 *Eisernes Kreuz II. Klasse.*
0.0.19__ *Verwundetenabzeichen*, 1939 *in Schwarz.*

Notes: Born into a farming family, Pölking mustered with the SA from late 1934 until 24 April 1935. Pölking fought with the *Germania* during the Polish, Dutch, Belgium and French campaigns. Wounded, he recovered in a Münster hospital for twelve weeks and was then posted to a reserve battalion at the SS-*Kaserne* Hamburg–Langhorn until he recovered. Here, Pölking was judged unfit for front service and transferred to the *HA* SS-*Gericht*, he was deployed at the Hamburg tribunal, (he lived on the court premises at Leinpfad 20). Marrying his fiancée Elfriede F. on 26 March 1941, a witness to the marriage was *Strm.* Paul Schneiders, a court colleague. The family settled in Harks/Heide and they had two children up to the point when records ceased in May 1945. In mid-May 1942 *Ostuf.* Spitz of the *HA* SS-*Gericht* asked their administration to provide Pölking's banking details. Hospitalised again, Pölking recovered and reported for duty at Danzig–Matzkau as an SS-*Beurkundungsunterführer* in July 1942. Pölking remained here until his transfer to the SS-*Straflager* Dachau in January 1945.[26]

Name: Josef Posch.
Last Rank SS-*Hauptscharführer.*
Born: 22.7.1920 in Hall, *Kreis* Innsbruck/Tirol.
SS-Nr.: (joined 1.4.1938).
Prewar Assignments:
Waffen-SS 1.4.1938.
Wartime Assignments:
SS-*Totenkopfdivision* 1939.
8. / SS-*Totenkopf-Infantrie*-Rgt. 1 on 17.9.1941.
SS-*Panzergrenadier-Ausbildung- und Ersatz*-Rgt. 12.5.1943–9.6.1943.
4. / 3. SS-*Panzergrenadier-Ersatz-Bataillon* 9.6.1943–4.10.1943.
SS-*Panzer-Grenadier-Ersatz-Bataillon* 3 (*Stab-Kompanie*) 4.10.1943–4.3.1944.

Strafvollzugslager der SS-*und Polizei* Danzig–Matzkau on 4.3.1944–1.1945.
SS-Rgt. *Kalthofen* in 1.1945.

Promotions:

1.4.1939	SS-*Sturmann der Waffen*-SS.
1.11.1939	SS-*Rottenführer der Waffen*-SS.
0.0.1943	SS-*Oberscharführer der Waffen*-SS.
0.0.1944	SS-*Hauptscharführer der Waffen*-SS.

Decorations & Awards:

0.0.19__	1939 *Eisernes Kreuz II. Klasse.*
30.9.1942	*Verwundetenabzeichen*, 1939 *in Schwarz.*
30.9.1942	*Verwundetenabzeichen*, 1939 *in Silber.*
3.8.1943	*Medaille 'Winterschlacht im Osten* 1941/42'.
1.10.1938	*Die Medaille zur Erinnerung an den* 1. Oktober 1938 (Sudetenland).

Notes: A student, Posch volunteered for the *Waffen*-SS in 1938 and committed himself to twelve years' service. Wounded on the Eastern Front while assigned to the *Totenkopfdivision*, Posch recovered and transferred from the Alzey *Reserve-Lazarett* to an infantry regiment in September 1941. A machine gunner, Posch returned to the front line and was wounded again in mid-1942. Leaving the Treptow *Reserve-Lazarett* for his former company on 5 September 1942, Posch was granted leave in Grabow between 26 November and 12 December 1942 and again between 31 December 1942 and 15 January 1943. Participating in the suppression of the Warsaw Ghetto in April/May 1943, Posch then transferring to a reserve regiment at Bitsch in May 1943. Returning from home leave on 5 June 1943, Posch received orders to join a reserve battalion in Warsaw in June 1943. As a guard, Posch found himself seconded to the SS and *Polizei* prison at Montelupich and remained in this post until ordered to Danzig–Matzkau in March 1944. They requested his personal papers from his last post on the 19 March. Probably assigned to the SS-Rgt. *Kalthofen* in February 1945, Posch has been missing since the war's end.[27]

Name: Friedrich 'Fritz' Wilhelm **Ringel.**
Last Rank: SS-*Obersturmführer.*
Born: 12.7.1908 in Marburg *an der* Drau, (Yugoslavia).
NSDAP-Nr.: 512.536 (joined 1.6.1931).
SS-Nr.: 9.352 (joined 1.6.1931).
HJ service: 1925 -1926 and from 7.1936

Prewar Assignments:

Tiroler *Heimatschutz* 1927–1930.
Österreichischen Legion 7.7.1933–1.1.1935.
II. / SS-*Standarte Deutschland* 1.1.1935–19.8.1936.
SS-*Bataillon Nürnberg* 30.9.1936–11.1.1937.
3. / SS-*Bataillon Nürnberg* 12.1.1937–9.1939.

Beurkundungsführer training course in Munich in 11.1938.
Offizier-Lehrgang SS-*Junkerschule* Bad Tölz 1938.
1. SS-*Artillerie-Abteilung* (Jüterbog) from 27.5.1939.
SS-VT *Hauptamt* SS-*Gericht* 15.8.1939–27.4.1945.

Wartime Assignments:

SS- *und Polizei-Gericht* XI, Stuttgart in 8.1940–28.5.1941.
SS- *und Polizei-Gericht* V, Dresden, branch court Breslau 28.5.1941–1.10.1941.
Strafvollzugslager der SS-*und Polizei* Danzig–Matzkau 1.10.1941–1.5.1944.
12th SS-*Panzer*-Division *Hitlerjugend* 1.5.1944–27.7.1944.
Strafvollzugslager der SS-*und Polizei* Danzig–Matzkau 27.7.1944–1.12.1944.
Leiter des Strafvollzugslager der SS-*und Polizei* Förrenbach 1.12.1944–2.4.1945.
Nr. 1 *Lagerführer Strafvollzugslager der* SS-*und Polizei* Förrenbach from 3.1945.
SS-*Straflager* Dachau, *Aussenstelle* Allach in 4.1945.
SS-*Gebirgs-Ersatz-Bataillon* 6 (Hallein), in 4.1945.

Promotions:

1.1.1935	SS-*Scharführer der Allgemeine*-SS.
15.8.1939	SS-*Untersturmführer der Reserve.*
20.4.1941	SS-*Obersturmführer der Waffen*-SS (*Aktiv*).

Decorations & Awards:

0.0.19__	SS-*Zivilabzeichen* (Nr. 11.160).
0.0.19__	SA-*Sportsabzeichen in Bronze.*
0.0.19__	SS-*Ehrenwinkel für alte Kämpfer.*
18.9.1939	*Die Medaille zur Erinnerung an den* 13. März 1938 (Austria).
25.4.1941	8. *Jähr Dienstauszeichnung der* SS.
20.4.1943	*Kriegsverdienstkreuz II. Klasse mit Schwertern.*

Notes: In his own words, Ringel described his formative years:

> Born as the second child of the *Oberbaurates* Josef Ringel and his wife Sophie von Curtius in Marburg, (Austria) on 12 December 1908, I studied successfully at the *Volksschule* from six years-old. My father was an engineer in the railway workshop in Marburg and my mother is [decended] from an old officer's family. As my father had taken to the field as an officer soon after the war began, I was the responsibility of my mother, who was born and educated in the greater German Reich. After completing *Volksschule* I then attended *Realschule.* After the collapse of the Austrian monarchy we remained in Marburg until its provisional inclusion in Yugoslavia. My father then decided on Germany–Austria and we had to leave Marburg and moved to Innsbruck, where I belatedly entered the *Realschule.* Due to the prevailing inflation and with regard to the costly study of my elder brother at the Academy of Fine Arts in Munich I had to return later and finished my studies after the completion of five classes. I then joined the construction company AUER and Co. in Innsbruck as an architectural draughtsman and clerk in 1926. In this year I joined the Nazi party as a consequence of advertising and on the urging of comrades in the

> *Heimatsschutzbewegung*, not through the *Hitlerjugend*, as indicated in the prosecuter's letter. I joined the *Heimatsschutzbewegung* in 1926, as at that time I violently opposed the Nazi movement and had lost interest in party politics.

Ringel studied at the Marburg *Volksschule* for five classes between 1914 and 1919 and then attended the Innsbruck *Realschule* for four classes. He broke his right elbow joint in October 1929. Speaking after the war, Edmund Baumgärtner was convinced that Ringel was the nephew of the *Gebirgsjägergeneral* Julius Ringel. Here, in his own words, Ringel explains his political leanings and reasons for engaging with the Nazi party:

> For their soldierly appearance I strongly favoured the emerging *Heimatsschutzbewegung* in 1927. This movement was initially apolitical and sworn in as auxiliary police for emergencies by the state government. However, over the years this organisation became political and drifted more and more into the monarchist fairway. This was against my socialist attitude and was the reason for my withdrawal in July 1930. In 1931 I came in contact with and entered for the first time the NSDAP. In accordance with my greater German attitude I saw in this movement through the eyes of an idealist and it fulfilled my political ideals. (An association of Germans, an ethnic community rather than class struggle, the common good before self-interest, National Socialism). I joined the party and the SS on 6 June 1931. I considered the *Allgemeine*-SS soldierly. Despite the violent political battles in Austria I never once was somehow in conflict with the law and punished. After the banning of the party, I and thousands of comrades from Austria received orders to escape across the border to Germany and I accepted a posting in a KL. Here took place our entrance in the Austrian Legion. I had to abandon my rank as an SS-*Scha* and start over again as a legionnaire. We were not clear about the meaning and purpose of the Legion, however, we thought we would soon return to Austria. A partial return only occured in 1938.
>
> The majority of the Austrian SS legion including myself was transferred to the SS-*Verfügungstruppe* on 1 January 1934. Voluntarily joining this military unit, I received notification to report to the communications section of the II. / SS-*Sta. Deutschland.* Already at this time the SS-VT was no party organization, but was a *Wehrmacht* attributed troop and recognised as such in the budget of the Reich. Recruitment was not successfully undertaken by political considerations but by the usual, but more stringent mustering conditions of the *Wehrmacht.* Service duties was carried out in accordance with the A.V.I. of the *Heeres* and the respective promotions did not occur as a result of political affiliation activity, but by duty and military service. The SS-VT did not participate in any political activities.

Finding himself unemployed in 1933, Ringel fled Austria for Germany and joined the Österreichischen Legion. Living and working in the SS-*Lager* Lechfeld until 1934, he lived at the SS-*Kaserne* Munich-Freimann until 1938. Becoming a radioman with the 3. *Nachrichtenzug* II. / SS-*Standarte Deutschland*, he then served with the *Nachrichtenzug* of the battalion *Nürnberg* until September 1939 (this unit became the *Panzer-Abwehr-Abteilung der* SS on 10.6.1939). Suffering an accident on duty in September 1936, Ringel underwent an operation to repair a ligament injury at the Hohenlychen SS-*Lazarett* in early 1937. Returning to the *Nürnberg* in February 1937, Ringel was judged unfit for active service and undertook a search for a non-combative post. Submitting a questionnaire to the department for old fighters at the NSDAP *Kreisleitung* Dachau in January 1938, Ringel was instructed to attend a specialised training courses in Munich and Bad Tölz in 1938. Marrying his fiancée Carola H., (b. 23.7.1915, Munich) on 12 August 1938, they had two children up to the point when records ceased in1945 and lived in a small apartment in Etzenhausen *bei* Dachau.

Participating in the *Anschluss* of Austria in 1938, Ringel was then seconded to an artillery unit at Jüterbog in May 1939 and trained with this unit in East Prussia. In preparation for the Polish campaign, the high command subordinated his regiment to the *Panzer*-Division *Kempf* on 7 July 1939 (it was observed at this time that he had undertaken specialised clerk training). Injured in a car crash on 24 July 1939, Ringel suffered a right forearm fracture, a compound joint fracture and concussion and was hospitalised in the Königsberg, Wismar and Dachau. Formally assigned to the *HA* SS-*Gericht* as a SS-*Beurkundungsführer* on 15 August 1939, Ringel was not discharged from the Dachau SS-*Lazarett* until 8 October the same year. Deployed at the *HA* SS-*Gericht* personnel department under Robert Pape from 23 November the same year, he then served as a certification officer with the Danzig, Stuttgart and Den Haag tribunals. A promotion recommendation was submitted for Ringel on 21 March 1941:

> He has been in his service post since 1 October 1939 and is an old reliable party member and SS man. The senior SS-*Richter* at the SS- *und Polizei-Gericht* XI, SS-*Stubaf.* Hoffmann, has judged Ringel a steady, diligent worker and noted that he takes care of his work in a satisfactory manner. In view of his long membership of the movement, his promotion to the rank of SS-*Ostuf.* is justified.

With General Scharfe's support of the application, the promotion was awarded in April 1941. As a SS-*Beurkundungsführer*, Ringel would claim after the war to have been seconded from the branch court Breslau to the SS-*Infantrie Ersatz-Bataillon Ost* in May 1941. Here, in his own words, Ringel describes his next posting:

> I arrived at the SS and *Polizei* prison camp in Danzig–Matzkau in 1942, but a more specific time I am unable to state more accurately. I had previously worked at the SS- *und Polizei-Gericht* Stuttgart as the leader of the office. Transferring to Danzig–Matzkau, I held the rank of SS-*Ostuf.* Here, in Danzig–Matzkau I became the *Wachkompanieführer.*

Ringel received orders to hand command of the office of the branch court Breslau to *Hscha.* Erich Hanf and report to Matzkau in late September 1941 and Dr Beelitz confirmed that he took command of the 1. *Wachkompanie.*[31]

Ringel suffered a serious concussion in Matzkau on 12 August 1943. Transferred to the troops in the summer of 1944, he fought as a *Zugführer* with a unit that he described as the SS-*Panzerjäger* *Kommando* 8 (12th SS-*Panzer*-Division *Hitlerjugend*) from the summer of 1944 and until he was wounded in the throat on 17 June. Ringel had returned to Matzkau by July the same year and was deployed at the prison on 7 September. Speaking in August 1968, Ringel claimed to have transferred to a prisoner camp at Hammelburg in Bavaria in early 1944 and acted as the *Lagerführer* there until the end of 1944. This statement is not reflected in his SSO file. Omitting his name from late 1944 Matzkau muster roster suggests that Ringel had been assigned to the *Zweiglager* Förrenbach from before December 1944 and he led this institution until Dr Beelitz's arrival in March 1945. Appointed the prisons Nr. 1 *Lagerführer*, the *Ergänzungsstelle Süd* (VII) issued Ringel a new ration book on 3.1.1945. Förrenbach was dissolved in April 1945 and Ringel transferred to the SS-*Straflager* Dachau, *Aussenstelle* Allach. Shortly before the capitulation, he reported to a reserve battalion and claimed to have been replaced in Dachau by an *Ostuf.*/*Ustuf.* Behrens.

Captured by US forces in Salzburg on 15 May 1945, Ringel was held as a prisoner of war in a camp near Bad Aibing. On 25 May 1945 the Bad Aibling CIC noted that he held the rank of *Hstuf.* and had formerly worked in what was described as the 'SS punitive camp'. Suspected of contracting typhus, he was hospitalised. Returning to Aibling on 12 July 1945, Ringel then transferred to Dachau and worked here as a painter between July 1945 and November 1946. Working willingly with an American work commando in Grünewald near Munich, he suffered a serious head injury and concussion on 3 November 1946 which resulted in Ringel suffering epileptic attacks on both sides of his brain which rendered him incapable of undertaking certain types of work. Arrested by the MID 320 on 12 July 1946, that same day Ringel reported to the CIE 29 Dachau and was placed in the Hammelburg Internment camp on 19/20 December 1946. Interrogated here by T/3 Joseph P. Galli on 15 April 1947, Ringel affirmed that he was a German national and had no recollection of voting for the Nazi party.

Writing to the Hammelburg camp leadership on 29 April and 15 May 1947, Ringel's wife requested her husband's release and reported that her parents had been bombed out of their home on 17 December 1944 and was living with her in great hardship (seven people lived in her home). Her entreaties hid an unpleasant surprise. Informed that his wife had given birth to a child that was not his in February 1947, Ringel applied successfully for home leave on 9 July to enable him to 'straighten things out'. Granting his request, he was authorised three days' travelling time, handed travel documents and food vouchers and was released from detention at 11.00 a.m. on 22 July with orders to return eight days later at 12.00 p.m. Returning home, Ringel received permission from the Munich *Polizei* on 29 July to extend his leave until 3 August and he then returned to Hammelburg. Writing to the court prosecuter on 28 October 1947, *Frau* Ringel asked for his case to be handled quickly on the grounds that the family was in financial difficulties. On 3 November Ringel suffered a serious epileptic fit that resulted in his transfer to the Langwasser internment camp eight days later. Admitted into the camp clinic on 13 November, here, he suffered two further fits, but had recovered sufficiently to be discharged from here on 29 November.

At this time the authorities froze the Ringel's Munich bank account. Receiving his indictment on 26 January 1948, Ringel submitted his rebuttal to the public prosecuter on 7 February the same year. His summary began with an explaination for joining the Nazi party and contains interesting justifications for his decision to join the Nazi party:

> [...] In the NSDAP I saw no organisation of tyranny, I believed and trusted its purely idealogical goals and believed that it always stood for fairness and openness. How should I, as a little-politically-trained man, believe in tyranny after the Nazis legally took over the government, when by international law it was recognised by all nations, and maintained normal diplomatic relations with foreign countries, who gave their consent by sending its diplomats to the Reich Party Rallies and completed the Vatican condordat. Yes, even statesmen such as Eden, Churchill, Halifax, Daladier, etc. conferred with Hitler. How should I, just a sworn soldier have later held any doubts about this regime's authenticity? I joined the movement in good faith and was used for operations, to which I had no control, and could not be held responsible. I myself have also possessed no knowledge of the handling, or the objectives to which the Nuremberg judgment placed the burden of criminality on the SS. This only stems from my military use since 1 September 1939. My units remained free of war crimes and crimes against humanity.
>
> Today, after almost three years of imprisonment and my multiple accidents with the military I am working disabled even after the recent accident in captivity in the American labour team and my future is in difficulty, especially as I am penniless with my family of five. My apartment in Etzenhausen in 1945 was plundered and all my all linen, clothes, etc. was stolen, along with a huge part of my furniture. Everything was taken from my wife and children.
>
> Since my stress and guilt are purely formal, I apply for you to classify me in group III, in order to give me the opportunity to build a new life with my sorely-tried and afflicted family. I submit another application and leave the decision fully to men of the chamber with a sense of justice.

To support his case, Ringel submitted a character statement, written by a former officer of the *Waffen*-SS:

> Arthur Erdmann, Hammelburg, dated 10.10.1948.
> As a former *Ostubaf.* of the *Waffen*-SS and a member of the Personnel Office of the *Waffen*-SS I can declare that the SS-*Verfügungstruppe* which was formed in 1934, was not associated with the party, but was funded from the budget of the *Wehrmacht*.
>
> Inductions were made not by political considerations, but by the stringent height measure alone and in accordance to the screening provisions of the *Wehrmacht*. The service operation and the training was carried out in accordance to the AVI of the army, and promotions were only awarded for soldierly achievements and service and not in accordance to political considerations or political activity.

In 1940 all armed units of the SS were combined to form a part of the *Wehrmacht* which was given the name *Waffen*-SS and was considered a fourth arm of the military. The *Hitlerjugend* Panzer Division fought within the organisation of the *Wehrmacht* and was subordinate administratively to the SS-FHA. Former SS-*Ostuf.* of the *Waffen*-SS Fritz Ringel was an active member of the *Waffen*-SS. His late promotion to SS-*Ostuf.* and no further promotion permits us the unconditional conclusion that Ringel did not excel.

The Hammelburg camp court (V) announced Fritz Ringel's judgement on 20 February 1948 and taking into account his half-year of forced labour, served by the existing internment, they ordered the confiscation of ten per cent of his existing assets, leaving him only the most necessary utensils and set the disputed amount at almost 4,000 *Reichsmark* (the usual work restrictions also applied). In its summation, the court questioned Ringel's inability to procure favorable witness statements from his family, former comrades and those who knew him when he lived in Innsbruck. In addition, the tribunal questioned his motives for joining the SS and voiced a suspicion that his time in the prison service had tainted his character:

> [...] On the other hand there are certain moments when he voices protective wording in the files, and from his time in Austria, we find that the person concerned was a particularly active fighter for Nazism. His greater-German attitude may explain some of this, but it cannot acquit him of all political accountability. The refutation of the presumption of guilt is not achieved, but rather hampered by the information supplied by the person concerned that he was employed as a company commander of a guard company in the SS prison camp at Danzig.

Declaring Ringel responsible and placing him in group II of the offenders, the tribunal also punished him with six months forced labour, which he had served in internment. Acknowledging that he was penniless, however, the court continued to demand a ten per cent asset collection. On 15 March 1948 the court determined that Ringel would remained in Hammelburg until a release date was determined. Unhappy with the courts sentencing, Ringel wrote to the appeals chamber for the region lower Franconia in Würzburg on 8 March the same year to appeal his judgement. Arguing against the legality of the sentence, Ringel then appealed to the tribunal's sense of fairness:

> The fact—that against me nothing negative has been presented, may prove at most, that there is nothing against me and that I am completely unknown. Never could you draw the conclusion from this fact that I was an active fighter for the National Socialism during my time Austria. Such a conclusion out of nowhere would open the floodgates to all possibilities. The implication of the chamber violates the principle of fundamental evidence. From nothing previous known, could then a little be inferred. Consequently, according to the generally recognized rules of evidence only no doubt must be decided

in my favor. Even after the chamber comes to the conclusion, that my personality as a whole, stands completely flawless, and in their own announcement with reference to Article 53 of the Act, they recommended the mitigation of the same in the clemency way, he could have classified me in the group of lesser offenders equally well under analogous application of Article 2 of the Act.

I enclose excerpts from the baptismal register of the Catholic parish church of St. Peter, St. Gabriel, St. John the Baptist in front of which it is apparent that my children have been baptized a Catholic. Hence my loyal attitude towards the church can be seen. I would also point out that in accordance to a medical examination I am only partially fit for work and a permanent outpatient observation is required.

In assessing the atonement I beg particularly to take into account that since my transfer from captivity in internment, I have lost everything because of the war and today possess only my wife and three little children. Resulting from an accident in captivity, with the American labor team in Grünwald near Munich, I am sick and incapable of work, so that the requirements of Article 19 apply to me.

The classification in group II of lesser offenders corresponds because it is the only justice that would be understood by me.

Ringel.

The authorities all in agreement, Ringel was finally released from Hammelburg on 25 March 1948 at 9.00 a.m. Returning to his family in Munich, Ringel found employment as a salaried salesman. Speaking in 1962, the former guard, R. M*ü*ller, recalled that Ringel was employed in the record keeping department of the *Landesversicherung* in Munich.

The Chairman of the Appeals Chamber for Munich considered a reduction of Ringel's sentence to 'lesser offenders' and then had to decide whether to impose a probation period of twelve months' duration. Later, declaring that Ringel's two years and two months of forced labour sufficient atonement, the Munich 4. *Senat* appeals chamber confirmed his sentence on 28 February 1949 and ordered him to bear the nearly 4,000 *Reichsmark* costs of the process, (his inability to produce witnesses to refute the prosecuter's statement hindered his application to reduce his sentence to 'lesser offender'). The State Office for asset management and reparation in Munich asked for permission to seize Ringel's property on 14 April 1949, but the court granted Ringel a temporary injunction against any confiscation on 11 October. The threat of seizure was not lifted until the asset management office returned the confiscation writ on 10 September 1949, on the grounds that it was no longer a legally enforceable.

Ringel's appeal was heard before the court of *Kassation* in the Bavarian Ministry for Special Affairs on 1 August 1949 and they decided to annul the 26 February 1949 judgement and ordered a reimplementation of the process. Transferring the case to the competent professional chamber in Munich, the tribunal accepted that his judgment had been based on presumtiveness and annulled the second announcement in order to determine Ringel's real motives for joining the Nazi party, to examine his church affiliations and permit him the opportunity to submit rebuttal evidence. Subsequent to this decision, the Munich appeals chamber confirmed that Ringel sought to be reclassified in the group III of the lesser offenders and acknowledged that he was seeking a probation period of one year (leaving any further atonement sanctions to the *Senat*). Compelled to present favourable witness statements to the court, two former senior officers of the *HA* SS-*Gericht*, including his last commander, stepped forward to write a character declaration for Ringel:

> Dr Günther Reinecke, dated 6.10.1949.
> At the war's end I was an *Oberführer* the *Waffen*-SS, the chief of the *Obersten* SS- *und Polizei Gericht* and the deputy Chief of the *HA* SS-*Gericht,* the headquarters of the military jurisdiction of the *Waffen*-SS and *Polizei.* In this capacity I was Ringel's immediate superior and I have known him personally since about 1938.
>
> At that time, Ringel applied for inclusion in the then under construction legal services of the *Waffen*-SS. After participating and passing the conducted competent judicial services exam in 1939, Ringel was accepted in the court service of the *Waffen*-SS as a SS-*Beurkundungsführer.* This career was defined by national law and corresponded to the average of judicial service within the civil jurisdiction.
>
> Since that time Ringel has been deployed in various courts exclusively as a specialist legal officer and was also only promoted to SS-*Ostuf.* as a specialist officer (of the judicial service). His later use in the prison camp Danzig corresponds to the activity of a judicial official in the criminal enforcement service. Ringel's activities within the *Waffen*-SS was therefore without any ties to the party or the *Allgemeine*-SS. Ringel has not visited any training courses that was required to achieve officer rank in the *Waffen*-SS, because he was only a specialist officer.

> Robert Pape, Munich, dated 28.3.1949.
> During the last war I was the personal case worker of the *HA* SS-*Gericht* and from this time I have known *Herr* Ringel, who belonged in the same office. Firstly, he was in use as a SS-*Beurkundungsführer* at the SS courts and was then transferred to the *Strafvollzugslager der* SS *und Polizei* in Danzig–Matzkau, an SS-own ran prison where he was employed as a *Kompanieführer.* Ringel revealed no initiative during the whole period of its membership in the *HA* SS-*Gericht,* so during the war the department only promoted him to the rank of SS-*Ostuf.* He is therefore likely regarded, by older people, to have held the lowest rank. In his service as a *Kompanieführer*, Ringel, as a good old soldier, has not attracted any particular evil attention. Charges of harassment, or even crimes against humanity by Ringel are unknown to me, I trust him not to undertake such an action because of his evident character.

Waiting for the court's decision, the public prosecutor wrote to Ringel on 28 April 1949 to inform him that he owed a two per cent interest charge on his almost 4,000 *Reichsmark* fine, he owed the costs of his appeal and was granted two weeks in which to pay just over 120 *Reichsmark*. The Munich 10. *Senat* appeals chamber published a favourable verdict on 7 November 1949 and granting his appeal, they reclassified Ringel in the group III of 'lesser offenders' and in addition to the usual caveats, they subjected him to a probationary period of one year (the costs of the appeal on the exchequer was fixed at almost 4,000 *Reichsmark*). Ringel was living with his wife anf family in May 1949 and received a new certificate from the Munich main chamber public prosecuter on 1 September 1950 which labelled him a 'follower' from this date. Interviewed by the Munich prosecutor in in connection with Hühn's murder allegations August 1968, Ringel explained that he was unable to help them with their enquiries:

> In 1947 I was in American captivity near Grünwald near Munich and was involved in a car accident and suffered a brain contusion. I was a long time receiving inpatient treatment. Since that time I have suffered from epileptic seizures and am therefore constantly under medical treatment. Because of these health concerns I was in 1949 or 1950 classified as heavily war injured (60 per cent).[28]

His court tribulations at an end, Fritz Ringel did not face any court sanction for his service in the *Waffen*-SS prison service and settled and worked in Munich.[29]

Name: Horst Ernst **Sack.**
Last Rank: SS-*Untersturmführer.*
Born: 31.12.1907 in Alt-Döbern.
NSDAP-Nr.: 4.861.216 (joined 1.5.1937).
SS-Nr.: (joined 1.3.1943)
Wartime Assignments:
Waffen-SS from 1.3.1943.
3. / SS-*Artillerie-Ausbildung- und Ersatz*-Rgt. 1.3.1943–30.4.1943.
SS-*Artillerieschule* I Glau (*Kommandostab*) 1.5.1943–12.1.1944.
Waffen-SS *Hauptamt* SS-*Gericht* 31.9.1943–8.5.1945.
Kommandostab RF-SS field court 1.3.–1.6.1944.
Transfer to the 15th *Waffen-Grenadier*-Division *der* SS field court on 1.6.1944 cancelled.
SS- *und Polizei-Gericht* IV, Danzig from 1.7.1944.
Verbindungsmann Danzig–Matzkau 8.1944–26.2.1945.
HA SS-*Gericht* z.b.V. from 26.2.1945.
Promotions:

0.0.1943	SS-*Sturmann der Reserve.*
20.4.1944	SS-*Oberscharführer der Reserve.*
1.10.1944	SS-*Standartenoberjunker der Reserve.*
9.11.1944	SS-*Untersturmführer der Reserve.*

Decorations & Awards:

0.0.19__	SA-*Sportsabzeichen in Bronze.*
30.1.1945	*Kriegsverdienstkreuz II. Klasse mit Schwertern.*

Notes: Attending *Volksschule* from 1912 for three classes, Sack obtained his *Abitur* from *Höhere Schule* in Easter 1926 (*Oberprima*). Studying jurisprudence at Königsberg University until passing his *Referendarexamen* on 2 August 1933, Sack then undertook his practical training in Frankfurt an Oder and then in Königsberg. Passing his *Assessorexamen* on 19 June 1937, he found employment as an *Assessor*, a department leader and deputy officer leader from May 1938. Mustering with the SA between 3 August 1933 and 1938, Sack joined the *Nationalsozialistische Rechtswahrerbund* and NSV on 6 February 1934. Marrying his fiancée Gerda P., (b. 8.5.1909 in Königsberg), the couple had one child up to the point when records ceased in1945 and lived in Dresden during April 1942. Joining the *Waffen*-SS in March 1943, Sack transferred to the *HA* SS-*Gericht* in September 1943 and was appointed a reserve SS-*Richter* on 20 April 1944. Deployed with the SS- *und Polizei-Gericht* IV, Danzig in July 1944, an officer's promotion recommendation was submitted for Sack on 10 September 1944:

> SS-*Oscha. der Reserve* Sack is a judge with the SS- *und Polizei–Gericht* Danzig. He possesses an open-minded in character and has a soldierly immaculate presentation. He possesses strong sense of duty and good judgment. As a reserve judge he promises to do well in all respects.

The recommendation supported by General Breithaupt, he was promoted in November 1944. Speaking in 1967, Rudolf Heiß confirmed that Sack's deployed with the Danzig tribunal and affirmed that he replaced Dr Beelitz in Matzkau in August 1944. Transferring from the Danzig tribunal to undertake special duties with the *HA* SS-*Gericht* in early 1945, Heiß recalled that Sack survived the war and corresponded with him from Heiligenkirchen *bei* Detmold.[30]

Name: Josef Schwaiger.
Last Rank: SS-*Obersturmführer*.
Born: 8.2.1910 in Bischofshofen, *Bezirk* St. Johann/Pongau-Salzburg/Österreich.
NSDAP-Nr.: 511.161 (joined 2.5.1931).
SS-Nr.: 139.449 (joined 29.6.1933).
Prewar Assignments
3. / II. / 37. SS-*Standarte* (Linz) 1933-1934.
SS-*Standarte Deutschland* from 19.12.1933.
SS-VT from 10.1934.
II. / SS-*Standarte Der Führer* in 1938.
Wartime Assignments:
SS-*Infantrie-Ersatz-Bataillon Der Führer* (Stralsrund) from 24.4.1942.
19. *Kriegslehrgang für Verwaltungsführer* in Dachau from 1.8.1942.
SS-*Straflager* Dachau 6.1.1943–27.4.1945.
2. *Kriegs-Beurkundungsführer-Lehrgang* in Dachau from 19.1.1943.
Waffen-SS *Hauptamt* SS-*Gericht* 22.1.1943–27.4.1945.

Promotions:

0.0.19__	SS-*Scharführer* der SS-VT.
1.1.1935	SS-*Hauptscharführer der* SS-VT.
22.1.1944	SS-*Hauptscharführer der Reserve.*
30.1.1944	SS-*Untersturmführer* of the *Waffen*-SS (*Aktiv*).
9.11.1944	SS-*Obersturmführer* of the *Waffen*-SS (*Aktiv*).

Decorations & Awards:

0.0.19__	SS-*Zivilabzeichen.*
0.0.19__	SA-*Sportsabzeichen in Bronze.*
0.0.19__	*Deutsches Reichssportabzeichen in Bronze.*
0.0.19__	SS-*Ehrenwinkel für alte Kämpfer.*
0.0.1938	*Die Medaille zur Erinnerung an den* 1. Oktober 1938 (Sudetenland).
0.0.1938	*Die Medaille zur Erinnerung an den* 13. März 1938 (Austria).
12.10.1940	*Kriegsverdienstkreuz II. Klasse mit Schwertern.*
0.0.19__	*Medaille* '*Winterschlacht im Osten* 1941/42'.

Notes: One of three children, his father was a Bischofshofen railway official. Attending *Volksschule* for five classes between 1 May 1916 and 16 September 1921, Schwaiger then attended *Hauptschule* for three classes until 12 July 1924 and studied at trade school for three classes between 1924 and 1927. Leaving full time education, Schwaiger was employed as a house painter and worked for various businesses in his trade until 1933. Mustering with the Bischofshofen SA from 1 August 1931 until 28 June 1933, he fled Austria for Bavaria in the wake of the aborted SS coup in 1933 and applied for political asylum on arrival. Joining the Austrian legion at Kloster–Lechfeld camp, he remained with this formation when it transformed into the *Deutschland* in December 1933. Assigned to the *Deutschland* when it morphed into the *Der Führer*, Schwaiger participated in the march into the Sudetenland and the *Anschluss* of Austria. In the wake of these events, Schwaiger's *Allgemeine*-SS unit was based in Radstatt near Salzburg and here, he trained in the use of the K98k rifle, the 08 pistol, both the SMG 08 and MG34. He occupied the positions of *Richtschütze*, *Gewahrführer*, and a machine gun *Gruppenführer* respectively from 1 October 1934 to 1 March 1938.

Marrying his fiancée Elfriede F., (b. 24.10.1905 in Plauen), on 16 March 1935, they had two children up to the point when records ceased in May 1945 and lived at Dachau, Vienna, Fasangarten SS-*Siedlung* and in Bischofshofen. The *Gruppenführer* of a machine gun section between 1 March 1938 and 1 July 1939, Schwaiger was the *Kammerunterführer* from 1 March to 1 July 1938 and then fulfilled the role of *Stabsscharführer* for the *Der Führer* fourth company. Holding this post until 20 February 1942, Schwaiger had responsibility for reporting disciplinary problems and accounting for weapons, ammunition and equipment. Taking part in the attacks on Holland and France in the spring of 1940, his company was on occupation duties in Holland between July and December 1940 and he took part in the 1941 Serbian campaign and in the assault on the Soviet Union from 22 June 1941. Wounded on 20 February 1942, Schwaiger recovered at the Viennese

SS-*Lazarett* between 27 February and 24 April the same year. Once recovered, Schwaiger transferred to a reserve battalion and was seconded to its administration office on 25 April 1942. Appointed an officer candidate for the WVHA on 1 June the same year, he deployed at the SS-*Straflager* Dachau in January 1943 and became an SS-*Beurkundungsunterführer* of the *HA* SS-*Gericht* the same month. A *Rapportführer* in Dachau, Schwaiger later occupied the post of 2. *Lagerführer*. A promotion recommendation was submitted for him on 15 January 1944:

> Schwaiger is an SS-*Beurkundungsführer* in a *Straflager* of the SS and *Polizei*. He is hard-working and his work performance is circumspect. Up until now there have been no complaints about his behaviour. His attitude is comradely and he is at one with SS values. His behaviour in and out of service remains impeccable.

The report supported by *Sta.* Dr Reinecke, his promotion to officer rank was conferred on him in January 1944. Probably replacing *Hstuf.* Sturmann as Nr. 1 *Lagerführer* on 8 November the same year, the former inmate Johann Ott recalled that Schwaiger acted as *Hstuf.* Albert's adjutant/administrative assistant and remained in this institution until fleeing a little ahead of the US occupation of Dachau in April 1945.[31]

His name placed on the 5th wanted list, Crowcass, central registry of war criminals and security suspects (Kew FO 371/51041, dated 11.12.1945), Schwaiger probably hid near Salzburg after the collapse. The Bischofshofen *Gendarmerie Posten Kommandant* and *Volksgerichtshof* prosecutor initiated a court's prosecution of Schwaiger *in absentia* in early 1948. Observing that his name appeared in the central police report list from the year 1933, if caught, the *Gendarmerie* announced their intention to recommend his prosecution for committing offences against paragraph § 58 of the *Strafgesetzes* (high treason). In addition, his name was also listed by the B.K. in St. Johann i.Tyrol from 15 September 1933. On 27 January 1948 the *Bundespolizeidirektion* Salzburg confirmed that Schwaiger's name had been printed in the Pongau-Bischofshofen central police wanted list from 1933 on suspicion of committing offences against paragraph § 58 STOP.

As a consequence of the police discoveries, a criminal investigation was then initiated against Schwaiger in accordance with paragraph § 11 of the *Volksgesetzes*, (*Verjährung*) and the *Bezkirkshauptmannschaft* St. Johann i. Tyrol re-published a wanted advert for him in the municipality of Bischofshofen from 15 September 1933. At this time the *Polizei* and state prosecuter did not have access to Schwaiger's NSDAP and SS files and had no idea where he had been born or was living. The *Volksgerichtshof* prosecutor convened a meeting in Bischofshofen on 10 February 1948 and submitted an indictment against Schwaiger to the Linz prosecutor on 12 February 1948. The first application by the prosecuter for indictment against Schwaiger was submitted on 18 February the same year in accordance with paragraphs § § 10, (örtlicher Geltungsbereich des Gesetzes) and 11, (*Verjährung*) of the *Volksgesetzes* (St. 428/1948). The *Landgericht* Linz initiated proceedings against Schwaiger on 20 February the same year, but decided to cancel the process in accordance with paragraph § 412 STPO. If brought for trial, this may have occurred on 20 March

1948, but it is by no means clear from surviving documents if this process was undertaken *in absentia*.[32]

Name: Wilhelm Sparwasser.
Last Rank: SS-*Obersturmführer*.
Born: 18.1.1905 in Frankfurt am Main.
NSDAP-Nr.: 30.034 (16.2.1926–30.9.1927).
2.395.620 (1.5.1933).
SS-Nr.: 53.276, (15.12.1932).
Prewar Assignments:
2. / 6. SS-*Sta*. (Frankfurt am Main) from 15.12.1932.
Wartime Assignments:
SS-TV from 6.9.1939.
3. SS-*Totenkopf-Infantrie*-Rgt. from 6.9.1939.
Waffen-SS *Hauptamt* SS-*Gericht* from 12.1940.
SS- *und Polizei-Gericht* IX, Oslo 1941.
Polizeidivison field court 2.4.1942–19.11.1943.
4th SS-*Panzergrenadier*-Division *Reich* field court 19.11.1943–7.7.1944.
SS- *und Polizei-Gericht* XI, Stuttgart 7.7.1944–26.10.1944.
Strafvollzugslager der SS *und Polizei* Danzig–Matzkau 26.10.1944–2.1945.
Strafvollzugslager der SS-*und Polizei* Förrenbach 1.2.–4.1945.
SS-*Straflager* Dachau in 4.1945.
Promotions:

15.12.1932	SS-*Anwärter*.
9.11.1941	SS-*Untersturmführer der Reserve*.
9.11.1942	SS-*Obersturmführer der Reserve*.
1.1.1944	SS-*Obersturmführer der Waffen*-SS (*Aktiv*).

Decorations & Awards:

0.0.19__	SS-*Zivilabzeichen* (Nr. 23.226).
0.0.19__	*Totenkopfring der* SS.
0.0.19__	SS-*Ehrenwinkel für alte Kämpfer.*
0.0.19__	*Ehrendolches des Reichsführer*-SS.
0.0. 19__	*Dienstauszeichnung der NSDAP in Gelb.*
0.0.19__	*Gauehrenzeichen*, (Nr. 23).
11.1942	*Kriegsverdienstkreuz II. Klasse mit Schwertern.*

Notes: Attending *Volksschule* between 1911 and 1919, Sparwasser studied at trade school for three classes and leaving full time education he found employment as a salaried office worker with the justice service in Frankfurt am Main, (the *Amtsgericht* from 10.11.1925). Passing his civil service examination for the justice service in May 1925, he joined the *Volkische Jugend* in 1923 and mustered with the SA between 1923 and 1932 (the SS noted that he spoke French and Norwegian). Sparwasser attended the 28 January 1923 party day in Munich, the 4 July 1926 meeting in Weimar and the 20 May 1927 and 2 September 1933 party days in Nuremberg. Volunteering for military training with the *Reichswehr* for three months between March and April 1925 (*Schütze*) he undertook a further eight weeks training with the *Wehrmacht Heer* in 1938. Marrying his fiancée, the couple settled in Frankfurt, but this union ended in divorce in October 1935 and had two children. He became engaged to his fiancée on 25.1.1944. Drafted into the SS-TV in September 1939, Sparwasser transferred to the *HA* SS-*Gericht* in December 1940 and became an SS-*Beurkundungsunterführer* on 1 January 1944. He had received orders to leave the Stuttgart tribunal for the *Strafvollzugslager der* SS *und Polizei* Danzig–Matzkau by October 1944 and then deployed with the staff company.[34]

Name: Franz Sturmann.
Last Rank: SS-*Hauptsturmführer.*
Born: 5.12.1909 in Voitsberg/Steiermark.
NSDAP-Nr.: 81.690 (joined 1.11.1927).
SS-Nr.: 60.666 (joined 1.8.1932).
Prewar Assignments:
1. III. / 38. SS-*Standarte*, (Graz) 1.8.1932–20.8.1933.
II. / SS-*Standarte Deutschland* from 9.1934.
SS-VT from 1.1.1935.
8. / SS-*Standarte Deutschland* 1.1.1935–20.8.1936.
4. M.G. *Kompanie* / K. / SS-*Bataillon Nürnberg* (Prittelbach) 1937.
Beurkundungsführer–Lehrgang SS-*Junkerschule* Bad Tölz in early 1938.
II. / SS-*Standarte Deutschland* from 11.1938.
Wartime Assignments:
SS-VT *Panzerjägerbataillon* from 9.1939.
SS-VT *Hauptamt* SS-*Gericht* 17.10.1939–8.11.1944.
Led the office of the SS- *und Polizei-Gericht* VI, Krakau in 12.1940.
SS-*Straflager* Dachau 6.1.1941–1.2.1944.
SS-*Lagerführer* SS-*Straflager* Dachau from 20.7.1941–1.2.1944.
Strafvollzugslager SS *und Polizei* Danzig–Matzkau 1.2.1944–late summer 1944.
Leiter des Zweiglager Ludwigsfelde 1.2.1944–late summer 1944.
SS-*Straflager* Dachau, *Aussenstelle* Allach until 8.11.1944.
SS-*Panzer-Grenadier-Ausbildung- und Ersatz-Bn.* 18 (Breslau) 8.11.1944–12.1.1945.
Offizier-Lehrgang Kienschlag SS-*Panzergrenadier-Schule* until 12.1.1945.
SS-*Rekruitdepot Kurmark* (Nieder-Lausitz) 12.1.–25.1.1945.
SS-*Kampfgruppe Kurmark* / 32. SS-*Freiwilligen-Grenadier*-Division *30. Januar* 25.1.1945–29.4.1945.
Promotions:
1.12.1927 SA-*Mann.*
0.0.19__ SS-*Rottenführer der Allgemeine*-SS.

24.12.1933 SS-*Unterscharführer der Allgemeine*-SS.
20.4.1936 SS-*Scharführer der* SS-*Verfügungstruppe.*
1.5.1937 SS-*Oberscharführer der* SS-*Verfügungstruppe.*
9.11.1940 SS-*Untersturmführer der Waffen*-SS (*Aktiv*).
30.1.1942 SS-*Obersturmführer der Waffen*-SS (*Aktiv*).
21.6.1944 SS-*Hauptsturmführer der Waffen*-SS (*Aktiv*).

Decorations & Awards:

0.0.19__ SS-*Zivilabzeichen* (Nr. 119.786).
0.0.19__ SA-*Sportsabzeichen in Bronze.*
0.0.19__ *Deutsches Reichssportabzeichen in Bronze.*
0.0.19__ SS-*Ehrenwinkel für alte Kämpfer.*
0.0.19__ *Totenkopfring der* SS.
0.0.19__ *Dienstauszeichnung der* NSDAP *in Bronze.*
0.0.19__ *Dienstauszeichnung der* NSDAP *in Silber.*
0.0. 19__ *Dienstauszeichnung der* NSDAP *in Gelb.*
0.0.19__ *Ehrendegen des Reichsführer*-SS.
0.0.19__ *Ehrendolch des Reichsführer*-SS.

Notes: Attending *Volksschule* and then *Bürgerschule* for three classes, Sturmann was taught the skills of an employed tradesmen at a specialist school for two years and then worked as a salesman with the Kleider, Wäsche *und* Modewaren in Köflach until August 1933. Mustering with the *Sturm* 11/ 27. SA-*Standarte* from 1 December 1927 until 1 August 1932, Sturmann fled Austria for Bavaria on 20 August 1933 and accepted a civilian post as an office clerk with the Österreich Legion in the SA-*Lager* Kloster–Lechfeld. Living in Dachau and employed as a civilian worker at the SS-*Hilfwerk* between 20 December 1933 and 1 October 1934, this former comrade explained the circumstance behind Sturmann's entry into the SS-VT in 1947:

> Sepp Willinger, Mosburg/*Arbeitskommando* 50, dated 12.9.1947.
> Arriving in Germany in 1933 *Herr* Franz Sturmann had no expectation of finding a position in his profession and so he had to adopt some other civilian position. Then Sturmann, who had already accepted he would seek civil employment, then had to solve his employment difficulties and so decided to report for duty at the SS-*Hilfwerk* Dachau. This service office then commanded over Franz Sturmann.
>
> Franz Sturmann and other comrades had been ensnared reluctantly and as a consequence many of them then received warnings and punishments. They threatened all members of that SS-*Hilfwerkes* with admission into the concentration camp when they stated their dislike of the arrangement. Against this pressure and ongoing threats of detention in the KL, Sturmann stood steady with his comrades. Also the above duty was denied to him.
>
> Three comrades, named Steinkogler, Brehm and Prechtl were detained in a concentration camp and the *Reichsführer*-SS ordered Sturmann and another group of

people to undertake five weeks punitive punishment drill under the supervision of the *Landespolizei*. Decrying this circle as mutineers, Sturmann then developed a long grudge against his treatment.

His transfer to the *Waffen*-SS (SS-VT) on 1 January 1935 was in response to taking advantage of economic coercion. This information and explanation I can confirm it because I have witnessed it myself.

Assigned to the SS-*Hilfwerks* command region in September or October 1934, Sturmann would claim to have 'hung around senselessly' in old uniforms over the winter of 1933/34 and more ominously to have 'occasionally' assisted the KL Dachau guard. Granted German citizenship in the wake of the September 1934 party day parade at Nuremberg, Sturmann married his pregnant fiancée Marta Magdalena H., (b. 21.7.1915 in Plauen) on 7 August 1937 and they had one child up to the point when records ceased in May 1945. The family lived in Dachau. When the couple applied to marry, their local *Gauleiter* furnished the SS with allegations that his bride's family were Social Democrats and claimed that his fiancée had been a member of a communist youth organisation, was untruthful and deceitful, had received warnings from the youth court for deception and avoided school attendance. In the wake of her father's death, the *Gauleiter* acknowledged that she had volunteered for service with the Leipzig *Arbeitsdienst* and recognised that her morals were wholly flawless.

Sturmann undertook military instruction for six months in 1938 and attended indoctrination classes at Bad Tölz in preparation for service in the yet to be formed SS and *Polizei* courts. Lectured on the Nazi version of German history, he participated in a great deal of sporting activities and at the courses conclusion he then undertook three months' training at the Munich public prosecutor's office. Undertaking a further six weeks' instruction at the *Landgericht* and *Justizplatz* at the end of 1938, he then returned to Bad Tölz to sit his final certification officer exam in November 1938. At the course's conclusion, Sturmann and his comrades were promoted to candidate rank and he then returned to the *Deutschland* in Dachau. Taking part in the 1939 invasion of Poland with an anti-tank battalion, Sturmann sustained a head wound fourteen days into the campaign and recovered in the Krakau SS-*Lazarett*. From here, he received orders to transfer to the *HA* SS-*Gericht* as an SS-*Beurkundungsführer* in October 1939 and reported to the SS-*Straflager* Dachau in January 1941. Later, Sturmann recalled remaining here, in 'outside service' until May 1943:

> […] My duties consisted of supervising the convicts' exercise and work duties, I had nothing to do with concentration camp prisoners. I was at the *Aussenstelle* Allach from May 1943 to the end of 1943 and there, as the administrator of suitable work, I was also at the same time the disciplinary superior of the SS and *Polizei* convicts, likewise for the members of the personnel of the SS who guarded the *Polizei* and SS convicts.

Transferred to Danzig–Matzkau by February 1944, Sturmann then found himself placed in charge of the *Zweiglager* Ludwigsfelde. He and thirteen other certification officers of the *HA* SS-*Gericht* were ordered to transfer to the SS-FHA on 15 March the same year, but his command was rescinded the following day and Sturmann remained in the prison service. Returning to Allach when the Ludwigsfelde branch prison was closed in the late summer of 1944, Sturmann was then transferred to the SS-FHA and found himself posted to a training and reserve battalion in November 1944. A medical examination judged him fit for battle and over two months until January 1945, his fitness to lead troops was judged until he had qualified as a *Kompanieführer*, Sturmann joined a reserve unit and then led a grenadier company of the *30. Januar* near Oppeln until becoming a Red Army prisoner of war at Vogelsang *an der* Oder on 29 April 1945. Escaping from captivity three days later, he made his way back to his family at Dachau and became a prisoner of the US Army on 8 May 1945. Detained in the *Schutzhaflager*, former camp prisoners denounced Sturmann for serving in the camp service and he was paraded before 20 former inmates to face accusations of mishandling prisoners. Successfully refuting their accusations, he was arrested in Dachau on 13 May 1945 and the local CIC ordered his internment on 18 May 1945. Detained in camp 8, at Garmisch–Partenkirchen, Sturmann laboured as a forester in Fürstenfeldbruck from 3 June to 15 July 1945, was a camp policeman from 30 August to 1 October 1945, worked as a lumberjack in Bad Aibling from 5 September to 9 October 1945 and undertook labouring tasks in Munich between 19 October 1945 and 30 August 1946. Transferred to the Moosburg camp in August 1946, here, he accepted voluntary work between 11 and 24 November 1946 and was then employed at the Überland Hoch-u, Tief- und Strassenbau Aktengesellschaft from 4 February 1947. Submitting a denazification document to the Dachau court on 21 June the same year, Sturmann handed 60 *Reichsmark* to the camp authorities for safe keeping on 17 November. On 9 May and 12 November 1947, *Frau* Sturmann appealed for clemency on the grounds of her husband's 70 per cent disablement and requested his immediate release from Moosburg. In a strange twist of fate, the BMW concern at Allach had begun employing Sturmann by August/September 1948. He had arranged the employment of SS and *Polizei* convicts at this factory between 1943/1945.

A convict and internee of the Moosburg camp, Heinrich Schregle, submitted an affidavit to the *Spruchkammer* on 20 November 1946 which described Sturmann in glowing terms:

> *Herr* Franz Sturmann, born 5 December 1909, I have known since January 1941 and at that time he was assigned to the *Straflager der* SS-*und Polizei* Dachau of the *HA* SS-*Gericht*, as the leader for outside duties. In this punishment camp was housed the already condemned delinquent members of the SS and *Polizei.* Located within the KL Dachau, this prison had no connection with that camp. Working here until May 1943, I got to know *Herr* Sturmann as a precise supervisor and as a man in these two years. His sense of justice and understanding of the needs of prisoners labeled him as the most popular supervisor and they repeatedly dubbed him 'the fatherly friend.'
>
> As the letter censor I had insight into the concerns and issues of prisoners who came to me with their requests. I often presented suggestions and requests to *Herr* Sturmann

> and found him at all times willing to listen. Whether it was to get permission to receive a packet, or arrange family visits, or vacations in urgent cases, Sturmann would help where he could, even at the risk of being reprimanded by the superior authority, which would occur.
>
> By all means he aspired to improve the food for the people and had many great successes. In his instruction hours he taught his subordinates to always refrain from ill-treating and assaulting the inmates. You will probably fail to find any former prisoners of the camp, who could accuse Sturmann of committing any assaults. By drafting the best leadership reports Sturmann succeeded in procuring many prisoners their freedom, long before the expiration of their sentence. Since the camp only held already condemned SS and *Polizei* officers members, he had no influence on the drafting of judgments. I am not related to *Herr* Sturmann, even by marriage.

The former inmate of the prison, *Polizei Hauptwachmeister a.d.* Georg Sterr also submitted a favourable statement to the court on 4 December 1946:

> *Herr* Sturmann was the deputy leader during my detention in the Dachau *Straflager der* SS *und Polizei* from 5 March 1942 to 28 March 1944. He treated the prisoners very mildly and in many cases he ensured parole by filing good leadership reports. Additionally, he obtained food and beer for the work commandos under the most difficult circumstances. At his own risk, Sturmann often did not inform his superiors about giving prisoners few days' leave to deal with bomb damage, deaths and serious illnesses of relatives. Eventually this became known to his superiors and they had initiated a disciplinary and court's process against him.
>
> Towards the convicts Sturmann has, to my knowledge, disseminated no National Socialist propaganda material. Lectures and teachings were only addressed in terms of performance and leadership. He has permitted visits and even care packages without the written permission of the supervisor's service office. You could approach *Herr* Sturmann with every request, without being rejected by him. He helped every prisoner whenever possible and in general was very popular. I have not been a member of the NSDAP nor one of its formations and I am increasingly hostile towards the National Socialist party.

Sceptical of such testimonials, it is evident that both these former convicts thought highly of Sturmann and were willing to portray him in the best possible light.

Judged 'less burdened' by the Dachau *Spruchkammer* in 1948, the Munich public prosecutor then lodged an appeal against this mild sentence. Receiving a copy of Sturmann's RuSHA file on 25 October 1948, the prosecutor noted that this contained a biography that he had submitted in 1937 which implicated him in the distribution of illegal propaganda and the planting of a bomb in Austria. Conducting an investigation into his wartime activities, the prosecutor wrote to the authorities in all the places he had claimed to have lived, worked, or undertaken crimes for the Nazi's and none was able to confirm his acts of subversion. Submitting himself for questioning in Dachau on 21 December the same year, the prosecutor showed Sturmann a copy of his 1937 biography with his claims of illegal activity and asked him to explain his claims. In response, Sturmann insisted that he had written the letter as a ruse to deflect attention away from the political activities of his wife's family. He then explained that he left Austria as a consequence of handing a man of four children his job and then failing to find employment in his native country. Concerned at the direction his case was heading, Sturmann questioned the necessity of the investigation and requested that a new court handled his case.

Further enquiries about Sturmann's activities in Austria revealed that Sturmann had been dismissed from Kleider, Wäsche *und* Modewaren in Köflach on the grounds of weak sales and poor office practice in August 1933 and on 24 January 1949 the Austrian Federal Ministry revealed that he had fled to Germany without his passport on 25 August 1933 in the wake of his released from three weeks' detention for membership of the banned NSDAP (flight case Nr. 16.607). Finding no evidence of his involvement in a bomb attack, or for distributing banned propaganda material, the Austrian authorities expressed their suspicion that Sturmann had committed offences against the 1947 prohibition act and revealed that they planned to seek more information about his prewar activities. As a consequence of these findings, Sturmann's details were referred to the *Landesgerichte* Graz to enable them to initiate a court investigation and the Austrian prosecutor stated his intention to apply to the American authorities to compel the Bavarian government to extradite him to Austria. Events, had now taken a more ominous turn for Sturmann, but his situation was to worsen. At this time the *Landesstelle der* VVN wrote to the court to demand more information about his involvement with the KL Dachau. When questioned on this subject, Sturmann 'disputing violently' that he had any disciplinary powers over camp prisoners, but admitted to have experienced minimal contact with them.

Sturmann expressed his happiness when the Munich-Land *Hauptspruchkammer* took over his case on 23 December 1948 and on the grounds of his SS and NSDAP membership, the prosecutor indicted Sturmann on 23 February 1949 and on the grounds of suspicion that he had, through his own admission, committed crimes in Austria he applied to have him placed in the group I category, the highest guilt classification. Writing to the Munich *Spruchkammer* on 4 March 1949, Sturmann replied to the charges brought against him on 23 February and explaining the reasons for his award of the NSDAP medal, he then turned his attention to the 1937 RuSHA letter. He again reiterated his earlier explanation for claiming to have spread propaganda and conducted a bomb attack and pointing to his willingness to work in internment, he submitted nine character statements to the court. Sitting on 3 September 1949, the Munich *Spruchkammer* accepted that Sturmann had lied about his political activities in Austria and convinced that he had left his country on economic grounds in August 1933, the chamber classifed him as a 'follower' and setting aside the imposition of expiation measure, the tribunal ordered Sturmann to bear the costs of the process. Here, the court comments on his wartime postings:

> [...] In pursuit of this service, he showed humanity towards the prisoners and attempted to give them every possible facilitation. It is this behavior that the chamber understands

as a sign that the person concerned was not inclined to violent methods. Already in 1937, he had worked at the request of an acquaintance to arrange the dismissal of a KL-prisoner. From another affidavit, which stated that he himself was politically active, that person was permitted to speak and disparage freely in front of him [Sturmann].

In his summary, the court chairman proffered the following observations:

[...] The person concerned was an early member of the Nazi movement, and also belonged to it during the time that it was banned in Austria and therefore was punished with three weeks' detention. Therefore his involvement was more than just a nominal Nazi. His decision to join the SS after fleeing into the German *Reich* must be regarded in this sense, so that the suspicion of activism cannot be refuted in a clear and unambiguous manner.

However, it is to his credit, that he was still youthfully immature during his employment in Austria and he was under the influence of his employer. Although the entry into the *Allgemeine*-SS and the entry into the *Waffen*-SS was undertaken voluntary, we accept that it was done under a certain pressure. As a professional soldier he was then no longer politically active. In consideration of his proper overall attitude and in the absence of any substantive responsibility, the chamber has classified him in the group of the 'responsible' and has then declared him a 'lesser offender' pursuant to Article 11 I 1.

The person concerned was interned from 13 May 1945 to 12 November 1947 and was released by way of disability (70 per cent maimed). He has already suffered through the considerable personal and economic restrictions. We have therefore refrained from the imposition of a probation and an expiation fee pursuant to Article 18 paragraph 3 in connection with Article 17 VIII. The amount in dispute would be determined according to afflict the scale of fees to 4,500 *Marks*. As a manual worker for one month at BMW the person concerned has only one monthly income of 162.00 *Marks*.

To apply a fee schedule under his completely changed economic circumstances would result in undue hardship. We therefore set the costs to twenty *Marks* in accordance to § 6 of the fee schedule in conjunction with the explanation to the fee schedule from 2 September 1948.

On 25 November 1954, the Munich appeals and main chamber reported that they had received copies of Sturmann's court documents from the *Amtsgericht* Dachau. It is not clear whether the Austrian authorities were successful in their attempt to extradite Sturmann, but given the time that had lapsed from his flight in 1933, the lack of evidence for committing a crime and the completion of his denazification process in Bavaria, he is highly unlikely to have been returned to his native country to face trial.[35]

Name: Alfred Hermann **Vollmer.**
Last Rank: SS-*Untersturmführer*.
Born: 15.5.1915 in Haslach, Kinzigtal/Baden.

SS-Nr.: 279.590 (joined 1.5.1935).
RAD service: 1.4.1936–26.9.1936.
Prewar Assignments:
11. SS-*Standarte* 86 (Wolfach) from 1.5.1935.
SS-VT 1.10.1936.
Wartime Assignments:
Waffen-SS *Hauptamt* SS-*Gericht* 1942.
SS- *und Polizei-Gericht* V, Dresden until 1.9.1942.
SS- *und Polizei-Gericht* III, Berlin 1.9.1942–22.5.1944.
Strafvollzugslager der SS *und Polizei* Danzig–Matzkau 22.5.1944–2.1945.
Promotions:

1.5.1935	SS-*Anwärter.*
0.0.19__	SS-*Oberscharführer der Reserve.*
1.7.1942	SS-*Hauptscharführer der Reserve.*
9.11.1944	SS-*Untersturmführer der Reserve.*

Decorations & Awards:

0.0.19__	SA-*Sportsabzeichen in Bronze.*
0.0.19__	*Deutsches Reichssportabzeichen in Bronze.*
0.0.19__	D.L.R.G.
0.0.19__	1939 *Eisernes Kreuz II. Klasse.*

Notes: His father retired from his post as a quarry foreman following an accident that resulted in the loss of an arm. Attending *Volksschule* for eight classes, Vollmer then trained at a trade school, apprenticed for three years and qualified as a clerk and stenographer. Employed with the DAF, Volmer became an honorary *Ortsjugendleiter* of this organisation. Marrying his fiancée Bertl. H., (b. 18.12.1913 in Elzach) on 1 March 1941, the couple had three children up to the point when records ceased in May 1945 and lived in Berlin. A member of the SS-VT from October 1936, Vollmer transferred to the *HA* SS-*Gericht* in early 1942. Qualifying as an SS-*Beurkundungsunterführer*, he received orders in May 1943 to report to Danzig–Matzkau and had become *Hstuf.* Dr Fritz Beelitz's adjutant in Matzkau by 24 October 1944. He almost certainly left this prison for Bavaria in March 1945.[36]

Name: Erich Wagner.
Last Rank: SS-*Unterscharführer.*
Born: 3.7.1920 in Rodewisch, *Kreis* Auerbach/Vogtland.
NSDAP-Nr.: 7.171.670 (joined 1.9.1939).
SS-Nr.: 364.163 (joined 1.9.1939).
HJ Service: 1.6.1933–18.3.1939.
Wartime Assignments:
SS-VT from 1.9.1939.
LSSAH in Berlin 7.11.1939–20.10.1941.

LSSAH *Ersatz-Bataillon* (Berlin) from 12.12.1942.
Strafvollzugslager der SS *und Polizei* Danzig–Matzkau in 1944.
Promotions:
1.1.1942 SS-*Sturmann der Reserve.*
1.11.1941 SS-*Rottenführer der Reserve.*
1.4.1944 SS-*Unterscharführer der Reserve.*
Decorations & Awards:
0.0.19__ *Schutzwallehrenzeichen.*

Notes: By profession a plumber in Rodewisch, Wagner mustered with the LSSAH in Berlin in 1939. Seeing front service until his wounding on 18 December 1941, Wagner returned to Germany and recovered in the Berlin SS-*Lazarett* between 8 September and 20 October 1942. Examined by a doctor on 1 December 1942, Wagner was declared no longer fit for front line service. Wagner married his fiancée Margarete S. on 6 February 1943 and living in Berlin, the couple later relocating to the Vogtland in spring of 1944. Wagner reported to the Danzig–Matzkau in mid-1944 and received 150 *Reichsmark* from the SS for the birth of his son on 7 September the same year.[37]

Name: Heimo Ludwig **Wurm.**
Last Rank: SS-*Obersturmführer.*
Born: 8.5.1908 in Erling, Andechs/Bavaria.
Died: 18.3.1968 in Munich.
NSDAP-Nr.: 695.126 (joined 1.11.1931).
SS-Nr.: 14.924 (joined 1.11.1931).
Prewar Assignments:
Reichsführung der SS, SS.-*Gericht* 20.3.1935–19.10.1938.
13. *Ersatz-Pionier-Kompanie* 17.3.–11.5.1936.
13. *Ersatz-Pionier-Kompanie* 4.6.–28.7.1936 (Reserve Office candidate).
Seconded to the investigative service of the SD-*Hauptamt* 15.2.–8.8.1938.
SD-*Oberabschnitt* (Munich) 3.1938-17.5.1938.
Pioneer exercise 1.6.–19.8.1939.
Wartime Assignments:
Luftwaffe 1.10.1939–1.11.1941.
Panzer-Pionier-Bataillon 27 (Ingolstadt) 1.6.–1.7.1941.
Luftwaffe-Ersatz-Aufklärungsgruppe (Weimar) 1.7.1–18.7.1941.
3. *Fernaufklärungs-Rer.-Nachstaffel* on the Eastern Front 18.7.–30.10.1941.
Waffen-SS *Hauptamt* SS-*Gericht Amt* III 23.12.1942–29.4.1945.
Strafvollzugslager der SS *und Polizei* Danzig–Matzkau 3.11.1942–15.2.1944.
SS- *und Polizei-Gericht* I, Munich 15.2.1944–29.4.1945.
Promotions:
0.0.1935 SS-*Oberscharführer der Allgemeine*-SS.
0.0.1936 *Gefreiter u. Reserve-Offizieranwärter.*

12.9.1937	SS-*Untersturmführer der Allgemeine*-SS.
1.4.1940	*Luftwaffe Leutnant der Reserve.*
1.7.1940	SS-*Untersturmführer der Reserve* (W.A.).
23.12.1942	SS-*Obersturmführer der Reserve.*

Decorations & Awards:

1.8.1934	*Blutorden* (Nr. 903).
0.0.19__	SA-*Sportsabzeichen in Bronze.*
0.0.19__	*Totenkopfring der* SS.
0.0.19__	*Kriegsverdienstkreuz II. Klasse mit Schwertern.*

Notes: His father was the Bavarian painter Armin Wurm. Attending a Munich *Volksschule* from 1915 to 1919, Wurm then studied at the Munich *Real* and *Oberrealschule* from 1919 and passed the *mittlere Reifprüfung* in 1927. Aged only fifteen, Wurm mustered with the 2. / SA-Rgt. *München* and marched alongside them during the Putsch on 1 November 1923 (his association with them ended that same day). Departing *Realschule*, Wurm then studied at the Dr Sabel trade school in Munich during 1927 and wishing to become a sports and gymnastics teacher, he trained at the Wolf Ferrari and Rea Glu sports and gymnastics schools in Munich between 1928 and 1930. Completing their courses, Wurm was unable to obtain employment in this field and so accepted work as a stage dancer at different venues in Germany and abroad from 1930 to 1 May 1933 (earning 4,500 *Reichsmark per annum*). Encountering obstacles to renewing his passport in 1933, Wurm was unable to obtain work abroad and began a search for work in the Bavarian capital. Accepting a post as an assistant and clerk in the *Reichsleitung der* NSDAP, (earning 130 *Reichsmark* per month), Wurm failed to obtain a pay rise in 1935 and so accepted a clerk's post with the *Reichsführung der* SS, SS.-*Gericht* on 20 March 1935 (employed under *Stubaf.* Meske, he earned just under 3,000 *Reichsmark per annum*). Marrying his fiancée Bertha Stadler, (b. 15.8.1912 in Munich) on 8 June 1937, they had one son and lived Gabelsbergerstraße—the same street where the SS.-*Gericht* had originally been located.

The *Gestapo* arrested Wurm on 9 August 1938 and the SS.-*Gericht* placed him on service leave until October the same year. Remaining in detention at the Briennerstraße *Gestapo* prison until 19 August 1938 and daily faced ten to twelve hours of interrogation. At first his questioners accused him of committing offences against paragraph § 175 of the RStGB some fifteen years previously, which Wurm could disprove, as he was only fifteen at that time. Then accused of conniving with foreigners to engage in espionage for Czechoslovakia, the witnesses were unable to identify Wurm and the *Gestapo* released him from detention after ten days of interrogation, (postwar, his wife acknowledged that this episode caused them both a great deal of mental strain). Suspended from his official position with the SS.-*Gericht*, Wurm was then subjected to an *Ehrenstrafe* and released from the SS for having an unsuitable character and for his political unreliability on 19 October 1938.

The consequence of this judgement was Wurm's discharge from his service position without notice and attempting without success to find a salaried job via the employment office, it was only after repeated consultations that they informed him that their office was unable to convey any position to him without his prior permission of the SD Leader and *Gestapo* Inspector, *Oberf.* Beutel. Offered and accepting a civilian position as an assistant, clerk and file leader in the personnel department of the *Lebensborn* e.V. on 1 April 1939, Wurm was paid a paltry 130 *Reichsmark* per month for his efforts. Despite this low salary, Wurm accepted the post, fearing that refusal would lead to him being labelled an asocial and result in his detention in a concentration camp. Remaining in their employment until 30 September 1939, Wurm joined the NSV in 1940.

Drafted into the *Luftwaffe* in October 1939, the following year Wurm found himself seriously injured in a plane crash. An observer on a Do 17 from the 1. (F)/*Aufklärungsgruppe* 123 on 7 April 1940, Wurm's aircraft came under attack from a French Morane MS 406 fighter on its return from a mission over the Laon area. The pilot of the stricken aircraft, flying with one engine, found himself unable to guide his plane to its base at Langendiebach, some 21 kilometres east-north-east of Frankfurt am Main, and so force-landed at the emergency airfield at Donauwörth. The only casualty of this manoeuvre was Wurm and admitted to hospital the following day, his injuries included a skull fracture, cuts to his skull and the eye, four bone breaks in his left upper arm, radial cracking, paralysis to the left upper arm, seven fractures in his right lower leg, severe trauma to both ankles, moderate damage to the left hand and severe flesh wounds to his right upper thigh. Operated at the surgical clinic of the Munich *Reserve-Lazarett* I, they wrote to the *Oberabschnitt Sud* on 11 September 1940 to inform them that Wurm was recovering well from his procedures and reported that his spirit and morale remained good. Interestingly, despite his earlier release from the SS, this letter noted that Wurm was assigned to the *Stab Reichsführer*-SS. As a consequence of his injuries, the hospital amputated Wurm's right foot and fitted a sleeve supporting prosthesis. Discharged from hospital on 1 June 1941, Wurm reported to a reserve formation in Ingolstadt and was then assigned to a *Luftwaffe* Reserve squadron. Applying to rejoin the SS in July 1941, Wurm reported to a reconnaissance squadron on the Eastern Front in July 1941 and 'constantly' flew missions until October the same year.

The *Luftwaffe*, discovering his earlier problems with the *Gestapo*, decided to discharge Wurm from their service on 1 November 1941. Returning home and faced with returning to the *Lebensborn* e.V., Wurm entrusted his advocate, *Herrn von* Sollmann, with clarifying his situation with the *HA* SS-*Gericht*. Admitted into the Munich *Reserve-Lazarett* (I) for a second operation on an arm injury on 1 June 1942, Wurm was discharged from hospital on 30 October the same year. At this time and on her own initiative, *Frau* Wurm wrote to the *HA* SS-*Gericht* to request her husband's admittance into the *Waffen*-SS and they accepted Wurm into the courts service in November 1942. Posted to the *Amt* III, Wurm immediately transferred to Danzig–Matzkau and was appointed the commandant's adjutant. A Bletchley intercept from confirms his deployment in the prison:

18. OLQ (Munich) the OLG for OLA (Danzig) 1101 185 12.1.1943
To the prison camp, for the attention of SS-*Ustuf.* WURM.

He is asked to immediately send the completed personnel questionnaire, as this is needed to create his pay book.
HA SS-*Gericht.*

Remaining in this post until his transfer to the *Stab HA* SS-*Gericht* on 15 February 1944, Wurm was employed as a *Beurkundungsführer* at the Munich tribunal on 15 February 1944 and remained in this post until the war's end (described as an active investigator on 20.12.1944).

Surrendering to US Army forces at Zell am See on 6 May 1945, Wurm was detained in the Hammelburg internment camp on 16 June 1945 and remained there until his release on 31 March 1947. Here, Wurm worked as a kitchen helper between 1 October 1945 and 31 March 1946 and volunteered to act as a *Stubenältester* between 15 January and 31 March 1947. Writing to the camp authorities on 12 December 1946, Wurm's wife claimed that he had joined the Nazi party at an early age from misguidedness. Granted special leave to visit his seriously ill 61-year-old mother between 27 February and 5 May 1947, Wurm underwent a medical examination by an American medical commission in Hammelburg on 31 March and this concluded that his wounds had left him 70 per cent war disabled (his left arm was lame and he wore a prosthesis on his right foot). Released from detention the following day, Wurm joined his wife and son with her parents in Munich and was employed as a menial worker, shoveling coal, stacking and cutting wood with a circular saw and undertaking other warehouse tasks with the wood and coal merchant Josef Stadler in Munich on 15 April 1947. Employed here a year later, his father in-law may have owned the business. Stating his profession as sports teacher, Wurm faced the *Spruchkammer* on 15 September 1948 and here, he claimed to have no idea why he had been awarded the *Blutorden*. Announcing that he joined the SS only for the employment opportunities, here, in his own words he explained his reasons for joining the Nazi movement and elucidated his political life:

> By casual acquaintance I came into the SA as a fifteen-year-old on 1 November 1923. I was an SA candidate from 1 November to 9 November 1923. Believing it was a good and decent thing, I was persuaded in a time of great unemployment to join the SS and the Nazi Party on 1 November 1931 and I was convinced that this would contribute to a clean and honest structure of the German state. Through my work as a professional dancer I had been almost permanently abroad until 1933 and was not at all active in politics. I was at this time only a nominal member of the SS and the party and I only paid the prescribed fees. After taking up my position with the *Reichsleitung der* NSDAP in April 1933, where I was busy with entries in land registers and the filling of temporary identity cards, I performed no further service with the SS and only after repeated requests and some appeals would I visit in the form of comradely evenings.
>
> Following my transfer to the *Reichsführung der* SS on 20 March 1935, I undertook no political service with the SS, but was only in use as a clerk and my salary was in accordance with the classification of an SS-*Oscha.* As a consequence of my derogatory

> utterances about the measures of the party and the state I was warned and threatened with penalties during work performance reviews. I transferred to SD-*Oberabschnitt* Munich in March 1938 and my salary was classified as that for a SS-*Ustuf.* Here, I also exercised only commercial activity as a clerk and travel companion. With the *Lebensborn* I functioned also only as a clerk without influence, or insight into the technical work of the department. During my military service and during the war I practiced no political activity. In my work with the *HA* SS-*Gericht* I handled the tasks of a certification officer and had no control over the announced judgments and decisions.

Unmoved by his statement, the court placed Wurm in the offender category I and ordering him to pay the costs of the trial, the tribunal also imposed a fine of 2,000 *Marks*. A review was undertaken by the Munich court II on 23 November 1948 and Wurm submitted ten character references that attested to his long criticism of the regime. One affidavit, composed by former SD *Hstuf.* and administrative lawyer Dr Max Irlinger, who claiming to have been a proven resister against Nazi tyranny, confirmed Wurm's good character:

> I have known *Herr* Heimo Wurm, born 8 May 1908 since 1937. During this time I was working as a trainee at the SS.-*Gericht* in Munich. The SS.-*Gericht* at that time edited disciplinary cases for SS members. At that time I retired from service in the SS, but remained in contact with *Herr* Heimo Wurm and with a small maintenance grant I was employed as a junior clerk while preparing for the bar exam. He was arrested by the *Gestapo* in 1938 under the pretext of suspicion of committing an offence under § 175 of the RStGB, but in reality, probably because he had come to the attention of the former head of the SD for being a 'so-called troublemaker' and for complaining about the political course of the regime. As I was constantly in touch with him the road for Heimo Wurm is known to me and he was detained. The basis of our connection was our common rejection of the party regime.
>
> I knew that he had been expelled from the SS in 1938 and finally went to the *Luftwaffe* in 1939 in order, as he himself told me at that time, to leave 'fate' to run wild. I visited him after his accident as a flier as he lay seriously injured in the surgical clinic in Munich in 1940. I did not hear from him again for a long time until bumping into him after my own detention in 1943 (on suspicion of undermining the war effort). He told me then that he had been inducted into the *Waffen*-SS and from there to the SS-*Gericht,* but informed me that his rejection of the Nazi regime had deepened. I can still well remember him telling me that he had not forgotten that he owed his damaged physical condition to the meanness of this regime.
>
> After my release from the *Gestapo* prison, when the SS and *Polizei* judicial court proceedings against me were dropped due to lack of evidence, there continued to run a disciplinary proceedings by the SS-*Gericht.* So concerned was I about damaging my professional existence as a senior civil servant, that I turned to *Herr* Wurm for help in 1944. Contrary to his official duty, Wurm orientated myself on the progress and status of

> my process and assured me in 1944 that he had succeeded in pushing my case aside. The fact that the planned expulsion process against me never took place until the collapse was a consequence of his help.

On the strength of this and other submissions, the *Spruchkammer* Munich III reduced Wurm's category to a 'lesser offender' on 23 November 1948. Writing to the court on 19 September the same year, Wurm complained that earning just 100 *Marks* per month he was experiencing difficulties paying his court fine. Heimo Wurm died in Munich in March 1968.[38]

Senior Matzkau Non-Commissioned Officers

Hscha. Fritz Bohn (b. 4.3.1915).
Hscha. Ernst Dallinger (b. 17.6.1916).
Stuscha. Alfred Engelhardt (b. 24.6.1897).
Stuscha. Flieger.
Hscha. Gaube (from 28.4.1944).
Hscha. Kilian Kranzmayr (b. 27.10.1908).
Stuscha. Morr.
Hscha. Heinrich Müller (b. 17.11.1913).
Hscha. Karl Münch (b. 11.2.1890).
Hscha. Reimelt.
Hscha. Gustav Rosengarth (b. 21.8.1888).[38]

4.2 The Postwar Denazification Process

The denazification process in Germany and Austria was initially undertaken by the occupying forces, but a special law transferred this legal process to civilian courts in occupied Germany from April 1946 and these tribunals were operated by German administrators until 1948. The denazification process for those interned in Germany concluded with their trial and punishment before the camp *Spruchkammer* (announcement chamber). The tribunals' judgement was achieved on the basis of SS and Nazi party records, police files, the internees work performance and testimonials. Depending on their culpability in Nazi crimes, the tribunal classified the guilty as 'major offenders', 'offenders', 'lesser offenders', and 'followers' and imposed fines, compulsory work orders and restricted the work the offenders were permitted to undertake during their period of probation. The court also denied offenders their legal claims to payments from public funds, pensions or annuities, denied them their right to vote and their eligibility for election. Banned from participation in any right wing political activities, the offenders were prohibited from belonging to a political party as a member. Banned from joining a union, or membership of an economic, or professional association for five years, the guilty were also prohibited from employment in a liberal profession, self-employed in a business, or operating a commercial operation of any kind. Forbidden from participating in a business or exercising a position of supervision or control over a business, offenders were prohibited from employment in any dependent position other than ordinary labour. The guilty were also excluded from working as teachers, preachers, editors, authors, or radio commentators and were subject to housing and residence restrictions.

Each offender had the right of appeal and judgments were automatically reviewed once the probationary period had ended to enable the offender's reclassification.

In Austria, the process was handed to civil administrators in February 1946 and prosecutions took place according to the tenets of the 1945 laws. These prosecutions took place according to the law from February 1947 to May 1948 and a time of amnesty existed between 1948 and 1957. Former members of the *HA* SS-*Gericht* are known to have faced trial for high treason before the Austrian *Volksgerichte* (People's Courts) for their membership of the NSDAP and SS prior to 1938. Those finding themselves detained in the Soviet Union also appeared before tribunals. Harsh sentences were commonly imposed and many years of hard labour in camps stood ahead of these prisoners. The majority of these 'war prisoners' were released and permitted to return to Germany by 1956.

5

Front Probation Units of the SS and *Polizei*

A history of the *Waffen*-SS *Strafvollzugslager* would not be complete without an examination of the front probation programme to which the vast majority of Himmler's felonious troops were subject. At the outbreak of war the German military jurisdiction, initially driven by a desire to reform those soldiers judged unworthy of belonging to what was described as a brotherhood of arms, predicated the entire legal jurisdiction to meet the ideological demands of the regime and the army's own practical military considerations. Punishing the vast majority of delinquent and criminal soldiers to part-prison, part-front probation penalties the Nazi leader hoped that giving these parolees the opportunity to face the enemy in dangerous situations would restore their honour on the battlefield or see them die in the attempt.

No longer satisfied to permit criminal and disobedient soldiers to languish safely in prison while disciplined troops fought for their lives at the front, the regime, fearing that a kind of Darwinian counter-selection would occur if so-called 'inferior' and 'asocial' convicts spent the war safe in prison, conceived a plan prior to the outbreak of war to grant suitable military convicts front probation. Filtering 'usable' soldiers through military penal institutions and back to the front in one capacity or another, the Nazi leadership hoped that the process itself would deter soldiers from offending. Conversely, the front probation method also channelled recalcitrant, or incorrigible soldiers to the front, usually those who resisted the oft draconian motivational effects of prisons and penal units. Modifying the prison/front probation punishment process during the war years, troops were provided from prisons to undertake dangerous front line duties and deploy against the partisans.[1]

5.1 Front Probation Procedure

Reaching an accord with the *Reichsjustizministerium*, the OKW issued orders on 28 May 1936 to establish the *Sonder-Abteilungen* (special battalions) for those troops judged unworthy to bear arms in isolated camps at Stablack, Altengrabow, Königsbrück, Münsigen, Grafenwöhr, Bergen and Münster (later relocated, seven special battalions had been established by October the same year). Accepting felons who exhibited difficulties with discipline, their number included alcoholics, those who posed a threat to discipline and troops punished by civil courts with a term of twelve months' *Gefängnis* or greater. The special battalions excluded conscripts punished by the military courts and using military drill, severe discipline and hard labour, it was the staff's task to re-educate non-conformists and enable their eventual return to the ranks of the armed forces as orderly, duty-conscious and honourable, fit soldiers.[2]

The parolees of the special battalions transferred to combat units in September 1939 and on their own initiative, the *Ersatzheer* replaced them with six new units. It was clear at this early stage of the conflict that the regime wished to reconfigure the military judiciary to ensure that the front probation process became a central tenet of the judicial method and the success of the special battalion's resulted in the majority of prison sentences investing service in the parole units from 1941.[3]

The realisation that the conflict would be a long-running affair, the Nazi leadership and military authorities expressed their determination to prevent the discharge of military offenders from active service once their prison sentences were complete. Announcing the publication of a succession of wartime decrees, these ensured that military criminals—including those deemed military 'pests'—would deploy at the front until they had proven worthy of rehabilitation and re-joining the people's community.[4]

Published by the *Chef* OKH on 23 August 1939, the 'Order for Clemency for the Army in the War and those in Special Deployment' observed that responsibility for all clemency decisions lay in the hands of Adolf Hitler in his capacity as *Der Oberbefehlshaber der Wehrmacht* (*Gerichtsherr*) and he alone was responsible for confirming all death sentences for all officers in accordance with paragraph *§§* 79 sections 1 & 80 of the KStVO. These authorisation powers were delegated to the various *Befehlshaber* (commanders) and also extended to the *Reichsführer* Heinrich Himmler on 17 October 1939.[5]

Announced on 1 and 9 September 1939, a *Führer* edict commanded front probation for members of the armed forces serving terms of *Gefängnis* and permitted the *Wehrmacht* and *Waffen*-SS *Gerichtsherrn* to send minor criminals to the front to atone for their delinquent or criminal behaviour.[6]

Planning the 1941 summer invasion of the USSR, the Nazi regime ordered a further codification of the front probation process to enable military convicts to play their part in the oncoming battle. Announced on 21 October 1940 and 12 March 1941, these *Führer* edicts authorised the establishment of the *Bewährungstruppe* (probation troops) for the armed forces and the *Polizei* and the German Army High Command received permission to establish the 500 *Bewährungstruppe* on 21 December 1940. Raised in Meiningen on 1 April 1941, this formation trained delinquent soldiers for frontline deployment. Demonstrating the requisite bravery in battle, the parolees of the 500 *Bewährungstruppe* earned their rehabilitation and returned to the troops, the blemish on their military record was expunged.[7]

Clemency legislation culminated in the spring of 1942 with a raft of new edicts that permitted military convicts of all types and from all service branches, to leave their cells and fight at the front.[8]

From February 1942 all clemency petitions for probationers were submitted to the *Befehlshaber* on the basis of their performance in the field. Codifying this process in April 1942, each military convict offered front probation was expected to perform hazardous tasks at the front in circumstances where a high possibility of death or injury would hang perpetually over the heads of the parolees. Turning the probation method into the proverbial 'sword of Damocles' it was only by exposing themselves to enemy fire could the felons prove themselves worthy of regaining their honour. Those judged medically incapable of imprisonment were usually dismissed from military service and sent to a civil jail or the KL Emsland to serve their sentence. The time spent in military jail was not deducted from the original sentence if the convict was subsequently transferred to a civil institution.[9]

By the winter of 1941/42 the Nazi leadership had accepted that their audacious offensive against the Soviet Union had failed to win a quick victory and the heavy losses suffered by frontline units and the need for additional security units to battle the growing partisan menace gave the regime added impetus for instituting a widespread front probation programme for military convicts, including those previously omitted from selection. By the spring of 1942 the resulting combined prison/field probation method had become the main focus of the military jurisdictions and convicts were routinely offered early release from gaol and front probation. Those refusing this offer risked incarceration in concentration camps (S.A.W.).

In his capacity as Chief of the *Ersatzheer* the probationary forces of the German Army fell under the command of the *Reichsführer* in July 1944. Seizing their potential, Himmler offered many hundreds of *Zuchthaus* category military convicts the opportunity to leave their cells for front service and they reported to the 36th *Waffen-Grenadier*-Division *der* SS. Integrated with Himmler's malefactors and camp prisoners, these military felons participated in the last desperate battles to defend Germany.[10]

The SS and *Polizei* judiciary initiated the process of 'funnelling' suitable malefactors to the front line in 1940 and expanding the method in 1941, the *Reichsführer* permitted a greater number of his convicts to deploy in the most dangerous sectors of the frontline.[11]

The principles of SS comradeship dictated that Himmler's errant troops were granted another chance to right their wrong and within a year of its creation, the SS jurisdiction had been re-orientated to offer virtually all SS and *Polizei* convicts a part-prison/part-front probation sentence.[12]

5.2 *Verlorenen Haufen*

Condemned as a criminal organisation by the postwar Nuremberg tribunal, at the beginning of the World War Two the SS-VT, to become known as the *Waffen*-SS (armed SS) was considered an elite force by the vast majority of the German nation. Setting itself the task of only selecting what they considered the best physical and racial candidates, the SS appeared at first glance to not require a part prison and front probation sentencing process, but drafting many tens of thousands of suitable racial and physical men from the *Allgemeine*-SS, the wider society and ethnic-German communities to their colours in the autumn of 1939, it soon become evident that amongst their number were the unwilling, delinquents and petty criminals who committed disciplinary and criminal offences that required their court martial and punishment. In an effort to forestall any thoughts of delinquency, the field court SS Judges disseminated educational legal material to the troops and during their induction all troops were warned that indiscipline was prosecuted with the full severity of the law.

From its inception in October 1939 it was the practice of the SS jurisdiction field courts to punish malefactors with a term of *Gefängnis* and *Zuchthaus* and completing their punishment, these convicts were then discharged from active service with the *Waffen*-SS. Though disgraced, Himmler's field army could ill-afford the loss of trained troops and the commander of the *Totenkopfdivision* became the first of Himmler's four divisional commanders to turn to the 21 October 1940 front probation edict to solve his disciplinary problems. Considered little more than a police formation, the *Totenkopfdivision* commander, the irascible *Gruf.* Theodore Eicke, was determined to prove his detractors wrong, but his force inducting a high number of draftees in September 1939, he struggled to deal with indiscipline in the ranks of his troops which threatened to damage the reputation of his division. Punishing indiscipline with tough penalties, including jail sentences, Eicke, conscious of the need to forestall a further erosion of 'bayonet strength' and suspicious that the insubordinate elements of his division had begun committing disciplinary offences in a deliberate effort to avoid military service, then sought ways to prevent the dishonourable discharge of convicts once their prison term had been served.[13]

Vexed and desperate, Eicke punished a handful of his undisciplined troops with imprisonment in the KL Buchenwald. Made aware of this measure, the *Reichsführer* ordered a halt to this practice, fearing the negative effect the measure would have on recruitment.[14]

Exercising his *Gerichtsherr* powers, Eicke suspended the jail sentences of court punished troops for service in the newly created *Sonderkommando* (special commando). Also known as the *Kommando* z.b.V. and the SS-*Strafkompanie* (punishment company), from 30 November 1939 General Eicke only permitted the incarceration of very serious offenders in civil jails and the remainder joined the *Sonderkommando* for an indeterminate period to perform dangerous labouring tasks until he judged them worthy of returning to his division. Himmler warmly embraced Eicke's concept and the name *Verlorenen Haufen* was coined for these parolees (the lost bunch/forlorn hope). A term from the Middle Ages, this described a unit of men created from sentenced felons who hoped to gain financial rewards and fame with the expectation of heavy losses.[15]

Leadership of the *Sonderkommando* was entrusted to *Ostuf.* Paul Monich, the leader of the 4. / SS-*Totenkopf-Pionier-Abteilung* and he accepted his first two delinquents at the end of January 1940.[16] Monich inducted an additional thirteen *Totenkopf* offenders on 6/7 February 1940.[17]

Naturally, the creation of the *Sonderkommando* did not totally eradicate delinquency and criminality in the *Totenkopfdivision*. Seconded to the military medical unit at Neustadt for training, at the conclusion of the course a handful of medical troops of the 1. / SS-*Totenkopf-Sanitätsabteilung* had stolen blankets, towels and other property. Informed of these thefts, the *Reichsführer* ordered their court martial before the field court. Judged guilty of the charges, two thieves received terms of *Gefängnis*, which were suspended in favour of service in the *Sonderkommando*.[18]

As the men of the *Totenkopfdivision* trained in the wintery terrain of Baden-Württemberg, the *Sonderkommando* accepted further malefactors into its ranks in February 1940 and the company had obtained a strength of around 100 men by spring the same year.[19]

At this time, the head of the SS again voiced his satisfaction with the parole concept and ordered its expansion. Inmates languishing in the KL Sachsenhausen SS-*Erziehungssturm*, who had served in all branches of the SS-VT and the *Hauptämter*, then underwent a medical to judge their fitness for front service with the *Verlorenen Haufen* and those judged suitable, with Himmler's approbation, then transferred to the 1. / SS-*Pionier-Ersatz-Bataillon* at the SS-*Kaserne* Wildermann in Dresden to undertake training to defuse enemy mines. Completing this training course, the probationary pioneers then received orders to join the *Sonderkommando*.[20]

Arriving at the *Totenkopfdivision*, the pioneer parolees were gathered into the *Verlorenen Haufen Zug*, which was also referred to as the *Pionier-Sonderzug* (special section) and also as the *Pionier-Abteilung* z.b.V. (special duties). Equipped with mine detection equipment, motorcycles and side cars, this platoon-sized unit was divided into two, or three sections and a disgraced officer took command of each. Given their task, these probationers could have been under no illusion that once deployed in battle, they faced an extremely high chance of death or serious injury.[21]

Deployed with the *Pionier-Abteilung* z.b.V., these following two former officers lost their lives during the 1940 French campaign. Born into a minor aristocratic family in Eichwerder on 28 June 1910, *Ostuf.* Rüdiger v.Bodungen was assigned to the SS-*Junkerschule* Bad Tölz in 1939 when he began an illicit love affair with another officer, the 25 years-old *Ostuf.* Rudolf Klaebe. Their relationship denounced to the school commandant, here, he confronted both officers in his office to answer the accusation around 25 August 1939. Confessing to engaging in sexual intercourse, v.Bodungen and Klaebe were arrested on a charge of possessing same sex inclinations towards a comrade. Cashiered, they were then expelled from the SS and Klaebe spent six months in the KL Flossenburg before joining v.Bodungen in the Sachsenhausen *Erziehungssturm*. A decision taken in late 1939 to release both cashiered officers for service in the *Verlorenen Haufen*, they then attended an enemy mine detection course in Dresden and at its conclusion, v.Bodungen and Klaebe then transferred to the *Pionier-Abteilung* z.b.V. and each took command of a three-man *Verlorenen Haufen Zug* within the *Sonderkommando* 3. *Sonderzug* (special section). Leading their small commands during the surprise attack on France during May 1940, *Stubaf.* Heinz Lammerading described their fates in his action report from 2 June 1940.

Between the hours of 9.00 p.m. and 1.00 a.m. on the morning of 26/27 May 1940 the first section of the 3. *Sonderzug* received orders to clear a route through an enemy minefield composed of S-mines north of Bois de Pacaut. The northern edge of the field was still in British hands, but despite the danger, both v.Bodungen and Klaebe led their small groups of pioneers from the cover of woods and into the minefield. Here, they begun the dangerous task of marking mines with small yellow flags and then created a safe path for an infantry attack. In the early hours of the morning, a mine explosion, or enemy bullet pierced v.Bodungen's skull and he died almost immediately. Abandoning their task, his men removed his shattered body from the scene of the explosion and a decision was then taken to return the rest of the pioneer company into the minefield. In the early hours of 27 May 1940, taking advantage of the pre-dawn darkness, Klaebe once again led his small group of probationer pioneers into the minefield and attempted to clear a safe route through the treacherous field. Advancing slowly, Klaebe's group was closest to the British positions when a mine detonated in that part of the field. Reaching the place of the explosion the surviving pioneers found Klaebe's smashed body alongside his three wounded comrades. Within a couple of hours of his former lover's death, Klaebe had stepped on a mine and was killed instantly. Thinking highly of Klaebe, *Stubaf.* Lammerading voiced his conviction that his death was intentional. Supporting Lammerading's recommendation for both officers' rehabilitation, General Eicke ensured that this was later granted and both v.Bodungen and Klaebe were buried in France.[22]

This disgraced high ranking SS officer joined the *Sonderkommando* in the winter of 1939/40: Born in Leipzig in 6.5.1902, Dr Lothar Beutel joined the Nazi party on 1.6.1929 (NSDAP-Nr.: 135.2380) and the *Allgemeine*-SS on 8.5.1930 (2.422). A member of the SD since 1932, *Brigadef.* Dr Beutel was placed in command of *Einsatzgruppe* IV (4th *Armee*) in Poland from August 1939 and was the *Befehlshaber der* SiPo *und des* SD 'Warsaw' between 13 September and 23 October 1939. Deploying his 'security force' in Bromberg in September 1939, here, his men conducted arrests, mass executions and deportations in an effort to eliminate the Polish intelligentsia. Relocating to the Polish capital, Dr Beutel plundered foreign currency and jewels from the vault of the 'Savoy' hotel and loading his booty in suitcases, he flew them home secretly by plane. Denounced for plundering, committing embezzlement and engaging in a sexual relationship with a Polish woman, the responsible SS and *Polizei* court, probably Berlin, was then tasked with conducting a court's investigation into his illegal activities. Demoted and expelled from the SS on 23 October 1939, Dr Beutel then attended a short mine disposal course at the SS-*Kaserne* Dresden and at its conclusion he served with the *Verlorenen Haufen* between 23 October 1939 and 9 November 1940. Judged to have redeemed himself during the disposal of enemy minefields in May/June 1940, Dr Beutel joined the *Waffen*-SS and was re-admitted into the SS and SD with his former rank on 9 November 1940. Appointed the department chief of the *Reichsapothekerkammer* until 1944, Dr Beutel was promoted to the rank of *Hstuf. der Reserve* on 9.11.1940.

Published as a *Führer* edict on 18 April 1940, the 'Exercising of Clemency Rights in Punishment Cases, which are the Responsibility of the Courts of the SS and *Polizei*' observed that all courts cases belonging to Himmler's jurisdiction now contained provisions on the law of clemency which were to be applied *mutatis mutandis*. At this time, the head of the SS announced that the right to decide in some cases that were usually reserved for Adolf Hitler had now been delegated to himself and made the following announcement on 23 May 1940:

> The *Führer* will no longer exercise clemency decisions in criminal cases which are reserved for the jurisdictional court of the SS and *Polizei* in accordance with paragraph § 114 section C of the KSSVO. I retain for myself those cases; where the blame for a censure penalty has been made against members of the SS and *Polizei* and where a punishment of greater than six months prison has been imposed against SS officers, officers of the *Ordnungspolizei*, or *Polizei* civil servants in officer rank. In all other cases, I authorise the Chief of the *HA* SS-*Gericht* to impose clemency rights in my name. In cases where the sentence has been mitigated by the confirmation of the judgment or where clemency request has already been refused by the *Führer*, then he [Scharfe] has to submit to me all further clemency decisions.

In an effort to permit him to keep up to date with the disciplinary affairs of the *Waffen*-SS the head of the SS ordered all cases of indiscipline and criminality to be submitted to the SS-VT inspector every ten months from May 1940.[24]

Committed to the battlefield during the French campaign, the men of the *Sonderkommando* constructed bridges under enemy fire across the Bethune canal and the River Loire near Roanne and at the end of the short, but gruelling campaign, which officially ended on 25 June 1940, the *Sonderkommando* and the surviving *Verlorenen Haufen* were billeted near Templeux la Fasse.[25]

From here, *Ostuf.* Paul Monich submitted rehabilitation requests for those killed in action, but although willing to rehabilitate those parolees who had died in action, General Eicke was reticent to release the survivors from their punishment and few, if any surviving probationers were rehabilitated at that time. During the occupation of France the *Sonderkommando* probationers undertook long hours of drill and conducted punishment duties.[26]

Despite the punitive threat of service with the *Sonderkommando*, the *Totenkopfdivision* and the other three *Waffen*-SS divisions, continued to report episodes of criminality and delinquency. Helping to swell the ranks of the *Sonderkommando* in the aftermath of the battle for France, was two troops who had been court martialled for committing serious sexual offences: Apprehended by an officer of the 4th *Panzer*-Division near Boulogne on suspicion of stealing from a French woman's house, 25 year-old *Anwärter* W. Mundt of the SS-*Totenkopf-Artillerie*-Rgt. faced trial on 31 May 1940 and the court convicted him of drunkenness and attempted rape. Judged guilty of the rape of French woman from Laventie and drunkenness while in charge of a divisional vehicle, the court punished 32 year-old *Strm.* Hans Kunkel of the 11. / SS-*Totenkopf-Infantrie*-Rgt. with a one year term of *Gefängnis*. Both men were expelled from the SS and their sentences was then set aside for indeterminate service in the *Sonderkommando*.[27]

'Creeps and scoundrels' declared Eicke angrily when he discovering that troops of the *Totenkopfdivision* were operating a complex financial fraud from the café 'Le Royal' in Nevers. From here, two Austrians and a north German had sold redundant pre-1923 inflationary *Marks* which had been printed in the millions, to German soldiers, and the buyers then used these notes to purchase goods from local shops and businesses. Their scheme exposed, Eicke ordered these fraudsters court martial before his field court. *Rttf.* Bruno Koslowsky of the 1. / SS-*Totenkopf-Artillerie*-Rgt. found himself judged guilty of fraud and punished with two years' *Gefängnis*, he was also expelled from the SS. His co-defendant, *Strm.* Emmerich Gigler of the same regiment's third company had used an invalid 20 mark note to purchase a haircut and the court punished him with a year's *Gefängnis* and expulsion. The trial judge, expressing doubts that Gigler was a professional criminal, set aside his sentence for service in the *Sonderkommando* for the duration of his punishment.[28]

Aware that the war situation in the summer of 1940 precluded the long term imprisonment of SS offenders, the *Reichsführer* begun planning the introduction of a probation process that offered rehabilitation to offenders who had proved themselves at the front. To meet this expectation, SS-*Richter* received sentencing guidance that instructed them to offer field probation for the majority of criminal cases on 12 June 1940. Himmler then turned his attention to the *Sonderkommando*. Ending Eicke's draconian authorisation powers over this unit on 15 August 1940, the head of the SS then ordered its disbandment on 18 August.[29]

Placing the entire *Verlorenen Haufen* rehabilitation process under the total control of the *Amt* III, henceforth, the *Reichsführer* entrusted *Stubaf.* Kegel and his successor, *Ostubaf.* Günther Burmeister, with coordinating the rehabilitation of errant troops. The SS-*Richter* and *Gerichtsherrn* received authorisation to recommend field probation sentences during the post sentencing process, but the final decision to permit parole and clemency was placed firmly in the hands of the SS leader and the *Amt* III.[30]

The *HA* SS-*Gericht* then turned their attention to dealing with the men languishing in the *Sonderkommando*. According to their own statistics, 47 of the 104 parolees were criminals and 57 military delinquents. Of these, 91, (87.5 per cent) had proved themselves in battle, five, (4.8 per cent) had failed to prove themselves completely during their *Sonderkommando* service, eight, (7.7 per cent) had been judged failures and 37 of the 91 parolees had committed offences such as theft, embezzlement, plundering, fraud, falsifying documents and bribery (52 of their number had been judged guilty of offences such as desertion, unauthorised absences, late from leave, threatening behaviour against a superior, drunkenness and drunkenness with insult and injury). Two of their number were guilty of sex crimes, five had no proven transgressions and the remaining eight men had not had any opportunity to prove themselves. The *Amt* III judged that 25 of the 104 probationers were suitable for immediate rehabilitation and admission back into the SS and they calculated that 90 probationers who had subsequently qualified for rehabilitation could joined the *Totenkopfdivision* on the condition that they had not committed another offence while on parole.[31]

Ten of the *Sonderkommando* probationers failed to qualify for rehabilitation and were sent under guard to the KL Sachsenhausen. The KL inspector obtained their detention order on behalf of the SS-FHA and a *Portepee* NCO—a non-commissioned officer without sword knot—and a handful of *Totenkopf* non-commissioned officers ushered the parolees aboard a truck and escorted them to Sachsenhausen. On arrival, the guards accepted a receipt from the camp commandant before they were discharged them from their duty, (these felons may have been detained in the *Erziehungssturm* for a period of observation to determine their future deployment).[32]

General Eicke did not accept the loss of the *Sonderkommando* lightly; in an effort to support the introduction of another new sentencing proposal, he and his divisional judge, *Hstuf.* Thum, submitted a detailed report about rising crime in the *Totenkopfdivision* to the *HA* SS-*Gericht* in March 1941. 'The SS-*Ehrenstrafe* has become a route out of military service' complained Eicke with some justification and voicing his conviction that the new parole process was not a deterrent for would-be offenders, he now proposed that SS men of his division who had committed sentences requiring less than twelve months' *Gefängnis* was no longer expelled from the division. His proposal would eventually be adopted by the entire jurisdiction.[33]

5.3 *Verlorenen Haufen* SS-*Pionier-Abteilung*

Himmler's decision to remove the *Sonderkommando* from General Eicke's control preceded the secret publication of a *Führer* edict on 21 October 1940 which authorised the military to establish armed field units from paroled convicts. 'During wartime the sharpest, drastic measures must be undertaken' commanded the Nazi leader and he now demanded that 'shirkers' no longer remained in prison and avoided their duty. Once again, Hitler permitted the military judiciaries to offer front probation to suitably willing military convicts. Released from jail, they would be sent to fight or perform manual work at the front in difficult, dangerous circumstances for the remainder of their sentence.[34]

Although the Nazi regime had failed to defeat Great Britain in 1940, its military forces continued their preparations for the invasion of the USSR in the summer of 1941. Early that same year, the SS leader sought to unify his parolees into formations that conformed to the October 1940 edict. Responding to this demand, the SS-FHA established the *Sondereinheit Verlorenen Haufen* on 19 February 1941 and suborned it's parolees to the SS-Division *Reich* with orders to undertake pioneer training. Implementing new principles for the imprisonment of inmates in the SS-*Straflager* Dachau, the *Reichsführer* then commanded the *HA* SS-*Gericht* to implement a new rehabilitation process for parolees. The SS-*Rechtamt* announced its intention in March 1941 to enter discussions with the head of the *Reichministerium für Bewaffnung-und Munitions*, *Ministerialrat* Dorsch and in an effort to avoid an expansion of the probation force he attempted to deploy *Gefängnis* convicts in heavy industry under the supervision of the Organisation Todt.[35]

An agreement between the parties failed to materialise, Himmler ordered the detention of *Gefängnis* offenders in the SS-*Straflager* Dachau and those convicts judged suitable for front probation were offered the chance of training to lift enemy mines in Dresden.[36]

The *Verlorenen Haufen* of the *Sonderkommando* who had qualified for rehabilitation in December 1940 remained with the *Totenkopfdivision* until 16 April 1941 and were then transferred to the *Verlorenen Haufen Zug* of the *Reich Pionier-Bataillon* in Dresden.[37]

Although the *Totenkopfdivision* had no front probation unit, probationers continued to languish in its reserve units. Wresting control of the *Totenkopfverbände* from Eicke, the SS-FHA then ordered the disbandment of its SS-*Sonderbataillon Prag* in Brünn on 5 January 1941 and its miscreants—troops who had been declared unfit for front probation—were then transferred to the SS-*Infanterie-Ersatz-Bataillon* near Goslar. This unit later transferred to Prague and provided a cadre for a new probation battalion.[38]

In the wake of his prosecution for military disobedience this discredited officer was assigned to the *Sondereinheit Verlorenen Haufen*:

Name: Karl Schäfer.
Last Rank: SS-*Mann*.
Born: 3.11.1918 in Herne/Westfallen.
SS-Nr.: 312.617 (joined 1.11.1937).
RAD Service: 1.4.1937–24.10.1937.
HJ Service: 1.6.1933–1.4.1937.
Prewar Assignments:
SS-VT 1.11.1937.
SS-*Standarte Germania* (Hamburg) from 1.11.1937.
Offizier-Lehrgang SS-*Junkerschule* Braunschweig 12.4.–9.11.1939.
Wartime Assignments:
Zugführer-Lehrgang until 20.12.1939.
5. *Hundertschaft des* SS-*Totenkopf-Rekruit*-Rgt. *Oberbayern* from 4.1.1940.
II. / SS-*Totenkopf-Infantrie*-Rgt 9 (Matzkau) in 1940.
9. / SS-*Totenkopf-Infantrie*-Rgt. 6 (Norway) in 1940.
SS-*Totenkopf-Ersatz-Bataillon* 'A' (Goslar) from 28.2.1941.
Verlorenen Haufen (Dresden) from 20.4.1941.
Promotions:
1.10.1939 SS-*Unterscharführer der Waffen*-SS.
1.10.1939 SS-*Standartenjunker*.
9.11.1939 SS-*Standartenoberjunker*.
20.4.1940 SS-*Untersturmführer der Waffen*-SS (*Aktiv*).
20.4.1941 SS-*Mann*.

Decorations & Awards:

0.0.19__ SA-*Sportsabzeichen in Bronze.*

0.0.19__ *Deutsches Reichssportabzeichen in Bronze.*

Notes: Attending *Volksschule* for four classes, Schäfer then obtained his *Abitur* from the *Humanistisches Gymnasium* (U-I). Judged fit for to undertake SS-VT officer training on 31 December 1938, Schäfer joined the *Oberbayern* in January 1940 and later mustered with the headquarters of this regiment's second battalion. A fitness report was submitted for Schäfer on 27 March 1940:

> SS-*St. OJ* Schäfer transferred from the service post FPNr. 10.461 for this service post as a *Zugf*ührer on 26 January 1940. Schäfer commands over a decent soldierly ability, not only in theory, but especially in a practical respect. In appearance he is sure and purposeful. At all times he has undertaken the tasks imposed on him with care and diligence. Towards the men he is strict, but fair and is a good role model as an SS officer. The view is that Schäfer, from his service, has increased in mass as an SS officer, which testifies about how he has voluntarily chosen the profession as a SS officer and he now approaches this task with lust and a love for this profession. His appearance within the Leadership Corps is flawless; and he never lack's the respect and his restraint towards older comrades, he is on the other hand a real comrade. He has already possesses a good SS officer-corps-spirit.

Chauffeured by his driver, SS-*Mann* Negwer, from Narvik to Stavern on 28 November 1940, Schäfer met a woman later that same night and injudiciously offered her a ride to Narvik in his service vehicle. During this journey the car was involved in a vehicle accident, injuring SS-*Mann* Berthold and two woman. Once the injured had been loaded into an ambulance for their journey to hospital, Schäfer continued on his way. Told the following day that the SS man had died, Schäfer begun to fear that his journey without movement orders, his use of service fuel for private means and wilful disregard of the ban on transporting civilian women in service vehicles would be discovered. As a consequence of his concerns, Schäfer submitted a false report about the affair and coerced Negwer to support his version of events. When his duplicity became common knowledge among the troops under his command, Schäfer's superiors instigated a court's investigation and arraigned him before the courts martial of the SS- *und Polizei-Gericht* IX, Oslo in Sandefjord on 10 January 1941. Here, he was indicted for offences against military disobedience in a sense of paragraph § 92 MStGB, for writing a false service report and inciting others to write a false service report (St. L. Nr. 148/1940). The court chairman, *Stubaf.* Dr Günther Reinecke was supported in his deliberations by *Hstuf.* Oscar Voss of the SS-*Totenkopf-Infantrie*-Rgt. 6 and *Ustuf.* Weber. *Hstuf.* Hans Latza prosecuted the case and the protocol officer was *Rttf.* Kurt Silbermann.

'The behaviour of the defendant in all three cases had caused great injury to [his] superior's authority' judged Dr Reinecke and expressing his conviction that Schäfer's duplicity had caused harm to the troops, the judge imposed a term of one week's *Gefängnis* on the young officer for committing military disobedience, three weeks' *Gefängnis* for submitting a false report and five months' *Gefängnis* for incitement to submit a false report; a total sentence of six months' *Gefängnis*. Although the court had not recommend his *Ehrenstrafe*, Schäfer was later expelled from the SS. Confirming the judgment on 4 March 1941, the *Reichsführer* set aside his prison punishment until the conclusion of the current war situation, and suspending him from officer rank he ordered Schäfer to accept a transfer to the *Sondereinheit Verlorenen Haufen*. The *HA* SS-*Gericht* commanded Schäfer to the *Verlorenen Haufen* at Dresden in March 1941.[39]

The *Verlorenen Haufen* were completing their preparations for the attack on the Soviet Union in Dresden when Himmler forbad them from wearing combat decorations or SS awards in May 1941. Warning that rehabilitation would only be offered to parolees who had proven themselves in battle, the SS leader placed the responsibility for determining all rehabilitation decisions with himself and informed them that to enable him to arrive at a decision, he would take into account the offences the parolee's had committed and their behaviour in action.[40]

The invasion of the USSR took place on 22 June 1941 and at this time the *Verlorenen Haufen* remained in the SS-*Kaserne* Wildermann until receiving orders to suborn themselves completely to the 4. / *Reich* SS-*Pionier-Abteilung* on 15 July 1941 (*FPNr.* 21.825). Arriving in Russia, *Ustuf.* Hans-Günther Schweigert took command of this small parole force as *Hstuf.* Rudolf Enselling's subordinate. At this time Enselling led the 3. / *Reich* SS-*Pionier-Abteilung*.[41]

At this time the *Verlorenen Haufen* included a cadre of pioneer non-commissioned officers who do not appear to have been punished for any offences. One of four non-commissioned officers of this unit awarded the EK I. *Klasse* on 1 August 1941 was *Oscha.* Willy Schumann. Promoted to officer rank on 9 November 1943, Schumann spent much of the war assigned to pioneer training posts.[42]

Prior to the deployment of the *Verlorenen Haufen* on the Eastern Front, the *HA* SS-*Gericht* gave further thought to the regulations governing the front probation process and published new sentencing guidelines for the parolees on 14 June 1941. The possibility of mercy and acceptance into the SS was now permitted for those criminals who had been judged guilty beyond question and assessed without reference to previous convictions and the *Amt* III demanded that parolees must have committed a 'one off' crime, (temporarily gone 'off the rails'). Habitual criminals and those involved in a major theft crime were excluded from this measure. The *HA* SS-*Gericht* also demanded that the criminal expressed his honest willingness to transfer to the parolee unit to fight the enemy in dangerous or difficult circumstances. Warning the troops of the *Verlorenen Haufen* not to desert, the *HA* SS-*Gericht* insisted that the parolees were mentally capable and remained at the front until wounded. Only those criminals suspended from the SS, or *Polizei* were considered for this service and felons judged unacceptable for deployment in the *Verlorenen Haufen* were whose presence was judged detrimental to the unit's discipline, those whose thoughtless behaviour prevented other troops from rehabilitation, those observed unduly influencing others and parolees found unsuitable for service in a military unit.[43]

Germany's armies in the east had encircled, captured and annihilated 300,000 Red Army troops armies in the Smolensk pocket and stood poised to lay siege the city of Leningrad when the military and *Waffen*-SS agreed in August 1941 that troops would no longer be automatically dismissed from military service for committing criminal offences, but would instead be offered front probation.[44]

Publishing new sentencing/front probation regulations in September 1941, the *HA* SS-*Gericht* now demanded that the responsible *Gerichtsherr* reviewed the criminal cases of those *Gefängnis* offenders who had not been immediately selected for probation and determine the length of their prison sentence. The *Abteilung Gefängnis* wing in Dachau was accepting *Gefängnis* convicts from March 1941 and prior to their admittance, the responsible *Gerichtsherr* was tasked with submitting an application for detention to the prison leader. The prison leader then supplied the *Amt* III with a convict's fitness report after four weeks' detention, which documented the inmate's behaviour. And this report formed the basis under which the prospective probationer's suitability was determined for probation. The *Amt* III placed the document in the inmate's punishment file to assist case officers with their decisions and if judged suitable, the felon then transferred to the pioneer school in Dresden to undertake a medical examination and specialist training. The short training course concluded, the probationers were then posted to the *Reich Pionier-Abteilung*. Those the prison judged unsuitable for parole remained incarcerated until the *Amt* III once again reviewed their case. An examination of court's daily letter book reveals that at least thirteen convicts submitted clemency requests per week.[45]

The parolees of the *Verlorenen Haufen* was excluded from some military policies: Concerned that the high casualty rate in frontline units would rob German families of their only sons, the SS-FHA adopted the policy of extracting last sons from *Waffen*-SS combat units on 4 August 1941. Writing to his former driver in early 1942, Friedrich Bielke, who was at that time assigned to the 13. / III. / SS-Rgt. *Deutschland* on the Eastern Front, Horst Bender confirmed that last sons of the *Bewährungsbataillon* were excluded from the last son programme.[46]

Amongst the probationers fighting on the central sector of the Eastern Front in 1941 was a disgraced officer who had been reduced to the ranks for contravening paragraph § 175 RStGB:

Name: Erich Bruns.
Last Rank: SS-*Untersturmführer*.
Born: 8.10.1907 in Golzwerder-Allendeich.
Died: 14.12.1941 in Nikeljewo.
NSDAP-Nr.: 136.445 (joined 1.5.1929).
SS-Nr.: 4.064 (joined 18.12.1930).

Prewar Assignments:
SD-*Hauptamt* from 4.4.1934.
Military training with the *Wehrmacht Heer* 21.10.1936–9.2.1937.
Military training with the *Wehrmacht Heer* 12.7.1938–21.1.1939.
Wartime Assignments:
Waffen-SS from 1.3.1940.
SS-*Artillerie-Bataillon* (Munich) in 1940.
5. / LSSAH *Artillerie*-Rgt. in 1941.
Lehrgang Pionierschule (Bechet *an der* Donau) until 19.3.1941.
Verlorenen Haufen in 1941.
Promotions:

4.7.1934	SS-*Untersturmführer der Allgemeine*-SS.
1.3.1940	SS-*Untersturmführer der Reserve.*

Decorations & Awards:

0.0.19__	SA-*Sportsabzeichen in Bronze.*
0.0.19__	*Deutsches Reichssportabzeichen in Bronze.*
0.0.19__	*Reiterssportsabzeichen in Bronze*
0.0.19__	*Totenkopfring der* SS.
0.0.19__	*Ehrendegen des Reichsführer*-SS.

Notes: Attending *Volksschule* for three classes and *Höhere Schule* for five classes, Bruns left full time education to work as a clerk/salesman. Marrying his fiancée Inge S., (b. 12.8.1911 in Berlin) on 24 September 1938, there appears to have been no issue from this union. He mustered with the SA from 1929 to December 1930.

A court's investigation was conducted against Bruns on suspicion of contravening paragraph § 175 RStGB while assigned to the LSSAH. Bruns attended a training course at a pioneer school and at its conclusion the staff organised a farewell party for the trainees in March 1941. Becoming extremely inebriated during the festivities, Bruns was then observed kissing and fondling an army officer and an NCO until the early hours of the morning. Reporting the incident to the LSSAH, *Gruf.* Dietrich ordered Bruns court martial (case Nr. St. L. 74/1941). Arraigned before the LSSAH tribunal, Bruns pleaded guilty to committing offences contrary to paragraphs §§ 330a and 175 RStGB and as a consequence of shaming the SS and behaving unnaturally while drunk, the court imposed a term of eighteen months' *Gefängnis* on Bruns on 29 March 1941. The court noted that he had participated in the defeat of the 'Röhm revolt' and had previously expressed of horror at the homosexual behaviour within the SA. When made aware of her husband's sentence Bruns wife applied for a divorce.

Post-sentencing, the *Chef* RSHA, *Gruf.* Reinhard Heydrich, interceded on Bruns behalf and appealed directly to the SS leader to have his sentence set aside for probation in the *Verlorenen Haufen*. At this time that those convicted of contravening paragraph § 175 RStGB were not automatically considered for parole, but the general's intervention was successful and the SS leader permitted the Amt III to offer Bruns front probation.

Following his transfer to the *Verlorenen Haufen* at Dresden, General Heydrich continued to express an interest in his former subordinate's predicament. Deployed with the 1. / 2. SS-*Pionier-Abteilung*, Bruns was killed in action at Nikeljewo in December 1941. His death qualified a posthumous rehabilitation and his awards, benefits and ranks were then re-instated to his family.[47]

Writing to General Heydrich in June 1941, the *HA* SS-*Gericht Amt* III explained the rehabilitation process for the disgraced SS parolees. Confirming that the end of an offender's original prison sentence did not result in an automatic rehabilitation, the *Amt* III explained that only the *Reichsführer* was responsible for determining whether those who later re-offended would be punished with a mix prison and front probation sentence. Only when the *Gerichtsherr* and the *HA* SS-*Gericht* were in agreement, did a transfer to a probation unit then take place. This process applied to thieves, but those convicted of contravening paragraph § 175 RStGB were not automatically selected for the *Verlorenen Haufen*. The *Amt* III then confirmed that criminals were not automatically transferred to a probation unit, a process of decision making had first to take place and if selected, it was made clear to the offender that parole with this unit was undertaken to regain their honour.[48]

This *Allgemeine*-SS officer joined the *Verlorenen Haufen* for embezzling funds from his SS units to pay personal debts:

Name: Johannes Zingler.
Last Rank: SS-*Untersturmführer*.
Born: 29.5.1901 in Forsthaus Dommatau/*Kreis* Putzig.
Died: 4.1962 in Frankfurt am Main.
NSDAP-Nr.: 544.378 (joined 3.1931).
SS-Nr.: 10.196 (joined 3.1931).
Prewar Assignments:
Annaburg *Militärknabenschule* from 1913.
Mölln and Potsdam *Unterführerschule* until 5.1920.
Infantrie-Rgt. 5 until 1.9.1920.
Schutzpolizei until 1.4.1928.
Ortsgruppe Olivia *Beim Organisation Wehrwolf* 1925–1928.
Führer-Lehrgang Munich 2.1932–7.1932.
Stabsführer der Abschnitt VII (Königsberg) 9.11.1931–8.2.1932.
Stabsführer der Gruppe Nord until 1.10.1932.
Führer beim Stab SS-*Gruppe Nord* until 30.1.1933.
Stabsführer der Abschnitt VII until 10.9.1933.
Stabsführer der Abschnitt VII until 1.2.1934.
Stabsführer der Oberabschnitt Nordost 25.11.1933–1.2.1934.
40. SS-*Standarte* 25.11.1933–12.3.1934.

Led the 40. SS-*Standarte* 12.3.1934–1.9.1934.
Led the 43. SS-*Standarte* (Frankenstein) 15.10.1934–30.5.1936.
Led the 45. SS-*Standarte* (Oppeln) 1.7.1936–30.1.1939.
Led the *Abschnitt* V (Essen) until 5.4.1941.

Wartime Assignments:

SS-*Pionierschule* Dresden 16.4.1941.
Verlorenen Haufen 16.4.1941.
SS-*Pionier-Abteilung Reich* in 12.1941.
SS-*Pionier-Abteilung* 23 in 1945.

Promotions:

3.1920	*Gefreiter.*
0.0.19__	*Unteroffizier.*
15.1.1932	SS-*Sturmführer der Allgemeine*-SS.
30.1.1939	SS-*Oberführer der Allgemeine*-SS.
21.11.1940	SS-*Mann.*
9.2.1942	SS-*Rottenführer der Reserve.*
29.12.1944	SS-*Unterscharführer der Reserve.*
5.1.1945	SS-*Untersturmführer der Reserve.*

Decorations & Awards:

0.0.19__	*Schleischer Adler* II. *Klasse.*
0.0.19__	SA-*Sportsabzeichen in Bronze.*
9.2.1942	*Kriegsverdienstkreuz II. Klasse mit Schwertern.*
0.0. 19__	*Dienstauszeichnung der* NSDAP *in Silber.*

Notes: His father was a state forester. Leaving full time education, Zingler worked as a craftsman and then embarked on a military career until accepted into the Berlin and Danzig *Schutzpolizei*. A courts investigation was initiated against Zingler on the suspicion of him committing embezzlement in 1940. When arrested, it was revealed that running up large private debts, he had paid them using funds stolen from all the regiments under his command. As a consequence of these allegations, Zingler found himself arraigned before the courts martial of the SS- *und Polizei-Gericht* III, Berlin and the court chairman, *Stubaf.* Günther Burmeister was supported in his deliberations by *Ostuf.* Hans Bauszus and *Staf.* Max Schneller. The case was prosecuted by *Hstuf.* Ullrich Dümichen. Judged guilty of the charges on 21 November 1940, the court imposed a term of 30 months' *Gefängnis* on Zingler and ordering his demotion to the rank of SS-*Mann*, they released him from the SS with shame. Spending eighteen weeks in goal, Zingler then accepted front probation in April 1941 and transferred to the SS-*Pionierschule* Dresden to undertake mine detection training. Here, Zingler underwent a medical examination that judged him physically unsuitable for combat. Detecting a heart murmur, the physician discovered that an old fracture had resulted in a significant loss of mobility in his right hand and arm. Despite these observations, Zingler was declared fit for combat on 26 June 1941 and then posted to the *Verlorenen Haufen Zug* of the *Reich Pionier-Abteilung* in Russia in late 1941.

Here, Zingler and his probationer comrades found themselves fighting in extreme winter weather conditions before the Soviet capital. Fending off numerous Red Army assaults, he survived his deployment at the front and earned his rehabilitation. Transferred to the HSSPF *Ostland* HQ in early 1942, Zingler then became involved in the mass murder of the Jews. His recommendation for a promotion was reported to the SS- *und Polizei-Gericht* XVI, Riga in February 1942 and passing this information to the Berlin tribunal, they forwarded this news to the SS-*Richter beim* RF-SS. Although the *Reichsführer* was unhappy with how exactly his probation had taken place, he permitted Zingler's further advancement on 9 February 1942. Promoted to officer rank in January 1945, Zingler ended the war fighting with a pioneer battalion. Surviving the collapse in May 1945, he died in Frankfurt am Main in April 1962.[49]

Exercising his disciplinary powers, the *Reichsführer* was permitted to send offenders to the *Verlorenen Haufen*. Prior to the outbreak of war a three year drinking alcohol ban had been imposed on *Oberleutnant der Schupo* Dr Hans Bachmann, but despite his pledge, he continued to drink Vermouth and Steinhäger to excess. Making a disrespectful remark to his commander at the Jens *Polizei-Schule* and assaulting a comrade on 27 March 1939, Dr Bachmann was sent home to Nördlingen to await a decision on his fate. As member of the *Allgemeine*-SS with the rank of *Ostuf.*, Dr Bachmann mustered with the *Fulda-Werra Bezirk* 47. His refusal to obey the alcohol pledge resulted in him receiving a strong warning on 26 March 1940 and his dismissal from the *Schutzpolizei* and SS.

Demoted to the rank of *Oscha.*, Dr Bachmann then found himself assigned to the *Verlorenen Haufen Abteilung* I (*Sonderkommando*) with orders to remain with this formation until considered for rehabilitation. 'Probably a death sentence' complained Dr Bachmann when he wrote to the head of the SS on 14 April 1940 to beg for his expulsion to be overturned to spare him the burdens this punishment would bring him in civilian life. Heeding his petition, the SS leader cancelled his expulsion on 29 April 1940. Despite his fears, Dr Bachmann survived the battle for France, but received a wound that required his hospitalisation. Recovered, he was then assigned to the LSSAH reserve battalion in Berlin and here, he obtained good fitness reports, but judged unsuitable for further frontline service, he was discharged from the *Waffen*-SS in June 1940. That same month he applied unsuccessfully for the return of his old *Polizei* and SS service ranks. Recommended for promotion to the rank of *Oscha.* of the *Allgemeine*-SS, Dr Bachmann was then posted to a service office close to home and his application for promotion was reconsidered after a year's submission of good reports.[50]

Struggling through the Russia *rasputitsa*, the German armies in the east stood poised to attack the city of Moscow when on 30 September 1941, the *Reichsführer* commanded the men of the *Verlorenen Haufen* to remain on probation until each had committed an honourable act. Only at this point would he be willing to consider their rehabilitation and only if by their behaviour they had proved themselves worthy of this decision. To aid his decision making, Himmler and his case workers demanded that the probationer's commander submitted probation reports that detailed the duration of engagement, included a battle report and a punishment case and gave reasons for the offender's transfer to the *Verlorenen Haufen*.[51]

In the autumn of 1941 the SS-*Richter* of the *Amt* III committed themselves to improving and introducing a faster clemency decision process and sought guidance from the SS leader about those *Verlorenen Haufen* clemency cases in which there was an issue of whether to rehabilitate if they fell, or had died as a result of wounds suffered. Writing to the SS-*Richter beim* RF-SS on this issue on 12 September 1941, *Ustuf.* Meder of the clemency office assumed that those transferring to the *Verlorenen Haufen* with a mitigated *Ehrenstrafe* could be restored to the SS when paroled, but was working under the impression that only those transferring from the *Verlorenen Haufen* to the newly established *Bewährungseinheit* and the *Arbeitsabteilung* Debica had the possibility of recovery via probation in the SS. Furthermore, Meder suggested granting full rehabilitation to *Verlorenen Haufen* who had fallen in battle and bringing about their rehabilitation early and expressed his belief that the family should be informed of the loss, so they could inform the circle of acquaintances of the family before the death of the fallen was announced in public. With all the interested parties agreeing that the rehabilitation process required acceleration, a demand was also raised to settle claims of salaries and welfare as a result of clemency decisions. It was noted at this time that a new regulation for the rehabilitation of *Polizei* officers—those who had fallen while fighting with the *Verlorenen Haufen* of the *Polizeidivision*—was required as changes to civil service law required the agreement of the *Chef Ordnungspolizei*.[52]

Himmler agreed that an accelerated process was necessary on 24 October 1941 and at this time, he reserved for himself the decision in important cases, particularly when it involved higher SS officers. Demanding that he was immediately informed about these cases by telephone or telex, the *Reichsführer* now commanded that those in the *Verlorenen Haufen* be classified into the following categories: Convicts whose re-entry into the SS was possible with probation; convicts whose probation was possible with a mitigation of the *Ehrenstrafe* and convicts that he intended to grant the possibility of a death with honour.[53]

Participating in the bloody winter battle before Moscow earned a significant number of the *Verlorenen Haufen* their rehabilitation. Following receipt of a clemency request from the *Totenkopfdivision* field court, the *Amt* III opened a clemency process for Max Weber on 20 October 1941 (case Nr. St. L. B 93/1940). *Hstuf.* Rudolf Enseling submitted a fitness report for Weber to the *Amt* III on 31 July and revealing that he had 62 parolees under his command, a provisional check revealed that 29 of their number were proven in battle and suitable for probation. In Enseling's opinion, just over a quarter of the remaining parolees would soon qualify for rehabilitation consideration. Receiving his report, the *HA* SS-*Gericht* then ordered Enseling to provide full fitness reports for those that he proposed for rehabilitation and demanded that his submission included details of their bravery before the enemy, the criminal act they had committed and any character observations. 'To create a lasting educational influence' on the rest of the probationers and encourage them to earn their rehabilitation, the *Amt* III proposed to publish quick decisions in these cases.[54]

The *HA* SS-*Gericht Amt* II initiated a discussion with the SS-FHA *Amt* III at the end of December 1941 to examine the possibility of rehabilitating further *Reich Verlorenen Haufen* and Enseling received orders to prepare the necessary rehabilitation reports in early January 1942. However, Enseling was unable to carry out this order as his unit was in constant action. To obtain the SS leaders opinion the *Amt* III demanded a general examination of the parolees files to be undertaken on 10 January 1942.[55]

On 19 January 1942 the SS-*Richter beim* RF-SS complained that the SS-FHA were 'foot dragging' and as a response to his dissatisfaction with the speed of the process, the *Amt* III wrote directly to Enseling and commanded him to prepare and submit fitness reports for the probationers Beller, Breyer, Hauptmann and Wittkowski. At this time the SS-FHA was reminded that they were to handle *Verlorenen Haufen* cases with urgency and in accordance to the November 1941 edict, then report when 'adequate' probation had occurred. Enseling's fitness reports for those who had fulfilled the requirements of probation were then passed to the field court and they supplied this information to the *Amt* III, who furnished copies to the SS-FHA *Amt* III on 22 January 1942.[56]

This SS man was selected to fight with the *Verlorenen Haufen* when it was revealed that he had killed a camp prisoner:

Name: Otto Andresen.
Last Rank: SS-*Hauptsturmführer*.
Born: 3.10.1890 in Hüxmark/Eckernförde
NSDAP-Nr.: 268.791 (joined 1.7.1930).
SS-Nr.: 18.865 (joined 1.10.1931).
Prewar Assignments:
Infantrie-Rgt. 9 (Potsdam) between 1.10.1911–14.11.1918.
SA-*Sturm* 19 in1930.
SA-*Sturm* 42 in 1930.
II. / 3. SA-*Standarte Niederschlesien* in 1931.
3. / I. / 8. SS-*Standarte* (Lauben) from 1.10.1931.
SS-*Junkerschule* Braunschweig (Ordnance officer) from 1.4.1935.
SS-*Wachbataillon* III (KL Sachsenhausen).
2. *Schutzhaftlager-Führer* KL Sachsenhausen in 1939.
Led the III. / 50. SS-*Standarte* (Flensburg) 29.6.1939.
Wartime Assignments:
Zugführer 3. / *Reich* SS-*Pionier-Abteilung* from 27.10.1942–8.1943.
2. / SS-*Pionier-Ausbildung- und Ersatz-Bataillon* 2 from 8.1943.
Stellvertreter des SS-*Pionier-Ausbildung- und Ersatz-Bataillon* 2 in mid-1943.
SS-*Pionierschule* Hradischko 20.1.–11.3.1943.
SS-*Pionier-Ausbildung- und Ersatz-Bataillon* III (Krakow) 11.3.1943–15.10.1943.
SS-*Junkerschule* Bad Tölz 15.10.–23.11.1943.

Kompanieführer SS-*Pionier-Ausbildung- und Ersatz-Bataillon* (Dresden) from 23.11.1943.
1. SS-*Pionier-Bau-Bataillon* in 6.1944.

Promotions:

1.10.1931	SS-*Anwärter.*
1.10.1931	SS-*Mann.*
16.12.1931	SS-*Truppführer der Allgemeine*-SS.
15.9.1932	SS-*Obertruppführer der Allgemeine*-SS.
24.12.1932	SS-*Sturmführer der Allgemeine*-SS.
26.5.1934	SS-*Obersturmführer der Allgemeine*-SS.
20.4.1934	SS-*Sturmhauptführer der Allgemeine*-SS.
9.11.1937	SS-*Sturmbannführer der Allgemeine*-SS.
9.1941	SS-*Hauptsturmführer der Reserve.*
4.3.1942	SS-*Mann.*
0.0.1943	SS-*Hauptsturmführer der Reserve.*

Decorations & Awards:

1914-18	*Eisernes Kreuz* I. *Klasse.*
1914-18	*Eisernes Kreuz* II. *Klasse.*
1914-18	*Verwundetenabzeichen in Schwarz.*
1914-18	*Ehrenkreuz für Frontkämpfer.*
00.0.19__	SA-*Sportsabzeichen in Bronze.*
00.0.19__	*Deutsches Reichssportabzeichen in Gelb.*
00.0.19_	*Totenkopfring der* SS.
00.0.19__	*Ehrendegen des Reichsführer*-SS.
18.10.1931	*Abzeichen des* SA *Treffens* Braunschweig 1931.
22.8.1942	*Spange Eisernes Kreuz* II. *Klasse.*
00.0.19__	*Medaille* '*Winterschlacht im Osten* 1941/42'.

Notes: Attending *Volksschule* for eight classes, Andresen was then employed as an apprentice at a fish company in Bremerhaven. A technical leader with the same company from 1 January 1906, he worked as a salesman between the wars and married. Mustering with the *Stahlhelm*, Andresen marched with the SA from July 1930.

In 1942, Andresen became the subject of an RSHA investigation into allegations he had murdered a camp prisoner, a former SA man. As a consequence, he found himself arraigned before the courts martial of the SS- *und Polizei-Gericht* III, Berlin on 4 March 1942 for contravening paragraph § 14 MStGB, the tribunal judged him guilty of murder and imposed a prison sentence on Andresen. Confirming the judgement, the *Reichsführer* commanded Andresen's demotion and transfer to the *Reich Pionier-Bataillon* (*FPNr.* 14.179). Writing to the *Oberabschnitt Elbe* on 11 January 1943, the *HA* SS-*Gericht* reported that the decision to send Andersen to the *Verlorenen Haufen* had been unanimously supported by all the departments consulted and the parolee was informed of the judgment on 10 June.

'It was not murder, but a political necessity' asserted Andresen from Dresden on 29 June 1942 and comparing his deed to the execution of the SA leadership in 1934, he expressed his belief that it had been his duty as an older SS member to help the camp administration murder the prisoner (for the part he had played in the Röhm affair, Andresen requested that his war disability pension payments continued uninterrupted). His training complete, Andresen left Dresden and deployed on the Eastern Front from October 1941. 'I have come to the judgement that the SS-*Mann* Andresen for me is an upright character, a dependable soldier and a true warrior' wrote *Hstuf.* Enseling when asked to comment on Andresen's performance and in the pioneer officers opinion, his subordinate was a supportive member of the unit, who had, despite his old wounds, taken command of the section for a short period when *Ustuf.* Hans-Günther Schweigert had fallen ill. Andresen's eventual rehabilitation was in no small part credited to his exemplary behaviour at the front. Released from the *Verlorenen Haufen* in late 1942, Andresen regained his former rank and ended the war assigned to a pioneer labour battalion in the Kurland pocket.[57]

In theory, the clemency decisions of the *Amt* III case workers and the *Reichsführer* were not influenced by entreaties of mercy from the offender or his family, but in practice, sentencing complaints and written appeals to Himmler, *HA* SS-*Gericht* and the Reichs Chancellery from the parolee, family and friends do appear to have influenced the subsequent clemency decision. Although not influencing the final rehabilitation decision, submissions did have the effect of bringing the offender's file to the attention of the SS-*Richter* case worker and led to action being taken to resolve the issue. The wife of a *Verlorenen Haufen* probationer, *Frau* Irmgard Koch, wrote directly to the head of the SS from her Berlin-Pankow home on 9 November 1941 to request clemency for her husband. A former member of the *Totenkopfdivision*, Koch had transferred to the *Sonderkommando* in 1940, (case Nr. St. L. 301/1940), but judged to have failed to proven himself during the French campaign, General Scharfe rejected his clemency request and commanded his transfer to the *Verlorenen Haufen* on 16 April 1941. Koch received orders on 30 May to remain with the *Verlorenen Haufen* until Himmler decided otherwise and this news provoked *Frau* Koch into submitting a new clemency request to the *Reichsführer* on 9 November. Burmeister ignored the appeal, but in expectation that they would have some influence on the process, the responsible court for Koch's case included this letter and earlier appeals in the case file they forwarded to the SS-*Richter beim* RF-SS on 10 December 1941 (Koch remained at the front during this process).

Leadership reports for *Uscha.* Heinz Heyden and Koch were forwarded to Himmler on 15 December 1941 and *Frau* Koch once again proffered a new clemency appeal to the SS-*Richter beim* RF-SS on 22 February 1942 which appears to have had some effect on her husband's case. Forwarding her letter to the *HA* SS-*Gericht* on 12 March, the SS-*Richter beim* RF-SS requested that they sent a progress report to the *Persönlichen Stabes* RF-SS and to deter *Frau* Koch from writing to him again, the case worker, Dr Wehser, wrote to her on 12 March to explain that her husband's rehabilitation, in the interest of uniformity, was the sole responsibility of the *Chef HA* SS-*Gericht*. Asking for her patience, he revealed that Koch had transferred to the *Bewährungsabteilung* and would remain there until a favourable fitness report had changed his status. On 26 March, the *HA* SS-*Gericht* revealed that they expected a decision in *Rttf.* Gerhard Koch's clemency case to be published soon (12.3.1942, case Nr. G. L 77/1942). A chance find in the Wiener institute's archive reveals that Koch was rehabilitated and he had transferred to the 5th SS-*Grenadier*-Division *Wiking* by April 1942.[58]

Amongst those of the *Verlorenen Haufen* under considering for rehabilitation in early 1942 was former officer, Friedrich Böhme. Assigned to this unit in August 1941, the SS-*Richter beim* RF-SS would intercede on his behalf with the *HA* SS-*Gericht* in January 1942. At this time, Himmler's advocate noted that his office had received rehabilitation applications from a number of other men of the *Verlorenen Haufen*.[59]

Ostuf. Böhme was one of a handful of cashiered officers who had been sent to the *Verlorenen Haufen* when their involvement in the theft of military vehicles and other offences came to light. Böhme's trial notes were placed in the file of his co-defendant:

Name: Paul Friedrich **Lindner.**
Last Rank: SS-*Sturmbannführer*.
Born: 28.8.1895 in Darmstadt.
NSDAP-Nr.: 60.021 (joined 14.4.1927).
SS-Nr.: 2.520 (joined Sept.1929).
Prewar Assignments:
2. Bavarian *Luftschiffabteilung* 17.8.1914–17.1.1915.
206. Bavarian *Ballonkraftzug* 17.1.1915–9.11.1918.
Freikorps Oberland 1.8.1922–1.4.1927.
Referent (Organisation) *Oberabschnitt Nordost* (Königsberg) in early 1936.
Led the II. / 63. SS-*Standarte* 1.11.1936–1.12.1939.
Wartime Assignments:
SS-RuSHA (Prague) from 1.12.1939.
Waffen-SS from 1.3.1940.
Zugführer 7. / SS-*Infantrie*-Rgt. 4 in 1940.
SS-*Infantrie-Ersatz-Bataillon Nord* from 15.4.1941.
Verlorenen Haufen in 4.1941.
Promotions:

9.11.1934	SS-*Sturmbannführer der Allgemeine*-SS.
0.0.19__	*Leutnant der Reserve.*
1.3.1940	SS-*Untersturmführer der Reserve.*
1.8.1940	SS-*Obersturmführer der Reserve.*
19.4.1941	SS-*Mann.*

Decorations & Awards:

1914-18	*Eisernes Kreuz* II. *Klasse.*
1914-18	*Bayerische Militär Orden Kreuz* II. *Klasse.*

1914-18	*Ehrenkreuz für Frontkämpfer.*
0.0.19__	*Blutorden.*
0.0.19__	SA-*Sportsabzeichen in Bronze.*
0.0.19__	*Totenkopfring der* SS.
0.0.19__	SS-*Ehrenwinkel für alte Kämpfer.*
0.0.19__	*Goldenes Ehrenzeichen der* NSDAP.

Notes: The son of a shoemaker. Lindner attended *Volksschule* for four classes and then studied at trade school for six classes and passed his final examinations. Prior to the Great War he worked as a clerk and took part in the abortive Munich Putsch on 9 November 1923. A *Polizei* employee until 1927, Lindner marched with the SA between 1 January 1927 and 1 September 1929. Suffering long periods of unemployment until 1933, he sold Nazi newspapers, performed menial work and was employed as a bookkeeper in 1933–34. Employed full time by the SS from 1934, Lindner married his fiancée Therese M., (b. 25.11.1908 in Munich) on 12 August 1933 and they had three children together up to the point when records ceased in May 1945. Voluntarily attending two military exercises in 1934, Lindner was questioned in October 1936 and asked to explain the circumstances of *Sta.* Karl Ostberg's injury of two men while driving a service vehicle many years previously. Reporting to the SS.-*Gericht*, at the SS-*Zentralkanzlei* in Munich on 17 May 1936, Lindner walked the investigator through the accident site and attempted to convince his questioner that Ostberg had ordered him to hand over the keys to his service vehicle when he expressed his desire to visit the III. / SS-*Standarte* 1. Complying with this order, Lindner explained that he travelled with him to the unit's location, but unbeknown to him, Ostberg did not possess a full driving licence, only a motorcycle licence. The only witness to the accident was a civil servant and he had been unable to identity of the car's driver. Though suspicion lingered that Lindner was in fact the driver, a lack of evidence precluded his punishment and the injured men received 1,500 *Reichsmark* compensation. As a consequence of his involvement in this case and for his injurious attitude towards secret duties, Lindner was demoted in December 1936, but returning to Munich, he became a salaried SS employee from 22 August 1939.

In the wake of the expulsion of his son from the *Nationalpolitischen Erzanstadt* Bensberg on 5 May 1938, Lindner received an invoice for boarding expenses. Disputing the 50 *Reichsmark* demand for payment, he wrote a strongly worded letter of complaint to their cash office and the NPEA leader which resulted in the SS.-*Gericht* investigating him for insulting behaviour. Subsequently apologising for his behaviour, the *Oberabschnitt Südwest* (Stuttgart) decided against further disciplinary action on 31 October 1938. Writing to the *Nationalpolitischen Erziehungsanstalt* Bensberg leader, *Gruf.* Wilf, on 30 August 1939, the SS.-*Gericht* Ib expressed their disapproval of Lindner's behaviour, but rejected his further punishment.

Appointed the vehicle officer of the II. / SS-*Infantrie*-Rgt. 4 in Assen from July 1939, a Zündapp motorcycle was placed at Lindner's disposal to carry out his tasks. On 18 November 1940 *Ostuf.* Gebhardt ordered all units to report their possession of motorcycles and this audit revealed that Lindner and other troops of this regiment had stolen many vehicles. The SS- *und Polizei-Gericht* X, Den Haag was then entrusted with the court's investigation and questioning Hoffelner about the activities of Fischer and others, he accused Lindner of embezzlement and of arranging for his Zündapp to be taken to his home when he had overseen the transport of cars to Linz. Denying Hoffelner's accusations, Lindner denounced him for committing the same crime. A trial for plundering and theft was then initiated against Lindner and his co-defendants on 18 January 1941, (St. L. 263/1940). The court chairman, *Stubaf.* Dr Hans Braußе was supported in his deliberations by *Stubaf.* Bellwied, (Walter Bellwidt?) and *Ostuf.* Hoffmann. *Hstuf.* Dr Rudolf Barth prosecuted the case and the *Beurkundungsführer* was *Oscha.* Bierwolf. Arraigned before the courts martial of the Den Haag tribunal for military embezzlement and committing perjury, (he had falsely accused Hoffelner of committing the crime), Lindner's explanation for the motorcycles absence was rejected.

Considering his previous service to the party, the court judged Lindner guilty of these charges and an act of bribery and imposed a term of three and a half years *Gefängnis* on Lindner and ordered his expulsion from the SS and demotion to the rank of SS-*Mann* on 19 April 1941. While he awaited a confirmation of his sentence, Lindner mustered with a reserve battalion from 15 April and then joined the *Verlorenen Haufen*.[60]

A total of four trucks and eleven motorcycles had been embezzled by the defendants. Born in Ketschendorf/Spree on 20 May 1914, Günter Fischer, the son of a *Regierungsinspektor*, attended *Mittelschule* for four classes, obtained his *Abitur* from *Gymnasium* in August 1933 and studied at the University Jena for two sessions. Joining the NS-*Schulerbund* in 1932, at the time of his trial Fischer was unmarried. Admitted into the *Allgemeine*-SS in March 1933, (SS Nr. 147.839), he joined the Nazi party a little while later (NSDAP Nr. 4.262.088). Mustering with the LSSAH in April 1934, Fischer attended an officer training course at the SS-*Junkerschule* Braunschweig in 1935 and received a promotion to officer rank on 20 April 1936. Then assigned to the SD, Fischer was simultaneously promoted to the rank of *Gefreiter der Luftwaffe* and *Oscha.* Joining the SS-*Standarte Deutschland* in the autumn of 1936, Fischer's superiors promoted him to the rank of *Ostuf.* on 30 January 1939. At the outbreak of war he found himself assigned to the SS-TV *Inspektion* in Berlin, where he obtained a driving licence. His career was not without blemish, Fischer was punished with a fourteen days' *Stubenarrest* for by-passing the chain of command (he had applied directly to the *Reichsführer* for a front deployment). Assigned to the SS-*Wachbataillon* in Prague, *Ostuf.* (*Aktiv*) Fischer then received orders to transfer to the SS-*Infantrie*-Rgt. 4 in Holland in mid-June 1940. Before leaving he decided to remove a writing desk, electrical fire, a screen, fruit bowl, a coloured jug, vase, numerous crockery and cooking utensils from his office and accommodation at the *Studentenheim Technischen Hochschule*.

Leading the fourteenth company of this regiment in 1941, Fischer received orders at this time to travel to France and buy vehicles. Purchasing vehicles and motorcycles, he then falsified their documents and sold them in Germany as his own possessions. Discovering that the regimental commander had ordered a vehicle audit in the summer/early autumn of 1940, Fischer submitted false reports and sales receipts to explain the vehicles absence. In addition to these crimes, Fischer committed two abuses of his supervisory powers during his tenure as company leader. Informed that a wallet belonging to *Rttf.* Doritz had been stolen from the washroom in September 1940, Fischer then ordered his company to stand to attention for two hours and threatened to leave them on parade until the culprit admitted his guilt (the culprit was not identified). On another occasion *Rttf.* Habersack and Stölting were both reported for drunkenness and for having tattoos applied to their bodies. The company was assembled on 24 October 1940 to watch Habersack and Stölting perform punishment exercises and drill in the cold weather (*Blutorden* holder *Rttf.* Wolf reported that the drill ended in a song). For avoiding the censure, Fischer punished *Uscha.* Thiel with three weeks' intensified arrest.

Arraigned before the Den Haag courts martial, Fischer initially denied the charges, but faced with evidence of his crimes he finally plead guilty to the charges. The court noted that with the collusion of Schneider and Brüne he had stolen a Citroën car and disguising its true ownership, he changed its number plates and sold the vehicle for profit. He was then judged guilty of plundering in the field, for embezzling a 200 cc BMW, stealing furniture from Prague, disobedience in connection with failing to submit a subordinate for punishable acts, falsifying orders, suppressing a complaint and for stealing the car and motorcycle with Böhme. In addition to these charges, Fischer was also judged guilty of attempting to commit perjury, for involving subordinates in motor vehicle theft and for mishandling subordinates with two hours of punishment drill. When announcing the sentence, the court acknowledged that Fischer had shamed the officer corps and *Waffen*-SS and voiced their conviction that he had been a 'disastrous influence' on Hoffelner, had wrongfully handled his subordinates, suppressed *Rttf.* Wolf's complaint and plundered. Imposing a term of five years' *Zuchthaus* on Fischer, the tribunal expelled Fischer from the SS and then sent him to the *Verlorenen Haufen. Ostubaf.* Burmeister acknowledged his rehabilitation request from 19 September 1942.[61] Fischer was later rehabilitated, returned to officer rank and led the I. / SS-*Gebirgsjäger*-Rgt. 13 in October 1944.[62]

Born in Dortmund on 21 January 1902, Friedrich Böhme, the son of a regional pit foreman, attended *Volksschule* and *Realschule* and worked as a *Praktikant* in an engine factory in Bergbau. Married with two children, he participated in the Kapp Putsch in 1921 and was politically active in Berbau until 1923 (resisting the French occupation in the Ruhr). Joining the *Polizei*, Böhme obtained officer rank, but was arbitrated out of the service in 1934 to work for his parents-in-law on their farm and bakery. Enjoying a disharmonious relationship with his in-laws, their death permitted Böhme to become active in the SD in 1936–37. Joining the Nazi party in 1932, (NSDAP Nr. 1.252.282), Böhm was accepted into the *Allgemeine*-SS in 1934 (Nr. 276.922) and would receive a warning for service neglect. Entered the *Waffen*-SS with officer rank on 4 January 1940, Böhme mustered with the SS-*Infantrie*-Rgt. 4 and became a *Zugführer* in Fischer's company. Leading the eleventh company in 1941, a court imposed a fine of just over 200 *Reichsmark* on Böhme for causing grievous bodily harm. Böhme appeared for trial before the SS- *und Polizei-Gericht* X, Den

Haag at the end of May 1942 and confessed to re-numbering two motorcycles with Dutch number plates and selling them for profit. Judged guilty of embezzlement, the tribunal punished him with a term of four years' *Gefängnis* and expelled him from the SS. Serving his prison sentence, Böhm then joined the *Verlorenen Haufen*. The SS-*Richter beim* RF-SS submitted a plea for clemency to the *HA* SS-*Gericht* for *Pionier* Böhme with a request that they undertook a review of his case. At this time, Horst Bender noted that Böhme had been wounded three times.[63]

Born in Weyer *an der* Ems on 27 October 1907, Karl Hoffelner, the son of a railway station master, was married with one child and had adopted two children born to his dead sister. Attending *Volks-und Bürgerschule*, he studied at the Salzburg state trade school in 1925 and worked as a motor mechanic until 1930. Between that time and 1933 he worked irregularly. Mustering with the Austrian SA in August 1929, Hoffelner joined the Nazi party in 1930, (NSDAP Nr. 196.474) and was accepted into the SS in 1930, (SS Nr. 2.569). Mustering with the LSSAH on 17 March 1933, he was active in Munich until July 1934 and then joined the SS-*Standarte Deutschland* as an officer and *Zugführer*. Degraded to the rank of SS-*Mann* following his participation in a brawl in March 1936, Hoffelner's punishment was set-aside by a *Reichsführer* clemency decision in July 1936 and he then mustered with the *Oberabschnitt West*.

Adjutant at the 19. SS-*Standarte*, Hoffelner left his salaried position in 1939 to join the *Gauleitung* in Innsbruck in 1939. Here, he took over his late sister's responsibilities and worked as a driving instructor. At the beginning of the war, Hoffelner joined the SS-*Infantrie*-Rgt. 8 and transferred to the SS-*Infantrie* Rgt 4 in May 1940. Entrusted with the formation and command of the motorcycle section of the fifteenth company, this unit was disbanded in the autumn of 1940 and *Ostuf.* Hofflener transferred to other duties. During the court's investigation it was revealed that Hofflener had embezzled a Harley Davidson motorcycle, given false orders to Tyschen and Peskoller, committed disobedience in the facts of the case with false orders, had encouraged *Rttf.* Brüne to commit perjury (he had helped to plunder a Citroën car and embezzled a 97 cc motorcycle which was given to Harms and Schwab, who had no idea that it was stolen). 'A weak character, who was practically inexperienced in the leadership of men' announced the court chairman and for committing these punishable acts, SS- *und Polizei-Gericht* X, Den Hague punished Hoffelner with three years' *Gefängnis*. Expelled from the SS, but acquitted of other accusations, Hoffelner then joined the *Verlorenen Haufen* for a short period of front probation. Reduced to the rank of *Ustuf.*, Hoffelner fought with the 18th SS-*Panzergrenadier*-Division *Horst Wesel* in September 1944 and was posted to the SS-StuG *Schule* in December the same year.

In connection with this case, twelve other NCO defendants were implicated in theft, embezzlement and forgery offences. Amongst their number included the brother of the Knights Cross winner, *Ostubaf.* Christian Tyschen. These men were punished with between four weeks' sharp arrest and eight months' *Gefängnis* for their part in the fraud and most were demoted. The *Reichsführer* confirmed the courts judgements on 19 April 1941 and Lindner's sentence was amended from expulsion from the SS to exclusion and cancelled the demotions of Schwarten, Möller, Tyschen, Peskoller, Miller, Göring and Harms. The three weeks Josef Miller spent on remand was subtracted from his sentence and Göring was ordered to serve his imprisonment in full. Böhm's punishment and that of Schneider, Schwarten, Möller, Münch, Tyschen and Peskoller were ordered to run concurrently and the remaining imprisonment sentences were set aside. The trial at an end, Böhm, Hoffelner and Lindner were ordered to report to the *Verlorenen Haufen*.[64]

Post war, Paul Lindner's name appeared on the Crowcass consolidated wanted list (this contained the names of men wanted for arrest in connection with war crimes). The Polish authorities believed he been the HSSPF *Sosnowice* and had ordered his arrest on suspicion of committing murder.[65]

The majority of those *Verlorenen Haufen* who died at the front were subsequently rehabilitated, received a posthumous pardon, or were permitted to re-enter the SS. The families of those posthumously rehabilitated then had to wait for the *Reichsführer* to decide the award of insurance and benefit payments:

Name: Wilhelm 'Willi' **Rudolf.**
Last Rank: SS-*Untersturmführer.*
Born: 28.12.1918 in Hümme/Kassel.
Died: 18.8.1941 in Smolensk.
SS-Nr.: 372.394 (joined 1.11.1938).
RAD Service: 11.4.1938-24.10.1938.
HJ Service: 1.9.1932-31.4.1938.
Prewar Assignments:
SS-VT 11.1938.
SS-*Totenkopf Ersatz-Bataillon* (Goslar) until 1.11.1938.
8. / LSSAH from 1.11.1938–3.9.1939.
Wartime Assignments:
Offizier-Lehrgang SS-*Junkerschule* Bad Tölz 1.11.–24.2.1940.
8. / SS-*Totenkopf-Infantrie*-Rgt. 6 from 9.11.1940.
SS-*Pionierschule* (Dresden) in 1941.
Verlorenen Haufen Zug (*FPNr* 10.879) in summer 1941.
Promotions:

24.2.1940	*Oberjunker der Waffen*-SS.
1.6.1940	SS-*Oberscharführer der Waffen*-SS (*Aktiv*).
9.11.1940	SS-*Hauptscharführer der Waffen*-SS (*Aktiv*).
9.11.1940	SS-*Untersturmführer der Waffen*-SS (*Aktiv*).
0.0.1940	*Pionier.*
18.8.1941	SS-*Untersturmführer der Waffen*-SS (*Aktiv*).

Decorations & Awards:

0.0.19__	SA-*Sportsabzeichen in Bronze.*
0.0.19__	*Deutsches Reichssportabzeichen in Bronze.*
0.0.19__	D.L.R.G. *in Bronze.*
0.0.19__	*Goldenes Hitler-Jugend Ehrenzeichen in Gelb.*
14.9.1939	1939 *Eisernes Kreuz II. Klasse.*
1.6.1940	1939 *Eisernes Kreuz I. Klasse.*
6.10.1939	*Verwundetenabzeichen,* 1939 *in Schwarz.*
15.7.1940	*Verwundetenabzeichen,* 1939 *in Silber.*

Notes: The son of a former *Oberleutnant*, railway official and the mayor of *Obervellmar bei* Kassel. Attending *Volksschule* for eight classes, Rudolf left full time education and found employment as a printer. Attending the Poetlin political high school, he volunteered for military service with the SS-TV in Kassel in November 1938. Wounded by a bullet in Poland on 3 September, Rudolf also received grenade splinters in his back near Kutno on 28 September. Hospitalised at the Lodsch *Feldlazarett* on the same day, he recovered and was then selected for officer training. Receiving good service reports from his Bad Tölz instructors, Rudolf was recommended for use as a *Zugführer* in a machine gun company. Appointed a *Zugführer* with an SS-*Totenkopf-Infantrie*-Rgt., Rudolf arrived in Norway on 10 June 1940 and was stationed in Oslo on 21 June the same year. Around the time of his promotion in November 1940, the SS- *und Polizei-Gericht* IX, Oslo ordered his remand detention for committing an unknown offence (case Nr. St. L. 123/40). That same the month the *Befehlshaber der Waffen*-SS conducted enquiries to discover whether his promotion would be awarded in view of the initiation of a court's investigation. In view of the court's process, his promotion was denied on 28 November 1940. Subsequently arraigned before the courts martial of the Oslo tribunal, Rudolf was judged guilty and punished with a term of three years' *Gefängnis*. The following year, Rudolf found himself undertaking training to deactivate enemy mines in Dresden. His instruction complete, he then joined the *Verlorenen Haufen* in time to participate in opening stages of the attack on the USSR. As the hot summer prepared to give way for the autumn rains, the *Reich* Division found itself part of the assault on the city of Smolensk. Here, the *Verlorenen Haufen* were clearing enemy minefields in August 1941 when Rudolf lost his life. Writing to his father on 2 August 1941, Enseling offered his condolences for his loss:

> I have to convey a deeply saddening communication to you that your son Willi carried out a storm troop mission on 18 August 1941 and heavily wounded, he was taken back to his unit and died. With rare devotion he fought and he was the best in the unit.
>
> Please accept my expression of deepest sympathies for the hard loss you have suffered.

'For giving his life in battle for the people and homeland the criminal's expulsion from the SS has been cancelled and his former service grade returned with effect from the date of his death' declared the *HA* SS-*Gericht Amt* III on 9 September 1941 and Willi

Rudolf was approved for clemency (case Nr. L. 137/1941). At that time a decision about the payment of his death insurance and welfare payments remained undecided, but these were later paid to his father and son, along with a posthumous promotion to officer rank.[66]

This probationer also atoned for his crime with his life:

Name: Markus Habben.
Last Rank: SS-*Sturmbannführer.*
Born: 26.10.1903 in Nordhausen.
Died: 21.9.1941 in Korowinzy.
NSDAP-Nr.: 71.617 (joined 5.12.1927).
SS-Nr.: 15.347 (joined 15.9.1931).
Prewar Assignments:
Jugland Deutscher Orden 1919–1922.
Gräfenhainichen SS-*Sportsschule* (fitness instructor) 1.7.1934.
SS-*Wachbataillon Elbe* (KL Lichtenburg) 1.3.1935.
SS- *Wachbataillon* IV *Ostfriedland* (KL Buchenwald) 1.3.1936–10.7.1937.
2. / IV. / SS-*Standarte Brandenburg* (KL Sachsenhausen) from 10.7.1937.
Led the III. / 82. SS-*Standarte* (Bielefeld) 1.5.1938–10.9.1939.
Wartime Assignments:
Waffen-SS from 10.9.1939.
Led the 6. / SS-*Totenkopf-Infantrie*-Rgt. 6 (Prague) on 15.11.1939.
KL *Inspektorate* HQ 24.4.1940–24.4.1941.
SS-*Wachbataillon* (Gusen) until 19.6.1941.
SS-*Pionierschule* Dresden in 1941.
Sonderzug II/ *Verlorenen Haufen* until 29.9.1941.
Promotions:

0.0.1925	*Wachmeister der Polizei.*
20.3.1934	SS-*Untersturmführer der Allgemeine*-SS.
15.9.1935	SS-*Obersturmführer der Allgemeine*-SS.
20.4.1936	SS-*Hauptsturmführer der Allgemeine*-SS.
10.9.1939	SS-*Sturmbannführer der Allgemeine*-SS.
15.11.1939	SS-*Hauptsturmführer der Reserve.*
19.6.1941	SS-*Mann.*
18.2.1942	SS-*Sturmbannführer der Allgemeine*-SS.
18.2.1942	SS-*Hauptsturmführer der Reserve.*

Decorations & Awards:

0.0.19__	SA-*Sportsabzeichen in Bronze.*
0.0.19__	*Totenkopfring der* SS.
0.0. 19__	*Dienstauszeichnung der* NSDAP *in Gelb.*
0.0.19__	D.L.R.G. *in Bronze.*

Notes: Attending *Mittlelschule*, Habben underwent an apprenticeship between 1920 and 1923 and was by profession a photographer. Training for the Prussian *Polizei* for six months at the Burg *Polizei-Schule*, Habben passed the course and once qualified he served as a policeman with the Wittenburg *Schutzpolizei* until 1925. Mustering with the SA from December 1927 to September 1931, he married his fiancée Walli B., (b. 21.10.1909 in Bittefeld) on 25 May 1936 and they had one child together up to the point when records ceased in May 1945. A fitness report, from November 1939, observed that Habben was unsuitable for military service and as a consequence of this report, he returned to the camp service. Commanding the guard battalion at the KL Gusen, Habben accepted an invitation for him and a few of his officers and non-commissioned officer's to attend a Labour Front party in Perg on 5 February 1941. The event was co-hosted by the Perg *Bürgermeister*, the *Kreisamtleiter* Anton Pilz and NSDAP *Kreigsgeschaftsführer* Josef Chudomel in the town sports hall and went without incident until around 11.00 p.m. when a drunken Habben began to demand repeatedly in a rude manner for the *Bürgermeister* to attend to him. The party ended two hours later, but Habben demanded the organisers kept the drinks coming. Denied an extension to the festivities, he then became obstreperous and threatening towards the organisers. A quarrel then broke out between the camp guards and the Nazi party officials and during the trade of insults, Habben threatened the party members with arrest. The *Polizei* were called to eject the SS men from the hall. Punching *Oberwachmeister* Brauner, Habben then slipped away to return to his quarters.

A little later, the local court formally indicted Habben for drunkenness on duty and for insulting behaviour (the police authorities demanded his prosecution for the assault on their officer). A court's investigation was then initiated against Habben and this recommended his trial for committing two counts of arrogance, for insulting behaviour, physical and threatening imprisonment (case Nr. St. I. 22/1941 F.). Arraigned before the courts martial of the SS- *und Polizei-Gericht* VII, Vienna on 24 April 1941, the court chairman *Stubaf.* Dr Klahre and the lay judges heard the evidence against him and as a consequence of his behaviour they judged him guilty of the offences on 30 April 1941 and imposed an entire sentence of 15 months *Gefängnis* and ordered his expulsion from the SS. Confirming the sentence on 19 June 1941, the *Reichsführer* ordered his incarceration until the end of the war. Sent to the SS-*Straflager* Dachau to serve his sentence, a little later the pugnacious Habben quickly accepted parole and then undertook minefield clearing training. Then posted to the *Verlorenen Haufen* of the *Reich* SS-*Pionier-Abteilung*, Habben was killed in action at Korowinzy while seconded to the 16. (Pi) / SS-*Totenkopf-Infantrie*-Rgt. 3 on 29 September 1941. His demise provoked the *Gauleiter* for *Westfalen-Nord*, Dr Alfred Meyer, to write to the *HA* SS-*Gericht* on 3 December 1941 to report that Habben's widow was in some distress and the family was in financial difficulty. However, before offering her financial assistance, the local Nazi party wished to know whether Habben, had by his honourable death in combat, been rehabilitated to his former rank and wanted to know if his death benefits were payable to the widow. The head of the SS subsequently ordered Habben's rehabilitation, the reinstatement of his former rank and his name was added to the list of fallen officers.[67]

Elsewhere, the original instigator of the front probation programme for the *Waffen*-SS, *Gruf.* Eicke, found his *Totenkopfdivision* completely enveloped by Red Army forces at Demyansk in Northern Russia in the winter of 1941/42. Suffering extremely high casualties, the intransigent Eicke unable, or unwilling to transfer his convicted felons out of the pocket to safety, decided to place those accused of cowardice, self-mutilation, desertion and other military offences into a field probation unit. These unlucky parolee's fought for three-days in the front line until they were wiped out to a man.[68]

Towards the end of 1941 the *HA* SS-*Gericht* was tasked with overseeing a radical change to the probation process. As part of these changes the leader of the SS forbad the further re-enforcement of the *Verlorenen Haufen* in early September 1941 and the surviving parolees transferred from the Eastern Front in early 1942 to the relative safety of the newly established *Bewährungsabteilung der Waffen*-SS in Chlum/Bohemia.[69]

5.4 *Non- Verlorenen Haufen Front Probation*

In addition to sending malefactors to the *Verlorenen Haufen Zug*, the *Reichsführer* also punished miscreants with front probation that was served among the troops. This punishment was carried out in reserve formations, or with regular field units at the front and their commanders submitted regular fitness reports to the *HA* SS-*Gericht* to determine whether the parolee had performed their duties satisfactory. Fulfilling their terms and length of service, the probationer then either return to his former unit or transferred to another post which was commensurate with his skills: Born in Freiburg/Brsg on 22 December 1916, Artur Grathwol mustered with the *Allgemeine*-SS since September 1934 (SS Nr. 372.382) and deployed with the *Wiking* Division between August 1941 and July 1944. Punished with a field judgement on 15 September 1943, *Hstuf.* Grathwol's negligence had led to an injury and a man's death which resulted in the court imposing a term of twelve months' *Gefängnis* on him and ordering his demotion to the rank of *Ustuf.* Confirming this punishment on 14 January 1944, the leader of the SS amended the sentence to front probation on 26 January. Grathwol led the 2. / SS-*Panzerjäger-Abteilung* 11 during August 1944 and commanded the I. / SS-*Panzer*-Rgt. 11 from February 1945 until the collapse of German resistance. During his military service Grathwol received the prestigious *Deutsch Kreuz in Gelb.*[70]

Name: Hubert Derda.
Last Rank: SS-*Sturmbannführer.*
Born: 12.2.1912 in Danzig-Langfuhr.
SS-Nr.: 190.937 (joined 14.8.1933).
Prewar Assignments:
10. / 36. SS-*Standarte* (Danzig) from 14.8.1933.
I. / SS-*Standarte Germania* from 1.9.1935.
I. / SS-*Standarte Germania Führeranwärter-Lehrgang* on 1.11.1935

Führeranwärter-Lehrgang SS-*Junkerschule* Bad Tölz 1.4.1936–31.1.1937.
Zugführer-Lehrgang Dachau 1.2.–20.4.1937.
Lehrgang für Verwaltungskunde SS-*Junkerschule* Bad Tölz 1.5.1937–12.3.1938.
Officer of the *Oberabschnitt Donau* (Vienna) from 1.4.1938–11.9.1938.
Officer of the *Abschnitt* XXXI (Vienna) from 11.9.1938–5.10.1939.

Wartime Assignments:
SS-*Polizeidivision* 5.10.1939–19.8.1940.
II. / SS-*Polizei*-Rgt. 1 5.10.1939- summer 1940
5. / SS-*Polizei*-Rgt. 2 from the summer of 1940.
9. / II. / LSSAH 19.8.1940-10.4.1942.
1. *Mitarbeiter des Division Intendanten, Divisions-Intendant der* SS-*Panzergrenadier*-Division *Wiking* from 15.4.1943.
Led the 5. SS-*Nachschubabteilung* until 1.8.1944.
Generalkommando der Waffen-SS XIII SS-*Armeekorps* from 1.8.1944.

Promotions:

20.4.1937	SS-*Untersturmführer der Allgemeine*-SS.
11.9.1938	SS-*Obersturmführer der Allgemeine*-SS.
5.10.1939	SS-*Obersturmführer der Reserve.*
31.7.1940	SS-*Schütze.*
9.1940	SS-*Obersturmführer der Reserve.*
20.4.1941	SS-*Hauptsturmführer der Reserve.*
9.11.1943	SS-*Sturmbannführer der Reserve.*

Decorations & Awards:

0.0.19__	SS-*Zivilabzeichen* (Nr. 91.276).
0.0.19__	SA-*Sportsabzeichen in Bronze.*
0.0.19__	*Reiterssportsabzeichen in Bronze.*
0.0.19__	*Deutsches Reichssportabzeichen in Bronze.*
0.0.1944	1939 *Eisernes Kreuz I. Klasse.*
0.0.19__	1939 *Eisernes Kreuz II. Klasse.*
0.0.19__	*Medaille 'Winterschlacht im Osten* 1941/42'.
0.0.19__	*Infanterie-Sturmabzeichen in Bronze.*
0.0.19__	*Verwundetenabzeichen,* 1939 *in Silber.*
0.0.19__	*Kriegsverdienstkreuz II. Klasse mit Schwertern.*
0.0.19__	*Kriegsverdienstkreuz I. Klasse mit Schwertern.*
0.0.19__	*Bulgarien orden* für Tapferkeit IV. *Stufe* II. *Klasse.*

Notes: Attending *Volksschule*, Derda obtained his *Abitur* from *Höhere Schule*, then studied mathematics and physics in Danzig and in Austria for six months. Serving as the administrative officer in the *Polizeidivision*, Derda committed an act of indiscipline that resulted in a spell of probation at the front. Without their commander's permission both Derda and *Ostuf.* Dr Lambert Lueb attended a party organised by officers of the second battalion at the Königsschafthausen public house on Sunday, 10 March 1940. Inebriated, they left the party shouting and then beat and attempted to steal two horses. Hearing about their escapade, the commander of the SS-*Polizei*-Rgt. 1 questioned both officers, but denying the allegations, Derda assured his commander that the owner of a nearby brewery would bear witness to their non-attendance at the party. The regimental ordnance officer investigated Derda's alibi and very soon discovered that both officers had lied (his investigation involved a line-up of officers from the 8. *Kompanie*). The regimental leader reported the affair to the divisional commander on 17 March 1940 and complaining that their actions were less that that expected of SS officers, he asked whether three days' close arrest for both officers was sufficient punishment. It was then left to the *Hauptamt Haushalt-und Bauten* to punish Derda. Transferring him to their headquarters in Berlin on 24 March 1940, the *Chef Verwaltungs-Hauptamt* interceded on his behalf with the head of the SS to mitigate the punishment. The *Reichsführer* commanded Derda to serve for between six and eight weeks at the front as a rifleman in the *Polizeidivision* for his deceit and drunkenness and the *HA* SS-*Gericht* confirmed this punishment on 31 July 1940. *Schütze* Derda then served his punishment with a combat unit. His company leader and divisional IIa expressing their satisfaction with his service and recommending his rehabilitation on 6 June 1940, Derda returned to the administrative service and remained with this branch of the *Waffen*-SS until the collapse in May 1945. His co-defendant, *Ostuf.* Dr. Lueb transferred to the *Stab Reichsarzt*-SS on 29 March 1940 and held the rank of *Hstuf.* when assigned to the 9th SS-*Panzer*-Division in the summer of 1944.[71]

Assigned to the HSSPF *Russland-Süd* in October 1942, SS-*Oberführer der Allgemeine*-SS Fischer-Schweder was denounced for drinking to excess in March 1943 and his superior complained that he had fired his service weapon in the Kiev casino. His behaviour reported to the HSSPF *Russland-Süd* on 8 September the same year, the results of this investigation were then presented to the *Reichsführer* who ordered Fischer-Schweder to the front for probation. Transferring to the *Waffen*-SS and the LSSAH *Ersatz-Bataillon* in Berlin in September 1943, *Ustuf.* Fischer-Schweder attended a *Zugführer* training course at the Kienschlag SS-*Panzergrenadierschule* in late 1944 and then led a grenadier company of the 12th SS-*Panzer*-Division *Hitlerjugend* from 16 January until seriously wounded in Austria on 11 April 1945.[72]

Send to the front for probation, this officer did not survive the experience:

Name: Erich Schulze.
Last Rank: SS-*Untersturmführer.*
Born: 26.2.1914 Görlitz/Schles.
Died: 22.1.1942 Bialystock.
SS-Nr.: 400.132 (joined 1.4.1938).

RAD Service: 1938.

Prewar Assignments:

SS-VT 1.4.1938.

SS-*Standarte Deutschland* 1.4.1938–15.1.1939.

Stab SS-*Standarte Deutschland* 15.1.-31.1.1940.

Wartime Assignments:

14. / SS-*Standarte Deutschland* 31.1.–30.7.1940.

Offizier-Lehrgang SS-*Junkerschule* Braunschweig 1.8.1940–20.4.1941.

Zugführer SS-*Lehrkompanie* SS-*Junkerschule* Braunschweig from 20.4.1941.

SS-*Infantrie-Ersatz-Bataillon Germania* 11.7.1941–21.1.1942.

Zugführer SS-*Standort* Warsaw 2.1.–21.1.1942.

SS-Division *Reich* 21.1.–22.1.1942.

Promotions:

1.4.1938	SS-*Mann*.
1.3.1939	SS-*Rottenführer der Reserve*.
0.0.1940	SS-*Standartenjunker*.
15.2.1941	SS-*Standartenoberjunker*.
20.4.1941	SS-*Untersturmführer der Reserve*.
15.12.1941	SS-*Unterscharführer der Reserve*.
21.1.1942	SS-*Untersturmführer der Reserve*.

Decorations & Awards:

0.0.19__	SA-*Sportsabzeichen in Bronze*.
0.0.19__	*Die Medaille zur Erinnerung an den* 1. Oktober 1938 (Sudetenland).
25.7.1940	*Kriegsverdienstkreuz II. Klasse mit Schwertern*.

Notes: Attending *Volksschule* for four classes and *Höhere Schule* (U-II), Schulze participated in the Western campaign. Schulze's commander in Braunschweig, *Hstuf.* Endemann, ordered *Ustuf.* Schorn, a future SS Judge, to undertake an investigation on 29 June 1941 to examine claims that that Schulze had visited places with his orderlies which were unsuitable for SS officers and shared the same woman. In addition, he was tasked with examining complaints that Schulze had handled a serious comrade theft case without having reported this occurance to his superiors. Questioning Schulze's nineteen year-old orderly, *Anwärter* Willi Swaton, he confirmed that he and Schulze had visited nightclubs on 20 occasions and had entertained the same women. He also affirmed that he had reported Schulze for committing theft. Giving *Staffelmann* Musmann his post office savings book, Swaton asked that he paid 85 *Reichsmark* into the account, but Musmann stole 285 *Reichsmark* and reported the book missing (Swaton reported its loss to the post office). Informed of the theft, Schulze questioned Musmann and obtaining his promise to return the money, he failed to report the embezzlement to his commander. Questioned on this matter on 5 July 1933, Schulze denied visiting nightclubs with Swaton, but admitted some knowledge of the theft case. Speaking with various witnesses, Schorn became convinced that they officer was lying and in the presence of *Hstuf.* Endemann, the witnesses again related their statements before *Ustuf.* Schulze. When they left the room, he again stuck to his original statement.

In the presence of Schulze, Schorn once again questioned Swaton on his oath and again Schulze denied having knowledge of the comrade theft case. Schorn presented his findings to Endemann on 30 June 1941 and Schulze was then called to his commander's service office. Here, in the presence of the *Gerichtsoffizier*, Endemann read out the accusatory statements and accused Schulze of untruthfullness. Aware that the *Reichsführer* had previously ordered Schulze not be sent to a field unit and had demanded to be informed of any changes to his service, Endemann, convinced of Swaton's version of events, then submitted the statements of all involved directly to Himmler with a request that Schulze be removed from Braunschweig on the grounds that it was common knowledge that he had made false statements, persisted in calling his men liars and had been judged an unsuitable SS officer.

Reporting to a reserve battalion in Arnhem as a *Zugführer*, on 25 July 1941, Schulze waited here for the outcome of the court investigation (St. L. II 205/1941). For failing to obey orders and reporting a comrade theft, Schulze was arraigned before the courts martial of the SS- *und Polizei-Gericht* X, Den Haag on 7 August 1941 and judged guilty of the charges, the tribunal sentenced him to a term of three months' *Gefängnis* and ordered his demotion to the rank of *Uscha.* The *Reichsführer* confirmed the sentence on 15 December 1941, but repealed the *Ehrenstrafe* and set-aside the punishment in favour of front probation as a *Gruppenführer.* Reporting to the Warsaw garrison administration on 2 January 1942, Schulze was posted to the *Reich* on 21 January 1942. However, the following day he passed away from scarlet fever in the Bialystock *Reserve-Lazarett* and the process for his full rehabilitation was initiated on 28 September the same year.[73]

In this instance, an officer's death sentence was set aside for front probation in 1943:

Name: Fritz Ferdinand **Maletta.**
Last Rank: SS-*Obersturmführer.*
Born: 30.1.1907 in Neutitschein.
Died: 31.7.1943.
NSDAP-Nr.: 6.658.710 (joined 1.11.1938).
SS-Nr.: 331.608 (joined 1.4.1938).
Prewar Assignments:
2. Pioneer Rgt. of the Czech Army 15.3.1932–29.6.1933 (he trained for 4 weeks each year until 1938).
5. / SS-*Standarte* 104.
Wartime Assignments:
Waffen-SS 2.1940–31.7.1943.
Pionier-Lehrgang SS-*Pionierschule* Dresden until 29.3.1940.
Led the *Pionierzug* / SS-*Totenkopf-Kavallerie* Rgt. 2 from 30.3.1940.
11. *Technisch Kompanie* / SS-*Totenkopf-Kavallerie*-Rgt. (Lublin) from 4.4.1940.

Zugführer with the 6. *Pionier-Schwadron* / SS-*Totenkopf-Kavallerie*-Rgt. 2 on 8.5.1941.
Led the 1. *Pionier Kompanie* of the SS-*Kavallerie*-Rgt. 1 in 1942.
2. / SS-*Pionier-Abteilung* 8 in 1942.
SS-*Kavallerie-Ersatz-Bataillon* (Warsaw) until 20.4.1943.
SS-*Totenkopfdivision* 20.4.1943–31.7.1943.
2. / SS-*Pionier-Abteilung* 3 from 2.5.1943–31.7.1943.

Promotions:

4.1940	SS-*Sturmann der Reserve.*
20.4.1940	SS-*Untersturmführer der Allgemeine*-SS.
20.4.1940	SS-*Untersturmführer der Reserve.*
9.11.1941	SS-*Obersturmführer der Allgemeine*-SS.
9.11.1941	SS-*Obersturmführer der Reserve.*

Decorations & Awards:

0.0.19__	SS-*Ehrenwinkel für alte Kämpfer.*
0.0.19__	1939 *Eisernes Kreuz I. Klasse.*
0.0.19__	1939 *Eisernes Kreuz II. Klasse.*
0.0.19__	*Infanterie-Sturmabzeichen in Bronze.*

Notes: His father was a master hairdresser. Maletta attended *Volksschule* for five classes, obtained his *Reiferprüfung* from *Realschule* after seven classes and then studied electronics at the German Technical University in Brno for seven years. A member of the *Deutschen Turnverband*, he joined the SDP in 1934, was a member of a German fraternity in Brno and was active in right-wing politics from early 1936. Maletta passed his first State Examination on 12 August 1931 and his second on 12 December 1941. Obtaining his engineering diploma, he worked without salary with the Neutitschein town hall technical department from December 1933 to mid-1935, (gas and water). Undertaking practical training at various companies in Neutitschein and Vienna, he returned to his home town and worked voluntarily for three months at the urban elecktrizitätswerk in Neutitschein. Maletta married his fiancée Elisabeth F., (b. 28.2.1914 in Neutitschein) on 20 November 1937 and they had two children. Managing the District Office for Technology from 1 January 1939, Maletta was drafted into the *Waffen*-SS in 1940, but quickly obtained leave to continue his university studies. Returning to active duty in the spring of 1940, his commander submitted a glowing fitness report for him on 18 April 1940:

> The 2. SS-*Totenkopf-Ersatz-Kompanie* in Dresden referred SS-*Ustuf.* Maletta to here with this rank on 29.3.1940 and he has been put to use here as an SS-*Ustuf.* and a platoon leader of the *Pionierzug*. Maletta is a quiet and prudent leader with good manners, and he commits with great zeal. His behaviour in and out of service is impeccable and is a good comrade. His military knowledge, as far as I can tell you, is satisfactory.

Maletta's superior submitted a fitness assessment for him on 8 April 1941:

> SS-*Ustuf.* Maletta's demeanour on and off duty is modestly certain and his attitude and military bearing is perfect. His essence is calm and balanced and his character is sincere and faithful.[...] His military tactics and technical weapons knowledge are judged comparatively good and he is excellent in pioneer technical areas. Maletta is also infantry trained. His presentation is clear, consistent and exhaustive, his theoretical military knowledge is good. Maletta is athletic and his world viewpoint is firmly grounded in Nazism. Because of his exemplary conduct SS-*Ustuf.* Maletta is a good educator and a pioneer *Zugführer.* His ability to command a unit is still lacking, although given the necessary experience and dilligence this will be achived in a matter of time. Maletta is thin and a little delicate.

His regiment requested his further promotion on 20 September 1941:

> I agree with the proposal of the SS-*Totenkopf-Kavallerie*-Rgt. 2. The SS-*Ustuf.* Maletta is to be recognised for his personal courageous behaviour in the various operations of the brigade by the awarding of the *E.K.* II class. His promotion to SS-*Ostuf.* is a well deserved recognition.

A court's investigative process was introduced against Maletta on the suspicion of cowardice while deployed at the front. His company beaten, Maletta once again received orders to attack and hold an enemy position with his Hungarian ethnic-German troops. Failing on two previous occasions to eject the enemy from their position, his raw troops had suffered 50 dead and 30 wounded in the attempts. Maletta, minus a finger, refused to lead his men back into action and suspecting that his subordinate had suffered a breakdown, Malletta's commander was entrusted him with taking the 40 survivors of his company to Tréhin (an attack by other troops secured the enemy position). Accused of cowardice, Maletta found himself arraigned before the courts martial of the divisonal field court on 9 December 1942 (St. L. 226/42).

At trial, his former commander, *Hstuf.* Ernst Imhof stated confidently that Maletta had swelling to the right side of his head on the day of the attack, suggesting his injury by a stray bullet or shrapnel and assured the court that he was a brave officer. Despite this support, the court judged Maletta guilty of two acts of cowardice and punished him with two capital sentences and ordered his expulsion from the SS. Responsibility for confirming the sentence was left to the *Führer*, but the *HA* SS-*Gericht* refused to proceed with the confirmation until it had been determined whether Maletta's head wound had affected his professionalism. Considering a suspension of the court's process, the *Reichsführer* ordered his advocate to detirmine Maletta's suitability for front probation with the rank of *Uscha.* 'Here, in a reasonable time' the SS leader was certain that it would be determined whether Maletta's actions related to acts committed out of cowardice, or had been the product of a complete nervous breakdown. The SS-*Richter beim* RF-SS received Maletta's punishment case file and one *HA* SS-*Gericht* specialist report on 25 January 1943 and the *Chef des Amt* IVb, Dr Braußе, raised concerns with the case the following month:

> [...] It does not seem appropriate to burden the Führer with this affair. Therefore I propose that the *Reichsführer*-SS orders an annulment and issues a provisional suspension of the proceedings, in order to give Maletta the opportunity to prove that he is not a coward.[...]

The Troppau *Gestapo* supplied the SS-*Richter beim* RF-SS with a detailed report about the Maletta family on 2 February 1943 which reported no 'political, criminal or racial anomalies'. Setting aside Maletta's court judgment on 11 February 1943 to determine whether he had committed his act in the state of free exercise of will, Himmler, in expectation that he would demonstrate whether the judgment had been a consequence of acts which had been committed out of cowardice, or were due to a complete nervous breakdown, then decided he would be sent to the front with the rank of *Uscha*. Firstly, the head of the SS arranged for Maletta to be placed under the care of *Gruf*. Prof. Dr Gebhardt at the Hohenlychen SS-*Lazarett* on 28 February. 'Bring him completely back to his feet' commanded Himmler and the SS-*Kavallerie*-Division was made aware by telex of these arrangements. Prof. Dr Gebhardt later recommended that Maletta, with NCO rank, recuperated in a *Gesungsheim des Waffen*-SS for three weeks and the SS-*Richter beim* RF-SS raised no objections to this arrangement on 11 March 1943, but observed that Himmler had commanded Maletta to take up residence in a small and secluded rest home and avoid contacting former comrades. Leaving Hohenlychen, Maletta reported to the Laag-Soeren *Sanitätsabteilung* on 17 March 1943 to permit them to deal with his injured ring finger. He was then sent to the *Gesungsheim des Waffen*-SS to recuperate.

The *HA* SS-*Gericht* agreed with Himmler's proposal on 25 March 1943 and receiving orders to join the *Totenkopfdivision* in April the same year, Maletta reported to their divisional HQ on 26 April and the following month he joined the pioneer battalion. Killed in action in July 1943, the *HA* SS-*Gericht* had then to decide whether by his death, Maletta had earned the right to be buried with his officer rank. An investigation into the circumstances of his death was conducted by the SS-*Richter*, *Ustuf.* Junge of the *Totenkopfdivision* field court and he submitted a report on his findings on 30 October 1943:

> Adjustment order.
> Concerning the investigation against the SS-*Ostuf.* Friedrich Ferdinand Maletta, of the 3. / SS-*Pionier-Abteilung* 3 of the SS-*Panzer-Grenadier*-Division *Totenkopf* for cowardice. [the sentence] shall be adjusted, on the grounds that the accused has been adjudged to be a hero during the attack on the height 213.9 on the Mius front on 31 July 1943. The company probation report from 14 August 1943, has revealed that Maletta was himself the *Gruppenführer* and had proven himself in deployment at that location. During the battles of Mius Front he was used to solve the most difficult tasks and his person was deployed recklessly to fulfil these orders. He was for his group a model of prudence and valor.

On 10 January 1944 the *Amt* IIIa revealed that they and the *Totenkopfdivision* field court had been unable to initiate a rehabilitation procedure for Maletta on the grounds that he had died with the rank of *Uscha.* (G.L.2447/43). However, this situation would change if Maletta's former officer rank was restored to him. It was left to Himmler to decide whether by his death, Maletta had earned the right to regain his former officer rank. Turning to this subject on 8 June, the SS-*Richter beim* RF-SS (Killing) confirmed that Maletta's rank as an *Ostuf.* had not been not revoked. Dying in posession of officer rank, the *Amt* III then set in motion a clemency process for Maletta and the SS-FHA wrote to the SS-*Pionier-Ausbildung- und Ersatz-Bataillon* 1 on 22 June to order an amendment of Maletta's personal papers to reflect his officer rank.[74]

Later in the war, *Waffen*-SS miscreants were offered front probation with divisional SS-*Strafkompanie* (Punishment Company): Born in Riga/Latvia on 1 August 1920, Harry Holtschak joined the *Waffen*-SS on 1 May 1940 and mustered with the 5. / SS-*Kavallerie*-Rgt. 1 during July 1941. Transferring to the 6. / SS-*Kavallerie*-Rgt. 2 during January 1943, Holtschak rose to the rank of *Uscha.* and obtained a promotion to officer rank in September 1943. Leaving the cavalry, he then undertook training at an artillery school and then trained with assault guns. Posted to the SS-*Truppenübungsplatz* Beneschau between 1 February and 31 May 1943, Holtschak then reported for service with the 1. / SS-*Panzerjäger-Abteilung* 54. Holtschak's *Gerichtsherr*, *Brigadef.* Jürgen Wagner, ordered his arraignment before the courts martial on the grounds of military disobedience for an unknown incident that occurred in Croatia the year previously and his trial took place on 7 April 1944, (case Nr. St. L. 27/1944). Judged guilty, Holtschak found himself fighting with the 23. *Nederland Strafkompanie*. 'A personal example to his unit,' stated the *Strafkompanie* leader when he submitted a request for Holtschak's transfer to the troops in 1944. Despite his wounding in action the application was denied, but later overturning this decision, Holtschak joined the SS-*Panzer-Abteilung* 4 in July 1944 and ended the war fighting with the II. / SS-*Panzergrenadier*-Rgt. 4.[75]

Born in Nikolajew/Ukraine on 12 January 1915, *Waffen-Ustuf.* Peteris Miervaldis Ziedins was leading the 13. / *Waffen-Grenadier*-Rgt. *der* SS 42 in the spring of 1944 when an evening of drunken exuberance landed him in trouble with the *HA* SS-*Gericht*. Insulting and punching an NCO in the face on the evening of 22 May 1944, Ziedins behaviour was reported to his superiors and the *Gerichtsherr* ordered his arraignment before the divisional courts martial. Judged guilty of conduct unbecoming of an officer and of mishandling a soldier under his command, the sentence is not known, but the *HA* SS-*Gericht* passed the case file to the *Reichsführer* for his consideration. Confirming the sentence on 1 July, the head of the SS ordered Ziedins demotion to the rank of *Waffen-Ustuf.* and commanded his deployment with the divisional *Strafkompanie* for three months. The divisional commander agreed with this judgement on 1 October and Ziedins then reported to the 19. *Strafkompanie* for probation. During this period it was decided that Ziedin's pay would continue to be sent to his family to prevent them suffering hardship. Dying 'a hero's death' in action at the front, the *HA* SS-*Gericht* closed Ziedin's case on 20 February 1945.[76]

5.5 12 November 1941 Edict

The campaign against the Soviet Union had failed to achieve total victory at the end of 1942 and the German Army security forces were proving incapable of handling the increasing threat of partisan attack on the military supply routes. The forces guarding the rear echelon requiring immediate reinforcement, the *Reichsführer* decided to select new troops for this task from among the criminals and delinquent elements of the *Waffen*-SS and *Polizei*. With Hitler's support, he secured an agreement with the military to establish a new generation of field probation units and the *HA* SS-*Gericht Amt* IIIb reached an accord with the German High Command on 31 October 1941, which for the duration of the war permitted the head of the SS, to send discharged *Waffen*-SS convicts to a special units, for continued military service. As a consequence of this agreement the *HA* SS-*Gericht* published new sentencing/probation guidelines for its courts.[77]

The *HA* SS-*Gericht* published a secret internal edict on 12 November 1941 which authorised their courts to punish new categories of offenders with part-prison and part-field probation sentences. Initially excluded from this process were those parolees of the *Verlorenen Haufen Zug*, who was deployed with the *Reich Pionierzug* z.b.V. in Dresden and had been sentenced before 11 June 1940. The *Amt* III published amendments to this edict on 24 January 1942 and these permitted the SS divisions to form their own punishment companies.[78]

Again, the *Reichsführer* continued to reserve for himself the right to review all cases, but the November 1941 edict placed responsibility for all reprieve, probation and rehabilitation cases involving malfeasants punished with a term of imprisonment to the clemency department of the *Amt* III. The courts and the responsible *Gerichtsherr* were permitted to add a part probation element to all sentences; including terms of *Festungshaft*, concentration camp punishments and to those handed a term of intensified arrest of six weeks, or greater. Those involved in this decision process were cautioned to judge moderately and wisely and their summations were to take into account the offender's party affiliations and state whether the defendant was well thought of by his superiors (the court judgment ignored previous crimes).[79]

At the time of sentencing, the offenders were denied their service grade and benefits and the *Gerichtsherr* and court were tasked with proposing a minimum sentence to be served prior to offering parole to enable the *Amt* IIIb and the *Reichsführer* time to present their objections to the punishment. If willing and judged appropriate for military service, the prison authorities then submitted a positive probation fitness report for the convict to the *Amt* III and if they concurred with this decision, the *Amt* III they sought the opinions of the offender's disciplinary superior, the *Gerichtsherr* and *HA* SS-*Gericht* before the trial period was finally granted. The opinions and views of all parties involved in the case were affixed to the convict's punishment book.[80]

The November 1941 edict permitted the suspension of the entire sentence for those punished with terms of *Gefängnis* of less than six months and the offender served this time in the *Waffen*-SS special units. In these cases, the probationer, including those expelled from the SS and *Polizei* who had been judged of no further use to the war effort, or denied their civil rights, would remain at the front until killed or rehabilitated. Inmates serving a term of six *Gefängnis* months, or greater were also offered probation once they had served at least one third of their punishment. Inmates incarcerated with long sentences had to serve a minimum of two-thirds of their punishment before parole was offered.

The *Reichsführer* appears to have personally reviewed all *Zuchthaus* cases to judge whether given the war situation warranted their amendment to a term of *Gefängnis*. *Zuchthaus* inmates recommended for probation at their sentencing, were informed of this decision by letter, separately of the punishment book. Receiving Himmler's sentencing recommendation, the *Amt* IIIb then determined whether a *Zuchthaus* inmate served his punishment in the *Straflager* Dachau, or another place of detention. The *Gerichtsherrn* were authorised to amend the original sentence from *Zuchthaus* to *Gefängnis*, convert unsuitable for the war effort judgements to battle worthy and return civil and honour rights to the convict. In cases where the original judgement stated that the offence had not been proved, or the defendant had been judged unsuitable for probation, then permission was granted to amend this decision to reflect their suitability for probation. In appropriate cases, the *Gerichtsherr*, *Amt* IIIb or SS-*Hauptamt* were authorised to recommend unsuitable convicts for front probation. At those times when the *Amt* III argued for a change in sentence, the case officer had to elucidate his reasons why probation was considered suitable and his report included the convict's level of proficiency and his fitness for deployment in dangerous or difficult circumstances. The opinions of all the interested parties gathered together, the *HA* SS-*Gericht* then handed the offender's case file to the SS-*Richter beim* RF-SS to obtain Himmler's final confirmation.[81]

The *Reichsführer*, in his capacity as *Gerichtsherr*, was responsible for deciding the inmate's length of punishment and his probation deployment. Even if the convict's presence was deemed detrimental to the unit's discipline, Himmler exercised the right to command felons to the parole units, judge in what capacity he was to be employed at the front and was authorised to overrule the objections of the trial judge. The decision made, the *HA* SS-*Gericht* forwarded the sentencing command to the relevant court and this informed all interested parties whether a decision had been taken to accept the probationer back in to the SS or *Polizei*. The *Amt* III recognised the importance of appeals for clemency and retaining them in the punishment file, it was accepted that they could aid a successful rehabilitation order. The writer was expected to express regret, highlight his loyalty to the SS and support for the party and announce his willingness to serve at the front to atone for his actions. The case worker usually replied to appeals and informed the sender of any changes to the sentence.[82]

The number of appeals sent to the *HA* SS-*Gericht Amt* III during the war was considerable; 169 reprieve cases passed through their hands during 1942 and this figure had risen to 369 cases by February 1943. A steady rise in the number of appeals was observed in the subsequent years and in that same period the courts imposed 86 death sentences of which three-quarters were successfully appealed and the punishment commuted to a term of imprisonment.[83]

For convict's who had fully served their gaol sentence, the prison commandant/leader arranged his transfer to the parole units or another unit to undertake a period of front probation. In theory, prior to leaving prison, every probationer received six to eight weeks military training and physical exercise, but Himmler's decision in 1943 to send inmates to factories resulted in inadequate battle preparation. As a consequence of this situation, the assessment of combat fitness was undertaken by the probationary unit and short-term probationers remained in Bohemia with the *Bewährungsabteilung* to undertake hours of back-breaking military drill and exercise. Their probation period fulfilled, the probationers then transferred to the troops or their former unit.[84]

The November 1941 edict ruled that only the recently expelled, including those SS and *Polizei* deployed with *Wehrmacht* units, were acceptable for probation and these parolees were commanded to either join a suitable troop unit, or the *Sondereinheit der Waffen*-SS. At this time this forces consisted of the *Bewährungsabteilung der Waffen*-SS, the *Arbeitsabteilung der Waffen*-SS and the *Sondereinheit* 'X' and recognised as part of the reserve army, these units were placed under the tactical command of the SS-FHA when deployed in the field. The head of the SS and the *HA* SS-*Gericht* held the final decision on the admission, exit and service of parolees serving in these units and the offender's time spent with these formations counted towards his military obligations (the units listed above replaced the *Reich Verlorenen Haufen*).[85]

The names and details of the felons transferring to the *Bewährungsabteilung* were recorded in both the SS-FHA punishment register and punishment book and each entry noted his crimes, his military delinquency, the court date and any other relevant information. Their names remained in the punishment book until they had transferred from the SS-FHA. *Bewährungsabteilung* parolees continued to receive basic pay, and benefits when Himmler had voiced concerns that his family would suffer as consequence of their withholding. The only awards permitted to be worn on the tunics of these disgraced men were the *Verwundetenabzeichen* and the *Medaille* '*Winterschlacht im Osten* 1941/42', but the *HA* SS-*Gericht* again forbad the awarding of all combat decorations in September of 1942.[86]

Lastly, the November 1941 edict observed that convicts suffering from diseases such as tuberculosis, the disabled, those suffering mental illness, or requiring another type of special medical care were to carry out their sentence in the institutions of the civil judiciary that had a medical hospital. During the pre-judging phase, the courts took into account the offender's medical needs and the trial judge would decide whether the felon was suitable for detention in an SS penal institution. Members of the *Allgemeine*-SS and *Polizei* serving with the military who obtained their punishment from military courts could be declared unsuitable for further use in battle and their punishment and the criminal case file then be sent to the appropriate military district commando. The department handling military reports then forwarded these files to the responsible SS and *Polizei* court and a decision was then taken whether to offer these offenders probation in a suitable SS or *Polizei* unit.[87]

On 13 December 1941 it was commanded, that those *Polizei* convicts judged unsuitable for combat would serve their probation with the *Arbeitsabteilung der Waffen*-SS and the

HA SS-*Gericht* received permission to establish a probation unit for the *Polizei* at the front. Receiving news that Himmler had retained the right to suspend an entire prison sentence for service in a field probation unit, the *HA* SS-*Gericht Amt* I then asked what to do with those who shirked from doing their duty at the front in a probation unit. 'Here in the SS-*Erziehungssturm* Sachsenhausen, or in the SS-*Straflager* Dachau they will have the blindfold removed from their eyes' announced Himmler unambiguously in reply.[88]

During discussions between the *Kanzlei des Führers der* NSDAP and *HA* SS-*Gericht* in November 1941, it was agreed that the SS and *Polizei* courts were competent to deal with clemency cases and both offices agreed to work together on the RSHA cases.[89]

Although concerned that the high casualties facing the German Army had resulted in some families losing their last surviving sons the SS-FHA reiterated their policy of denying last son status to probationers assigned to the *Bewährungsabteilung*.[90]

5.6 Clemency and Rehabilitation Edicts

The 12 November 1941 edict was quickly superseded by further probation, clemency, rehabilitation legislation in the spring of 1942 which enabled the *HA* SS-*Gericht* to establish a uniform method of permitting clemency for military offenders who had regained their honour at the front. These edicts prioritised the front probation process within the SS jurisdiction until virtually all types of offender were urged to accept part prison/part probation court sentences.[97]

In 1941 the leader of the SS had decided that the process to determine a convict's suitability for front probation would be undertaken by three judges of the *HA* SS-*Gericht Amt* III prior to the conclusion of a third of his sentence. All parties involved in this process were advised to submit their applications quickly and the *Amt* III asked that the offender's punishment book was returned to the original sentencing court to enable the appropriate *Gerichtsherr* to submitted their probation or clemency recommendation, (in an effort to speed up the process, these opinions were relayed via radio messages). With everyone's opinions submitted, the punishment book was delivered to the *Reichsführer* for his confirmation and the *Amt* III appear rarely, if ever, to have disagreed with his final decision.[91]

The clemency, rehabilitation process was only undertaken once the probationer had served between three and six months in the *Bewährungsabteilung*, or had demonstrated exceptional bravery, received a wound or had died on the battlefield. To initiate a clemency process, the parolees *Kompanieführer* submitted a truthful, detailed after action report to the *HA* SS-*Gericht* which described the tactical situation, the probationer's actions, how his behaviour had affected the battle and explained the dangers the probationer had faced. The *Amt* III accepting the reports assessment, the probationer was rehabilitated and permitted to return to the troops, or another part of the service. When determining their decision, the *Amt* III took into account whether the probationer was long time member of the *Waffen*-SS, or *Polizei* and had been an officer with a low SS number.[92]

The families of probationers killed in action were notified of the parolee's fate by letter and this document informed them whether his death had resulted in rehabilitation. If by death he had exonerated himself, then the head of the SS authorised the return of his former rank, his name was re-entered in the SS membership list and widow's benefits, such as a death payments and pensions were usually, but not always supplied in full.[93]

How large was the pool of potential probationers? The *HA* SS-*Gericht* estimated that between 500 to 600 convicts were eligible for service in the *Bewährungsabteilung*, the SS-*Infantrie-Ersatz-Bataillon Ost* and other probation units deployed on the Eastern Front between February and March 1942.[94]

By March 1943, the number of available parolees leaving Matzkau each month was estimated at between 200 and 250 inmates, not including those transferring to the probation unit from other sources. In an effort to reduce the size of the prison population those SS divisions fighting on the Eastern Front, with large numbers of non-German troops, received permission to form *Strafkompanie* which were composed of their own delinquents, punished with short sentences.[95]

Becoming aware that it was common knowledge among the prison convicts that a transfer to the *Bewährungsabteilung* was a veritable death sentence, the *HA* SS-*Gericht* also received reports that inmates, fearing leaving prison for the dangers of the front, had begun to refuse to apply for probation. In response the *Amt* III demanded that prison authorities delivered a 'pep' talk to those selected for service in the *Bewährungsabteilung* and made every effort to present the transfer in a positive light. During this discussion, both the prison leader and commandant were commanded to impress on the prospective candidate that parole was an opportunity for redemption and warn them not to become involved in any activity which would warrant a return to prison. Escorted under guard to the *Bewährungsabteilung*, those parolees refusing the offer of probation were transferred to the concentration camps as prisoners.[96]

The 'Measures to be adopted for those Members of the *Wehrmacht* who had purchased with their Courage Re-admittance in an Honourable Place within the Peoples Society' was published as a *Führer* edict on 26 January 1942 and came into force on 21 March 1942. This legislation delegated the right to remove an offender's offence from the punishment register from the head of state to the Chief of the German High Command and permitted probationers with extensive good behaviour reports, or having performed their duties dutifully for a long period of time to be considered for clemency (this condition was waived for those who had suffered heavy wounds). The authorisation to decide clemency decisions outside of Germany was conferred on the *Oberbefehlshaber der Wehrmachtsstelle* on 21 March 1942.[98]

'Due to the requirements of the changing war situation new measures were required for the imposition of probation on the Eastern Front' announced the *Führer* on 2 April 1942 and commanding suitable military convicts, the so-called 'weak characters,' to deploy on the harshest sectors of the front and serve their sentence in dangerous circumstances, the German leader now wished for those convicts judged unsuitable for battle and the irredeemable to leave the safety of their prison cells and join probationary units to labour in dangerous circumstances (the *Bewährungsbataillon* would be reserved for those capable of improvement). Those judged unsuitable for detention in the *Straflager* were ordered into the care of the *Gestapo* and incarcerated in a KL. The *Reichsführer* announced this *Führer* edict to the *Waffen*-SS on 2 April 1942 and considering the parole units reserve units of the *HA* SS-*Gericht*, he demanded that the commanders of these formations monitored the probationers for signs of improvement, or a deterioration in their conduct and then forward these fitness reports to the SS-*Richter beim* RF-SS to permit him to judge whether the parolees sentence should be amended.[99]

Analysing both the 26 January and 2 April 1942 *Führer* edicts, the *Amt* III prepared to draft new regulations for the preparatory process of the rehabilitation process on 17 April 1942. Prior its publication, the *Chef HA* SS-*Gericht* proposed that all clemency/probationary orders emanating from his *Hauptämter* be included in the offender's probation recommendation and to avoid delays during the preparatory phase, he demanded that the parolee's unit leader's reports included all relevant information about their conduct and the circumstances of their wounding or death. At this time, General Scharfe revealed that the head of the SS had entrusted to him the authorisation power to determine the clemency of fallen probationers and from this time the *Reichsführer* would only handle cases of special interest.[100]

General Scharfe also proposed that only part-punished malefactors, those judged to have unsuitable personalities which rendered them unsuitable for continued service in the SS, should in future face an *Ehrenstrafe*, be released from service and removed from the SS. All others would remain in the *Waffen*-SS as troops for the war's duration. Lastly, Scharfe proposed that probationers judged unsuitable would remain in the *Waffen*-SS parole units with no prospect of rehabilitation. His proposals were then presented to the *Chef Ordnungspolizei*, the *Chef* SiPo to determine whether the civil service laws permitted the removal of offenders in this fashion and the *HA* SS-*Gericht* was asked if a milder punishment was appropriate for these types of offender.[101]

'For the Exercise of Mercy Rights in Criminal Law Cases Pertaining to the Jurisdiction of the SS and *Polizei* courts' was published by the *HA* SS-*Gericht* on 2 April 1942 and came into force on 17 April. Supplanting the *Führer* edict from 18 April 1940 and all previous legislation on this matter, the clemency sentencing process was commanded to be implemented according to 'SS suitability' to enable the atonement and retribution for wrongdoing and permit the condemned their fullest possible reintegration into society. Reiterating the demand that clemency was achieved as a result of the felon's re-education in prison, this edict authorised pardons from punishment, the imposition of a criminal penalty and permitted the amendment of judgments, including their abrogation or mitigation. Retaining clemency rights and pardons, the *Führer* reserved the right to exercise clemency in the cases in which the *Oberste* SS and *Polizei* Court had imposed the penalty, where an officer, or *Polizei* administrator with officer rank had been sentenced to death, cases involving an officer, or *Polizei* administrator with officer rank who had committed a crime, or had abused his official authority and was awaiting sentencing and cases where the German leader had expressed a reservation in general, or had expressed an interest in particular single cases and had conferred these powers to the *Reichsführer*. Himmler exercised these rights in cases in which a member of the SS, or *Polizei* faced the death penalty, when officers, or *Polizei* officials with officer rank had been penalised with a prison sentence of six months or greater, where the Führer had already expressed a negative decision and when a renewed request for clemency had been submitted. Authorised to intercede in cases where the *Chef HA* SS-*Gericht* had already reduced the sentence at the confirmation stage, the head of the SS exercised this right when he had himself reserved the pronunciation in general, or in rehabilitation cases of special importance. In all other clemency concerns, Himmler conferred upon General Scharfe the right to exercise clemency in his name. The effect of a pardon was to set aside a death sentence without any legal disadvantages and a special clemency decision set aside an already occurred legal action. The parole unit's leaders were responsible for immediately reporting to the *HA* SS-*Gericht* the names of those who failed to serve their probation properly and reiterating previous regulations, this legislation commanded the clemency process for convicts to be initiated by a service office in writing in the form of a clemency petition and its merits was assessed on the basis of the criminal's personal development; in particular his behaviour in prison. For formal registration, the appeal was submitted to the courts that had imposed the sentence and checking its merits, the responsible tribunal then handled the preparatory part of the process. Applications seeking only to change a sentencing decision remained the responsibility of the *Gerichtsherr* in accordance to § 104 KStVO and the edict of 12 November 1941, but these applications of this type could not be handled as petitions for clemency.

A written order was required from the *Gerichtsherr* in cases where he had rejected a change of execution and this, or at the very least a judicial memorandum, was submitted to the court's official records with his stated his reasons. The courts forwarded pardon petitions to the *HA* SS-*Gericht Amt* III and they exercised the final say in sentencing decisions. The *Gerichtsherr* accepted clemency cases for pardon and it was left to his discretion whether to forward the file to the *Amt* III (if he believed that a part, or full pardon would result from his decision, the *Gerichtsherr* had the authority to temporarily suspend the execution of a sentence in clemency proceedings). All applications seeking to adopt an early redemption of court punishments and disciplinary sanctions were forwarded to the *Amt* III for preliminary processing and included cases in which rehabilitation occurred following the probationer's death before the enemy. Completing its assessment, the *Amt* III then sent the clemency application file back to the responsible court. This docket included a probation report, the offender's combat record, his acts before the enemy, reported evidence of any outstanding behaviour, a summary assessment from the disciplinary superior, the date of his wounding, the nature and location of the injury and the address of his next of kin. The tribunal then forward its response to the *Amt* III and if granting clemency, then the 2 April 1942 legislation permitted the competent court to amend, or strike the probationer's details from the punishment register. For all SS and *Polizei* on probation with the troops, but not deployed with the parole units, the *HA* SS-*Gericht* demanded that the unit commander submit a copy of his report to the responsible court, the SS-FHA and to themselves. In all other cases, the rehabilitation and the preparation of the clemency process was the responsibility of the sentencing SS and *Polizei* court.[102]

Completing the preparatory process, the courts then sought a clemency decision from the *Führer*, *Reichsführer*, or from the *Chef HA* SS-*Gericht* respectively. Again, the final decision in these cases was determined on the contents of the offender's clemency folder, which contained the court record and the opinions of each service office involved in the decision-making process. In principle, parole and probation were only granted for front deployment, but if this proved impossible, or inappropriate, such as for physically unfit offenders, then the *HA* SS-*Gericht* was authorised to approve the felon an 'exceptional opportunity' to serve his probation in the civil sector for a correspondingly longer duration. The suspended sentence was dependent on special stipulations and conditions and the 2 April edict demanded that the final clemency process was undertaken by the *Amt* III within three months before the expiry of the probation period. The probationer's court file, clemency folder and the *Gerichtsherr* statement was then submitted to the *Amt* III case worker for him to decide whether to suspend the punishment and adopt a new sentence. A suspended sentence could be revoked at any time by the providing office and the court was notified by letter when an appeal for clemency had been rejected. The 2 April edict ended with special provisions for field court clemency proceedings. When these cases had been judged to be against the locally adopted replacement court regulation from the *HA* SS-*Gericht Amt* IIa from 6 May 1942, then those field courts deployed with divisions, or brigades could refrain from creating a clemency instruction if it resulted in a processing delay, (a note to this effect was attached to the clemency process cover letter before forwarding to the *HA* SS-*Gericht* for decision). Warning that the judicial opinion would always be based on the clemency case presented to the judge, the April 1942 edict prohibited the filing of dispatches which sought the advice of the involved trial chairman and observed that a request for the *Gerichtsherr* opinion could be waived in cases where he had not expressively reserved his opinion. SS-*Richter* were advised that when the division, or brigade had relocated, it remained his duty to find and obtain indispensable statements from other service offices, in particular to obtain the fitness records from the *Straflager der* SS *und Polizei* Dachau and the *Strafvollzugslagers der* SS *und Polizei* Danzig-Matzkau. Obtaining such statements was always undertaken when the court had suggested sending this file. The *HA* SS-*Gericht* demanded that the applying division, or brigade court sent the criminal file and the clemency request to them by the quickest route and commanded all communications to pass through their service office.[103]

The 2 April 1942 edict formed the basis for all subsequent clemency/probation legislation and amendments, or additional commands were published in the *Mitteilung des Hauptamt* SS-*Gericht*, *Hinweis des* SS-*Richter* and other SS publications. Analysing both the 26 January and 2 April 1942 edict and the *Verordnungsblatt der Waffen*-SS from 21 April the same year, Burmeister observed on 4 May 1942 that the vast majority of clemency appeals were actually handled by the head of the SS and General Breithaupt and only a very few cases were submitted directly to the *Führer* to obtain his decision. To ensure a uniform process, Burmeister determined that both the views of the *Reichsführer* and General Scharfe were required in these cases, but from this time, the clemency section of the *Amt* III would handle these types of cases.[104]

The 15 May 1942 edition of the *Verordnungsblatt der Waffen*-SS contains an *HA* SS-*Gericht* ordinance which announced that seriously wounded probationers were permitted to receive clemency while still alive. The *Bewährungsabteilung* commander had orders to submit all rehabilitation appeals and recommendations directly to the *Reichsführer* and *Amt* III and to ensure a quick and accurate process, the *Amt* III handled cases where there was an imminent prospect of death, (i.e. risk to life injuries or deadly disease). The divisional commander had orders to send a telex directly to the SS-*Richter beim* RF-SS to request that he sought the SS leader's decision to preserve the parolee's life. His decision was communicated to the divisional commander and *HA* SS-*Gericht* and they supplied rehabilitation comments.[105]

A draft of the 'Delegation of the Criminal Expiation Law' which transferred the right to amend the punishment register for SS and *Polizei* courts convictions from the *Reichsjustizministerium* to the *Reichsführer*'s jurisdiction was prepared on 25 April 1942. Although Hitler supported the transfer of these powers to Himmler, the *Reichsjustizministerium* expressed their desire to retain the criminal expatiation rights for the SS jurisdiction, as it did with the existing judiciaries, fearing that making an exception for the SS would result in the military jurisdiction demanding the same rights. An agreement reached between the various parties, the right to erase entries for SS and *Polizei* criminals in the punishment register were transferred from the *Führer* to the *Reichsführer* on 17 October 1942 and from this time, the *HA* SS-*Gericht* was now virtually free to run its own legal affairs without the interference of the civil judiciary.[106]

In July 1942, the head of the SS commanded those judged unworthy to bear arms to transfer to a field probation unit to fight partisans. Expanding on this policy in late 1942, Himmler ordered the prison 'old timers', those serving long terms of *Zuchthaus* and those handed a suspended death sentences to be given the opportunity to redeem themselves in a probation unit. Offering the vast majority of this category of miscreant a chance to fight at the front, those accepting the proposal were transferred to the SS-*Sonderbataillon Dirlewanger* in Belorussia.[107]

In stark contrast to previous regulations, in November 1942 the *Reichsführer* begun accepting clemency applications from parents, spouses and children in criminal cases involving ethnic-German SS men, those whose punishments exceeded two years in length. Hoping to foster a good feeling in the ethnic-German community and strengthen their debt to the SS, Himmler proposed ending these convicts' prison sentences if he had obtained favourable prison fitness report, the inmate had been recommended for probation against the enemy and those cases in which he was convinced that the felon would not relapse into delinquency again and held no hard feelings for his mistreatment.[108]

Seeking to make well his losses and buttress the front line with fresh troops following the German Army's defeat at Stalingrad, Adolf Hitler then delegated to the *Chef* OKW the clemency decision for all offences, except death sentences, or concerns of a fundamental importance to the *Reichkriegsgericht* (National war court). Made aware of this legislation, the SS-*Richter beim* RF-SS immediately initiated negotiations with the *Reichsjustizministerium* with the purpose of conferring these same clemency rights to the SS leader. Himmler then instigated negotiations with the *Reichsjustizminister* to obtain these powers on 11 March 1943 and commanding all clemency decisions to be undertaken by an SS-*Richter*, he ordered offenders to be thoroughly instructed and if granted a clemency decision then be told that they must prove worthy in future. Judges assessing clemency for non-SS offenders, such as members of the *Polizei* in the occupied areas of Europe had instructions to act sensitively, but make tough decisions where necessary for fear that leniency was wrongly interpreted as weakness.[109]

In June 1943 the SS-FHA demanded that their disciplinary office supplied a transfer letter prior to probationers leaving the courts, or prisons for the *Bewährungsabteilung*, and this contained the judgement and sentencing order. The SS-FHA determined in December 1943 that those offenders judged with diminished mental ability be permitted to join the parole units at the front, or deploy against the partisans.[110]

'Face the consequences of their act and be punished' announced the head of the SS on 23 July 1943 and commanding criminals to make amends for their shame, he ordered unhealthy convicts to the front. Those felons who had previously been wounded in battle could avoid front service, but Himmler demanded that they be sent to Russia to fight partisans. Dr Braußе composed a draft edict titled 'Limitations for the Punishment and Probation for Members of the SS and *Polizei*' on 26 August 1943 and a final draft was announced on 29 September:

> [...] Following the act the criminal has to bear the punishment. He alone is responsible for his situation. It is appropriate for me to demand from him that he pulls himself together and finds a solution for his own shame. If a criminal is unfit for combat, then it is appropriate that a suitable probation is found for him, or he serves his [prison] sentence. I demand from the criminal that he, without consideration for his fitness, proves himself during his deployment at the front or in the rebel partisan regions. The determining factor is the principle of health of the convict at the time of the offence. If he was healthy enough to commit a crime then he is also healthy enough to, by appropriate deployment, to atone by completely serving his punishment. If the criminal was wounded in the field prior to the offence, or had suffered damage in service then this may of course be taken into account.[111]

The *Reichsführer* turned his attention again to the subject of clemency for SS, *Polizei* and *Polizei* administrators and now wished to obtain authorisation to rehabilitate all *Polizei* probationers. The 'Officials Law for the Rehabilitation of Severely Maimed Police who are Situated in Probation Deployment' was published in the form of a *Chef Ordnungspolizei* circular on 22 July 1943 and included special regulations for the rehabilitation of *Polizei* administrators punished with front probation deployment. On a case by case basis, this legislation permitted Himmler to reinstate *Polizei* officials with a legal rehabilitation when they had been severely maimed in probation deployment. Exceptions to this ruling were the ranks of *Major* and *Regierungsrat* and upwards respectively, the right to rehabilitate officers and officials remained in the hands of the Interior Minister and the power to pardon was reserved for the *Führer*. To ensure the rapid implementation of the amnesty law in all appropriate cases, the *Chef Ordnungspolizei* recommended that divisional commanders, for the appropriate rank, submitted their rehabilitation request directly to the *Reichsführer* and their message included the current military rank of the severely disfigured and his last police service rank. Concerning follow up questions about re-employment to the division commanders, it was suggested that the head of the SS carried out this deed by telephone, radio, or telegram respectively. For legal and practical considerations it was recommended that a template be created for all messages, including for those leaving hospitals. Himmler was served with a full removal notice for cases involving the reinstatement of *Majors/Regierungsrat* and upwards and the most seriously wounded, the *Chef Ordnungspolizei* suggested that Himmler was served with a full removal notice. To enable his offices to take measures for further implementation, all copies of re-employment orders were sent to the *Chef Ordnungspolizei* and his office was kept abreast of any further developments. In additional discussions between the *HA* SS-*Gericht* and the *Ordnungspolizei* it was agreed to draft a new regulation for the civil service rights for the rehabilitation of severely disabled members of the *Polizei* on 3 August 1944. This regulation was subsequently published in the *Anordnungsblatt der* SS- *und Polizeigerichtsbarkeit* and the *Verordnungsblatt der Waffen*-SS on15 May 1942:

Possibility of Rehabilitating via Probation.

1.) Concerning punished SS members the unit leaders are to recommend to the court a clemency measure if:
a) He had behaved well for a long time and in particular has excelled with exemplary commitment.
b) The convicted is severely wounded, killed or died from the effects of wounding.

The same applies to a limited rehabilitation. This includes men, whose SS-*Ehrenstrafe* has been converted into a simple services release for the duration of the war only and continued military service in the *Waffen*-SS.

The submitted applications are to include a probation report from the unit to the responsible SS and *Polizei* courts that prepared them and then these are forward these to the *HA* SS-*Gericht*.

2.) In urgent cases: (for example, risk to life caused injury or disease) the division commander will immediately report the probation proposal to the SS-*Richter beim* RF-SS by telegram to enable him to obtain the immediate decision of the *Reichsführer*-SS. He must also submit reports concerning all those men with an SS-*Ehrenstrafe* and those with restricted rehabilitation.

3) The probation report shall contain:
a) The criminal's past battles, any special combat, other evidence of his use against the enemy or outstanding probation of another kind,
b) The nature of the wound and place of current wound,
c) The address of his next of kin.

4) To apply for the adoption and the early redemption of the disciplinary provisions accordingly. The probation report, a copy of the disciplinary penalty order, an extract of the criminal book and a copy of the main card must be accompanied by self-written biography of the punished. These documents must be sent from the SS and *Polizei* courts along with any resulting files to the appropriate unit that is responsible for forwarding them to the *HA* SS-*Gericht*.[112]

During the second half of the war the *HA* SS-*Gericht* became increasingly preoccupied with simplifying and speeding up this convoluted clemency process. Discussing ways to clarify the clemency instructions with *Hstuf.* Fritz Killing in Munich in December 1943, Günther Burmeister concluded that the clemency evidence should only contain personal information about the convicted criminal and include the exact computation time and the *HA* SS-*Gericht* proposal. He then suggested that everything else, especially criminal records and assessment appreciations be presented to the SS-*Richter beim* RF-SS at another time, so long as the general aspiration was to simplify business traffic. Leaving the detailed arrangements to the *HA* SS-*Gericht*, along with the corresponding clemency system instructions, Burmeister advised retaining clemency evidence in files sent to the *Führer* at the *Reich* Chancellery.[113]

Accepting that the war situation required a simplification of the clemency, rehabilitation and criminal eradication process, the *HA* SS-*Gericht* desired that the troops witnessed the quick imposition of punishments and wished to relieve the work burden on its case workers. As a consequence of these needs the *Amt* III published further clemency regulations on 21 January 1944 that offered time savings in these proceedings. Both at the clemency and rehabilitation stage of the process this regulation limited the right of the local *Gerichtsherr* to question the leader of the SS in clemency to death penalty cases, officer cases, criminal cases, trials in which the *Gerichtsherr* had reserved his opinion and issues in which an immediate suspension of sentence had occurred or had been achieved by a decision in the clemency case. The SS and *Polizei* courts received orders to enter the date of notification, the date they had informed the parole units of processes introduction and make five copies of the offender's fitness report, which listed his misconduct and punishment. All copies of the clemency, or sentencing file was then sent to the *Amt* III and they demanded that all clemency evidence from earlier processes be submitted to them in triplicate. The SS-*Richter beim* RF-SS was warned to avoid duplicating clemency paths if he chose to write to directly to the SS and *Polizei* courts during the preparatory process.[114]

A new clemency regulation was drafted for Himmler's jurisdiction on 3 March 1944 that applied a clemency decision for death sentence cases to enable their front probation:

> […] As you are aware, the *Reichsführer*-SS has clearly decided, that attempts to obtain his clemency decision by telegram, which presents the facts, can only be attempted in very urgent case decisions and must include the signature of the respective, responsible court *Chefrichter*. For this measure the SS leader has decided to ensure the suspension of an immediate execution of death sentences and other offences for those who are still worthy of a front probation and put them to immediate use. I request that this agreed judicial responsibility arrangement for the *Reichsführer*-SS also be extended to the clemency responsibilities of the *Chef HA* SS-*Gericht*. The deployment of the *Zuchthaus* criminal must be permitted immediately once the confirmation of the decision has been received by the *Gerichtsherrn* of the troops, or when the *Chef HA* SS-*Gericht* has given his consent by telegram.[115]

Discussions had taken place between the *Reichsjustizministerium* and the *HA* SS-*Gericht* since early 1943 to enable the transfer of powers held by the *Führer* to the *Reichsführer* in cases where the German leader was the first point of call in the clemency process. Acknowledging that these cases were rare, the SS-*Richter beim* RF-SS nevertheless considered it necessary to formulate a new regulation to enable a transfer of these clemency rights to Himmler and regulate all legal entities. With Hitler's approbation, the *Reichsjustizministerium* agreed to this transfer of powers without the need to publish an edict. It was agreed that when a *Führer* pardon had been judged appropriate, unless the specific nature of the case prohibited his suggestion, then he would be permitted to submit a further clemency decision.[116]

In late 1944 the *HA* SS-*Gericht* proposed to deploy almost all types of SS and *Polizei* convicts to the front, prior to the completion of the clemency process, to undertake probation. On 28 November the same year the SS-*Richter beim* RF-SS suggested all *Zuchthaus* and capital punishment convicts were in future sent to the SS-*Straflager* Dachau immediately after sentencing, to enable the prison *Leiter* to observe their behaviour and prepare a fitness report while they waited for confirmation of the punishment. In cases where a term of *Zuchthaus* and *Gefängnis* had been imposed, it was recommended that in those punished with *Gefängnis*, though few in number, be offered probation immediately and the clemency process enacted while he fought at the front (a throwback to the *Sonderkommando* process in 1940). On 16 December the SS-*Richter beim* RF-SS demanded that sentenced offenders be sent directly to prison to awaiting confirmation of the punishment and this opportunity was used to educate and observe the inmates with the intention of arranging a quick opportunity for their front probation.[117]

It was inevitable, given the convoluted appeals process that mistakes were made during the case file's course through the judiciary. One case highlights the lack of cooperation that existed between the SS-*Richter beim* RF-SS and the *Amt* III in 1944. *St.OJ*. Rother's wife visited the *HA* SS-*Gericht* in Munich to speak with her husbands' case worker on 25 October 1944. Here, *Stubaf.* Dr Folkerts, assured the convict's wife that the head of the SS had yet to confirm her husband's death sentence and voiced his certainty that he would soon be reprieved. Unfortunately, Himmler confirmed Rother's execution on

20 November and informed of this decision, *Frau* Rother met with the SS-*Richter beim* RF-SS at his Berlin office to demand an explanation for the misinformation and appeal for clemency. Her petition for mercy fell on death ears and Rother's execution was carried out. As a consequence of this muddle, the SS-*Richter beim* RF-SS was commanded to work closely with the *Amt* III to produce a simplified rehabilitation process that would prevent such mistakes occurring again.[118]

Later, it was decided that only the *HA* SS-*Gericht*, or the relevant court was entitled to send a letter of sentence confirmation, or reprieve to the offender's relatives and the *HA* SS-*Gericht* case officer became solely responsible for the reprieve decision. In addition, it was agreed that Himmler alone would confirm death sentence and punishment cases and he reserved the right to impose a final opinion. New regulations were published with these procedural changes and from this time, the courts were authorised to issue a reprieve verdict which the *Amt* III reviewed. In order to save time and the duplication of work, two expert officers of the *Amt* III were tasked with completing the finished punishment book and completing this business, the file was sent to the SS-*Richter beim* RF-SS with all the relevant appendices for him to add his observations (he then sought the opinions of the relevant departments involved in the case).[119]

Writing to the SS-*Richter beim* RF-SS on 22 December 1944, the *Amt* III suggested establishing a standard form of reporting *Ehrenstrafe* punishments. Noting that mistakes were 'frequent' in these cases, they complained that these mishaps prevented the promotion of *Waffen*-SS members who had received restricted rehabilitation orders. In future, the *HA* SS-*Gericht* asked that clemency decision applications for a limited rehabilitation included the offenders name, the date of release from the remaining punishment, the date of the *Ehrenstrafe* punishment and his service rank.[120]

5.7 *Bewährungsabteilung der Waffen*-SS

Initially known as the *Straf-und Bewährungsabteilung* (punishment and probation battalion) the *Reichsführer* commanded the establishment of what became known as the *Bewährungsabteilung der Waffen*-SS on 2 July 1941 to provide suitable paroled convicts with military training for the remaineder of their court sentence. Establishing a single rifle company at the SS-*Kaserne* Heinrich Himmler in Prague-Rusin on 1 November 1941, the SS-*Infanterie-Ersatz-Bataillon Deutschland* provided support and training. Transferring to Dublowitz bei Seltscham in December the same year, the battalion was placed under the command of the SS-*Wachbataillon Prag* the following year. Probationers—known as riflemen, not SS riflemen—initially wore two blank collar patches on their tunic collars and omitting the national eagle from the upper left arm of the jacket, a crossed grenade, over rifle collar patch had been issued to the troops of the Dirlewanger battalion on 29 January 1943 and was worn by all parolees. The structure and equipping of the battalion was identical to a field unit and the SS-FHA *Amt* IIa and IIb supplied the staff cadre, equipment and vehicles.[121]

Born in Frankfurt am Main on 25 May 1925, Max Kümmel joined the *Waffen*-SS in May 1942 and had been an inmate in the *Strafvollzugslager der* SS *und Polizei* Danzig-Matzkau from May 1943. Transferring to the *Bewährungsabteilung* during October 1943, at that time he recalled that located in Chlum, it was composed like a normal infantry battalion with 1,000 men and command of the battalion lay in two officers' hands (Böhm).[122]

Transferring to Graf Schwarzenberg's *Schloss* Chlum at Dublowitz near Seltscham on 10 June 1942, a town 40 kilometres from Prague, the battalion had grown to a strength of 500 troops by October the same year and eventually became an independent command under the SS-*Truppenübungsplatz* Böhmen-Mähren.[123]

Later, the *Bewährungsabteilung* split into two separate training battalions and non-German parolees were segregated into a separate section. Delinquent parolees were subject to the disciplinary regulations of then SS and *Polizei* jurisdiction and disobedience was punished with punishment drill, detention, or a return to prison. Probationers committing a serious offence faced prosecution before the SS- *und Polizei-Gericht* VIII, Prague.[124]

Short term and long term parolees reported to the *Bewährungsabteilung* for military training and remained with this holding unit until returned to their original unit, a front formation or a divisional *Strafkompanie.* Those paroled from long prison sentences could find themselves attached to independent *Bewährungszug* (parolee sections) which were assigned with one of the three HSSPF in the occupied eastern territories. These probationers conducted long range patrols and fought against the partisans until their death or rehabilitation. The SS-*Grenadier-Ausbildung- und Ersatz-Bataillon Ost* in Breslau provided the *Bewährungszug* with a home depot. The *Bewährungsabteilung* also supplied troops for both the SS-*Fallschirmjägerabteilung* 500, the SS-*Sonderverbände Friedenthal* from 1943 and additionally for the SS-*Jäger-Bataillon* 502, later the SS-*Jäger-Bataillon Mitte* and the SS-*Sonderregiment Dirlewanger*. The relationship with the latter force resulted in the *Bewährungsabteilung* becoming the reserve battalion of the 36. *Waffen-Grenadier*-Division *der* SS in early 1945.[125]

Name: Karl Mercinsky.
Last Rank: SS-*Untersturmführer*.
Born: 9.8.1916 in Mannheim.
NSDAP-Nr.: 2.571.125 (joined 1.10.1935).
SS-Nr.: 270.826 (joined 1.4.1935).
HJ Service: 1929-1934.
Prewar Assignments:
LSSAH 1.4.1935–1.4.1937.
SS-VT LSSAH from 15.7.1938.
Wartime Assignments:
Kraft. Tech. Lehrabteilung der SS 30.1.-6.7.1942.
2. *Instand Abteilung* / SS-*Panzer-Grenadier*-Division *Das Reich* 6.7.1942–25.9.1942.
SS-*Kraft-Ersatz-Bataillon* 25.9.1942–21.1.1943.

Bewährungsabteilung in 1.1943.
SS-*Sonderregiment Dirlewanger* in 1944.
Promotions:
30.1.1942 SS-*Untersturmführer der Reserve.*

Notes: Attending *Volksschule* for four classes, Mercinsky left full time education and was employed as a clerk/salesman. While assigned to the *Das Reich* maintenance battalion, Mercinsky was accused of committing self-mutilation and placed in remand detention until transferred to a reserve battalion to await his trial. Arraigned before the courts martial of the SS- *und Polizei-Gericht* X, Den Haag on 21 January 1943, the tribunal judged Mercinsky guilty of the charge and punished him with five years' *Zuchthaus*, ordered his expulsion from the SS and declared him unworthy to bear arms (the year spent on remand was subtracted from the sentence). Confirming the judgement, the *Reichsführer* set the punishment aside for a term of *Gefängnis* of the same duration, less time served. Revoking his unworthiness to bear arms, Himmler offered Mercinsky the opportunity for probation, which he accepted. Transferred to the *Bewährungsabteilung* in January 1943, Mercinsky, by a circuitous route was eventually assigned to the SS-*Sonderregiment.* Publishing the confirmation order on 20 August 1944, the time elapsed between his sentencing announcement and sentence was not discount from his punishment.[126]

Name: Hans Mickeleit.
Last Rank: SS-*Hauptsturmführer.*
Born: 19.3.1898 in Werdohl Kreis Altena/Hagen.
NSDAP-Nr.: 862.154 (joined 1.12.1931).
SS-Nr.: 37.237 (joined 15.2.1932).
Prewar Assignments:
Jungdeutschen Orden Siegerland 1920–1926.
4. / III. / 30. SS-*Standarte* (Bochum) 1.12.1932–24.8.1933.
Two year *Offizier-Lehrgang* SS-*Junkerschulen* Möllen, Braunchweig and Essen 1933/1934.
III. / 30. SS-*Standarte* 69 30.11.1933-1.5.1934.
Adjutant III. / 30. SS-*Standarte* until 29.11.1933.
Adjutant III. / 25. SS-*Standarte* (Essen) until 1.5.1935.
Adjutant 25 SS-*Motorsturm* 1.6.1934-25.1.1935.
Led the 6. / II. / 5. SS-*Motorsturm* 26.1.-25.4.1935.
Adjutant KL Columbia Haus 26.4.1935-31.10.1935.
Stab SS-TV from 1.11.1935 (*Gruf.* Eicke's personal secretary).
Schützhaftlagerführer des KL Sachsenhausen 1.8.1938–1.4.1940.
Wartime Assignments:
Hauptfürsorge-und Versorgungsamt der SS in 1940.
SS-*Fürsorgeführer* for Elbe, (IV) (Dresden) in 1940.
Officer of the *Oberabschnitt Warthe* (Posen) until 20.2.1940–1.5.1942.
FF Warthe SS-*Standort*ältester Posen 7.8.1941–1.5.1942.

*Bewährungsabteilung der Waffen-*SS 1942.
SS-*Infantrie-Ersatz-Bataillon Ost* 8.1942–13.8.1943.
Stab Oberabschnitt Ukraine from 13.8.1943.
Stab SSPF *Lublin* in 1943
Stellvertreter Tomaschow SS-*Landwachschule* 1.12.1943–10.1.1944.
Stellvertreter Streibel Bataillon 11.1.1944–1.11.1944.

Promotions:

0.0.1920	*Gefreiter.*
20.4.1934	SS-*Untersturmführer der Allgemeine-*SS.
15.9.1935	SS-*Obersturmführer der Allgemeine-*SS.
30.1.1936	SS-*Hauptsturmführer der Allgemeine-*SS.
12.9.1937	SS-*Sturmbannführer der Allgemeine-*SS.
9.11.1940	SS-*Obersturmbannführer der Allgemeine-*SS.
30.6.1942	*Schütze.*
1.10.1944	SS-*Untersturmführer der Reserve.*
2.10.1944	SS-*Obersturmführer der Reserve.*
3.10.1944	SS-*Hauptsturmführer der Reserve.*

Decorations & Awards:

1914-18	*Eisernes Kreuz II. Klasse.*
1914-18	*Verwundetenabzeichen in Schwarz.*
0.0.19__	SS-*Zivilabzeichen* (Nr. 22.890).
0.0.19__	SA-*Sportsabzeichen in Bronze.*
0.0.19__	*Deutsches Reichssportabzeichen in Silber.*
0.0.19__	SS-*Ehrenwinkel für alte Kämpfer.*
0.0.19__	*Totenkopfring der* SS.
0.0.19__	*Ehrendegen des Reichsführer-*SS.
0.0.1938	*Die Medaille zur Erinnerung an den* 1. Oktober 1938 (Sudetenland).
0.0. 19__	*Dienstauszeichnung der* SS III. *Stufe.*
13.5.1943	*Spange zum Eisernen Kreuz* II. *Klasse.*
0.0.19__	*Tapferkeitsauzeichnung für Ostvolker* I.I *Klasse in Silber.*
0.0.19__	*Kriegsverdienstkreuz II. Klasse mit Schwertern.*
0.0.19__	*Bulgarien Kriegserinnerungsmedaille.*
0.0.19__	*Ungarischen Kriegserinnerungsmedaille mit Schwertern.*

Notes: Attending *Volksschule* for seven classes and then trade school, Mickeleit mustered with the Guard Foot Rgt. at the end of 1916 and was wounded in the upper thigh on 30 August 1918. Leaving hospital in 1920, Mickeleit was then employed at his father's business. Marrying his fiancée Leni J., (b. 7.2.1898 in Siegen) on 19 March 1923, they had three children up to the point when records ceased in May 1945. He mustered with the Eisserfeld SA in December 1931.

Mickeleit and his family left the city of Dresden in February 1941 and lived at the Posen Continental Hotel from 27 March to 17 April 1941 which was owned by *Ustuf.*

Helmut Schmidt. Mickeleit was appointed to the SS-*Standort* Posen in August 1941. Accepting an invoice from Schmidt on 20 June 1941, Mickeleit submitted this to the administration office to enable his reimbursement for his expenses. Realising that Mickeleit had overcharging for his accommodation costs, it was later discovered that he had lived with another officer and created a false invoice. *Hstuf.* Maier then denounced Mickeleit for embezzlement and a court's investigation was then initiated on suspicion of him committing fraud. Ordered to return to the welfare headquarters in Berlin on 6 December 1941, the charge substantiated, Mickeleit was arraigned before the courts martial of the SS- *und Polizei-Gericht* III, Berlin on 18 February 1942 (case Nr; St. L. II 366/1941). The court chairman *Stubaf.* Wetzling was supported in his deliberations by *Staf. Erich* Giebeler and *Ostubaf.* Albert Uhlig. *Hstuf.* Heinz Meurin prosecuted the case. Judged guilty of the charges, the tribunal punished Mickeleit with eight months' *Gefängnis* and ordering his demotion, the court recommended front probation and the restoration of his rank in the future. The *Reichsführer* confirmed his sentence on 30 June 1942 and permitted the offer of front deployment. Released from the *Warthe* welfare office in May 1942, Mickeleit served part of his punishment in the *Strafvollzugslager der* SS *und Polizei* Danzig-Matzkau before accepting front probation.

The *Bewährungsabteilung* forwarded Mickeleit to the front in August 1942 and as a rifleman, he fought with the III. / SS-*Infantrie*-Rgt. 10. Earning his rehabilitation with an SSPF on 20 November 1943, Mickeleit's superiors submitted positive fitness reports to the court that noted that he had fought against partisans. As a consequence, his commander expressed his full support for promotion to officer rank and this was conferred on Mickeleit in October 1944. The SS pay office was notified of his change in circumstances on 4 October and the former parolee reported to the *Ausbildunglager der* SS *Trawniki*, where his duties included the training of Baltic, Russian and Ukrainian auxiliary guards for the concentration camps in the East. Through his participation in the partisan war and the Nazi's genocidal actions in the east, Mickeleit once again served as an officer, but his re-admittance into the SS remains doubtful.[127]

The allocation of older officers to the *Bewährungsabteilung* resulted in accusations of lazy leadership and a belief that this situation hampered the parolee's rehabilitation. Writing on this subject in May 1943, Himmler commanded the SS-FHA to provide better trained officers and non-commissioned officers for the unit and an experienced front line field commander was selected to lead the battalion. Born in Berlin on 17 January 1894, *Ostubaf.* Friedrich Schröder, (SS Nr. 78.641), had formally led the 2. / SS-*Totenkopf-Infantrie*-Rgt. 9 and took command of the *Bewährungsabteilung* in 1944.[128]

5.8 *Arbeitsabteilung der Waffen*-SS

Depending on which source is viewed, the *Arbeitsabteilung der Waffen*-SS was established in the KL Oranienburg in June 1941, or at the SS-*Truppenübungsplatz* Debica on 1

September 1941 for probationers declared unworthy to bear arms, judged incapable of fighting, possessing unsuitable personalities for service in a military unit, or had committed crimes so terrible that their presence in a combat unit was detrimental to that unit's morale. The battalion also inducted convicts who had not completed their military obligation, but had been judged suitable for service in this unit. Equipped in accordance to a field unit, the SS-FHA *Abt.* IVC supplied horses to the *Arbeitsabteilung* for its single *Baukompanie* (labour company). The *Arbeitsabteilung* troops wore uniforms without any insignia in accordance with SS order Nr. 16 from 1 September 1941, (Nr. 348), [129]

The leader of the SS-*Wachbataillon* Debica, *Ostubaf.* Hans v.Feil, was responsible for the probationers' training and he maintained discipline in accordance with the SS-DBO. Delinquent probationers were subject to the punishments of the SS and *Polizei* judiciary and persistent offenders returned to prison to complete their sentence. Those committing a crime while assigned to this formation faced trial and punishment before the SS- *und Polizei-Gericht* VI, Krakau.[130]

Once established, the SS-FHA demanded that the *HA* SS-*Gericht* only transferred felons to the *Arbeitsabteilung* once they had served a minimum of twelve months of their prison sentence.[131]

The Debica branch prison was created in early 1943 to detain the men of the *Arbeitsabteilung* and offenders awaiting trial or serving short detention sentences. Initially, these parolees built barracks and new facilities for the Debica works leader and later laboured for the local *Polizei*. In time, enough parolees had been assigned to the battalion to establish two *Baukompanie* and a *Werkstattkompanie* (workshop) and legionary convicts were segregated into their own section. Reversing an earlier decision, Himmler prohibited *Polizei* probationers from transferring to the *Arbeitsabteilung* on 4 December 1941.[132]

Zuchthaus category military convicts were permitted to serve their probation with the *Arbeitsabteilung* in late 1944.[133]

A 52 man-strong group of *Arbeitsabteilung* parolees left Debica for the HSSPF *Rußland-Mitte Nachschubkommando* in April 1942 and here, they constructed accommodation, a kitchen, shooting range and farmed the land. Later in the same year a handful of parolees formed small patrol groups to defend local railways and roads. In the spring of 1942 the *Arbeitsabteilung* was declared an independent force under the control of the SS-FHA and the battalion commander was appointed the disciplinary superior.[134]

In the wake of the *Arbeitsabteilung* transferring to the command region of the HSSPF *Rußland-Mitte Nachschubkommando* a decision was taken to establish an *Ersatzkompanie* (reserve) for the battalion in the SS-*Truppenübungsplatz* Debica. Remaining in Debica until July/August 1944, the *Ersatzkompanie* then transferred to Danzig-Matzkau.[135]

The commander of the *Arbeitsabteilung* in the spring of 1942, *Ostuf.* Richard Harzer had been born in Gelenau/Erzgebirge on 6 May 1895, (SS Nr. 47.166). Musering with an SS-*Infantrie*-Rgt. in November 1941, he was assigned to the SS-*Truppenübungsplatz Böhmen-Mähren* in November 1944. Not every parolee assigned to the *Arbeitsabteilung* proved entirely happy with their assignment. On 22 June 1943 the HSSPF *Rußland-Mitte* informed the *HA* SS-*Gericht* that the deserter *Schütze* Gerhard Rockstroh had been apprehended by the SS-*Artillerie-Ausbildung- und Ersatz*-Rgt. in Munich and had been detained. His case was subsequently handed to the SS- *und Polizei-Gericht* Munich for investigation. Concluding their enquries, the tribunal indicted Rockstroh for desertion.[136]

Released from the *Zweiglager* Ludwigsfelde, SS-*Mann* Gunther Goerke then joined the *Arbeitsabteilung*. Prior to his sentencing, Goerke had served as a radio man in the SS-*Nachschub* HQ (*FPNr* 22.825).[137]

The success of the Red Army summer offensive ejected the German forces from Soviet territory and the probationer's war against the Soviet partisan was finally at an end. Their *raison d'être* no longer applicable, Himmler announced the dissolution of the *Arbeitsabteilung* on 6 June 1944 and regardless of age and suitability, they entire compliment was ordered to the SS-*Sonderbrigade Dirlewanger*. It was left to the brigade commander to decide for himself which of their number were fit for frontline fighting. Events on the Eastern Front precluded the battalion's immediate transfer to Dirlewanger. The Red Army summer offensive over-run the SS-*Truppenübungsplatz* Moorlager *bei* Bereza Kartuska in occupied Poland in July 1944 and forced to retreat to Brest-Litovsk, the men of the *Arbeitsabteilung* and finally gathered themselves in the SS-*Truppenübungsplatz Böhmen–Mähren*. Here, they laboured at the hydroelectric plant at Lohmen *bei* Pirna, south of Dresden, until the battalions disbandment was again ordered in January 1945. The *Arbeitsabteilung* parolees, excluding the rehabilitated, then received orders to report to the *Bewährungsabteilung* at Dublowitz.[138]

At this time, the *Bewährungsabteilung* had been appointed the training and reserve formation for the 36. *Waffen-Grenadier*-Division *der* SS.[139]

5.9 *Polizei Zug*

By the outbreak of war the SS and *Polizei* had not yet completely merged into one force, but policemen deployed at the front line, or engaged in security duties were subject to court's punishment in accordance to the 17 October 1939 edict. Forming a combat division from troops of the SS-VT, *Ordnungspolizei* and *Wehrmacht* in 1939, this formation, the SS-*Polizeidivision*, participated in the invasion of France during the spring/summer of 1940. In early 1941 the *Chef Ordnungspolizei* demanded and received permission to establish a probation unit for the *Polizeidivision*, which was known as the *Polizei Sondereinheit*, (Police special unit) and its candidates undertook pioneer training with the 1. / SS-*Pionier-Ersatz-Bataillon* in Dresden. Recognising their existence, the November 1941 edict contained provisions for the probation of *Polizei* convicts.[140]

Polizei offenders serving part of their sentence could, if judged suitable, then apply for front probation. If accepted, the parolee relinquished his service grade to the rank of rifleman. The agreement of the *Chef Ordnungspolizei* and *Chef* SiPo-*und* SD was required to transfer of officers, police officials of officer rank before their transfer a probation unit and all interested parties in the process added their opinions to his punishment file. Consensus obtained between the various department chiefs, the offender's punishment file was forwarded to the *Reichsführer* for him to decide whether to impose a probation order. If it had been decided that the offender's entire prison punishment was to be served in its entirety, then the miscreant transferred to the *Strafvollzugslager der* SS *und Polizei* Danzig–Matzkau to serve his sentence. If judged unsuitable for front line service, the *Polizei* convict then joined the *Arbeitsabteilung*. However, it appears that every effort was made to assign this category of parolee to the *Polizei* probation unit.[141]

Established in 1941, the Following a suggestion from the *Chef der Ordnungspolizei* on November 12th 1941 policemen on probation from gaol sentences; men who had committed a wide variety of crimes, from comrade theft to murder and corruption to military disobedienceAAA*Polizei Sondereinheit Zug*, also known as the *Sondereinheit* 'K', was subordinate to the *Polizei Pionier-Abteilung* on the Leningrad Front (*FPNr* 05.429) and accepted felons who had committed offences ranging from desertion to theft. Their commander tolerated no acts of comrade theft and acts of bravery were not rewarded with medals. The probationer's only exit from the *Sondereinheit* 'K' was the receipt of a serious wound or their death in action. Would be deserters returned to prison to await trial.[142]

By all accounts the *Sondereinheit* 'K' probationers were well treated by their pioneer comrades and performed dangerous tasks such as reconnaissance missions/attacks and recording and destroying enemy minefields. Destroying enemy tanks with hand held magnetic mines, the *Polizei* probationers are thought also to have been tasked with the execution of enemy prisoners. Given their exposure to these dangers, casualties in this unit were inevitably high. It is believed that the *Polizei Pionier-Abteilung* commander coined the name *Pionier* 'X' for the parole unit in December 1941 and on one occasion, a senior non-commissioned officer led around 50 probationers into the trenches along the Kolpino Front during winter of 1941.[143]

In August 1942 the parolees fought alongside the *Polizei-Schützen*-Rgt. 3 near Kolpino where many were killed or wounded. 'Weak characters who were basically good fellows' is how the physician of the *Polizei Pionier-Abteilung*, *Hstuf.* Dr Hans Pichler, recalled the troops of the *Sondereinheit* 'K' and noted that amongst the parolees was a former *Polizei* officer and 1936 Olympic gold medal winner. The physician would recall the parolee's lonely and deadly deployment: 'Night after night they went off on patrol to reconnoitre hostile enemy positions and take action against enemy minefields. The mines often caused many casualties. Of the 28 probationers that set off on patrol only five remained, the rest were killed or wounded.' When nine of the probationers were commanded to disable a Red Army tank with 120 kg of explosives on 27 November 1942, Dr Pichler recalled that only six of their number survived the attack. Three parolees were blown apart completely and their remains remained unidentifiable.[144]

Name: Heinz Nellen.
Last Rank: SS-*Obersturmführer*.
Born: 27.11.1913 in Hamburg–Altona.
Died: 16.4.1943 in Kolpina.

NSDAP-Nr.: (joined 1932).
SS-Nr.: 237.909 (joined 1932).
Prewar Assignments:
SS-VT *Nachrichten-Bataillon* (Berlin–Aldershof) 1.2.1935–30.6.1936.
Berlin *Schutzpolizei* from 30.6.1936.
Wartime Assignments:
1. / I. / *Polizei-Schützen*-Rgt. 1 spring/summer of 1940.
Polizei Sondereinheit/Pionier X 1.1943–4.1943.
Promotions:

0.0.1935	SS-*Sturmmann der* SS-VT.
30.6.1936	SS-*Unterscharführer der Allgemeine*-SS.
0.0.19__	SS-*Untersturmführer der Reserve.*
0.0.19__	SS-*Obersturmführer der Reserve.*
4.6.1942	SS-*Mann.*
15.4.1943	SS-*Obersturmführer der Allgemeine*-SS.
15.4.1943	SS-*Obersturmführer der Reserve.*

Decorations & Awards:

0.00.1940	1939 *Eisernes Kreuz II. Klasse.*

Notes: Married with two children, Nellen was formally released from the *Allgemeine*-SS to the Berlin *Schutzpolizei* in the summer of 1936. Spending four months in hospital suffering from bronchitis from 5 November 1938, Nellen recovered and was then released to a reserve unit. Nellen participated in the 1939 Polish and 1940 French campaign, but a court's investigation was initiated against him on suspicion of committing military disobedience in 1941 and this recommend his trial (case Nr. St. L. II 279/1941). Arraigned before the SS- *und Polizei-Gericht* X, Den Haag on 2 April 1942, the court judged Nellen guilty of the charges and punished him with a term of six years' *Zuchthaus* for an absence without leave offence and for contravening paragraph § 92 MStGB. The *Reichsführer* confirmed the sentence on 4 June 1942 and ordered Nellen's immediate detention in the SS-*Straflager* Dachau until the end of the war (the *HA* SS-*Gericht* acknowledged this judgment on 18.4.1942). Receiving a positive fitness report from the prison leader, Nellen was considered for front probation after six months detention. Writing to the Den Haag tribunal on 20 November the same year, the *HA* SS-*Gericht* reported that Nellen's appeal was underway and they were waiting for the *Reichsführer* to announce his final decision. Nellen received orders on 10 January 1943 to serve in the front probation unit of the *Polizeidivision* for one year before consideration would be given for his rehabilitation. Falling in action at Kolpina in April 1943, the *HA* SS-*Gericht* noted that he had bravely given his life for leader, people and nation in June the same year and judged him to have atoned for his offence during his deployed against the enemy. As a consequence of his sacrifice, Nellen's expulsion order was rescinded on 15 April 1943 and his old service grade and his old SS number were returned posthumously.[145]

The *Pionier* X was probably disbanded at the end of 1943, but it is thought that the SS-*Pioneer-Abteilung* 4 established a section-sized probation unit when sufficient parolees were available to fill its ranks.

Name: Eugen Bauer.
Last Rank: SS-*Untersturmführer.*
Born: 22.4.1906 in Schärding.
NSDAP-Nr.: 6.198.325 (joined 1.12.1936),
(re-joined 1.5.1938).
SS-Nr.: 413.719 (joined 1940).
Prewar Assignments:
Reichsheer 1.4.1925–9.6.1930.
NSKK 3.1938-11.1940.
Wartime Assignments:
Waffen-SS from 19.2.1943.
SS-*Polizeidivision* from 19.2.1943.
Promotions:
0.0.19__ *Leutnant der Polizei.*
15.11.1941 SS-*Untersturmführer der Allgemeine*-SS.
Decorations & Awards:
0.0.19__ SA-*Sportsabzeichen in Bronze.*
0.0.19__ *Deutsches Reichssportabzeichen in Silber.*
0.0.19__ SS-*Ehrenwinkel für alte Kämpfer.*

Notes: Attending *Volksschule* for five classes and trade school for two classes, Bauer was by profession a carpenter. Joining the *Polizei* on 10 June 1930, Bauer married his fiancée Maria P., (b. 24.5.1911 in Urfahr bei Linz) on 13 June 1934 and they had three children up to the point when records ceased in May 1945. Arraigned before the courts martial of the SS- *und Polizei-Gericht* VI, Vienna for theft on 2 February 1943, the tribunal heard the evidence against Bauer, judged him guilty of the offence on 30 April 1943 and ordered him to serve a term of four months' *Gefängnis* (his expulsion from the SS was ordered). Confirming this sentence, the *Reichsführer* amended the punishment to four weeks *Stubenarrest* and commanded the remaining punishment be served with a suitable *Polizei* unit on the Eastern Front. The responsible *Gerichtsherr* received orders to abandon the sentencing decision until a later date and the court received this decision on 20 April 1943. The delinquent Bauer transferred to the *Waffen*-SS and to the *Polizei Sondereinheiten* on 19 February 1943.[146]

Polizei parolees also served their punishment in regular *Polizei* units: *Revieroberwachmeister der Schutzpolizei* Obst served a period of probation with the 3. / SS-*Polizei-Schützen*-Rgt. 11 in 1943. *Leutnant der Schupo* Hoffmann wrote to the SS- *und Polizei-Gericht* XVIII, Kiev on 15 September 1943 to report that Obst was a good, proven and determined soldier in the battle against the partisans.[147]

Polizei probationers, those who were also members of the *Waffen*-SS, are known to have been assigned to the *Bewährungsabteilung*: Born in Lübeck on 7 July 1914, former *Ustuf.* Hans Dunkelmann was a long serving member of the *Waffen*-SS who had served with the LSSAH in 1934. Demoted to the rank of rifleman while fighting with the 10. / SS-*Polizei-Schützen*-Rgt. 3 in 1943, Dunkelmann served as a parolee with the *Bewährungsabteilung* in August 1944.[148]

On 26 September 1943 it was announced that the commanders of units with *Polizei* probationers under their command could in future, in exceptional cases, such as life-threatening wounds, request that their divisional commander send a short letter stating the facts of the case to the responsible chief judge, who without delay would forwarded a probation report to the *Reichsführer*. To enable the SS leader to make his decision, the judged were instructed to include the offender's former police and military service grade in his report. Himmler's decision was then relayed to the corps, divisional, brigade judge and *Gerichtsherr*.[149]

5.10 SS-*Ersatz Bataillon Ost*

Though not a probation battalion per se, the SS-*Infantrie-Ersatz-Bataillon Ost*, the reserve unit of the *Kommandostab* RF-SS, accepted troops into its ranks who were under investigation, had committed disciplinary offences or accepted front probation. Established in the city of Breslau during 1941, the *Ost* is known to have provided military training for *Bewährungszug* assigned to the three HSSPF on the Eastern Front from 1942. Later, the *Ost* armed and equipped former camp prisoners who had volunteered for the SS-*Sonderbataillon*/*Sonderregiment Dirlewanger* in Belorussia. During the Russian campaign, the *Ost* underwent a number of name changes, was divided, provided the basis of a field force to partisans for the HSSPF and was reformed into a combat unit. Its relationship with the probation force was further solidified when the 4. *Schützen-Ersatz-Kompanie* was established for the *Ost* with parolees on 21 December 1942.[150]

Interestingly, the SS-*Infantrie-Ersatz-Bataillon Ost* accepted a handful of judges and fourteen *Beurkundungsführer* of the *HA* SS-*Gericht* on to its muster rolls in March 1944. Assessed for their suitability for front line deployment, those selected for *Zugführer* positions was then assigned to other units. In February 1945 a further 79 SS-*Richter* and *Beurkundungsführer* mustered on the *Ost* battalion's roles while preparing for front line deployment.[151]

The final derivative of the *Ost* was the SS-*Panzergrenadier-Ausbildung- und Ersatz-Bataillon* 18 Breslau. Aside from inducting, equipping and training *Waffen*-SS parolees, this formation also accepted a large group of volunteer camp prisoners in the spring of 1945. While training, these camp parolees lived and in block five of the SS-*Kaserne* Langenhorn. Armed with rifles on 1 May 1945, they then marched to the Hamburg Front.[152]

Probationers assigned to the SS-*Infantrie-Ersatz-Bataillon Ost* were usually transferred to the troops once their sentence was complete: The SS- *und Polizei-Gericht* XV, Breslau ordered the release of 23 year-old *Rttf.* Heinz Steppe from the SS-*Panzergrenadier-Ersatz-Bataillon Ost* 31 in Breslau on 29 January 1944. At this time they requested that the SS- *und Polizei-Gericht* XVIII, Luzk supplied them with a copy of his field judgement.[153]

For failing to supervise his troops, this officer was cashiered and sent to the front to fight partisans with the *Ost* Battalion's front line derivative, the SS-*Panzergrenadier Ersatz-Bataillon Ost* 31:

Name: Franz Maier.
Last Rank: SS-*Unterscharführer.*
Born: 12.1.1906 in Passau/Bavaria.
Died: 26.3.1944 in Balta.
NSDAP-Nr.: 60.050 (20.4.1927).
SS-Nr.: 4.483 (joined 1.12.1934).
Prewar Assignments:
4. / II. / 34. SS-*Standarte* (Weilheim) 12.1930.
SS-*Ausbildungkommando München* in 4.1933.
SS-*Standarte Deutschland* (military training) in 1933.
KL Columbia *Haus* from 15.8.1934.
SS-*Totenkopf-Standarte Brandenburg* 1.4.–1.9.1935
Zugführer SS-*Totenkopf Sturmbann Ostfreisland* from 1.9.1935–31.10.1938.
Wartime Assignments:
Officer of the 21. SS-*Standarte* (Magdeburg) from 15.9.1939.
Wachabteilung der Wirtschaftlichen Forschungsstelle (Wi-Fo) (Munich, Bernsdorf-Thüringen) 10.1939–1.12.1940.
Officer of the 3. / 47. SS-*Standarte* (Jena) 1.12.1940–8.5.1945.
Waffen-SS from 7.4.1942.
SS-TV *Inspektorate* 7.4.1942.
KL Auschwitz 7.4.1942–15.4.1943.
Led the 2. / SS-*Wachbataillon* KL Auschwitz 6.1942–15.4.1943.
SS-*Panzergrenadier-Ersatz-Bataillon Ost* (Breslau) from 15.4.1943.
SS-*Panzergrenadier-Ausbildung- und Ersatz-Bataillon* 31 from 4.–8.11.1943.
10. *Panzer-Nahbekämpfslehrgang* at Kienschlag SS-*Pz.-Gren.-Schule* 8.11.–15.11.1943.
SS-*Totenkopfdivision* 15.11.1943–26.3.1944.
Promotions:

20.4.1937	SS-*Untersturmführer der* SS-TV.
7.4.1942	SS-*Untersturmführer der Reserve.*
10.4.1943	SS-*Unterscharführer der Reserve.*

Decorations & Awards:

0.0.19__	SS-*Zivilabzeichen* (Nr. 2.203).
0.0.19__	SA-*Sportsabzeichen in Bronze.*
0.0.19__	SS-*Ehrenwinkel für alte Kämpfer.*
0.0.19__	*Ehrendegen des Reichsführer*-SS.

0.0.19__ *Totenkopfring der* SS.
0.12.1930 *Dienstauszeichnung der* NSDAP *in Gelb.*

Notes: Attending *Volksschule* for seven classes, Maier left full time education and was employed as a carpenter. Mustering with the SA from April 1927 to December 1934, he married a woman with three children from a previous marriage in April 1938. Following an incident in which he assaulted a civilian, Maier left the SS-TV and was employed with the border guard from 31 October 1938. Deployed in the KL Auschwitz from April 1942, Maier's superior punished him with ten days' *Stubenarrest* for an unknown infraction on 6 September 1942. The SS- *und Polizei-Gericht* XV, Breslau initiated a court's investigation against Maier in the spring of 1943 and recommended his trial for the neglect of his duties. Instigating an all day card game with a handful of senior non-commissioned officers of his company in April 1943, Maier was aware that this was forbidden activity and large amounts of money were gambled during the card school games. During the course of the day, Maier neglected to attend to his duties and ordered the other players to do likewise and continue playing. Their activities were then reported to the guard commander, who informed the camp commandant and the courts martial of the Breslau tribunal initiated an investigation against Maier on suspicion of participating in a forbidden card game, instigating the game and preventing his men from their duties in April 1943 (case Nr. St. L. IV 25/1943). His court martial took place in the *Kommandantur* KL Auschwitz on 10 April 1943 and the court chairman, *Ostuf.* Bredehöft, was supported in his deliberations by the camp administration officer, *Stubaf.* Wilhelm Burger, and *Ustuf.* Gerhard Crommes. *Ustuf.* Dr Heppner prosecuted the case. Judged guilty of the charges, the tribunal punished Maier with a term of seven months' *Gefängnis,* imposed three months' probation, levied a 100 *Reichsmark* fine on him, imposed a six weeks' intensified arrest order for the guard duty transgression and ordered his temporary expulsion from the SS. Confirming the judgement, the *Reichsführer* suspended the prison sentence in favour of field probation and demoted Maier to the rank of *Uscha.* He then fought partisans on the Eastern Front until his rehabilitation in November 1943. Fighting with the SS-*Panzergrenadier*-Rgt. 6 in November 1943, Maier died as a result of a head wound in March 1944.[154]

In the last weeks of the war a former battalion commander was himself court martialled and sent to a probation unit:

Name: Karl Burkhardt.
Last Rank: SS-*Obersturmbannführer.*
Born: 17.7.1900 in Schmalkalden/Thüringen.
NSDAP-Nr.: 44.728 (joined 15.10.1926).
SS-Nr.: 52.909 (joined 10.7.1932).
Prewar Assignments:
Garde Schützen Korps in 1919.
SS-*Wachtruppe Weimar* 30.10.1933–30.9.1936.

Officer of the *Abschnitt* XXXII (Augsburg) from 1.4.1936.
SS-TV from 1.4.1936.
KL service until 6.4.1937.
Led the II. / 45. SS-*Standarte* (Neu Ruppin) 1937–1938.
SS-*Offizier-Lehrgang* in Berne 23.1. 12.2.1938.

Wartime Assignments:

1. / SS-*Totenkopf-Infantrie*-Rgt. 11 from 10.10.1939.
Waffen-SS from 3.1940.
SS-*Grenadier-Ersatz-Bataillon Ost* (Breslau) in 1940.
SS-*Ersatz-Bataillon* (Brünn) in 1941.
Led the II. / SS-*Totenkopf-Infantrie*-Rgt. 7 (*Kampfgruppe Nord*) until 6.1941.
Led the SS-*Grenadier-Ersatz-Bataillon Ost* (Breslau) from spring of 1942.
SS-FHA reserve list from 6.1942-10.8.1942.
7th SS-*Gebirgsjäger*-Division *Prinz Eugen* 20.8.1942–26.4.1944.
SSPF *Italien-Mitte* 26.4.1944-11.1944.
36th *Waffen-Grenadier*-Division *der* SS in 1945

Promotions:

4.6.1934	SS-*Untersturmführer der Allgemeine*-SS.
9.11.1935	SS-*Obersturmführer der* SS-TV.
30.1.1937	SS-*Hauptsturmführer der* SS-TV.
20.4.1938	SS-*Sturmbannführer der* SS-TV.
16.9.1935	SS-*Obersturmbannführer der* SS-TV.
1.3.1940	SS-*Sturmbannführer der Reserve*.
16.6.1943	SS-*Obersturmbannführer der Waffen*-SS.
12.1944	SS-*Mann*.

Decorations & Awards:

0.0.19__	*Blutorden*.
0.0.19__	SA-*Sportsabzeichen in Bronze*.
0.0.19__	*Ehrendegen des Reichsführer*-SS.
0.0.19__	*Dienstauszeichnung der* NSDAP *in Gelb*.
0.0.19__	*Totenkopfring der* SS.
0.0.19__	1939 *Eisernes Kreuz I. Klasse*.
0.0.19__	1939 *Eisernes Kreuz II. Klasse*.
0.0.19__	*Kriegsverdienstkreuz II. Klasse mit Schwertern*.

Notes: Attending *Volksschule* for eight classes, Burkhardt was drafted into the army during 1918. Working as a travelling salesman and hospital worker from 1920 until 1933, he then suffered long periods of unemployment. Marrying his fiancée Gertrud K. on 27 September 1922, they had two children up to the point when records ceased in May 1945. Burkhardt participated in four Nazi demonstrations between 1927 and 1934 and guarded the *Reichsstatthalter*, *Ogruf.* Fritz Saukel, in Weimar between October 1933 and September 1936. Wounded in action in Finland during June 1941, he recuperated in Berlin and was then judged 30 per cent disabled by his wounds. Declared fit for duty in November 1941, Burkhardt raised a reserve ethnic-German unit in Panschova during 1942. Commanded to the SSPF *Italien–Mitte* in the spring of 1944, Burkhardt became the deployment commander for the *Gendarmerie Hauptmannschaft* in Padua, Italy. Here, his German and Italian personnel was responsible for patrolling the Venetian Region, hunting partisans and capturing resisters to the Nazi occupation. Burkhardt's further promotion was denied by the SS-FHA in October 1944 in the wake of his commander submitting a glowing testimonial that voiced his concerns that Burkhardt did not possess a convincing SS manner, he doubted his sincerity and considered him unworthy for further promotion. Postwar, Burkhardt claimed that he was accused of theft in October 1944 and was then arraigned before the courts martial of the SS- *und Polizei-Gericht* XXXI, Verona in December the same year. Judged guilty of the charge, the tribunal punished Burkhardt with a term of eighteen months' *Gefängnis*, a 1,000 *Reichsmark* fine, demotion and expulsion from the SS with a recommendation that he was expelled from the Nazi party. As an alternative to prison, Burkhardt was commanded to the 36th *Waffen-Grenadier*-Division *der* SS in 1945 and fought with *Stubaf.* Ewald Ehlers regiment.[155]

5.11 *Front Probation Case Studies*

The following probation cases are presented to explain how the front probation and clemency process:

Name: Fritz Göttling.
Last Rank: SS-*Untersturmführer*.
Born: 19.3.1913 in Obergebra/Bleicherode/Harz.
NSDAP-Nr.: 4.866.920 (1.5.1937).
SS-Nr.: 223.789 (joined 1933).
Prewar Assignments:
7. / 67. SS-*Standarte* (Erfurt) 1933.
Panzerjäger-Abteilung 4 in the late summer/autumn of 1937.
Panzerjäger-Abteilung 4 on 12.8.1938.
Wartime Assignments:
Waffen-SS from 18.9.1939.
SS-*Panzerjäger-Ersatz-Bataillon* 18.9.1939.
5. SS-Division *Wiking* 1940–1941.
Führer-Lehrgang in 2.1942.
II. / SS-*Panzer*-Rgt. *Totenkopf* in 1943.
11. / 2. SS-*Panzerjäger-Abteilung* spring/summer 1943.
SS-*Panzer-Ausbildung- und Ersatz*-Rgt. 1.10.1944.
SS-*Panzer*-Rgt. 9 late 1944-8.5.1945.

Promotions:

1.9.1942	SS-*Untersturmführer der Reserve.*
29.4.1943	SS-*Oberscharführer der Reserve.*
1.5.1944	SS-*Untersturmführer der Reserve.*

Decorations & Awards:

0.0.19__	SS-*Zivilabzeichen.*
0.0.19__	SA-*Sportsabzeichen in Bronze.*
0.0.19__	*Deutsches Reichssportabzeichen in Bronze.*
0.0.19__	1939 *Eisernes Kreuz I. Klasse.*
0.0.19__	1939 *Eisernes Kreuz II. Klasse.*
0.0.19__	*Verwundetenabzeichen*, 1939 *in Schwarz.*
0.0.19__	*Infanterie-Sturmabzeichen in Bronze.*

Notes: His father died during the Great War. Attending *Volksschule* for eight classes and then trade school, Göttling became a member of the NSV and NSF in May 1937 and married his fiancée Ell K., (b. 18.6.1913 in Obergebra) on 23 September 1934. They had two children up to the point when records ceased in May 1945 and lived in Obergebra. Fighting with the *Wiking* until wounded at Dnepropetrovsk in 1942, *Ustuf.* Göttling and *Ustuf.* Gerhard Warnecke received orders in 1943 to take a convoy of tanks by rail from Achse to Angouleme via Perpignan, where the new tank regiment was forming in La Braconne, but handed only two days' rations for the estimated five or six-day journey, continued delays resulted in both officers going without rations for three days, (Warnecke's wife later stated that her husband experienced two weeks' of irregular food distribution over the previous four weeks with this command and at the time of his offence he was in great hunger). Both officers attempt to purchase food from a French railway garage rebuffed when they were unable produce ration stamps, Göttling then attempted to telephone the necessary authorities in Bordeaux to complain about his situation. Striking up a conversation with a German railway official and explaining his situation, the railwayman listened to Göttling's grievances and pointing out twenty unguarded boxes and packages in the railway station that he claimed some *Luftwaffe* soldiers had stolen food and alcohol from and had not been caught and punished. Encouraged by this news Göttling and Warnecke, surreptitiously picked two locks on the cases and stole some cans of sardines in oil, which they consumed on the spot. Encouraged by their success, they then proceeded to open two more boxes and stole a number of items including a leather case, leather coat and a bottle of rum. Unfortunately for Göttling and Warnecke, the railway official later reported these items stolen and the theft was reported to their commander.

The *Totenkopfdivision* field court conducted a court's investigation against the two delinquent officers and both were arraigned before its courts martial on 11 January 1943 (case Nr. St. L. 22/1943). Judged guilty of the charges, the tribunal punished Göttling with two years' *Zuchthaus* for theft and the case report was then sent to the *HA* SS-*Gericht* and the *Reichsführer* for their confirmation. Fearing the worst, Göttling contacted his wife to explain his predicament and she wrote an impassioned letter to the SS leader: 'Please release my husband to the front where he will help bring about victory' she pleaded and describing him as a good father, *Frau* Göttling explained that in addition to his fate becoming a harsh punishment on her children, she mentioned that as her husband's best friend had died at the front on 7 January 1943, she expressed her certainty that he would wish to avenge his death at the front (her letter contained a photograph of herself and their children).

Receiving Göttling's punishment book on 1 March 1943, *Ostubaf.* Dr Klahre of the *HA* SS-*Gericht* declared that although both officers had dishonoured the SS in the eyes of the railway, the military and the *Feldgendarme*, both he and the *Gerichtsherr* agreed that the court punishment was too harsh and given their previous good service, they considered it appropriate that both stood a chance of a reprieve. Querying the evidence that the officers had broken into the boxes, or had stolen the leather goods, the *HA* SS-*Gericht*—on the grounds of what was good for 'National Socialism'—recommended the original sentence was reduced to two years' *Gefängnis* on 22 March 1943 and declaring Göttling unworthy to bear arms, they recommended he served one year's imprisonment and face a year's suspension of membership from the SS. It was then proposed that both officers receive probation at the front to atone for their one-off transgression and a report was ordered composed to determine their fate after they had spent six months at the front. With the agreement of all the parties, this sentence was confirmed on 1 April 1943 and Göttling was formally reduced to the rank of *Oscha.* on 29 April the same year. Posted to the anti-tank unit of the *Kampfgruppe Das Reich*, Göttling fought at the front for four months before receiving a serious wound in his right thigh. As a consequence of this injury, the *HA* SS-*Gericht* sent his punishment file to the *Reichsführer* for a case review on 10 March 1944. Commanding Göttling's rehabilitation on 5 April, Himmler permitted his return to officer rank on 1 May. Fully recovered from his injuries, Göttling was then posted to a training unit in October and they assigned him to a Panzer regiment, where he remained until the war's end.[156]

Name: Gerhard Warnecke.
Last Rank: SS-*Untersturmführer.*
Born: 10.4.1910 in Aschersleben.
Died: 14.11.1943 in Biala Zerkoff.
NSDAP-Nr.: (joined 1932).
Wartime Assignments:
Waffen-SS from 1939.
II. / SS-*Panzer*-Rgt. *Totenkopf* in 1943.
11. / 2. SS-*Panzerjäger-Abteilung* spring 1943–14.11.1943.
Promotions:

30.1.1943	SS-*Untersturmführer der Reserve.*
29.4.1943	SS-*Oberscharführer der Reserve.*
13.11.1943	SS-*Untersturmführer der Reserve.*

Notes: A student at university and active sportsman, Warnecke did not smoke cigarettes and prior to the outbreak of war, he taught sport for the *Hitlerjugend*, the NSRL and the National Socialist School and had taken part in sports competitions. Working in a factory during 1939, Warnecke volunteered for the *Waffen*-SS that same year and alongside *Ustuf.* Göttling, was arraigned before the courts martial of the *Totenkopfdivision* field court for committing military theft on 11 January 1943 (case Nr. St. L. I 22/1943). Judged guilty of the charges, the court punished Warnecke with two years' *Zuchthaus*. 'A harmless character, a good comrade at Bad Tölz and proven front soldier' wrote his wife from her Halle home and pleading for clemency, she expressed concern that her husband's sentence for stealing alcohol was incorrect as he was a teetotaller. At this time she asked the head of the SS to consider in his judgment that at that time of the offence, her husband had not eaten for three days and concluded her letter with an appeal for front probation and a special clemency decision. Confirming the judgement on 1 March 1943, the *Reichsführer* set aside the prison sentence and he commanded both officers to undergo fourteen days' intensified *Stubenarrest*. Setting aside the *Ehrenstrafe* and unworthiness to bear arms judgment, Himmler directed both officers to the *Reich* for front probation with the rank of *Oscha.* and demanded regular reports be submitted about their performance and behaviour. A rehabilitation process was ordered once both men had spent six months' of good performance at the front and if no problems had been reported by their command officers.

Formally reduced to the rank of *Oscha.* on 29 April 1943, Warnecke then joined the *Kampfgruppe Das Reich* on the Eastern Front. Killed in action in November 1943, Himmler was informed of Warnecke's demise on 9 December the same year. For his 'courageous deployment' the *Amt* III initiated a rehabilitation process on 23 December 1943, the chief judge of the *Kampfgruppe Das Reich*, *Hstuf.* Okrent, supplied a fitness report for Warnecke on 1 January 1944. Granting Warnecke a full rehabilitation on 14 January, his part sentence was cancelled and his former rank and SS number were returned (the sentence was erased from the punishment register on 13.11.1943). Giving birth to a boy on 1 March 1944, *Frau* Warnecke wrote to her husband's case worker at the SS-*Richter beim* RF-SS in March 1944 to enquire how his case was progressing. His reply on 18 March reported no progress as the head of the SS was deployed at the front and wished to deal with her case personally. Sending the facts of the case to the welfare leader of the *Oberabschnitt Elbe* on the last day of that same month, the SS-*Richter beim* RF-SS demanded that their office looked after the widow and her child's welfare. Commanded on 5 May to send a report about Warnecke's surviving family to the SS-*Richter beim* RF-SS, the *Elbe* welfare officer carried out this order and reported that the widow was in financial dire straits. Writing on 19 May, *Scha.* Stosius, reported that *Frau* Warnecke had borrowed almost 360 *Reichsmark* from the Merseburg *Regierungspräsident*, with a promise that she would re-pay the loan within three months. Disgruntled with her treatment, Stosius approach to *Frau* Warnecke to offer financial assistance was refused.[157]

This officer, prosecuted on two separate occasions for two different offences, was fully rehabilitated following his death:

Name: Jakob de Vries.
Last Rank: SS-*Hauptsturmführer.*
Born: 21.2.1906 in S'Gravenhage/Den Haag.
Died: 31.7.1944 in Waiwara.
SS-Nr.: 372.321 (joined 8.8.1940)
Prewar Assignments:
Dutch Army in 7.1940,
Attended an officer school training course for nine months in 1925.
Wartime Assignments:
Waffen-SS from 8.1940.
Special political course at Berchtesgaden 13.–31.8.19840.
SS-*Infantrie*-Rgt. *Westland* until 10.9.1940.
1. / SS-*Artillerie-Ersatz-Bataillon* 10.9.–15.11.1940.
Batterieführer 4. / SS-*Artillerie Ersatz-Bataillon* 15.11.–1.12.1940.
2. / SS-*Artillerie-Ausbildung- und Ersatz*-Rgt. (Dachau) 10.3.1941.
Batterieführer III. / SS- *Artillerie-Ausbildung- und Ersatz*-Rgt. (Dachau) in 1941.
Ib / SS-*Artillerie*-Rgt. *Nord* on 1.5.1942–1943.
4. / SS-*Polizei-Artillerie-Ersatz-Bataillon* (Amersfort) in 1943.
Batterieführer SS-*Panzer-Artillerie*-Rgt. 10 from 2.3.1943.
Led the 1. / SS-*Panzer-Artillerie*-Rgt. 10 in 1943.
Led the 8. / SS-*Panzer-Artillerie*-Rgt. 10 until 16.8.1943.
III. SS-*Panzerkorps* from 16.8.1943.
Bewährungsabteilung in 1944.
11. SS-*Panzer-Grenadier*-Division *Nordland* 1.5.1944–31.7.1944.
7. / I. / SS-*Panzer-Artillerie*-Rgt. 11 on 30.7.1944–31.7.1944.
Promotions:

2.12.1939	*Hauptmann.*
8.8.1940	SS-*Hauptsturmführer der Waffen*-SS.
17.11.1943	SS-*Untersturmführer der Waffen*-SS.
9.1.1945	SS-*Hauptsturmführer der Waffen*-SS (R.D.A. 30.7.1944).

Notes: His father was a Voorburg businessman. Studying at business school for two years, de Vries then worked as a clerk until entering the Dutch Army in October 1925. Active in nationalist politics from 1929, de Vries married his fiancée Menna B. and they had one child. An artillery officer in the Dutch Army, de Vries fought at Helenaven u. Asten between 10 and 11 May 1940. Assigned to a *Waffen*-SS artillery reserve battalion in Amersfort when a disciplinary investigation was initiated against de Vries to examine his behaviour under fire. As a result of his findings the commander of the *Nord* recommended de Vries face trial for cowardice in the face of the enemy on 29 September 1943. Leading an artillery convoy to the front on 12 September 1942, de Vries was informed that partisans had attacked elements of the division fourteen miles from his position and then decided to order his convoy into the surrounding forest to hide until the threat had evaporated.

His behaviour reported, the field court initiated an investigating for his dereliction of duty for displaying fear in the face of the enemy in contravention of § 84 MStGB and his case was subsequently transferred from the *Nord* field court to the SS- *und Polizei-Gericht* X, Den Haag for trial (case Nr. St. L. II 410/1942). Arraigned before the courts martial on 18 February 1943. Although he had admitted destroying his after action report, the court chairman, *Stubaf.* Härtel, discharged de Vries from a punishment and the *Reichsführer* confirmed his sentence on 19 March 1943 and de Vries then returned to the front.

Assigned to the III. SS-*Panzerkorps* in the summer of 1943, de Vries committed a disciplinary offence that once again required his court martial. He, *Ustuf.* Walter Spieth, *Ustuf.* Rudolf Schmied, and *Oscha.* Otto Ränsle of the SS-*Panzer-Artillerie*-Rgt. 10 were accused of launching an unauthorised artillery attack on the French village of Salies de Beam on 4 September 1943 (case Nr. St. L. 414/1943). Arraigned before the courts martial of the *Frundsberg* field court on 5 August 1943, the court chairman was *Hstuf.* Schön. Hearing the evidence, the tribunal judged all three guilty of drunkenness and ordering an artillery bombardment that destroyed a French village. Punishing de Vries with a nine months' *Gefängnis*, the court imposed three months *Gefängnis* on *Ustuf.* Walter Spietz, *Ustuf.* Rudolf Schmied served a four weeks' period of intensified arrest and *Oscha.* Otto Ränsle was ordered to suffer two weeks' intensified arrest. The SS-FHA supported these judgements on 26 September and de Vries, with the agreement of the *HA* SS-*Gericht*, was demoted to the rank of *Ustuf.* in November 1943. Agreeing with this decision on 2 December, the *Reichsführer* amended the judgement to two months' *Gefängnis* on 23 December 1943. With all the interested parties in agreement on 18 January 1944, it was decided to punish de Vries with a total of ten months' *Gefängnis* of which three months would be served in prison and seven on probation in the *Bewährungsabteilung*. His sentence completed in May 1944, de Vries then transferred to the *Nordland*. His battery was stationed close to the Waiwara railway station when de Vries was killed by Red Army artillery in July 1944 (his body was interred at a graveyard near Jöhwi). 'He died for a better Europe' explained his commander, *Hstuf.* Otto Kroll in a letter to his widow on 6 August 1944. His co-defendant, Walter Spieth was later deployed with the SS-*Panzer-Artillerie*-Rgt. 17 and attached to the 4. / SS-*Panzer-Artillerie*-Rgt. 10, *Ustuf.* Rudolf Schmied died in action near the town of Malot on 11 July 1944.[158]

5.12 Marriage Regulations for Probationers

Parolees of the *Bewährungsabteilung* were entitled to apply for permission to marry. The *Verordnungsblatt der Waffen*-SS from 15 November 1942 made note of this regulation and warned that home leave was only permitted for felons and probationers for the purpose of engagement and marriage. Written permission was required from the *Reichsführer* and RuSHA before the convict could submit a request for marriage leave.[159]

These two probationers applied to marry while imprisoned or attached to a probation unit: Born in Köln on 14 March 1920, Heinz Willerscheid had been a member of the *Hitlerjugend* from 25 May 1932 until July 1938 and prior to joining the Weimar *Schutzpolizei*, he was employed as an apprentice builder. Remaining with the *Polizei* until 14 March 1940, Willerscheid later joined the *Waffen*-SS and deployed on the Eastern Front from June 1941 to January 1942. Wounded in November 1941, Willerscheid, a recipient of the *E.K.* II. *Klasse*, was arraigned before the courts martial of a divisional field court for an unspecified crime in January 1942. Judged guilty, he was punished with four years' *Gefängnis* and sent to Danzig-Matzkau for two years, Willerscheid then reported to the 2. / *Bewährungsabteilung* in Chlum on 2 February 1944. From here he applied to the SS-*Pflegstelle* 108, (Prague) on 9 June 1944 to marry his fiancée Anni P., (b. 5.11.1921 in Höxster/Westfal.). His application was supported by *Hstuf.* Kayser and his medical examination was conducted by *Ostuf.* Dr Viktor Lewe on 19 August. Writing again to the SS-*Pflegestelle* 108, Willerscheid expressed concern that his application had not been approved and requested that they processed his application quickly before his deployed to the front. Replying to Willerscheid's letter on 2 March 1945, *Hstuf.* Dr Hans Trischkat of the RuSHA informed him that the war situation prevented them from processing his application any faster and warning that his application did not contain details of his criminal offence, the RuSHA then requested that his fiancée provide him with her application immediately. When Willerscheid received this reply he would have already been assigned to the SS-*Sonderbrigade* which was deployed along the River Niesse.[160]

Born in Leiden/Holland on 28 March 1923, Cornelius Lancel, found himself arraigned before the courts martial of the *Wiking* Division for an unspecified offence on 23 October 1944 and judged guilty, he was punished with six months' *Gefängnis* with a recommendation that part of the sentence was served on probation. Detained in the divisional *Strafvollstreckungszug*, Lancel received approval from the SS-*Pflegestelle* 152 on 3 November 1944 to marry his German fiancée Sophia S., (b. 8.3.1924 in Willich). Noting that Lancel had been released from the *Strafvollstreckungszug* on 21 January 1945, the *Pflegestelle* observed that the remainder of his prison sentence had been set aside in favour of field probation with the SS-*Panzer-Pionier-Abteilung* 5.[161]

The *HA* SS-*Gericht* supported the demand that the wishes of dead probationers were carried out with consideration for their ex-wife and children. Following the publication of a new marriage statute, the SS-*Richter beim* RF-SS (Killing) observed that this new ordinance did not contain any references to the expulsion from the 'SS clan,' failed to mention the unfaithfulness of the wives of men who had died a 'hero's death', or contained any reference to the effect that this law would have on the surviving children. Following discussions with the *Reichsjustizministerium*, Killing reported that the new edict permitted the dead man's spouse to receive his inheritance and benefits if his will came to light after his death. In cases where the ex-wife had been judged at fault during the divorce, it was agreed that their applications would be examined by the *Reichsjustizministerium* on a case by case basis to rule out any reasons to change the dead man's wishes.[162]

5.13 Front Probation Regulations for the Non-German Offenders of the *Waffen*-SS

The rapid expansion of the *Waffen*-SS was achieved by recruiting men born outside the 1938 German borders and from non-German countries. Their recruitment resulted in an exponential increase in the number of disciplinary and criminal cases, which the SS leadership attributed partly to the recruitment of men raised in countries with a long tradition of democratic governments. Noting that few of these recruits had previously served in a military service with a strict discipline comparable to the German military, Himmler accepted that these men were not conversant with the absolute discipline demanded of the *Waffen*-SS. Though punishable in accordance with the statutes of his jurisdiction, the head of the SS demanded that his *Gerichtsherrn* and SS-*Richter* treated non-German offenders with greater sensitivity and leniency, fearing that bad publicity would result negatively on recruitment.[163]

Instructing his courts to punish Germanic volunteers with less vigour than imposed on German soldiers, the *Reichsführer* commanded the *Gerichtsherrn* and SS-*Richter* of non-German formations to separate the non-German felons from other convicts in prison and permit their admission in front probation units which was composed of their own kind.[164]

Discussing this issue with Himmler in the summer of 1942, the HSSPF *Norwegen* and the chief judge of the SS- *und Polizei-Gericht* IX, Oslo wished to know what measures they could bring to bear against the increasing number of Norwegian SS and *Polizei* convicts held in detention by the civil authorities and the Holmestrand *Ersatz-Bataillon*.[165] As a consequence of these concerns, the *Reichsführer* instructed the SS-*Richter beim* RF-SS on 8 July 1942 to ensure that convicted Germanic SS and Norwegian Legionaries, of all categories, were no longer sent into the civil prisons and commanded him to verify that their detention occurred in a separate unit within the Dachau and Danzig–Matzkau (his order was brought to the attention of the HSSPF *Norwegen*).[166]

Ordering non-German legionaries and members of the *Schutzmannschaften* judged guilty of an offence by his courts to serve their punishments in the *Strafvollzugslager der* SS *und Polizei* Danzig–Matzkau from the autumn of 1942, Himmler demanded consideration was given for war recruits to receive immediate probation in a Germanic SS divisional *Strafkompanie*, the *Bewährungsabteilung*, or the *Arbeitsabteilung*. In addition to this measure, the *Amt* III received instructions to offer work service in the Reich for non-SS Legionnaires, or release them to their homeland. Members of the *Schutzmannschaften* punished with up to six months' prison for light offences, were permitted to accept the offer of parole.[167]

'For those members of the legion and Germanic volunteers of the *Waffen*-SS, who do not belong to the SS; the SS-FHA is to order the formation of a special probation unit in the 2. SS-*Infantrie*-Brigade (mot) and they are to go here directly' commanded the *Reichsführer* in August 1942 and he once again demanded that Germanic soldiers receive field parole in their own national units at the front. In addition, the courts were instructed to avoid punishing the criminals and delinquents of the *Schutzmannschaft*, Legion, *Schutzpolizei* and auxiliary police with prison sentences and where possible send them directly to a separate unit within the *Arbeitsabteilung*.[168]

Protesting against this decision, the *Chef* SS-FHA and the *HA* SS-*Gericht* voiced their preference to imprison these malfeasant elements in Danzig–Matzkau, or in Salaspils, where they could be properly assessed for rehabilitation. Rejecting their plea, Himmler once again demanded that the national formations of the *Waffen*-SS sent their delinquents to their own *Strafkompanie* to earn back their honour, but conceded that serious criminals, those whose presence in the unit proved detrimental to discipline, to be incarcerated in Salaspils.[169]

Evidence for leniency towards non-Germans is evident in the following two cases. This officer committed murder, but avoided a gaol sentence and was sent to the front: Born in Eidsvoll/Norway on 28 May 1905, *Ostuf.* Dr Ingier, a qualified medical doctor, was married with two children and fought with the *Freiwilligen*-Legion *Norwegen* from May 1942 and received the *E.K.* II. *Klasse* and *Ostmedaile* 1941/42. In the company of other members of the unit and local villagers, Dr Ingier proceeded to drink a bottle of schnapps in his Duderho quarters on 31 December 1942 and during this impromptu party, he became completely drunk and stabbed a fellow drinker, a Russian, with a knife. So serious did he consider the incident, that Dr Ingier's commander referred the incident to the SS- *und Polizei-Gericht* XII, Hamburg and their court's investigation recommended he faced trial for aggravated assault (case Nr. St. L. 186/1943). Arraigned before the courts martial of the Hamburg tribunal on 9 October 1941, Dr Ingier was judged guilty of the 'cold blooded' offence of causing bodily harm and mishandling a weapon and punished with a term of six months' *Festunghaft* under intensified arrest conditions. The *Gerichtsherr* and the HSSPF *Nord* supported the sentence, but confirming the court's decision, the *Reichsführer*, in the belief that Dr Ingier's act was mitigated by his drunkenness, amended the judgement to two weeks' intensified arrest and ordered him to spend one week's probation at the front as a rifleman. The *HA* SS-*Gericht* confirmed this judgment on 12 April 1943. Surviving the collapse in May 1945, Dr Ingier died in Norway on 22 August 1978.[170]

In this instance the *Ehrenstrafe* was applied to a non-German volunteer and serving his prison sentence, he was then recommended for work in the Reich. Born in Senlin/ Croatia on 3 March 1893, Christoph Bellanovich, an ethnic-Austrian, was born into an old frontier guard and military family and had formally served in the Austrian Army during the Great War, obtaining the rank of *Leutnant*. Volunteering his services to the *Gestapo* in the wake of the 1941 invasion of Yugoslavia, Bellanovich was employed as an interpreter until joining the *Waffen*-SS with the rank *Ostuf.* in April 1942. In Belgrade, Bellanovich ran office of the National Socialist People's Welfare organisation. Assigned to the 4. / SS-*Gebirgsjäger-Ersatz-Bataillon* 7 in early 1943, Bellanovich was drinking alcohol in a Serbian–Banat café when he became inebriated and molested a woman sitting at another table. Other officers removed Bellanovich from the café and placed him in the senior con-commissioned officer's office, but attempting to escape, he was caught, tied with rope and locked in the office. Falling to sleep, Bellanovich was then taken to his quarters and the incident was reported to higher authorities.

Arraigned before the courts martial of the SS- *und Polizei-Gericht* XIX, Belgrade to answer charges of drunkenness and shaming the SS on 11 February 1943, (case Nr; St. L. 13/1943), the tribunal judged Bellanovich judged guilty of disobedience and drunkenness in contravention of paragraphs §§ 92 MStGB and 80 MStGB and punished him with two months' *Gefängnis* and recommended his expulsion from the SS. Supported by the *HA* SS-*Gericht*, the *Gerichtsherr* recommended Bellanovich undertook six weeks' *Stubenarrest* and supported his dismissal from the SS. Submitting his confirmation on 19 April 1943, the SS-*Richter beim* RF-SS upheld the sentence and with the support of the plenipotentiary for the economy in Serbia, he demanded Bellanovich worked in a factory or workshop in Germany. Unhappy with this decision, Bellanovich appealed to the *HA* SS-*Gericht Amt* IVb to permit his entry into the Croatian Army with his present rank. His request was forwarded to the SS-*Richter beim* RF-SS on 19 September 1943 and he agreed with the proposal. The *Reichsführer* concurred on 4 December and serving his punishment, Bellanovich then joined a Croatian Infantry Division to undertake front service.[171]

5.14 Divisional Front Probation Units

From 1942, offenders of front line divisions sentenced to a term of *Gefängnis* of up-to three months' duration usually had their punishment amended to front probation with the *Strafkompanie* (punishment company), or a field probation unit subordinate to the divisional pioneer battalion. Here, they undertook dangerous or onerous tasks.

1st SS-*Panzer*-Division *Leibstandarte*-SS *Adolf Hitler*
***Feldpostnummer*:** 05.113
Established: Eureux/France on 24 September 1942
Notes: Its commander, *Ostuf.* Willi Heinrich, died in action on 3 August 1941.[172]

2nd SS-*Panzer*-Division *Das Reich*
***Feldpostnummer*:** 14.179
Established: July 1941
Notes: Participated in the campaign on the Eastern Front and remained with the *Reich* until the unit's disbandment in the spring of 1942.[173]

3rd SS-*Panzer*-Division *Totenkopf*
***Feldpostnummer*:** 16.192
Established: Nov.1939
Notes: The *Sonderkommando* and a mine detection section participated in the 1940 summer campaign in the west and was disbanded in the summer of 1940. Its successor was established on 30 January 1942 and known as the *Einsatzkommando* z.b.V. this unit was led by *Ustuf.* Hans Endreß.[174]

4th SS-*Panzergrenadier*-Division *Polizei*
***Feldpostnummer*:** 05.429
Established: mid.1941
Notes: The *Sondereinheit* 'X' deployed on the Leningrad Front with the *Polizei* SS-*Pionier-Abteilung* and suffered heavy casualties during the winter of 1941/42 and probably disbanded in 1943.[175]

5th SS-*Panzer*-Division *Wiking*
***Feldpostnummer*:** 44.189
Established: 1944
Notes: Led by *Ustuf.* Rudolf Meder (SS Nr. 475.423)—he is thought to have previously led a company in the SS-Rgt. *Westland*—and was killed in action near Wieliszew on 16 October 1944.[176]

1st SS-*Infanterie*-Brigade
***Feldpostnummer*:** 16.441
Established: 1942
Notes: Accepting ethnic-German probationers, this *Strafkompanie* was carried over to the 18th SS-*Panzergrenadier*-Division *Horst Wessel* in December 1943.[177]

2nd SS-*Infanterie*-Brigade
***Feldpostnummer*:** 43.500
Established: 1942.
Notes: Accepting ethnic-German probationers, this *Strafkompanie* was carried over to the 15. *Waffen-Grenadier*-Division *der* SS during March 1943.[178]

11th SS-*Panzergrenadier*-Division *Nordland*
***Feldpostnummer*:** 33.316
Established: 17.7.1943
Notes: The 11. SS- *Strafkompanie*, subordinate to the SS-*Panzer-Pionier-Abteilung* 11, accepted probationers of Scandinavian and Western European origin.[179]

13th SS-*Freiwilligen-Gebirgsjager*-Division *Handschar*
***Feldpostnummer*:** 56.975
Established: June 1944
Notes: The 13. SS-*Strafkompanie*, subordinated to the SS-*Gebirgsjäger-Pionier-Abteilung* 13 and fought under the command of *Waffen-Ustuf.* Slawko Oresic.[180]

14th SS-*Grenadier*-Division *Galizien*
***Feldpostnummer*:** 29.826
Established: late 1944.
Notes: The 14. *Strafkompanie* accepted Ukrainian nationals.[181]

15th *Waffen-Grenadier*-Division *der* SS
***Feldpostnummer*:** 34.400
Established: 15.9.1944
Notes: The 15. SS- *Strafkompanie* formed as part of the SS-*Grenadier-Ausbildung- und Ersatz-Bataillon* 15 for Latvian probationers and was led by *Hstuf.* Peteris Mardoks.[182]

18th SS-*Grenadier*-Division *Horst Wessel*
***Feldpostnummer*:** 16.441
Notes: The 18. SS- *Strafkompanie* was established from the former 1. SS-*Infantrie*-Brigade (mot) *Strafkompanie* and accepted ethnic-German probationers.[183]

19th *Waffen-Grenadier*-Division *der* SS
***Feldpostnummer*:** 43.500
Established: March 1943
Notes: The 19. SS- *Strafkompanie* was established from the former 2. SS-*Infantrie*-Brigade (mot) *Strafkompanie* and accepted Latvian parolees.[184]

Waffen-Hstuf. Peteris Miervaldis Ziedins is known to have spent time with this *Strafkompanie.*[185] [18[

20th *Waffen-Grenadier*-Division *der* SS
***Feldpostnummer*:** 59.340
Established: 1944
Notes: *Waffen-Hstuf.* Voldemar Salumäe, (b.5.10.1901 in Estonia) led the SS-*Bau-Pionier-Bataillon* 3 when ordered to serve a three month period of probation in this *Strafzug* for committing an unknown offence in 1944.[186]

23rd SS-*Freiwilligen-Panzergrenadier*-Division *Nederland*
***Feldpostnummer*:** 58.308
Established: 1943
Notes: Established when this formation was at brigade strength and existed in the spring of 1944.[187]

27th *Freiwilligen-Grenadier*-Division *Langemarck*
***Feldpostnummer*:** 64.116A
Established: March 1945
Notes: Established for Flemish delinquents on the Berlin Front in the last weeks of the war, was subordinate to the divisional SS-*Pionier-Abteilung* 27 and led by *Ustuf.* Roger Groenvynck.[188]

28th SS-*Freiwilligen-Panzergrenadier*-Division *Wallonien*
***Feldpostnummer*:** 38.918
Established: Summer 1944

Notes: Established for the 5. SS-*Freiwilligen-Sturmbrigade Wallonien*, it accepted French speakers from Belgium, and its parolees fought in the Ukraine in 1944 and Germany in 1945.[189]

31st *Freiwilligen-Grenadier*-Division
***Feldpostnummer*:** 19.970
Established: February 1945
Notes: Established for this division from ethnic-German parolees.

33rd *Waffen-Grenadier*-Division *der* SS *Charlemagne*
***Feldpostnummer*:** 65.448
Established: Winter 1944-45
Notes: The 33. *Strafkompanie* was established in the *Truppenübungsplatz* Greifenburg for French delinquents and its parolees fought under the operational command of the SS-*Pionier-Abteilung* 33.[190]

35th SS-*Polizei-Grenadier*-Division
Notes: Elements of the 500. *Wehrmacht Bewährungsverbände* were attached to this division in the spring of 1945.[191]

III. SS-*Germanische-Panzerkorp*
***Feldpostnummer*:** 57.575
Established: 1944
Notes: A *Strafzug* was established for the III. SS-*Panzerkorps-Pionier-Abteilung* and the 103. SS-*Strafkompanie*, (*FPNr*. 35.194) which had been established in Chlum, fought alongside this corps at Grenadier Hill in June 1944. The survivors were rehabilitated at the conclusion of this brutal battle and in their entirety then transferred to the SS-*Panzergrenadier*-Rgt. 24 *Danemark*.[192]

5.15 *Einsatzgruppen* Probation

In some circumstances, the criminal and disciplinary offenders of the RSHA, including those from the SiPo and SD, accepted probation with an *Einsatzgruppen* on the Eastern Front:

Name: Friedrich Kockerols.
Last Rank: SS-*Untersturmführer*.
Born: 27.6.1904 in Ichendorf.
Died: 1995.
NSDAP-Nr.: 738.328 (joined 1.12.1932).
SS-Nr.: 280.239 (joined 1936).

Prewar Assignments:
Polizei z.b.V. Wecke 14.10.1925–26.7.1934.
Wartime Assignments:
SD *Einsatzgruppe* 1943.
Einsatzkommando B 1944.
Armeegruppe Wohler (AOK. 8) (*FPNr.* 44.644S) 5.1.1945.
Promotions:
9.11.1938 SS-*Untersturmführer der Allgemeine*-SS.
Decorations & Awards:
0.0.19__ SA-*Sportsabzeichen in Bronze.*
0.0.19__ SS-*Ehrenwinkel für alte Kämpfer.*
0.0.19__ *Deutsches Reichssportabzeichen in Bronze.*
0.0.19__ D.L.R.G. *in Bronze.*

Notes: Attending *Volksschule* for four classes, Kockerals obtained his *Abitur* from *Höhere Schule* and fought as a pioneer during the Great War. A policeman by profession, Kockerols was employed as a *Polizeibeamter* for the *Kriminalpolizei Grenzpolizei Kommission* and then joined the Hohensalza *Gestapo*. Kockerals married his fiancée Anneliese D., (b. 4.1.1914 in Petersdorf) on 1 April 1935 and the couple had three children up to the point when records ceased in May 1945. Deployed in Poland, Luxemburg, Holland and Belgium during his SD service, Kockerols was punished with a strong warning for behaviour unbecoming of an SS man on 29 January 1941. A subsequent court's investigation recommended his indictment and Kockerols found himself arraigned before the courts martial of the SS- *und Polizei-Gericht* III, Berlin on 5 June 1942. Judged guilty of stealing departmental property, Kockerols was punished with a term of two years' *Gefängnis* and expelled from the SS. Confirming the sentence on 6 November 1942, the *Reichsführer* amended the judgment to a term of four months' *Gefängnis* and suspended him from the SS. Serving his sentence in Danzig–Matzkau, Kockerols then undertook a period of probation with an SD murder squad on the Eastern Front. Retaining his former rank, he then joined *Brigadef.* Erich Naumann's *Einsatzkommando* in the central sector of the Eastern Front and then deployed in Romania in January 1945. Surviving the war, Kockerols was employed as a policeman and does not appear to have undergone a prosecution for his service in the *Einsatzgruppen*. He died in 1995.[193]

This police officer was punished for committing offences against the military. Born in Lötzen on 10 April 1911, Helmut Grusa, by profession a car locksmith, was employed by the Königsberg *Gestapo* with the rank of *Kriminal-Assessor-Anwärter* and accepted into the SS in May 1933 (SS Nr. 63.909), he joined the Nazi party in December 1934 and was promoted to officer rank on 13 September 1936 (RSHA). Completing his compulsory military training with the *Infantrie*-Rgt. 1 between 1 October 1936 and 30 September 1937, (*Gefreiter* d.R.), a court's investigation was conducted against Grusa on 31 July 1941 to establish his culpability in the injury caused to two military personnel while driving a car in drunken state. Arraigned before the courts martial, they judged Grusa guilty of the charge and punished him with three months' *Gefängnis* on 2 July 1942 (two months recommended served on probation). The *Reichsführer* confirmed this sentence on 6 November 1942 and commanding Grusa to serve with an *Einsatzgruppe* of the SD in the East for the remaining month of punishment, he also imposed a two years' alcohol ban on him from 16 December. Records in the Wiener library indicate that Grusa was indicted or convicted for committing war crimes in the post 1955 trials and is thought to have died in 1977.[194]

One might expect that RSHA men refusing to partake in the murderous activities of the *Einsatzgruppen* would then face court martial for committing an act of disobedience, but it appears to have been common practice to transfer refusers to other service posts without punishment. *Uscha.* Matthias Graf was attached to 6. *Einsatzkommando* in 1941 when he was ordered to take command of a commando in September 1942. Refusing to lead this murder squad, his superior then recommended him undergo a disciplinary process, but released from detention, the charges against him were dropped.[195]

This odious officer of the RSHA was punished with a prison sentence which was later amended to probation in a force engaged in the elimination of all traces of the holocaust:

Name: Paul Otto Radomski.
Last Rank: SS-*Sturmbannführer.*
Born: 21.9.1902 in Mewe *Kreis* Marienweder/West Prussia.
Died: 14.3.1945 near Székesfehérvár/Hungary.
NSDAP-Nr.: 96.942 (joined 1.5.1928).
SS-Nr.: 2.235 (joined 1.1.1930).
Prewar Assignments:
I. / 28. SS-*Standarte*, (Hamburg) from 1.1930.
Officer of the 28. SS-*Standarte* in 4.1934.
Officer of the 23. SS-*Standarte* (Gleiwitz) from 20.2.1937.
Wartime Assignments:
Waffen-SS from 1940.
Seconded to the Brandenburg *Volksdeutsche Mittelstelle* on 14.3.1941.
SD-*Leitabschnitte* Stettin in summer of 1942.
Led the *Zwangsarbeitslager* Kiev (Syrets) from 2.6.1942.
Verwaltungsführer Einsatzgruppe C from 2.6.1942.
Befehlshaber der Sipo Griechenland on 26.10.1943.
Lagerkommandant Chaidari *Arbeitserziehungslager* (Athens) from 26.10.1943.
Staatspolizeileitstelle Hamburg in 1943.
SS-*Sonderkommando* 1005 from 2.1945.
1. / SS-*Panzer-Grenadier-Ausbildung- und Ersatz-Bataillon* 5 (Bergedorf) in 1945?
Promotions:
24.11.1932 SS-*Truppführer der Allgemeine*-SS.
20.4.1934 SS-*Untersturmführer der Allgemeine*-SS.

20.7.1935 SS-*Obersturmführer der Allgemeine*-SS.
10.9.1939 SS-*Hauptsturmführer der Allgemeine*-SS.
0.0.1940 SS-*Hauptsturmführer der Reserve.*
30.1.1942 SS-*Sturmbannführer der Reserve.*
24.1.1945 SS-*Oberscharführer der Reserve.*

Decorations & Awards:

0.0.19__ SA-*Sportsabzeichen in Bronze.*
0.0.19__ *Deutsches Reichssportabzeichen in Bronze.*
0.0. 19__ *Dienstauszeichnung der* NSDAP *in Bronze.*
0.0. 19__ *Dienstauszeichnung der* NSDAP *in Silber.*
0.0.19__ *Totenkopfring der* SS.
0.0.19__ *Gelb Parteiabzeichen.*

Notes: His family moved from Mewe to Hamburg in his teens and leaving *Volksschule*, Radomski found employment at the Hamburg electric works from 1923. Undergoing periods of self-employment, Radomski marched with the 50. SA-*Sturm* between February 1928 and 30 December 1929 and his personnel file alludes to a street fight in Saale around this time which resulted in his wounding. Coming to the attention of the head of the SD in Hamburg, Reinhard Heydrich, he found a place in his organisation for Radomski's thuggish talents and his predilection for violence resulted in him receiving a term of eighteen months' *Gefängnis* from a civil court in 1932 for his part in the murder of a political opponent (he served six months). Posted to the Stettin in 1942, he took command of the Stettin–Bredow prisoner of war camp at Marchandstraße 34 and is known to have vented his sadistic personality on his prisoners. Ordered to the Syrets camp in the Ukraine in June 1942, Radomski once again indulged in his predilection for committing acts of sadism and became notorious for whipping, torturing and killing prisoners. Marrying his fiancée on 20 September 1943, the couple had one child up to the point when records ceased in 1945 and lived at Billhorner. Appointed a camp commandant for a Greek *Arbeitserziehungslager* in October 1943, Radomski once again indulged his inclination to terrorise prisoners.

Attending a small birthday party in Chaidari on 17 February 1944, Radomski and four other members of the camp staff consumed three bottles of cognac and two bottles of Samos before an extremely drunk Radomski called for his orderly, SS-*Mann* Valentin Nedler, (an ethnic-German and Croatian national) to take him to his room at 11.00 p.m. Arriving at his quarters, the irascible camp commandant became frustrated by his lack of success in his attempt to find his key to open the door and begun berating his orderly. 'Open the door you sows head!' Shouted Radomski, but annoyed at Nedler's inability to carry out this command, he then punched his orderly twice on the chin and followed these blows with two further punches to his head. 'You'll see your family no more, I'll shoot you!' Threatened Radomski to which Nedler retorted 'if I deserve it, then shoot me!' At that point two non-commissioned officer's arrived on the scene and attempted to pacify their commander. A search of Radomski's pockets produced the 'missing' key and unsurprisingly the incident was reported to higher authorities.

As a consequence of his behaviour, Radomski left Athens for Hamburg–Altengamme in February 1944 and was probably assigned to the *Staatspolizeileitstelle* Hamburg, (subordinate to the RSHA IV B4). A subsequent court's investigation recommended Radomski's prosecution and he was then arraigned before the courts martial of the SS- *und Polizei-Gericht* III, Berlin on 25 August 1944. Judged guilty of mishandling a subordinate, the tribunal imposed a term of six months' *Gefängnis* on Radomski. His *Gerichtsherr*, General Dr Kaltenbrunner, approved the sentence on 21 September, but the *HA* SS-*Gericht* disagreed with the court's assessment and declaring the sentence too mild, they forwarded the case to the *Reichsführer* for his decision.

'Exceptionally simple with a primitive mental ability' and 'wholly primate in his thinking and not suitable as an SS officer' are the words Dr Wehser used to describe Radomski in his report to the SS leader on 2 December and acknowledging that he had expressed remorse for his actions, the judge noted that the court had failed to take into account his six months' detention in 1932 for a political murder. As a result of this omission, he recommended Radomski's transfer to a RSHA *Einsatzgruppe* for a period of probation with the rank of *Oscha.* The *Reichsführer* approved this course of action on 24 January 1945 and also imposed a three year alcohol ban on Radomski. Shortly after the confirmation of his sentence, Radomski transferred to a SS-*Sonderkommando* in Riga and took charge of a unit of forced Jewish labour who exhumed victims of the *Einsatzgruppe* from mass graves, cremated the corpses and crushed their remains to dust, (many of those engaged in this gruesome task were murdered shortly before the Red Army overrun their camps). Radomski is thought to have ended the war assigned to a reserve battalion and perished before the collapse. In 2005 the Hamburg public prosecutor revealed to the Ukrainian authorities that Radomski had died in March 1945 near Székesfehérvár in Hungary.[196]

The discharging of a firearm during an impromptu party resulted in front probation for this SD officer:

Name: Arno Groebel.
Last Rank: SS-*Hauptsturmführer*.
Born: 16.3.1911 in Friedeberg/Saale.
NSDAP-Nr.: 1.399.803 (joined 1.12.1932).
SS-Nr.: 257.757 (joined 30.1.1930).
Prewar Assignments:
Hermann Göring 9.4.1930–1.5.1934.
LSSAH 1.5.1934–30.11.1936.
LSSAH 17.9.–22.10.1938.
Wartime Assignments:
Adjutant Kds Warsaw in 8.1944.
RSHA *Amt* VI FH (Havelinstitute) in 10.1944.
RSHA *Sonderkommando* from 26.2.1945.

Promotions:

30.1.1938	SS-*Untersturmführer der Allgemeine*-SS.
9.11.1939	SS-*Obersturmführer der Allgemeine*-SS.
30.1.1941	SS-*Hauptsturmführer der Allgemeine*-SS.

Decorations & Awards:

0.0.19__	SS-*Zivilabzeichen* (Nr. 132.145).
0.0.19__	SA-*Sportsabzeichen in Bronze.*
0.0.19__	*Deutsches Reichssportabzeichen in Bronze.*
0.0.19__	D.L.R.G. *in Bronze.*
0.0.19__	SS-*Ehrenwinkel für alte Kämpfer.*
0.0.19__	*Totenkopfring der* SS.

Notes: By profession a policeman, Groebel was admitted into the RSHA in 1936 and married his fiancée on 5 February 1938. The couple had two children up to the point when records ceased in May 1945. Punished with an alcohol ban on 7 August 1941, Groebel spent much of the early years of war assigned to a SiPo *Sonderkommando* on the Eastern Front. Participating in the 1944 battle for Warsaw, Groebel transferred to Berlin at its conclusion and during a visit to the home of *Stubaf.* Faßbender early one morning in April 1944 he accepted an alcoholic drink from his host and quickly became inebriated. He then proceeded to shoot out one of Faßbender's windows, surprising his host's Polish house maid and his frolicking completed, Groebel then fell into a sound drunken sleep. Though Faßbender does not appear to have been upset at his behaviour the incident reached the ears of higher authorities and the Sipo and SD investigator examined the allegation and recommended his trial (case Nr. St. L. I 345/1944). Groebel was then arraigned before the courts martial of the Berlin tribunal and judged guilty of disobedience, a term of three months' *Gefängnis* was imposed on Groebel on 7 September. Although the *Gerichtsherr*, *Ogruf.* Heissmeyer, initially concurred with the judgement, he then ordered the sentence amended to front probation on 26 January. Examining the case, *Stubaf.* Dr Bruno Heger of the *HA* SS-*Gericht Amt* Ie argued for Groebel to serve six months' *Gefängnis*, but when the interim judgement was agreed on 14 February 1945, Dr Heger's advice was ignored and a reduced punishment and front probation was recommended. The entire affair was put in the hands of the *Reichsführer* and confirming the sentence on 26 February, Himmler commanded Groebel to join an RSHA *Sonderkommando* to fight so-called bandits. An alcohol ban was imposed on him on 13 March and Groebel was warned that if he resumed drinking again the jail sentence would be imposed. Informed of this decision, Dr Heger again disagreed with the sentence and expressed his concern that the punishment would be perceived wrongly in the troop's minds.[197]

This odious officer, who was deeply involved in the murderous activities of the *Einsatzgruppe*, was punished with a prison sentence for black market activities:

Name: Friedrich Pradel.
Last Rank: SS-*Sturmbannführer*.
Born: 16.4.1901 in Berlin.
NSDAP-Nr.: 5.499.960 (1.6.1937).
SS-Nr.: 290.450 (joined 3.1.1938).
Prewar Assignments:
SD-*Hauptamt* from 1.3.1938.
Led the RSHA *Amt* II D3a (*Kraftfahrwesen der Sipo*) 1.3.1938.
Wartime Assignments:
SS-*Polizeidivision* 1.7.–31.7.1940.
Waffen-SS from late 1942,
Polizei-Schützen-Rgt. 1 *Ersatz-Bataillon* 12–20.12.1942.
SS-*Polizeidivision* from 20.12.1942.
LSSAH *Intendant-Bataillon* 1 on 20.2.1943.
SS-*Panzergrenadier-Ausbildung- und Ersatz-Bataillon* 1 (Berlin) 1.5.–7.5.1943.
Waffen-SS from 5.2.1945.
Promotions:

0.0.19__	*Polizeikommissar*.
0.0.19__	*Hauptmann der Polizei*.
3.1.1938	SS-*Mann der Allgemeine*-SS.
1.3.1938	SS-*Hauptsturmführer der Allgemeine*-SS.
1.1.1942	*Major der Schutzpolizei*.
1.1.1942	SS-*Sturmbannführer der Allgemeine*-SS.
12.12.1942	SS-*Sturmbannführer der Reserve*.

Decorations & Awards:

0.0.19__	SS-*Zivilabzeichen* (Nr. 160.365).
0.0.19__	SA-*Sportsabzeichen in Bronze*.
0.0.19__	*Ehrendegen des Reichsführer*-SS.
0.0.19__	*Kriegsverdienstkreuz II. Klasse ohne Schwertern*.
0.0.19__	*Deutsche Olympia-Ehrenzeichen* II. *Klasse*.
0.0.19__	*Deutsches Reichssportabzeichen in Silber*.
0.0.1938	*Die Medaille zur Erinnerung an den* 1. Oktober 1938 (Sudetenland).
0.0.1938	*Die Medaille zur Erinnerung an den* 13. März 1938 (Austria).

Notes: Attending *Volksschule* for four classes, Pradel obtained his *Abitur* from *Höhere Schule* and studied national economics at university for four sessions. Working as a salesman for three years, Prager joined the *Schutzpolizei* in October 1925 and married his fiancée Gertrud G., (b. 18.1.1910 in St. Petersburg) on 21 November 1932. The couple had at least one child up to the point when records ceased in May 1945 and lived in Berlin–Reinickendorf–Ost. Pradel contributed to the NSV and was assigned to the SD-*Hauptamt* from the spring of 1938. In his post as *Kraftfahrreferent der* SiPo, Pradel was responsible for technical affairs and cared for the vehicles of the SD and part of his duties entailed coordinating with other SS offices to establish motor pools in occupied countries. In cooperation with other agencies, Pradel became involved in the development and construction of gas killing vehicles in November 1941 (the vehicles were procured from the Wentritt Gaubschat in Berlin–Neukölln). Feeding exhaust fumes from the vehicle's engine via an exhaust hose into a sealed van body, the van was loaded with its victims and then driven to a burial site. Filling the van body with car exhaust fumes, the victims were suffocated during its journey. Tested in the KL Sachsenhausen, Pradel's killing machines were used to deadly effect by the *Sonderkommando* 4a and the Chelmno death camp.

Transferred to the *Waffen*-SS in late 1942, the SS-FHA agreed to Pradel's return to the RSHA on 29 April 1943 and he re-joined the SD with the rank of *Stubaf.* The SD investigator at the Potsdam branch office initiated a court's investigation against Pradel and others in early 1944 on suspicion of committing corrupt acts. During his queries, he discovered that Pradel and two other men had abused their service positions to collude to supply fuel to the black market. Recommending Pradel face trial, the investigator noted on 11 February 1944 that he required the *Reichsführer*'s decision on how to proceed against Pradel and his co-defendants. Subsequently arraigned before the courts martial of the SS- *und Polizei-Gericht* III, Berlin and their guilt ascertained, Pradel was punished with a prison sentence (unconfirmed in his personal file). Thought to have been released from detention on 13 January 1945, he then returned to the SiPo-*und* SD. Pradel's application to re-join the *Waffen*-SS was accepted in early 1945 and at this time the departments involved in Pradel's case were awaiting a decision by the SS-*Hauptamt* about his fate. Surviving the collapse in May 1945, Pradel returned to police service and worked in lower Saxony. Brought to account for his wartime crimes, the *Landgericht* Hannover punished him with a seven year prison sentence on 6 June 1966 for his part in the construction of the vehicles that murdered Jews, Gypsies and the mentally ill (case Nr. 2 Ks 2/65).[198]

5.16 Field Probation against the Partisans

Prior to the invasion of the USSR in July 1941 the *Reichsführer* accepted responsibility for providing rear echelon security for those *Wehrmacht* forces deployed on what would become the Eastern Front. Establishing the *Kommandostab* RF-SS in May 1941, this command formation accepted responsibility for controlling security units protecting the military's lines of communication, battled partisans and isolated Red Army troops. Onerously, the forces subordinate to the *Kommandostab* RF-SS, consisting of three brigades and a myriad of smaller formations, assisted the *Einsatzgruppen* in their murderous task to eliminate those judged enemies of the Reich from within the civil population, which included ancient Jewish communities. The *Kommandostab* RF-SS and the SS murder unit's orgy of death and destruction earned the force and its members the mantle of a criminal organisation at the postwar Nuremberg trial.[199]

Suffering grievous casualties during the first Russian winter campaign, Himmler had no choice but to transfer the combat elements of the *Kommandostab* RF-SS to the frontline to bolster his sorely pressed *Waffen*-SS forces. Their absence left a vacuum in the rear echelon that partisan forces hurried to fill. The remaining security forces proved unable to secure the lines of communications and had no choice but to recruit an indigenous *Polizei* force. Unfortunately for Himmler, these men proved less than reliable against the highly motivated partisan forces and rising resistance to the German occupiers in the newly conquered territories and the need to replace the forces that had been sent to the front resulted in the decision to deploy *Waffen*-SS and military parolees against the partisans.[200]

To coordinate the security forces in the occupied lands of the USSR, the *Reichsführer* commanded the establishment of three HSSPF under the leadership of a senior SS general. It was their task to exterminate Baltic and Soviet Jews and coordinate the battle against the partisans. 'He is one of the cleverest persons. Even in the party I only used him for the most difficult jobs' explained Himmler when describing *Gruf.* Erich v.dem Bach-Zelewski's capabilities and it was this craven character that the SS leader appointed to the post of HSSPF *Rußland-Mitte und Weißruthenien* in May 1941. Von dem Bach is usually credited with suggesting the deployment of SS and *Polizei* probationers against the partisans.[201]

Insurgency warfare of this type is psychologically hard; both sides frequently ignore internationally recognised rules of war and fight in harsh environments. The partisan battle on the Eastern Front witnessed some of the toughest, most brutal fighting of its type and the partisans proved a tenacious foe. Appointing v.dem Bach to the post of 'Authority for the Bandit battle' on 23 October 1942, Himmler issued orders for him to coordinate the German forces against the partisans in Northern Russia. 'The most important precondition to combat the ways of the bandit are strong nerves, a fearless heart, the will and capability to attack the enemy with very small forces and necessity to maintain the initiative, rather than leave it to the enemy, who are a poorer quality' announced Himmler in his 21 June 1943 bandit war edict. At this time he revealed the existence of the *Bandenkampfverbände*, (bandit-combating formations) and explained that v.dem Bach would coordinate these anti-partisan forces.[202]

As a direct consequence of the April 1942 *Führer* edict, a small group of men from the *Arbeitsabteilung* transferred from Debica to Bobruisk in Belorussia during April 1942 and the *Bewährungsabteilung* also created section-sized probationary forces for deployment with each of the HSSPF. These parolees participated in arduous long range patrols, nerve-wracking ambushes and seek-and-destroy combat patrols against the partisans. Long hours of inactivity were punctuated with short, but violent skirmishes with the partisans and those captured by either side, could expect little sympathy from their captors. In between conducting patrols, the probationers terrorised the local inhabitants who they suspected of supporting the partisans and also stole produce and livestock from the locals. Into this brutal, unforgiving world, Himmler ordered his very worst offenders with the intention that they either amended their personalities, or died in the attempt.[203]

The partisans were rarely pinned down in open battle and it is estimated by one author that 40 per cent of the ironically named *Himmelsfahrtskommandos* (ascension to heaven commandos) were killed, or wounded during this no-holds barred conflict.[204]

Parolees assigned to the *Bewährungsabteilung* were authorised to fight partisans on the Eastern Front from 25 August 1942 and as a consequence of this order the *Bewährungsabteilung* in Bohemia contributed 45 man-sized combat sections, later company sized formations, to participate in this fight on the Eastern Front until they qualified for clemency or rehabilitation.[205]

Probationers sent to the HSSPF *Rußland-Mitte* are known to have patrolled the road between Minsk, Slutz and Bobruisk and a probation unit is known to have held the Klitschi collective farm against partisan attacks. The 20, 21, and 22 *Strafzug* was deployed on the Eastern Front on 9 April 1943.[206]

In February 1943 the *Arbeitsabteilung* laboured to expand the SS-*Feldrekruten Depot* Moorlager, which was also known as SS-*Waldlager* 'Bobruisk' and later as the SS-*Truppenübungsplatz* 'Moorlager', and this base became the central supply depot for the anti-partisan forces for *Rußland Mitte* (SS-*Jäger-Bataillon*). Comprising of a number of fortified camps in forests along the Minsk–Bobruisk railway line, the Moorlager included training facilities, military supply warehouses, stores of equipment and confiscated food stuffs. The site also included a forestry processing plant, peat storage and a garage for vehicles. Here, in the SS-*Waldlager*, the probationers of the *Arbeitsabteilung* were tasked with the construction of a firing range, barracks and building a kitchen for the guerrilla specialists. One source reveals that *Arbeitsabteilung* probationers guarded Soviet prisoners of war and participated in the confiscation of agricultural products from local farmers.[207]

5.16.1 SS-*Sonderkommando Dirlewanger*

Despite its size and effectiveness in the anti-partisan battle, since the end of the Second World War the SS-*Sonderkommando* 'Dirlewanger' has become synonymous with this irregular conflict. A parolee unit, initially composed of Austrian and German convicted poachers who had been prosecuted for hunting with rifles, had been conceived in 1940 to permit this category of felon the opportunity to redeem themselves on the hardest sectors of the battlefield. Quickly proving an unsustainable source of manpower, the recruitment of incorrigible miscreants of the *Waffen*-SS, *Polizei* and volunteers from the concentration camps had been undertaken for this formation by 1942 and Dirlewanger's formation was accepting the vast majority of court-punished *Waffen*-SS and military probationers by the autumn of 1944, especially those under sentence of death or punished to a term of *Zuchthaus*.[208]

The *Waffen*-SS and the *Reichsjustizministerium* entered into negotiations to create this fighting force on 23 March 1940 and quickly establishing its terms of reference, the recruitment centres, *Polizei*, civil jails, the various *Land* and State administrators and *Polizeipräsidenten* compiled a list of possible candidates which was submitted to the *HA* SS-*Gericht* and *Reichsjustizministerium* for their scrutiny. Identifying suitable candidates, the SS-*Hauptamt Abt.* B I approached 300 poachers to offer them the opportunity to join the *Waffen*-SS. 86 felons accepted this offer and the RSHA then issued a protection order to permit their detention in the KL Sachsenhausen. Each volunteer received the same terms of service as offered to foreign wartime volunteers in the *Waffen*-SS and clad in the steel grey uniform without SS runes, they received combat decorations and promotions. In addition they received benefits such as family support, welfare and war injury insurance. The poacher's service in the *Waffen*-SS counted towards their military obligations, but home leave was forbidden and they remained at the front unless seriously incapacitated or killed in action.[209]

Gathered together in the KL Sachsenhausen barrack 36 between May and June 1940, the *Wilddiebkommando Oranienberg* (poacher commando) was activated on 14 June and their military training was supervised by troops of the I. / SS-*Infantrie*-Rgt. 5. Subordinate to the SS-*Hauptamt*, the *Wilddiebkommando* commander and disciplinary superior, *Ostuf.* Oskar Dirlewanger, himself a rehabilitated convict, rejected 55 volunteers on 1 July, but these losses were replaced by 27 convicts on 30 August. Four long-serving non-commissioned officers of the SS-*Infantrie-Ersatz-Bataillon Germania* joined their ranks the following month. Completing their basic training, the *Wilddiebkommando* was placed under the direct authority of the HSSPF Lublin and then deployed as guards at the Dzikow–Stary *Arbeitslager* at Grabenhaus on the River Bug. Here, the parolees of the SS-*Sonderkommando Dirlewanger* watched over Jewish forced workers digging trenches for the Otto line south of Belzec. In addition, 42 poachers deployed with various local companies to prevent sabotage.[210]

The poacher parolees were exempt from taking the oath of allegiance, but this condition appears to have been waived during the last weeks of the war for those appearing before the divisional court martial.[211]

In the late summer of 1941 General Berger supplied Dirlewanger with 3,000 *złoty* to establish a welfare fund for parolees who for no fault of their own, found themselves in financial crises. In 1941, Dirlewanger explained that this support was required as many of his men reported directly to his command from prison and had saved no money prior to their incarceration, received no support from their families and did not send their pay home.[212]

Remaining in Poland for eighteen months, Dirlewanger was denounced by anonymous letters on 24 July 1941 for his involvement in black market dealings and for engaging in sexual relations with two Jewish woman assigned to his unit canteen. The matter was reported to the SS- *und Polizei-Gericht* VI, Krakau and an investigative judge, Dr Konrad Morgen, undertook an inquiry to confirm the allegations. Obtaining Himmler's approbation, the HSSPF intervened in this matter and squashed the investigation using his *Gerichtsherr* powers. The SS-*Hauptamt* then arranged for the *Sonderkommando* to transfer to the *Kommandostab* RF-SS Belorussia, where they would engage in the anti-partisan battle.[213]

Recognised as part of the SS-FHA on 1 September 1941, the *Sonderkommando* was quickly re-supplied, re-armed and arrived in Minsk on 10 February 1942, (*FPNr.* 00.512). The 1 April 1943 issue of the *Verordnungsblatt der Waffen*-SS (Nr. 7) announced that *Sonderkommando* troops had the previosu month received permission to apply the crossed rifles/grenade insignia to their tunic collars. Remaining in Belorussia until the summer of 1944, apart from a brief period in the winter of 1943/44, Dirlewanger's troops participated in the tenacious, cruel battle against the partisans, stole foodstuffs from the local population and were active participants in the Nazi regime's murderous racial policies in the east.[214]

Subordinate to the HSSPF *Rußland-Mitte und Weißruthenien*, the *Sonderkommando* equipment and supplies were stored at the KL Sachsenhausen and the SS-*Infantrie-Ersatz-Bataillon Ost* was appointed its reserve depot. For many months this reserve unit provided a staging post for camp volunteers, but on 20 February 1944, Dirlewanger arranged for some former camp inmates to spend two hours with the SS-*Panzer-Grenadier-Ersatz-Bataillon* 35 at the SS-*Truppenübungsplatz* Westpreußen.Die Masse der Angehörigen waren straffällig gewordene Militärangehörige der Waffen SS und Polizei. Westpreußen on the proviso that they did not stay overnight.[215]

During the first week of October 1944 the *Hauptzeugamt der Waffen*-SS complained that due to the lack of storage space, the weapons and uniforms for the SS-*Sonderbrigade Dirlewanger* would no longer be permitted to store their equipment on their premises (these stores had been gathered in the camp since 30.10.1943). As a consequence of this decision, a collection commando was established to transport the stores directly to the brigade. The regimental supply unit was later based in the KL Auschwitz and this formation supplied the new recruits with their military papers and equipment.[216]

Growing from a small company-sized unit to a regimental-sized formation by 1944, the parolees of the SS-*Sonderregiment* found themselves subordinate to *Kampfgruppe Von Gottberg* and earmarked for front service in the summer of 1944. However, Dirlewanger skilfully avoided encirclement at Minsk and led his troops westwards to Grodno, passing through Ziechenau, Lida and Lomscha. Losing only their artillery unit and pioneers, the survivors escaped capture and finally reported to the SS-*Truppenübungsplatz* Ayrs in East Prussia at the end of July 1944 and undertook a period of rest and re-equipping. As the felons rested, the Polish Home Army in Warsaw fought to retake the capital city from the German occupiers. To deal with this crisis and provide the German defenders with immediate reinforcements, the *Reichsführer* commanded Dirlewanger to deploy his felons in the stricken city. This order marked the end of the unit's involvement in the partisan war.[217]

5.16.2 Rehabilitation and Recruitment Policies for the SS-*Sonderkommando*

The poachers remained with the *Sonderkommando* until pardoned and Dirlewanger had personal responsibility for submitting individual rehabilitation requests to the SS-*und Polizei-Gericht* XV, Breslau and later to the SS- *und Polizei-Gericht* XVIII, Minsk. Himmler conferred *Gerichtsherr* authorisation powers to *Ogruf.* v.dem Bach for single deserving rehabilitation cases of the *Sonderkommando Dirlewanger* on 19 May 1943.[218]

Surviving the winter battles of 1943/44, Dirlewanger announced his intention to recommend the rehabilitation of 337 probationers to the SS- *und Polizei-Gericht* XVIII, Minsk on 7 February 1944 and this occurred on 18 March. In view of the fact that only poachers were entitled for rehabilitation consideration; Dirlewanger, given the high number of submissions, had certainly ignored this regulation and recommended clemency for former camp prisoners. Though exonerated, these troops remained with the *Sonderkommando* until their wounding or death.[219]

On 16 April 1944, the SS-*Hauptamt* commanded the SS-*Sonderregiment* to send copies of medical reports for hospitalised probationers to the *HA* SS-*Gericht* for them to determine whether they were capable of undertaking further combat.[220]

1942 witnessed the beginning of the second distinct stage in the personnel development of the SS-*Sonderregiment* and not long after its deployment in Belorussia, the *Chef* SS-*Hauptamt*, General Berger, begun sending unpunished officers to Dirlewanger to enable them to satisfy the call for *Fronthilfe* (front assistance). These administrators volunteered for 'active' service with the SS-*Sonderbataillon* for a short period and their deployment satisfied the call for front assistance and offered the potential to earn combat decorations. Applying for front assistance with Dirlewanger in November 1942, *Hstuf.* Erwin Walser reported for duty as a specialist officer with the rank of *Oscha.* on 10 January 1943. Following a successful tour as an administrator, he returned to the SS-*Hauptamt* in the spring of 1944 with a clutch of combat decorations attached to his tunic.[221]

This manpower relationship between Dirlewanger and the SS-*Hauptamt* resulted in General Berger taking the decision to begin sending his recalcitrant and undisciplined officers to the SS-*Sonderbataillon* to undertake a short period of front probation. Accused of theft in 1942, this SS-*Hauptamt* officer was one the first to join Dirlewanger to prove himself worthy of remaining in the bodyguard:

Name: Werner Kurt Gerhard **Blessau.**
Last Rank: SS-*Hauptsturmführer.*
Born: 18.5.1918 in Beeskow-Storkow.
NSDAP-Nr.: 3.807.016 (joined 1.5.1937)
SS-Nr.: 290.636 (joined 15.7.1937).
HJ Service: 1.11.1931–30.1.1938.
RAD Service: 4.4.1938–25.10.1938.
Prewar Assignments:
RSHA 15.7.1937 – 31.3.1938.
6. / LSSAH 1.11.1938–12.9.1939.
Wartime Assignments:
LSSAH *Genesungkompanie* (Berlin) until 1.4.1941.
Stab SS-*Hauptamt* 1.4.1941–12.6.1943.
SS-*Sonderbataillon Dirlewanger* 12.6.1943–7.8.1943
Stab SS-*Hauptamt* 7.8.1943–8.5.1945.

Promotions:

20.4.1941	SS-*Untersturmführer der Allgemeine*-SS.
0.0.1941	SS-*Oberscharführer der Reserve.*
15.10.1941	SS-*Untersturmführer* (*Fachführer*).
20.4.1942	SS-*Untersturmführer der Reserve* (R.D.A. 1.4.1942).
9.7.1942	SS-*Obersturmführer* (*Fachführer*).
20.4.1943	SS-*Obersturmführer der Allgemeine*-SS.
20.4.1943	SS-*Obersturmführer der Reserve.*
30.1.1944	SS-*Hauptsturmführer der Allgemeine*-SS.
30.1.1944	SS-*Hauptsturmführer der Reserve.*

Decorations & Awards:

0.0.19__	SS-*Zivilabzeichen* (Nr. 172.730).
0.0.19__	SA-*Sportsabzeichen in Bronze.*
0.0.19__	*Goldenes Hitler-Jugend Ehrenzeichen* (Nr. 37693).
0.0.19__	*Deutsches Reichssportabzeichen in Bronze.*
12.3.1939	*Die Medaille zur Erinnerung an den* 1. Oktober 1938 (Sudetenland).
18.2.1940	*Verwundetenabzeichen*, 1939 *in Schwarz.*
12.6.1940	*Spange Erinnerungs-Medaile Prager Burg.*
19.6.1940	*Erinnerung-Medaile an den* 1. Oktober 1938.
1.6.1940	1939 *Eisernes Kreuz II. Klasse.*
17.9.1940	*Deutsch Schutzwall Ehrenzeichen.*
1.9.1941	*Kriegsverdienstkreuz II. Klasse mit Schwertern.*
26.6.1943	*Tapferkeitsmedaile für Ostvölker* I. *Kl. in Silber.*
8.8.1943	1939 *Eisernes Kreuz I. Klasse.*
14.8.1943	*Infanterie-Sturmabzeichen in Silber.*
0.0.1944	*Kriegsverdienstkreuz I. Klasse mit Schwertern.*
0.0.1944	*Verwundetenabzeichen*, 1939 *in Silber.*

Notes: Attending *Volksschule* for eight classes between 1924 and 1932, and trade school for three classes between 1 April 1932 and 5 April 1935, Blessau then qualified as an administrative assistant and undertook an apprenticeship at the *Kreissusschuß des Kreis* Luckau between 1 April 1933 and 31 December 1935. Working as a salaried employee at this business until 15 July 1937, Blessau remained unmarried up to the point when records ceased in May 1945. Participating in the opening stages of the invasion of Poland in 1939 with the LSSAH, Blessau was severely wounded in the upper left thigh on 12 September 1939 and claimed that his injuries were the result of a *Dum-Dum* bullet. Recovering from his wound at the Meißen, Gottleuba and Freiburg hospitals until 16 February 1940, Blessau then recuperated with a reserve battalion until April 1941. Declared fit only for garrison duties, Blessau was then appointed an adjutant to the office of the *Chef* SS-*Hauptamt* in Berlin with the rank of *Oscha*. and appointed a specialist leader of the *Ergänzungs* in October 1941.

Drinking with comrades in the 'Filmhof' public house on Mollendorf-Platz on 4 July 1942, Blessau invited *Frau* Ilse Erdmann to his table to drink with him. Departing the establishment for another public house at 11.00 p.m., the couple ended the night at her room at the Hotel 'Pension Eder' (later Blessau would claim to have slept alone on a sofa). The following morning *Frau* Erdmann noted that her jewellery, including a diamond ring was missing from her nightstand and undertaking fruitless search of the room, Blessau then left the hotel for his own lodgings. In his absence, *Frau* Selma Rudolf informed the *Polizei* of the theft and blamed the loss on the shoulders of an '*Ustuf.* Pensow'. She submitted a written statement to the *Kriminalpolizei* on 8 July and their inquiries revealed that the main suspect was Blessau and facing a cross-examination before the SS-*Hauptamt Gerichtsoffizier*, Dr Walter Hennings, in September 1942, he denied the theft. Speaking with *Frau* Rudolf on 8 and 10 September, she denied that *Frau* Erdmann had stolen her own jewellery and Dr Henning elicited from her an accusation against the hotel chambermaid.

At the conclusion of his investigation, Dr Hennings voiced his doubts that the ring had been stolen and judged that there was no evidence to initiate a courts case against Blessau. The *Reichsführer* was supplied a report on the affair in October 1942 and this cleared Blessau of any impropriety and observed that the process had failed to establish any other suspects. Writing to *Frau* Erdmann on 22 October, the SS-*Hauptamt Amt* I 3 reported that they had failed to recover the jewellery. Concluding that Blessau's absentmindedness had limited the scope of the investigation the investigator then informed her that he had decided to end his enquiry. Although doubts existed about Blessau's involvement in the theft, an investigative suspension order was commanded by the *Chef* SS-*Hauptamt* on 25 September 1942. However, doubts about Blessau's integrity persisted and General Berger commanded him to undertake front deployment with the SS-*Sonderregiment* in 1943. Arriving at his new post, Blessau became the battalion adjutant and his new commander submitted this glowing report for him on 29 December 1943:

> During the time of 12.6.1943 to 7.8.1943, SS-*Ostuf. der Reserve* Blessau was ordered to this unit by the SS-*Hauptamt* Chief. Tasked with the leadership of a company, he has participated in all engagements of the unit, amongst them two large endeavours against Bolshevik bandits and has proven to be a circumspect, daring and brave soldier. Despite the injuries sustained during the Polish Campaign which still cause him problems in walking, he marched and stormed at the front of his company against the enemy and always set a good example to his men. His military know-how and his youthful dare-devil behaviour often led to great success. To his non-commissioned officers and men below him he was always an example of courage and bravery. Because of his correct, military and open comradely behaviour, within a very short time he gained the confidence of his superiors and the entire officer corps. Likewise he was always appreciated and respected by the non-commissioned officers and men subordinate to him. For extraordinary bravery against the enemy, SS-*Ostuf.* Blessau was awarded the *Tapferkeitsmedaile für Ostvölker I. Kl. in Silber* on 26.6.1943 and on 8.8.1943 he was awarded the *Eisernes Kreuz*

> *II. Klasse.* For a successful assault attack, he was awarded the *Infanterie-Sturmabzeichen in Silber* on 14.8.1943. As far as his character is concerned, Blessau exemplifies fully the requisites of an SS officer. His premature transfer back to the SS-HA on 7.8.1943 was due to injuries he had sustained.

Severely wounded during the destruction of eleven villages on 7 August 1943, Blessau recovered from his wounds and transferred back to the SS-*Hauptamt* in Berlin.[222]

Alongside the SS-*Hauptamt* decision to send their undisciplined to Dirlewanger, the head of the SS then decided that the very worst sadists, perverts and psychotics of the *Waffen*-SS and *Polizei* would join the SS-*Sonderbataillon* and permit its enlargement to a regimental sized formation. Envisaging the unit as a last resort repository for all those sentenced to terms of *Zuchthaus* and *Gefängnis*, Himmler left it to Dirlewanger to determine whether disgraced officers were placed into positions of authority or fought as ordinary infantrymen.

Joining the SS-*Sonderregiment* in July 1943 was possibly one of the most sadistic and disreputable member of the *Waffen*-SS. His arrival heralded a new page in the unit's history:

Name: Kurt Weiße.
Last Rank: SS-*Sturmbannführer.*
Born: 11.10.1909 in Ehrenfriedersdorf, Erzgebirgskreis/Sa.
NSDAP-Nr.: 563.159 (joined 1.7.1931).
SS-Nr.: 129.822 (joined 1932).
Prewar Assignments:
SS-*Sonderkommando Sachen* 1933.
3. SS-*Standarte Dresden* in 1934.
B.m.d.F der 17 *Hundertsch.* 16.2.1935–10.7.1937.
29. / SS-*Totenkopfverbände Thüringen* 10.7.1937–1.11.1937.
II. / 3. SS-*Totenkopf-Infantrie*-Rgt. *Thüringen* 1.11.1937–1.3.1939.
I. / 4. SS-*Totenkopf-Infantrie*-Rgt. *Ostmark* 1.3.1937–1.1.1941.
Wartime Assignments:
III. / SS-*Totenkopf-Infantrie*-Rgt. 11 from 1.11.1939.
Led the 9. / SS-*Infanterie*-Rgt. *Deutschland* 1.12.1940–1.4.1941.
Led the 3. / SS-*Infanterie*-Rgt. *Deutschland* 1.4.194–2.3.1942.
SS-*Infantrie-Ersatz-Bataillon Deutschland* 2.3.1942–15.5.1942.
Nachschub Kommandantur der SS *und Polizei Russland Nord* 15.5.–25.8.1942.
Aufstellungsstab / SS-*Totenkopfdivision* 25.8.1942–1.7.1943.
Led the 9. / SS-*Panzergrenadier*-Rgt. 3 25.8.1942–1.7.1943.
SS-*Sonderregiment Dirlewanger* 1.7.1943–8.5.1945.

Promotions:

16.2.1935	SS-*Untersturmführer der Allgemeine*-SS.
13.9.1936	SS-*Hauptsturmführer der Allgemeine*-SS.
10.1939	SS-*Hauptsturmführer der Reserve.*
23.1.1943	SS-*Mann.*
1.7.1943	SS-*Hauptsturmführer der Reserve.*
1.8.1944	SS-*Sturmbannführer der Reserve.*
0.0.1945	SS-*Obersturmbannführer der Reserve?*

Decorations & Awards:

0.0.19__	SA-*Sportsabzeichen in Bronze.*
0.0.19__	SS-*Ehrenwinkel für alte Kämpfer.*
0.0.19__	*Totenkopfring der* SS.
0.0.19__	*Ehrendegen des Reichsführer*-SS.
0.0.19__	*Kriegsverdienstkreuz I. Klasse mit Schwertern.*
0.0. 19__	*Dienstauszeichnung der* NSDAP *in Bronze.*
0.0.19__	1939 *Eisernes Kreuz II. Klasse.*
7.8.1941	*Verwundetenabzeichen*, 1939 *in Schwarz.*
25.4.1941	*Verwundetenabzeichen*, 1939 *in Silber.*
20.11.1943	*Infanterie-Sturmabzeichen in Bronze.*
7.12.1943	*Nahkampfspange in Bronze.*
13.12.1943	1939 *Eisernes Kreuz I. Klasse.*
9.9.1944	*Kriegsorden des Deutschen Kreuzes in Gelb.*
0.0.19__	*Ostvolk Tapferkeit Abzeichen* 2. *Klasse*,
0.0.19__	*Ostvolk Tapferkeit Abzeichen* 1. *Klasse.*
0.0.19__	*Bandenkampfabzeichen in Bronze.*

Notes: A foreign language correspondent by profession, Weiße mustered with the prewar SA and marrying his fiancée on 27 May 1939, this union ended in divorce in December 1942. The *Ostmark* regimental commander punished Weiße and *Anwärter* Max Kielhorn with a reprimanded and a term of *Stubenarrest* for committing an unknown offence on 28 March 1939. While assigned to the SS-*Infantrie*-Rgt. 11, Weiße become drunk in Arnhem on the night of 28 June 1940 and was later discovered passed out, with his trousers undone, on the bed of the hotel owner's ten year-old son. The child was unhurt by the incident, but Weiße behaviour was reported to higher authorities and the SS-*Richter*, *Ustuf.* Heinz Meurin of the *Totenkopfdivision* field court conducted an investigation to determine the facts of the case. As a consequence of his enquiry, Weiße was arraigned before the courts martial of the SS- *und Polizei-Gericht* X, Den Haag on suspicion of committing an offence in contravention of paragraph §176 RStGB (case Nr. St. L. 22/1940). A doctor's report, prepared for the trial, concluded that Weiße was psychologically unstable and suffered from a nervous disorder. Convinced that he had intended to assault the child, but had failed to carry out his intention, the court judged Weiße guilty of drunkenness in uniform on 19 July 1940 and punished him with fourteen days' intensified arrest. Leaving Holland with his regiment for occupied Poland, Weiße was wounded by a shell splinter in his lower leg in September 1941 and transferred to a reserve battalion to recover. Wounded in the knee during February 1942, Weiße remained in hospital until May the same year and was then assigned to a reserve battalion to recuperate. His redeployment to a supply office in Riga was recommended on 15 May 1942 and assigned to the HSSPF *Russland-Nord*, Weiße remained in this post until 8 August 1942.

Leading a grenadier company at the Sennelager troop training ground from August 1942, Weiße was an extremely damaged individual by this time, a man who enjoyed exercising sadistic tendencies on the young soldiers of his command. Irritated by reports of thefts occurring in his company, Weiße ordered *Grenadier* Wilhelms to his office on 19 December 1942 to accuse him of stealing two post office packets containing sweets. When the young soldier arrived at his office, Weiße immediately began to abuse him for the theft of bread. 'You swine, you'll get a slap!' Shouted Weiße when Wilhelms denied the accusation and then proceeded to hit him three times about the head and shoulder with a blue rubber truncheon. As Wilhelms cowered before him, Weiße placed another ten blows across his back before permitting him to leave (Wilhelms was still in pain from the assault when questioned by the court many weeks later). The subsequent court investigation later revealed that least two or three other soldiers of his company were accused of the same accusation and had been beaten similarly in December 1942.

Weiße's fondness for beating his men culminated in an assault that resulted in the death of a young soldier. During a meeting with two of his officers and a few of his senior non-commissioned officers on 17 January 1943, Weiße was notified that *Grenadier* Barthel had committed 30 cases of comrade theft. Ordering Barthel to report to his office, Weiße boasted to his cronies that he would beat him when he appeared. Entering the office, Barthel was immediately subjected to a barrage of abuse and repeated blows from Weiße's rubber truncheon. 'You swine, you have discredited the company!' Shouted Weiße and repeatedly questioned him about the thefts while hitting him. Shocked by the assault, Barthel admitted stealing cigarettes and bread, but his disclosure only infuriated Weiße further and he proceeded to beat him again for fifteen minutes, landing twelve hard blows on his head and body. Finally released from his torment, Barthel returned to his room with a bloody nose and recounting the beating to his roommate, he remained on his bed for fourteen hours. When made aware of the assault, Barthel *Zugführer* assured his young trainee's that he wouldn't strike a man of possessing a dirty belt!

Later that same day a seriously concussed Barthel struggled to report to the parade ground for a drill session. In an effort to revive him, his comrades poured cold water over him before dragging him to the parade ground. The drill session concluded, Barthel returned to his room, passed out on the floor and messed himself. With help, his roommate, *Strm.* Bockhop, placed Barthel on a board and carried him to the washroom to clean him up. Convinced that he was drunk, his comrades left Barthel in the barrack cells and he remained here, lying on the floor for the remainder of the night. The following morning the guard discovered that Barthel had died and a criminal investigation was initiated to discover what had occurred prior to his death (case Nr. St. L. 52/1943). When questioned about Barthel's death on 18 January 1943 Weiße denied any knowledge of the incident and laying the blame for the soldiers' bruises on others, *Ustuf.* Fritz Kröker and *Stabscharführer* Obermeier of the fifth company confirmed Weiße's version of events. When questioned, the other company officers and non-commissioned officer's contradicted Weiße's version of events.

Arraigned before the courts martial of the *Totenkopfdivision* field court on 23 January 1943, the court chairman, *Stubaf.* Dr Barth, was supported in his deliberations by *Ostubaf.* Lammerading and *Hstuf.* Karl-Horst Arnold. *Ustuf.* Karl Heinz Klinter, from the regimental staff prosecuted the case and the protocol officer was *Rttf.* Schoel. Judged guilty of negligent homicide on 23 January 1943, the court sentenced Weiße to a term of *Zuchthaus* life imprisonment for mishandling in two cases and imposed an additional four years' *Gefängnis* for assault and perjury. Declaring him unworthy to bear arms, the tribunal denied him his civil rights, stripped him of his honour and ordered his expulsion from the SS. Weiße's co-defendants, *Ustuf.* Kröker and *Stabscharführer* Obermeier were punished for committing perjury. 'The case was without equal' and 'Barthel was a sacrifice to a sadist,' exclaimed Dr Barth in his summation and expressing his conviction that Weiße was a significant contributing factor in his death, the judge warned that Weiße should not be entrusted with men's lives in future. Conceding that he was a satisfactory officer, who enjoyed military life, was knowledgeable about military affairs and had been a good officer when part of the occupying force in Holland, the judge observed that Weiße was an violently angry man, who had developed a 'weak character' and displayed 'unrefined behaviour.'

The trial concluded, In February 1944 In shameInWeiße was then incarcerated in the *Strafvollzugslager der* SS *und Polizei* Danzig–Matzkau to await confirmation of his sentence. Remaining here for seventeen weeks, he then transferred to the SS-*Sonderregiment* in July 1943 and on arrival, Dirlewanger placed him in command of the first company with the rank of *Hstuf.* The qualities that made Weiße an unsuitable sadistic officer were precisely those required by his new superior to manage the former camp prisoners serving in his unit. The *Reichsführer* confirmed the courts judgment on 2 September and amending his punishment to a term of *Gefängnis*, he also set aside his *Ehrenstrafe* and ordered him to undertake front probation. In time, Weiße became Dirlewanger's deputy commander and was known as his trusted right hand. Former members of the unit would recall that Weiße deputised for Dirlewanger during his absences and brought to mind that his sadistic tendencies and violent behaviour knew no bounds. Feared by the *Sonderkommando* troops, Weiße name would become synonymous for brutality and ruthlessness.[223]

Rising to command a battalion, Weiße was appointed the operations officer when the SS-*Sonderbrigade* converted into a division. Thought to have survived the war by disguising himself as a soldier of the *Wehrmacht*, Weiße may have been interned by British forces in May 1945 and escaped from custody on 5 May 1946. It is alleged in some postwar publications that Weiße worked for the postwar Gehlen intelligence organisation and was eventually murdered.[224]

Another malfeasant character to join the SS-*Sonderregiment* in the summer of 1943 was a medica' officer who was expelled from the SS when he exhibited signs of mental illness:

Name: Dr med. Heinrich Wehninck.
Last Rank: SS-*Untersturmführer.*
Born: 25.7.1909 in Anholt.
NSDAP-Nr.: 4.837.758 (joined 1.5.1937).
SS-Nr.: 372.362 (joined 1940).
Prewar Assignments:
Trained with the *Infantrie-Ersatz-Bataillon* 45 (Elbling) 7.1.–7.3.1936.
Trained with the *Infantrie-Ersatz-Bataillon* 44 (Bartenstein) 8.6.–8.8.1936.
SS-*Sanitätsabteilung* 26 (Cologne) 22.2.–4.4.1937.
Wartime Assignments:
Waffen-SS from 1940
Assistant physician with the Munich & Stettin SS-*Ergänzungsstelle* from 10.1940.
SS-TV *Sanitätsabteilung* (Prague) 1940–25.2.1941.
Einwandererzentralstelle in Litzmannstadt 26.5.–10.6.1941.
SS-*Sanitätsabteilung* (Stettin) from 10.6.1941.
SS-Division *Wiking* 7.1941–5.10.1941
SS-*Polizeidivision Ersatz-Bataillon* 5.10.1941–27.8.1942.
SS-*Infantrie-Ersatz-Bataillon Germania* 27.8.–7.11.1942.
SS-*Totenkopf Sanitätsabteilung* 7.11.1942–16.1.1943.
SS-*Sanitätsabteilung* (Berlin) from 12.11.42.
Einwandererstelle Litzmannstadt 17.6.1943.
HSSPF *Russland-Mitte* 17.6.1943–15.1.1944.
SS-*Sanitätsabteilung* (Berlin) 15.1.1944–6.6.1944.
Promotions:
0.0.1937 *Feldwebel der Reserve.*
9.11.1940 SS-*Untersturmführer der Reserve.*

Notes: Attending *Volksschule* for four classes, Wehninck obtained his *Abitur* from *Höhere Schule* and against the wishes of his family he studied medicine until qualifying in 1937. Dr Wehninck was then employed by the medical service of the Organisation Todt and mustered with the SA from 4 November 1933 to 31 December 1938. Dr Wehninck was transferred to the Berlin medical reserve as a consequence of a court's investigation which had been initiated to examine his activities the previous November while attached to the 1./ SS-*Sanitätsabteilung* 3.

Receiving orders in November 1942 to make his way to the *Totenkopfdivision* in Angoulême in France, Dr Wehninck decided not to travel directly to the division, but he detoured to purchase a new uniform and visit a former service office. Arriving in Angoulême on 21 November, he was asked to explain his absence from 16–21 November

1942. Explaining the reasons for his tardiness, his superiors noted that he had no comprehension as to why his late arrival was a problem. While awaiting for a decision in his case, Dr Wehninck reported to the Würzburg *Sanitätsabteilung* on 18 December 1942 and the *Totenkopf* court investigator recommended his trial for his unauthorised absence on 4 January 1943 (case Nr. St. L. IV 226/1942). Arraigned before the courts martial of the SS- *und Polizei-Gericht* III, Berlin, the tribunal judged Dr Wehninck guilty of the offence on 16 February 1943 and punished him with four months' *Gefängnis* for contravening paragraph § 64 MStGB. The *Gerichtsherr* then recommended his case was sent to the SS leader for his opinions and writing on 1 March 1943, *Ostubaf.* Dr Klahre of the *HA* SS-*Gericht Amt* IV declared that his trial and punishment was correct and condemned him for failing to meet the disciplinary demands required of an officer.

Cutting a poor figure in court, Dr Wehninck, was placed in the Würzburg SS-*Lazarett* for observation on the date of his judgement and undertook psychological tests until 17 June 1943. Speaking with Dr Wehninck the SS-*Richter beim* RF-SS made the following observation on 3 April 1943: 'He is an inscrutable character, although he had regular medical service supervision and training, he is a loner whose training is greatly lacking.' The SS leaders advocate then observed that Dr Wehninck continued to express no comprehension of what he done wrong and warned that he possessed an 'abnormal personality' which was the result of mental illness (informed of this assessment, Dr Wehninck expressed surprise that he had been judged a psychopath). The *Gerichtsherr* and *HA* SS-*Gericht* upheld the court judgement and expressed the view that he should no longer serve as an officer. Confirmed the sentence, the *Reichsführer* ordered Dr Wehninck to undergo three weeks' intensified *Stubenarrest* and then join a medical post in a concentration camp for nine months. The Würzburg physician observing Dr Wehninck recommended his expulsion from the SS, but at the time of confirming the sentence, Himmler had refused to act on this advice and preferred to offer him special deployment in the east. The head of the SS agreed to consider expulsion at a later date, once he had received the court's fitness reports.

Posted to the HSSPF *Russland-Mitte*, the SS- *und Polizei-Gericht* XVII, Minsk was instructed to compile and submit regular fitness reports, which recorded his mental state during this deployment. The author French L. Mclean reports that the HSSPF seconded Dr Wehninck to Dirlewanger's command in June 1943 and while assigned to this unit, he was punished with fourteens days' arrest for engaging in sexual intercourse with a captured Polish prisoner. This punishment is not recorded in Dr Wehninck's *Führerkarte*, but writing on 15 January 1944, the Minsk tribunal reported that the doctor had been taken into custody following an accusation of comrade theft and the slaughtering of a goose. These events were reported to the SS-*Richter beim* RF-SS and pending a new trial, Dr Wehninck was held on remand in Berlin. Released from investigative detention on 14 February, the doctor returned to the Würzburg SS-*Lazarett* and remained under observation until the following day. Transferred to care of the specialist psychiatric team at the Gießen SS-*Lazarett* on 28 February, Dr Wehninck then underwent a further two days' observation. On 14 April Dr Klahre of the *Amt* IV revealed that the doctor was due to appear before the Berlin tribunal to answer a charge of theft (St. L. 434/1943). Further psychiatric tests were then arranged for Dr Wehninck and at their conclusion, Himmler ordered a halt to his court process on 6 June 1944. Discharging Dr Wehninck from the *Waffen*-SS, the *HA* SS-*Gericht Amt* Ie was entrusted with arranging the cancellation of his trial. Fearing the safety of his future patients, the *HA* SS-*Gericht* contacted the National Physicians Chamber to inform them of his mental illness and ask that they prevented Dr Wehninck's further use as a doctor in civilian practice. The Düsseldorf physician chamber undertook proceedings to ban the Dr Wehninck from practising in accordance with paragraph § 5 of the *Reichsärztekammerordnung* on 28 July 1944 and Dr Reinecke of the *Amt* I supervised these processes and reported on the proceedings' progress to the SS leader.[225]

Born in Unterböbingen on 31 August 1914, *Ustuf.* August Zeller had formally been attached to the SD-*Leitabschnitt Stuttgart*. He undertook military training with the SS-*Standarte Deutschland* in 1935 and fought with the SS-*Aufklärungsabteilung* 4. Sentenced to five months' imprisonment, the head of the SS confirmed Zeller's judgement and commuted it to a four weeks' *Stubenarrrest* on 11 August 1943. His punishment served, Zeller was then sent to the SS-*Sonderregiment Dirlewanger* for a period of probation in November 1943, Zeller died in Kosari, north of Cherykaw in Belorussia on 13 November 1943.[226]

From early 1943, the SS leader had selected offenders for front probation with the SS-*Sonderregiment* as an alternative to a prison sentence:

Name: Heinrich Willmann.
Last Rank: SS-*Untersturmführer*.
Born: 21.6.1917 in Kirchheimbolanden.
Died: 1.8.1944 in Warsaw/Narew bridgehead.
NSDAP-Nr.: 4.137.282 (joined 1.5.1937).
SS-Nr.: 288.565 (joined 4.1938).
RAD Service: 10.1937–4.1938.
HJ Service: 3.1.1930–22.3.1934.
Prewar Assignments:
SS-VT from 1938.
SS-*Totenkopfstandarte* 2 *Brandenburg* in 12.1938.
Wartime Assignments:
6. SS-*Gebirgsjäger*-Division *Nord* in 1942.
SS-Rgt. *Dirlewanger* in 6.1944.
7./ SS-*Panzergrenadier*-Rgt. 9 in 7.1944.
Promotions:

11.9.1938	SS-*Untersturmführer der Allgemine*-SS.
0.0.1939	SS-*Untersturmführer der Waffen*-SS.

0.0.1942 *Schütze.*
0.0.1944 SS-*Oberscharführer der Reserve.*
21.6.1944 SS-*Untersturmführer der Waffen*-SS.

Decorations & Awards:
0.0.19__ SA-*Sportsabzeichen in Bronze.*
30.8.1944 1939 *Eisernes Kreuz I. Klasse.*
0.0.19__ 1939 *Eisernes Kreuz II. Klasse.*
0.0.19__ *Goldenes Hitler-Jugend Ehrenzeichen.*
0.0.19__ SS-*Ehrenwinkel für alte Kämpfer.*

Notes: Attending *Volksschule* for four classes, Willmann studied at *Höhere Schule*, (U-I) and mustered with the SA between 28 September 1934 and 31 April 1936. Visiting Africa with the merchant fleet from December 1935 to February 1936, he sailed to Holland, England, France, Portugal and Madeira between October 1935 and December 1936. Returning to Germany, Willmann then mustered with the *Totenkopfverbände*. Assigned to the *Nord* when a punishment process was inititated against him on 23 January 1942 for committing an act of gross disobedience in the field and for issuing false orders. Arraigned before the *Nord* courts martial, the tribunal judged Willmann guilty of the charges and punished him with two year's *Gefängnis* and loss of his service grade. The *Reichsführer* confirmed the sentence on 15 May 1942, but suspended the prison sentence until the war's end and commanded Willmann to the *Bewahrungseinheiten* with the rank of *Schütze*. Fighting with the SS-*Sonderregiment Dirlewanger* in the summer of 1944, he then reported to a SS-*Panzergrenadier*-Rgt. with the rank of *Oscha.* in August the same year. Bearing the *E.K.* II. *Klasse* on his chest, Willmann had evidently proven his bravery and earned his full rehabilitation. Reported missing in action at the Warsaw/Narew bridgehead on 1 August, Willmann had been killed in action and was buried in the Pulawy cemetery. The IIa of the *Wiking* announced Willman's receipt of a posthumous combat decoration on 8 September and opening a clemency case on 6 December, the *HA* SS-*Gericht* ensured his rehabilitation and backdated Willmann's officer rank to 21 June 1944.[227]

Name: Dr med. Jan Schreuder.
Last Rank: SS-*Hauptsturmführer.*
Born: 31.5.1898 in Reeuwijk/Holland.
SS-Nr.: 393.396 (1.4.1941).
Wartime Assignments:
Waffen-SS from 4.1941.
SS-*Infantrie-Ersatz-Bataillon Ost* 2.4.1941–18.3.1942.
SS-*Infantrie-Ersatz-Bataillon Westland* 18.3.–1.6.1942.
SS-*Sonderbataillone* from 4.1944.
Seconded to the *Osttürkische Waffen-Verbände der* SS from 12.1944.

Promotions:

0.0.19__	*Leutnant der Reserve.*
1.4.1941	SS-*Obersturmführer der Reserve.*
20.4.1942	SS-*Hauptsturmführer der Reserve.*
20.8.1942	SS-*Obersturmführer der Reserve.*
Dec.1944	SS-*Hauptsturmführer der Reserve.*

Notes: Attending *Höhere Schule*, Schreuder obtained his *Abitur* from *Höhere Schule* and studied medicine at university until passing his final exam in 1923. Married in 1927, this union ended in divorce in 1932 and Dr Schreuder married his fiancée Elisabeth R. (b. 16.8.1905 in Apeldorn) on 5 July 1933. Dr Schreuder had three children from these two marriages and prior to the invasion of his country in May 1940, he had served in the Dutch Army and reached officer rank. Volunteering for military service with the *Waffen*-SS in the spring of 1941, Dr Schreuder was assigned to various SS-*Lazarett* from the summer of 1942. Arraigned before a courts martial on 20 August 1942, the SS tribunal judged Dr Schreuder guilty for an unknown incident that occurred the previous day and punished him with six months' *Gefängnis* and commanded his demotion. Confirming the sentence, the *Reichsführer* amended the punishment to six weeks' intensified arrest and loss of rank. Ordered to the SS-*Sonderregiment* in April 1944, an investigation had been undertaken by Munich authorities in February the same year when a neighbour had reported that Dr Schreuder's wife was suffering from a mental breakdown. Rehabilitated in December 1944, Dr Schreuder then reported to a non-German formation.[228]

Without waiting for the result of his trial, Himmler ordered this offender to the SS-*Sonderregiment*:

Name: Ernst-Günther Heidelberg.
Last Rank: SS-*Sturmbannführer.*
Born: 1.5.1908 in Beuthen O/S.
NSDAP-Nr.: 1.684.932 (joined 1.4.1933).
SS-Nr.: 209.649 (joined 2.1933).
Prewar Assignments:
Oberschlesien *Selbstschutz* Pissarski 7.5.–11.7.1921.
Landesschütze Oberschlesien
Reichswehr in 4.1931.
Reichswehr in 1.1933.
Stab II. / 8. SS-*Standarte* (Hirschberg i./Schlesien) from 2.1933.
Infantry training 3.11.–24.11.1934.
Pioneer training 12.10.–11.12.1935.
Pioneer training 1.4.–12.4.1937.
Wartime Assignments:
Stab V.u. W.-Hauptamt 1.4.–18.9.1940.
Bauten im Hauptamt Haushalt und Bauten, *Chef des Amtes* II 18.9.1940–1.9.1941.

SS-FHA from 1.9.1941.
*Nachschubkommando der Waffen-*SS *und Polizei Russland-Süd* 1.5.–15.9.1942.
SS-*Infantrie-Ersatz-Bataillon Ost* 15.9.-5.11.1942.
*Nachschubkommando der Waffen-*SS *und Polizei Russland-Nord* 5.11.1942-30.10.1943.
VI. SS-*Freiwilligen-Armeekorps* 30.10.-15.11.1943 (R.D.A. 30.10.1943).
SS-*Truppenübungsplatz* Böhmen *und* Mähren 15.12.1943.
VI. SS-*Freiwilligen-Armeekorps* 15.11.1943-17.3.1944.
SS-*Sonderregiment* from 17.3.1944.

Promotions:

11.12.1935	*Gefreiter der Reserve.*
1.4.1940	SS-*Unterscharführer der Reserve.*
1.4.1940	SS-*Sturmbannführer der Reserve.*

Decorations & Awards:

0.0.19__	*Schlesischer Adler* II. *Klasse.*
0.0.19__	*Sudetenkreuz.*
0.0.19__	SS-*Zivilabzeichen* (188.163).
0.0.19__	SS-*Ehrenwinkel für alte Kämpfer.*
21.2.1944	*Totenkopfring der* SS.

Notes: Attending the Beuthen *Volksschule*, Heidelberg received his *Abitur* from the Beuthen *Oberrealschule* and then studied engineering and architecture at university. His family destitute as a result of hyperinflation, Heidelberg paid his own fees and took his finals exams over the winter of 1932/33. Heidelberg received his diploma in March 1933 and employed as an assistant at the *Strassenbau-Forschungslaboratorium* for a short period, he was then appointed the Special Representative for job creation in Lauban (*Baurat*). Becoming the leader of the regional works department on 1 April 1934, Heidelberg was engaged in various building projects on the Westwall, Sudetenland and Poland from 1937 to 1940 and was injured in April 1937 while undertaking pioneer training. In occupied Warsaw, Heidelberg was tasked with supervising the repair of the cities infrastructure and he was then appointed to the Warsaw district building department. At the end of his university studies, Heidelberg married his fiancée Annliese K., (b. 16.3.1908 in Scharley O/S) on 12 February 1934. The couple had two children up to the point when records ceased in May 1945. Heidelberg was then employed at the architect's office of the Warsaw governor in the spring of 1940. Falling ill while assigned to the HSSPF *Russland-Süd*, Heidelberg recovered in a Berlin SS-*Lazarett*.

As a consequence of *Kriminalsekretär* Heinrich Nett's investigation, criminal proceedings were initated against Heidelberg, *Ostubaf.* Erwin Leckebusch and sixteen other SS officers at SS-*Truppenübungsplatz* Debica (an investigator of the *Kriminalpolizei*, Nett investigated corruption in public offices). The SS- *und Polizei-Gericht* VI, Krakau initiated Heidelberg's court martial for military service disobedience and dereliction of duty on 13 July 1942, but assessing that the entire legal process against him was too complicated to continue, the *Reichsführer* commanded Heidelberg to the

SS-*Sonderregiment* in March 1944. Reporting to Dirlewanger, Heidelberg took command of the fourth company. On 28 June 1944 the SS-*Rechtsamt* observed that they had not yet completed the court's procedure against Heidelberg from 7 May and the process had still not been concluded in October the same year.[229]

In 1944, Himmler also extended probation in the SS-*Sonderregiment* to non-German officers. Born in Poerwakarta/Dutch East Indies on 3 July 1910, Anthonius Ammerlaan had served as an army officer in the Dutch East Indies prior to volunteering for military service with the *Waffen*-SS. Promoted to officer rank on 2 November 1942, the SS-*Hauptamt* ordered *Ustuf.* Ammerlaan to leave his SS-*Pionier-Abteilung* on 2 March 1944 and report to Dirlewanger for six to eight weeks' front probation. It is not known what disciplinary offence he committed, but a letter dated 7 April 1944, confirms that Ammerlaan's transfer was the consequence of committing a disciplinary offence. Appointed a *Zugführer* in the first section of the second company, the SS-FHA ordered Ammerlaan to the SS-*Panzergrenadier-Ersatz-Bataillon* 11 in Graz on 3 June and he was granted six weeks leave to return to the *Reich* and report to his new posting. Ammerlaan was called to the Berlin civil courts during November 1944 to declare his paternity of a child.[230]

This disgraced *Ordnungspolizei* officer was amongst those sent to fight with Dirlewanger:

Name: Dr jur. Hans Heinsen.
Last Rank: SS-*Sturmbannführer*.
Born: 28.12.1907 in Braunschweig.
NSDAP-Nr.: (joined 1931).
SS-Nr.: 313.914 (joined 9.11.1938).
Prewar Assignments:
Feldjäger in spring of 1933.
Stab SS-*Hauptamt* 1938.
Wartime Assignments:
SS-*Personalhauptamt* from 9.11.1939.
Hellerau *Polizei-Waffenschule* in late 1943.
SS-*Sonderregiment* in 1944.
Promotions:

0.0.1938	*Hauptmann der Gendarmes.*
9.11.1938	SS-*Hauptsturmführer der Allgemeine*-SS.
0.0.1942	*Major der Gendarme*
21.6.1942	SS-*Sturmbannführer der Allgemeine*-SS.

Decorations & Awards:

0.0.19__	SS-*Zivilabzeichen* (Nr. 172.440).
0.0.19__	SA-*Sportsabzeichen in Bronze.*

0.0.19__ *Ehrendegen des Reichsführer*-SS.
0.0.19__ *Deutsche Olympia-Ehrenzeichen* I. *Klasse.*
0.0.19__ *Totenkopfring der* SS.

Notes: The son of a builder, Heinsen studied jurisprudence at university from 1927 and until he received his law doctorate in 1934. Studying aboard from April to October 1929, Heinsen lived in France between September and 9 October 1929. Once qualified, he worked as an assistant judge and *Gerichtsassessor* in an *Amtsgericht.* Joining the *Gendarmes*, Dr Heinsen's superiors later seconded him from the *Standort Hauptamt Ordnungspolizei* to the *Reichsjustizministerium* and he worked at the National Interior Ministry in Berlin during 1942. Mustering with the SA in 1931, he marched with the 10. SA-*Standarte* in Goslar from 1 March 1933 to 31 January 1935. Dr Heinsen left the *Feldjäger* for the *Gendarmerie* in 1933 and applied for admittance into the *Allgemeine*-SS on 19 July 1938. Marrying his fiancée Margerete D., (b. 9.4.1915 in Siegen) on 8 May 1936, the couple had three children up to the point when records ceased in May 1945 and lived in Berlin-Hohenschönhausen. Deployed in France from 5 October 1942, first as commander of the *Ordnungspolizei* in the area of the military commander in Poitiers, (*FPNr* 16.834S), Dr Heinsen was then assigned to a Toulouse task force in the summer of 1943 (*FPNr* 144.13). In this post he is thought to have been involved in the deportation of Jews from France to concentration camps. Reported for taking an unauthorised leave and committing an act of military disobedience while assigned to Hellerau in late 1943, a court's investigation was also initiated against Dr Heinsen to examine allegations that he had engaged in an affair with a Frenchwoman (case Nr. St. L. 267/1943). Recommending his trial, Dr Heinsen was arraigned before the courts martial of the SS- *und Polizei-Gericht* V, Dresden on 12 December 1943. The court chairman was *Hstuf.* Anton Baumgartl. Judging Dr Heinsen guilty of the charges, the tribunal punished him with nine months' *Gefängnis* and ordered his expulsion from the SS. The *Reichsführer* confirmed this judgment on 29 May 1944, but cancelled Dr Heinsen's *Ehrenstrafe* and reducing the sentence to a term of six months' *Gefängnis*, the head of the SS set this punishment set-aside to permit Dr Heinsen's immediate probation with a suitable probation unit. Reserving the right to amend this sentencing decision, Himmler commanded Dr Heinsen to the SS-*Sonderregiment* in Belorussia. Surviving the war, Dr Heinsen was employed in the West Berlin judiciary for 21 years (*Landgerichtsdirektor*).[231]

This officer's continuous incompetence earned him a place in the ranks of SS-*Sonderregiment*:

Name: Paul Löffler.
Last Rank: SS-*Standartenoberjunker.*
Born: 7.6.1920 in Darmstadt.
SS-Nr.: 421.084 (v) (joined 10.9.1939).
RAD Service: 15.11.1932 –?

Wartime Assignments:
Waffen-SS from 10.9.1939.
3. / LSSAH *Ersatz-Bataillon* from 10.9.1939.
1. / LSSAH from 15.6.1940.
5. *Kriegs-Junker-Lehrgang* SS-*Junkerschule* Bad Tölz 1.5.–15.9.1941.
Zugführer 1. / SS-*Aufklärungsabteilung Reich* from 16.9.1941.
SS-*Kradschützen-Ersatz-Bataillon* (Ellwangen) from 15.1.–15.6.1942.
Led the 2. / SS-*Aufklärungsabteilung Reich* 15.6.–20.4.1942.
2. SS-*Panzergrenadier*-Division *Das Reich* until 23.9.1942.
SS-*Kradschützen-Ersatz-Bataillon* (Ellwangen) 23.9.1942–4.2.1943.
Zugführer 1. / 3. SS-*Aufklärungsabteilung* 4.2.1943–9.1943.
Zugführer 1. / 3. SS-*Aufklärungsabteilung* 20.1.–24.5.1944.
SS-*Aufklärungs-Ersatz-Abteilung* (Seelager) 24.5.–10.7.1944.
SS-*Aufklärungsabteilung* 22 (Kisber/Hungary) 10.7.–11.1944.
Aufklärungskompanie 36 11.1944–4.1945.

Promotions:

15.9.1941	SS-*Standartenoberjunker der Waffen*-SS.
30.1.1942	SS-*Untersturmführer der Waffen*-SS *der Reserve*.
25.2.1943	SS-*Standartenoberjunker der Waffen*-SS.
1.1.1944	SS-*Untersturmführer der Waffen*-SS *der Reserve*.
17.3.1944	SS-*Standartenoberjunker der Waffen*-SS.

Decorations & Awards:

0.0.1942	*Verwundetenabzeichen in Schwarz.*

Notes: The son of staff veterinarian, Löffler had mustered with the *Hitlerjugend* and the NSKK. Fighting on the central Russian Front with a reconnaissance battalion until wounded in his left leg by shell splinters, Löffler recovered at the Elisabethstift *Reserve-Lazarett* in Darmstadt until 15 January 1942 and then joined a reserve unit. Receiving an injury that required hospitalisation in the spring of 1942, Löffler's punishment for an unknown offence at this time was reduced to a term of three days' *Stubenarrest*. While the division was reforming in France, Löffler and some of his subordinates visited a brothel on 21 August 1942 and here undertook a 24 hour drinking binge. At some point in the evening's revelry, *Oscha.* Kellermann and Frey, became embroiled in an argument over who was next to visit a prostitute. Both men refused to stop and Löffler pulled out his service pistol and proceeded to hit them about the head causing injuries that required a visit to a medical orderly. Both Kellermann and Frey were then dragged to a *Wehrmachtgefängnis* and held under arrest until they had sobered up. As a consequence of his actions the *Das Reich* field court then conducted a court's investigation into the affair and Löffler was arraigned before its courts martial on 28 August 1942 for assaulting his subordinates and misusing his rank (case Nr. St. L. II 254/1942). Löffler's guilt ascertained, he was punished with six months' *Gefängnis* and demoted to the rank of *Hscha.*

Posted to a reserve battalion to awaited confirmation of his sentence in September 1942, Löffler was here on 13 January 1943. During the confirmation stage of the legal process the *Gerichtsherr* and *HA* SS-*Gericht* both observed that Löffler had expressed guilt about his behaviour and feared an *Ehrenstrafe*. Confirming the sentence, both offices recommended he undertake probation, the imposition of a mild punishment and his demotion to the rank of *Uscha*. Prior to presenting the case to the SS leader, all parties agreed to demote Löffler to the rank of *Oscha.* and send him to front for probation once he had served his punishment. Confirming the sentence on 4 February 1943, the *Reichsführer,* noting the poor conditions existing in military prisons, decided to amend Löffler's sentence to four weeks' intensified arrest, demoted him to the rank of *Standartenoberjunker* and order him to the front for six months' probation. Confirming this decision on 25 February, the *HA* SS-*Gericht* ordered his reduction in rank from this date and unfortunately for Löffler, they commanded regular behavioural reports from his superiors which would prove his undoing. His earlier leg wound troubling him, Löffler sought medical attention in the *Totenkopfdivision Feldlazarett* at Weutitschein between September and the end of November 1943.

The leader of the SS confirmed his reduction to the rank of *Sta.OJ* on 4 December 1943, but mistakenly promoted to officer rank on 1 January 1944, Löffler was once again demoted on 17 March and his unit was informed that his disciplinary file remained active. Reporting to the *Totenkopf* reconnaissance battalion in January 1944, at this time his battalion commander reported that his troublesome subordinate was very insecure, too soft with his men, did not communicate orders properly and had not gained his men's trust. In addition, his commander complained that the men under Löffler's command had complained that Löffler had failed to follow explicit orders in a critical situation. 'Stupid!' Declared the SS-*Richter* beim RF-SS when he read this fitness report on 11 August and doubting the battalion officer's motives for making these comments, Dr Wehser demanded that he wrote and explained himself. Rejecting Löffler's reprieve at this time, Dr Wehser ordered the officer candidate to another reconnaissance unit to learn to communicate properly as a field commander.

The poor performance report composed by the commander of this reconnaissance battalion resulted in Löffler's transfer to a reserve battalion to undertake further training and they seconded him to a training unit at Majorhof-Seelager on 25 May. Ordered to a new reconnaissance battalion in Hungary in July 1944, Löffler's officer skills were once again reassessed and his new commander also formed a low opinion of his new subordinate's abilities. Reporting his findings to the SS-*Richter beim* RF-SS, Dr Wehser expressed his exhaustion with Löffler's 'absolute stupidity' and convinced that he had failed to fulfil the demands expected of an officer, the judge wrote to the *HA* SS-*Gericht* on 2 September to arrange his immediate transfer to the SS-*Sonderbrigade Dirlewanger* in Slovakia. On arrival, Dr Wehser demanded that Löffler was reminded that if he continued to behave stupidly then he would face expulsion from the SS with all the uncertainty that this punishment entailed. Ordering Löffler to remain with the SS-*Sonderbrigade* for one year, Himmler again demanded regular fitness reports about his behaviour. Reporting to Dirlewanger in November 1944, Löffler fought alongside former *Oberst* Momm and the former SS-*Richter* Willy Osthues. Finding himself at Forsthaus Lübben in April 1945, here, Löffler observed his officers deserting and he and Osthues decided to follow suit. Surviving the war, Löffler was incarcerated in the Darmstadt internment camp on 9 September 1946.[232]

Wishing to increase his strength and replace losses, Dirlewanger wrote to the head of the SS in 1942 to suggest recruiting concentration camp prisoners into his unit and expressed his willingness to accept the regimes political enemies and incorrigible criminals. At this time, Himmler had already decided, whatever their crime, to offer SS and *Polizei* convicts detained in concentration camps the opportunity of probation with *Bewährungsabteilung* and *Sondereinheiten* and deploy them against the enemy in difficult circumstances, or in situations where there existed a high chance of death or mutilation, but the number of suitable candidates for this scheme remained small.[233]

Accepting Dirlewanger's concentration camp recruitment proposal in the summer of 1942, the head of the SS also commanded that prisoners in civil jails, serving *Zuchthaus* sentences or facing capital punishments, should be offered chance to fight with the SS-*Sonderregiment*. In early 1943 the *HA* SS-*Gericht* begun the task of identifying former SS and *Polizei* camp prisoners for parole with Dirlewanger and selecting four of these inmates languishing in the KL Sachsenhausen for service with the SS-*Sonderregiment* on 10 February 1943, the SS-*Ergänzungsamt* commanded that these parolees report directly to the SS-*Infantrie-Ersatz-Bataillon Ost* in Zhitomir to undertake basic infantry training. When this training had been completed was all four former convicts then joined the SS-*Sonderregiment*.[234]

The policy of recruiting political and so-called asocial concentration camp prisoners into the SS-*Sonderbataillon*/*Sonderregiment* was implemented in the latter half of 1942 and during camp roll calls, the *Schützhaftlagerführer* appealed to the camp prisoners' patriotism to volunteer for military service, but omitted to mention that they would join the *Waffen*-SS. Those accepting this offer were then segregated from the remainder of the prisoners, underwent disinfection and faced a medical examination. Issued an SS uniform—minus runes and rank insignia—the parolee's photograph was taken and SS pay books were prepared for them. Weapons were not usually issued at this time and the volunteers drilled and exercised while awaiting transport to Belorussia.[235]

The policy of accepting camp prisoners was quickly extended to non-German inmates. In February 1943 the WVHA authorised the *Ergänzungsamt* to recruit amongst Croatian and Romanian ethnic-German camp prisoners and in September the same year the SS-*Sonderregiment* inducted a batch of camp prisoner parolees who had completed their basic training with the SS-*Grenadier-Bataillon Ost* in Breslau.[236]

The recruitment of former camp prisoners and serious offenders from civil penal institutions enabled Dirlewanger to expand the size of his formation from a battalion to a regiment and by early 1944, the *Reichsführer* was seeking to recruit more parolees from camp sources. For the purpose of rehabilitation with the SS-*Sonderregiment*, the

Reichsführer announced on 19 February 1944 that German 'asocials and criminals' aged between seventeen and 40 was recruited from the camps and as a consequence of this order, Himmler expected to recruit between 1,000 and 1,200 camp prisoners for Dirlewanger. By the following month some 800 camp prisoners had been recruited. Writing on 29 April, *Ostubaf.* Dr Wilhelm Wolff of the SS-*Hauptamt Amt* C I 3, (3b) ordered a batch of these camp recruits to gather at Lobositz on the Elbe with their escort. Permitting them to bring extra blankets, musical instruments, games and photographs, Wolff warned the parolees to possess no more than one *Reichsmark* worth of tobacco. The collection commando escorting these volunteers to Belorussia consisted of one non-commissioned officer and three SS men. In addition to the recruitment of camp prisoners, the *Arbeitsabteilung* in Bobruisk and *Bewährungsabteilung* in Prague received orders on 20 May 1944 to select and send 200 suitable parolees to Dirlewanger.[237]

5.16.3 Punishment Regime within the SS-*Sonderkommando*

From its inception in 1940, Dirlewanger was granted the authorisation powers of a *Gerichtsherr* and possessed the authority to punish or recommend the rehabilitation of all of his soldiers below the rank of *Hstuf.* Undisciplined miscreants of the *Waffen*-SS faced punishment in accordance to the principles of the SS-DBO and statutes of the MStGB. Those sentenced to short terms of intensified detention served their incarceration in the KL Sachsenhausen camp arrest and completing his punishment, the offender returned to the SS-*Sonderbataillon/Sonderregiment.* In addition to these powers, Dirlewanger was granted authorisation to punish poachers and former camp prisoners with capital punishments (by firing squad, hanging in a KL or the field and summary neck shooting). Possessing the power of life and death over the former camp prisoners, Dirlewanger, Weiße and his officers are known to have rewarded signs of indiscipline with sadistic cruelty. Dirlewanger's summery powers did not extend to members of the *Waffen*-SS, these parolees accused of committing serious offences faced court martial before the SS-*und Polizei-Gericht* XVII, Minsk.[238]

A member of the SS-*Sonderbataillon* recuperating in a Mogil'ov hospital for two weeks in October 1942 was denounced for contracting to a sexual disease and Dirlewanger accepted the physician's recommendation that his patient was punished with a six months' leave ban for disobedience.[239]

The publication of a special order of the day on 11 May 1944 sheds an interesting light on how Dirlewanger handled indiscipline within his formation. Lodging with *Ostuf.* Egyd Ingruber's first company in Russian village for one night, the *Sonderbataillon* commander was shocked to discover that his troops lived cheek-by-jowl with 22 Russians, (their number included 20 women who cleaned the accommodation and cooked meals). 'To clean officers' boots, serve their food and be lorded over' admonished Dirlewanger and informed his men that this situation had occurred in direct contravention of an order of the head of the SS. Demanding an end to this 'hair-raising state of affairs,' Dirlewanger could not imagine the effect of this situation on the new recruits and commanded that the Russians leave their accommodation and warned his men in future to only employ Russians for construction work. Demanding that his troops cleaned their own military accommodation, the *Sonderbataillon* commander warned that he intended to keep an eye on this situation and if this problem arose again, Dirlewanger threatened to send the offenders to a concentration camp. He then instructed his troops to report such incidents to the regimental headquarters immediately and cautioned his non-commissioned officers that if they permitted this state of affairs to occur again then they would risk punishment for negligence—even those who had not personally shared accommodation with 'native women' (Dirlewanger evidently feared that his troops were cohabitating with the women).[240]

Absorbing large numbers of camp prisoners into the regiment from late 1942, Dirlewanger and his officers treated these parolees, who included habitual criminals and political prisoners, with great harshness and did not hesitate to impose summary executions to maintain discipline. With fifteen guards under his command, *Hstuf.* Rudolf Stöweno left the KL Sachsenhausen on 2 July 1943 with 321 former camp prisoners to undertake an eight day rail journey to the city of Minsk. The column then marched the 50 km to Lahoysk and on arrival the group was designated the 2. *Rekruit-Kompanie* (German). Before retiring to their billet, a village school building, the company assembled before Stöweno to witness the summary execute of one of their number. During training, he selected two rifleman of his company for execution.[241]

The cane was commonly imposed on undisciplined former camp prisoners. For a first time offence, the offender was placed across a wooden stock and received 25 lashes across his lower back and buttocks. 50 lashes was imposed for committing a repeat offence and parolees were beaten 100 times for committing a serious breach of discipline. A particularly nasty punishment associated with the SS-*Sonderbrigade* was the so-called '*Stehbunker*' (standing bunker). Also known as the 'Dirlewanger box', this penalty is thought to have been introduced by Kurt Weiße in Prlevidza/Slovakia during January 1945. Sealed into a standing coffin-shaped box, the parolee had no ventilation, or wriggle room to turn and they were unable to bend their knees for anything between three days to three weeks' duration. This punishment also resulted in the swelling of the ankles, making standing very painful. A five minute break was permitted each day to eat and to use the toilet.[242]

The selection of 'unsuitable' camp prisoner recruits proved a source of aggravation to Dirlewanger. Writing to *Gruf.* Berger on 21 August 1943 the *Sonderregiment* commander complained that the arrival of one transport had caused him a 'mild shock' when he discovered that 44 of their number were homosexuals and Gypsies. Returning these men to the camps, he then demanded that these types of volunteers were no longer sent to him. In future, he asked that parolee's personnel files accompanied them to his unit. As a deterrent for would be deserters, Dirlewanger revealed that he planned to send these offenders to the KL Mauthausen—considered to be the worst camp in the system. Despite his demand that the camps refrained from accepting paragraph § 175 volunteers, these prisoners appear to have continued stepped forward for service in the SS-*Sonderbrigade*.

According to one source, discovering that three troops had committed offences in contravention of paragraph § 175 during the winter of 1944/1945. Dirlewanger ordered them stripped of their winter uniforms at night and pink pieces of cloth were sewn to their tunics and trousers. Then taken forcibly to a nearby forest and tied to trees, their guards roundly abused them before leaving them to die from exposure. Quickly discovered by a Red Army patrol, the freezing SS men were led back to the Soviet headquarters and questioned about the meaning of the pink patches. Fearing further retribution, all pleaded ignorance about their significance and their lives were saved by an Armenian doctor, who ordered them taken to a hospital to recover from frostbite.[243]

Turning his attention to the disciplinary concerns of the SS-*Sonderbrigade Dirlewanger* on 20 February 1944, Himmler clarified the legal status of its men:

> The *Einsatz-Bataillon* Dirlewanger consists of German men who have been previously convicted of poaching. The nucleus is considered to be good and even very good: concentration camp prisoners who are suitable for the assignment; former members of the SS, who, after having served their time, are then assigned to front service for rehabilitation purposes. In combat the commander has jurisdiction over life and death over all the members of these battalions, which consists of various components. The rehabilitation of the former poachers is undertaken, without the participation of the *HA* SS-*Gericht*, through SS-*Ogruf.* Berger and SS-*Gruf.* Nebe of the RSHA through the *Reichsjustizministerium*. The accomplished rehabilitation will be reported to the *HA* SS-*Gericht*. The commander of the battalion, SS-*Ostubaf.* Dirlewanger possesses jurisdiction over the life and death of the concentration camp prisoners in rest areas and the field garrison. The poachers will remain under SS jurisdiction after their rehabilitation. As long as they have not been rehabilitated, the commander also possesses the power of life and death in the rest area and the field garrison. Former SS men, assigned for rehabilitation, remain under SS jurisdiction in rest areas and the field garrison.

In battle deployment, the SS-*Sonderregiment* commander had the right of life and death over all men. Once rehabilitated, the poacher and SS probationers remained with Dirlewanger until the *Reichsführer* personally decided their release. Case files involving poachers who had been wounded in action were passed to the *HA* SS-*Gericht*, the SS-*Hauptamt* and RSHA to obtain a mutually agreed rehabilitation decision. At this time, the head of the SS refused to permit the rehabilitation of former camp prisoners and ordered them to remain in the SS-*Sonderregiment* until their death. Simply cannon fodder, the former camp prisoners fought under a suspended death sentence.[244]

There is evidence that in the latter half of 1944 the *HA* SS-*Gericht* had become convinced that Dirlewanger was flouting Himmler's 20 February order and failing to adhere to the clemency process. 'Imploring' *Ostuf.* Klumm of the SS-*Hauptamt* to inform him exactly what court had confirmed the capital punishment of three *Sonderbrigade* parolees on 29 October 1944, the SS-*Richter beim* RF-SS, (Dr Wehser) complained that it was 'unusual' for the *Chef* SS-*Hauptamt* to confirmed these three court-sentenced cases directly to Dirlewanger without informing his office and now demanded that Klumm furnish him with further case details, the names of the condemned and an explanation for how this situation had been permitted to occur.[245]

Given the *Sonderbrigade*'s complicated disciplinary needs, the *HA* SS-*Gericht* decided at the end of 1944 to assign an SS-*Richter* to their headquarters. When told of this decision, Dirlewanger expressed his preference for *Ostubaf.* Horst Kaminski to the post of chief judge on 3 December 1944, but unavailable, the *HA* SS-*Gericht* substituted him for *Hstuf.* Dr Bruno Wille with orders to ensure that SS and military probationers were properly assessed for rehabilitation in accordance with the military legal code. Arriving at the SS-*Sonderbrigade* in December 1944, Dr Wille introduced himself to its commander and then proceeded to undertake his task. In the short time he spent with this formation, Dr Wille grew convinced that the dregs of the Nazi prisons fought with Dirlewanger and estimating that 30 per cent of the brigade's personnel were former camp prisoners, who in his opinion were little more than 'cannon fodder' and he witnessed the execution of twenty of their number in January 1945. Here Dr Wille relates his short experience with the brigade in 1946:

> In neither its composition nor in its leadership was the formation an SS unit; few of their number wore an SS uniform; all matters concerning Dirlewanger were regulated directly with Himmler or his intimate friend SS-*Gruf.* Berger who did everything for him. Justice in the brigade was shocking, Dirlewanger handled this task personally and was responsible for discipline within the whole unit, which was based only on beatings. When I pointed out to Dirlewanger what was happening in the brigade, he threatened me with murder and I was then transferred to another place of safety for reasons of my own personal.[246]

Fleeing from the brigade to report his treatment to the SS-*Gericht des Dt. Befehlshabers in der Slowakei* and the *HA* SS-*Gericht*, Dr Wille returned to the 16th SS-*Panzergrenadier*-Division 'RF-SS' and in the absence of a qualified SS-*Richter*, a brigade non-commissioned officer handled the court's business until *Ostubaf.* Horst Kaminski was appointed the chief judge of the 36th *Waffen-Grenadier*-Division *der* SS in March 1945.[247]

5.16.4 *Sonderbrigade Dirlewanger* and the 36th *Waffen* Grenadier Division of the SS

Narrowly escaping destruction during its retreat from Belorussia in the summer of 1944, Dirlewanger settled his survivors in at the SS-*Truppenübungsplatz* Ayrs in East Prussia and then travelled to Berlin to visit General Berger. Here, he discovered that the Polish Home Army had begun their attempt to retake Warsaw from the German occupiers on 1 August 1944. Entrusting the head of the SS with quelling this uprising, Hitler permitted him to recruit fresh troops from the *Ersatzheer* and Himmler commanded Dirlewanger to deploy his troops in Warsaw on 5 August.[248]

Dirlewanger directed a battalion-sized unit under the leadership of *Ustuf.* Meyer to deploy along the Wolska in the east of the city and the parolees then fought their way into the city centre. Discovering that Dirlewanger was still in Berlin on 8 August, the *Reichsführer* angrily ordered him to immediately leave the capital for Warsaw.[249]

In Warsaw the parolees of the SS-*Sonderregiment* sought to establish a corridor to trapped German forces and in the process they unleashed a wave of murder, rape and plunder on the unarmed citizens. Woman and children were among their victims, but the probationer's genocidal behaviour only served to stiffen the Polish fighters' resolve and prolonged the battle. Ironically a ceasefire was only facilitated once Dirlewanger's troops had been ordered out of the city in the last week of September 1944.[250]

A crony of Dirlewanger, this officer lost his life fighting in Warsaw:

Name: Max Schreiner.
Last Rank: SS-*Untersturmführer.*
Born: 21.6.1899 in Eßlingen a. N.
Died: 6.9.1944 in Warsaw.
Promotions:

9.6.1943	SS-*Hauptscharführer der Reserve.*
2.8.1944	SS-*Untersturmführer der Reserve.*

Decorations & Awards:

1914-18	*Eisernes Kreuz II. Klasse.*
1914-18	Württemberg *Tapferkeitsmedaile in Silber.*
12.2.1944	*Spange* 1939 *Eisernes Kreuz II. Klasse.*
0.0.19__	*Kriegsverdienstkreuz II. Klasse ohne Schwertern.*
18.8.1944	1939 *Eisernes Kreuz I. Klasse.*
0.0.19__	*Tapferkeits- u. Verdienstauszeichnung f. Angehörige der Ostvölker in Silber.*
0.0.19__	*Infanterie-Sturmabzeichen in Silber.*
0.0.19__	*Bandenkampfabzeichen in Bronze.*
0.0.19__	*Verwundetenabzeichen,* 1939 *in Silber.*

Notes: A decorated Württemberger Great War veteran, Max Schreiner, appears to have joined the SS-*Sonderbataillon* at the behest of Dirlewanger on 9 June 1943, but little is known about Schreiner before he arrived in Belorussia, but from his collection of combat decorations, he appears to have been an active participant in the anti-partisan battle. Escaping the Byelorussian encirclement, Schreiner was promoted to officer rank in August 1944 and appointed a *Kompanieführer.* Killed in action on 6 September while leading his company during an attack on a defended Warsaw riverside apartment block, Dirlewanger recommended his posthumous award of the *Deutsches Kreuz in Gelb* and his application was supported by both *Gruf.* Reinfarth and *Ogruf.* v.Bach. The award submission noted that Schreiner had attacked an enemy anti-tank position near the River Drissa on 7 November 1943, had fought near Conibar southwest of the Newel on 13 November and was wounded while attacking an enemy position on 14 November (he returned to unit eight days later). Leading an attack on partisan positions between Minsk and Usda on 22 February 1944, Schreiner reportedly forced the defenders to retreat with heavy casualties. Assessed to have ensured few losses during the retreat between Rakow and Lida on 3 July and having prevented the Home Army forces from retreating from the Markthalle on 8 August, Dirlewanger claimed that Schreiner's actions enabled the regiment to advance on the Palais Brühl and although wounded four days later, Schreiner continued to lead his troops despite the injuries to his lower-jaw and led an attack against a barricaded position on the Dlugastraße. The *Reichsführer* rejected the recommendation for this award on 16 November 1944.[251]

While Dirlewanger's regiment struggled to overcome the Warsaw defenders, a decision was taken to expand the regiment to a brigade-sized formation. This demand and a need to replenish the regiments losses suffered in Poland led the head of the SS to conduct an intense search for reinforcements and to issue a command to the *Strafvollzugslager der* SS *und Polizei* Danzig–Matzkau to prepare 1,500 inmates for immediate transfer to the SS-*Sonderregiment* in Warsaw on 20 August 1944.[252]

In addition to these reinforcements, the SS-*Straflager* Dachau and its branch prisons were combed through for suitable parolees and the SS-*Hauptamt* renewed their efforts to recruit more camp prisoners. Collected together at the Radom *Luftwaffe Truppen*übungsplatz, these new parolees received uniforms, equipment and arms before joining the regiment. During the battle for Warsaw an estimated 2,500 replacements reinforced Dirlewanger's regiment and he reported 2,700 losses.[253]

As a direct consequence of the 20 July 1944 assassination plot, Adolf Hitler had handed command of the *Ersatzheer* to the control of the *Reichsführer*. This was the military organisation responsible for the recruitment and training of new troops, and oversaw the implementation of the military judiciary.[254]

The decision to place the head of the SS in command of the *Ersatzheer* permitted Himmler to select around 500 military convicts from the Torgau–Anklam and Bruschsal *Wehrmachtgefängnis* for probation with the SS-*Sonderregiment* and these parolees arrived in time to participate in the battle for Warsaw. Discussing the transfer of additional military convicts to Dirlewanger in the autumn of 1944, the SS-*Richter beim* RF-SS arranged with the military to select *Zuchthaus* inmates serving sentences of fifteen years or greater and those who had been punished with suspended capital punishments. Concluding his negotiations the SS-*Richter beim* RF-SS would note ruefully that this was 'an unattractive arrangement' for these men. On 12 December 1944 it was announced that officer offenders posted from military gaols to the SS-*Sonderbrigade* would not automatically transfer to the *Waffen*-SS:

> There are two ways of entering the brigade and this depends on the seriousness of the crime that they have committed:

1. They are dismissed from the Army and enter the *Waffen*-SS only for the duration of the war and,
2. Dirlewanger permits them to join the *Waffen*-SS in which case he notifies the Army personnel department via the SS-PHA.

In addition to these proposals, the armed military probationers of the *Wehrmacht* 500 and 999 formations were also transferred in their entirety to the SS-*Sonderbrigade*. 'On the orders of the *Reichsführer*, those military criminals going to Dirlewanger will do so as if they were receiving probation with the *Heer*' commanded the SS-*Richter beim* RF-SS and at this time he revealed that the SS-*Sonderbrigade* had become the final destination for all military convicts, even enemies of the state, who had been judged eligible for field probation.[255]

As a result of these measures an estimated 1,000 military convicts transferred to the *Bewährungsabteilung* at the SS-*Truppenübungsplatz Böhmen-Mähren* by the late autumn of 1944 to prepare for military service in the SS-*Sonderbrigade*. Amongst those parole units absorbed into the brigade at this time were the troops of the *Bewährungsabteilung Fischer* (part of the *Ersatz*-Rgt. 500) and a total of 3,250 *Wehrmacht* probationers had reported to the brigade by the end of the year. Leaving Warsaw, the brigade survivors then joined probationers training with the *Ersatz-Kompanie* at Krakau, Fischerstraße 16. By the winter of 1944 enough manpower had been sourced from military gaols to establish a brigade with two infantry regiments. Deploying the SS-*Sonderbrigade* near Brünn in late September/early October 1944, here, Dirlewanger's troops participated in the suppression of the uprising in Slovakia and at the conclusion of this short campaign the brigade rested in and around the town of Diviaky to train and absorb new recruits.[256]

This disgraced officer transferred to the SS-*Sonderbrigade* when it was discovered he had embezzled company stores:

Name: Eugen Haiber.
Last Rank: SS-*Untersturmführer*.
Born: 30.7.1914 in Aalen/Wttbg.
NSDAP-Nr.: 2. 091.716 (joined 20.3.1933).
SS-Nr.: 113.802 (joined 1.6.1933).
Prewar Assignments:
SS-VT 1.10.1934–1.10.1938.
II. / SS-*Standarte Deutschland* from 1.10.1934.
Gruppenführer 6. / III. / SS-Rgt. *Germania* 1.5.1935-31.10.1938.
Training course at the Wündsorf *Heer Sportsschule* in 1938.
Wartime Assignments:
Waffen-SS from 1.8.1939.
Gruppenführer 11. / III. / SS-Rgt. *Germania* from 1.8.1939.
Kriegs-Reserve-Führeranwärter-Lehrgang SS-*Unterführerschule* Radolfzell 2.3.–23.7.1941.

Zugführer 4. / SS-FLAK-*Abteilung des Kommandostab* RF-SS from 1.9.1941.
'RF-SS' *Begleitbatallion* in the summer of 1942.
Lt. Artillerie Kolonne / Kommando RF-SS FLAK *Abteilung* 8.1942.
SS-FLAK *Ersatz-Bataillon* 5.12.1942.
Unterführerlehrgang SS-FLAK-*Ersatz*-Rgt. (Arolsen) in early 1.1942.
FLAK *Lehrgang* Munich *Krieg* FLAK-*Artillerieschule* in 1942.
Led the 1. *Batterie* (2cm) / 14. / SS-*Panzergrenadier* Rgt. 19 from 28.2.–11.8.1943.
Ordnance officer SS-FLAK-*Abteilung* 9 from 11.8.1943.
SS-*Sonderbrigade Dirlewanger* from 7.7.1944–8.5.1945.

Promotions:

1.10.1934	SS-*Anwärter*.
1.10.1934	SS-*Mann*.
25.4.1935	SS-*Sturmann der Allgemeine*-SS.
15.9.1935	SS-*Rottenführer der Allgemeine*-SS.
20.4.1936	SS-*Unterscharführer der Allgemeine*-SS.
1.6.1941	SS-*Oberscharführer d. R. u. Führeranwärter*.
1.9.1941	SS-*Untersturmführer der Reserve*.

Decorations & Awards:

0.0.19__	SS-*Zivilabzeichen*.
0.0.19__	SA-*Sportsabzeichen in Bronze*.
0.0.19__	4 *Jähr Dienstauszeichnung der* SS.
0.0.19__	*Die Medaille zur Erinnerung an den* 1. Oktober 1938 (Sudetenland).
0.0.19__	*Die Medaille zur Erinnerung an den* 13. März 1938 (Austria).
0.0.1939	1939 *Eisernes Kreuz II. Klasse*.
0.0.19__	*Medaille* '*Winterschlacht im Osten* 1941/42'.
0.0.19__	*Deutsches Reichssportabzeichen in Bronze*.
0.0.19__	D.L.R.G (*Lehrschein*).

Notes: The son of a *Reichsbahninspektor* from Aalen/Wttbg. Attending *Volksschule* for three classes, Haiber obtained his *Abitur* from the Arolsen *Mittel/Höhere Schule* in Easter 1933 (nine classes) and then undertook training in a bank for one year (*Bankbeamter*). Signing a twelve year contract with the SS-VT on 1 October 1934, Haiber left this service for a salaried post with the NS-*Jugendleiter bei der Kreisamtsleitung* Kassel, but drafted into the *Waffen*-SS in August 1939 and he participated in the Polish and Western campaigns. Haiber married his fiancée Margarit K., (b. 25.11.1917 in Arolsen) on 10 June 1939 and they had one child up to the point when records ceased in May 1945.

For committing offences against good soldierly conduct and discipline the SS-FHA *Amt* V punished Haiber and *Hscha*. Kurt Benkel with a strong warning on 6 January 1943, (ended 25.7.1943). An audit of the fourteenth company canteen and company funds revealed unexplained losses in their fuel levels and special *Panzer* rations. As a consequence of these findings, the field court arranged for *Hscha*. Benkel's detention in the *Strafvollstreckungszüge* on 26 August 1943 and Haiber joined him on 3 September 1943.

Remaining in remand custody until 20 September, Haiber was hospitalised during his incarceration and permitted recovery leave. Questioned about the discrepancies, Haiber claimed to have lost the receipt acknowledgment and cash book and revealed that he had destroyed old invoices because they had become superfluous to his calculations (these invoices would have been useful for reconstructing the cash fund). Wishing to make sense of his book keeping, the court arranged for a forensic accountant to examine the surviving records and assuming an intrinsic 20 per cent profit margin, he estimated a 1,700 *Reichsmark* shortfall in the canteen cash box. Questioned about this loss, Haiber explained that he had sold many products without a profit margin, some even below cost and given away out of date stock.

Questioning other troops in the fourteen company, the investigator discovered that while in charge of the canteen stock both Haiber and Benkel had become fascinated by the special *Panzer* rations, especially the Scho-ka-kola which was wrapped in individual packages. Within a four/six week's period Haiber had stolen at least fifteen packs of Scho-ka-kola and Benkel one pack. The division relocating from Belgium to France, two members of the company reported the theft of Scho-ka-kola from an opened package to the courier. Questioned about this loss, Haiber explained that the sweet may have been damaged in transit or had spilled in liquid form. He then attempted to convince the judge that he had encountered problems storing food properly, especially the Scho-ka-kola, and had had experienced difficulty preventing them from rotting away. In actual fact, Haiber had arbitrarily increased the number of supposedly worthless packs to hide the thefts. In addition to the theft of the sweets, Benkel was accused of conducting auctions during room reviews and accepted bids for surplus found equipment he had found in the lockers of men, regardless whether the bidder was missing these items, or not. The proceeds of these auctions went into the company cash box, but Benkel was impeached for abusing his service authority.

Confronted with the accusation that he had misused company fuel stocks, Haiber claimed that he had only used petrol to drive his car during his official duties, an explanation the judge accepted. However, Haiber was unable to explain why he induced subordinates to cover up the amount of fuel that he had used and the judge therefore indicted him for abusing his service authority. In addition to these offences, four witnesses accused Haiber and Benkel of taking cigarettes whenever they wanted them. Permitted three cigarettes a day, Haiber explained that he omitted to take his daily allocation, but waited until he had accumulated a full box of cigarettes before taking his ration. As a consequence of this theft, both Haiber and Benkel were indicted for abusing their service authority.

Arraigned before the courts martial of the 9th SS-*Panzer*-Division *Hohenstaufen* at Amiens on 10 December 1943 (St. L. 601/43), Haiber was indicted for document suppression, for committing military embezzlement, inciting subordinates and failing to report subordinates' offences. The trial judge, *Hstuf.* Dr Franz Marx, was supported in his deliberations by *Hstuf.* Lofmann of the 5. / SS-*Panzergrenadier* Rgt. 19 and *Ostuf.* Schiffer of the SS-*Nachrichtenabteilung* 9. *Ustuf.* Dr Georg Mörtel prosecuted the case, the

Beurkundungsführer was SS-*Panzer-Obergrenadier* Vetter (22 officers, non-commissioned officers and other ranks attended the trial as witnesses). Judged guilty of the charges, the tribunal punished Haiber with fifteen months' *Gefängnis* and ordered his expulsion from the SS, (four months for document destruction, three months for military embezzlement of Scho-ka-Kola, five months for failing to report the theft of the chocolate, three months for his misuse of service authority in the matter of the cigarettes and two months for falsely claiming prohibited material things). The court punished Benkel with seven months' *Gefängnis* for document destruction, military theft and his misuse of his service authority (four months for document suppression, two months for the military theft of Scho-ka-Kola and two months for the abuse of service authority). The court was unable to impose an *Ehrenstrafe* on Benkel. The time both men spent on remand was not subtracted from their sentences.

His trial completed, Haiber returned to his prior post to await the confirmation of his sentence. The *Gerichtsherr* submitted his opinion to the *Reichsführer* on 6 February 1944 and recommended that Haiber's sentence be reduced to one year's *Gefängnis* and requesting his expulsion was cancelled, he supported his demotion to *Oscha*. Turning to Benkel, the *Gerichtsherr* decided that he had mitigated his sentence by crediting pre-trial detention and via the disciplinary path and therefore requested his demotion to the rank of *Uscha*. The *Korpsrichter* of the II. SS-*Panzerkorps* field court submitted a specialist report to the head of the SS r on 24 February and confirming both judgements, the *HA* SS-*Gericht* supported Benkel's demotion to the rank of *Uscha*. Haiber's commander judged him unfit for independent command on 3 June, but while awaiting for a decision about his fate, he was seriously wounded while serving as an Ordnance officer on 30 June 1944.

Elsewhere, the SS-*Richter beim* RF-SS case worker presented the facts of the case to the *Reichsführer* on 14 June and expressed his belief that it had been proven in at least one case that Haiber had sold stolen cigarettes at above the usual purchase price and this explained why he had not been sentenced for embezzlement, but only for document destruction. In the case workers opinion, the judgement was legally incorrect, as a conviction for document destruction would not have been made if this theft had occurred with the intent to inflict another disadvantage. Concerning Benkel, the case worker noted that he was in charge of the company cash box and it was a new *Kompanieführer* who had discovered irregularities. Since the documents were in a poor state and incomplete, the case worker considered it impossible to establish proof of their untruthfulness, but was convinced that Haiber needed to 'free himself from his non-commissioned officer attitude:

> [...] Concerning the punishment against Haiber and Benkel it would be unjustified to impose a four months' jail sentence on both for the suppression of documents. On the other hand, the judgement against Benkel and Haiber corresponds to the level of criminal acts they have committed. Concerning the punishment for the unauthorized document destruction a cancellation must be introduced. Both Haiber and Benkel are already back in action, specifically in the division *Strafvollstreckungszüge*, which for Haiber, as an officer, is improper. Therefore, I set aside the judgment against Haiber

and Benkel and the appropriate punishment to be introduced against Haiber is eleven months in *Gefängnis* with a demotion, and against Benkel, five months in *Gefängnis* and a demotion.

The *Reichsführer* confirmed both men's sentences on 20 June 1944 and commanded the two months spent on remand be included in Benkel punishment. Through the clemency path, the SS leader subtracted the time spent in detention between the sentencing and confirmation stage and the remaining prison time was set aside for his probation in the SS-*Sonderregiment Dirlewanger*. Himmler then instructed the *HA* SS-*Gericht* to amend the sentence and handle the clemency decision. Demoted to the rank of *Uscha.* on 4 August, Benkel's punishment was confirmed on 7 July and he then reported to Dirlewanger for one year's front probation. Avoiding a prison sentence, Haiber held a minor command position in the SS-*Sonderbrigade* in the autumn of 1944. One former probationer recollected that prior to the brigade converting to a division, a '*Zugführer* Haiber' gathered his men around him in January 1945 to discuss taking the oath of allegiance.[257]

Prosecuted for desertion, this officer's trial was set aside in favour of joining the SS-*Sonderbrigade*: Born in Berlin-Zehlendorf on 31.5.1899, *Brigadef.* Rudolf Vincent Weiß joined the Nazi party on 1.5.1930 (NSDAP Nr.: 237.711) and the SS on 1.5.1930 (SS Nr.: 4.299). The *Polizeipräsident* Metz from January 1944, Weiß's nerve broke as the US Army stood poised to attack the *Fortress* Metz and fled his post by car at 3.00 a.m. on 1 September 1944. Later that same day, he reported to the Saarbrücken *Gauleiter*, SA-*Staf.* Jansen, and claimed that he had abandoned the city when becoming aware that US troops threatened to advance into the city. His actions reported to the head of the SS, Himmler commanded the *Obersten* SS- *und Polizei-Gericht* to initiate an investigating against Weiß on suspicion of desertion and the case was placed in the hands of *Ostubaf.* Hinderfeld of the *HA* SS-*Gericht* in Munich (case Nr. St. L. 74/1944). Within days of leaving Metz, Weiß received orders to report to the SS-*Ergänzungsstelle* Rhein, but Himmler countermanded this instruction and commanded him to report to the SS-PHA in Berlin at 11.00 a.m. on 19 September. Here, Weiß was permitted 24 hours to report under escort to the SS-*Sonderregiment* in Warsaw with the rank of *Uscha.* Weiß left the capital an hour later in the company of *Ostuf.* Klumm and reported to the SS-*Sonderbrigade* in Krakau. In his absence, the *Reichsführer* ordered the court proceedings against him suspended until the war's conclusion. Participating in the Slovakian campaign, the battles in Hungary and the retreat to the German border, Weiß was killed in action at Lieberose near the city of Cottbus on 22 February 1945.[258]

Name: Julian Scherner.
Last Rank: SS-*Hauptsturmführer.*
Born: 23.9.1895 in Baczamajo/German East Africa.
Died: 28.4.1945 near the town of Märkisch Buchholz.

NSDAP-Nr.: 865.027 (joined 31.12.1931).
SS-Nr.: 39.493 (joined 15.4.1932).
Prewar Assignments:
Bund Oberland 1.10.1921–1.5.1930.
5. / II. / 1. SS-*Standarte* (Munich) from 25.10.1932.
Led the 5. / II. / 1. SS-*Standarte* (Munich) 31.7.1933–1.3.1934.
Led the II. / 1. SS-*Standarte* (Munich) 1.3.–1.2.1934.
Led the 1. SS-*Standarte* (Munich) 12.8.–9.1.1935.
Offizier Lehrgang I. / *Infantrie*-Rgt. 19.4.–6.934.
Lehrgang Münsingen 3.8.–15.8.1934.
Gasschutz-Lehrgang in 11.1935.
Stabsführer Oberabschnitt Südost (Brieg/Breslau) from 9.1.1935.
Stabsführer Oberabschnitt Nordost (Königsberg) until 15.2.1936.
Lehrgang 28.9.–10.10.1936.
Stabsführer Abschnitt XIV (Bremen) 15.2.1936–1.1.1937.
Led the *Abschnitt* XIV (Bremen) until 1.10.1937.
Led the SS-*Führerschule* Dachau 9.11.1937.
Wartime Assignments:
Led the SS-*Totenkopf-Infantrie*-Rgt. 6 from 28.8.1939.
Led the SS-*Totenkopf-Rekruit*-Rgt. from 1.11.1939.
Led the SS-*Junkerschule* Bad Tölz 1.3.–11.7.1940.
Led the SS-*Totenkopf-Infantrie*-Rgt. 8 11.7.1940–10.1.1941.
Offizier z.b.V. *Kommando der Waffen*-SS (Berlin) 1941.
Stab SS-*Standort* Prague 1941.
Led the SS-*Truppenübungsplatz Beneschau* from 20.1.1941.
SS-FHA 2.8.–4.8.1941.
SSPF *Distrikt* Krakau 4.8.1941–1.3.1944.
Stab Kompanie HSSPF *Ost* from 1.11.1942.
Ordnungspolizei from 1.11.1943.
Officer of the SS-PHA on 1.3.1944–16.10.1944.
SS-*Sonderbrigade Dirlewanger* 16.10.1944-28.4.1945.
Promotions:

20.6.1932	*Anwärter*.
19.9.1932	*Staffelmann der Allgemeine*-SS.
1.11.1932	SS-*Unterscharführer der Allgemeine*-SS.
1.2.1933	SS-*Oberscharführer der Allgemeine*-SS.
31.7.1933	SS-*Sturmführer der Allgemeine*-SS.
24.12.1933	SS-*Obersturmführer der Allgemeine*-SS.
1.3.1934	SS-*Hauptsturmführer der Allgemeine*-SS.
12.8.1934	SS-*Sturmbannführer der Allgemeine*-SS.
1.1.1935	SS-*Obersturmbannführer der Allgemeine*-SS.
30.1.1936	SS-*Standartenführer der Allgemeine*-SS.

12.9.1937	SS-*Oberführer der Allgemeine*-SS.
1.3.1940	SS-*Oberführer der Reserve der Waffen*-SS.
0.0.1944	SS-*Hauptsturmführer der Reserve.*

Decorations & Awards:

0.10.1914	*Eisernes Kreuz* II. *Klasse.*
1914-18	*Verwundetenabzeichen in Schwarz.*
1914-18	*Ehrenkreuz für Frontkämpfer.*
0.0.19__	Coburg *Abzeichen.*
20.11.1933	*Blutorden* (Nr. 175).
0.0.19__	SS-*Zivilabzeichen* (Nr. 22.258).
0.0.19__	SA-*Sportsabzeichen in Bronze.*
0.0.19__	SS-*Ehrenwinkel für alte Kämpfer.*
3.6.1937	*Ehrendegen des Reichsführer*-SS.
0.0.19__	*Ehrendolch.*
0.0.19__	*Totenkopfring der* SS.
10.5.1941	*Kriegsverdienstkreuz II. Klasse mit Schwertern.*
0.0.1943	*Kriegsverdienstkreuz I. Klasse mit Schwertern.*
0.0.1938	*Die Medaille zur Erinnerung an den* 1. Oktober 1938 (Sudetenland).
0.0.1937	*Ungarn Medaille* Für *Verdienst.*

Notes: His father was a *Hauptmann* of the Colonial *Schutztruppe*. Living in German East Africa until he was two years old, Scherner attended the Karlsruhe i.B. *Kadettenanstalt* between 1 October 1905 and 1911 and then studied at the Berlin-Lichterfelde *Kadettenanstalt* between 1911 and 1914 (UJ). Mustering with the *Infantrie*-Rgt. 114 between 15 March 1912 and 10 August 1914, Scherner obtained the rank of *Fähnrich* in April 1914, was promoted to officer rank on 5 August the same year and fought as a *Zugführer* and *Kompanieführer*. Wounded by shell splinters in the head and rifle fire in his right ankle in 1914. Hospitalised in various hospitals until 1 January 1915, Scherner returned to his regiment and was captured by French forces in May the same year. Released in 1919, the military discharged Scherner from the army on 30 March 1920, (*Oberleutnant* 20.10.1920). Employed as a bank clerk between 1920 and 1924 and as a shop assistant until 1930, Scherner was a partner in a merchant's business until 1934. Marrying his fiancée, Rosita S., (b. 1.5.1889, Mainz) on 1 May 1924, the couple had two children. Participating in the abortive November 1929 Munich Putsch and injured and arrested during the fracas, Scherner was detained by the civil authorities on two further occasions until March 1924. Attending the party days in 1923 and between 1933 and 1937, Scherner became a salaried officer of the SS from June 1934. Involved in a vehicle accident on 1 December 1936, he injured his head and left knee and fell from a horse, injuring his left knee on 29 June 1939. Appointed to the post of the SSPF *Krakau* in 1941, Scherner become instrumental in the creation of the Płaszów *Arbeitslager* and the Bełżec *Vernichtungslager*.

Meeting the 'talented' *Oscha.* d.R. Heinz Klare in Dachau in 1940, Scherner renewed his acquaintance with him during his many visits to Krakau. In 1941 the two would meet in

Prague and in Munich to carouse and eat together. His business concluded in early 1941, Klare asked and received Scherner's help to extend his work leave. Scherner also eased his entry into the *Waffen*-SS, arranged his posting to the SS-*Standort* Prague in April 1941 and ensured that Klare received sick leave on the grounds of a heart condition. Relocating to Krakau, Scherner then arranged for Klare to join his staff as his ordnance officer and he became his personal adjutant on 15 December 1941. Against standing orders, Scherner borrowed 3,500 *Reichsmark* from Klare's company expense account to help him pay his living expenses and accepted another loan of 3,000 *Reichsmark* from the same source in the summer of 1941. Later, Scherner borrowed a further 500 *Reichsmark* from Klare's own pockets and he paid Scherner's rent and coal invoice for three months. Renting an apartment in the vicinity of Scherner's accommodation, Klare received three weeks' home leave in the winter of 1941-42.

In late 1941 Scherner and Klare were denounced for living indecently and possessing illegal food and spirits. Made aware of the accusations, the *Reichsführer* commanded the SiPo to investigate the allegations and they proceeded to arrest Klare on suspicion of his involvement in black market dealings in December 1941 and again in March 1942. A search of Klare's apartment revealing food, luxury items, fuel coupons and military documents, the SS- *und Polizei-Gericht* VI, Krakau initiated an investigation and over seven nights, *Stubaf.* Dr Pohl interviewed both men in the SS officer's club (at this time that Scherner was involved in the forced evacuation of the Tarnow ghetto in March 1942 and the survivors were incarcerated in the Płaszów *Arbeitslager*). When questioned, Klare made damaging allegations against his friend and claiming that he was owned money for purchases he had made on Scherner's behalf, the examining SS-*Richter* discounted his assertion's on the grounds that Scherner obtained foodstuffs from the officer club. Establishing that Scherner had self-catered, the judge confirmed that requiring additional food for guests, such as for comrades travelling to the front, or eggs for his sick wife, Scherner had obtained these items from the TWL Krakau, the SS-*Truppenübungsplatz* Debica, the Krakau department of Nutrition and Agriculture and from the covered market (on Scherner's behalf Klare had distributed preserves, coffee, fruit and chocolate). The judge then turned his attention to the allegation that Scherner had misused his service vehicle. Assuring him that *Ogruf.* Krüger had given him an exception card granting him permission to use the car in exceptional cases and for private purposes, Scherner denied Klare's allegation that he owned money for furniture purchased from his former company, (the judge confirmed that Pätz's furniture had been paid from Scherner's SS expenses account). Discounting Klare's allegation that Scherner had beaten his orderly, *Rttf.* Klas, the examining judge gave no credence to the accusation that Scherner received military pay from the *Waffen*-SS, as did other services members, or increments from the EWGG Krakau district. However, he expressed his conviction that Klare had loaned monies to his commander in return for very generous leave entitlements, but had been unable to establish whether the loans and food purchases were linked to Klare's absences.

Visiting Krakau on 13 March 1942, the *Reichsführer* met with Scherner to rebuke him for leading an excessive lifestyle, for his excessive food expenditure, his errant ways, the misuse of fuel and the use of the removal van with Klare and Pätz in Krakau. Punishing him with a serious warning, Himmler then commanded the court that same day to initiate a court's process against Scherner in an effort to get to the bottom of his dealings. *Hstuf.* Dr Jansen of the *Wiking* field court was then tasked by the *HA* SS-*Gericht* to investigate whether Klare had paid for special considerations and submitting his report on 30 June 1943, this described the sequence of events leading to their relationship. In his role as *Gerichtsherr*, *Ogruf.* Krüger, who had known Scherner from his early youth, expressed his view that Scherner was a victim of Klare's 'winning personality' and submitted a fitness report which attempted to explain his subordinate's behavior:

> He [Scherner] is very companionable and helpful towards everyone. He gets close very quickly to every person, but unfortunately he does not possess the ability to recognise and comply with the prescribed boundaries that apply to him in his official position towards subordinates.

Convinced that Scherner was party to a deliberate attempt to assist Klare to avoid the military draft, the *HA* SS-*Gericht* expressed their satisfaction that he had employed his subordinate in the knowledge that he would be absent from his duties for ten months. Acknowledging that such leaves in the *Generalgouvernement* were commonplace, the judge concluded that Scherner had not acted with the correct sense of duty and expressed his belief that he had abused his service post when borrowing monies and enjoying other economic advantages. However, the judge accepted that no evidence or assumption existed to prove that Klare had given the loans with the intention to leading Scherner into wrongful acts and concluding that their financial relationship was the consequence of a friendliness and not linked to offenses of active and passive bribery, the judge voiced his conviction that Scherner had accepted the money as an act of SS comradeship. On the grounds that Klare left him in the dark about monetary affairs the examining judge set aside the charge of passive military corruption for accepting gifts and other benefits, but partially upheld the accusation that Scherner had engaged in active bribery.

Unconvinced that Scherner had committed an act of disobedience in contravention of the *Reichsführer*-SS edict of 5 March 1937 and had not lost his authority over Klare when accepting the loans, the judge did not support his prosecution for disobedience, (Himmler's edict forbad SS men from entering into debt obligations, which could not be paid back, with certainty over a period of three months and without affecting the personal and family maintenance). Finding no link between Scherner and Klare's private deals and the provision of work and sick leaves, the *HA* SS-*Gericht* remained unconvinced that Scherner had hoarded luxury goods. Recommending his disciplinary punishment for misconduct, the SS-*Richter* noted that as an old fighter and member of the *Allgemeine*-SS, Scherner was very affable and companionable towards his subordinates and as consequence, he had failed to separate SS camaraderie from conduct that was expected to exist between the superior and his subordinates.

The investigation completed, the case file was then handed to the SS-*Richters beim* RF-SS on 25 June. Accepting the findings and agreeing that no evidence existed to suggest that Scherner had committed a court punishable offence, the *Reichsführer* then imposed a punishment of fourteen days' *Stubenarrest* for wrongful behaviour. Writing to the *Reichsführer* on 2 September 1943, *Ogruf.* Krüger expressed his concern that Scherner had become the victim of double jeopardy and asked that the imposition of a fourteen days' *Stubenarrest* be set-aside in view of his involvement in bandit fighting during the recent months. In addition, he cautioned against placing a disciplinary order in his personal file in case it hindered his future opportunities for promotion. Responding to this letter on 5 October 1943, Himmler denied that Scherner was the victim of double jeopardy as he had accepted a warning from himself on 13 March 1942 and the *Stubenarrest* had been imposed for Scherner making a personal friend of an ordnance officer, for his incorrect machinations when recruiting Klare into the *Waffen*-SS and for granting permanent leave and for borrowing money. Agreeing that Scherner had proven himself in the 'bandit war,' Himmler suspended his punishment for the duration of the war (interestingly, the SS-*Richters beim* RF-SS also argued against the imposition of this second disciplinary punishment). Confirming the judgement against Scherner for the abuse of his service powers on 25 August 1943, the *Oberste* SS- *und Polizei-Gericht* passed the disciplinary order to *Ogruf.* Krüger with a recommendation that the process was concluded.

Remaining in his post, Scherner continued to enjoy its corrupt benefits and is known to have received payments from business concerns (notably from Oskar Schindler).
Tasked with making his way to the KL Płaszów to investigate allegations of corruption, *Ustuf.* Dr Karl Eckert, a WVHA investigator, questioning the camp commandant's book keeper, Mietek Pemper and discovered the full depth of Amon Göth's corruption. As a consequence of Pemper's disclosures, Dr Eckert almost certainly became aware of Scherner's close relationship with Göth and linked him to the many malfeasant practices emanating from Płaszów. Although it does not appear that an investigative process was undertaken specifically against Scherner for corruption, he was released from his post on 13 February 1944 and the Krakau tribunal is thought to have initiated an investigation against him for drunkenness between 16 February and 20 March 1944 and Scherner transferred to the SS-PHA as a consequence of this attention. Suspending the trial process, Himmler commanded Scherner to leave Berlin for the front with the rank of *Hstuf.* on 13 October 1944. Reporting to the *Ersatz-Kompanie* of the SS-*Sonderbrigade Dirlewanger* in Krakau that same month, Scherner then joined the brigade in Slovakia and became the divisional adjutant when the brigade became a division in February 1945. Scherner died in action near the town of Märkisch–Buchholz in April the same year. At this time the 9th *Armee* was desperately attempting to escape from the Spreewald-Halbe pocket.[259]

The SS-S*onderbrigade Dirlewanger* found itself subordinate to the 8th *Armee* in the wake ofList the brutal suppression of the Slovakian uprising and during the second week of December 1944 its disparate forces deployed between Ipolysag and Levice on the Slovakian–Hungarian border. Spread north and south of this town, a large number of disaffected probationers of the III. / SS-Rgt. 2 took this opportunity of front deployment to desert and surrender to units of the 6th Guards Tank Army. Crossing the frontline from the morning of 12 December, groups and individual parolees continued to desert to the Soviet forces over the next few days. Amongst their number was *Hstuf.* Langelotz, a demoted Austrian *Heer* officer and commander of the tenth company. He successfully led former Matzkau and KL Sachsenhausen inmates over to the Red Army on 16 December and was then detained as a prisoner of war.[260]

To discourage further desertions from the brigade, the loyal components of the SS-Rgt. 2 opened fire on the would-be absconders and one of those killed while attempting to reach the Red Army trenches was a former training school officer:

Name: Georg Wild.
Last Rank: SS-*Untersturmführer.*
Born: 7.4.1915 in Baden near Vienna.
Died: 17.12.1944 in Palast/Hungary.
SS-Nr.: 423.850 (v) (joined 7.4.1941).
Prewar Assignments:
Austrian Army 1.10.1937–10.1938.
Wehrmacht Heer 10.1938–7.4.1941.
Wartime Assignments:
Waffen-SS 7.4.1941–17.12.1944.
SS-*Totenkopf-Infantrie-Ersatz-Bataillon* II. 7.4.–1.9.1941.
5. *Kriegs-Res.-Führeranwärter-Lehrgang* SS-*Junkerschule* Bad Tölz 1.9.1941–26.1.1942.
Führer-Lehrgang SS-*Junkerschule* Bad Tölz 26.1.–20.4.1942.
SS-*Infantrie*-Rgt. *Der Führer* 20.4.–6.7.1942.
SS-*Hauptamt Amt* I 6.7.1942–26.2.1943.
Reichsschule der Sicherheitspolizei und des SD Prague 6.–15.11.1942.
SS-*Polizei-Infantrie*-Rgt. 1 of the SS-*Polizeidivision* 26.2.–13.7.1943.
SS-*Grenadier-Ausbildung- und Ersatz-Bataillon* 4 from 13.7.1943.
12th SS-*Panzer*-Division *Hitlerjugend* from 17.7.1943.
15th *Waffen-Grenadier*-Division *der* SS (*Lett.* Nr. 1) from 13.6.1944.
Zugführer-Lehrgang Kienschlag SS-*Panzergrenadierschule* 18.10.–8.11.1944.
SS-*Sonderbrigade Dirlewanger* 8.11.–17.12.1944.
Promotions:

7.4.1941	SS-*Mann.*
0.0.19__	SS-*Unterscharführer der Reserve*
26.1.1942	SS-*Oberscharführer der Reserve*
26.1.1942	*Reserve-Führeranwärter der Waffen*-SS.
20.4.1942	SS-*Untersturmführer der Allgemeine*-SS.
20.4.1942	SS-*Untersturmführer der Reserve.*
9.12.1944	*Grenadier.*

Decorations & Awards:

0.0.1940 1939 *Eisernes Kreuz II. Klasse.*
0.0.19__ *Deutsches Reichssportabzeichen in Bronze.*
0.0.19__ D.L.R.G. *in Bronze.*

Notes: Attending *Volksschule* for five classes, Wild obtained his *Abitur* from *Gymnasium* after eight classes and studied law at university for two sessions. His studies incomplete, Wild mustered with the Austrian Army *Infantrie*-Rgt. 34 on 1 October 1937 and was inducted into the *Wehrmacht Heer* on 1 November 1938. A member of the *Hitlerjugend* until accepted into the *Allgemeine*-SS and *Waffen*-SS on 7 April 1941, Wild married his fiancée Gertrude Sachau, (b. 20.7.1919) on 27 December 1941 and the couple lived in Witswort über Husam/Schleswig-Holstein (the marriage remained childless). Posted to the Kienschlag SS-*Panzergrenadier-Schule* in October 1944, here, Wild led the *Lehrgruppe* A, (14. / 15. *Oberjunkerlehrgang*) until the school commandant expressed his dissatisfaction with his performance. On the grounds of two incidents of disobedience, the commandant requested his transfer for unsuitability on 7 November and concurring with this decision, the SS-FHA judged Wild unfit for further use in the SS. Without doubt the matter was reported to the *HA* SS-*Gericht* and presenting the affair to the SS-*Richter beim* RF-SS, he commanded Wild to Dirlewanger's command in November 1944. Demoted to the rank of *Grenadier* in the second week of December, Wild mustered with the 9. / III. / Rgt. 2, but fearing that his personal situation had become precarious, he decided to desert to the Red Army. In the early hours of 17 December, Wild made his bid for freedom, but was shot dead near Palast. The RSHA, SS-FHA and *HA* SS-*Gericht* were informed of his death on 16 January 1945.[261]

Of the 770 former camp prisoners assigned to SS-*Sonderbrigade* in December 1944, some 480 successfully deserted to the Red Army at this time and half of those remaining with the brigade were killed or wounded in action on the Hungarian Front.[262]

An estimated 500 parolees deserted from the SS-*Sonderbrigade* to the Red Army between 11 and 18 December 1944 and their loss resulted in the disbandment of the entire III. / SS-Rgt. 2. Those successfully escaping Dirlewanger's grasp were eventually detained in a prisoner of war camp near Molotov in the Urals.[263]

This junior officer was killed in action on the Ipolysag and Levice Front at the end of 1944:

Name: Siegfried Polack.
Last Rank: SS-*Untersturmführer*
Born: 31.7.1899 in Sommerfeld/East Prussia.
Died: 27.12.1944 near Budapest.
NSDAP-Nr.: 75.148 (joined 1928).
SS-Nr.: 25.720 (joined 11.3.1932)

Prewar Assignments:
SS-*Rangführer Abschnitt* XXIII (Berlin) from 31.5.1932.
Wartime Assignments:
Waffen-SS 21.9.1943–27.12.1944.
31. SS-*Grenadier-Ausbildung- und Ersatz-Bataillon* 21.9.–20.11.1943.
SS-*Sonderregiment Dirlewanger* 20.11.1943–27.12.1944.
Promotions:

31.5.1932	SS-*Sturmbannführer der Allgemeine*-SS.
30.11.1935	SS-*Mann.*
21.9.1943	*Leutnant der Reserve* a.D.
24.11.1943	SS-*Untersturmführer der Reserve.*

Notes: Attending *Realgymnasium*, Polack then studied at the *Haupt-Kadettenanstalt Groß-Lichterfelde* and participated in the Great War with officer rank. Post-war, Polack worked as a clerk and editor in Nowawes and was married with two children. Employed as the *Gaugeschäftsführer der Gauleitung Kurmark der* NSDAP from 1933, Polack remained in this post until the *Reichsführer* ordered his degradation and expulsion from the SS on 30 November 1935. The NSDAP representative for the constituency 4 (Potsdam I) from November 1933 to March 1936, (his *Führerkarte* indicates his expulsion from the Nazi party), at the outbreak of war Polack joined the *Wehrmacht* and was promoted to officer rank on 21 September 1943. Assigned to the SS-*Sonderregiment* in November 1943, Polack was promoted to officer rank four days after his arrival and led the second company in April 1944. Though there is no evidence that Polack had committed an offence warranting his transfer to the SS-*Sonderregiment*, the *HA* SS-*Gericht* enquired his wherabouts on 7 June 1944. Polack was either killed in action on the Hungarian–Slovakian border, or died in captivity in December 1944.[264]

Refusing to defend his positions when the Red Army began their offensive against the 8th *Armee* during the winter of 1944/45, Dirlewanger conducted a fighting withdrawal to the Slovakia border and extricating his brigade from the disaster unfolding in Hungary, his troops crossed the German–Czech border in the second week of February 1945 and deployed near Kulm and Guben. Here, the brigade absorbed fresh replacements from military prisons and concentration camps and at this time Dirlewanger received orders to take command of the *Arbeitsabteilung* and *Bewährungsabteilung* at Olmütz. Seeking to create a divisional-sized formation which would become the main repository for all military probationers to fight the front line, Adolf Hitler agreed to establish the 36th *Waffen-Grenadier*-Division *der* SS on 14 February 1945 and the appropriate order was issued three days later. As part of these plans, the *Bewährungsabteilung* was disbanded in March 1945 and became the divisional reserve battalion.[265]

Appointed to Dirlewanger's divisional staff as a tactical advisor with orders to oversee its conversion and improve its fighting ability on 17 February 1945, *Brigadef.* Fritz Schmedes arrival witnessed little change to the brutal disciplinary regime and the summary execution of former camp prisoners did little to prevent further desertions. A little after Schmedes appointment, Dirlewanger left the Division to return to his home in Esslingen and took with him his accumulated loot and booty.[266]

Evacuating the population of Dublowitz from their homes, around 400 former camp prisoners found themselves billeted in and around the town on 8 April 1945 to undertake battle training with the divisional reserve battalion. A security cordon with trusted troops was thrown around the villages and those caught attempting to desert were tied to a stake and summarily executed. Beatings in this training company were commonplace, so common in fact that the unit doctor complained that those beaten were unfit for combat. A few weeks later the reserve battalion relocated to Jamlitz, east of Guben, a position close to the divisional headquarters and surrendered to the Red Army on 7 May 1945 near the village of Pirna, south of Dresden.[267]

Placed under the tactical command of the XXXX. *Panzerkorps*, the bulk of the 36th *Waffen-Grenadier*-Division *der* SS trained around the town of Guben on 1 March 1945 and established a tank destruction school in the town for SS instructors to teach new recruits how to handle *Panzerfausts*. A large group of probationers attempted to desert from this school on March 1945 and the following day their SS instructors summarily executed those they re-captured.[268]

The constituent parts of the 36th *Waffen-Grenadier*-Division *der* SS were subordinated to the V. SS-*Armeekorps*, (9th *Armee*) on 20 March 1945 and in expectation of the Red Army spring offensive, the parolees dug emplacements and laid minefields along the River Niesse, near the towns of Forst and Spreewald. Despite *Brigadef.* Schmede's warning that those attempting to desert would be shot on sight, the number of attempts increased when combat elements of the division took their place in the front line. The divisional headquarters was located in Weissagk when the Soviet spring offensive finally smashed into the division on 19 April 1945.[269]

The same day, 30 probationers deserted to the Red Army near Horno and 40 others abandoned their positions near Heinersbruck. Under constant bombardment much of the division disintegrated, but in some places the parolees and their military comrades fought well. In Guben a handful of probationers fought stubbornly alongside the town commandant Werner Theermann and his local *Volkssturm*. To stiffen their resolve, the Theermann unleashed a *Standgericht* on the townsfolk and summarily executed those who attempted to leave the town without permission or revealed an unwillingness to fight the enemy. Ordering the execution of 40 parolees caught attempting to desert, Theermann's draconian measures did little to stem the tide of battle. Guben was finally overrun by the Red Army on 24 April 1945.[270]

Elements of the 36th *Waffen-Grenadier*-Division *der* SS successfully extricated themselves from the shattered front on 21 April 1945, but the artillery and pioneer battalions disintegrated during the retreat. Within hours, Schmede's troops were surrounded near Peitz and it was at this point that former jail inmates and camp prisoners began to surrender in large numbers to the Red Army.[271]

Foolishly surrendering to the Red Army with his troops, this senior officer then faced the deadly retribution at the hands of former camp prisoners:

Name: Ewald Ehlers.
Last Rank: SS-*Sturmbannführer.*
Born: 3.1.1910 in Leim, *Kreis* Helmstedt.
Died: 28.4.1945 in Märkisch-Buchholz.
NSDAP-Nr.: (joined 1.10.1938).
SS-Nr.: 309.725 (joined 1.10.1938).
Prewar Assignments:
Alten Heere 3. *Reiter*-Rgt. 1.10.1928–19.11.1934.
Luftwaffe 18.11.1934-1.10.1938.
2. *Nachrichtenkompanie* / RLM *Nachrichtenabteilung* (Potsdam–Eiche) from 1.1.1938.
SS-TV from 1.10.1938.
SS-*Totenkopf-Infantrie*-Rgt 3 *Thüringen* (Weimar) 1.10.1938–20.10.1939.
Wartime Assignments:
1. *kl. Kraftwagenkolonne / Nachschub/* SS-*Totenkopfdivision* 20.10.–14.11.1939.
SS-TV *Inspectorate* from 14.11.1939.
SS-*Totenkopf-Infantrie*-Rgt. 5 (Oranienburg) in 11.1939.
1. / 12. *Totenkopf-Infantrie*-Rgt. 10.11.1939–1.9.1940.
SS-*Totenkopf-Infantrie*-Rgt. 8 from 1.9.1940.
6. / II. / SS-*Totenkopf-Infanterie*-Rgt. *Kirkenes* 1.9.1940–1.9.1941.
6. / SS-*Totenkopf-Infantrie*-Rgt. 9 (regimental adjutant) 1.9.1941–1.4.1942.
SS-*Gebirgsjäger-Ersatz-Bataillon Nord* (Trauentau) 1.4.1942–10.2.1943.
SS-*Rekrutendepot* Debica 10.2.–1.5.1943.
SS-*Polizei-Panzergrenadier*-Rgt. 1 (Milowitz) 1.5.-10.7.1943.
3rd SS-*Panzergrenadier*-Division *Totenkopf* 10.7.-1.10.1943.
SS-*Infantrie-Ersatz-Bataillon Ost* 1.10.1943-7.7.1944.
31. SS-*Grenadier-Ausbildung- und Ersatz-Bataillon* 1.10.1943.
4th SS-*Polizei-Panzergrenadier*-Division 7.7.-15.9.1944.
SS-*Sonderregiment Dirlewanger* 15.9.1944–28.4.1945.
Led the II. / *Waffen-Grenadier*-Rgt. *der* SS 73 until 1.1945.
Led the *Waffen-Grenadier*-Rgt. *der* SS 73 from 1.3.1945.
Promotions:

0.0.19__	*Wachtmeister.*
0.0.19__	*Oberfeldwebel der Lufwaffe.*
1.10.1938	SS-*Bewerber.*
1.10.1938	SS-*Mann.*
1.10.1938	SS-*Untersturmführer der Waffen*-SS (*Aktiv*).
30.1.1940	SS-*Obersturmführer der Waffen*-SS (*Aktiv*).
1.9.1941	SS-*Hauptsturmführer der Waffen*-SS (*Aktiv*).
0.0.19__	SS-*Sturmbannführer der Waffen*-SS (*Aktiv*).

Decorations & Awards:

0.0.19_ _ *Deutsches Reichssportabzeichen in Bronze.*
0.0.19__ *Kriegsverdienstkreuz II. Klasse mit Schwertern.*
0.0.19__ *Infanterie-Sturmabzeichen in Bronze.*
0.0.19__ *Medaille 'Winterschlacht im Osten* 1941/42.'

Notes: Attending *Volksschule* for four classes and concluding his studies at *Gymnasium*, (U-II), Ehlers, with a schoolboy's grasp of English and French, mustered with the cavalry and *Luftwaffe* communications branch in the prewar period and enjoyed good fitness reports. Marrying his fiancée Annelies R. on 3 January 1936, the couple later lived in Weimar and had two children. Applying to join the *Waffen*-SS in 1938, his admittance was permitted on the proviso that he joined a combat formation. In July 1939 Ehler's superiors observed that he was a good trainer of men. Punished with five days' *Stubenarrest* for committing a traffic violation, Ehlers reported to the SS-TV *Inspektorate* at the KL Oranienberg in November 1939 and received good fitness reports for his handling of his troops in various infantry regiments. A court's process was initiated against Ehlers on 14 April 1942 for the suspicion of showing cowardice before the enemy in Finland and he was arraigned before the courts martial of the SS- *und Polizei-Gericht* XV, Breslau on 17 August 1942 (St. L. I 301/42). The court announced its decision against Ehlers on 29 January 1943:

> A final determination of the charges against the accused can only be accomplished by comparison with SS-*Hstuf.* Arnold of the 6. / SS-*Kradschützen*-Rgt. *Thule*. However, this comparison is not possible with respect to the currently existing front conditions. Therefore, the preliminary opinion of the investigator is to give the accused an opportunity to prove his courage and demonstrate his moral attitude at the front seems appropriate to rebut the allegations.

This provisional judgement was announced in accordance with paragraph § 47 KStVO and Ehlers mustered with a reserve unit while awaiting the court to conclude its business. Here, he assisted with the formation of a new formation and his commander, *Ostubaf.* Pannier made the following observations about his subordinate on 18 May 1943:

> SS-*Hstuf.* E. has a small, powerful appearance and possesses an open character. He imposes value on a groomed exterior. E. He has a good theoretical knowledge that he translates into practice. During his good recruit training service he has earned his men's trust in him and looks after them with diligence and prudence. Suggestions and teachings fall on fertile ground with him. Spirited and busy in a good sense, he is respected by comrades and he engages his subordinates and men with his fresh, carefree attitude. E. fulfills his position adequately.

Joining the SS-*Sonderbrigade* in September 1944, postwar, the former members of Ehler's command alleged that he behaved brutally towards his subordinates. His regiment become a component of the 36th *Waffen-Grenadier*-Division *der* SS on 19 December 1944. Surrendering to Red Army forces with his troops in late April 1945, former camp prisoners denounced Ehlers to their captors on 28 April and the Soviet guards stood aside as the parolee prisoners pushed him from a stool and hung their former commander by his neck from a tree in Weissagk. Ehler's corpse was then set alight and later interred in Märkisch–Buchholz.[272]

Elements of the 9th *Armee* successfully broke out of the Red Army trap around Hammer on 29 April and the few remaining cohesive parts of the 36th *Waffen-Grenadier*-Division *der* SS retreated from Peitz to Neuendorf via Schlepzig–Lübbenau. This manoeuvre was the division's last gasp and it had effectively ceased to exist by 24/25 April 1945. In an effort to escape capture by the Red Army, a handful of troops continued to resist near Sperrenberg–Mennikendorf bei Zesch and Kummersdorf until 2 May 1945 and the divisional staff and some loyal troops ended the war in the town of Märkisch–Bucholz. Here, they disguised themselves as military officers and attempted to flee westwards, or surrendered to the Red Army alongside regular military units.[273]

5.18 Das dürfte das Ers.Btl in Breslau gewesen sein, das Bataillon wurde aber Angang 1943 in Ersatz- und Ausbildungsbataillon mit verschiedenen Standorten (Breslau für das Ersatz und Shitomir für das Ausbildungs-Bataillon) getrennt, später mit der Nummer "31" und zuletzt, ab Januar 1944 mit der Nummer "18" versehen.* * * * *SS-*Fallschirmjägerabteilung* 500

Seeking to deploy convicts against the Yugoslav partisans at the end of 1942, the *Reichsführer* demanded that these parolees participated in highly dangerous operations in the Balkans' with little chance of survival. A battlefield heavily contested by nationalists, partisans and Axis security forces, both sides suffered high casualties on what is now considered the most brutal of all the irregular Second World War fronts. As a consequence of Himmler's command to create a parachute trained probation battalion in early 1943 the *HA* SS-*Gericht* identified 600 court punished miscreants to undertake specialist airborne training.[274]

Commanded to select inmates standing between 160 cm and 185 cm tall, who were younger than 30 years-old and not prone to air sickness or stuttered, the Danzig–Matzkau commandant, Dr Ernst selected 100 inmates for deployment to the new unit during the first weeks of February 1943 and at that time, he explained his selection process to the SS-*Richter beim* RF-SS:

> Their selection and deployment followed my examination of the photographs in the first instance and then studying the case file and using my personal knowledge, I then

> judged the eventual deployment capability of the named from the reliability of his character. Under these circumstances and using my own self-understanding judgement, I then gauged their behavioural suitability and judged the men impartially to determine whether they had committed violations of the camp rules, for example, the smoking ban. I did not select from these special cases. I excluded men from the selection who had repeatedly committed transgressions, like the cigarette ban or some other thing in the camp and whether his character had failed to show signs of improvement. Against this, I also had to determine from the judgement the behaviour and value he had exhibited in the troops, especially in a deployment situation. When this judgement was not especially significant, then I then determined from the beginning of the list if it was relevant that his behaviour had undergone an inner adjustment in the camp.

Those selected for parachute training left Matzkau for the *Bewährungsabteilung* in Chlum to undertake special training with the *Pionierschule* at the Beneschau SS-*Truppenübungsplatz*.[275]

It is by no means clear that those volunteering for this unit was fully aware of the dangers awaiting them. Most may have simply have been relieved to leave prison where they had been working to clear enemy bomb damage in Danzig.[276]

Writing to the *Amtschef des Amt* III on 8 May 1943, the SS-*Richter beim* RF-SS revealed that the convict parachute candidates selected by Dr Ernst had faced the scrutiny of the RSHA and from the original 100 volunteers, the security service had concluded that only 31 of them were suitable for front probation.[277]

Despite the concerns of the RSHA, the head of the SS ordered the probationers to undertake parachute training in Chlum. Discussing the issue with the SS-FHA on 9 August 1943, the SS-*Richter beim* RF-SS delineated Himmler's order to establish an airborne assault unit from paroled SS men. As an insufficient number of convicts had been identified as suitable for service in this battalion, Himmler had then proposed that half of the parachute unit was established from *Waffen*-SS volunteers and commanded former convicts be restored to their earlier ranks and integrated throughout the new unit. The appropriate orders issued by the SS-FHA, the SS-*Fallschirmjägerabteilung* 'Chlum' was officially established in the Bohemian town by that name on 6 September 1943 (*FPNr* 15.814A). Locating its headquarters in Chlum castle, the battalions various constituents were scattered across different towns and villages in the region.[278]

Convicts from the SS-*Straflager* Dachau also volunteered for the new unit and among their number were Scandinavian felons. The *Amt* III persuaded further convicts to volunteer for the SS-*Fallschirmjägerabteilung* in late 1943 and amongst their number was SS-*Mann* Paul Spitt, a former member of the *Heimwehr Danzig* and the *Wiking*. Selected for parachute training while detained in the *Zweiglager* Ludwigsfelde, Spitt arrived in Chlum during October 1943 and later in the war volunteered for commando missions with the SS-*Jagdverbände Mitte*.[279]

According to one source, 70 parolees of the second company refused to undertake parachute training and was returned to the *Bewährungsabteilung*. A former convict alleged that three of their number were executed. The SS-*Fallschirmjäger-Ersatz-Kompanie* remained in Chlum while the battalion deployed in the Maturuschk–Banka region. Here, the battalion undertook advanced parachute training at the *Luftwaffe Fallschirmschule* III at Kraljewo in Croatia.[280]

Receiving the prefix 500 and issued a new field post number in May 1944 (*FPNr.* 28.933), the 850-strong SS-*Fallschirmjägerabteilung* had completed its training by the summer of 1944 and then undertook anti-partisan operations in Yugoslavia (Operation *Maypole*). Operation *Knights Move* had been conceived as a grand airborne and ground assault operation and was reminiscent of the early war assaults. Intended to destroy the headquarters of the partisan leader Josip 'Tito' Broz in the mountains near Drvar, the German assault against this well-defended base took place on 25 May 1944. Despite achieving initial surprise, the partisans conducted a spirited counterattack and the men of the SS-*Fallschirmjägerabteilung* suffered crippling casualties. At the end of the intensely savage battle only 292 of the paratroopers remained alive or uninjured from almost a 1,000 troops that had begun the attack. Following the bloody assault at Drvar the prisons no longer selected large groups of probationers for this unit, but selected individuals to serve in its ranks. On 1 October 1944 the head of the SS commanded those convicts deserving probation in suicidal units to no longer report to the SS-*Fallschirmjägerabteilung* 500, but fight instead with the SS-*Sonderbrigade*.[286]

Surviving the battle for Drvar in May 1944, this disgraced officer earned his rehabilitation:

Name: Wilhelm 'Willi' **Schmidl**.
Last Rank: SS-*Obersturmführer*.
Born: 4.5.1910 in Eger.
Died: 10.2.1945.
NSDAP-Nr.: 986.460 (joined 1.2.1932).
SS-Nr.: 44.413 (joined 19.6.1932).
Prewar Assignments:
Stahlhelm 3.1929-9.1929.
Reichswehr Schwarz RW III. / *Infantrie*-Rgt. 20.
Reichsschule der Sicherheitspolizei und des SD on 29.11.1937.
5. / LSSAH (Berlin) on 19.10.1938.
3. SS-*Totenkopfstandarte Thüringen* in 11.1938.
Wartime Assignments:
3. SS-*Totenkopfstandarte Thüringen* in 7.1941.
SS-*Fallschirmjägerabteilung* 500 in 1943.
Promotions:
1.11.1938 SS-*Untersturmführer der* SS-VT.
21.6.1941 SS-*Obersturmführer der Reserve*.
1.11.1944 SS-*Obersturmführer der Reserve*.

Decorations & Awards:
0.0.19__ SA-*Sportsabzeichen in Bronze.*
0.0.19__ *Totenkopfring der* SS.
0.0.19__ *Deutsches Reichssportabzeichen in Silber.*
0.0.19__ *Ehrendegen des Reichsführer*-SS.

Notes: Attending *Volksschule* for four classes and then studying at *Höhere Schule*, (OI), Schmidl failed to complete his university course. A member of the NSDStB from September 1929 to 10 August 1932, he marched with the SA from February until 1 August 1932. A prewar member of the SD, Schmidl mustered with the LSSAH and with the *Thüringen* in July 1941. For reasons that are not clear, *Hstuf.* Schmidl found himself degraded to the rank of *Hscha.* and expelled from the SS in 1942. Schmidl then undertook training with the newly forming SS-*Fallschirmjägerabteilung* 500 in 1943. Surviving Operation *Knights Move*, he appears to have been rehabilitated and promoted to the rank of *Ostuf.* in November 1944. Schmidl was a *Kompanieführer* in the SS-*Fallschirmjägerabteilung* 600 when killed in action in February 1945.[282]

Imprisoned for many years, this former communications officer volunteered for parachute training in 1943:

Name: Wilhelm Blank.
Last Rank: SS-Untersturmführer.
Born: 27.2.1916 in Stockerau near Vienna.
Died: 26.5.1944.
NSDAP-Nr.: 1.672.77 (joined 5.4.1934).
SS-Nr.: 270.319 (joined 5.4.1934).
R.A.D Service: 1.10.1936-24.3.1937.
Prewar Assignments:
SS-VT from 1.6.1937.
2. / SS-*Nachrichtenabteilung* (Aldershof/Unna) in 1937.
Offizier-Anwärter-Lehrgang SS-*Infanterie*-Rgt. *Germania* (Arolsen) 1939.
Offizier-Lehrgang SS-*Junkerschule* Braunschweig 13.4.–1.9.1939.
Lehrgang Heeresfachschule Halle 1.11.1939–25.1.1940.
Wartime Assignments:
Stab LSSAH in 4.1940.
SS-*Nachrichtenabteilung* (Unna) in 1940.
II. / *Reich* SS-*Nachrichtenabteilung* from 1.9.1940.
Nachrichtenzug / IV. / SS-*Artillerie*-Rgt. in 1941.
SS-*Artillerie-Ersatz-Bataillon* (Berlin) in 1941.
II. / SS-*Nachrichten-Ersatz-Bataillon* 2 (Nuremberg) from 10.4.1941.
SS-*Fallschirmjägerabteilung* 500 from 2.1943.

Promotions:

5.4.1934 SS-*Bewerber*.
16.6.1935 SS-*Mann der Allgemeine*-SS.
1.12.1933 SS-*Sturmann der* SS-VT.
1.10.1933 SS-*Unterscharführer der* SS-VT.
17.10.1939 SS-*Scharführer der* SS-VT.
3.11.1939 SS-*Hauptscharführer der* SS-VT.
20.4.1940 SS-*Untersturmführer der Waffen*-SS (*Aktiv*).

Decorations & Awards:

0.0.19__ SS-*Zivilabzeichen* (Nr. 167.277).
0.0.19__ SA-*Sportsabzeichen in Bronze*.
0.0.19__ *Deutsches Reichssportabzeichen in Bronze*.
0.0.19__ SS-*Ehrenwinkel für alte Kämpfer*.

Notes: Attending *Volksschule* for five classes and *Bürgerschule* for four years, Blank worked at the hotel am Sammering for three years and remained unmarried. Fleeing Austria for Germany in 1935, Blank reported to the Lechfeld camp and attended the 1935 and 1937 party days in Nuremberg. A communications officer, Blank participated in the attack on France and Yugoslavia with the LSSAH. Blank ran afoul of military regulations for incompetence and drunkenness on duty in 1941 and as a consequence of his behaviour, *Gruf.* Dietrich ordered his transfer from the regiment. 'Thoughtless on countless occasions, he had been reprimanded on countless occasions for incompetence' complained *Ostubaf.* Staudinger and alleged that Blank had been repeatedly ordered to refrain from drinking alcohol with the men under his command and been found drunk at 9.00 a.m. Replaced by *Sturmscharführer* Saul, Blank then transferred to a reserve artillery formation. Investigating an allegation that Blank had contravened paragraph § 175a, the unit *Gerichtsoffizier* in Nuremberg recommended Blank's trial and the SS-*Richter*, *Ustuf.* Dr Neukam of the SS- *und Polizei-Gericht* I, Munich visited the city to conduct a court's investigation. Submitting his report on 12 May 1941, Neukam recommended Blank's trial. Unrelated to this allegation, Blank was punished with fourteen days *Stubenarrest* for undisciplined behaviour with a military officer on 12 March 1941. Blank served the penalty between 23 April and 5 June 1941 (confirmed on 7.5.1941).

The *Reich* was stationed in south-eastern France in December 1940 when the officers and men of the second communications company at Echenos held a party to celebrate New Year's Eve. *Funker* Eberhard Stiehler visited Blank's room with a cookware full of mulled wine at around 00.15 a.m. and the pair finished off this beverage and then consumed a flask of *Sekt*. Copulating until around 1.30 a.m., although under the age of 21, Stiehler permitted Blank to penetrate and ejaculated inside of him. Later, denounced for committing an act of theft, Stiehler revealed his sexual encounter with Blank and was indicted for committing an act in contravention of paragraph § 175 RStGB. Blank and Stiehler were arraigned before the courts martial of the SS- *und Polizei-Gericht* I in Nuremberg on 28 April 1941 to answer a charge of committing *Widernatürlicher Unzucht* (case Nr. St. L. I. 173/1941). The court chairman, *Ustuf.* Neukam, was supported in his deliberations by the signals officer *Hstuf.* Karl Krüger and *Ustuf.* Wilhelm Klein, from the SS-Rgt. *Westland.* The SS-*Richter, Oscha.* Ernst Alexander prosecuted the case and the *Beurkundungsführer* was *Ustuf.* Erwin Denner. At trial, Stiehler alleged that he had been coerced and only with the greatest reluctance had he agreed to undress and have sex with Blank in return for special leave. Judging Stiehler's statement a clear attempt to mitigate his own behaviour, the court chairman's summation judged both guilty of the charge:

> Blank intended to have anal intercourse with Stiehler and to misuse him in fornication. This determination has been made on the basis of Blank's and Stiehler's proven abuse of a subordinate relationship. Blank is an SS-*Ustuf.* and the platoon superior of Stiehler, who as an SS radio operator and a member of Blank's section should always comply with the orders and penalties in service concerns. Blank has achieved his purpose with Stiehler on the grounds of this subordinate relationship and with the resulting dependency. The fact that he himself enquired on the personal circumstances of Stiehler while drinking enabled him to realise, that drinking with him, Blank could advocate special leave if he was docile and willing to engage in fornication.
>
> Although Blank may not explicitly promised Stiehler leave, he could still expect that he would receive leave, if he acceded to Blank's wishes. In addition, Stiehler, whose volition was weakened by the copious alcohol consumption in comparison with his superior, did not dare offer serious resistance and thus has tolerated, albeit unwillingly, to permit himself to have sex with Blank. Blank himself was well aware that he was taking advantage of the subordinate relationship and from this expectation he forced Stiehler to fornicate with him. His desire and handling stood outside his official powers and represents an abuse of the same. He is thus guilty of a crime contrary to paragraph § 175a section 2 RStGB.
>
> Contrary to the adoption of the indictment, it cannot be ascertained on the basis of the trial outcome that Blank had seduced Stiehler to fornication and thereby the court will sentence him in accordance to § 175a section 3 RStGB. Aware that Stiehler was not yet 21 years old, he used the concept of seductive action to strengthen his determination to go ahead with the enticement. By awakening sensual desires, or other ideas, the seduction is a propensity to enable the will of an unanswered desire to fornicate. However, Blank's motivation is not known. There is a lack of information and at least more is required. In other respects, the military relationship of the two concerning the seduction cannot be determined. Although Stiehler is still a minor, we can consider him a soldier but this case speaks less of a seduction within the meaning of the § 175a section 3 RGtGB.
>
> Blank had enjoyed plenty of alcohol on New Year's evening and yet contends that his senses were clear and he was not drunk while committing the offense. However, the court agrees that Blank was fully sober when the act was committed. Although I have observed that the excessive consumption of alcoholic drunk by Blank had removed certain inhibitions, which would have normally kept him from committing the offence. However, his behaviour in the act reveals that he had behaved with necessary insight and

determination of will. He deliberately steered the conversation with Stiehler to girls, to his personal circumstances and then raised the possibility of awarding him a special leave.

He also admits to have at once felt remorseful about his actions in the morning after the fact. He would not, if his senses would not have been strong, since if he had been completely drunk then he would be unable to recall in detail any of the facts committed. Finally, both were stripped completely naked, which they certainly could not do if they were completely drunk. According to experience they would have laid in a drunken sleep as they were and not just stripped off completely; this includes a certain amount of consideration that cannot be applied to complete drunkenness. Blank has committed the offense with consideration and is thus responsible for his actions.

Turning our attention to the criminal extent of the accused, he admitted to the offence immediately upon discovery. Without further grounds for suspicion we must also assume that it was for him a one-time lapse. Finally, Blank, as an Austrian National Socialist, has more than fulfilled his duty and gave up his job rather than reveal his [Nazi] attitude. The court therefore does not impose a *Zuchthausstrafen* and the defendant is granted leniency. Blank, however, has to be sentenced to a term of *Gefängnisstrafe*. It is a serious aberration for an SS officer to carry out such acts. Blank knew that the National Socialist State and particularly the SS impose the sharpest means action against homosexual offenders. Therefore as an SS officer he faces a harder punishment. We cannot excuse him the excess use of alcohol. He should know as an SS officer, how far he can get drunk and still be able to control his alcoholic state.

Failing to contest Stiehler's evidence, the tribunal judged Blank guilty of engaging in sex with his subordinate and the court punished him with three years' *Gefängnis* and ordered his expulsion from the SS. Assuming Blank was an NSDAP candidate, the tribunal recommended that his party application was blocked and his local party office in *Kreis* Herne–Castrop–Rauxel debated this topic until it was decided that his behaviour had damaged the reputation of the party. His expulsion from the party was ordered on 6 November 1941. Once sentenced, Blank reported to the SS-*Straflager* Dachau to serve out his sentence. Applying successfully for front probation, this was granted to Blank during the first weeks of February 1943 and he then reported to the newly forming SS-*Fallschirmjägerabteilung*. Prior to participating in the air assault component of Operation *Knights Move*, he undertook three months specialist paratrooper training. Jumping near Drvar on 26 May 1944, Wilhelm Blank was killed storming Tito's headquarters and as a consequence of his sacrifice, the *Reichsführer* almost certainly permitted his posthumous rehabilitation.[283]

5.19 *Sonderverbände z.b.V. Friedenthal* and *Jagdverbände*

Continuing his search for dangerous front probation for his convicts, the *Reichsführer* conceived a plan in 1944 to offer felons the opportunity to redeem themselves by volunteering to fight with the *Sonderverbände* z.b.V. *Friedenthal* (special unit for special duties) a commando unit designed to undertake near suicidal missions with the almost certain risk of death.[284]

Suffering from gallstones in 1942, *Ostuf.* Otto Skorzeny left the front to report to the Berlin SS motor pool while the SS- *und Polizei-Gericht* III, Berlin investigated him on the suspicion of cowardice (he successfully refuted this accusation). Skorzeny served a period of *Stubenarrest* and was then placed on probation in the wake of a drunken episode in a Parisian bar and for abusing a military *Polizei* patrol. *Ostuf.* Skorzeny received orders on 18 April 1943 to establish what was termed the *Oranienberg Sondereinheit*, a commando unit of the SD *Ausland* (foreign) and was tasked with establish 'stay behind' formations, training troops to undertake reconnaissance and sabotage missions behind enemy lines and develop new ways to fight the enemy in their rear echelon. Promoted eighteen days later, Skorzeny named his unit section 'S' (*schule*) and he established his headquarters in an office at Berlin, 32 Berkarstraße.[285]

Recruiting experienced officers from the SS and the military, Skorzeny also accepted foreign specialists and hit upon the idea of enlisting men that were willing to take part in missions with little chance of survival. Considering convicts suitable for this task, Skorzeny approached the *Chef* RSHA, General Dr Kaltenbrunner, to requested that he negotiated with the *HA* SS-*Gericht* to obtain a list of suitable candidates and obtain permission for their release. So taken was General Breithaupt with this concept, that he requested permission to send suitable candidates directly to Skorzeny's unit without prior consultation, a request that was ultimately denied.[286]

Commando Candidates for Skorzeny were then selected from convicts in prisons and probationers in the *Bewährungsabteilung*. The initial nine convicts identified for this duty had all served jail time in the SS-*Straflager* Dachau and only two were finally selected for special duties. The rejected felons transferred to the SS-*Sonderbrigade*.[287]

Amongst those selected to join Skorzeny was the following former officers: Born in Berlin on 20 April 1912, *Hstuf.* Dietrich Bernhardt had served with the WVHA in July 1941. Accused of stealing wood in Norway, he was arraigned before the courts martial of the SS- *und Polizei-Gericht* III, Berlin on 10 February 1942 to answer charges of embezzlement, (case Nr. St. L. I 2/1942). Judged guilty of the offences, the court punished Bernhardt with four years' *Gefängnis* and denied him his honour. Ordered to serve this punishment in the SS-*Straflager* Dachau, Bernhardt spent 22 months here, before considered for rehabilitation on 1 April 1944. Transferred to the *Bewährungsabteilung* in the summer of 1944, *Schütze* Bernhardt then reported to the SS-*Jagdverbände* in October the same year.

Born in Berlin on 16 March 1903, *Ostuf.* Hans Hempel, a member of the *Allgemeine*-SS (SS Nr. 62.878), was assigned to the 1. / SS-*Wachbataillon Böhmen-Mähren* when he was arraigned before the courts martial of the SS- *und Polizei-Gericht* VIII, Prague to answer accusations of disobedience (he had engaged in coitus with wives of serving soldiers), for procuring an abortion, stealing military food and been involved with the black market (case Nr. St. L. 90/1942). Judged guilty of the offences, the tribunal imposed a four years and two months term of *Gefängnis* on Hempel in January 1941. Detained in the SS-*Straflager* Dachau, Hempel failed to prove himself a model prisoner, but the prison leader would eventually report a significant improvement in his behaviour to enable his release to the *Bewährungsabteilung* in January 1944.

Born on 6 March 1915, *Ustuf.* Albert Priess was accused of obtaining money under false pretences from girlfriends and various acquaintances and committing embezzlement and found himself arraigned before the courts martial of the SS- *und Polizei-Gericht* III, Berlin on 17 May 1943 (case Nr. St. L. II 107/1942). Promising to marry two or three women, Priess swindled money from them and disappeared. In addition he stole 1,600 *Reichsmark* from one man and 1,200 *Reichsmark* from his service office. Judged guilty of the offences, Priess served fourteen months inside the SS-*Straflager* Dachau before accepting probation. He remained with the *Bewährungsabteilung* for 25 months before considered for service with Skorzeny's force. *Schütze* Priess was assigned to the SS-*Jagdverbände* in the summer of 1944.

Born on 22 November 1915, Andreas Daroß, a member of the *Allgemeine*-SS (SS Nr. 286.806), had led the Lemberg SS-*Kurierstelle* until the end of 1941. A post of immense trust, Daroß stole toiletries and a fur coat and began a relationship with a Polish woman in October 1941. Journeying to Berlin in January 1943, he visited the city of Essen, delaying his delivery of mail by three days. Returning to his service post, Daroß attempted to claim the costs of this private journey, but his embezzlement was later uncovered and a court's investigation recommended his trial for committing comrade theft, race crimes and embezzlement, (fearing exposure when a new leader was appointed, Daroß set light to the unit records, which made his successor's task more difficult). Arraigned before the courts martial of the SS- *und Polizei-Gericht* VI, Krakau on 15 May 1942, (case Nr. St. L. I 217/1941), the tribunal judged him guilty of the crimes and punished Daroß with ten years' *Zuchthaus* on 15 May 1942 and ordered his expulsion from the SS. Serving fifteen months of his sentence in the SS-*Straflager* Dachau, Daroß was then accepted for front probation and reported to the *Bewährungsabteilung* on 15 June 1943. Remaining here for two years and five months, Daroß was considered for service in the SS-*Jagdverbände* in the spring of 1944, but his candidacy was rejected on the grounds of his conviction for theft and he then transferred to the SS-*Sonderbrigade*.

The remaining candidates were former *St.OJ* Karl Gebauer, indicted for drunkenness on duty, attempted rape and rape and former *Ostuf.* Heinz-Paul Sieling, who had been brought for trial for the unauthorised use of service funds, misuse of service rank, the falsification of official papers, theft and the mishandling a subordinate. Lastly, former *Bewerber* Hans Steinfurth had been indicted for committing an act of corruption.[288]

Those selected for service in the SS-*Jagdverbände* then reported to the SS-*Kaserne* Adolf Hitler in Berlin–Lichterfelde to undertake a four week training course alongside *Kreigsmarine* and *Luftwaffe* candidates. Those recruited to Skorzeny's troops remained on probation until they had proved their bravery and prior to their arrival in Berlin, *Ostubaf.* Günther Burmeister requested that *Sta.* Werner Scholtz dressed them in SS uniforms with the rank of *Rttf.* attached to the collars to prevent the army and navy volunteers discovering that they were criminals on parole. However, discovering that their SS comrades were 'jailbirds', the naval officers complained to their superiors, forcing Himmler to re-think the whole concept. Considering the matter, the head of the SS then demanded that the case files of those volunteering from Danzig–Matzkau and other disciplinary units be in future examined in greater detail to judge their suitability.[289]

Undeterred by the lack of suitable convicts, Skorzeny then advertised to all units, including prisons and those assigned to Dirlewanger on 5 June 1944, to call for volunteers to join his unit for what was described as 'near suicide missions'. So successful was his announcement, that Skorzeny was then able to establish a staff and a three company battalion, which he titled the 502. *Jäger-Bataillon* and re-located his headquarters to Friedenthal.[290]

The men of the 502. *Jäger-Bataillon* carried out commando-style operations behind the allied front lines and provide resistance in occupied territories. Interrogated by Allied forces, Matr Wuchterl, a former member of this unit, revealed under questioning that 34 year-old Estonian *Ostuf.* Udo Vielhaek (SS Nr. 455.697) had led the 5. *Strafkompanie* / 502. *Jäger-Bataillon*, which was composed almost entirely from former convicts and probationers. Succeeded by 36 year-old China born *Hstuf.* Werner Hunke (SS Nr. 324.950), he was himself succeeded in turn by *Hstuf.* Hoyer, who had formally led a *Bewährungsabteilung* in Croatia. Wuchterl recollected that an *Rttf.* Seifert led a small section of Banat and Balkans ethnic-Germans who had refused to swear the oath of allegiance to the *Führer* and called to mind that a large group of parolees from this unit transferred to the Lübeck–Steinkoppel navy pioneer barracks on full pay in the last months of the war with orders to keep quiet about their time in gaol. Placed under the commander of the Plön U-boats training department, the probationers then undertook specialised torpedo training. Recalling that 100 SS and *Polizei* parolees was absorbed into the 250–300 strong Linsen *Flotilla*, Wuchterl stated that this unit was led by *Leutnant zur see* Martin, a former *Uscha.*[291]

Not all the former convicts were happy with their new assignment: Deserting from the SS-*Jagdverbände*, twenty five year-old *Scha.* Jean Poignet was questioned by Allied interrogators and claimed to have been held in the 'KL Dachau' during November 1943. From there, he volunteered for military service the SS-*Grenadier*-Brigade *Charlemagne* in 3 December 1944, but accepted into the Skorzeny troops, he was then subordinated to *Ostuf.* Pavel. Tasked undertaking a reconnaissance/intelligence gathering mission in January 1945, Poignet and 42 year-old *Scha.* Goerges Tostain used this mission as an opportunity to desert to the 7th US Army near Seltz, (Hagenau).[292]

His death sentence for theft amended to a *Zuchthaus* sentence, this disgraced officer then transferred to Skorzeny's troops:

Name: Hans Ammon.
Last Rank: SS-*Untersturmführer.*
Born: 23.5.1912 in Nuremberg

NSDAP-Nr.: 5.031.701 (joined 1.3.1937).
SS-Nr.: 209.146 (joined 23.2.1934).
Prewar Assignments:
Freikorps Brigade *Ehrhardt*.
SS-VT (Ellwangen) from 23.2.1934.
SS-*Standarte Germania* (Arolsen) from 1.5.1935.
LSSAH 1935–1.2.1937.
SS-*Bataillon Nürnberg* (Prittelbach) on 1.2.1937.
LSSAH (administrative leader) in 5.1939,
SS-*Artillerie-Ersatz-Bataillon* (administrative leader) in 1939.
Wartime Assignments:
Verwaltungsführer-Lehrgang in 11.1939.
SS-*Lazarett* Berlin (3. administrative officer) in 1939.
SS-*Lazarett* Krakau 20.4.–3.11.1941.
SS-*Lazarett* Vienna (1. administrative officer) from 3.11.1941.
SS-WVHA in spring 1942.
Bewährungsabteilung 29.6.1943.
Sonderverbände z.b.V. *Friedenthal* from 10.7.1944.
Promotions:
5.1937 SS-*Unterscharführer der* SS-VT.
30.1.1940 SS-*Untersturmführer der Waffen*-SS (*Aktiv*).
Decorations & Awards:
0.0.19__ SS-*Zivilabzeichen* (Nr. 53.917).
0.0.19__ SA-*Sportsabzeichen in Bronze*.
0.0.19__ *Deutsches Reichssportabzeichen in Bronze*.

Notes: His father was an electrician/machine worker. Attending *Volksschule* for four classes and *Höhere Schule* (O-II), Ammon left full time education and found employment as a salesman. Ammon never married, but had a child out of wedlock in 1941. Suffering an injury as a result of a motorcycle accident at Prittelbach in 1938, Ammon undertook training as an administrative candidate in May the same year and reported to the Krakau SS-*Lazarett* in April 1941. Here, *Brigadef.* Dr Frank ordered his transfer from the Polish city with an admonishment for unsatisfactory behaviour, (he had hit about the head an official of the military and fired his service weapon in the air when drunk). Transferred to the SS-*Lazarett* Vienna in November 1941, here, the chief physician, *Stubaf.* Dr Heinrich Röttger, purchased one 100 flasks of *Sekt* for his patients from hospital stores and handed these to Ammon for safe keeping. Deceitfully, Ammon and two members of his staff then conspired to pilfer the alcohol and falsified the stock book to give the appearance that the alcohol had been used for medicinal reasons. Stealing 28 flasks, Ammon drank his share with a woman in his room, became drunk and then fired his service pistol at a light bulb. The theft discovered, the SS- *und Polizei-Gericht* VII, Vienna was tasked with conducting a court's investigation. Recommending Ammon's trial, he was detained in the Vienna *Polizeigefängnis* on 17 January 1942 (case Nr. St. L. I 336/1941).

Both Ammon's co-defendants, Werner Feuerstein and Kurt Weymann faced trial for their part in the theft. All three were arraigned before the courts martial of the Viennese tribunal on 11 April 1942 and judged guilty, a sentence of four years and eight months *Zuchthaus* was imposed on Ammon along with his expulsion from the SS. Refusing to confirm this judgement, the *Reichsführer* ordered their retrial and this took place before *Stubaf.* Brinkmann of the Vienna tribunal on 26 November 1942. Pleading guilty to the charges, Ammon also asked the court to take into consideration an offence of driving without undue care, he admitted committing an earlier act of indiscipline in Krakau and confessed to the theft of a radio part and the deception of a school child (the court noted that *Stubaf.* Dr Heinrich Röttger had expressed dissatisfaction with Ammon's work). Noting that Ammon came from a good home and that his father had received a bravery award during the Great War, the court complained of his carelessness, but accepting his remorsefulness, the judge voiced his conviction that only a prison term could change his ways. All three defendants again declared guilty of military theft for stealing the bottles of Sekt, the tribunal declared Ammon a people's pest, assessed him guilty of serious document forgery and decided against him for committing two cases of actual bodily harm for the earlier assault on an *Oberzahlmeister* in Krakau. Adjudicating him guilty for two misuses of his service pistol, the court declared him military unworthy and imposed two years' *Zuchthaus* on Ammon for committing fraud, three months' *Gefängnis* for self-injury, six weeks' close arrest for the misuse of his service weapon and sentenced him to death for theft. Writing to the SS-*Richter beim* RF-SS on 28 November 1942, *Ustuf.* Brinkmann informed him that the trial had concluded that very day and Ammon had been sent back to Nuremberg.[293]

The *Gerichtsherr, Gruf.* Dr Kaltenbrunner, confirmed their sentences and noting that Ammon was a deceiver, careless and a doubtful character of little value, he upheld the *Zuchthaus* punishment and recommended probation with a demand that Ammon was never again employed as an administrator. Observing that Ammon came from a high standing family, Dr Kaltenbrunner noted that he had previously offered good services and was the first in his family to drink Sekt. The *HA* SS-*Gericht* recommended that Ammon's sentence was amended to fifteen years' *Zuchthaus* with a loss of honour and civil rights for ten years, or the war's end and judged him suitable for front probation. Concurring with the views of the *Gerichtsherr* and *HA* SS-*Gericht* the *Reichsführer* then sent Ammon's case file to the Reich Chancellery for the *Führer* to review the officer's case and arrange his reprieve.

Confirming Ammon's sentence, the *Führer* set aside the death penalty and amended the judgement to fifteen years' *Zuchthaus* on 18 May 1943. The *Reichsführer*, the *Gerichtsherr* and the *HA* SS-*Gericht* agreed to this decision on 15 June and recommended that Ammon served six months of his jail sentence. With all parties in agreement on 29 June 1943, Ammon then mustered with the *Bewährungsabteilung* that same month. Writing to the *HA* SS-*Gericht* on 26 September 1944, Ammon's father inquired after his son's welfare and received notification from his case worker on 4 October that his son would soon be rehabilitated. The SS-*Richter beim* RF-SS approved Ammon's selection for the Skorzeny commando troops in Berlin in July 1944 and commanded him to participate in near death missions.[294]

5.20 103. SS-*Bewährungskompanie*

Also known as the 103. SS-*Sturmkompanie*, this formation was raised from parolees of the *Bewährungsabteilung* in Dublowitz during the summer of 1944 (FPNr. 35.194). Subordinate to the III. *Germanic* SS-*Panzerkorps*, these probationers participated in the battle for Narva in July 1944. Under the leadership of *Hstuf.* Adolf Klocker, the 103. SS-*Sturmkompanie* deployed at Grenadier Hill and during the battle for this sector of the front, Klocker replaced the wounded *Hstuf.* Josef Bachmeier as commander of all the SS units on this sector of the front on 5 August. In the aftermath of this brutal battle the surviving parolees were rehabilitated and transferred in their entirety to the 24. SS-*Panzergrenadier* Rgt. *Danemark.*[295]

5.21 SS-*Bewährungsabteilung Thomalla*

One of the last known probation formation raised from former *Waffen*-SS convicts was the SS-*Bataillon Thomalla*, which fought north of Berlin under the command of the III. III. Germanic SS-*Panzerkorps* in the last days of the conflict.[296]

Decimated following the retreat from Pomerania, the III. SS-*Panzerkorps* required an induction of fresh troops to flesh out its depleted ranks. To facilitate the rebuilding of his shattered units, the corps commander, *Gruf.* Steiner, ordered all the reserve units for every divisions under his command to amalgamate into one field training unit. As a consequence of this decision, the 103. SS-*Ausbildung- und Ersatz*-Rgt., later brigade, was established the command of *Ostubaf.* Lang in March 1945 near Gramzow north-west of Schwedt. In February, Lang established the *Unteroffizierlehrkompanie* (NCO demonstration company), or the ULK, a front probation unit, which became the third company of the *Hstuf.* Franz Thomalla's command.[297]

The first two companies of the *Thomalla* were comprised of trainees and convalescents from the 11th SS-*Panzergrenadier*-Division *Nordland* and both were led by 34 year-old *Ustuf.* Hans Hecker. An SS man since November 1936, Hecker had previously fought with the *Deutschland.* The 80-man strong third company was composed of former parolees of the ULK and was led by *Ustuf.* Klostermann, the former Ordnance officer for the 103. SS-*Ausbildung- und Ersatz*-Rgt.[298]

Thomalla's battalion entered the front line positions and prepared to lead the attack of the 3. *Marine-Infanterie*-Division along the Hohenzollern canal position on 22 April 1945. With no prior reconnaissance, the troops of the *Thomalla* left their positions at 5 a.m.

on 24 April 1945 and began their assault against Red Army positions near Klosterfelde (Hecker's companies advanced on the right flank, Klostermann's on the left). The attack was repelled in the face of tough Red Army resistance and the survivors were forced to retreat to Alt and Neu-Ruppen on the 30 April 1945. Hoping to reach the demarcation line before the Red army tank spearheads, the survivors of the *Thomalla* battalion retreated through Lindow, rested one kilometre from Stolpe on 1 May 1945 and then continued their journey to Tramnitz. From here, they proceeded to Karnow and at this point in time all trace of the parolees disappeared from history.[299]

5.22 SS-*Bewährungsregiment Ludwigsfelde*

'Established from the members of the SS prison Ludwigsfelde into a battlegroup near Hammer, it was deployed east of Liebenwalde. They went down with the battalion *Thomalla*' wrote Horst Voight, in *Die Verlor'nen Haufen* and stating the existence of a three battalion, 1,200 strong SS-*Bewährungsregiment Ludwigsfelde/Marienfelde*', Voight then reveals that this parole formation fought with the 12th *Armee* near Forst and then placed under *Generalleutnant* Reyman's command in the southern suburbs of Berlin, it fought alongside the 1st FLAK Division near Siethen in Potsdam and Gro*ß*-Beeren until destroyed by the Red Army.[300]

Other sources reveal that this regiment, listed in the SS-DAL of 1 March 1945, was composed of delinquents who had previously worked in the Daimler-Benz factory at Tetlow. Fighting to defend Berlin, this regiment ended the war fighting under the XX. *Korps* of Wenck's 12th *Armee* in April 1945.

It is interesting to note that this regiment is not specifically mentioned in either of Tony Le Tissier's exhaustive books on the battle for Berlin and it is omitted from both Wilhelm Tieke's *The End between Elbe and Oder* and Wolfgang Benz and Angelika Konigseder's *Der Ort des Terrors*. As far as I have been able to ascertain, the *Reichsführer*, via *Stubaf.* Herbert Marienfeldt, commanded the establishment of a grenadier regiment from convicts detained in Berlin–Teltow in the spring of 1945. The *Zweiglager* Ludwigsfelde had closed in September 1944 and we are left to assume that this message refers to parolees recruited from the myriad of remand institutions located in and around Berlin. It remains uncertain whether Marienfeldt's command led directly to the creation of a SS-*Bewährungs*-Rgt. *Marienfelde*, or the establishment of the SS-*Bataillon Thomalla*.

5.23 SS-*Standarte Mauthausen*

On Sunday, 27 March 1945 the *Kommandanteur des* KL Gusen and Mauthausen reported a combined strength of 9,808 men all ranks and 80 per cent of these troops had been judged fit to fight at the front in a combat unit. The subsequent field formation created from this levy was known as the SS-*Standarte Mauthausen*.[301]

At this time a decision was also taken to recruit camp prisoners for a probation company for the SS-*Standarte Mauthausen*. Those volunteering for this unit numbered more than a company's worth of infantry and issued uniforms, SS pay books, equipment, a rifle and 60 rounds of ammunition, they marched from the *Schutzhaftlager* on 5 March 1945.[302]

The following day the former camp parolees received the blood tattoo, was divided into companies and fifteen man sections which were led by SS troops, who received orders to instruct them in the use of the rifle. The regiment was probably reinforced with convicted Viennese firemen from the Mauthausen camp arrest.[303]

While training, the former camp prisoners dug trenches and bunkers in the eastern quadrant of the camp, but desertions was commonplace. 200 German and Austrian camp prisoners replaced these losses on 14 April and these parolees were issued green *Afrika Korp* uniforms and SS pay books. Receiving a blood type tattoo, they were then handed their equipment and armed.[304]

Additional strength then arrived in the form of recruits from the *Hitlerjugend*, *Luftwaffe*, *Polizei*, SD, *Volkssturm* and at least 250 *Kriegsmarine* personnel joined this regiment on 28 April. Leaving the camp environs, the estimated 5,000 troops of the '*Mauthausen*' marched towards Leibnitz and arriving in Peggau, the regiment was placed under the command of the *Ausbildung- und Ersatz*-Division 487 near Amstettin.[305]

Deployed at the front, the *Mauthausen* became the *Kampfgruppe Oberdonau*, then later the SS-*Panzerjäger- und Zerstörer*-Rgt *Oberdonau*. Its sub-units fought US Army armoured units along a line Gallneukirchen–Gramastetten–Offenheim on 3 May and in the face of overwhelming enemy superiority, this formation lost cohesion and then disintegrated. Its surviving elements, including the former camp probationers, surrendered to the US Army near Radstatt, Wagrain and Kleinarl.[306]

5.24 SS-*Bewährungsabteilung Nürnberg*

One source reports that selected convicts of the defunct SS-*Zweiglager Hammerweg* reported to the SS-*Kaserne* Nuremberg in April 1945 and accepting front probation, they formed the SS-*Bewährungsabteilung Nürnberg* and defended the city against the 45th US Army Division. The SS-*Kaserne* Nuremberg fell to forces of the US Army on 20 April and at that time the surviving parolees of the *Nürnberg* battalion surrendered to the US Army.[307]

5.25 SS-*Kampfgruppe Matingen/Pavian*

The *Polizei* authorities controlling the Mantelupich prison in Krakow established the SS-*Kampfgruppe Matingen/Pavian* from suitable offenders at the end of May/beginning June 1944. Armed and equipped, these parolees then fought partisans operating around Krakow.[308]

It is estimated that between 60 and 70 prison inmates were selected for front probation with the *Matingen/Pavian* and these were led by non-commissioned officers of the SS-*Panzergrenadier- und Ausbildung Ersatz-Bataillon* 3. This *ad hoc Kampfgruppe* also included SS officers, VoMi officers, Polish ethnic-Germans, *Generalgouvernment Polizei* and a handful of Russian and Ukrainian volunteers; a total of 180 men.[309]

Fighting with *Oberst der Gendarmerie* Felix Bauer's SS-*Polizei*-Rgt. 23 in three separate groups, the first and second battalions battled partisan groups in Oberschlesien, while the third battalion, composed of parolees, manoeuvred around Krakow and fought around Wisloka near Debica until the end of July 1944. The *Kampfgruppe Pavian* was then deployed against Polish/Ukrainian partisans in Galicia and in the Beskydy mountains from September to December 1944. Tessin states that at the end of the war this unit fought alongside with the 1,500 strong *Grossjägdverband*, (FPNr. 57.508).[310]

5.26 *Polizei-Bewährungskompanie Einbrodt*

While deployed in Slovenia, the *Sonderzüge* of the SS-*Polizei*-Rgt. 13 and 14 were commanded to combine and establish one parolee company:

> As its company commander, the SS-FHA has seconded SS-*Hstuf.* Herbert Einbrodt. SS-*Hstuf.* Einbrodt will be assigned to the *Polizei-Gebirgsjägerkompanie Alpenland* for instruction and training in mountain warfare until 28 February 1945. The combination of the *Sonderzüge* into a probation company will have been completed by 1 March 1945. A full report on the implementation of this order to the *Abt.* Ia will be undertaken by the company commander.[311]

Endnotes

Introduction

1 Hans Buchheim, *Anatomie des SS-Staates, Die SS- das Herrschaftsinstrument*, Walter-Verlag, 1965, pp.154-155.

2 Letter *HA* SS-*Gericht* to the SS-*Richter beim* RF-SS, dated 1.2.1943: BA NS 7/365, pp. 46-52.

Chapter 1: The Disciplinary Punishment of SS Men

1 SS-Disziplinarstraf- und Beschwerdeordnung: IfZ-Archiv Munich, DC 002.019.

2 SS-Befehl des Reichsführer-SS tGB. nR. a/ 9434, dated 9.11.1935.

3 SS-Disziplinarstraf-und Beschwerdeordnung für den mobilen Zustand: D.C NARA microfilm publication T-580, roll 212.

1.1 Pre-war Concentration Camp Detention

4 Peter Padfield, *Himmler Reichsführer*-SS, Cassel & Co 2001, pp. 124-125.

5 Martina Steber/Bernhard Gotto, *Visions of Community in Nazi Germany: Social Engineering and Private Lives*, OUP Oxford 2014, p. 20-25.

6 Barbara Distel/Ruth Jakusch, *Concentration Camp* Dachau, Com. International de Dachau; edition 1978, p. 91. See Peter Padfield, '*Himmler...*', op cit.; pp. 183-184.

7 SS-*Richter* Dr Konrad Morgan, Die Unrechtsbekampfung in Konzentrationslager durch SS-Richter, dated 21.12.1945, pp. 57–68: NARA BDC, SSO Personalakte Dr Konrad Morgan.

8 Charles W. Sydnor Jr., *Soldiers of Destruction*, PUP edition 1990, p. 315. See Eugen Kogon, *The Theory and Practice of Hell*, Farrar Straus Giroux; revised edition 2006, p. 22. 'Several times' Kogon claimed to have witnessed former camp guards parading before their company and having their heads shaved bald, then were whipped 25 times and given a concentration camp uniform, before being sent into a concentration camp.

9 Peter Padfield, '*Himmler...*' *op cit.;* p. 138. See Barbara Distel, '*Concentration Camp...*' op cit.; p. 58.

10 Heinz Höhne, *the Order of the Deaths Head*, Secker & Warburg 1969, p. 138. Höhne claims that eleven prewar SS officer were sent to the camps for refusing to sign their oath of loyalty.

11 Paul Martin Neurath, *The Society of Terror; inside Dachau and Buchenwald Concentration Camps*, Routledge 2005, p. 67.

12 Brittany N. Austin, *Persecuted Homosexuals in Nazi Germany* HIST 542 Research paper, p. 9. See G.J. Giles, *The Denial of Homosexuality: Same-Sex Incidents in Himmler's SS*, Journal of the History of Sexuality, Vol. 11, No. 1 (202).

13 Padfield, '*Himmler…*', op cit.; p. 138; George C. Bowder, *Foundations of the Nazi Police State*, Kentucky 1990, p. 122/123.

1.2 Emslandlager

14 Nikolas Wachsmann, *KL: A History of the Nazi Concentrations Camps*, Little, Brown 2015, p. 49.

15 Seidler, '*Die Militärgerichtsbarkeit…*' op cit.; p. 124.

16 *Ibid*, pp. 124-128.

17 *Ibid*, pp. 124-128.

18 *Chef des HA* SS-*Gericht* edict 'Concerning the Teaching of the Special Judiciary to the SS and *Polizei* and Subordinate SS and *Polizei* members respectively': D.C. NARA Washington microfilm T-580, roll 213. See letter SS-*Richter beim* RF-SS to *HA* SS-*Gericht*, dated 18.5.1942: BA NS 7/378, p. 32.

19 The wooden barracks of the Esterwegen *Strafgefanggenenlager* near Papenburg are also known as *Lager* VII and held a variety of different categories of prisoners from its opening in 1933. Become a sub-camp of the KL Neuengamme in 1941.

1.3 SS-Erziehungssturm

20 Hans-Peter Klausch, *Die Bewährungstruppe 500* (Ed. 1995), pp. 19, 33-40.

21 *Ibid*, pp. 33-40. The prisoners referred to Richard Bugdalle as 'Brutalla.' Joining the SS in 10.1931, Bugdalle was a *Blockführer* from 1937 and then led the *Strafkompanie* and particularly enjoyed punching prisoners to death. Sent for front line training in 1942, he ended up incarcerated in an SS prison for assaulting his commander who found fault with his military bearing. Post-war, Bugdalle's name appeared on the Crowcass consolidated wanted list. The Belgium authorities believed he had been a *Blockführer* in the KL Neuengamme between 1940-1944 and wanted him arrested on suspicion of committing murder, (central registry of war criminals and security suspects part 1 & 2; Kew WO 309/1704, (195831) dated 3.1947). See Christel Trouvé, *Richard Bugdalle, SS-Blockführer im Konzentrationslager Sachsenhausen*, pp. 37-41; *Landgericht* Bonn judgement 6.2.1959 JNV Vol. 15; p. 422.

22 Jens-Christian Wagner, *Produktion des Todes. Das KZ Mittelbau-Dora*, Wallstein Verlag 2004, pp. 429-430.

23 *Reichsführer* edict, dated 21.7.1938: NCC, doc. 161: Odt. VOL. 3 & 33.

24 Wolfgang Benz/Barbara Distel/Angelika Königseder, *Der Ort des Terrors: Ort des Terrors: Geschichte der nationalsozialistischen Konzentrationslager. Band 2 Frühe Lager Dachau, Emslandlager*, C.H.Beck 2005, p. 33. See Erziehungssturm im Konzentrationslager Sachsenhausen AS R 49/1 (Abschrift der ZStA, Film-Nr. 3335): Vopersal: BA NS 756/283b.

25 Harry Naujoks, *Mein Leben im KZ Sachsenhausen 1936–1942*, Röderberg-Vlg., Köln 1990, pp. 64, 68, 131 & 150.

26 Leo Baeck Institute: LBI Archives, 15 West 16th Street, New York, NY 10011, USA.

27 NARA BDC, SSO Personalakte Rudiger v.Bodungen.

28 The punished were: *Strm.* Willi v.Dahlen, (*Stab Ersatz-Kp.*), SS-*Mann* Alexander Simon, (1. *Ersatz-Kp.*), *Strm.* Hans Pessiner, (1. *Ersatz-Kp.*), *Rttf.* Fritz v.Sturm, (3. *Ersatz-Kp.*), *Scha.* Erich Stichnoth, (5. *Ersatz-Kp.*) and *Uscha.* Franz Effland, (5. *Ersatz-Kp.*): BA RS 4/1692.
29 Letter *Kommandeur des Panzerspahzugskompanie* Berlin Lichterfelde to the *Kommandeur des* LSSAH *Ersatz-Bataillon*, dated 5.3.1940: BA RS 4/1692.
30 *Ibid.*
31 Letter dated 17.9.1940: BA RS 4/1641.
32 Letter SS-*Richter beim* RF-SS to the *HA* SS-*Gericht*, dated 13.12.1941: D.C. NARA microfilm publication T-580, roll 212.
33 NARA BDC, SSO Personalakte Willi Prager.

1.4 Sondergerichtsbarkeit der SS und Polizei

34 Roland Freisler, *Strafgerichtsbarkeit der SS und des R.A.D. in Deutsche Justiz 100 (1938) Ausgabe A Nr. 9*, dated 4.3.1938, p. 352-353. See Höhne, *the Order…*' op cit.; p. 149.
35 *Reichsführer* edict, dated 19.3.1943: D.C. NARA Washington microfilm; T-580, roll, 213.
36 Seidler, '*Die Militärgerichtsbarkeit…*' op cit.; p. 202.
37 Vieregge, *Der Gerichtsbarkeit…*' op cit.; p. 95.
38 Erlasse des Hauptamtes SS-Gericht (Sammlung) Juli.-Dez. 1942: BA NS 7/5.
39 *Ibid.*
40 *Ibid.*
41 Letter *Gruf.* Scharfe, dated 19.2.1941. For further details see letter Dr Reinecke, dated 16.5.1944: D.C. NARA Washington microfilm; T-580, roll 213.
42 *Erlasse des Hauptamtes* SS-*Gericht* (Sammlung) 7.1942–12.1942: BA NS 7/5. See NARA BDC, SSO Personalakte Dr Günther Reinecke.
43 Vieregge, '*Der Gerichtsbarkeit…*' ob cit.; p. 148.
44 *Ibid*, p. 150.
45 NARA BDC, SSO Personalakte Horst Bender; undated letter 63292.
46 Sydnor Jr., '*Soldiers…*' op cit.; p. 132.
47 Seidler, '*Die Militärgerichtsbarkeit…*' op cit.; pp. 39-51.
48 *Ibid*, p. 42.
49 Dr Günther Reinecke statement, dated 27.4.1965: *StA* Munich: 13 Js 9/66 /W; Landeskriminalamt Bayern III a/SK, pp. 399-402.
50 Interrogation of *Hstuf.* Richard Neun by allied intelligence, dated 26.10.1945: Kew WO 208/3149.
51 The Hotel zum 'Kronprinz' is now a health clinic and is called the Medicalpark Klinik Kronprinz. The Hotel zum 'Chiemsee' is now the clinic Schön Klinik GmbH: Gabi Oberloher at the Kur & Tourismusbüro, Priener Tourismus GmbH; Prien am Chiemsee, Alte Rathausstrasse 11, dated 16.9.2011.
52 Vernehmung des Zeugen Günther Burmeister: 1. Frankfurter Auschwitz Prozess: Strafsach gegen Mulka and others << 4 Ks 2/63 Landgericht Frankfurt am Main, dated 26.3.1965.

1.5 Wartime Disziplinarvorgesetzte and Arrest Punishments

53 *HA* SS-*Gericht* edict, dated 17.10.1939: NSD 41/39. Published in the *Reich* law gazette on 1.9.1939 (Seite I, page 1336) and came into force on 17.10.1939.

54 Letter SS-*Richter beim* RF-SS to the *HA* SS-*Gericht*, dated 6.8.1940. See letter SS-*Richter beim* RF-SS (Dr Wehser), dated 15.9.1942: D.C. NARA microfilm publication T-81, roll 213.

55 *Ibid.*

56 *Ibid.*

57 *Ibid.*

58 *Ibid.*

59 *HA* SS-*Gericht* edict, dated 17.10.1939: BA NSD 41/39.

60 NARA BDC, SSO Personalakte Rodiger v.Bodungen.

61 Letter SS-*Richter beim* RF-SS to the *HA* SS-*Gericht*, dated 8.10.1942; SS-*Richter beim* RF-SS to the *HA* SS-*Gericht*, dated 6.1.1943; letter SS-*Richter beim* RF-SS to Eberhard Hinderfeld, dated 8.1.1943: D.C. NARA Microfilm T-580, roll 214.

62 Letter SS-*Richter beim* RF-SS to *Gruf.* Breithaupt, dated 26.3.1944. See SS-*Richter beim* RF-SS the *HA* SS-*Gericht*, dated 29.9.1944: D.C. NARA Microfilm T-580, roll 214.

63 Letter *Stubaf.* Burmeister to the SS-*Richter beim* RF-SS, dated 26.10.1944; *Gruf.* Breithaupt to the SS-*Richter beim* RF-SS, dated 8.12.1944: D.C. NARA Microfilm T-580, roll 214.

64 Phil Nix/Georges Jerome, *The Uniformed Police Forces of the Third Reich 1933–45*, Leandoer and Ekholm 2008, pp. 40-47.

65 *Ibid*, p. 12.

66 NARA BDC, SSO Personalakte Hans-Dietrich Grünewald. See *HA* SS-*Gericht* edict, dated 17.10.1939: NSD 41/39.

67 Message Kew WO 208/3616; interrogation of P.W, (b. 1902, Oberschwarzbrunn/Sud.); Vopersal collection: BA NS 756/283a.

68 *Ostuf.* Wilhelm Gogalla, (b. 30.5.1901 in Frankfurt on Oder, SS Nr. 50.941): http://www.tagesspiegel.de/berlin/prinz-albrecht-gelaende-zentrale-des-schreckens/1814996.html.

1.6 Untersuchungshaft

69 Letters SS-*Rechtamt* to the SS-*Richter beim* RF-SS, dated 5.8.1940/15.11.1940: D.C. NARA Washington microfilm, T-580, roll 213.

70 Remand Prison list, dated 7.2.1945: BA NS 7/1, p. 212. *Strm.* Tischler, *Strm.* Szarensky, *Strm.* Jünemann, *Schütze* Roth, *Schütze* Schrode, *Schütze* Hobert, *Schütze* Ouchinger, *Schütze* Meuser and *Schütze* Kroll. *Schütze* Geldmacher transferred from this post directly from the SS-*Straflager* Dachau.

1.7 Standort Arrestanstalt

71 Archiv Vopersal: BA NS 19/1913; WVHA memorandum, dated 29.4.1942: BA NS 7/362, p. 4; NARA BDC, SSO Personalakte *Ustuf.* Karl-Heinz Schröder.

72 Archiv Vopersal: BA NS 19/1913. See SS-*Richter beim* RF-SS memorandum, dated 21.3.1942: BA NS 7/362, pp. 1-5.

73 Letter SS-*Richter beim* RF-SS to *Ogruf.* Pohl, dated 22.3.1944: BA NS 7/362, pp. 2-5.

74 SS-*Richter beim* RF-SS memorandum, dated 21.3.1942: BA NS 7/362, pp. 1-5.

75 SS-*und Polizei-Gericht* VI, *Zweiggericht* Lublin, undated: USHMM RG-15.034M –Reel 2.

76 Archiv Vopersal: BA NS 19/1913. See letter *Gruf.* Breithaupt to the RFSS, dated 1.2.1944: BA NS 7/369, pp. 2-4.

77 BDC, SS Personalakte Gustav Layer. See letter *Ogruf.* Frank, HSSPF *Böhmen und* Mähren dated 20.7.1944: Narodi Archiv: 109-6155/69.

1.8 Strafvollstreckungszug

78 Seidler, '*Die Militärgerichtsbarkeit...*', op cit.; p. 166.

79 Letter *Stubaf.* Denzel, chief judge of the 12th SS-*Panzergrenadier*-Division *Hitlerjugend*, dated 8.2.1944: John Moore archive dated 3.11.2012. Published by the *Panzerarmeekommando 2 Abt.* III on 13.9.1943, the *Aufstellung von Strafvollstreckungszugen* authorised one officer, two non-commissioned officers and a soldier to each prison and divided the institution into two parts, the first for court sentenced convicts and the second for disciplinary cases.

80 *Ibid*, dated 14.2.1944.

1.9 Wartime Incarceration of SS men in Concentration Camps

81 NARA BDC, SSO Personalakte SS-Führer: Rüdiger v.Bodungen. Born on 15.12.1915 in Magdeburg, *Ostuf.* Rudolf Klaebe (SS Nr. 257.553) died in action with the *Verlorenen Haufen* in France during 1940.

82 Sydnor Jr., '*Soldiers...*', op cit.; p. 62. See '*Totenkopf Nachschub* daily order Nr. 56, dated 29.12.1939: BA RS 3 3/27, p. 121. See Chris Mann, *SS Totenkopf; The History of the Deaths Head Division* 1940-45, Motor books International 2001, p. 49.

83 Letter SS-*Richter beim* RF-SS to the RSHA, dated 25.10.1942: BA NS 756/283a. The differences between the camps could be marginal and not consistent and while food supplies may be better in one camp, they may not be improved a month later. A camp was usually graded by the work it provided, the harder and more difficult the work, the more prisoners that died: Kogon, '*The Theory...*', op cit.; pp. 26-27.

84 Letter SS-*Richter beim* RF-SS to the RSHA, dated 25.10.1942: BA NS 756/283a.

85 Daily Report *Gestapo* Vienna No. 1, between 1.–4.3.1944; Helmut Bouzek: Wien and its Fire Department, Vienna and Ernst Toman: '... for I fear not death!' Vienna Fire Department in the Resistance against Fascism, Wien 1986.

86 Franz-Otto Hühn statement: *Abteilung*; BA Ludwigsburg: B 162/829. See letter *HA* SS-*Gericht Amt* III to the WVHA *Amtsgruppe* D, dated 10.9.1942: D.C. NARA Washington microfilm, T-580, roll 213.

87 Seidler, '*Die Militärgerichtsbarkeit...*' op cit.; pp. 230-231.

88 Letter *HA* SS-*Gericht Amt* III to WVHA *Amtsgruppe* D, dated 10.9.1942: D.C. NARA Washington microfilm, T-580, roll 213.

89 Letter *HA* SS-*Gericht* IIIb 320/6, dated 22.9.1942: BA NS 756/283a, p.156. See Hans Maršálek's, *Die Geschichte des KZ Mauthausen*, Wien 1995, p.333.

90 Letter *HA* SS-*Gericht Amt* IIIb 320/6, dated 22.9.1942: BA NS 756/283a, p. 156

91 Source; Kew TNA, HW 16/40, dated 21.4.1944.

92 NARA BDC, SSO Personalakte Ewald Kimenskowski. *Stubaf.* Werner Peterseim, (b. 27.2.1899 in Mülhausen/Thüringen, SS Nr. 93.744).

93 NW M-1079 Roll II B, 652f; Benz, '*Der Ort* des...', op cit.; pp. 355-442. See Wagner, '*Konzentrationslager...*' op cit.; pp. 68 & 426.

94 Wachsmann, '*KL*', op cit.; p. 217. See deposition of Heinrich Schäfer by the British Field Investigation Section, War Crimes Group (NWE) at the Essen *Polizeipräsidium* on 12.10.1947. *Uscha.* Heinrich

Schäfer, (b. 10.6.1907 in Essen). Admitted into the *Allgemeine*-SS in May 1933 and the Nazi party in 1938, Schäfer mustered with the *Genesungkompanie* / SS-*Panzer-Grenadier-Ersatz-Bataillon Totenkopf* I (Warschau) during April 1942 when ordered to transfer to the FKL Ravensbrück canteen. Surviving the war, Schäfer faced interrogation by the British field investigation section, war crimes group at the Essen *Polizeipräsidium* in October 1947. Here, he admitted to participating in the execution of nine to ten female prisoners on three separate occasions: National Archives, reference WO 311/511.

Non-German Concentration Camp Prisoners

95 Letter SS-*Richter beim* RF-SS to the *Chef des Stabes des Kommandostabes* RF-SS, dated 7.1.1942: D.C. NARA Washington microfilm, T-580, roll 215.

96 Letter *Ogruf.* Rauter to the SS-*Richter beim* RF-SS, dated 9.2.1944: D.C. NARA Washington microfilm, T-580, roll 215.

97 Letter Dr Wehser to *Ogruf.* Rauter, dated 1.3.1944: D.C. NARA Washington microfilm, T-580, roll 215.

98 Message Kew TNA, HW 16/40, dated 2.5.1944.

99 Torsten Schäfer, *Jedenfalls Habe ich auch Mitgeschossen*, LIT; Auflage: 1., Aufl. 2007, p. 190, (J.z., StA Frankfurt/Main, 4K51/71, Bd 7 cross examination dated 6.8.1962).

1.10 Entwöhnungsaufenhalt.

100 Letter *HA* SS-*Gericht Amt* III, dated 18.11.1941: D.C. NARA microfilm publication T-580, roll 212. Born in Plumenai in the Sudetenland on 25.3.1899, Kamilo v.Knorr-Krehan was assigned to the KL Sachsenhausen when promoted to the rank of *Hstuf.* in Nov.1944. He ended the war as camp commandant of the *Außenlager* Eisberg.

101 *Ibid.*

102 Letter *HA* SS-*Gericht Amt* III dated 18.11.1941: D.C. NARA microfilm publication T-580, roll 212.

103 NARA BDC, SSO Personalakte Otto Friedrich.

104 Letter SS-*Richter beim* RF-SS to the *HA* SS-*Gericht Amt* III, dated 5.1.1942: D.C. NARA microfilm publication T-580, roll 212.

105 Letter SS-*Richter beim* RF-SS, dated 25.11.1942: D.C. NARA microfilm publication T-580, roll 212.

106 NARA BDC, SSO Personalakte Rudolf Röder.

1.11 Disciplinary Case Studies

107 NARA BDC, SSO Personalakte Heinz Gloger; letter *HA* SS-*Gericht*, dated 27.1.1944.

108 Letter *HA* SS-*Gericht*, dated 27.12.1944: NARA BDC, SSO Personalakte Eduard Johannes Limion.

109 NARA BDC, SSO Personalakte Quinus de Veer.

110 NARA BDC, SSO Personalakte Enn Sirvet.

111 NARA BDC, SSO Personalakte Jan Wesel.

Chapter 2: *Strafvollzugslager der SS und Polizei*; Origin, Structure and Activities

2.1 Wartime Imprisonment Provisions of the SS- und Polizei-Gerichtsbarkeit

1 Seidler, '*Die Militärgerichtsbarkeit…*' op cit.; pp. 220-224.

2 *Ibid*, p. 222.

3 Letter *Hstuf.* Thum to the *HA* SS-*Gericht*, dated 3.3.1940: BA RS 3-3 3/28.
4 NARA BDC, SSO Personalakte Paul Löffler.

2.2 Festungshaft

5 Seidler, '*Die Militärgerichtsbarkeit…*' op cit.; p. 221.
6 Letter *Chef des HA* SS-*Gericht* to the OKW, dated 11.3.1940: D.C. NARA microfilm publication T-580, roll 212.
7 Letter SS-*Rechtamt* and the SS-*Richter beim* RF-SS, dated 11.8.1942: D.C. NARA microfilm publication T-580, roll 212.
8 BA WS 191/1916, p. 133.
9 Letter *HA* SS-*Gericht Amt* IIIb to the SS-*Richter beim* RF-SS, dated 11.9.1942: D.C. NARA microfilm publication T-580, roll 212.
10 NARA BDC, SSO Personalakte Eduard Voorwinden.

2.3 Strafvollzugslager der SS und Polizei Dachau

11 Seidler, '*Die Militärgerichtsbarkeit…*' op cit.; pp. 97-127.
12 *Ibid*, p.135-138.
13 Seidler, '*Die Militärgerichtsbarkeit…*' op cit.; 251.
14 Rudolf Absolon, *Die Wehrmacht im Dritten Reich: 19. Dezember 1941 bis 9. Mai 1945*, Oldenbourg Wissenschaftsverlag 1996, p. 574.
15 *Führer* edict, dated 18.4.1940: D.C. NARA Washington microfilm, T-580, 213.
16 Letter SS-*Richter beim* RF-SS, dated 21.8.1940: BA NS 7/384.
17 The argument for the creation of a *Waffen*-SS and *Polizei* prison differed little from those espoused for the creation of the SS jurisdiction in 1938. For more details see Vieregge, 'Die Gerichtsbarkeit…' op. cit.; pp. 10-12
18 *Totenkopfdivision* daily order Nr. 30, dated 6.2.1940: BA RS 3 3/17, pp. 289 & 281
19 Given how the institution operated, the *Reichsf*ührer evidently envisioned an SS-*Erziehungssturm*-type prison.
20 Barbera Distel, *Concentration camp Dachau 1933-1945*, pp.46-47.
21 *Ibid*, pp. 41-42.
22 *Ibid*, p. 77.
23 Hans-Günther Richardi, *SS-Geiseln in der Alpenfestung* (Bozen Ed. Raetia 2005), p. 130.
24 http://www.scrapbookpages.com/DachauScrapbook/KZDachau/Bunker/
25 aus: Werner Thalheim, Dachau, wie ich es erlebte und überlebte. Werner Thalheim, *Dachau, as I Experienced It and Survived*: Manuskript KZGDa.KzGD manuscript, p. 36. Born in Beuerberg on 20.5.1897, *Ostuf.* Johann Kantschuster's, (SS Nr. 58.541) behaviour eventually led to his transfer from the camp arrest to the KL Ravensbrück and here, he violently abused the female inmates which led to his eventual transfer to the KL Mauthausen. Here, Kantschuster aimed his service pistol at a fellow officer during a drunken incident and as a consequence was sent to an SS physician to under go a psychological test. Declared clinically insane, he was sent to the KL Sachsenhausen where it was determined that his alcoholism made him unfit for service in the SS. Despite this verdict Kantschuster remained in the *Totenkopfverbände* and was assigned to the KL Breendonk in Sept.1942 where he continued to drink heavily and abuse prisoners. In Apr.1943, Kantschuster transferred from Breendock and disappeared from the record.

While assigned to the KL Dachau camp arrest Kantschuster murdered the prisoner Alfred Strauss on 24.5.1933 prompting the Bavarian state judiciary to attempt to arrest him. This and other murder cases occurring in Dachau resulted in a stand-off between the civil judiciary and the SS leader. The SS refused to co-operate with the courts and the situation was only resolved when the legal responsibility for crimes committed in the concentration camps was removed from the state judiciary. *Hscha.* Joseph Seuss then took command (b. 3.3.1906 in Nuremberg)

26 The prison was commonly referred to as the SS-*Straflager der Waffen* SS-*und Polizei.*

27 NARA BDC, SSO Personalakte Wolfgang Walther.

28 Letter SS-*Richter beim* RF-SS, Dr Hans Braußе, Hinderfield and Wetzling dated, 11.1940: D.C. NARA microfilm publication T-81, roll 212.

29 Letter *HA* SS-*Gericht Amt* Id to SS-PHA, dated 4.5.1944. See Dirk Riedel communication, dated 16.6.2011. There remains a possibility that the SS used the camp arrest in 1938 to hold convicts requiring detention for short punishments.

30 NARA BDC, SSO Personalaktes Erich Albert/Franz Sturmann.

Prison Headquarters

31 NARA BDC, SSO Personalaktes Edmund Baumgärtner/Otto Langer/Franz Sturmann.

32 *StA* Munich *Spruchkammerakten* K1811: Franz Sturmann, b. 5.10.1909.
Hstuf. Albert's *de factotum* in 1944/1945 was *Hscha.* Seipel until 27.4.1945.

33 Johann Ott, SAIC/PIR/49, dated 21.9.1945 & 245, dated 27.8.1945.
Hscha. Seipel escaped from Dachau before its occupation, and identified by Johann Ott in the Heilbronn PWTE, he reported Seipel's presence in this camp to the 17th CIC Detachment.

34 NARA BDC, SSO Personalakte Dr Cassio Castelpietra.

35 Johann Ott, SAIC/PIR/49 dated 21.9.1945 & 245, dated 27.8.1945. In addition to the mentioned SS staff, Ott claimed that the following inmates were assigned to the *Lager Krankenrevier*: B-*Schütze* Dr Rupp; a 38 years-old a German national in 1945, was sentenced to death, but subsequently pardoned. He fled Dachau with Dr Castelpietra. B-*Schütze* Dr Honig; a Dutch national, he spoke English and German. Sentenced to death, Dr Honig was later reprieved and last seen by Ott on 29.4.1945. Ott believed that in the wake of Dachau's liberation, Dr Honig continued to work at the *Lager Krankenrevier*. B-*Schütze* Dr Arco; a 38 year-Old Italian national, (Tyrolean), he was a surgeon by profession. Ott recalled that Dr Arco spoke broken German and had also been previously sentenced to death but was later pardoned.

36 NARA BDC, SSO Personalakte Karl Martins.

37 NARA BDC, SSO Personalakte Johann Ott. For further details see Johann Ott SAIC/PIR/49 dated 21.9.1945 & 245 dated 27.8.1945.

38 Attending *Volksschule* and *Höhere Schule* (O-II), Rieth left full time education to work as a teacher at the Pforzheim *Volksschule*. Drafted into the Army on 16 May 1916, Rieth fought with the *Infantrie*-Rgt. 113 on the Western Front on 10 July 1917 and became a prisoner of war of the French Army on 3 August the same year. Remaining in captivity until 20 February 1920, Rieth returned to Pforzheim when released and married his fiancée *Frau* Frida S., (b. 21.4.1897) on 23 March 1921. There appears to have been no issue from this union. Promoted to the rank of *Ustuf.* on 9.11.1943 and Ostuf on 9.11.1943, Rieth was a recipient of the 1914-18 *Ehrenkreuz für Frontkämpfer*, SS-*Zivilabzeichen* (87.320), SA-*Sportsabzeichen in Bronze* and *Die Medaille zur Erinnerung an den* 1. Oktober 1938 (Sud.): NARA BDC, SSO Personalakte Artur Rieth.

39 *Reichsjustizministerium* edict concerning the sentencing of convicts, dated 20.9.1940. See letter SS-*Rechtamt* to the SS-*Richter beim* RF-SS, dated 7.4.1941: D.C. NARA microfilm publication T-580, roll 214.

Induction

40 Letter *Gruf.* Breithaupt, *HA* SS-*Gericht Amt* IIIb 320/6, dated 22.9.1942: BA NS 756/283a, p. 156. For further details see Gaby Sikorski, *Kriechen hab Ich nie Gelernt*, My Story Verlag 2005, pp. 70-82. William Nagel, a rifleman in the SS-*Krad-Schütze-Bataillon Reich*, deserted from his unit during the winter of 1941/1942. When caught, Nagel faced trial, was punished with a term of two years *Gefängnis* and served this punishment in the SS-*Straflager* Dachau.

41 Seidler, '*Die Militärgerichtsbarkeit…*' op cit.; pp. 124-128.

42 Letter Dr Hans Brauße to the SS-*Richter beim* RF-SS, dated 27.4.1940: D.C. NARA Washington microfilm T-580, roll 214. See letter SS-*Richter beim* RF-SS to the *Hauptfürsorge-und Versorgungsamt* SS, dated 30.1.1942; letter *Gruf.* Jungclaus to the RuSHA, dated 10.1.1944: D.C. NARA microfilm publication T-580, roll 212.

43 Karl Hirsch statement, dated 29.4.1969: BA Ludwigsburg; B 162/829, p. 209-214. See Robert Jung statement, dated 20.9.1969: BA Ludwigsburg; B 162/829, p. 244.

44 Sikorski, '*Kriechen…*' op cit.; pp. 70-82.

45 BA NS 756/283a.

46 Letter SS-*Richter beim* RF-SS to the *HA* SS-*Gericht*, dated 14.2.1943: D.C. NARA microfilm publication T-580, roll 214.

47 Johann Ott, SAIC/PIR/49, dated 21.9.1945 & 245, dated 27.8.1945.

48 *StA* Munich: Rudolf Heiß statement, dated 8.3.1967: Akt.-Zeichen 13 Js 9 a-e/66, pp. 101-109.

49 Karl Lang statement to the Polizeidirektion Augsburg Kriminalpolizei I.K Tgb. Nr, 929/47, dated 20.8.1947: *StA* Landgericht Munich II vor dem Landgericht Trauenstein Strafkammer; Verfahren gegen Karl Lang wegen der Tötung von Franz Breithaupt, (Az I Ks 21-23/49).

50 NARA BDC, SSO Personalakte Franz Zeber.

Daily Life

51 *Ibid*, p. 70-82. See letter *HA* SS-*Gericht*, dated 25.6.1942: BA NS 7/378, p. 42.

52 Reitlinger, '*The SS…*' op cit.; pp. 256-257. For more details concerning SS business I recommend reading Francis R. Nicosia, *Business and Industry in Nazi Germany*, Berghahn Books 2004 and Paul Martin Neurath's, *The Society of Terror: Inside the Dachau and Buchenwald Concentration Camp*, Routledge 2005, p.26.

53 Sikorski, '*Kriechen…*' op cit.; pp. 45, 70-82. See letter *HA* SS-*Gericht* dated 15.5.1942: BA NS 7/365, p. 8.

54 *Ibid*, pp. 70-82.

55 *Ibid*, p. 70-82. For further details see Neurath, '*The Society of Terror…*' op. cit.; p. 37.

56 Interrogation of *Hstuf.* Richard Neun, dated 28.10.1945: Kew national archives WO 208/3149.

Abteilung Gefängnis

57 *HA* SS-*Gericht Amt* III undated leaflet titled 'Transition of Abteilung Gefängnis from SS-und Polizei Strafvollzugslager Dachau to SS-und Polizei Strafvollzugslager Danzig-Matzkau': BA NS 7/378. p.14.

58 Seidler, '*Die Militärgerichtsbarkeit...*' op cit.; p.251. *Ostuf.* Karl Weitzel (b. 15.12.1901 in Frankfurt am Main, SS Nr. 8.247).

59 *Ibid.*

60 *HA* SS-*Gericht Amt* III, undated leaflet titled 'Transition of Abteilung Gefängnis from SS-*Straflager* Dachau to the St. V. L. d. SS-u. Pol. Danzig-Matzkau': BA NS 7/378, p. 14.

61 Sikorski, '*Kriechen...*' op cit.; pp. 70-71.

1941–43

62 Letter SS-*Richter beim* RF-SS to the RFSS, dated 22.5.1942: BA NS 7/378.

63 Letter dated 21.7.1938: BA NS 756/283a.

64 https://www.jewishvirtuallibrary.org/jsource/Holocaust/dachauhimmler.html

65 Versorgungsamt Dortmund II/I-HHG 25/2, dated 9.1.1960.

66 Yad Vashem image_ Item 1477 of 93359 (Edgar A. Ansbacher collection).

67 NARA BDC, SSO Personalakte Edmund Baumgärtner.

68 Fritz S. *StA* Frankfurt am Main, 4Ks1/71, Bd 65, Hauptverhandlung 26. Verhandlungstag am 10.III.1972, Bl. 545). See Fritz .S. StA Frankfurt am Main 4Ks1/71, Bd. 15, Vernehmung vom 5.21963, Bl. 2852. See Message Kew TNA, HW 16/22, dated 12.1942.

69 Holger Lessing, *Der Erste Dachauer Prozess* (1945/46) Baden-Baden 1993. For further details see also the Spokesman Review from 29.5.1946, p. 1.

70 NARA BDC, SSO Personalakte Walter Dieterle.

71 Message Kew HW 16/19, dated 1.10.1942.

72 http://service.virtuos.uni-osnabrueck.de/wikifarm/fields/stolpersteine/index.php/Main/DetersFriederich.

73 SS-*Richter beim* RF-SS memorandum, dated 10.2.1943: BA NS 7/365, p. 61. See Otto Langer statement, dated 9.3.1970: BA Ludwigsburg B 162/ 26452.

74 geboren am 25.05.1901 in OsnabrücUniversity of Osnabrück; state Archives: Political persecution, Rep accent n 304 430 Dec. 2003/036 573, (filed 15.5.2013).

75 The inmates were Adolf Bender (b. 19.12.1923), Leo Blanke (b. 26.2.1923), Wolfgang Keonig (b. 31.2.1923) and Otto Koester (b. 30.5.1923): Source; Kew HW 16/19, dated 4.6.1942

76 Message Kew TNA, HW 16/19, dated 6.8.1942.

77 Message Kew HW 16/21, dated 20.8.1942, 1.10.1942; Kew HW 16/36, dated 10.1942.

78 Letter *Ostubaf.* Dr Ernst to the *HA* SS-*Gericht*, dated 10.2.1943: BA NS 756/283a.

79 Message Kew HW 16/22, dated 15.12.1942.

80 NARA BDC, SSO Personalakte Josef Schwaiger / Edmund Baumgärtner.

81 SS-*Richter beim* RF-SS memorandum, dated 10.2.1943: BA NS 7/365, p. 61.

82 Mordecai Paldiel, S*aving the Jews: Amazing Stories of Men and Women Who Defied the 'Final Solution'* Schreiber Publishing 2000, p. 241.

83 Henry Friedlander, *The Origins of Nazi Genocide: From Euthanasia to the Final Solution*, University North Carolina Pr; 3 edition 1995, p. 244.

84 Letter *HA* SS-*Gericht* to the SS-*Richter beim* RF-SS, dated 22.4.1944: BA NS 7.

85 *Reichsführer*-SS *Verfügung* for Edgar Kühnel, dated 11.8.1943: Author's archiv.

86 Letter SS-*Richter beim* RF-SS to *Ostubaf.* Günther Burmeister, dated 2.8.1943; letter *Ostubaf.* Burmeister to SS-*Richter beim* RF-SS, dated 9.8.1943: BA NS 7/366, pp. 1-2.

87 NARA BDC, SSO Personalakte Johann Engelke; BOAR/37711/221/a (ps4) Dachau: Interrogation of Heinrich Nett 1945: Kew WO 309/2042.

88 Letter SS-*Richter beim* RF-SS to the *HA* SS-*Gericht* on 22.4.1944: BA NS 7.

89 NARA BDC, SSO Personalakte Georg van Kempen.

90 Letter *Ostubaf.* Dr Brauße to SS-*Richter beim* RF-SS, dated 2.10.1943: BA NS 756/283a.

91 A. M. Wittman, *Mutiny in the Balkans: Croat Volksdeutsche, the Waffen-SS and Motherhood*, East European Quarterly; September 2002, Vol. 36 Issue 3, p255. For more details see George Lepre, *Himmler's Bosnian Division*, Schiffer Publishing, Ltd.; First Edition 1997, p. 107.

92 NARA BDC, SSO Personalakte Albert Breh.

93 NARA BDC, SSO Personalakte Carl Juels.

94 NARA BDC, SSO Personalakte Ludwig Bahrke.

95 Message Kew HW 16/38, Nr. 23, dated 27.8.1943.

1944–45; the Years of Defeat

96 Undated Verteidigungs- und Entlastungsschrift: Staatsarchiv Munich: SpK A 1280: Osthues, Wilhelm.

97 *HA* SS-*Gericht* transfer order, dated 28.2.1945: BA NS 7/1, p. 216.

98 NARA BDC, SSO Personalakte Karl Ernst Gebauer.

99 Brendel's co-defendant, *Scha.* Willi Medenbach, appeared alongside him before the Metz tribunal on 25.10.1943 (case Nr. St. L. I 26/1943). Judged guilty of committing an act of military disobedience in contravention of paragraphs § 92 MStGB and § 140 MStGB, the court punished Medenbach with a term of 30 months' *Gefängnis*, expelled him from the SS, declared him unworthy to bear arms and denied him his honour and civil rights. The *HA* SS-*Gericht* confirmed his sentence on 12.1.1944 and the *Gerichtsherr*, the HSSPF *Rhein-Westmark*, concurred with this decision on 21.1.1944 the same year. Medenbach almost certainly served his penalty at Danzig–Matzkau.
Around this time, *Uscha.* Fenohel, a guard at the KL Hinzert, was brought before the courts martial of the Metz tribunal on 25.10.1943 and declaring him a 'pest to the people,' the court punished Fenohel with six years' *Zuchthaus*, ordered his expulsion from the SS with disgrace, declared him unworthy to bear arms and denied him his civil and honour rights for six years. His trial finished, Fenohel transferred from the Trier gaol to the SS-*Straflager* Dachau: BA NS 4/Hi/13, p. 6. See teleprinter KL Hinzert to the KL Stutthof dated 26.10.1943: BA NS 4/Hi/13, p.58.

100 NARA BDC, SSO Personalakte Heinz-Paul Sieling.

101 Letter *Chef des HA* SS-*Gericht* to the *Reichsführer*, dated 1.2.1944: BA NS 7/369. For further details see KZ-Gedenkstaette-Dachau DA 18442.

102 Message Kew TNA, HW 16/40, dated 27.7.1944. This inmate received some good news in the summer of 1944: Wilhelm Kohn's, (b. 27.5.1922 Phibswareden/Oldenburg) release from the prison was ordered on 2.7.1944 and contacting the SS-*Straflager* Dachau on 22.7.1944 the same year, the SS and *Polizei* Court XXII, Kassel requested they supply them a fitness report on the convict Alfred Helsinski, (b. 27.9.1925).

103 Letter *Reichsführer* to *Ogruf.* Pohl, dated 1.1.1943: BA NS 7/365, p. 549.

104 Bruno M.: Von Gedenken zum Handeln; http://www.erport-do.de/wiki/index.php/Hauptseite.

105 Holger Lessing, *the First Dachau Trial* (1945/46) Baden-Baden 1993.

106 *StA* Landgericht Munich II vor dem Landgericht Trauenstein Strafkammer; Verfahren gegen Karl Lang wegen der Tötung von Franz Breithaupt, (Az I Ks 21-23/49). *Meister der Schutzpolizei* Johannes Häse lived in Meissen.

107 NARA BDC, SSO Personalakte Edmund Baumgärtner.

108 NARA BDC, SSO Personalakte: Ernst Schumacher. The *Gerichtsoffiziere* in this case was *Ostuf.* Kurt Gündisch, (b. 28.12.1915 in Elisabethstadt/Ungarn). At this time Gündisch led the 3. / SS-FLAK *Abt.* 7 and acted as the adjutant of the SS-FLAK *Abt.* 22 in 9.1944.

109 Anton Krug (b. 21.1.1926 in Hamborn), Franz Bordeufel (b. 23.7.1924 in Köln), Hermann Rietz (b. 26.5.1923 in Johannesburg/ Ostpreußen) and Otto Günther (b. 23.1.1920 in Gottesburg/Sil.): Message Kew TNA, HW 16/41, Nr. 17, dated 28.7.1944; message Kew TNA, HW 16/42, Nr. 5.

110 NARA BDC, SSO Personalakte Julius Mülthaler.

111 SS-*Mann* Langer conversation with Kursteiner, dated 1.8.1944: WO208/4138-589.

112 *HA* SS-*Gericht Brieftagbuch* entry dated 8.9.1944: Wiener Library for the Study of the Holocaust & Genocide.

113 Dr H.N recollections to Mr John Moore: e-mail communication, dated 30.6.2013.

114 NARA BDC, SSO Personalakte Otto Raab.

115 Klausch, '*Antifaschisten...*' op cit.; p. 193. The source for the death of Langlotz is contained within a letter written by the ex-KZ prisoner Willi Eifler to A.M. Kraskiewiczs on 5.7.1990, (Klausch, 'Antifaschisten...', ob cit.; p. 247). Langlotz was reportedly killed by German gunfire while attempting to desert in Dec.1944.

116 NARA BDC, SSO Personalakte SS-Führer: Franz Sturmann.

117 NARA BDC, SSO Personalakte SS-Führer: Sascha Bibrich

1945; the Last Months and Dissolution

118 Paul Goetze (b. 26.12.1925) & Emil Senvas (b. 16.12.1919): Message Kew TNA, HW 16/21; message Kew TNA, HW 16/43, dated 29.3.1945.

119 Wolfgang Benz, *Der Ort des Terrors: Geschichte der Nationalsozialistischen KZ Vol. 4*, p. 137 (Aussage Felix Marszalek, in; *StA* Nuremberg, Staatsanwaltschaft beim Landgericht Nuremberg-Fürth 2637 Ia, p. 29 R f.). For more details see NARA BDC, SSO Personalakte Fritz Ringel.

The transferees included: *Uscha.* Stanko, *Rttf.* Göttfert, *Schütze* Dunschen, *Schütze* Sperber, *Schütze* Schäller, *Schütze* Wild, *Schütze* Grieger, *Schütze* Elischer, *Schütze* Heine, *Schütze* Bönlein, *Schütze* Beck, *Schütze* Tams, *Schütze* Heumann, *Schütze* Bäro, *Schütze* Heuser, *Schütze* Rosenfeldt, *Schütze* Brandes, *Schütze* Koch, *Schütze* Polz, *Schütze* Zureck, *Schütze* Leopld, *Schütze* Hartmann, *Schütze* Telge, *Schütze* Kornelsen, *Schütze* Klein, *Schütze* Meyer and *Schütze* Teschner: *Beurkundungsunterführer* transfers to *Straflager* Dachau, dated 7.2.1945, pp. 211-213: BA NS 7/1,

120 Summery report Nr. 976, dated 22.3.1945: Source; TNA, HW 13/42.

121 Interrogation of Heinrich Nett 1945; BOAR/37711/221/a (ps4) Dachau: Kew WO 309/2042.

122 Richardi, '*SS-Geiseln...*' ob cit.; pp.128-130. The convict Brenner recalled that *Ostuf.* Stiller was the *Fürsorge Offizier*. Held in the SS-*Straflager* Dachau from 1941 until 1945, Brenner described his cell block as the *Kommandeur-Heim-Arrestbau* (KA), which was the camp arrest building and worked in the camp kitchen: Staatsarchiv Munich: SpK A 1280: Osthues, Wilhelm.

123 Ibid. See also *StA* Munich STAnW M I J VSG 25/2 investigation and interview of Friedrich Engelke by Landgericht II Munich on 23.7.1952. See Ian Sawyer Archive; Ref. *StA* 34475/2, p. 114 and reverse (2 pages): *StA* Munich.

124 Herbert H. report, dated 8.10.1945: *StA* Kassel, A 5.55, NT. 67; BA-ZNS, Kriegsgerichtsunterlagen Herbert H.

125 Dachau, G-2 section US 7th Army, Marriam Press 1988.

126 Interrogation of Heinrich Nett; BOAR/37711/221/a (ps4) Dachau: Kew WO 309/2042. See Vopersol Archive: BA NS 756/283a.

127 NARA BDC, SSO Personalakte Alfred Bauer. For further details see IWM, FO 945 Box 163, US interrogation of Georg Mair dated 3.9.1945 (BBL 53/1942). His execution is mentioned in U.S. NARA, RG 65 – Entry A1-136P – Box 188. USFET CI Consolidated Interrogation Report No. 15 (CI-CIR/15), dated 14.3.1946. The execution took place in 4.1945: message TNA Kew, WO 235/427.

128 NARA BDC, SSO Personalakte Dr Sigmund Rascher.

129 Reitlinger, '*The SS…*', op cit.; p. 261. See *StA* München STAnW M I J VSG 25/2 investigation by Landgericht II Munich and the interview of Friedrich Engelke on 23.7.1952. See CI Consolidated interrogation report (CI-CIR_ No 10 Military intelligence service centre APO 757, dated 6.12.1945; interrogation of Ernst Wagner and Friedrich Karl *Freiherr* v.Eberstein the HSSPF *Wehrkreis* VII).

Hscha. Theodor Bongartz died in Heilbronn in US Army captivity on 15.5.1945: http://www.georg-elser-arbeitskreis.de/texts/bongartz-grab.htm).

130 Nikolas Wachsmann, '*KL…*', op cit.; p. 432 (DaA, Nr. 7566 K. Schecher, *Rückblich auf Dachau n.d.*, p. 249). Writing on 16.3.1946, the former Dachau prisoner, Johann Neuhäusler, revealed that the disgraced SS-*Richter*, *Hstuf.* Willy Osthues spoke to Dr Rascher in the SS-*Arrestanstalt* Munich-Freimann in 12.1944 and found him in a very depressed state of mind: Statement Johann Neuhäusler, dated 16.3.1946: *StA* Munich: SpK A 1280: Osthues, Wilhelm.

131 Reitlinger, '*The SS…' ob cit.;* p. 261. See Landgericht II Munich: *StA* Munich STAnW M I J VSG 25/2 and the interview of Friedrich Engelke, dated 23.7.1952; CI Consolidated interrogation report (CI-CIR_ No 10 Military intelligence service centre APO 757, dated 6.12.1945; interrogation of Ernst Wagner and Friedrich Karl *Freiherr* v.Eberstein the HSSPF *Wehrkreis* VII.

132 Heiß, Rudolf interview with the Landpolizei Oberbayern, dated 3.6.1947: *StA* Munich Spruchkammerakten K668.

133 LKA-NW Düsseldorf interrogation of Albert Müller, dated 7.5.1962: *StA* Munich: 13 Js 9/66 /W (*StA* Munich), pp. 261-271. See Johann Ott, SAIC/PIR/49 & 245 report, dated 27.8.1945/21.9.1945. See NARA—Records of the Army Staff (Record Group 319) College park, Maryland 270/84/01/01-270/84/19/07 Investigative Records Repository (IRR) Personal Name Files, 1939-1976; XE004042, Erich Albert.

134 Records of the Army Staff (Record Group 319) Investigative Records Repository (IRR) Personal Name Files, 1939-1976 Gottfried Biedermann XE101203/664, (declassified on 24.4.2000).

135 P. Koppenhofer article: KL Dachau Museum. *Ustuf.* Heinrich Wicker, (b. 30.6.1921 in Gansbach, SS Nr. 320.280).

136 http://www.scrapbookpages.com/DachauScrapbook/NaziPrison.html.

137 For more details see Joshua M. Greene, *Justice at Dachau: The Trials of an American Prosecutor*, Publishers Group UK Oto; 1 edition 2003.

Post-War Investigation

138 Source; 7th US Army interrogation centre APO 758; Final interrogation report: SAIC/FIR/49, dated 21.9.1945 & FIR/245, dated 27.8.1945.

139 *Ibid*: The *Chefarzt* at the Dachau *Revier* was the American born *Ustuf.* Dr Hans-Georg Eckert.

140 *Ibid.*

141 *Ibid.*

2.2 Strafvollzugslager der SS und Polizei Dachau, Aussenstelle Allach

142 Letter *Reichsführer* to *Ogruf.* Pohl, dated 3.2.1943: D.C. NARA microfilm publication T-580, roll 212.

143 SS-*Richter beim* RF-SS memorandum, dated 10.2.1943: BA NS 7/365, pp. 61-64.

144 SS-*Richter beim* RF-SS memorandum, dated 10.2.1943; BA NS 7/365, p. 61.

145 Dr Fritz Beelitz statement, dated 14.4.1959: BA Ludwigsburg; B 162/829, p. 133.

146 NARA BDC, SSO Personalakte Theodor Janssen. See letter SS-*Straflager der* SS-*und Polizei* Dachau, *Aussenstelle* Allach to the BMW, Werk Allach, Munich 68, Karlsfeld, dated 11.12.1944: Archiv Dachau.

147 Description based on the Henri Gayot drawing; http://www.hdbg.de/dachau/pdfs/10/10_02/10_02_02.PDF. See letter *Reichsführer* to *Gruf.* Pohl, dated 1.1.1943: BA NS 7/365, p. 54. See letter *Chef des HA* SS-*Gericht*, dated 1.2.1944: BA NS 7/369.

148 Harold Marcuse, *Legacies of Dachau; the uses and abuses of a concentration camp 1933*-2001, Cambridge University Press; Reissue edition 2008, p. 43.

149 Ludwig Eiber, *Dachauer Hefte 12; KZ-Aussenlager in München*, 1996, p. 62. For further details see Constanze Werner, *Kriegswirtschaft und Zwangsarbeit bei BMW: Im Auftrag von MTU Aero Engines und BMW Group* (Perspektiven, Band 1), De Gruyter Oldenbourg, p. 222. Here, Werner states that 29 per cent of the entire work community were German, a minority of the total workforce. In addition to the concentration camp workers were 564 SS convicts, 1, 340 Russian prisoners of war, Eastern workers and forced labourers from about 30 different countries, but predominantly from west European nations.

150 Karl Lang statement to the Polizeidirektion Augsburg Kriminalpolizei I.K Tgb. Nr, 929/47, dated 20.8.1947: *StA* Landgericht Munich II vor dem Landgericht Trauenstein Strafkammer: Verfahren gegen Karl Lang wegen der Tötung von Franz Breithaupt, (Az I Ks 21-23/49).

151 The work hours for each convict was calculated on the basis that an average of 61 convicts, working ten hours had each earned 8,540 *Reichsmark* (3.11.–16.11.1944, or fourteen days) and an average of 70 convicts, working ten hours each earned 9,800 *Reichsmark.* (17.11.–30.11.1944, or fourteen days). Therefore the 287,989.25 work hours was multiplied by 62 *pfennigs* for each inmate, totalling 178,553.34 *Reichsmark* owed per convicts labour: Letter SS-*Straflager der* SS-*und Polizei Dachau, Aussenstelle* Allach to BMW, Werk Allach, Munich 68, Karlsfeld, dated 11.12.1944: Archive Dachau

152 Letter *Gruf.* Breithaupt to *Reichsführer*-SS, dated 1.2.1944: BA NS 7/369. For further details see KZ-Gedenkstaette-Dachau DA 18442. *Hscha.* Dick transferred from the *HA* SS-*Gericht* HQ to the SS-*Straflager* Dachau on 19.11.1943: BA NS 7/1, p. 151.

153 Otto Langer deposition to the *StA* Dortmund, dated 23.9.1970: *StA* Düsseldorf 8 I Js 974/62/IV 117 AR 438/62: BA Ludwigsburg B 162/26452.

154 Friedrich Koch, (b. 15.4.1923 in Neudorf/Romania): Message Kew TNA, HW 16/42, dated 21.10.1944.

155 Message Kew TNA, HW 16/43, Nr. 5, dated 27.3.1945.
156 KZ-Gedenkstaette-Dachau DA 188442. http://www.scrapbookpages.com/DachauScrapbook/DachauLiberation/Allach.html.
157 BOAR/37711/221/a (ps4) Dachau: Interrogation of Heinrich Nett 1945; Kew WO 309/2042.
158 Otto Langer deposition to the *StA* Dortmund, dated 23.9.1970: *StA* Düsseldorf 8 I Js 974/62/IV 117 AR 438/62: BA Ludwigsburg B 162/26452.
159 KZ-Gedenkstaette-Dachau DA 188442.

2.5 Strafvollzugslager der SS und Polizei Dachau, Zweiglager Hammerweg

160 *Streitsache Frau* Angels Marschell, Manastur Nr. 5 Judetul Arad, Rumania. Letter from the Landessozialgericht für das Land Nordrhein-Westfalen 9. Senat to the Innenministerium Baden-Württemburg, dated 28.3.1974. Their reply Nr. III 301/16, dated 1.4.1974: Landesarchiv Baden-Württemberg: EA2/303 Bü 23, pp. 31-32.
161 Necklarz Museum. For further details see the Vopersol archive; *Straflager der* SS-*und Polizei* Mosbach Baden: BA NS756/283a
162 Der Speigel/ J.R Mette article
163 *Hscha.* Knecht was replaced in the wake of an air raid in Mosbach on 8.12.1944. SS-*Vertragsarzt* Dr Bergemann: NARA BDC, SSO Personalakte Max Dolles.
164 Johann Ott, SAIC/PIR/49 & 245 report, dated 21.9.1945/27.8.1945.
165 http://crailsheim-geschichte.de/115.html.
166 Ivan Stumiek (b. 4.4.1920): Kreuzberger Gedenktafel für Opfer des Nazi Regimes 1933–1945 (Bruno Rudolf).
167 Peter Koppenhoefer article; H.Marcuse 2001, S.5. Vgl. auch Juergen Zarusky 1997, S.53 über eine moegliche Erschiessung von Wicker.
168 Straflager der SS-und Polizei Mosbach Baden, Vopersol archive: BA NS756/283a.
169 HIAG search 25.9.1954: BA NS 756/283a.
170 'De Waarheid', dated 1.8.1945 Nr. 74, p. 2 (Inlichtingen Verzocht Omtrent).
171 Message Kew Archive: Mill-Niesen; WO 309/1775 BAOR detention report Alfred Mueller, (31 G.6 556 246).
172 Communication with Martina Rantasa, Große Kreisstadt Mosbach Stadtarchiv dated 6-7/2010. See Hildegard Radolko, *erinnert sich an die letzten Kriegstage im Gebiet um Mosbach* (Published 4.7.2013); *Plötzlich nahm der Panzer unser Haus ins Visier*: Rhein Neckar Zeitung Samstag, dated 29.8.2015.

Chapter 3: *Strafvollzugslager der SS und Polizei* Danzig-Matzkau

1 http://webpages.milwpc.com/phygulgow/courtly_gulgowsk; authored and researched by their highnesses Commodore Prof Dr Paul W. Margrave Gulgowski-Doliwa and Dame Heide Anna Maria Margravine Gulgowski-Doliwa in 2000.
The site buyer may have been *Oberf.* Hellmuth Willich. For more details see Peter Piotrowski, *Historia. History, Zapomniany obóz w Gdańsku Maćkowych Forgotten camp in Gdansk Maćkowych*, Classifieds G.W (Gdańsk), No. 97, edition *of GDG 25/04/2003ŚLEDŹ TE PARTIES*, p. 10. See also Michaelis, *Die SS-Heimwehr Danzig in Polanfeldzug*, p. 18.

2 'The SS barracks in Matzkau': The Danziger Vorposten Wednesday, dated 18.10.1939.

3 *Ibid.*

4 *Ibid.*

5 Pamięć I Sprawiedliwość Pismo Instytutu Pamięci Narodowej 2 (18) 2011: Jan Daniluk—*Obóz karny SS i policji w Maćkowach pod Gdańskiem*, p. 218. Unsubstantiated reports, suggest that the *Einsatzkommando* 16 (Eimann) was stationed in Matzkau from 12.9.1939.

6 Marek Orski, *Filie Obozu Koncentracyjnego Stutthof w Latach 1939-1945*, p. 122-126. *Oscha.* Hans Rach, (b. 5.6.1905, SS Nr. 66.301).

7 M. Sikorska, *W-Gdansku-karano-SS-Mannow*. For further details see http://ofiaromwojny.republika.pl/teksty/historiastutthof.pdf.

Slave labourers from Matzkau returned to Stutthof to labor for the *Leiter des* SS-*Bauleitung* in Stutthof *Oscha.* Otto Neubauer, (later replaced by *Oscha.* Leo Spark). These prisoners were supervised the SS guards Paul Lutz and Joseph Leising.

8 Marek Orski, *Niewolnicza praca więźniów obozu Koncentracyjnego Stutthof w Latach 1939-1945*, Gdańsk 1999. See letter *Reichsführer*, dated 24.4.1940—*Der Generalinspekteur der verst. SS-Totenkopf Standarten* 12/40 geh v.

9 Reitlinger, '*The SS:' ob cit.;* p. 129.

'Like a great many welfare organisations in the most over governed era in the history of man, it, grew into a tyranny and VoMi ended up as a pressgang for any Germanic looking individual in any occupied country': Luman, *Himmler's Auxiliaries: The Volksdeutsche Mittelstelle and the German National Minorities of Europe, 1933-1945*, UNC Press Enduring Edition 2010, p. 163. The head of the WVHA in Zoppot at this time was *Ostuf.* Henry Bösche: BA NS 49/3083 & 47/69. For more details see Annaberger Annalen, *Eine Familie-Sieben* Staate (19/2011)

10 The work of the NS-Frauenschaft Danzig-Land, dated 17.10.1941, (author's collection).

11 Letter *HA* SS-*Gericht* dated 1.2.1943: BA NS 7/365, p. 45; *Bauleitung* Danzig-Matzkau to *Hauptamt Haushalt-und Bauten Amt* II, dated 30.7.1941: BA NS 3/164. See undated leaflet *HA* SS-*Gericht Amt* III titled; 'Transition of Abteilung gefängnis from SS-und Polizei Strafvollzugslager Dachau to SS-und Polizei Strafvollzugslager Danzig-Matzkau': BA NS 7/378, p. 14

12 *HA SS-Gericht Amt* II bulletin, dated 12.8.1941: BA NS 7/1, pp. 30–31. See letter *HA* SS-*Gericht* 15.6.1942 Tgb Nr 364/42 geh: BA NS 7/365, p. 15.

13 Letter *Bauleitung* Danzig-Matzkau, dated 15.9.1941: BA NS 1649356. See letter *Bauleitung* Danzig-Matzkau to the *Reichsführer* & *Hauptamt Haushalt-und Bauten Amt* II, dated 30.7.1941: BA NS 3/1649. See letter *Bauleitung der Waffen*-SS Matzkau, dated 18.10.1941: BA NS 3/1656.

14 NARA BDC, SSO Personalakte Paul Scharfe.

15 Letter *Bauleitung* Danzig-Matzkau to *Reichsführer* & *Hauptamt Haushalt-und Bauten Amt* II, dated 19.7.1941: BA NS 3/1649. For more details about the general's movements see NARA BDC, SSO Personalakte Paul Scharfe,

16 Letter *Hauptamt Haushalt-und Bauten, Amt* II to *Leiter Bauleitung* Danzig-Matzkau, dated 8.8.1941: BA NS 3/1649. See letter *Hauptamt Haushalt-und Bauten Amt* II to the *Leiter Bauleitung* Danzig-Matzkau, dated 16.9.1941: BA NS 3/1649.

17 NARA BDC, SSO Personalakte SS-Führer: Franz Ott.

18 NARA BDC, SSO Personalakte Dr Ing. Rudolf Götze.

19 Letter SS-FHA, dated 19.2.1942; BA NS 3/1656.

20 Alexander Jeske (b. 27.2.1908): Letter *Stubaf.* Dr Leo Ernst to the *HA* SS-*Gericht*, dated 10.2.1943: BA NS 756/283a.

21 Letter *Bauleitung* Danzig-Matzkau, dated 15.9.1941; letter *Bauleitung* Danzig-Matzkau to the *Reichsführer*, dated 30.7.1941: BA NS 3/1649.

22 Letter *Verwaltung* Danzig-Matzkau to the *Hauptamt Haushalt-und Bauten* II B1, dated 20.2.1941: BA NS 3/1649.

23 Letter *Bauleitung der Waffen*-SS, dated 25.9.1941: BA NS 3/1656.

24 *Bauleitung der Waffen*-SS, dated 28.10.1941: BA NS 3/1656.

25 NARA BDC, SSO Personalakte Dr Leo Ernst.

26 Letter *Bauleitung* Danzig-Matzkau to the *Reichsführer* and the *Hauptamt Haushalt-und Bauten Amt* II, dated 27.11.1941: BA NS 3/1649

27 Letter SS-*Richter beim* RF-SS to the *HA* SS-*Gericht*, dated 1.2.1943: BA NS 7/365, p. 48.
Interestingly, the *Reichsführer* had visited the KL Stutthof on 23.11.1941.
One wonder's whether he found time in his busy itinery to include a tour of Matzkau?

28 Letter *Chef der Amt Allgemeine* SS-*Bauwirtschft*, dated 24.2.1942: BA NS 3/1649. See letter *HA* SS-*Gericht*, dated 1.2.1943: BA NS 7/365, pp. 45-48.

29 *Ibid.*

3.2 Command Structure and Teething Problems

30 LKA-NW Düsseldorf; witness statement Albert Müller, dated 7.5.1962: *StA* Munich: 13 Js 9/66 /W (*StA* Munich), pp. 261-271.

31 BA Ludwigsburg: B 162/829, p. 57. The former inmate was Franz-Josef Letzel, (b. 8.6.1907 in Blumenau, Kreis Waldenburg).

32 Rudolf Heiß statement, dated 8.3.1967: *Akt.-Zeichen* 13 Js 9 a-e/66: *StA* Munich, pp. 101-109. A farmer by profession, *Uscha.* Hans Kötterl (b. 3.6.1910) lived in Niederleierndorf near Regensburg. Surviving the war, this former Matzkau guard settled in Straubing, or Landschut in Bavaria. *Strm.* Heinz Becker (b. 23.2.1924).

33 LKA-NW Düsseldorf; witness statement Albert Müller, dated 7.5.1962: *StA* Munich: 13 Js 9/66 /W: *StA* Munich, pp. 261-271.

34 *StA* Munich II: statement Rudolf Heiß, dated 14.3.1967: Case file 13 Js 9 a-e/66: *StA* Munich.

35 Friedrich Wilhelm Ringel statement, dated 13.8.1968: Case file 13 Js 9/66 /W: *StA* Munich.

36 NARA BDC, SSO Personalakte Gottfried Biedermann; personal application of Gottfried Biedermann to the *HA* SS-*Gericht*, dated 30.4.1944. For more details see *HA* SS-*Gericht* dated 15.5.1942: BANS 7/365, p. 8

The Matzkauer *Wachkompanie* numbered 183 men on 4 January 1943, of these, sixteen had non-German sounding names, (Dutch and Scandinavian). Amongst their number was the Dutchman Jan Robertson. Nine non-commissioned officers, all born after 1900 and 108 junior NCOs and riflemen were deployed with the *Wachkompanie* on 1 July the same year and only two had non-German sounding names (Dutch). On 4 August 1943 the prison reported that twelve senior non-commissioned officers' and 105 junior non-commissioned officers and riflemen composed the *Wachkompanie* and two of these had non-German sounding names (Scandinavian). Writing on 4 September the same year, the prison announced that eleven senior non-commissioned officers and 108 junior non-commissioned officers and men comprised the guard unit and of these only one had a non-German sounding name

(Scandinavian). The last report from this year, from 4 December, established that twelve senior and 114 junior non-commissioned officers and men composed of the Matzkau *Wachkompanie*. None appear to have been non-German members of the *Waffen*-SS: Liste der Wachkompanie, dated 4.1.1943 Danzig-Matzkau, Liste der Wachkompanie, dated 1.7.1943 Danzig-Matzkau, Liste der Wachkompanie, dated 4.8.1943 Danzig-Matzkau, Liste der Wachkompanie, dated 4.9.1943 Danzig-Matzkau and Liste der Wachkompanie, dated 4.12.1943 Danzig-Matzkau: Source: BA R70-Polen-355.

37 LKA-NW Düsseldorf; witness statement Albert Müller, dated 7.5.1962: *StA* Munich: 13 Js 9/66 /W, pp. 261-271: *StA* Munich.

38 *Ibid.*

39 *Ibid. Uscha.* Lage, (b. Danzig circa 1912). A druggist from civilian life, post-war, Lage lived in southern Germany and founded at a *Kommunalverwaltung*. According to Rudolf Mueller, Lage was later employed highly in the IG-Farben-*Werke*. An *Uscha.* Lage is mentioned acting as a courier for the commandant in February 1943. He carried a letter from the commandant to the SS-*Richter beim* RF-SS, with the list of convicts suitable for probation in the new parachute unit.

40 NARA BDC, SSO Personalakte Walter Dieterle. See Karl Hirsch statement, pp. 209, 214-221: BA Ludwigsburg B 162/829.

41 NARA BDC, SSO Personalakte Otto Langer.

42 NARA BDC, SSO Personalakte Stefan Golda.

43 Edmund Baumgärtner statement, dated 4.6.1968 to Bundesministerium für Innernes Abteilung 18: BA Ludwigsburg; B 162/829, p. 181. See Karl Hirsch statement, dated 29.4.1969, B 162/829, p. 214: BA Ludwigsburg. See Robert Jung statement, dated 20.9.1969: BA Ludwigsburg; B 162/829, p. 244.

44 Hans Kopplow (b. 3.5.1921). *Gren.* Philip Manz (b. 18.10.1907): Message Kew TNA, HW 16/22, dated 7.11.1942. See Kew TNA, HW 16/41, Nr. 12, dated 29.6.1944.

45 NARA BDC, SSO Personalakte Dr Frank Müller.

46 NARA BDC, SSO Personalakte Dr Karl Flothmann.

47 NARA BDC, SSO Personalakte Dr Viktor Schode. For further details see Wolfgang Vopersal; Leaders of the junior department medical corps of the *Waffen*-SS: BA MA N 756, p. 1. See undated transfer order titled *Vorkommando* Hersbruck! Source: BA R70-Polen-355, p.5.

48 Edmund Baumgärtner statement to Bundesministerium für Innernes Abteilung 18, dated 4.6.1968: BA Ludwigsburg; B 162/829, p. 181. See Karl Hirsch statement, dated 29.4.1969: BA Ludwigsburg; B 162/829, p. 214. See Robert Jung statement, dated 20.9.1969: BA Ludwigsburg; B 162/829, p. 244.

49 NARA BDC, SSO Personalakte Johannes Eggert. A date of 1.3.1933 for membership of the Nazi party is written on his SS Personalakte which is incorrect. For a short time, Eggert may have mustered with the LSSAH. See BA Ludwigsburg: B 162/829, pp. 185-187.

50 Dr Fritz Beelitz statement BA Ludwigsburg: B 162/829, p. 143. Albert Müller witness statement to the LKA-NW Düsseldorf, dated 7.5.1962: 13 Js 9/66 /W (*StA* Munich), pp. 261-271.

51 *Uscha*. Manhard Barthelmi (b. 3.9.1919): Albert Müller witness statement to the LKA-NW Düsseldorf, dated 7.5.1962: 13 Js 9/66 /W (*StA* Munich), pp. 261-271. *Uscha*. Manhard Barthelmi, (b. 3.9.1919 in Oberhausen-Sterkrade) transferred to the SS-*Panzer-Grenadier Ausbildung- und Ersatz-Bataillon* 9 (Stralsund) on 27.10.1944: BA R70-Polen-355.

3.3 Opening and Daily Routine

52 Edmund Baumgärtner statement, dated 4.6.1968 to Bundesministerium für Innernes Abteilung 18: BA Ludwigsburg; B 162/829, pp. 181, 209-214.

53 Albert Müller witness statement to the LKA-NW Düsseldorf, dated 7.5.1962: 13 Js 9/66 /W (*StA* Munich), pp. 261-271.

54 Edmund Baumgärtner statement to Bundesministerium für Innernes Abteilung 18, dated 4.6.1968: BA Ludwigsburg; B 162/829, p. 181. See Karl Hirsch statement, dated 29.4.1969: BA Ludwigsburg; B 162/829, p. 214. See Robert Jung statement, dated 20.9.1969: BA Ludwigsburg; B 162/829, p.244.

55 B 162/829, pp. 185-187: BA Ludwigsburg:

56 Dr Beelitz *Lebenslauf*: BA Ludwigsburg; B 162/829, p. 133.

57 Source; Kew WO 208/3616, interrogation of P.W., (b. 1902, Oberschwarzbrunn/Sud.) captured 12.3.1945. The source of the information for the prison compound is derived from the architects drawings submitted to the WVHA during 1941/42: BA NS 3/1649.

German graves are mentioned in Peter Piotrowski, Historia. History, Zapomniany obóz w Gdańsku Maćkowych, Classifieds G.W (Gdańsk), No. 97, edition *of GDG 25/04/2003ŚLEDŹ TE PARTIES*, p. 10

58 Letter *HA* SS-*Gericht*, dated 17.1.1942: BA NS 7/365, p. 11; *Reichsführer*-SS edict – VII IIIb 320/4, dated 8.4.1942; letter SS-*Richter beim* RF-SS to the *HA* SS-*Gericht*, dated 1.2.1943: BA NS 7/365, p. 47. See Otto Langer statement, dated 9.3.1970: BA B 162/ 26452.

59 Letter SS-*Richter beim* RF-SS to the *HA* SS-*Gericht*, dated 7.4.1941; letter *Reichsminister der Justiz*, dated 20.9.1940: D.C NARA Washington microfilm, T-580, 213.

60 *HA* SS-*Gericht* to the SS-FHA, dated 15.7.1942: BA NS 7/365, p. 15.

61 *Ibid.* The *Wehrmacht* gaol may have been located inside the Dubno castle.

62 Letter *Kommandant* of *Wehrmachtgefängnis* Torgau to the SS-*Richter beim* RF-SS, dated 28.9.1944: BA NS 7/371, p.1-3.

63 SS-*Richter bei* RF-SS, dated 10.8.1942; BA NS 7/365, p. 21.

64 Letter *Chef der Ordnungspolizei* to *Chef des HA* SS-*Gericht*, dated 17.7.1942: BA NS 7/365, p. 20. See letter *HA* SS *Gericht*, dated 15.6.1942: BA NS 7/365, pp. 7-15.

65 Letter *HA* SS-*Gericht*, dated 15.6.1942: BA NS 7/365, p. 15 (*Stubaf.* Fritz Nordmann led the SS-*Truppenübungsplatz* Westpreußen in 1.1945). See letter *Ostubaf.* Günther Burmeister to the SS-*Richter beim* RF-SS, dated 5.8.1942: BA NS 7/365, pp. 18-27.

A study of surviving Matzkau Wachkompanie muster documents reveals that only a few Belgium and Dutch soldiers remained in the prison by the summer of 1943.

66 NARA BDC, SSO Personalakte Jan Robertson; Robertson statement in Vuran, dated 18.9.1946: Bob Gerritsen archiv 25.4.2011.

67 Statement Pieter Alburtus Gerhardus Willems, dated 18.10.1972, p. 270: BA Ludwigsburg: B 162/829.

68 Karl Hirsch statement, dated 29.4.1969: BA Ludwigsburg; B 162/829, pp. 209-214. See R. Jung statement, dated 20.9.1969: BA Ludwigsburg; B 162/829, p. 244.

69 BA Ludwigsburg: B 162/829, pp. 209-214.

70 *Ibid.* See also R. Jung statement, dated 20.9.1969: BA Ludwigsburg; B 162/829, p. 244.

71 B 162/829, p. 209-214: BA Ludwigsburg:

72 *Ibid.*

73 Karl Hirsch statement, dated 29.4.1969: BA Ludwigsburg; B 162/829, pp. 209- 214.

74 NARA BDC, SSO Personalakte Walter Dieterle.

75 R. Jung statement, dated 20.9.1969: BA Ludwigsburg; B 162/829, p. 244.

76 Seidler, *Die Militärgerichtsbarkeit…*', op cit.; pp. 253-261.

77 Letter *HA* SS-*Gericht* dated 15.2.1942: BA NS 7/365, p. 48-49. See letter SS-*Richter beim* RF-SS, dated 1.2.1943: BA NS 7/365, pp. 45-66. See letter *HA* SS-*Gericht*: - BA NS 7/365, p. 13, 5 & 8.

78 Seidler, '*Die Militärgerichtsbarkeit…*' op cit.; pp. 253-261.

79 Robert Jung statement, dated 20.9.1969: BA Ludwigsburg; B 162/829, pp. 209-214. See Franz Kurowski, *Hitler's Last Bastion*, Schiffer Publishing, Ltd 2004, p. 279.

80 Jan Daniluk, *Instytut Pamieci narodowej w Gdansku*; Kew national archives WO 208/3695—M.I 19 (R.P.S)/1164, dated 4.1.1943.

81 Letter *HA* SS-*Gericht*, dated 15.2.1942; letter SS-*Richter beim* RF-SS to the *HA* SS-*Gericht*, dated 1.2.1943: BA NS 7/365, pp. 48-49. See letter SS-*Richter beim* RF-SS, dated 1.2.1943: BA NS 7/365, pp. 45-66. See letter *HA* SS-*Gericht,* dated 15.5.1942: - BA NS 7/365, p. 13, 5 & 8.

82 Family archive of Franz Müller, correspondents with author 12.2013.

83 Courtesy of the Klaus Böhme archive. Reproduced with permission, © copyright preserved.

Discipinary Punishments

84 *StA* Munich B 162/829, pp. 209-214: BA Ludwigsburg.

85 Friedrich Wilhelm Ringel statement, dated 13.8.1968: case file 13 Js 9/66 /W.: *StA* Munich.

86 Letter *HA* SS-*Gericht* IIIb 320/6, dated 22.9.1942: BA NS 756/283a, p. 156.

87 NARA BDC, SSO Personalakte Walter Dieterle.

88 Letter *letter, dated 26-6-42 HA* SS-*Gericht*: - BA NS 7/365, pp. 13 & 5.

89 Communication with *Herr* Kurt Grawe, dated 1.8.2014.

90 NARA BDC, SSO Personalakte Walter Dieterle.

Capital Punishments

91 13 Js 9/66 /W.: *StA* Munich.

92 Rudolf Heiß statement to the *StA* Munich, dated 14.3.1967: *StA* Munich II; 13 Js 9 a-e/66.

93 B 162/829, pp. 209-214: BA Ludwigsburg.

94 LKA-NW Düsseldorf; witness statement Albert Müller, dated 7.5.1962: *StA* Munich: 13 Js 9/66 /W, pp. 261-271: *StA* Munich.

95 *Ibid.*

96 *StA* Munich: 13 Js 9/66 /W., dated 11.1.1971: BA Ludwigsburg.

97 Friedrich Ringel statement, dated 13.8.1968: Case file 13 Js 9/66 /W: *StA* Munich

98 Sikorski, '*Kriechen…*' op cit.; letter *HA* SS-*Gericht* dated 15.5.1942: BA NS 7/365, p. 8.
For indiscipline in the SS-*Straflager* Dachau, Wilhelm Nagel found himself transferred to the KL Sachsenhausen and worked in the camp bakery. Nagel survived the war. The fate of former KL Stutthof guard *Strm.* Albert Richard Wagner is sourced from Marek Orksi, *Obywatele francuscy w obozie koncentracyjnym Stutthof w latach 1941-1945*, ediction Gdansk 2010, p. 87 using source: HQ order Troop Order Nr 78, dated 16.11.1944.

99 *23 SikorskiIbid.* For further details see *Das Lager Danzig-Matzkau, Strafvollzugslager in der Waffen-SS* and Jan Daniluk, *Obóz karny SS i policji w Maćkowach pod Gdańskim, „Pamięć i Sprawiedliwość*", ediction Gdansk 2011, nr 2 (18), p. 217.

100 *StA* Munich B 162/829, pp. 209-214: BA Ludwigsburg.

3.4 The First Years

101 Letter *HA* SS-*Gericht* to the SS-*Richter beim* RF-SS, dated 1.2.1943: BA NS 7/365, p. 46. A breakdown of the monthly growth of the Matzkau inmate population in 1942:

January	-	347
February	-	393 (+46)
March	-	378 (-15)
April	-	654 (+276)
May	-	728 (+74)
June	-	850 (+122)
July	-	985, (+135)
August	-	1,286 (+301)
September	-	1,412 (+126)
October	-	1, 640 (+228)
November	-	1,776 (+136)
December	-	1, 858 (+82)

102 Alfred Hubrig statement, dated 1.5.1966: B 162/829, p. 164, BA Ludwigsburg.

103 Letter *HA* SS-*Gericht* to the SS-*Richter beim* RF-SS, dated 1.2.1943: BA NS 7/365, pp. 46 & 52. See Personal Antrag, dated 30.4.1944: NARA BDC, SSO Personalakte Gottfried Biedermann.

104 Letter SS-*Richter beim* RF-SS to the *HA* SS-*Gericht*, dated 25.7.1942: D.C. NARA Washington microfilm, T-580, roll 214.

105 Letter *HA* SS-*Gericht* to the SS-*Richter beim* RF-SS, dated 25.6.1942: D.C. NARA Washington microfilm T-580, roll 214. *Stubaf.* Burmeister would discover that a total of 182 convicts languished in civil gaols (106 in *Gefängnissen*, 29 in *Zuchthäusern* and 47 in *Strafgefangenenlagern*). The prescription included those judged ineligible for military service, declared incapable of improving, those pronounced or assessed homosexual, habitual criminals and quitters from military service. Burmeister called on these inmates to be sent to the KL Sachsenhausen. Acknowledging that the head of the SS would have to confer the authorisation rights on General Scharfe to enable such offenders to be sent directly to the concentration camp, i.e. without recourse to obtaining a protective warrant from the RSHA, Burmeister also proposed that he monitored the sentencing time as well as any subsequent order for release via a clemency or sentencing decision command. Concluding his letter with a demand that the decision of the *Chef HA* SS-*Gericht* be binding for the concentration camps, Burmeister then requested that the SS-*Richter beim* RF-SS and himself discuss his proposals by 17.6.1942 to ensure they obeyed any subsequent decision of the *Reichsführer.*

106 *Der Polizeipräsident* in Berlin to the OKW, dated 20.12.1943: Author's Archive. *Rttf.* Hans Beuthner (b. 22.8.1922 in Dux). A brave infantryman, Beuthner had been awarded the *E.K. 2. Klasse*, the *Verwundetenabzeichen in Schwarz* and the *Infanterie-Sturmabzeichens in Bronze.*

107 Letter SS-*Richter beim* RF-SS to the RFSS, dated 1.2.1943: BA NS 7/365, pp. 46-47.

108 The prison received instructions on 1.5.1942 to release the convict *Uscha.* Will Kornrumpf (b. 9.10.1916) and send him to the *Arbeitsabteilung der Waffen*-SS to serve the probation part of his sentence. Telexing the prison on 29.5.1942, the Berlin tribunal commanded a prison guard named

Oscha. Herbert Paris to attend an officer training course at the SS-*Junkerschule* Bad Tölz. That same day, the SS- *und Polizei-Gericht* VI, Krakau ordered the release of the convict Josef Kantscheider Josef Kantscheider (b. 10.9.1922) (case Nr. St. L. II 76/1942). The Berlin tribunal requested that the prison prepared a fitness report for *Schütze* Karl Wieken (b. 8.12.1920 in Dortmund). In particular, the court wished to know whether Wieken was suitable for front probation (case Nr. St. L III 176/1942): Message Kew TNA, HW 16/18, dated 1.5.1942.

109 Letter *HA* SS-*Gericht*, dated 15.5.1942: BA NS 7/365, p. 5 & letter, dated 22-8-42 to RFSS Tg nr 100/42 g - 45-52.

110 Letter *HA* SS-*Gericht Amt* III to the WVHA, dated 25.2.1943: BA NS 7/365, p. 65.

111 At this time *Stubaf.* Burmeister's recommendations for how to handle sick convicts had evidently not been widely received. The SS and *Polizei* Court XIII, Posen contacted Matzkau on 9.6.1942 to ask where to send *Zuchthaus* offenders afflicted with T.B. Replying the same day, the SS-*Straflager* Dachau leader informed the court that inmates with health problems could be admitted into their clinic: Message Kew TNA, HW 16/18, dated 1.5.1942; message Kew HW 16/18, dated 29.5.1942; message Kew HW 16/19, dated 9.6.1942; message Kew TNA, HW 16/18, dated 3.6.1942 & message Kew HW 16/19, dated 9.6.1942.

112 Communication with Herr Kurt Grawe, dated 1.8.2014. Born in Bischofsburg/East Prussia on 18.2.1911, Hans Woellke had served with the Berlin police force. A shot-put athlete, Woellke won a gold medal in the men's shot put competition on the first day at the 1936 Summer Olympics in Berlin. A *Hauptmann* in the SiPo, Woellke led the 1. / *Schutzmannschaftbtl.* 118 with the rank of *Major* when killed by partisans on 22.3.1943 in Guba near Minsk (Belarus). At this time Woellke's unit was operating in conjunction with the 1. / SS-*Sonderbataillon Dirlewanger* to commit mass murder in the village of Kosyri, 1 km west of Chatyn. His death precipitated the destruction of Khatyn by *Polizei* forces and Dirlewanger's force on 22.3.1943.

113 Writing on 24.6.1942, Dr Müller informed the Prague tribunal that the inmate Reinhold Konrad (b. 20.4.1922) was fit for combat. The felon Alfred Wollmann (b. 7.7.1921) arrived in Matzkau from the SS-*und Polizei-Gericht* VI, Krakau on 26.6.1942. On the day of his arrival the prison requested that Krakau tribunal sent them his personal papers. The following day the Viennese court ordered a fitness report for Heinz Fienschbetz (b. 24.11.1923). Fienschbetz then received orders to report to a *Sondereinheiten* on 24.8.1942. At this time the Vienna court ordered the prison to release *Zugwachmeister der Schupo* Fritz Wesselbaum (b. 29.4.1913). Sent to the *Pionier-Ersatz-Kompanie* of the *Polizeidivision* in Dresden, here, Wesselbaum trained for his eventual service in the *Polizei-Sondereinheit*, which was fighting outside the city of Leningrad.

The same day, the chief judge of the Viennese court ordered the release of *Schütze* Franz Stieber (b. 15.10.1924). Ordered to release Hans Hohman on 29.6.1942, the prison carried out this instruction and Hohman reported to the *Sondereinheit* on 8.7.1942. Contacting the prison on 3.7.1942, the SS-*und Polizei-Gericht* XIII, Posen requested that the prison prepared a fitness report for Johan Paus (b. 28.6.1905). If found fit for front service, the tribunal planned to send Paus to the *Sondereinheit-Polizei* with his previous service grade.

The *Amt* III ordered the release SS-*Mann* Fritz Spitz from detention on 30.6.1942. Leaving prison, Spitz reported to the SS-*Infantrie-Ersatz-Bataillon* I *Totenkopf* and remained with this formation until they determined his fate. Following his sentencing by the Den Haag court, Heinrich Schledener arrived in Matzkau on 31.7.1942 (case Nr. St. L. I. 111/1942). Taking two week to report to the prison, the Dutch court was informed of Schledener's arrival on 14.8.1942. The Viennese tribunal ordered the prison to release Helmut Salman, (b. 23.11.1923), to the SS-*Feldersatz-Bataillon Westland* at Klagenfurt on 6.8.1942. Gerhard Blockhaus, (b. 5.12.1914) reported to the prison from the same court on 14.8.1942 and in order to determine his fitness for combat, the *Amt* III ordered the garrison physician to supply a medical report for August Meurer on 24.8.1942: Message Kew TNA, HW 16/21, dated 26.8.1942; message Kew HW 16/19, dated 24.6.1942; message Kew HW 16/19, dated 27.6.1942; message Kew TNA, HW 16/20, Kew HW 16/21 dated 24.8.1942; message Kew HW 16/20 30.6.1942.

114 Letter letter from Ernst to the *Hauptamt* SS-*Gericht* dated 10-2-1943- BA NS 756/283a & SS-*Richter beim* RF-SS to the *HA* SS-*Gericht*, dated 9.8.1943: BA NS 756/283a. See SS-FHA memorandum dated 9.5.1943: BA NS 7/365, p. 92. See letter *Stubaf.* Dr Ernst to the *HA* SS-*Gericht*, dated 10.2.1943: BA NS 756/283a.

115 NARA BDC, SSO Personalakte Dr Leo Ernst. The *Reichsführer* considered the wearing of SS uniforms in church a serious breach of order and discipline. The *Regierungspräsident* Hildesheim, *Oberf.* Dr Hermann Muhs was *ausgestoßene aus der* SS on 2.2.1941 for committing this very act of military disobedience.

116 Letter SS-*Richter beim* RF-SS to the *HA* SS-*Gericht*, dated 18.8.1942: D.C. NARA Washington microfilm T-580, roll 214.

117 *Reichsführer* draft copy of regulations concerning the punishment process for *Waffen*-SS and police units subordinate to the *Heer* dated 2.1942: D.C NARA Washington microfilm, T-580, roll 213. See letter SS-*Richter beim* RF-SS to the *HA* SS-*Gericht*, dated 8.3.1942: D.C NARA microfilm publication T-580, roll 215. See letter SS-*Richter beim* RF-SS to *Ostubaf.* Burmeister, dated 12.8.1942: BA NS 7/365, pp. 22-25. See message Kew TNA, HW 16/21, dated 24.8.1942. See letter *Ogruf.* Erich v.dem Bach-Zelewski to the *Reichsführer*, dated 26.8.1942: BA NS 7/365, pp. 28-29. See letter SS-*Richter beim* RF-SS to the *HA* SS-*Gericht*, dated 27.8.1942: BA NS 7/365, p. 30, 35 & 34.

118 Letter SS-*Richter beim* RF-SS, dated 12.8.1942: BA NS 7/379.

119 NARA BDC, SSO Personalakte Harald Svenke.

120 Seidler, '*Die Militärgerichtsbarkeit…*' op cit.; p. 260. See letter SS-*Richter beim* RF-SS to the *HA* SS-*Gericht*, dated 12.8.1942: BA NS 7/379, p. 8.

121 Letter *Reichsführer* to *Ostubaf.* Günther Burmeister, dated 19.10.1942: BA NS 7/365, p. 36, 38, 40, 50, 41-42.

122 The transferees were: *Reiter* Reinhard Geist of the SS-*Kavallerie*-Rgt. 3, *Kannonier* Johann Horvath and Gerhard Wothe of the SS-*Kavallerie-Artillerie*-Rgt. 8, *Reiter* Georg Seibert of the SS-*Kavallerie*-Rgt. 1 HQ and *Strm.* Karl-Heinz Muller of the bakery company).

The release of Heinz Fieschuetz was demanded on 24.8.1942, (b. 24.11.1923) (case Nr. St. L. 122/41) and that same day a doctor's examination was requested for the inmate August Meurer. Telexing on 14.9.1942, the SS-*und Polizei-Gericht* VII, Vienna refused to order the release of a convict named Blasius Muth (b. 26.12.1923) and the *HA* SS-*Gericht* ordered a fitness report for the inmate named Gerhard Schlegel on 29.9.1942. The Den Haag tribunal ordered a medical examination of former *Rttf.* Fritz Kalisch (b. 1.12.1920) on 9.10.1942 and the following day, having served four months of his sentence, the release of Heinrich Gruemmer (b. 10.4.1906) was received (case Nr. St. L. II. 52/1942). An inmate named Arthur Engler arrived in the prison on 14.10.1942 (case Nr. St. L. 120/1942) and on this same day, the Prague tribunal ordered the release of Gunther Suelpner (b. 28.3.1924) and requested a medical report for the inmate Friedrich Scholz (b. 12.11.1914).

Ordering a fitness report for Hans Thorn (b. 2.5.1923) on 23.9.1942, this was supplied to the SS-*und Polizei-Gericht* I, Munich on 27.10. The *Amt* III contacted Matzkau on 27.10.1942 to warn that the convict Ewald Schipper (b. 9.5.1919), would soon complete his part punishment and inform them that his release required the approval of the *Gerichtsherr* (case Nr. St. L. 110/1941). Two days later the prison reported that undergoing a medical examination, Heinrich Wagner (b. 12.7.1903), had been declared fit for front line service. The Vienna court ordered the release of a former policeman named Huebner on 16.10.1942 (b. 19.6.1903) and directed him to the *Sondereinheit Polizei* to undergo front probation.

Having served part of his sentence, Waldemar Raether (b. 6.4.1912) received orders to leave the Matzkau the following day to undertake a period of probation (case Nr. St. L. II 387/1941). Around this time the Viennese tribunal wrote to Matzkau to notify them that the punishment of TD-*Mann* Franz Salcher's (b. 4.6.1921) had ended on 19.10.1942 and this enabled his release. Writing to the prison on 20.10.1942, the Den Haag court requested that the prison supply them a fitness report for the following inmates: Walter Roediger (b. 2.5.1924), Richard Stober (b. 1.7.1924) and Horst Neumann, (b. 12.2.1925). If judged fit for front service, the court ordered all to report to the *Bewährungsabteilung der Waffen*-SS: Letter unidentified SS-*Beurkundungsführer* of the court service office 17.771, dated 3.9.1942: BA NS 756/283a. See message Kew TNA, HW 16/21, dated 23.8.1942; message Kew TNA, HW 16/21, dated 21.9.1942; message Kew TNA, HW 16/19, dated 9.10.1942/16.10.1942; message Kew TNA, HW 16/22, dated 24.11.1942; message Kew TNA, HW 16/19, dated 9.10.1942/16.10.1942; message Kew HW 16/22, dated 20.10.1942.

123 Letter *Chef HA* SS-*Gericht* to the *Chef* RSHA dated 18.4.1942: D.C. NARA Washington microfilm, T-580, roll 213. See letter *HA* SS-*Gericht Amt* III, dated 4.11.1942: BA NS 756/283a. See letter SS-*Richter beim* RF-SS to the *HA* SS-*Gericht*, dated 1.2.1943: BA NS 7/365, p. 47.

124 Letter SS-*Richter beim* RF-SS to the *HA* SS-*Gericht*, dated 1.2.1943: BA NS 7/365, p. 48.

125 NARA BDC, SSO Personalakte Otto Heinen.

126 The SS-*und Polizei-Gericht* I, Munich issued a release order for a convict named Englisch on 11.11.1942. The same court ordered a fitness report for *Kannonier* Gustav Schulze, (b. 21.5.1925) on the same date and ordered the release of the inmate Wilhelm Immig (b. 11.3.1921) on the same day. Serving part of a five month sentence, Immig then received front probation. On 11.11.1942 the *Wiking* field court ordered the release of the convict Kiefer. Contacting the prison on 12.11.1942, the Viennese tribunal informed them that Heinrich Schridder (b. 5.12.1922) had been sentenced to a term of eight months *Gefängnis* on 13.7.1942 and was due for release on 12.11.1942 the same year (at this time this court ordered a fitness report for Alfred Kleinsorge).

Writing on 18.11.1942 the SS-*und Polizei-Gericht* XIV, Metz reminded the prison that the inmate Werner Stitz (b. 13.8.1920), formally of the *Wiking*, had served part of his six month sentence on 19.11.1942 and was released from gaol on 25.12.1942 (case Nr. St. L. I. 57/1942). The SS-*und Polizei-Gericht* VII, Vienna commanded the release of Legion *Schütze* Marcel Petit on 20.11.1942 (case Nr. St. L. II 242/1942) and telexing the prison on 24.11.1942, the SS-*und Polizei-Gericht* XIV, Metz warned that having served part of his sentence, the convict August Appenzeller (b. 12.8.1904) was now due for release (case Nr. St. L. I. 71/1942). The Viennese tribunal authorised the release of Thomas Petrasch, (b. 28.9.1891) on 26.11.1942 and ordered to return home, Petrasch was commanded to report for probation with the *Wehrmacht*. The Prague court commanded the release of the inmate Geea-Ladislaus Pronay (b. 18.8.1907) on 2.11.1942. Serving part of his punishment, Pronay was permitted to leave the prison on 3.11.1942 (case Nr. St. L. 273/1942).

At this time, the SS-*und Polizei-Gericht* VIII, Prague tribunal ordered the release of Josef Teufel (b. 1.7.1922). Formerly of the SS-Division *Reich*, Teufel had served his full punishment on 30.11.1942 (case Nr. St. L. I. 269/1941). That same day, an inmate named Fritz (b. 27.10.1920) was ordered to the *Bewährungsabteilung* (case Nr. St. L. I. 269/41). At this time the Vienna tribunal requested the prison supplied a fitness report for the convict Werner Lehmann (b. 2.11.1920) (case Nr. St. L. 287/1942): Message Kew TNA, HW 16/21, dated 2.11.1942 (*Rttf.* Wesseller); message Kew TNA, HW 16/22, dated 24.11.1942; message Kew TNA, HW 16/22, dated 3.12.1942.

127 Message Kew TNA, HW 16/22, dated 8.12.1942; message Kew TNA, HW 16/22, dated 9.12.–6.12.1942.

128 Ludwig Wallner (b. 31.10.1922). The inmate Panny was commanded to be released from Matzkau for probation with the on 10.12.1942 and telexing the prison on 10.12.1942, the SS-*und Polizei-Gericht* VI, Krakau court ordered the release of Bruno Kunkel, (b. 23.1.1913) and instructed him to report to his home in Tierschtiegel. Telexing the 12.12.1942, the Vienna tribunal ordered the release of TENO-*Hscha.* Karl Harnesch, who had originally faced trial before the Prague court for committing an unauthorised leave offence (case Nr. St. L. 654/1942). The Posen court ordered a fitness report for the convict named Porenski on 15.12.1942. They required this document to enable them to process his appeal for leave to visit Juellini for seven days. A telex reached the prison on 16.12.1942, which informed them that *Revieroberwachtmeister* Richard Knoblach, who had been expelled from the *Schutzpolizei*, was recommended for probation pending the approbation of the head of the SS (this arrived the following day). The *HA* SS-*Gericht* commanded probation for the inmate *Uscha.* Paul Wiruschewski (b. 4.2.1916) on 4.1.1943 and he was commanded to the *Bewährungsabteilung*. The Den Haag tribunal ordered the release of Heinz Hannemann, (b. 19.12.1923) on 16.1.1943 and he received a command to undergo a period of probation at the front (case Nr. St. L. 1/1941): Message Kew TNA, HW 16/22, dated 8.12.1942.

129 Message Kew TNA, HW 16/22, dated 13.12.1942. See NARA BDC, SSO Personalakte Willi Prager.

130 Message Kew TNA, HW 16/23, dated 12.1.1943.

131 Telexing the prison on 18.1.1943, the Posen court informed them that the convict Walter Marquardt (b. 22.10.1911) had served part of his punishment and was eligible for release on 19.1.1943. This court also commanded that Hubert Frech (b. 20.3.1925) be released the same day. Serving part of his punishment, the SS-*und Polizei-Gericht* I, Munich ordered the release of Walter Tettenbaum (b. 6.1.1920) enabling him to undertake probation (case Nr. St. L. II 130/1942). Two days later the SS-*und Polizei-Gericht* VII, Vienna reported that the *Polizeigefängnis* Vienna was sending to the prison the personal effects of *Schütze* Arpad Tapalage (his mess kit, coat and armband). This court advised the prison on 20.1.1943 that Tapalage had left the *Polizeigefängnis* Vienna for Matzkau. Telexing on 19.1.1943, the Metz court ordered the release of Kurt Grossmann (b. 15.3.1921). He'd originally faced trial before the *Wiking* field court (case Nr. St. L. I 502/1941).

Contacting Matzkau, the Munich tribunal noted that a medical examination of the former SS-*Funker* Willi Frey (b. 10.4.1924), which was conducted on 1.1.1943, had judged him suitable for combat and they requested that the prison provide them with a parole suitability report. Having served part of his sentence, the prison was ordered to release the convict Erwin Clerici (b. 17.8.1920) to a probation unit on 26.1.1943. Telexing the Krakau tribunal on 26.1.1943, the Matzkau commandant queried the release of Georg Ularick (b. 24.4.1920). The following day, the SS-*und Polizei-Gericht* VII, Vienna requested a fitness report was produced for *Hauptwachmeister d. Schupo* Emil Krischke (case Nr. St. L. 470/1942) and ordering Jacob Moersch (b. 14.7.1902) to the *Sondereinheit Polizei* on 26.1.1943, the Den Haag tribunal demanded that he arrived at his new post within two days. The *Amt* III telexed the prison on 3.3.1943 to order the release of the inmate *Schütze* Hans Flohr (b. 15.1.1925). Leaving Matzkau, Flohr was then posted to the *Sondereinheit der Waffen*-SS. Incarcerating *Scha.* Albert Gotthardt (b. 6.3.1888) on 10.1.1943In the first week of January 1943 SS *Obersturmführer* Biedermann was transferred from the SS *Straflager* Dachau to the SS-*und Polizei Strafvollzugslager* Danzig-Matzkau as *Lagerführer* to replace SS *Hauptsturmführer* Albert. , the prison noted that the sentencing had been undertaken by the Metz tribunal on 15.12.1942 for committing comrade theft (case Nr. St. L. I 134/1942).

Judged guilty on 4.1.1943, Gotthardt found himself punished with six months *Gefängnis*. Writing to the SS-*Sonderlager* Hinzert on 27.1.1943, the prison requested Gotthardt's personal papers and requested details of his destination once his sentence was complete. Replying on 12.2.1943, the SS-*Sonderlager* Hinzert had decided, in view of his crime and sentence, to refuse him re-entry to the KL Hinzert once he'd served his gaol term. When his sentence was complete, the decision whether to transfer Gotthardt to the *Bewährungsabteilung* was left to the *Amt* III to decide: Message Kew TNA, HW 16/23, dated 16.1.1943–26.1.1943; BA NS 4/Hi/13, p. 111.

132 'The *Reichsführer*-SS approves your view, that unworthy convicts, especially cases involving convicts who had planned/attempted an escape, but not carried it out are to be punished for committing an unauthorised leave in the sense of § 64 MStGB': *Reichsführer* edict, dated 24.2.1943: D.C. NARA Washington microfilm, T-580, roll 213.

133 *HA* SS-*Gericht* memorandum, dated 29.1.1943: BA NS 7/365, pp. 43, 50-52, 54, 73 & 54. See letter *Reichsführer* to *Ogruf.* Pohl, dated 3.2.1943: D.C. NARA Washington microfilm, T-580, roll 212.

134 If the plan to establish a new shell basket and ammunition box workshop inside Matzkau proved unfeasible, the WVHA recommended establishing a new branch prison inside the KL Buchenwald, or another camp, and putting the convicts to work in the war industry: *Ostubaf.* Maurer memorandum, dated 10.2.1943: D.C. Washington microfilm, T-580, roll 212. For more details see letter *Reichsführer* to *Gruf.* Pohl, dated 1.3.1943: BA NS 7/365, pp. 54 & 62-65.

135 *Ostubaf.* Günther Burmeister memorandum, dated 30.1.1943: BA NS 7/365, pp. 44 & 75.

136 Letter *Ostubaf.* Dr Ernst to the *HA* SS-*Gericht*, dated 9.3.1943: BA NS 756/283a.

The SS men were: *Reviermeister* Arthur Stuwe (b. 3.3.1912; judged guilty of disobeying leave orders on 19.5.1942, *Polizei Anwärter* Ewald Luther (b. 9.5.1915); judged guilty of office theft on 12.9.1942, *Scha.* Martin Wimmer (b. 10.11.1911); judged guilty of military disobedience on 14.4.1942, *Scha.* Ernst Kliehm (b. 29.11.1909); judged guilty of revealing secrets on 30.9.1942 and *Anwärter* Franz Ruber (b. 30.9.1912); judged guilty of extortion and receiving stolen goods on 29.8.1942.

137 NARA BDC, SSO Personalakte Fritz Uhrig.

138 Message TNA, HW 16/41, dated 1.3.1943.

139 SS-*Richter beim* RF-SS memorandum, dated 10.2.1943: BA NS 7/365, p. 61, 54 & 93.

140 Verordensblatt der Waffen-SS, 2943, Nr. 8, dated 15.4.1943 Nr 148: BA NS 756/283.

141 Dr Beelitz Lebenslauf; B 162/829, p. 133; BA Ludwigsburg; BA NS 7/1, p. 119.

142 Letter SS-*Richter beim* RF-SS (Dr Wehser) to the *HA* SS-*Gericht*, dated 21.7.1943: D.C. NARA Washington microfilm T-580, roll 214.

143 Letter SS-*Richter beim* RF-SS to *HA* SS-*Gericht*, dated 21.6.1943: BA NS 7/365, pp. 78, 71-72.

144 Letter SS-*Richter beim* RF-SS to the *HA* SS-*Gericht*, dated 21.6.1943: BA NS 7/365, pp. 78, 71-72.

145 Letter SS-*Richter beim* RF-SS to the *HA* SS-*Gericht*, dated 9.8.1943: D.C. NARA Washington microfilm, T-580, roll 214.

146 *HA* SS-*Gericht Brieftagbuch* dated 26.8.1943: Wiener Institute. See message Kew HW 16/19.

147 B 162/829, dated 21.11.1963: BA Ludwigsburg.

148 NARA BDC, SSO Personalakte Wolfgang Plaul.

149 Letter *HA* SS-*Gericht* to the SS-*Richter beim* RF-SS, dated 7.11.1943: BA NS 7/365, pp. 80-81.

150 Message Kew TNA, HW 16/39, Nr. 41, dated 6.12.1943.

151 Letter *HA* SS-*Gericht* dated 1.2.1944: BA NS 7/369.

152 Richard P. 1951 report: *StA* Kassel, A 5. 55, Nr. 67; RP Darmstadt, WG-Akte Richard P.

153 NARA BDC, SSO Personalakte Anton Mennen.

3.5 The 1943 Brutality Scandal

154 NARA BDC, SSO Personalakte Walter Dieterle: Court-martial record SS and *Polizei* Court IV, Danzig, (case Nr. St. L. II. Nr 155/43), dated 17.9.1943.

155 NARA BDC, SSO Personalakte Dr Leo Ernst. See also BA NS 756/283a.

156 Telegram *Reichsführer* to the *Chef HA* SS-*Gericht*, dated 8.3.1944: BA NS 19-1256.

3.6 The Schloß Hornburg Project

157 Letter *Chef HA* SS-*Gericht* to the *Reichsführer*, dated 1.2.1944: BA NS 7/369, pp. 2-4, (*Ostuf.* Rudlieb Görcke led SS-FHA *Amt* C VII from 6.1944); letter *Ostubaf.* Günther Burmeister to the SS-*Richter beim* RF-SS, dated 1.2.1944: BA NS 7.

3.7 First Half of 1944

158 Liste des Kommandantur-Stabes Danzig-Matzkau, dated 4.2.1944: BA R70-Polen-355, p. 3 (this number excludes the men of the Wachkompanie).

159 Letter *HA* SS-*Gericht* IIIb to the SS-*Richter beim* RF-SS, dated 20.1.1944: BA NS 7/1189, pp. 93-95.

160 13 Js 9 a-e/66, dated 13.8.1968, p. 533-535 & 5.8.1969, pp. 683-685: *StA* Munich.
This posting is evident from the Dienststellen im Bereich des SS-Oberabschnitt Weichsel: BA NS 47/69. For more details see Edmund Baumgärtner's SSO file. For further details of the NCO's movement order see *HA* SS-*Gericht* transfer order, dated 25.1.1945: BA NS 7/1, pp. 159–161. The non-commissioned officers were: *Oscha.* Bernhard Kunze, Arno Müller and Layer.

161 B 162/829, p. 173 & B 162/829, pp. 185-187: BA Ludwigsburg.

162 NARA BDC, SSO Personalakte Josef Malkmus.

163 Telexing the prison on 29.1.1944, the Metz court informed them that the convict Richard Schwichter would have served part of his punishment on 12.2.1944 and was therefore ordered to the SS-*Panzergrenadier-Ausbildung- und Ersatz-Bataillon* Seelager troop training ground to undergo front probation. Messaging to the SS-*und Polizei-Gericht* VI, Lemberg on 30.1.1944, the SS and *Polizei* Court XX informed them that the *Pionier* Helmut Blech would transfer from the *Kreigwehrmachthaftanstalt* Lemberg to Matzkau with his personal papers. At this time, a convict named Berthold Knopp (b. 21.5.1912) was close to completing part of his punishment only required the SS- *und Polizei-Gericht* XIV, Metz to decide what type of parole he'd undertake.
Contacting the prison on 2.2.1944, the Stettin court ordered a fitness report for Eugen Becking on 2.2.1944 (b. 31.8.1923) and on the same day, the Metz tribunal informed the prison that the felon Johann Spaeter had served three months of his punishment and therefore was ordered to report to the *Schutzpolizei* in Saarbrücken on 16.2.1944. *Wachtmeister* Jakob Taiber left the SS-*und Polizei-Gericht* XXVIII, Agram to Matzkau to serve his prison sentence on 5.2.1944. Fearing he

suffered psychological problems, the Nikolajew tribunal telexed the prison on 24.2.1944 to order the immediate release of the inmate Seidel (b. 4.10.1919) into the care of the Stettin SS-*Sanitätsabteilung*: Message Kew HW 16/40, dated 14.1.1944/29.1.1944, Nr 2; message Kew HW 16/40, Nr 20, dated 5.2.1944 to 24.2.1944.

164 Letter *Ogruf.* Berger, dated 20.3.1944: BDC SS-HO 2422; Gottlieb Berger evidence Nuremburg case IX NO 2723 & NO 2061. See letter SS-*Richter beim* RF-SS to the *HA* SS-*Gericht*, dated 6.6.1944 (NO 2061). See letter SS-*Richter beim* RF-SS to the *HA* SS-*Gericht*, dated 6.6.1944: BA NS 756/283a.

165 Stephan Moravck (b. 10.8.1925): Message Kew TNA, HW 16/40, Nr. 4, dated 22.4.1944.

166 Military Tribunal NO II Case 4, USA v Oswald Pohl, Nuremburg trial.

167 Otto Klink (b. 27.5.1916), Heinz Galick/Garlick (b. 28.7.1921): Message Kew TNA, HW 16/40, dated 3.5.1944; message Nr. 18. Kew HW 16/41, dated 20.5.1944 Nr. 9.

168 Rolf Michaelis, *SS-Fallschirmjäger-bataillon 500/600*, Schiffer Publishing Ltd (US) 2008, p. 8.

3.8 The 20 July 1944 Plot.

169 NARA BDC, SSO Personalakte Edmund Baumgärtner; letter *HA* SS-*Gericht*, dated 18.8.1944.

3.9 Second Half of 1944

170 Dr Beelitz *Lebenslauf*, p. 133; Dr Beelitz statement, dated 14.4.1959: B 162/829: BA Ludwigsburg

171 Dr Beelitz statement, dated 14.4.1959; B 162/829: BA Ludwigsburg.
In late 1944 the *Stabkompanie des Strafvollzugslager* Danzig-Matzkau consisted of nine officers, one officer candidate, nine senior NCO's, 108 lower ranked NCO's and men and 34 convicts, of which four were policemen: Stabkompanie des Strafvollzugslager Danzig-Matzkau, dated late 1944: Source: BA R70-Polen-355.

172 Dr Beelitz *Lebenslauf*; B 162/829, p. 133 BA Ludwigsburg.

173 NARA BDC, SSO Personalakte Albert Knobelspieß.

174 NARA BDC, SSO Personalakte Max Jumpertz.

175 NARA BDC, SSO Personalakte *Hscha.* Malkmus (b. 11.12.1920). Released from Matzkau at the end of 8.1944. Letter *Ostubaf.* Günther Burmeister to the SS-*Richter beim* RF-SS, dated 15.6.1944: D.C. NARA Washington microfilm, T-580, roll 213.

176 Letter SS-*Richter beim* RF-SS to Dr Günther Reinecke, dated 27.7.1944: D.C. NARA Washington microfilm; T-580, roll 213.

177 Dr Flothmann family archive 22.7.2011.

178 NARA BDC, SSO Personalakte Kurt Korngiebel; letter *HA* SS-*Gericht* dated 1.2.1945: Case Number III 7976/44 GL.

179 Letter *Gerichtsoffizier des* SS-*Grenadier*-Rgt. 2, SS-Brigade *Charlemagne*, dated 10.10.1944: BA NS 756/283a. The head of the SS took personal responsibility for punishing French volunteers from 7.1944. 47 of the French prisoners were later forwarded to the *Arbeitsdurchgangslager* Berlin-Wilhelmshagen: Letter SS-*Richter beim* RF-SS, dated 19.7.1944: BAB NS 7/73.

180 Letter *Brigadef.* Rode of the *Kommandostabes* RF-SS 20.9.1944: BA NS 756/283a (Vopersal archive).

181 Klausch, 'Antifaschisten…' op cit.; p. 123. See letter *Hstuf.* Dr Zolly, dated 30.9.1944: BA NS 7/365.

182 The two parolees were *Bauhilfsarbeiter* Viktor Zerfass, (b. 5.9.1923 in Kimpolung/Rümanien) and *Heilgymastiker* Josef Stoll (b. 26.3.1909 in Neukirchen/Mosbach): Dr Beelitz statement, dated 14.4.1959; B 162/829 BA Ludwigsburg.

183 SS-*Nachtrichten-Ersatz-Abteilung*, (Eichstäatt) Abteilungs-Tagesbefehl, dated 22.1.1945.

184 Klausch, '*Antifaschisten…*' ob cit.; p. 453.

185 Letter *HA* SS-*Gericht* to *Hstuf.* Dr Zolly, dated 20.9.1944: BA NS 7/365, p. 85.
During the autumn of 1944 the SS-*Truppen*übungsplatz Westpreußen.Die Masse der Angehörigen waren straffällig gewordene Militärangehörige der Waffen SS und Polizei.Westpreußen absorbed the redundant Heidelager staff personneland the concentration camp Herzogenbosch). [9].

186 *Ogruf.* Katzmann to the SS-*Richter beim* RF-SS, dated 25.9.1944: BA NS 7/365, p. 82-84.
The *Reichsführer* had considered sending elements of the *Ersatz-Bataillon* of the 20. SS-Division to Matzkau when it was discovered that the *Truppen*übungsplatz Hammerstein was full to capacity with elements of the 15th *Waffen-Grenadier*-Division *der* SS: BA NS 7/365, pp. 82-83.

187 NARA BDC, SSO Personalakte Kirsti; letter *HA* SS-*Gericht* to the *Reichsführer*, dated 9.1.1945. At this time the SS- *und Polizei-Gericht* XVI, Riga branch court Reval had deployed in Matzkau.

188 NARA BDC, SSO Personalakte Willi Baier.

189 Piontrowski, *HZapomniany obóz w Gdańsku Maćkowych Forgotten camp in Gdansk Madko*, Trojmiasto No 97 issue 25.4.2003.

190 Message Kew TNA, HW 16/43 Nr 49. See NARA BDC, SSO Personalakte Waldemar Ueltzhöffer.

191 *Strafvollzugslager der* SS *und Polizei* Danzig-Matzkau Tagesbefehl 79/44, dated 21.10.1944: BA R70-Polen-355, p. 12.

192 *Ibid*, p. 24.

193 Letter SS-*Richter beim* RF-SS, dated 17.12.1944: BA NS 7/367, p. 2.

194 SS-*Nachtrichten-Ersatz-Abteilung* (Eichstäatt) Abteilungs-Tagesbefehl, dated 22.1.1945 (*Rttf.* Arthur Fritz): BA NS 756/283a.

3.10 Denouement

195 Heinz Guderian, *Panzer Leader*, (Penguin World War II Collection) Paperback 2009, p. 403. For further details see Reitlinger, '*SS Alibi…*' ob cit.; *p*. 400 – 407. See Wilhelm Tieke, *The Tragedy of the Faithful*, Fedorowicz (J.J.), Canada 2001, pp. 221, 345-346.

196 Message Kew TNA, HW 16/42. The *Auffanglager* Graz was probably connected to the Liebenau *Arbeitslager*. Its barracks usually held prisoners of war and forced labour, but by this time it probably held refugees displaced by the war.

197 Horst Voigt, *Die 'Verlor'nen Haufen; Sondertruppen zur Frontbewährung im 2. Weltkrieg, Teil VIII'*, p. 450.

198 *Ibid*, pp. 448-455. See also Landwehr Siegrunen, No 23, 27 & 46.

199 NARA BDC, SSO Personalakte Hans-Heinrich Kalthofen (b. 24.4.1909 in Riesa/Elbe SS Nr. 22.226).

200 Letter *HA* SS-*Gericht Amt* III to the HSSPF *Weichel*, dated 10.2.1945: D.C. NARA Washington microfilm; T-580, roll 214.

201 Seidler, '*Die Militärgerichtsbarkeit…*' op cit.; p. 261. The induction of paragraph § 175 offenders into the *Kalthofen* is mentioned in Giles, '*The Denial of Homosexuality…*' For deployment of *Kalthofen* see telegram HSSPF *Weichel* to the *Reichsführer und Ob. Weichel* dated 7.2.1945: Hoover Institution Archives, Stanford, CA, 94305-6010.
Stubaf. Paul Schneeberger (b. 10.7.1913 in Furth/Bavaria, SS Nr. 124.533). Prior to this appointment, Schneeberger had been assigned to the SS-*Truppen*übungsplatz Westpreußen.Die Masse

der Angehörigen waren straffällig gewordene Militärangehörige der Waffen SS und Polizei. Westpreußen. No disciplinary problems are recorded in his personal file.

202 Vopersol archive: BA NS 756/283a.

203 NARA BDC, SSO Personalakte Bjørn Elith Binnerup.

204 NARA BDC, SSO Personalakte Friedrich-Wilhelm Meier.

205 NARA BDC, SSO Personalakte Ernst Michael.

206 NARA BDC, SSO Personalakte Jörgen Salskov.

207 NARA BDC, SSO Personalakte Geert Ziegler.

208 Undated letter titled Vorkommando Hersbruck: BA R70-Polen-355, p. 5. The *Vorkommando* Heiß also included *Rttf.* Oesten as *Rechnungsführer*, *Rttf.* Wagner as cook, *Schtz.* Dobrindt as *Bekl.-Km.-Wart* (a convict) and *Uscha.* Hans Kötterl as the clerk.

209 Rudolf Heiß statement dated 8.3.1967: *StA* Munich, Akt.-Zeichen 13 Js 9 a-e/66, pp. 101-109. See Rudolf Heiß statement to the Landpolizei Oberbayern dated 3.6.1947: *StA* Munich Spruchkammerakten K668.

210 BA NS 7/6 BI.28. See also Vopersol archive: BA NS 756/283a.

211 Message Kew TNA, HW 16/43 Nr. 4, dated 9.2.1945.

212 Vopersol *Archiv* and also the 'Orientierung' Katholische Blätter für Weltanschauliche dated 30.11.1979, Zurich Nr. 22, 43 Jahrgang.

213 Richardi – 'SS-Geiseln...' ob cit.; p. 65.

214 *Ibid*, pp. 66, 70-71.

215 *Ibid*, p. 71.

216 *Ibid*, pp. 71-72.

217 *Ibid*, p. 72.

218 Horst Voigt, *Die Verlor'nen Haufen; Sondertruppen zur Frontbewährung im 2. Weltkrieg, Teil VIII*, p. 286. See Landwehr Siegrunen, No 23, 27 & 46. For more details see Pantenius, *The Last Battle of the Eastern Front*, pp. 190-191, 195-207. See Richard Landwehr's Siegrunen Nr. 41, p. 35. The author Antonio Munoz identifies these trainees as Greek *Hiwis*, assigned to the SS-*Polizeidivision*. Formally members of the Ethnikos andartikos sinaspismos andikommunistikis draesos, or EASAD, this paramilitary organisation was created from nationalists, anti-communists and farmers by the SD in Thessaly during March 1944. Led by Takis Makedon, their HQ was in Karditsa and by end of April 1944 he had eigtheen companies formed spread out over 13/15 locations with a thousand members armed with rifles. They wore civilian clothing and a green armband and fought with Greek *Gendarmes* and security forces. When the Germans left Greece, they gave the EASAD the choice to fight on as guerrillas, disband or join the German army. Some deserted to communists rather than leave with the SS. Two company sized units joined the SS-*Polizeidivision* in late August 1944 and were dispersed amongst division as *Hiwis*: Antonio Munoz, *Herackles and the Swastika*, Axis Europa Books 2000, p. 27. Some surrendered in Danzig 1945: Tomos Defteros, *to hroniko tou agona – sta armata! Sta armata!*: Historicas tis EASAD self-published in Paris, p, 104.

219 Dr Beelitz *Lebenslauf*, B 162/829, p. 133: BA Ludwigsburg.

220 *Herr* T. Beelitz archive; letter *Frau* Anna Kögel to Dr Beelitz, dated 16.8.1973; letter Dr Beelitz to *Sozialgericht* Kassel, dated 3.9.1973.

Rottwachtmeister der Luftschutzpolizei Gustav Kögel was an inmate at Danzig-Matzkau and using surviving letters, his wife believed that her husband had transferred to Hersbruck in late in Feb.1945. Kögel reportedly died at Hersbruck on 3.3.1945. Writing on 2.1.1963, Dr Beelitz would reiterate again that he left Matzkau in Mar.1945: B 162/829, 7 AR 261/62, dated 1.2.1963: BA Ludwigsburg.

221 Franz Kurowski, *Hitler's Last Bastion*, p. 274.

222 Letter from *Frau* Anna Kögel, dated 16.8.1973; letter Dr Beelitz to the *Sozialgericht* Kassel, dated 3.9.1973: *Herr* T. Beelitz Archiv:

223 Rudolf Heiß statement, dated 8.3.1967; Akt.-Zeichen 13 Js 9 a-e/66, pp.101-109: *StA* Munich.

224 Horst Voigt, *Die 'Verlor'nen Haufen; Sondertruppen zur Frontbewährung im 2. Weltkrieg, Teil VIII*, pp. 448-455; Pantenius, *The Last Battle of the Eastern Front*, pp.190-191, 195-207.

225 Born in Mariampol/Lithuania on 20 July 1919, *Uscha.* Waldemar Schinck had served with the *Waffen*-SS since 1941 and had seen service with the supply company of the *Kommandostab* RF-SS. Assigned to the SS-*Gebirgs-Ersatz-Bataillon* 7 *Prinz Eugen*, he then undertook medical orderly training at the SS-*Sanitätsabteilung* at Gießen in July 1943. Completing the course, Schinck was then declared fit for combat. Assigned to the SS-*Truppenübungsplatz* Westpreußen.Die Masse der Angehörigen waren straffällig gewordene Militärangehörige der Waffen SS und Polizei. Westpreußen in February 1944, Schinck then deployed with Schneeberger's company and his family believe that he was captured by Red Army troops during the battle near Dirschau–Pelpin and held as a prisoner of war in the Vortkuta camp: HIAG report, dated 18.12.1959: BA NS 756/283a.

226 Martin Hoffmann: BA NS 756/283a.

227 John Erickson, *the Road to Berlin: Stalin's War with Germany Vol. 2*, Cassell Military Paperbacks 2003, p. 523. For further details see Guderian, '*Panzer Leader…*' op cit.; p. 392.

228 M. Sikorska, *W-Gdansku-karano-SS-Mannow*.

229 Peter Piotrowski, *Historia.History, Zapomniany obóz w Gdańsku Maćkowych Forgotten camp in Gdansk Maćkowych*, Classifieds G.W (Gdańsk), No. 97, edition *of GDG 25/04/2003ŚLEDŹ TE PARTIES*, p. 10 (with assistance of the journalist Werner Hertz).

230 M. Sikorska, *W-Gdansku-karano-SS-Mannow*.

3.11 Strafvollzugslager der SS und Polizei Danzig-Matzkau, Zweiglager Ludwigsfelde

231 NARA BDC, SSO Personalakte Erich Albert. For further details see letter *Reichsf*ührer to *Ogruf.* Pohl dated 1.1.1943: BA NS 7/365, p. 549 & 54.

232 Letter *HA* SS-*Gericht* to the SS-*Richter beim* RF-SS, dated 25.2.1943: BA NS 756/283a.

233 Stephen Jegielka, *Das Kz Außenglager Genshagen*, p. 40.

234 J. Werner, *Kreigswirtschaft und Zwangsarbeit bei BMW*.

235 Writing to his Cottbus home in 1943, the convict Herbert Gullarch was assigned to the Ludwigsfeld 4. *Kompanie*: Klausch, '*Antifaschisten…*' op cit.; p. 95.
The director of Daimler-Benz, *Herr* Werner Romstedt was personally known to *Gruf.* Berger from 1941. For more details of the SS plot to remove Jewish board members from the company see Neil Gregor, *Daimler Benz in the Third Reich*, Yale University Press 1998, p. 172.

236 Vincenz Oertle, "*Sollte ich aus Russland nicht zurückkehren…". Schweizer Freiwillige an deutscher Seite 1939-1945: Eine Quellensuche*, Thesis 1997, p. 228.

237 Julius Rogers (b. 3.8.1914): Message Kew TNA, HW 16/40, Nr 14, dated 25.2.1944.

238 NARA BDC, SSO Personalakte Gunther Goerke. SS-*Mann* Goerke had trained at the SS-*Nachrichten-Ersatz-Bataillon* (Nuremberg).

239 Herbert Loewe, (b. 16.7.1925): Source; Kew HW 16/40, dated 27.4.1944

240 NARA BDC, SSO Personalakte Erich Albert / Otto Langer

241 Message TNA, HW 16/41, dated 22.7.1944.

242 Gregor, '*Daimler Benz…*' op cit.; pp. 218-219. For further details see Frederic Gümmer, *Die Rolle der Untertageverlagerung in der Deutschen Rüstungsproduktion 1943-1945*, Grin Verlag 2013.

243 Stephen Jegielka, *Das Kz Außenglager Genshagen*, Tectum—Der Wissenschaftsverlag 2011, p. 39. For further details see letter *Reichsf*ührer to *Gruf.* Pohl, dated Feb.1943: BA NS 7/365, p. 66.

244 NARA BDC, SSO Personalakte Helmut Bufe.

245 Jegielka, '*Das Kz Außenglager…*' op cit.; p. 39.

3.12 Strafvollzugslager der SS und Polizei Förrenbach

246 Nicole Czelhan, *The Camp Förrenbach*, Documentationsstätte Kz Hersbruck e.v 2006. See Joel E. Dimsdale, *Survivors, Victims and Perpetrators; Essays on the Nazi Holocaust*, Taylor & Francis 1980, pp. 259, 260.

247 Benz, '*Der Ort des Terrors…*' op cit.; p. 137 (Aussage Felix Marszalek, in; *StA* Nuremberg, *StA* beim Landgericht Nuremberg-Fürth 2637 Ia, p. 29 R f.).

248 Czelhan, op cit. For further details see Bauplan des Lagers Förrenbach vom 26. Juli 1944: Quelle Gemeindearchiv Happurg. For further reading see Bauten in Nürnberg: http://www.bauzeugen.de/hersbruck.htm

249 Message Kew TNA, HW 16/43, dated 27.3.1945. Neither *Ustuf.* Wilhelm Lippmann, (b. 3.10.1907 in Nordboegge, SS Nr. 235.030), or *Ustuf.* Wolfgang Lippmann, (b. 15.3.1920 in Mauthausen, SS Nr. 318.988) appear to have seen service in Förrenbach.

250 Conversation with *Herr* Dr Thomas Beelitz, dated 22.7.2014.

251 BA NS 7/6, p. 261 BI.28.

252 Message Kew TNA, HW 16/43, dated 4.2.1945.

253 *Meister Gendarme* Otto Kadner (b. 7.1.1903), *Meister Gendarme* Johan Hacker, (b. 9.4.1926) and finally Heinrich Kunstmann (b. 9.11.1909): Message Kew TNA, HW 16/43, Nr 5, dated 27.3.1945.

254 NARA BDC, SSO Personalakte Fritz Ringel. Ringel left Matzkau for Förrenbach prior to 10.1944.

255 Gerhard Faul, *Sklavenarbeiter für den Endsieg: KZ Hersbruck und das Rüstungsprojekt Dogger*, Hersbruck: Dokumentationsstätte KZ Hersbruck, ©2003. p. 78.

256 NARA BDC, SSO Personalakte Fritz Baumeister.

3.13 The Post-War Investigation

257 AR Z 47/1958 B 162/829, page 99: BA Ludwigsburg.

258 *Ibid*, p. 106 (AR-Z 47/58). See Dr Fritz Beelitz statement, dated 14.4.1959: B 162/829 BA Ludwigsburg.

259 *Ibid*: p. 106 (AR-Z 47/58).

260 *Ibid*: B 162/829, p. 111.

261 *Ibid.*

262 *Ibid*: B 162/829, p. 190-191.

263 *Ibid*: B 162/829.

264 *Ibid*: B 162/829, dated 18.1.1962 & 22.2.1962.

265 *Ibid*: B 162/829; Franz-Otto Hühn statement. *Hstuf.* Hans-Ulrich Pfensig, (b. 12.12.1906 in Hamburg, SS Nr. 50.358).

266 Witness statement Albert Müller to the LKA-NW Düsseldorf, dated 7.5.1962: 13 Js 9/66 /W (*StA* Munich); pp. 261-271: *StA* Munich.

267 *Ibid*, pp. 261-271.

268 *Ibid*, pp. 261-271.

269 *Ibid*, pp. 261-271.

270 *Ibid*, pp. 261-271.

271 B 162/829, dated 21.11.1963: BA Ludwigsburg.

272 *StA* Munich: 13 Js 9/66 /W., dated 11.1.1971: BA Ludwigsburg.

273 Letter dated 6.6.1966 & 2.8.1964: B 162/829 BA Ludwigsburg.

274 *Ibid*: (Az. 24 Js 3/66 (z)). According to Hühn, *Uscha.* Schulz, a native of Danzig, was aged 27-years old in the summer 1944. The non-commissioned officers identified with this name in Matzkau are *Uscha*. Helmut Schulz, (b. 19.6.1921) and *Uscha*. Otto Schulz, (b. 18.12.1921), who was deployed in Matzkau in Jul.1943 and transferred to the SS-*Panzergrenadier-Ersatz-Bataillon* 9 (Stralsund) on 28.10.1944.

275 Ibid: B 162/829 BA Ludwigsburg.

276 Dr Reinecke statement to the *StA* Munich, dated Munich 27.4.1965; 13 Js 9/66 /W; Landeskriminalamt Bavaria III a/SK, pp. 399-402: *StA* Munich:

277 *Ibid*, pp. 399-402.

278 *Ibid*, pp. 399-402.

279 *Ibid*, pp. 399-402.

280 B 162/829 BA Ludwigsburg.

281 *Ibid*, p. 164. Alfred Hubrig (b. 6.11.1924 in Dresden).

282 *Ibid*, p. 133 (Dr Beelitz Lebenslauf).

283 *Ibid*, p. 143.

284 *Ibid*, pp. 185-187.

285 *Ibid*, pp. 185-187.

286 *Ibid*, pp. 185-187.

287 *Ibid*, pp. 185-187.

288 *Ibid*, pp. 185-187.

289 *Ibid*, pp. 185-187.

290 Rudolf Heiß statement dated 8.3.1967: Akt.-Zeichen 13 Js 9 a-e/66, pp. 101-109: *StA* Munich.

291 *Ibid*, pp. 101-109.

292 *Ibid.*

293 *Ibid.*

294 *Ibid.*

295 *Ibid. Oscha.* N. Schulz was either *Uscha*. Helmut Schulz, (b. 19.6.1921), or less probably, *Uscha*. Otto Schulz. Recalling König, Rudolf Heiß was almost certainly referring to *Uscha.* Heinrich Köning, (b. 19.5.1911).

296 Friedrich Ringel statement, dated 13.8.1968: case file 13 Js 9/66 /W.: *StA* Munich.

297 Letter dated 28.2.1968: B 162/829, p. 203: BA Ludwigsburg.

298 Using the *Reichsführer* edict from 20.4.1944, concerning the judiciary's involvement with the SS-*Sonderbrigade Dirlewanger Ersatz-Bataillon* and probation at the front, the court found living former convicts to contact as witnesses. Amongst them was Dr Med. dent. Walter Zeppenfeld (b. 31.12.1901 in Gelsenkirchen, SS Nr. 256.727) was assigned to the *Stab* SS-*Sonderegiment Dirlewanger* in Apr.1944 and Dr Med. dent. Walter Escher (b. 18.7.1909 in Lengfeld/Odenwald,

SS Nr. 145.563) who had fought with the II. / SS-*Panzer* Rgt. in Apr.1944 and reported to the SS-*Sonderregiment* in August the same year. The investigators also identified three surviving inmates from the autumn 1944 Dirlewanger draft: Wilhelm Brinkmann (b. 13.5.1903 in Meinerzhagen), the former *Kriminalsekretär* Albert Richter (b. 24.10.1897 in Reudnitz/Greiz) who had been detained in Matzkau in early 1944 and finally, Nikolas Ellert, held in Matzkau during 1943-44. All five men were identified as potential witnesses in 1969: Letter Landgericht Munich II, dated 28.10.1968: Dr Beelitz statement, dated 14.4.1959: B 162/829, pp. 194-195: B 162/829 BA Ludwigsburg.

299 (As. S 13 Ja 9/66): B 162/829, p. 210: BA Ludwigsburg.

300 *Ibid*, pp. 209, 214-221 (Karl Hirsch).

301 *Ibid*, pp. 209, 214-221.

302 These were Willi Schwarz (b. Bremen) of the SS-*Standarte Brandenburg* and Willi Steinperl (b. Vienna). An SS man since 16 April 1938, Steinperl was executed on the orders of the SS- *und Polizei-Gericht* VII, Vienna. Hirsch claimed Schwarz was shot in Danzig-Matzkau and two barracks with 400 convicts witnessed his death: Ibid, pp. 209, 214-221.

303 The SS physician mentioned in Matzkau in 1942 was *Hstuf.* Frank Müller: Robert Jung statement, dated 20.9.1969; B 162/829, p. 244: BA Ludwigsburg.

304 *Ibid.*

305 The states prosecutor acknowledged that the defendants challenged Hühn's testimony, Baumgärtner claimed that during his tenure as commandant no executions had been carried out in Matzkau, Dr Beelitz, accepted that executions had taken place in Matzkau, but explained that these were capital punishments imposed by SS and *Polizei* courts as part of the SS and *Polizei* jurisdiction and asserted that the court judgments were always read to the condemned. Declaring that he had occasionally participated in the executions to monitor the legality of sentence enforcement, *Herr* Weiß accepted that Dr Beelitz had neither imposed a death sentence nor arbitrarily arranged a shooting in the prison. Observing that the defendants denied any involvement in the alleged killings of individual prisoners during 'drill' and remained adamant that no inmates had died during drill, *Herr* Weiß noted that they had all declared that no unworthy treatment of inmates and the punishments had been imposed on convicts for breaches of the camp regulations of a minor nature: *StA* Munich 13 Js 9/66 /W., dated 11.1.1971: BA Ludwigsburg.

306 *Ibid.*

307 *Ibid*: Amongst the witnesses asked to contribute to the investigation were the former SS Judges, Dr Reinecke and Horst Bender. Both expressed their certainty that no *Lagergericht* had taken place in the *Lager* Danzig-Matzkau and the legal jurisdiction was exclusively in the hands of the SS and *Polizei* courts.

310 *Ibid.*

311 *Ibid*: Writing on 25.7.1973, the Zentrale Stelle der Landesjustizverwaltungen in Ludwigsburg observed that three investigations had been conducted involving Matzkau. The first had been suspended, (203 AR 261/62 Z St = 13 J 9/66 *StA* Munich II against Dr Beelitz among others) and the second, the *StA* Berlin against Dr Beelitz had been suspended after the indicter had withdrawn his accusations. The testimony of the witness Hühn from 22.2.1962 had led to the introduction of a further investigation, which were also suspended when it was revealed that Hühn was not a reliable witness. The final investigation had been conducted by the *StA* Wiesbaden against the former Matzkau guard Elsner, (203 R 1120/67 ZSt = 7 1405/67 *StA* Wiesbaden against Elsner). Initiating the investigation on the basis of an anonymous accusation against Elsner, the Zentrale

Stelle observed that he had been been a member of the *Bewachungsmannschaft* at Matzkau from 1.1942-7.1942 and this courts process was suspended on 7.3.1968. The Zentrale Stelle noted that the complaint of former convict, Robert Jung (I 110 AR 50/70) cf. Bl 3) was also heard in the process 203. AR 261/62: B 162/829, p. 277: BA Ludwigsburg & I 110 AR 622/73, dated 25.7.1973: BA Ludwigsburg.

3.14 Gefängnis Debica

312 Message Kew TNA, HW 16/18.

2311313 Online article: http://szaropiotr.ubf.pl/viewpage.php?page_id=30 & http://pustkow.republika.pl/historia.html.

314 Letter SS-*Richter beim* RF-SS to the *HA* SS-*Gericht*, dated 1.2.1943: BA NS 7/365, pp. 49-52, 41 & 50.

315 Message Kew TNA, HW 16/22, dated 24.11.1942.

316 Message Kew TNA, HW 16/22, dated 15.12.1942. This message almost certainly refers to *Ustuf.* Dr Helmut Großnigg, (b.5.5.1912 in Wien). A Viennese *Rechtsanwalt* and SS-*Reservefährer* in 8.1943, he died in action with the SS-StuG-*Abteilung* 8 on 21.8.1943.

317 Message Kew TNA, HW 16/23, dated 14.1.1943.

318 Letter Początkowo zostali oni umieszczeni w jednej z hal "Lignozy" Po wybudowaniu kilku garaży na ringu 1, zostali tam przeniesieni.32SS-*Richter beim* RF-SS to Danzig-Matzkau, dated 30.9.1944: BA NS 7/365, p. 85.

3.15 SS-Aussenstelle Kolberg

319 Memorandum, dated 4.1945: BA NS 756/283a & MIRS.

3.16 Polizeigegfängnis -und Arbeitserziehungslager Kurtenhof

320 *Ostubaf.* Burmeister to the WVHA, dated 5.11.1942: BA NS 7/368, pp. 3-4, 1-2, 14 & 5.

321 Gerchäftsverteilungplan, dated 1.3.1941: BAP, R 58/840.

322 Letter SS-*Richter beim* RF-SS to the *HA* SS-*Gericht*: BA NS 7/368, pp. 7-8, 12 & 10.

323 Letter SS-*Richter beim* RF-SS to the *HA* SS-*Gericht*, dated 18.2.1943: BA NS 7/368, p. 13.

324 Letter *Stubaf.* Günther Burmeister to the RSHA, dated 29.3.1943; D.C. NARA Washington microfilm T-580, roll 214.

325 Andrej Angrick/Peter Klein, *Die Endlösung" in Riga: Ausbeutung und Vernichtung 1941-1944*, Wissenschaftliche Buchgesellschaft 2011, pp. 201, 254-255, 256-257 and 269.

326 BA WS 191/1916, p. 133.

327 *Reichsführer* undated edict; letter SS-*Richter beim* RF-SS to the RSHA, dated 7.9.1943: D.C. NARA Washington microfilm, T-580, roll 213.

328 Letter *HA* SS-*Gericht Amt* IIIb to the SS-*Richter beim* RF-SS (Dr Wehser), dated 17.11.1944: D.C. NARA Washington microfilm; T-580, roll 214.

329 Okupācijas muzeja in Riga: Hoover Institution Archives (USA, Stanford University).

330 Telegram *Hstuf.* Dr Zolly to the *HA* SS-*Gericht*, dated 30.9.1944: BA NS 7/365, p. 85. See *HA* SS-*Gericht Amt* IIIb to the SS-*Richter beim* RF-SS, dated 17.11.1944: NS 7/ 368, p. 26.

331 Seidler, '*Die Militärgerichtsbarkeit…*' op cit.; p. 27.

332 Authors correspondents with *Herr* Kurt Grawe, dated 5.6.2014.

3.17 SS-Strafgefanggenenlager Vught

333 Letter SS-*Richter beim* RF-SS to Danzig-Matzkau, dated 30.9.1944: BA NS 7/365, p. 85.

Chapter 4: SS-*Richter* and SS-*Beurkundungsführer*

1 NARA BDC, SSO Personalakte Horst Bender; letter from *HA* SS-*Gericht* chief to *HA* SS-*Gericht* Personal office, dated 6.6.1939.

2 NARA BDC, SSO Personalakte Wilhelm Meske.

3 NARA BDC, SSO Personalakte Richard Zentler/Walter Dieterle/Franz Sturmann.

4 Amongst these were Erich Albert, Edmund Baumgartner and Franz Sturmann.

4.1 Biographies

5 Undated document titled Übersicht, (15.2.1945): D.C. NARA microfilm publication T-580, roll 214.

6 NARA BDC, SSO Personalakte Erich Albert. See also NARA—Records of the Army Staff (Record Group 319) College park, Maryland 270/84/01/01-270/84/19/07 Investigative Records Repository (IRR) Personal Name Files, 1939-1976; XE004042, Erich Albert.

7 NARA BDC, SSO Personalakte Fritz Baumeister

8 NARA BDC, SSO Personalakte Edmund Baumgärtner. See B 162/829, p. 173 & 181: BA Ludwigsburg.

9 Dr Fritz Beelitz statement, dated 14.4.1959; B 162/829: BA Ludwigsburg.

10 NARA BDC, SSO Personalakte Dr Fritz Beelitz; Kew WO 208/684, dated 23.11.1943. See Dr Fritz Beelitz statement, dated 14.4.1959: BA Ludwigsburg; B 162/829, p. 133: BA Ludwigsburg.

11 NARA BDC, SSO Personalakte Gottfried Biedermann. See NARA—Records of the Army Staff (Record Group 319) Investigative Records Repository (IRR) Personal Name Files, 1939-1976 Gottfried Biedermann XE101203/664, (declassified on 24.4.2000). See Nordrhein-Westfalen 1005-G42 Nr. 649 Gottfried Biedermann.

12 NARA BDC, SSO Personalakte Walter Dieterle. See Signature: EL 902/4 Bü 2298; Walter Dieterle: BA Ludwigsburg.

13 NARA BDC, SSO Personalakte Max Dolles.

14 NARA BDC, SSO Personalakte Dr Leo Ernst.

15 NARA BDC, SSO Personalakte Synesius Hahn.

16 NARA BDC, SSO Personalakte Rudolf Heiß. See Rudolf Heiß statements, dated 2.3 & 14.3.1967, pp. 101, 6783-685, dated 5.8.1969: 13 JS 9 1-e/66; Spruchkammerakten K-668; Rudolf Heiß 21.1.1919: *StA* Munich.

17 NARA BDC, SSO Personalakte Theodor Janssen.

18 NARA BDC, SSO Personalakte Heinrich Köning.

19 NARA BDC, SSO Personalakte Artur Kretzschmar

20 NARA BDC, SSO Personalakte SS-Führer: Erich Laimgruber.

21 NARA BDC, SSO Personalakte Otto-Leo Langer. See Spruchkammerakte case Nr. D.Lg. XI/P/4210/47, Otto Langer: Protokoll dated 3.10.1947: Hessisches Hauptstaatsarchiv.

22 NARA BDC, SSO Personalakte Edmund Mansbach.

23 NARA BDC, SSO Personalakte Emil M*ä*rtins.

24 NARA BDC, SSO Personalakte Dr Hans-Georg Mayer; Michael Alberi, *Die Verfolgung und Vernichtung der Juden im Reichsgau Wartheland 1939-1945*, Wiesbaden 2006, p. 211 (quoting Elzbieta Kobierska-Mota, *Ekstradycja przestępców wojennych do Polski z czterech stref okupacyjnych Niemiec*, p. 160).

25 Detention report Alfred Mueller, (31 G.6 556 246): Kew Archive: Mill-Niesen; WO 309/1775 BAOR.

26 NARA BDC, SSO Personalakte Fritz Pölking.

27 NARA BDC, SSO Personalakte Josef Posch.

28 B 162/829, p. 179: BA Ludwigsburg.

29 NARA BDC, SSO Personalakte Fritz Ringel. See Fritz Ringel statements, dated 13.8.1968 & 5.8.1969, pp. 533-535, 683-685: 13 JS 9 1-e/66 *StA* Munich.

30 NARA BDC, SSO Personalakte Horst Sach. See Rudolf Heiß Akt.-Zeichen 13 Js 9 a-e/66, pp. 101-109: *StA* Munich.

31 Message Kew TNA, HW 16/43, dated 29.3.1945.

32 NARA BDC, SSO Personalakte Josef Schwaiger; p04160611_dated 1.6.2015.pdf Download: Josef Schwaiger: OÖ. Landesarchiv.

33 NARA BDC, SSO Personalakte Anton Sorg. See Liste des Kommandantur-Stabes Danzig-Matzkau, dated 4.2.1944: BA R70-Polen-355.

34 NARA BDC, SSO Personalakte Wilhelm Sparwasser. See document titled Stabkompanie des Strafvollzugslager Danzig-Matzkau, dated late 1944: BA R70-Polen-355.

35 NARA BDC, SSO Personalakte Franz Sturmann; Spruchkammerakten K1811 Sturmann, Franz * 5.10.1909: *StA* Munich.

36 NARA BDC, SSO Personalakte Alfred Vollmer. See document titled Stabkompanie des Strafvollzugslager Danzig-Matzkau, dated late 1944: BA R70-Polen-355.

37 NARA BDC, SSO Personalakte Erich Wagner.

38 NARA BDC, SSO Personalakte Heimo Wurm. See message Kew TNA, HW 16/22, dated 12.1.1943. See Lagerspruchkammer Signatur: SpKa K 2019 Wurm Heimo Geb. 8.5.1908.

39 Matzkau senior NCO list: BA R70-Polen-355, pp. 1 -23.

Chapter 5. Probation Units of the SS and *Polizei*

1 Erlass des Führer des Oberbefehlshaber Führerhauptquartier der Wehrmacht 21.12.1940.

5.1 Front Probation Procedure

2 *Ibid*, p. 18.

3 Seidler, '*Die Militärgerichtsbarkeit…*' op cit.; p. 67.

4 Hans-Peter Klausch, *Die Bewährungstruppe 500*, Edition Temmen 1995, p. 19.

5 *Gnadenordnung für die Wehrmacht*: (W Gn O): vom 1.7.1938; *HA* SS-*Gericht* edict dated 17.10.1939—NSD 41/39.

6 Rudolf Absolon, *Die Wehrmacht im Dritten Reich: 19.12.1941 bis 9.5.1945*, Boldt Verlag 1969, p. 574.

7 Klausch, '*Die Bewährungstruppe…*' op cit.; p.164.

8 For further details concerning probation decrees see Rudolf Absolon, *Die Wehrmacht im Dritten Reich*, Boldt Verlag 1969.

9 David Raub Snyder, Scott C. Patchan—*Sex Crimes under the Wehrmacht*, University of Nebraska Press 2007, pp. 67-78.

10 Padfield, '*Himmler…*' op cit.; p. 14. See Klausch, '*Antifaschisten…*' ob cit.; pp. 122-131.

11 *Der Chef des HA* SS-*Gericht* edict, dated 41942: D.C. NARA Washington microfilm; T-580, roll 213; *Reichsführer* edict A II (3) IIIb 320/2, dated 12.11.1941: BA NS 7/365, p. 69.

12 Überstellung SS-und Polizeigerichtlich verurteiler zur Bewahrungseinheit 'VH', dated 14.6.1941: BA NS 756/283a. See *HA* SS-*Gericht* edict published 17.10.1939: NSD 41/39. See letter *Reichsführer* to the SS-FHA, dated 31.10.1941: BA NS 7/378, p.1.

5.2 Verlorenen Haufen

13 NARA BDC, SSO Personalakte Dr Leo Ernst; Totenkopf daily orders: BA RS 3 3/17.

14 Totenkopf Nachschub daily order Nr. 56, dated 29.12.1939: BA RS 3 3/27, p.121.

15 A judge of the *HA* SS-*Gericht* would describe the term *Verlorenen Haufen* a 'false concept and an SS lie' on the grounds that service in the probation unit led to many deaths or mutilations in enemy minefields: For further details see letter *HA* SS-*Gericht*, dated 25.3.1942: BA NS 7/385, p. 1.

16 *Ostuf.* Paul Monich (b. 26.3.1913 in Nuremberg, SS Nr. 120.904). Ending the war with the rank of *Stubaf.*, Monich was killed in action at Tun on 18.8.1944 while leading the SS-*Pionier-Abteilung* 9.

17 SS-*Mann* Bruno Bissa, of the *Stab.* / I. / SS-*T.Inf.*Rgt. 3 earned himself a ten days *Geschäfte Arrest* in Jan. 1940 for extinguishing a cigarette in a petrol canister and SS-*Mann* Werner Hasenohr of the 2.gr.Kw.Kol was suspended from the SS for six months. For shaming the SS in the eyes of the *Wehrmacht* the following men of the 6. / SS-*T.Inf.*Rgt. 2 joined the *Sonderkommando* on 6.–7.2.1940: SS-*Mann* d.R. Franz Springer and SS-*Mann* Willi Fletzke were punished with a fourteen days *Geschäfte Arrest*, SS-*Mann* Ludwig Tintner, (b. 10.3.1921) of the 9. Kl. Kw. Kol was punished with an eighteen months *Gefängnis* sentence and expelled from the SS for swearing at an NCO. *Rttf.* Heinz Staub of the 7. / SS-*T.Inf.*Rgt. 3 received an eighteen months *Gefängnis* sentence, *Rttf.* E. Kröhler, *Sturmann* H. Lenger and *Anwärter* G. Engels from the 13. / SS-*T.Inf.*Rgt. 3 were all held responsible for a fire that broke out in their garage and was punished with a three days *geschäfte Arrest*. *Scha.* H. Eckert of the divisional motorcycle section was spared a *Gefängnis* sentence, but handed a five days *geschäfte Arrest*. SS-*Mann* d.R. Edmund Rabe of the light pioneer column was judged guilty of embezzlement, was expelled from the SS and punished with a year's *Gefängnis*. *Anwärter* Stefan Grzembski of the 14. / SS-*T.Inf.*Rgt. 3 was punished with a three weeks *Geschäfte Arrest*. *Scha.* Karst and SS-*Uscha.* Wolf of the 3. / SS-*T.Pi.Abt.* was punished with three weeks and six days *Geschäfte Arrest* for drunkenness and the theft of a sausage. *Rttf.* Karl Kaltner of the *Stab* III. / SS-*T.Inf.*Rgt. 1 was punished with a two weeks *Geschäfte Arrest* for reporting six hours late from leave and drunkenness: Totenkopf daily order Nr. 30, dated 6.2.1940: BA RS 3 3/17, p. 289. Totenkopf daily order, dated 27.1.1940: BA RS 3 3/17, p. 278. Totenkopf daily order, dated 30.1.1940: BA RS 3 3/17, p. 281.

18 Stealing from the *Wehrmacht* Neustadt medical unit, *Scha.* Arno Wolf was sentenced to a month's *Gefängnis* and SS-*Mann d. R.* Walter Weitzenmann to two months *Gefängnis*, (both suspended in favour of service in the *Sonderkommando*). A few days later *Strm.* Mayrhofer of the 12. / SS-*T.Inf.* Rgt. 2 was judged guilty of an unknown offence, was punished with a five months *Gefängnis* and

expelled from the SS on 13.2.1940. Myerhofer's sentence was suspended and he was sent to the *Sonderkommando*: *Totenkopf* daily orders Nr. 33, dated 9.2.1940: BA RS 3 3/17, p. 294.

19 As the SSTK trained in the wintery terrain of Baden-Württemberg *Anwärter* Lothar Miesler of the 9. / SS-*T.Inf.*Rgt. 3 were judged guilty of stealing half a pound of butter and 50 cigarettes from an SS NCO and punished with three months *Gefängnis* and expulsion from the SS. Receiving a similar sentence for military disobedience, *Rttf.* Otto Petereit of the 1. SS-*T.Inf.*Rgt. 2 and Miesler joined the *Sonderkommando* on 17.2.1940. Punished with a four months *Gefängnis* for swindling, *Anwärter* Siegfried Hohlfeld of the 2. / *Totenkopf* SS-*Panzerabwehrabteilung* was discharged from the SS and then posted to the *Sonderkommando* in 5.1940: Totenkopf daily orders Nr. 41, dated 17.2.1940: BA RS 3 3/17, p. 310; Totenkopf daily orders Nr. 51, dated 1.3.1940: BA RS 3 3/17, p. 331.

20 NARA BDC, SSO Personalakte Rudiger v.Bodungen; letter dated 22.12.1939.

21 *Ibid*:

22 *Ibid*:

23 Beutel studied pharmacy, economics and art history at the University of Leipzig and passing his state examinations was then employed as a chemist in Chemnitz. A councilman for the city of Chemnitz from 1935 to 1936, he was unsuccessful in his attempts to enter the *Reichstag* as a representative in 1938. A member of the *Führungskreises des* NS *Altherrenbundes der Deutschen Studenten* from 5 May 1938. Beutel was the SD-*Oberabschnittsführer* for Sachsen when he was thought to have led a death squad during the so-called Röhm-Putsch in 1934. Denounced for verbally abusing the Chemnitz police and for drunkenness in the Chemnitz SD officer club, (he had attempted to pull the table cloth from a table laden with beer glasses), the *Reichsführer* commanded the initiation of a disciplinary process against him. Adamant that his behaviour was correct and proper for an officer, Beutel refused to apologise and as a consequence of his attitude, Himmler ordered his transfer to the SD-*Abschnitt* III (Chemnitz) in October 1932. Prewar, Beutel served in a variety of SS posts: SD-*Abschnitt* III (Chemnitz) until 10.1.1934, *Stellvertretenden Reichsapothekerführer* in 1933, salaried officer of the SD-*Hauptamt* 10.1.1934-23.10.1939 and the SD-*Oberabschnittsführer* Sachsen in the summer 1934. Beutel led the SD-*Oberabschnitt Süd* (Munich) 1.1.1935.-1.10.1936, he led the *Stapoleitstelle* Munich 1936–20.4.1937 and was the *Inspekteur der SiPo und des* SD Bavaria (Munich/ Nuremberg) 15.12.1937–8.1939. He became the *Stellvertretenden Abteilungsleiters für den Bereich Polizei und eines Referenten in beim Bayerischen Staatsministerium des Innern* in1938.

Assigned to a combat unit in 1944, Beutel was wounded during the fighting in Hungary and captured by Red Army forces in Berlin in 1945, he remained in Soviet captivity until October 1955. Settling in West Berlin, Beutel worked as an *Apotheker*. Although the Berlin public prosecutor was aware of his wartime activities, the former SD officer remained untroubled by the authorities, (his name was recorded in documents concerning the events in Bromberg and had been mentioned during the Nuremberg process). The part he played in the suppression and murder of Poles in 1939 came into sharp focus during the Ulm *Einsatzgruppe* trial in 1957/58. The accounts of his wartime activities published in national newspapers, the Berlin judiciary came under intense pressure to investigate him. Undertaking a preliminary investigation in 1960, the court spent the next five years examining allegations and gathering witness statements. Taken into custody on 20 May 1965, Beutel's guilt was ascertained and the tribunal judged him guilty of the charges on 29 May 1965. His appeal before the *Landgericht* Berlin cited a lack of evidence and the court dismissed all charges against him on 26 March 1971. Dr Beutel died in Berlin-Steglitz on 16.5.1986: NARA BDC, SSO Personalakte Dr Lothar Beutel.

For further details see: http://verwaltungshandbuch.bayerische-landesbibliothek-online.de/beutel-lothar. In his post-war interrogation, Dr Johannes Hermann Müller (b. 30.8.1895 in Gotha) reported that Dr Beutel and his adjutant were punished for plundering in Warsaw: IFZ Munich 948/56, p. 4.

24 *Führer* edict dated 18.4.1940, (signed by A. Hitler/H. Himmler and Dr Lammers): D.C. NARA Washington microfilm, T-580, 213.

25 Seidler, '*Die Militärgerichtsbarkeit…*' op cit.; p. 223.

26 Sydnor, '*Soldiers…*' op cit.; pp. 59, 97–99.

27 Joining the *Sonderkommando* at this time was *Anwärter* Schwann of the 14. / SS-*T. Inf.*Rgt. 3. *Ausgesloßen aus* SS on 13.6.1940 for committing a paragraph § 175 offence, Schwann's prison sentence was subsequently set aside and he joined the 3. *Zug*/ 4. / SS-*T.Pi.Abt.* Convicted of assaulting an NCO, *Rttf.* Martin Breiter, (b. 12.1.1914) of the 1. / SS-*T.Inf.*Rgt. 1 was degraded and *ausgesloßen aus* SS: Totenkopf Nachschub daily order Nr. 104, dated 1.7.1940: BA RS 3 3/27; p. 262; Totenkopf Nachschub daily order 102, dated 13.6.1940: BA RS 3 3/27, p. 259.

28 Totenkopf Nachschub daily order 104, dated 1.7.1940: BA RS 3 3/27, p. 262.

29 Seidler, '*Die Militärgerichtsbarkeit…*' op cit.; p. 234.

30 Letter SS-*Richter beim* RF-SS, dated 21.8.1940: BA NS 7/384.

31 NARA 75/615, 616, Tgb Nr A/35/52/40. *Stubaf.* Dr Brandt of the *Persönlicher Stab* RF-SS forwarded a letter from the *Kommando der Waffen*-SS, dated 19.8.1940 to the SS-*Richter beim* RF-SS, on 30.8.1940, which contained a report about the probationers serving in the SS-*Totenkopfdivision*: D.C NARA Washington microfilm, T-580, roll 214.

32 The *Sonderkommando* probationers sent to the KL Sachsenhausen in 1940 were: Martin Breiter (b. 12.12.1914), Bruno Koslowski (b. 28.6.1916), Rudolf Meyer (b. 4.4.1913), Fritz Leibner (b. 14.3.1906), Otto Müller, (b. 10.11.1912), Hans Öllerich (b. 7.10.1916), Gerhard Schwann (b. 19.6.1913), Harold Tschernich (b. 3.4.1921), Wilhelm Wagerer (b. 11.7.1920) and Karl Weiss (b. 25.3.1920): Totenkopf Nachschub daily order Nr. 132 dated 15.8.1940: BA RS 3 3/27, p. 318.

33 SS-*Totenkopfdivision* HQ; activity report dated 3.3.1941: BA RS 3-3 3/28.

5.3 Verlorenen Haufen SS-Pionier-Abteilung

34 The Führer & Oberbefehlshaber Führerhauptquartier der Wehrmacht, dated 21.12.1940.

35 Letter *Stubaf.* Kegel to SS-*Richter beim* RF-SS, dated 11.3.1941: D.C. NARA microfilm publication T-580, roll 212.

36 *HA* SS-*Gericht Amt* III, undated leaflet titled; 'Transition of Abteilung Gefängnis from SS-Straflager Dachau to the St. V. L. d. SS-u. Pol. Danzig-Matzkau': BA NS 7/378, p. 14.

37 NARA BDC, SSO Personalakte Erich Bruns; letter SS-FHA to *Persönlicher Stab* RF-SS dated 14.5.1941.19.Febr.

38 Seidler, '*Die Militärgerichtsbarkeit…*' op cit.; p. 234. See letter chief judge of the SS and *Polizei* Court VIII, Prague. *Stubaf.* Burmeister reported that two men of this battalion were prosecuted for offences on 6.1.1941: Narodi Archiv 109-6155/69.

39 NARA BDC, SSO Personalakte Karl Schäfer.

40 Letter RFSS to the *HA* SS-*Gericht*, dated 30.5.1941: BA NS 7/378, p. 28.

41 NARA BDC, SSO Personalakte Otto Andresen. *Ustuf.* Hans-Günther Schweigert (b. 22.10.1919 in Hohensalza, SS Nr. 400.160). *Hstuf.* Rudolf Enselling (b. 30.8.1914 in Karlsruhe, SS Nr. 237.303).

42 NARA BDC, SSO Personalakte Willy Schumann. SS-Division *Reich* Einsatz Russland;

Verleihungsliste des SS-Pionier-Bataillone über die Verliehung von 13 *Eisernen Kreuzen* I. *Klasse*. Members of the V.H. awarded this decoration was *Oscha.* Willy Schumann (b. 19.2.1915 in Dresden), *Uscha.* Kurt Matterne (b. 21.9.1920 in Hirschberg), *Rttf.* Heinz Tornaw (b. 10.10.1919 in Radwitsch) and *Rttf.* Heinz Kretschmar (b. 9.8.1918 in Chemnitz).

43 Überstellung SS-und Polizeigerichtlich verurteiler zur Bewahrungseinheit 'VH', dated 14.6.1941: BA NS 756/283a.

44 Letter SS-FHA to all units, dated 4.8.1941: D.C. NARA Washington Microfilm, T-580, roll 213.

45 Letter *HA* SS-*Gericht, Amt* III titled 'Conscription of SS and Police Court Convicts', dated 16.8.1941: BA NS 7/384. See *HA* SS-*Gericht Brieftagbuch*: Wiener Institutes NSDAP archive.

46 Letter SS-*Richter beim* RF-SS to the *Dienststelle FPNr.* 21.867D: D.C. NARA Washington Microfilm, T-580, roll 213.

47 NARA BDC, SSO Personalakte Erich Bruns.

48 Letter SS-*Richter beim* RF-SS to the *HA* SS-*Gericht* IIIb 365/2, dated 14.6.1941; letter RSHA chief to the *Chef des HA* SS-*Gericht* dated 17.6.1941: NARA BDC, SSO Personalakte Eric Bruns. General Heydrich inquired after SS-*Mann* Bruns welfare when he was punished with a term of eighteen months prison.

49 Hamburg 14 1 Js 534/1960, p. 60. For further details see Mark C. Yerger, *Allgemeine SS: Commands, Units and Leaders of the General SS*, Schiffer Military History 2004, p. 124.

50 Letter *der Reichsführer-SS und der Chef der Deutschen Polizei im Reichministerium des Innern*, dated 29.4.1940: Authors collection.

51 Letter RFSS to *HA* SS-*Gericht*, dated 30.9.1941: D.C. NARA Washington microfilm, T-580, roll 213.

52 Letter *HA* SS-*Gericht Amt* IIIa, (*Ustuf.* Meder) to the SS-*Richter beim* RF-SS, dated 12.9.1941: D.C NARA Washington Microfilm, T-580, roll 214.

53 Letter SS-*Richter beim* RF-SS to the *HA* SS-*Gericht*, dated 24.10.1941: D.C. NARA Washington Microfilm, T-580, roll 214.

54 Clemency case Max Weber *HA* SS-*Gericht* letter to SS-FHA, dated 10.11.1941: D.C. NARA Washington microfilm, T-580, roll 213.

55 Letter SS-FHA *Abt.* III to the *HA* SS-*Gericht Amt* III, dated 7.1.1942: D.C. NARA Washington microfilm, T-580, roll 213.

56 Letter *HA* SS-*Gericht Amt* III to the SS-Division *Reich* field court, dated 19.1.1942: D.C. NARA Washington microfilm, T-580, roll 213.

57 NARA BDC, SSO Personalakte Otto Andresen.

58 Letter *Persönlicher Stab* RF-SS to the *HA* SS-*Gericht*, dated 17.11.1941; letter SS-*Richter beim* RF-SS (Dr Wehser) to the *HA* SS-*Gericht*, dated 12.3.1942; letter *Stubaf.* Günther Burmeister to the SS-*Richter beim* RF-SS, dated 26.3.1942: D.C. NARA Washington microfilm, T-580, roll 213.

59 Letter SS-*Richter beim* RF-SS to the *HA* SS-*Gericht Amt* III, dated 10.1.1942: D.C. NARA Washington microfilm, T-580, roll 213.

60 NARA BDC, SSO Personalakte Paul Friedrich Lindner.

61 Message Kew TNA, HW 16/21, dated 15.11.1942.

62 Message Kew HW 16/19, dated 4.6.1942; message Kew HW 16/21, dated 20.8.1942/1.10.1942; message Kew HW 16/36, dated 10.1942.

63 Message Kew TNA, HW 16/18, dated 30.5.1942.

64 NARA BDC, SSO Personalakte Paul Friedrich Lindner. His co-defendants were; *Scha.* d.R.

August Schneider (b. 8.4.1909 in Rottweil am Neckar), *Rttf.* d.R. Willy Schwarten (b. 28.6.1905 in Ahrensburg), *Rttf.* d.R. Walter Möller (b. 3.6.1921 in Neumünster), *Uscha. d.R.* Alfred Münch (b. 3.6.1921 in Ulm a. d. Donau), *Uscha.* d.R. Kurt-Bernhard Nikolai Tyschen (b. 10.2.1912 in Flensburg), the brother of *Ostubaf.* Christian Tyschen, the Knights Cross winner, *Uscha.* d.R. Jakob Peskoller (b. 3.8.1917 in Au-Hallertau), *Rttf.* d.R. Emil Brüne (b. 5.4.1910 in Kassel), *Rttf.* d.R. Hermann Heinrich Paul Schulze (b. 26.2.1925 in Hovedissen/Lippe), *Uscha.* d.R. Karl-Heinz Trübert (b. 1.3.1922 in Hagen/Westf.), *Scha.* Josef Miller (b. 9.4.1918 in Dietramszell), *Rttf.* d.R. Gerhard Göhring (b. 15.8.1909 in Strehlen/Schles.) and *Strm.* d.R. Rudolf Harms (b. 28.9.1912 in Hamburg).

65 Central registry of war criminals and security suspects part 1 & 2: Kew WO 309/1704, (188411) dated 3.1947.

66 Letter *Hstuf.* Rudolf Enseling to Christian Rudolf, dated 21.8.1941; letter *HA* SS-*Gericht Amt* III (*Ustuf.* Meder), dated 9.9.1941: D.C. NARA Washington archive, T-580, roll 213.

67 NARA BDC, SSO Personalakte Markus Habben.

68 Letter SS-*Richter beim* RF-SS dated 12.8.1942: BA NS 7/379, p. 11.

69 Letter *HA* SS-*Gericht*, dated 8.9.1941: Archiv Wolfgang Vopersal. See letters between the RFSS *Persönlicher Stab*, the *HA* SS-*Gericht* and SS-*Richter beim* RF-SS (Dr Wehser) to *Frau* Irma Koch/ Günther Burmeister to the SS-*Richter beim* RF-SS, dated between 17.11.1941-26.3.1942: D.C. NARA Washington microfilm, T-580, roll 213.

5.4 Non-'Verlorenen Haufen' Front Probation

70 NARA BDC, SSO Personalakte Artur Grathwol.

71 NARA BDC, SSO Personalakte Hubert Derda.

72 Born in Berlin-Spandau on 12.1.1904, Bernard Fischer-Schweder joined the Nazi Party on 28.8.1925 and the Allgemeine-SS on 15.8.1941. A member of the *Freikorps Fürstner* in 1921 and the Black *Reichswehr* in 1923, he marched with the SA from 29.8.1925, obtained the rank of SA-*Oberführer* in 1934 and joined the *Polizei* in 1932 (*Beamter*). Arrested by the *Gestapo* during the so-called Röhm Putsch, he was detained in the dreaded KL Columbia Haus and Lichtenberg until 21.9.1934. Released when no evidence surfaced of his involvement in the 'plot', Fischer-Schweder then deployed with the Breslau *Gestapo* until 1940. Posted to the *Polizeipräsidium* Memel, he became its *Polizeipräsident* in Jan.1941. Ordered to provide a cordon around the Lithuanian town of Garsden on 24.6.1941, Fischer-Schweder, on his own recognisance, instructed *Major der Polizei* Günther and ten or twelve of his men to enter the village to execute around 100 Jews. In the wake of this mass murder, Fischer-Schweder was then involved in the murder of the Tilsit Jewish community. Assigned to the HSSPF *Russland-Süd* from 22.10.1942 (R.D.A. 10.10.1942), he was the SSPF *Rostow* until dismissed from this post for drunkenness.

Held in captivity by US forces near Linz for six weeks, Fischer-Schweder was interned in Bavaria, changed his name and birthdate to avoid prosecution for war crimes. Attending his *Spruchkammer* at Bad Neustadt/Saale on 5.3.1946, the tribunal discharged him without penalty. For much of the next four years he worked as a labourer, a clerk and salesman in Bad Neustadt. Working as a vacuum salesman in Stuttgart from Jan.1952, the amendment to article 131 of the Basic Law in 1951 enabled him to apply for civil service posts using both his real and imaginary names. Employed by the state from 18.1.1954, he was the director of an Ulm camp until denounced in Jun.1954. The Württemberg authorities then examined his past with greater alacrity and terminated his employment on 13 April

1955. The state failing to find him alternative employment, Fischer-Schweder sought redress in court for wrongful dismissal on 18 April 1955. Rejecting his plea, the employment tribunal burdened him with the 2,000 *Reichsmark* costs of the process.

The publicity surrounding the case resulted in the Stuttgart police passing a dossier of evidence to the Ulm prosecutor on 13.6.1955 which contained accusations by Fischer-Schweder's former secretary that he had committed war-crimes in Memel. However, the Ulm prosecutor was unsuccessful in his attempts to prove Fischer-Schweder's complicity in the mass murders, but convinced of his involvement in mass shootings at Garsden, Krottingen and Polangen, he questioned the former SS officer again on 2.5.1956. Admitting knowledge of the shootings, Fischer-Schweder claimed they had been carried out against partisans. Arrested the following day, his trial was undertaken by the *Landgericht* Ulm for his complicity in the murder of the Jews of Memel on 5.7.1957. Judged guilty of accessory to the murder of nearly 4,000 people on 29.8.1958, the court punished Fischer-Schweder with a ten years' term of prison and he died in detention during Nov.1960: NARA BDC, SSO Personalakte Bernard Fischer-Schweder.

73 NARA BDC, SSO Personalakte Erich Schulze.

74 SS-*Pionier-Ausbildung- und Ersatz-Bataillon* 1 to the SS-FHA IIa II W I – Abt. 1, dated 15.5.1944: NARA BDC, SSO Personalakte Friedrich Maletta;

75 NARA BDC, SSO Personalakte Harry Holtschak; letter from *Gericht der Dienstelle* Nederland Brigade FPNr. 57.720, dated 7.3.1944.

76 Letter from *HA* SS-*Gericht* to *Stubaf.* Dr Wehser: NARA BDC, SSO Personalakte Peteris Miervaldis Ziedins;

5.5 12 November 1941 Decree

77 Letter SS-FHA to *HA* SS-*Gericht*, *Amt* IIIb, dated 31.10.1941: BA NS 7/378, p. 15.

78 Edict collection, the *HA* SS-*Gericht*, published 17.10.1939: NSD 41/39; letter *Reichsführer* to the SS-FHA, dated 31.10.1941: BA NS 7/378; p. 1.

79 *HA* SS-*Gericht* edict, dated 12.11.1941: BA NS7/ 378, p. 1-13.

80 *Ibid.*

81 *Ibid.*

82 *Ibid.*

83 BA WS 191/1916, p. 133.

84 Letter *HA* SS-*Gericht Amt* III to the SS-*Richter beim* RF-SS, dated 25.2.1943.

85 NARA 75/615, 616, Tgb Nr A/35/52/40; *HA* SS-*Gericht* edict, dated 12.11.1941: BA NS7/ 378, pp. 1-13.

86 The interrogation of P. W, (b. 1902, Oberschwarzbrunn/Sud.): Kew National Archive; WO 208/3616.

87 *HA* SS-*Gericht* edict, dated 12.11.1941: BA NS7/ 378, pp. 1-13. See letter *Stubaf.* Günther Burmeister to the SS-*Richter beim* RF-SS, dated 25.2.1943: BA NS 7/365, p. 69.

88 *Oberf.* Dr Günther Reinecke to the SS-*Richter beim* RF-SS, dated 12.11.1941: BA NS 7/378, p. 29 & 36.

89 Letter *Kanzlei des Führers der* NSDAP and *HA* SS-*Gericht*, SS-*Rechtamt*, dated 11.1941: D.C. NARA microfilm publication T-580, roll 213.

90 Letter *Chef des HA* SS-*Gericht*, *HA* SS-*Gericht* IIIb 320/6, dated 22.9.1942: BA NS 756/283a, p. 156. See letter SS-FHA to all units, dated 4.8.1941; letter SS-*Richter beim* RF-SS to the SS-*Standarte Deutschland*: D.C. NARA Washington Microfilm; T-580, roll 213.

5.6 Clemency and Rehabilitation Edicts

91 *Führer* edicts, dated 26.1.1942, 21.3.1942 & 17.4.1942; letter *Stubaf.* Günther Burmeister to the SS-*Richter beim* RF-SS, dated 27.3.1942: D.C. NARA Washington microfilm, T-580, roll 213.

92 *Chef HA* SS-*Gericht* edict, dated 4.1942: D.C. NARA Washington microfilm; T-580, roll 213.

93 Letter *HA* SS-*Gericht Amt* III to the SS-*Richter beim* RF-SS, dated 22.12.1944: D.C. NARA Washington microfilm, T-580, roll 213.

94 *HA* SS-*Gericht* edict, dated 4.1942: D.C. NARA Washington microfilm: T-580, roll 213.

95 Letter *HA* SS-*Gericht* to the SS-*Richter beim* RF-SS, dated 1.2.1943 to *Reichsf*ührer-SS: BA NS 7/365, p. 46.

96 Seidler, '*Die Militärgerichtsbarkeit…*' op cit.; pp. 245-248.

97 Sammlung von Erlassen des *HA* SS-*Gericht*, Bd. 3, Jan.-Jul. 1942: BANS 7/4; Sammlung von Erlassen des *HA* SS-*Gericht*, Bd. 4, Jul.-Dec. 1942; Sammlung von Erlassen des *HA* SS-*Gericht*, Bd. 5, 1943-1945: BA NS 7/6.

98 The *Führer* and Head of the Armed Forces, Berlin, dated 2.4.1942: BA NS 7/378, p. 31. See *Führer* edict dated 2.4.1942; letter Martin Bormann to all party offices, dated 24.6.1942: D.C. NARA microfilm publication T-580, roll 212. See letter *Stubaf.* Günther Burmeister to the SS-*Richter beim* RF-SS, dated 25.2.1942: BA NS 7/365, p. 69.

99 Letter *Chef HA* SS-*Gericht* to the SS-*Richter beim* RF-SS, dated 3.4.1942: D.C. NARA Washington microfilm, T-580, roll 213.

100 *Ogruf.* Scharfe edict, dated April 1942: D.C. NARA Washington microfilm; T-580, roll 213; *Reichsführer* edict A II (3) IIIb 320/2, dated 12.11.1941: BA NS 7/365, p. 69.

101 *Führer* edict, dated 26.1.1942 & 21.3.1942 & 17.4.1942; letter *Stubaf.* Günther Burmeister to the SS-*Richter beim* RF-SS, dated 27.3.1942: D.C. NARA Washington microfilm, T-580, roll 213.

102 Letter *Chef HA* SS-*Gericht* to the SS-*Richter beim* RF-SS, dated 3.4.1942: D.C. NARA Washington microfilm, T-580, roll 213.

103 Letter *Stubaf.* Dr Hans Braußе, dated 2.4.1942: D.C. NARA Washington microfilm; T-580, roll 213.

104 SS-*Richter beim* RF-SS memorandum, dated 11.5.1942: BA NS 7/378, p. 35.

105 *Verordnungsblatt der Waffen*-SS, dated 15.5.1942: D.C. NARA microfilm archive T-175, Roll 178/79.

106 SS-*Richter beim* RF-SS memorandum (Dr Wehser), dated 1.6.1942; letter *HA* SS-*Gericht Amt* III to the SS-*Richter beim* RF-SS, dated 22.6.1943; *Führer* edict concerning the exercising of rights clemency with regard to officials and former officials, dated 2.10.1939; letter *Stubaf.* Günther Burmeister to the *HA* SS-*Gericht*, dated 16.6.1943; SS-*Richter beim* RF-SS memorandum (Gießelmann), dated 19.7.1943; letter *Hstuf.* Gießelmann to *Major* Bourier, dated 20.7.1943; SS-*Richter beim* RF-SS memorandum, dated 19.2.1942, letter SS-*Richter beim* RF-SS to the *HA* SS-*Gericht*, dated 17.10.1942, letter SS-*Richter beim* RF-SS to Dr Ficker at the *Reichskanzlei*, dated 17.10.1942; edict *Der Oberbefehlshaber des Heeres im Auftrage* Keitel. *Heeres-Verordnungsblatt*, dated 11.12.1942, 24.Jahrgang, 66 Edition, part B, 29: D.C. NARA Washington Microfilm publication T-580, roll 213.

107 Letter *Stubaf.* Günther Burmeister to the SS-*Richter beim* RF-SS, dated 25.2.1943: D.C. NARA Washington microfilm, T-580, roll 211.

108 Letter SS-*Richter beim* RF-SS to the *HA* SS-*Gericht*, dated 19.11.1942: D.C. NARA microfilm publication T-580, roll 213.

109 SS-*Richter beim* RF-SS memorandum, dated 8.2.1943; SS-*Richter beim* RF-SS memorandum (Dr Wehser), dated 26.3.1944 & 25.10.1943; SS-*Richter beim* RF-SS to *HA* SS-*Gericht*, dated 30.6.1943: D.C. NARA Washington microfilm, T-580, roll 213.

110 *Verordnungsblatt der Waffen*-SS 227, dated 15.6.1943; letter SS-FHA *Amt* V, *Abt* III. (4), dated 1.12.43: BA NS 756/283a.

111 Letter SS-*Richter beim* RF-SS to *Stubaf.* Dr Hans Brauße, dated 23.7.1943; letter SS-*Richter beim* RF-SS to the *HA* SS-*Gericht*, dated 29.9.1943; *Reichsführer* edict titled 'Limitations for the Punishment and Probation for Members of the Police and SS', dated 29.9.1943: D.C. NARA Washington microfilm, T-580, roll 213.

112 Letter SS-*Richter beim* RF-SS (Gießelmann) to Major Dr Dippelhofer, *Hauptamt Ordnungspolizei*, dated 14.8.1943; draft *Schnellbrief* composed by the *Ordnungspolizei* chief dated 22.7.1943; letter SS-*Richter beim* RF-SS to the *Chef der Ordnungspolizei*, dated 3.8.1944; Verordnungsblatt der Waffen-SS entry, dated 22.6.1943 (*HA* SS-*Gericht Amt* III): D.C. NARA Washington microfilm, T-580, roll 213.

113 Letter SS-*Richter beim* RF-SS to *Ostubaf.* Günther Burmeister, dated 30.12.1943: D.C. NARA Washington microfilm, T-580, roll 213.

114 Letter *Ostubaf.* Günther Burmeister to the *HA* SS-*Gericht*, dated 21.1.1944: D.C. NARA Washington microfilm, T-580, roll 213.

115 Letter SS-*Richter beim* RF-SS, dated 3.3.1945: D.C. NARA Washington microfilm, T-580, roll 213.

116 Letter Dr Lammers to the SS-*Richter beim* RF-SS, dated 4.4.1944; letter SS-*Richter beim* RF-SS to Dr Lammers, date obscured (4.1944): D.C. NARA Washington microfilm, T-580, roll 213.

117 Letter SS-*Richter beim* RF-SS to the *HA* SS-*Gericht*, dated 16.12.1944: D.C. NARA Washington microfilm, T-580, roll 213.

118 Letter SS-*Richter beim* RF-SS to *Stubaf.* Günther Burmeister, dated 11.3.44: BA NS 7/352, p. 1.

119 Letter *Stubaf.* Günther Burmeister to the SS-*Richter beim* RF-SS, dated 16.1.1945: BA NS 7/352, p. 4. See letter SS-*Richter beim* RF-SS to *Stubaf.* Burmeister undated: BA NS 7/331, p. 1; letter *HA* SS-*Gericht* to the RFSS, dated 2.9.1942: BA NS 7/365, p. 31.

120 Letter *HA* SS-*Gericht Amt* III to the SS-*Richter beim* RF-SS; letter SS-FHA *Amt* V *Abteilung* III, dated 22.12.1944: D.C. NARA Washington microfilm; T-580, roll 213.

5.7 Bewährungsabteilung der Waffen-SS

121 Seidler, '*Die Militärgerichtsbarkeit…*' op cit.; p. 236 (Vopersal Archive: BA MA N 756/345b, dated 31.10.1941). See Der Freiwilligen 1978); p. 16 (Wolfgang Vopersal).

122 B 162/829, p. 164: BA Ludwigsburg.

123 *Reichsführer* edict AII (3) IIIb 320/2, dated 12.11.1941: BA NS 7/365, p. 69. See Voigt, *Sondertruppen zur Bewahrung im* WW2, p. 286. See Kew WO 208/3616, interrogation of P.W, (b. 1902, Oberschwarzbrunn/Sud.).

124 Seidler, '*Die Militärgerichtsbarkeit…*' op cit.; p. 238.

125 Letter *Ostubaf.* Dr Ernst to the *HA* SS-*Gericht*, dated 10.2.1943: BA NS 756/283a. For more details see NARA BDC, SSO Personalakte August Zeller.

126 NARA BDC, SSO Personalakte Karl Mercinsky.

127 NARA BDC, SSO Personalakte Hans Mickeleit.

128 Letter SS-*Richter beim* RF-SS, dated 19.5.1943: Archiv Vopersal.

5.8 Arbeitsabteilung der Waffen-SS

129 Letter SS-FHA to the *HA* SS-*Gericht Amt* IIIb, dated 31.10.1941: BA NS 7/378, pp. 156-7 & 15.

130 Letter SS-FHA to the *HA* SS-*Gericht Amt* IIIb, dated 31.10.1941: BA NS 7/378, p. 15.

131 Letter RFSS, dated 8.7.1944: BA NS 7/380.

132 *Ibid*. For further details see Horst Voigt, *Die 'Verlor'nen Haufen; Sondertruppen zur Frontbewährung im 2. Weltkrieg, Teil VIII*, p.286.

133 Seidler, '*Die Militärgerichtsbarkeit…*' op cit.; p. 259.

134 *Ibid*, p. 238.

135 Telegram SS-*Hstuf.* Dr Zolly to the *HA* SS-*Gericht*, dated 20.9.1944: BA NS 7/365, p. 85.

136 Message Kew TNA, HW 16/21 dated 22.6.1943.

137 Seidler, '*Die Militärgerichtsbarkeit…*' op cit.; p. 241.

138 Verordnungsblatt der Waffen-SS, dated 1.2.1945, p. 23. See letter SS-*Richter beim* RF-SS the *HA* SS-*Gericht*, dated 6.6.1944 (NO2061): BA NS 756/283a. For more details see Klausch, '*Antifaschisten…*' op cit.; pp. 291-292, 289.

139 Rolf Michaelis, *Die SS-Sturmbrigade "Dirlewanger": Vom Warschauer Aufstand bis zum Kessel von Halbe*, Dörfler Verlag GmbH, 2011, p. 14.

5.9 Polizei Sonderheiten Zug

140 *HA* SS-*Gericht* edict, dated 12.11.1941: BA NS7/ 378, pp. 1-13. See Voigt, '*Die 'Verlor'nen…*' op cit.; p. 287. See letter *Reichsführer* to *HA* SS-*Gericht* IIIb, dated 12.11.1941: BA NS 7/378 BIS.

141 Letter *Reichsführer* to the SS-FHA, dated 31.10.1941; *Verordnungsblatt der Waffen*-SS 15.3.1942 Nr. 6: BA NS 756/283a. See letter *Reichsführer* to *HA* SS-*Gericht*, dated 4.12.1941: BA NS 7/378, p. 28. The decision to send *Polizei* probationers to the *Arbeitsabteilung der Waffen*-SS would be reversed in later years.

142 Seidler, '*Die Militärgerichtsbarkeit…*' op cit.; p. 244.

143 Letter *HA* SS-*Gericht* to the SS-*Richter beim* RF-SS, dated 4.12.1941: D.C NARA microfilm publication T-580, roll 212. See letter *Reichsführer* to *HA* SS-*Gericht*, dated 4.12.1941: BA NS 7/378.

144 Hans Pichler, *Truppen Artz und Zeitzeuge, Heilen und Helfen im Krieg*, Villach 1988, p. 153-156. *Hstuf.* Dr Hans Pichler (b. 30.3.1912 in Villach, SS Nr. 32.831) served as doctor with the *Polizei-Pionier-Bataillon* in October 1942.

145 NARA BDC, SSO Personalakte Heinz Nellen.

146 NARA BDC, SSO Personalakte Eugen Bauer.

147 Message Kew TNA, HW 16/38, Nr. 6, dated 15.9.1943.

148 NARA BDC, SSO Personalakte Hans Dunkelmann.

149 *Anordnungsblatt*; rehabilitation of police officials; letter *HA* SS-*Gericht Amt* III to the SS-*Richter beim* RF-SS, dated 28.9.1943: D.C. NARA Washington microfilm, T-580, roll 213.

5.10 SS-Ersatz Bataillon Ost

150 Siegrunen Nr. 79, pp.103-106; Wolfgang Vopersal, SS-*Infantrie-Ersatz-Bataillon Ost*: BA NS 756/339a. See letter Dirlewanger to the SS-FHA, dated 28.2.1944: BA RS3 36/10, p. 145.

151 Undated document titled Übersicht (15.2.1945): D.C. NARA microfilm publication T-580, roll 214.

152 Siegrunen Nr. 79, pp. 103-106. For further details see Klausch, '*Anti-fascists…*' op cit.; p. 324.

153 Message Kew TNA, HW 16/40, Nr 2, dated 29.1.1944.

154 NARA BDC, SSO Personalakte Franz Maier.

155 NARA BDC, SSO Personalakte Karl H. Burkhardt. Surrendering to Red Army forces in the Halbe pocket in the spring of 1945, troops of Ewald Ehler's former command who had beeb camp prisoners murdered him in Hermsdorf on 28.4.1945 and reportedly hung him from a tree and set his body alight.

5.11 Front Probation Case Studies

156 NARA BDC, SSO Personalakte Fritz Göttling.

157 NARA BDC, SSO Personalakte Gerhard Warnecke.

158 NARA BDC, SSO Personalakte Jakob de Vries.

5.12 Marriage Regulations for Probationers

159 Letter *HA* SS-*Gericht*, dated 22.4.44; Verordnungsblatt der Waffen-SS dated 15.11.1942: BA NS 756/283a.

160 NARA BDC, SSO Personalakte Heinz Willerscheid. Possibly Max Kayser, (b. 23.3.1913, Tilsit, SS Nr. 354.115).

161 Cornelius Lancel: John Moore archive, dated 10.2.2013.

162 *Hstuf.* Fritz Killing memorandum; letter Killing to the *Ministerialdirektor* Dr Altstätter of the *Reichsjustizministerium*: D.C. NARA Washington microfilm, T-580, roll 213.

5.13 Front Probation Regulations for the Non-German Offenders of the Waffen-SS

163 Seidler, '*Die Militärgerichtsbarkeit…*' op cit.; pp. 245-246.

164 Wilhelm Tieke, *The Tragedy of the Faithful: 3rd SS Panzer Corps*, Fedorowicz (J.J.),Canada 2001, pp. 432-434 (Court-Martial practice in the III. (Germanisches) SS-*Panzer-Korps* from 1943-45 Lennart Westburg). See letter SS-*Richter beim* RF-SS to *HA* SS-*Gericht* dated 12.8.1942: BA NS 7/379, p. 8.

165 Letter *Gruf.* Rediess to the SS-*Richter beim* RF-SS, dated 8.7.1942: BA NS 756/283a.

166 Letter SS-*Richter beim* RF-SS to the *Reichsführer*, dated 12.8.1942: BA NS 756/283a.

167 Letter *HA* SS-*Gericht* IIIb 320/6, dated 22.9.1942: BA NS 756/283a; p. 156.

168 Letter *Reichsführer* to the *Chef HA* SS-*Gericht*, dated 18.7.1944: BA NS 7/380 Bl.7.

169 *Reichsführer* edict dated 30.9.1944. Evacuating Salaspils convicts to the *St. V. L. d. SS-u. Pol.* Matzkau, this decision had been provoked by an appeal from I.S. Hoogeboom to the *Reichsführer* for mercy that same month: BA NS 7/365, p. 85. See letter SS-*Richter beim* RF-SS dated 14.2.1943: D.C. NARA Washington microfilm T-580, roll 214.

170 NARA BDC, SSO Personalakte August Ingier.

171 NARA BDC, SSO Personalakte Christoph Bellanovich.

5.14 Divisional Front Probation Units

172 *Ostuf.* Willi Heinrich, (b. 28.11.1917, SS Nr. 308.444). Punished for attempting to desert, the SS- *und Polizei-Gericht* VI, Krakau assigned *Oscha.* Voß to this *Strafkompanie* in Sept.1942: Message Kew HW 16/21, dated 24.9.1942.

173 Seidler, '*Die Militärgerichtsbarkeit…*' op cit.; p. 242.

174 Charles Trang, *Totenkopf*, Heimdal 2008, pp. 178-179. *Ustuf.* Hans Endreß, (b. 5.7.1911 in Stuttgart, SS Nr. 225.734).

In Russia, the *Einsatzkommando* z.b.V. fought with the SS-*Totenkopf-Infantrie*-Rgt. 1 and when Endreß was the adjutant for the *Kampfgruppe Kleffner*, (SS-*Kradschütze-Bataillon* 3), his probationers failed to re-take Dubowizy on 10.6.1942: Letter *Gruf.* Theodore Eicke, dated 30.1.1942: BA NS 7/385, p. 1.

Deployed north of the main road between Biakowo and Wassiljewtschina, the *Einsatzkommando* z.b.V. then occupied the so-called 'finger position' some 600 metres from the Soviet lines. The chief judge of the *Totenkopfdivision* field court later alleged that these parolees fought the enemy for three days and were annihilated during savage fighting: Letter *Oberstrichter* Freiherr Hugo v.Dörnberg, dated 10.9.1942: *Wehrmacht Justiz im Dritten Reich; von Newel bis Remagen, Historisch Reihe der Forschungsgemeinschaft das andere Deutschland* (Hannover 1948), p. 9. See Seidler, '*Die Militärgerichtsbarkeit...*' op cit.; p. 245.

On 20.8.1944 the *Bewährungsabteilung* received orders to prepare 500 probationers for front service with the *Dirlewanger* formation, which was fighting in the city of Warsaw. Two companies, each with 250 men, departed for the front on 9 or 10 September and were led by *Hstuf.* Baumann and 22- year-old *Ustuf.* Eberhard Kunikowski respectively. Kunikowski had formally fought with the 15. / SS-*Pz.-Gren.*-Rgt. 3 *Totenkopf* in Mar.1942 and was promoted to officer rank in Sept.1943. Prior to leaving for Warsaw he had led the 3. *Bewährungskompanie*: Baumann's identity remains a mystery. For further details see Voperal archive, *Soldaten, Kampfer, Kameraden bd Vb* (Ed. 2005), p. 399.

Suffering heavy casualties defending its positions between Czrna Duza and Nadma between 5.8.-4.9.1944, the III. / SS-*Pz.-Gren.*-Rgt. *Totenkopf* required immediate reinforcement. During their journey to Warsaw, the two parole companies were diverted to the hard pressed SS-*Pz.-Gren.*-Rgt. *Theodore Eicke* near Jzabelin on 15.9.1944. Reporting to the regimental HQ, the probationers received SS rune collar patches to sew onto their tunics and Baumann's company joined the *Totenkopf* and Kunikowski's company found itself posted to the III. / *Theodore Eicke* near Jzabelin. Fighting off Red Army attacks for five days, the parolees suffered a high number of casualties. Baumann revealed on 19.9.1944 that only 51 men of his company was left unwounded, or killed and Kunikowski reported 195 men fit for battle. The Red Army offensive finally shuddered to a halt four weeks later on 21.9.1944 and the former probationers were all declared rehabilitated: Klausch, '*Antifaschisten...*', op cit.; p. 453.

The *Totenkopfdivision* almost certainly re-established a *Strafkompanie* for its undisciplined elements in 1944 and some 400 *Wehrmacht* probationers of the *Bataillon* z.b.V. 560, fought alongside the III. / SS-*Panzer*-Rgt. 3 *Totenkopf* in northern Poland during October 1944: Vopersol archive – *Soldaten, Kampfer, Kameraden bd Vb*, p. 399.

175 *HA* SS-*Gericht* edict, dated 12.11.1941: BA NS7/ 378, pp. 1-13. See Voigt, '*Die 'Verlor'nen Haufen...*' op cit.; p. 286.

176 Seidler, '*Die Militärgerichtsbarkeit...*' op cit.; p. 239.

177 *Ibid.*

178 *Ibid.*

179 *Ibid.* See also letter *HA* SS-*Gericht* IIIb 320/6, dated 22.9.1942: BA NS 756/283a, p. 156.

180 Oresic deserted to Tito's Partisans during Jan.1945 and *Rttf.* Wilhelm Roth accepted provisional command of the unit. Roth joined the *Waffen*-SS in Ma.1941, trained with an SS-*Infantrie*-Rgt. in Brünn and was wounded during Nov.1942 while assigned to the *Kampfgruppe Nord* in Finland. Recuperating in a military hospital in Graundenz, Roth recovered and was assigned to the *Aufstellungsstab des* 13th

SS-*Gebirgs*-Division *Handschar* and was later posted to the 13. *Strafkompanie* as a 'cadre' member. Roth took command after Oresic's desertion in Apr.1945, but was never formally named company leader. Subsequently promoted to the rank of *Uscha.* Roth was promoted again three times further and surviving the war, he then studied dentistry and obtained his doctorate in dentistry: Electronic conversation between Mr George Lepre, Mr John Moore and this author between 9.1.2011 & 11.1.2011.

181 Born in Tirschenreuth on 15.1.1895, *Hstuf.* Hans Haubner transfered from the SS-*Bewährungsabteilung* to the *Sonderkompanie* of the SS-*Pionier-Bataillon* 14 in Jul.1944 and was killed in action the following month at Sklabina (earning him the *E.K.* I. *Klasse*): Voigt, '*Die 'Verlor'nen Haufen…*' op cit.; p. 286.

182 Seidler, '*Die Militärgerichtsbarkeit…*' op cit.; p. 239. *Hstuf.* Peteris Mardoks, (b. 13.1.1898.

183 *Ibid.*

184 *Ibid.*

185 Latvian Legionnaires, sentenced by the SS- *und Polizei-Gericht* XVI, Riga for offences such as absence without leave were assigned to a *Bau-Bataillon* from 19 May 1944. A second battalion was established on 20 September 1944 and accepted one 120 offenders: Okupācijas muzeja in Riga: The Hoover Institution Archives, (USA Stanford University). This material consists of post-war testimony from former inmates. *Ostuf.* Johann Maier, (b. 5.9.1887 in Tettenweis, SS Nr. 314.959). The 19. SS-*Strafkompanie* appears not to have been the only front parolee formation established for the 19th *Waffen-Grenadier*-Division *der* SS. *Standartenoberjunker* Kimsnis died in action while fighting with the *Strafzug* of the *Waffen-Grenadier*-Rgt. *der* SS 42 on 24.12.1944.

186 NARA BDC, SSO Personalakte Voldemar Salumae.

187 Seidler, '*Die Militärgerichtsbarkeit…*' op cit.; p. 239.

188 *Ibid*, p. 239. *Ustuf.* Roger Groenvinck (b. 28.7.1921 in Ostende/Belgium, SS Nr 28.721). A member of the Belgium Army from 1939 to 1940, Groenvinck then enlisted in the *Waffen*-SS. Passing an officer's course at the SS-*Junkerschule* Bad Tölz on 30.5.1943, with the rank of *St. OJ*, he fought with *Kampfgruppe* Reymann during the battle for Orphanage hill. Deployed east of Grenadier hill, this is where the probationers of the 103. *Bewährungskompanie* also fought. At the conclusion of the battle on 29.7.1944, only 37 of 400 men survived the fighting without wounds or loss of life.

189 See Voigt, 'Die 'Verlor'nen Haufen…' op cit.; p. 448.

190 Robert Forbes, *Pour L'Europe: The French Volunteers of the Waffen-SS*, Aberdeen Bookstore; First Edition 2001, p. 145. See Voigt, '*Die 'Verlor'nen Haufen…*' op cit.; p. 286.

191 Seidler, '*Die Militärgerichtsbarkeit…*' op cit.; p. 276.

192 Tieke, '*The Tragedy…*' op cit.; pp. 126-127.

5.15 Einsatzgruppen Probation

193 NARA BDC, SSO Personalakte SS Friedrich Kockerols.

194 NARA BDC, SSO Personalakte Helmut Grusa.

195 Musmanno, Michael A., U.S.N.R, Military Tribunal II, Case 9: Opinion and Judgment of the Tribunal. Nuremberg: Palace of Justice. 8.4.1948, pp. 225-227 [original mimeographed copy] from http://www.nizkor.org/hweb/orgs/german/ … /graf.html.

196 NARA BDC, SSO Personalakte Paul Otto Radomski.

197 NARA BDC, SSO Personalakte Arno Groebel.

198 NARA BDC, SSO Personalakte Friedrich Pradel. Pradel's co-defendant were: *Obersekär* Gustav Kemper (b. 15.7.1904 in Hamm/Lippe-Detmold) and *Ostuf.* Fritz Niederhausen. Born in Berlin-

Hohenschönhausen on 15.7.1902, Fritz Niederhausen had worked as a locksmith prior to joining the *Polizei* on 3 January 1924. A Nazi party member (NSDAP Nr 873.189), he married his fiancée in 20.5.1939. A Technical Inspector of the RSHA, Niederhausen joined the *Allgemeine*-SS on 1.10.1941 (SS Nr 408.413) and was promoted directly to the rank of *Ostuf.* on 1.10.1942 (RSHA). Niederhausen was assigned to the RSHA *Amt* IIC3 when he became the subject of a court investigation and court martial for his part in supplying fuel to the black market. The *Gerichtsherr* ordered his release from detention on 13 January 1945.

5.16 Field probation against the Partisans

199 Nazi Conspiracy and Aggression: Opinion and Judgement, 102 IMT, 22:158-162.

200 Probationers would be sent to the most dangerous sectors of the front: The *Führer* and Head of the Armed Forces, Berlin, dated 2.4.1942: BA NS 7/378, p. 31.

201 Letter SS-*Richter beim* RF-SS to the *HA* SS-*Gericht*, dated 19.5.1943: BA NS 756/283a.

202 Einrichtung der Dienstelle 'Der Reichsführer-SS und Chef der Deutschen Polizei –to the Chef der Bandenbekämpfung' durch Umwandlung der Dienstelle des 'Bevollmächtigten für die Bandenbekämpfung' SS-Befehl, dated 21.6.1943: BA NS 19/291 / NS 19/1706.

203 Philip W. Blood, *Hitler's Bandit Hunters; the SS and the Nazi Occupation of Europe*, Potomac Books 2008, p. 85.

204 Letter SS-*Richter beim* RF-SS, dated 19.5.1943; Archiv Wolfgang Vopersal.

205 *Ogruf.* Scharfe edict: D.C. NARA Washington microfilm; T-580, roll 213.

206 Seidler, '*Die Militärgerichtsbarkeit…*' op cit.; p. 238. The existence of the 20, 21, and 22. *Bewährungszug* are recorded in NARA BDC, SSO Personalakte Willi Prager.

207 Seidler, '*Die Militärgerichtsbarkeit…*' op cit.; p. 238. For further details see Blood, '*Hitler's…*' op cit.; pp. 155-157, 162-165.

5.16.1 SS-Sonderkommando Dirlewanger

208 French L. Maclean, *The Cruel Hunters; SS-Sonderkommando Dirlewanger*, Schiffer Publishing Ltd (US) 1998, p. 42. See Klausch, '*Antifaschisten…*' op cit.; p. 126. See NARA BDC, SSO Personalakte Kurt Weiß.

209 Klausch, '*Antifaschisten…*' op cit.; pp. 27-35. See letter *Ostubaf.* Burmeister to the SS-*Richter beim* RF-SS, dated 25.2.1943: BA NS 7/365, p. 69. See letter SS-*Hauptamt* to the *Ergänzungsstellen*, SS-FHA & *Ost Bataillone*, dated 3.9.1943: BA RS 3 36/10, p. 79.

210 Letter *Kommando der Waffen*-SS/IIb/ dated 28.8.1940: Washington D.C. National Archives Microfilm Publication T-354, roll 650, BA RS 3 36/10, p. 162. See Mclean, '*The Cruel Hunters…*' op cit.; p. 58.

211 Klausch, '*Antifaschisten…*' op cit.; pp. 284-304, (Statutory Declaration Karl Gerber 24.6.1947 IFZ: NO 4137).

212 Cross-examination of Dirlewanger by Dr Friedrich of the SS-*Hauptamt Zentralamt* I 3 (*Gerichtsoffiziere*) on 26.8.1941; USHMM Washington; RG-15.034M Reel 2.

213 *Vernhemung* Dr Konrad Morgen dated 6.12.1946 (Nuremberg): Ifz-München 1236-2, p. 4. It had been alleged that a sixteen year-old female Jewish servant slept next to Dirlewanger's bedroom. Visiting Dirlewanger's headquarters, an SS officer was introduced to the girl and pressurised into drinking from her glass, the visitor was then told that his companion was Jewish. Insulted, the officer complained about Dirlewanger's behaviour and a courts investigation was initiated by the

SS- *und Polizei-Gericht* VI, Krakau to determine whether a race crime had taken place. The case was later transferred to the SS- *und Polizei-Gericht* XV, Breslau and they spent the next couple of years pursuing Dirlewanger with no success.

214 Klausch, '*Antifaschisten...*' op cit.; p. 58.

215 Mclean, '*The Cruel Hunters...*' op cit.; pp. 59-172.

216 Letter SS-*Hauptamt Amt* A I AI 2b-Az 18d-Ke/gi, dated 24.4.1944: BA RS 3 36/10, p. 17.

217 Letter Dirlewanger to SS-FHA, dated 28.2.1944; letter Dirlewanger to SS-FHA dated 28.2.1944: BA RS 3 36/10, p. 145.

5.16.2 Rehabilitation and Recruitment Policies for the SS-Sonderkommando

218 Klausch, '*Antifaschisten...*' op cit.; p. 90. Telegram message, dated 7.2.1944: MA RS 3-36, p. 19. See *StA* Nuremberg Process; Case XI A-80 protocol of Dr Walter Hennings from 9.6.1948, p. 8067.

219 *Ibid.*

220 Letter Dirlewanger to the SS-*Hauptamt*, dated 16.4.1944: BA RS 3 36/10, p. 50.

221 NARA BDC, SSO Personalakte Erwin Walser.

222 NARA BDC, SSO Personalakte Werner Blessau.

223 *Kriminalpolizei* questioning of P.D. on 4.7.1962: ZL Nr 492.

224 FAS Project on Government Secrecy, Vol. 2006 issue No. 67 dated 7.7.2006. This group was controlled by the US Army between 1945 until 1948. Then taken over by the Central Intelligence Agency under the command of Colonel James Critchfield until 1955-56, it was then led by the Federal Government of Germany and renamed the Bundesnachrichtendienst (BND) or State Intelligence Service). For more details see NARA BDC, SSO Personalakte Kurt Weiße.

225 NARA BDC, SSO Personalakte Dr Heinrich Wehninck.

226 NARA BDC, SSO Personalakte August Zeller; letter *Reichsführer* to *HA* SS-*Gericht* dated 14.9.1943: MA RS 3-36, p. 8.

227 NARA BDC, SSO Personalakte Heinrich Willmann.

228 NARA BDC, SSO Personalakte Jan Schreuder; letter SS-*Fursorgeführer Süd*, *Stubaf.* Sehmerel, in Munich, dated 18.2.1944.

229 NARA BDC, SSO Personalakte Ernst-Günther Heidelberg.

The officers under investigation were; *Ostubaf.* Erwin Leckebusch, *Stubaf.* Franz Blasé, *Sta.* Paul Nositz, *Hstuf.* Otto von u. zu der Tann, *Ustuf.* Friedrich-Wilhelm Meier, *Ustuf.* ? Kurtz (SS-*Bau-Btl.*), *Hstuf.* Michael Gerstmayr (*Kommandantur-Verwaltung*), *Ustuf.* Erich Ascher (*Zentral-Bauleitung*), *Ostubaf.* Friedrich Schumacher (SS-*San. Amt*), *Ustuf.* Reimer-Walther Reimers (San. *Zweiglager* Krakau), *Ustuf.* Franz Robl, *Ustuf.* Helmut Landau, *Ustuf.* Ludwig Pröscholdt, *Ostuf.* Johann Gerstenberger, *Ustuf.* Fritz Meisner (*Verwaltung* Debica). *Ostubaf.* Leckebusch had been executed by Jul.1942 and his file was stricken from SS records. *Ustuf.* Friedrich-Wilhelm Meier died in Mar.1945 while fighting with the SS-Rgt. *Kalthofen*. For further details see BOAR/37711/221/a (ps4) Dachau: Interrogation of Heinrich Nett 1945; Kew WO 309/2042.

230 NARA BDC, SSO Personalakte Anthonius Ammerlaan & BA RS 3-36/10, p. 58.

231 NARA BDC, SSO Personalakte Dr Hans Heinsen; Der Spiegel Nr. 11/1972; 'Feldpost 168.34 S'. This magazine article claimed that the West Berlin Landgericht Judge Dr Hans Heinsen had misled them about his Nazi past.

232 Standing alongside Löffler in court for refusing to obey an order was *Oscha.* Josef Frey. Born in Laiz-Sigmaringen on 14.2.1914, Frey was a former mechanic, who had completed two years' service in the

military and joined the SS-VT in 1938. Frey had fought in the West, Balkans and Russia as a troop and then *Zugführer*. Wounded, he received both classes of the *Eisernes Kreuz* and the *Infanterie Sturmabzeichen*. The court punished Frey with three months' *Gefängnis* and noting that he did not bear a grudge against Löffler, Frey recognised his guilt and drunkenness and expressed his hope that this affair would not prevent him becoming an officer. Josef Frey's sentence was later reduced to six weeks' sharp arrest and he was ordered to serve front probation for the remainder of his sentence: NARA BDC, SSO Personalakte Paul Löffler.

233 'The death toll in the *Bewährungsbataillone* was more than average; many men were literally burned': Seidler, '*Die Militärgerichtsbarkeit…*' op cit.; p. 250.

234 Source: AR-Z 85/60, p. 296.

235 Klausch, '*Antifaschisten…*' op cit.; p. 262.

236 Letter SS-*HA* to the WVHA, dated 5.12.1942: RS-3 36/10, p. 118; letter Dirlewanger dated 13.2.1943; letter Dirlewanger to the HSSPF *Russland Mitte*, dated 14.8.1943: BA RS 3 36/10.

237 Letter SS-*Hauptamt Amt* C I 3 (3b), dated 29.4.1944: BA RS 3 36/10, p. 26; German police decodes No 1 traffic; 27.5.1944 FF Nr 2 LYZ de DRY 1753 SSD LYP6 Nr. 9 1640 154 DQH.

5.16.3 Punishment Regime within the SS-Sonderkommando

238 Klausch, '*Antifaschisten…*' op cit.; p. 82. See also BA RS 3-36/10, p. 107.

239 Letter SS-*Richter beim* RF-SS to the *HA* SS-*Gericht*, dated 19.5.1943: D.C. NARA microfilm archive T-580, roll 212.

240 SS-*Sonderregiment* order, dated 11.5.1944: BA RS 3 36/10, p. 34. The *Kompanieführer* was *Ostuf.* Egyd Ingruber (b. 14.4.1920 in Mittersill/Salzburg, SS Nr 317.056). Ingruber earned the *E.K.* 1. *Klasse* and ended the war assigned to the HSSPF *Alpenland*.

241 Klausch, '*Antifaschisten…*' op cit.; p. 134. *Hstuf.* Rudolf Stöweno, (b. 11.4.1901 in Wollstein, SS Nr. 16.489). Dying on 14.11.1943, Stöweno received a posthumous *Julleuchter* on 28.4.1944: RS 3-36/10; p. 14.

242 Klausch, '*Antifaschisten…*' op cit.; p. 294. See Seidler, '*Die Militärgerichtsbarkeit…*' op cit.; p. 281.

243 Letter Dirlewanger to *Gruf.* Berger, dated 21.8.1943: MA RS 3-36, p. 95. See Klausch, '*Antifaschisten…*', op cit.; p. 440.

244 Mclean, '*The Cruel Hunters…*' op cit.; p. 154.

245 SS-*Richter beim* RF-SS memorandum (Dr Wehser), dated 30.10.1944: D.C. NARA Washington microfilm, T-580, roll 214.

246 NARA BDC, SSO Personalakte Dr Bruno Wille. For further details see Helmuth Auerbach, *Die Einheit Dirlewanger* (Vierteljahrshefte für Zeitgeschichte 1962). See Klausch, '*Antifaschisten…*', op cit.; pp. 126-134.

247 NARA BDC, SSO Personalakte Horst Kaminski.

5.16.4 Sonderbrigade Dirlewanger and the 36th Waffen-Grenadier-Division der SS

248 Voigt, '*Die 'Verlor'nen Haufen…*' op cit.; p. 286. See Mclean, '*The Cruel Hunters…*' op cit.; p. 179.

249 NARA BDC, SSO Personalakte Oskar Dirlewanger; telegram dated 4.8.1944 *Personalstab* RFSS Akt Nr Geh 1286.

Born in Bochum on 24.10.1914, *Ustuf.* Kurt-Heinz Meyer (SS Nr. 268.018) had served as an SS-*Mann* with the 11. / LSSAH in 1.1935, an *Uscha.* with the 12. / LSSAH in Jul.1941 and an *Ustuf.* with the I. / SS-*Geb.*-Rgt. 14 in 1.1943. Disgraced in 1943, Meyer joined the SS-*Sonderregiment* in 2.1945 and died with rank of *Schütze* on 24.2.1945.

250 Mclean, '*The Cruel Hunters…*' op cit.; p. 196. For a pictorial view of the destruction wrought on Warsaw I can recommend viewing Stefan Starba Baluk's, *Poles on the Fronts of WWII*, pp. 368-384.

251 NARA BDC, SSO Personalakte Max Schreiner.

252 Letter *Brigadef.* Rode of the *Kommandostabes* RF-SS 20.9.1944: BA NS 756/283a (Vopersal archive); SS-*Richter beim* RF-SS to the Danzig-Matzkau commandant, dated 30.9.1944: BA NS 7/365, p. 292. See telegram *Hstuf.* Dr Zolly to the *HA* SS-*Gericht*, dated 30.9.1944: BA NS 7/365, p. 85.

The figure of 1,400 or 1,500 was stated during the evidence of *Stubaf.* Karl Radl at the Nuremburg trial: 'Fact is, Himmler's order on 20.8.1944 calculated that there were 1,500 available inmates in Matzkau available for the Dirlewanger formation fighting in Warsaw, but according to one author only 1,400 men had arrived in Warsaw on the 24.8.1944': Klausch, '*Antifaschisten…*', op cit.; pp. 140-164.

253 *Ibid*, pp. 453-454.

254 Padfield, '*Himmler*', op cit.; p. 509.

255 Letter SS-*Richter beim* RF-SS to the SS-PHA, dated 31.12.1944; letter SS-*Richter beim* RF-SS to the *HA* SS-*Gericht*, dated 18.10.1944: Archiv IfZ Munich: Fa-146). See Klausch, '*Antifaschisten…*' op cit.; p. 445.

256 Klausch, '*Antifaschisten…*' op cit.; pp. 310-318 & 131.

257 Born in Speyer/Pfalz on 31.3.1917, Benkel was the son of a factory worker who undertook a two year stonemason's apprenticeship when he left *Volksschule*. Then employed as a registered printer, Benkel undertook his compulsory RAD training between 1.10.1935-28.9.1936 and signed a twelve years contract with the SS-VT on 1.10.1936. Promoted to his last rank on 1.8.1942, he fought with the SS-*Aufkl*ärungs*sabteilung* during the Polish campaign, the *Reich* for the Western campaign and the *Wiking* for the attack on the USSR. Mustering with the 14. / SS-*Pz.-Gren.*-Rgt. 19 on 21.4.1943, Benkel was subordinate to Haiber in the post of *Stabsscharführer*. Marrying his fiancée Klara G. on 25.4.1904, they had one child until the collapse. During his military service, he received the *Medaille zur Erinnerung an den* 1.10.1938, *die Medaille zur Erinnerung an den* 13. März 1938, *E.K.* II. *Klasse*, the K.v.K II *Klasse mit Schwerten* and the *Medaille* '*Winterschlacht im Osten* 1941/42': NARA BDC, SSO Personalakte Eugen Haiber. For further information see Klausch, '*Antifaschisten…*' op cit.; p. 284 (Statutory Declaration Karl Gerber 24.6.1947 IFZ: NO 4137).

258 A veteran of the Great Wear and *Freikorps*, Weiß was employed at the post office from Nov.1919 and married his fiancée Gertrude S., (b. 18.3.1901 in Berlin) on 12.6.1926. The couple had two children and lived in Ruhpolding bei Seehuber. Employed at the *Deutsch Reichspost Hauptfunkempfangsstelle* at Berlin–Zehlendorf, Weiß became an *Obertelegraphensekretär* on 1.7.1927. Appointed a councillor in the National and Prussian Interior Ministry after 30.1.1933, he became a Berlin city councillor in March 1933 and entering parliament in Nov.1933 (a city alderman the following year).

Punished with a written warning in Sept.1934 for ignoring a *Polizei* officer's orders during a march in Jun.1934, the head of the *Oberabschnitt Ost* punished Weiß with another serious warning on 2.10.1934 the same year for his involvement in an argument that had broken out between four SS officers and an American-German named Karl Schäfer and his companion, the nephew of Lord Astrid in the Schari-Wari Bar in Berlin. Questioned after the event, Weiß was adamant that the Americans started the argument and was settled amicably and quickly. The incident brought to the attention of the US Ambassador, he submitted an official complaint and the SS received orders to make enquiries into the affair. The *Gerichtsoffizier* for the *Oberabschnitt Ost* the investigation and despite Weiß's protestations, his superiors judged him to have disobeyed a *Führer* order concerning individuals in the party to respect foreigners and as a consequence he received a severe reprimand. Granted leave from his post in the ministries to work full time with the SS between 1.1.1935 and 1.4.1939, Weiß caused an injury while driving at great speed and the local a court punished him with a four day jail sentence on 10.12.1935.

Promoted to the rank of *Brigadef.* on 30.1.1939, Weiß had led numerous SS units in Berlin until Jan.1935, he was the *Landesgruppenführer des Reichsluftschutzbunds Landesgruppe Westfalen* from 1934 to Nov.1944. Leading the *Abschnitt* XXIX (Mannheim) 7.1.1935–Mar.1936, Weiß was an officer of the *Stab Reichsführer*-SS from 10.12.1938 and served with the *Wehrmacht Heer* 1.12.1942–31.8.1943. Entering the *Waffen*-SS on 31.8.1943, he joined the *Kommandant Hauptamt Ordnungspolizei* on 12.10.1943, was the SSPF *Nikolajew* 10.10.1943–21.3.1944 and then the *Polizeipräsident* Metz. An officer of the SS-*Personalhauptamt* from 11.4.1944, he reported to the SS-*Sonderbrigade* Sept.1944. His awards included the 1914-18 *Eisernes Kreuz* II. *Klasse*, the 1914-18 *Verwundetenabzeichen in Schwarz*, SS-*Zivilabzeichen*, SA-*Sportsabzeichen in Bronze*, *Deutsches Reichssportabzeichen in Bronze* and the *Reiterssportsabzeichen in Bronze*. Weiß also received the *Totenkopfring der* SS on 24.12.1933, the *Ehrendegen des Reichsführer*-SS, both classes of the *Kriegsverdienstkreuz II. Klasse mit Schwertern, the Luftschütz Ehrenzeichen* and *Dienstauszeichnung der* NSDAP *in Bronze*: NARA BDC, SSO Personalakte Rudolf Weiß.

259 NARA BDC, SSO Personalakte Julian Scherner.

The *Spruchkammerkate* for Willy Osthues contains statements that link Scherner to the prosecution of his *Stabsführer*, *Stubaf.* Willy Haase, (b. 17.5.1906 in Berlin SS Nr. 1077).

Born in Bielefeld on 28.10.1910, Heinz Klare was employed at his father's furniture workshop as salesman and dealer in his home town. Joining the Nazi Party, (NSDAP Nr. 2.479.531) and admitted into the *Allgemeine*-SS in 1933, Klare was drafted into the *Waffen*-SS in September 1939. Released from active service on 2.9.1940, he returned to work at his father's business and visited Prague in the spring of 1941 to 'Aryanise' an existing business and relocate his firm in the province. At that time Scherner arranged for Klare to join the *Waffen*-SS and contrived for him to receive medical leave (hospitalised until 15.12.1941). Joining Scherner's staff in Krakau at the end of 1941, Klare loaned his commander a substantial amount of money from his business and personal accounts, was owed money for the purchase of luxury food and spirits, received generous leave entitlements, purchased 200 *Reichsmark* worth of porcelain for Scherner and accused his superior of misusing his service vehicle and complained. Further, Klare claimed that he was owed for 20 *Reichsmark* of perfume and claimed that Scherner and the officers *Kasino* owed him payment for 100 *Reichsmark* worth of beer and cold plates. He then alleged that Scherner had flouted the *Führer* edict which limited vehicle use without permission, to undertake numerous trips for private family concerns and complained that he had helped his business friend Pätz to deliver furniture to Krakau in Sept.1941 and re-directed a bedroom set to Scherner, for which he yet to receive payment (this furniture was later returned to Klare).

As part of their investigation of Scherner the SiPo arrested Klare on 1.12.1941 and again on 1.3.1942. Interrogating Klare over two days, *Kriminalkommissar* Müller became convinced that the financial loans made to Scherner were in exchange for his extended work and medical leave. In each instance, Klare alleged that he had invoiced his superior for these goods, but had not received any payments and additionally, he alleged that Scherner had flouted the *Führer* edict limiting vehicle use without permission, to undertake numerous trips for private family concerns. Presented with these accusations, Scherner conceded that the food and beverage invoices were outstanding, but affirmed that the majority of his trips had been conducted for business purposes and was paid in full from his 300 *Reichsmark* expenses account. He then explained that Klare had not received any payments on the grounds that he had failed to submit invoices to the *Rechnungsführer*. Acknowledging the 3,500 *Reichsmark* loan, Scherner claimed that this was paid in full with a bank loan when Klare's company was sold and his successor terminated the loan. The examining judge would estimate that Scherner owed Klare 800 *Reichsmark*.

Prior to his arrest, Klare was to have reported to the 6th SS-*Gebirgsjäger*-Division *Nord* in Finland. Released from custody on 2.9.1942, he was once again added to the front transfer list, but was posted to the 10th SS-*Panzer*-Division as a column leader, (Kfz) in Apr.1943. The *HA* SS-*Gericht* did not recommend Klare's punishment for hoarding the food stocks, military tickets, petrol vouchers and the luxury items in his apartment, but on the basis of this accusation, Klare had been held under arrest for six months and in the courts opinion, this detention was wrongly imposed. However, the court recommended a further investigation was conducted into allegations that he had engaged in fraud and had misused military and petrol vouchers (the SS Judge observed that Scherner's own home had not been searched for such goods). *Hscha.* Heinz Klare was on medical leave until 8.7.1943 and then returned to his duties. As a consequence of the court investigation, Klare later received a reprimand for the misuse of a service vehicle.

260 Klausch, '*Antifaschisten…*' op cit.; pp. 225-226. *Hstuf.* Erich-Adolf Langelotz, (b. 12.1.1896 in Kojetitz). A Viennese accountant by profession, Langlotz was arrested by the Vienna *Gestapo* on 13.1.1944 and was detained in the KL Dachau between 9.7.-10.11.1944. Posted to the SS-*Sonderbrigade* in November the same year. *Hstuf.* Langelotz successfully crossed over to the Red Army on 16.12.1944 and was detained in a prisoner of war camp in the Ural Mountains, (7 207 / L district Molotov).

261 NARA BDC, SSO Personalakte Georg Wild.

262 Seidler, '*Die Militärgerichtsbarkeit…*' op cit.; p. 283. See Klausch, '*Antifaschisten…*' op cit.; p. 262.

263 Seidler, '*Die Militärgerichtsbarkeit…*' op cit.; p. 267. See Klausch, '*Antifaschisten…*' op cit.; p. 225.

264 NARA BDC, SSO Personalakte Siegfried Polack; message Kew HW 16/40, dated 7.7.1944.

265 Letter, dated 14.2.1945: Bundesarchiv MA RS 3-36/12, p. 12; Michaelis, '*SS-Sturmbrigade…*', op. cit.; p. 14. See Hellmuth Auerbach, *Die Einheit Dirlewanger* (Ifz-München 1962).

266 Mclean, '*The Cruel Hunters…*' op cit.; p. 216. See Klausch, '*Antifascisten…*' op cit.; pp. 303-306.

267 Klausch, '*Antifaschisten…*' op cit.; pp. 285, 290-293.

268 *Ibid*, p. 306.

269 Mclean, '*The Cruel Hunters…*', op cit.; pp. 221-222. See Klausch, '*Antifaschisten…*' op cit.; p. 312.

270 Related by Hans Georg Lengauer in a special issue of 'Gubener Heimatbriefs' published in 1998, *Hauptmann* Werner Theermann may have been the former leader of the I. / *Pz.-Art.*-Rgt. *Gross Deutschland* and holder of the prestigious *Deutsches Kreuz Gold*.

271 Klausch, '*Antifaschisten…*', op cit.; p. 283.

272 NARA BDC, SSO Personalakte Ewald Ehlers. See Klausch, '*Antifaschisten…*' op cit.; p. 314.

273 Mclean, '*The Cruel Hunters…*' op cit.; pp. 222-223.

5.17 SS-Fallschirmjägerabteilung 500

274 Letter *HA* SS-*Gericht* to the SS-*Richter beim* RF-SS, dated 5.2.1943: NS 756/283a.

275 Letter *Ostubaf.* Dr Ernst to the *HA* SS-*Gericht*, dated 10.2.1943: NS 756/283a.

276 Rolf Michaelis, *Das SS-Fallschirmjäger-bataillone 500/600*, Schiffer Publishing Ltd (US) 2008, p. 15.

277 Klausch, '*Anti-Fascists…*' op cit.; p. 454.

278 Michaelis, '*Das SS-Fallschirmjäger…*' op cit.; p. 12.

279 Vopersol archive: BA NS 756/283a.

280 Interrogation Reports C.S.D.I.C. (UK) S.I.R. 1591-1640: the National Archives: WO208/3616. S.I.R. 1597 6.4.1945 Kew WO 208/3616, interrogation of P.W. Matr Wuchterl, (b. 1902, Oberschwarzbrunn/Sud.). Wuchterl was captured off the port of Zeebrugge on 12.3.1945.

281 Letter *Chef* SS-*Hauptamt*, dated 20.3.1944: BDC SS-HO 2422, Berger evidence Nuremberg case IX NO 2723/NO 2061. See letter SS-*Richter beim* RF-SS to the *HA* SS-*Gericht* dated 6.6.1944: (NO 2061); letter SS-*Richter beim* RF-SS to the *HA* SS-*Gericht*, dated 6.6.1944: BA NS 756/283a. For further details I recommend reading Siegfried Milius's, *Fallschirmjager der Waffen-SS im Bild* (Joachim Peiper and Karl von den Driesch), Rolf Michaelis, *Das* SS-*Fallschirmjäger-bataillone* 500/600 and Antonio Munoz's, *Forgotten Legions: Obscure Combat Formations of the Waffen-SS.*

282 NARA BDC, SSO Personalakte Willi Schmidl.

283 NARA BDC, SSO Personalakte Wilhelm Blank.

5.18 SS-Sonderverbände z.b.V. 'Friedenthal' and the Jagdverbände

284 Perry Biddiscombe, *The SS Hunter Battalions*, The History Press 2006, p. 23/24.

285 NARA BDC, SSO Personalakte Otto Skorzeny. See Otto Skorzeny, *Skorzeny's Special Missions: The Memoirs of the Most Dangerous Man in Europe*, Greenhill Books 1997.

286 Letter *Chef* SiPo- *und* SD to *Amtschef* VI, dated 13.3.1944. VI S AZ; 378/44 gRs; letter *HA* SS-*Gericht* to the *Reichsführer*-SS 13.3.1944: BA NS 756/283a.
Stubaf. Günther Burmeister agreed to the transfer of convicts to Skorzeny's unit and *Sta.* Scholtz arranged for the volunteers to report to the SS-*Kaserne* Berlin-Lichterfelde.

287 Letter *HA* SS-*Gericht* to the RFSS, dated 22.4.1944.

288 *Ibid.*

289 *Ibid.*

290 Biddiscombe, '*The SS* Hunter…' op cit.; p. 25.

291 Interrogation Reports C.S.D.I.C. (UK) S.I.R. 1591-1640: the National Archives: WO208/3616. S.I.R. 1597 6.4.1945 Kew WO 208/3616, interrogation of P.W. Matr Wuchterl, (b. 1902, Oberschwarzbrunn/Sud.).

292 HQ 7th US Army reports marked secret 0107642, dated 21.1.1945.

293 Message Kew TNA, HW 16/22, dated 28.11.1942.

294 Born in Berlin on 7.6.1901, Werner Feuerstein was by profession a textile merchant in his father's business. Married in 1927, the couple had four children together. Joining the NSRB on 1.7.1933 and the Nazi party on 1.5.1936, Feuerstein received orders to join the *Waffen*-SS on 1.11.1939 and obtained a promotion to the rank of *Uscha.* on 24.11.1939. Assigned to the Krakau SS-*Lazarett* in Oct.1940, Feuerstein then joined the KL Oranienburg staff in Sept.1941. Transferred to the Viennese hospital in November the same year, Feuerstein then deployed as an SDG with the SS-*Kraftfahrschule* in Vienna and worked under Ammon in the wash and uniform department of the hospital. He had no previous disciplinary problems.
Born in Schönlanke/Ostpreußen on 13.4.1911, Kurt Weymann's father was carpenter and he left full time education to work as a watch makers apprentice until 1933. From that time, Weymann

worked as a self-employed watch maker and joined the Nazi party in Oct.1929 (NSDAP Nr. 153.558). Mustering with the SA, he joined the *Allgemeine*-SS during 1932 (SS Nr. 46.830) and found employment with the Schönlanke district office on 1.12.1934. Appointed the *Regierungsekr des Regierungsdirektor* of Schönlanke in the summer of 1939, Weymann married in 1936 and three children followed from this union. Drafted into the *Waffen*-SS on 25.11.1939, he served as a rifleman in the SS-*T.-Inf.*-Rgt. 9 and then as a radioman in the SS-*T.-Inf.*-Rgt. 10. *Rttf.* Weymann had formally worked in the Krakau SS-*Lazarett* and at the time of the offence, he worked alongside Feurerstein in the uniform wash room and store. The court noted that Weymann had a chronic gastritis which required doctor's treatment:

The court imposed a sentence of five years' *Zuchthaus* on Feuerstein for committing serious military theft and declared him a pest to the people. Punished with a one year *Zuchthaus* for fraud, the court ordered Feuerstein's total of six years and two months' *Zuchthaus* to be served in the SS-*Straflager* Dachau. At trial *Rttf.* Weymann denied the charges, but the tribunal judged him guilty of committing serious military theft and fraud and ordered him to serve 22 months *Zuchthaus* and declared him a pest to the people. In addition to these punishments, all three defendants were expelled from the SS, judged militarily unworthy, denied their civil rights and were commanded to the SS-*Straflager* to await the confirmation of their sentences. In view of his ill health, Weymann served his punishment in a KL clinic.

On 24.2.1943, Himmler commanded *Uscha.* Feuerstein serve a twelve months *Zuchthaus* and then accept front probation. Accepting that *Rttf.* Weymann had not instigated the theft of the alcohol, the *HA* SS-*Gericht* cancelled his sentence and he transferred to an SS-*Lazarett* to treat his stomach complaint. Prior to considering him for front probation, the SS leader commanded Feuerstein to serve nine months imprisonment: NARA BDC, SSO Personalakte Hans Ammon.

5.19 103. SS-Bewährungskompanie

295 Wilhelm Tieke, *The Tragedy of the Faithful*, pp.126-127. According to the Norwegian author Egil Ulateig, ('Jakten på Massemorderne'), Scandinavian volunteers and former *Wehrmacht* and *Waffen*-SS soldiers were assigned to the 103. SS-*Bewährungskompanie.* In Sept.1944 the survivors of the battle for Grenadier Hill were gathered at Pertatze near Johvi when they were overrun by a Red Army assault.

Hstuf. Adolf Klocker (b. 28.4.1905 in Paternion/Kärnten, SS Nr. 299.566). *Hstuf.* Josef Bachmeier (b. 27.10.1908 in Dinggolfing, SS Nr. 96.239)

5.20 SS-Bewärhungsabteilung 'Thomalla'

296 Werner Vopersol Archiv; SS-*Kampfgruppe*: BA NS 756/283a. For more details see Wilhelm Tieke's, *Das Ende zwischen Oder und Elbe, Der Kampf um Berlin 1945*, Motorbuch Verlag 2000.

297 *Hstuf.* Franz Thomalla, (b. 25.10.1917 in Essen-Borbeck, SS Nr. 365.106) spent the first part of the war fighting with the SS-Rgt. *Westland*, had led the SS-*Infantrie-Ersatz-Bataillon* from Sept.1942 and the SS-*Panzergrenadier-Ausbildung- und Ersatz-Bataillon Nordland* from Sept.1944.

298 *Soldaten, Kampfer, Kameraden, bd Vb S 399* (Ed. 2005): Vopersal archive; Horst Voigt—*Sondertruppen zur Bewahrung im WW2*, p. 286: BA NS 756/283a.

299 Tieke, '*Das Ende…*' op cit.; p. 453. See Voigt, '*Die 'Verlor'nen Haufen…*' op cit.; pp. 286-287: BA NS 756/283a.

5.21 SS-Bewährungs-Regiment 'Ludwigsfelde'

300 Voigt, '*Die Verlor'nen Haufen…*' op cit.; pp. 450-451: BA NS 756/283a.

5.22 SS-Standarte 'Mauthausen'

Die Masse der zersplittert eingesetzten Kampfgruppe „Oberdonau" geriet bei den Absetzbewegungen über die Enns und damit die amerikanisch – russische Demarkationslinie in amerikanische Gefangenschaft und wurde im Raum Radstatt – Wagrain – Kleinarl gesammelt.301 Wolfgang Benz, *Der Ort des Terrors. Geschichte der nationalsozialistischen Konzentrationslager. Gesamtwerk: Bd. 4*: *Flossenbürg, Mauthausen, Ravensbrück*, C.H.Beck 2006, p. 297.

302 Hans Maršálek, *Die Geschichte des KZ Mauthausen* Edition Mauthausen 1995, p. 333.

303 Brought to trial in 3.1944, these Vienesse firemen were then incarcerated in the z.Zt *Zug des Lagerarrest.*

304 Maršálek, '*Die Geschichte…*' op cit.; p. 333. For further details see Memorandum and Resistance: A report on the solidarity and resistance in the Mauthausen concentration camp from 1938 to 1945 edition: vom Komitee d. Antifaschist.The Committee of Antifascists. Widerstandskämpfer d. DDR, S. 155fResistance d. DDR, p. 155.

305 *Ibid.* For further details see Benz, '*Der Ort des Terrors…*' op cit.; p. 297.

306 Wolfgang Vopersal, *Smoke Steiner, War in Austria*, p. 285: BA MA N 756; Paul Wagner, *Activities and struggles of the Division in 487. EuA Litschel, Spear, Sword and Helmet*, 1968, p. 133.

5.23 SS-Bewährungsabteilung 'Nürnberg'

307 Vopersal Archive: BA NS 756/283a.

5.24 SS-Kampfgruppe 'Matingen/Pavian'

308 Seidler, '*Die Militärgerichtsbarkeit…*', op cit.; p. 261.

309 Vopersal Archive: BA NS 756/283a, b, c.

310 Seidler, '*Die Militärgerichtsbarkeit…*' op cit.; p. 266.

5.25 Polizei-Bewährungskompanie Einbrodt

311 Der HSSPF *im Wehrkreis* XVIII to the *Führungsstab für Bandenbekämpfung*, dated 9.1.1945, (Tagesbefehl Nr. 2/45; Nr. 4. *Bewährungskompanie*); Ende des 2 Seitigen Auszuges: Archiv RS AS 1621 Fasc 93.

Born in Eisenach on 13.12.1906, *Hstuf.* Herbert Einbrodt (SS Nr. 1.510) deployed with the 1. / 2. SS-*T.Inf.*Rgt. in Apr.1941 and mustered with the SS-*Truppen*übungsplatz *Böhmen-Mähren* in Apr.1944. Bolstered with Slovene recruits, the *Sonderzüge des* SS-*Polizei*-Rgt. 14 is thought to have been active with the HQ of the III. / SS-*Polizei*-Rgt. 14 around Großlaschitz (Velike Lašče) in Laibach province from the summer of 1944. Subordinate to the newly established V. (*Alarm*) *Bataillon der Slowenische Landwehr* in Nov.1944, the *Bewährungskompanie* XVIII was also assigned to this battalion, with *Podnarednik* Karol Jurjevčič leading the Slovene personnel of the company.

APPENDIX 1

SS Ranks Comparison Chart

SS Ranks

RFSS: SS-Reichsführer -	National Leader
SS-Obgruf.–	SS-Oberstgruppenführer–Colonel General
SS-Ogruf.–	SS-Obergruppenführer–General
SS-Gruf.–	SS-Gruppenführer–Lieutenant General
SS-Brigadef.–	SS-Brigadeführer–Major General
SS-Oberf.–	SS-Oberführer -Brigadier General
SS-Sta.:	SS-Standartenführer–Colonel
SS-Ostubaf.–	SS-Obersturmbannführer–Lieutenant Colonel
SS-Stubaf.–	SS-Sturmbannführer–Major
SS-Hstuf.–	SS-Hauptsturmführer–Captain
SS-Ostuf.–	SS-Obersturmführer–First Lieutenant
SS-Ustuf.–	SS-Untersturmführer–Second Lieutenant
SS-Sturmscharführer-	Sergeant Major
SS-Stabsscharführer–	Sergeant Major
SS-Hscha.–	SS-Hauptscharführer–Master Sergeant
SS-Oscha. -	SS-Oberscharführer–Senior Sergeant
SS-Scha.–	SS-Scharführer–Staff Sergeant
SS-Uscha.–	SS-Unterscharführer–Corporal
SS-Rttf.–	SS-Rottenführer–Lance Corporal
SS-Strm.–	SS-Sturmmann–Private First Class
SS-Schütze -	Private
SS-Mann–	Private
SS-Anwärter –	Candidate
SS-Bewerber–	Candidate

Police Ranks

Generalfeldmarschall–	Field Marshal
Generaloberst–	Colonel-General
General–	General
Generalleutnant–	Lieutenant-General
Generalmajor–	Major-General
Oberst–	Colonel
Oberstleutnant–	Lieutenant-Colonel
Major–	Major
Hauptmann–	Captain
Oberleutnant–	1. Lieutenant
Leutnant–	2. Lieutenant
Obermeister–	Warrant Officer
Meister–	Warrant Officer
Hauptwachtmeister–	Sergeant Major
Zugwachtmeister–	Sergeant Major
Oberwachtmeister–	Colour Sergeant
Wachtmeister -	Sergeant
Rottwachtmeister–	Senior Corporal
Unterwachtmeister–	Corporal
Anwärter–	Lance Corporal

APPENDIX 2

Lexicon

Abwicklungsstelle—Demobilisation office

Amtgericht—Magistrates court

Assessor—Lay Judge

Außenkommandos—Prisoner unit deployed outside a Concentration camp

Bataillone—Battalion, *abbr. Btl.*

Bewährungs—Probation

Einsatzgruppen—Special Action Group

Erlaß—Edict, a legal announcement

Ersatz Bataillone—Reserve battalion

Feldpostnummer—Field Post Number

Gefängnis—Prison sentence

Gerichtassessor—Courts adjudicator

Gerichtsherr—Chief Lord Justice

Gestapo—Secret Police

Gnadenwesen—Pardons

Hauptamt SS-Gericht—SS Main Office for legal matters, *abbr.* HA SS-Gericht

Höhere SS-und Polizeiführer—The senior SS and Police leader, *abbr.* HSSPF

Höchster SS-und Polizeiführer—The supreme SS and Police leader, *abbr.* HöSSPF

Kommandant—Commandant

Konzentrationslager Concentration Camp, *abbr.* KL.

Lagerführer—Camp Leader

Landgericht—District court

Lebensborn e.V—The Well of Life Society

Militärgerichtsbarkeit—Military Jurisdiction

Militärgesetzbuch—Military Law Manual

Nationalsozialistische Arbeits Partei—National Socialist Workers Party, *abbr.* Nazi Party

Oberstes SS- und Polizeigericht—highest SS and police Court

Polizei—Police, *abbr.* Pol.

Rechtsanwalt—Lawyer/legal council

Rechtreferent—Legal secretary

Referent—Secretary

Reichsjustizministerium—National Justice Ministry, *abbr.* RJM

Reichsführer-SS—Nation Leader of the SS, *abbr.* RFSS

Reiter—Cavalry

Reichsicherheitshauptamt—The Reich Security Main Office, *abb*r. RSHA

Reichskommissars für die Festigung des Deutschen Volkstums—Reich Commissioner for the Consolidation of German nationality *abbr.* RKFDV

Sturmabteilung—Storm Battalion ('Brown shirts'), *abbr.* SA

Sicherheitsdienst—SS Intelligence Service, *abbr.* S.D

Sicherheitspolizei—Security Police *abbr.* SiPo

Schutzstaffel—Protection Squad

SS-Führungshauptamt—SS Main Office for Leadership, *abbr.* SS-FHA

SS-Gerichtamt—SS Legal Office

SS-Gerichtsbarkeit—SS jurisdiction

SS-Hauptamt—SS Main Office

SS-Kaserne—SS Barracks

SS-Korp—SS Corp.

SS-Oberabschnitt—Higher District

SS-Panzergrenadier-Ausbildung-und Ersatz-Bataillon—SS Armoured Grenadier Training and Replacement Battalion, *abbr.* SS-Pz.-Gren.-Ausb.-u. Ers.-Btl.

SS-Personalhauptamt—SS Personal Office, *abbr.* SS-PHA

SS-Richter beim RF-SS—SS Judge for the RF-SS (Himmler's advocate)

SS-Standgericht—SS Summary Court

SS-Strafgefangenen—SS convicts

SS-Straflager—SS Punishment Camp

SS-Soldbuch—SS Pay Book

SS-Sonderkommando—SS Special Commando

SS-und Polizeigerichte—SS and Police Courts

SS-und Polizei Feldgerichte—SS and Police Field Court

SS-und Polizeigerichte z.b.V—non-permanent SS Tribunal for secret trials

SS-und Polizei Strafvollzugslager—SS and Police Prison camp

SS-Richter—SS Judge

SS-Sträflinge—SS Convicts

SS-Truppenübungsplatz—SS Troop Training Area, *abbr.* SS-Tr.Üb.Pl.

Staatspolizeileitstelle—Secret Police Regional Office

Standarte—Regiment, *abbr.* Sta.

Strafgefangene—Convict

Totenkopfverbände—Deaths Head formations

Truppen—Troops

Untersuchungsführer—Court Investigations Officer

SS Verfügungstruppe—SS Disposal Troops

Verlorenen Haufen—The Lost Bunch / Lost Fellows

Volksdeutsche Mittelstelle—Ethnic-German Resettlement Office, abbr. VoMi

Waffen-SS—Armed–SS

Weltanschauung—World Vision (Nazi Ideology)

Wirtschafts und Verwaltungshauptamt—Economic and Administrative Main Office *abbr.* WVHA

Zur Besonderen Verwendung—For Special Duties, *abbr.* z.b.V.

Zuchthaus—hard labour prison sentence

Zug—Infantry section

Zweiggericht—Branch court

APPENDIX 3

Abbreviations

Btl.—Bataillon

Ers.-Abt.—Ersatz Bataillon

FPNr.—Feldpostnummer

Gren.—Grenadier

HA SS-Gericht—Hauptamt SS-Gericht

HöSSPF—Höchster SS-und Polizeiführer

HSSPF—Höhere SS-und Polizeiführer

KL—Konzentrationslager

LssAH—Leibstandarte-SS Adolf Hitler

MStGB—Militärgesetzbuch

Nazi—Nationalsozialistische

Oberstes SS- u. Pol.-Ger.—Oberstes SS- und Polizeigericht

Pz.—Panzer

Pol.—Polizei

RFSS—Reichsführer-SS

RSHA—Reichssicherheitshauptamt

RKFDV—Reichskommissars für die Festigung des DeutschenVolkstums

SA—Sturmabteilung

SD—Sicherheitsdienst

SiPo—Sicherheitspolizei

SS—Schutzstaffel

SS-FHA—SS-Führungshauptamt

SS-HA—SS-Hauptamt –

SS-Pz.-Gren.-Ausb.-u. Ers.- Btl.—SS-Panzergrenadier-Ausbildung-und Ersatz Bataillone

SS-PHA—SS-Personalhauptamt

SS-u. Pol.-Ger.—SS-und Polizeigerichte

SS-Regt—SS-Regiment

SS-Sta.—SS-Standarte

SS-Tr.Üb.Pl.—SS-Truppenübungsplatz

SS-TV—SS-Totenkopfverbände

St. V. L. d. SS-u. Pol.—Strafvollzugslager der SS-und Polizei

SS-VT—SS-Verfügungstruppe

VoMi—Volksdeutsche Mittelstelle

WVHA—Wirtschafts und Verwaltungshauptamt

z.b.V—Zur Besonderen Verwendung

Select Biography

Books and Magazines

ANGRICK, Andrej—*Die Endlosung in Riga* (Darmstadt, 2006)

AUERBACH, Helmuth—*Die Einheit Dirlewanger* (Göttingen, 1955)

BIDDISCOMBE, Perry—*The SS Hunter Battalions* (Tempus, 2006)

BLOOD, Philip W.—*Hitler's Bandit Hunters: The SS and the Nazi Occupation of Europe* (Potomac Books, 2008)

BROSZAT, Martin—*Anatomie des SS-Staates Band 2* (dtv dokumente Okt.1984).

CHRISTENSEN, Claus—*The Danish Volunteers in the Waffen SS -and their Contribution to the Holocaust and the Nazi War of Extermination*

DANILUK, Jan—*Obóz karny SS i policji w Maćkowach pod Gdańskim*, „Pamięć i Sprawiedliwość" 2011, nr 2 (18)

EBERHARDT, P.—*Political Migrations in Poland 1939 to 1948* (Warsaw, 2006)

ERICKSON, John—*The Road to Berlin* (1983)

FAUL, G.—*Slave Labourers for the Final Victory* (Heersbruck, 2003)

FEST, Joachim. C.—*The Face of the Third Reich* (Penguin Books Ltd, 1988)

FISCHER, Thomas—*Soldiers of the Leibstandarte* (Fedorowicz (J. J.) Canada, 2008)

FRIEDLANDER, Saul—*The Years of Extermination* (Phoenix, 2007)

GILES, Geoffrey J.—*The Denial of Homosexuality: Same-Sex Incidents in Himmler's SS* (University of Texas Press, 2002)

GILES, Geoffrey J.—*Homophobia and Sexual Politics in Nazi Germany* (University of Texas Press, 2001)

GILES, Geoffrey J.—*The Most Unkindest Cut of All: Castration, Homosexuality and Nazi Justice* (University of Texas Press, 1992).

GLANTZ, David M.—*From the Don to the Dnepr* (Routledge, 1998).

GRUCHMANN, Lothar—*Justiz im Dritten Reich 1933–1940: Anpassung und -Unterwerfung in der Ära Gürtner* (Oldenbourg, 2002)

GUDERIAN, Hans—*Panzer Leader* (Penguin, 1999)

HERBERT, Ulrich– *Die Nationalsozialistischen Konzentrationslager* vol. 1 (Wallstein, 1998)

HELEMANN, Micaela, nee Loewen,Meine Jahre im Osten *My years in the East, March 1945 to October 1949*

HERZOG, Dagma—*Sexuality and German Fascism* (Berghahn, 2004)

HÖHNE, März 1945 - Oktober 1Hans—*The Order of the Deaths Head* (Secker & Warburg, 1980)

HORMANN, Jorg M.—*Das Verordnungsblatt der Waffen SS Bund 1* (Hannover, 1980)

JELLONEK, Burkhard—*Homosexualle unter dem Hakenkreuz* (Paderborn, 1990)

JEGIELKA, Stephen—*Das KZ Außenglager Genshagen* (Ed. Tectum Verlag Marburg, 2005)

JESKE, Gerhard—*Free City of Danzig before First of September 1939*

KASHUBIAN, Zwarra Bruno—*Najbardziej znaną książką Zwarry są kilkutomowe "Wspomnienia gdańskiego bówki". Memories bówki Gdansk Zwarra pochodzi z kaszubskiej rodziny, która przyjechała do Gdańska za chlebem. vol. III* (Gdańsk, 1986)

KERSTEN, Felix—*The Kersten Memoirs 1940–1945* (Hutchinson, 1957)

KLAUSCH, Hans Peter—*Antifaschisten in SS Uniform* (Temmen, 1993)

KLEE, Ernst—*Das Personenlexikon zum Dritten Reich* (Fischer Taschenbuch Verlag, 2013)

KLEITMANN, Kurt George—*Die Waffen SS: eine Dokumentation* (Osnabrück, 1965)

KOGEN, Eugen—*The Theory and Practice of Hell—The German Concentration Camps and System behind Them* (Farrar Straus Giroux, 2006)

KUROWKSI, Franz—*Panzer Aces* (Fedorowicz (J. J.) Canada, 2004)

LANGBEIN, Hermann—*People in Auschwitz* (The University of North Carolina Press 2005)

LEPRE, George—*Himmler's Bosnian Division* (Schiffer Military History, 2007)

LUMAN, Valdis. O.—*Himmler's Auxiliaries* (The University of North Carolina Press, 1993)

LUMSDEN, Robin—*A Collector's Guide To: The Allgemeine SS* (2001)

MARKOWITSCH, Tobias—*Goldfisch und Zebra. Das Konzentrationsaußenlager Neckarelz. Mosbach* (KZ-Gedenkstätte Neckarelz e.V. Selbstverlag, 2005)

MEHNER, Kurt—*Die Waffen-SS und Polizei 1939–1945* (Militar-Verlag, 1995)

METTKE, Jorg. R.—Der Spiegal 15/1986 article—*Sie haben etwas Gutzumachen*

MCLEAN, French—*The Camp Men*, (Schiffer Military History, 1999)

MCLEAN, French—*The Field Men*, (Schiffer Military History, 1999)

MEYER, Bruenn—*Dienstalterliste der Waffen-SS—SS-Obergruppenführer bis SS-Hauptsturmführer* (Biblio Verlag—Osnabrück 1987)

MILIUS, Siegfried—*Fallschirmjäger der Waffen-SS im Bild* (Verlag, Osnabrück, 1986)

MICHAELIS, Rolf—*SS-Heimwehr Danzig im Polenfeldzug* (Winkelried-Verlag, 2007)

MICHAELIS, Rolf—*SS-Fallschirmjager-Bataillon 500/600* (Schiffer Publishing, 2008)

Müller, j.—*Homosexuelle Männer im KZ Sachsenhausen* (Verlag pink triangle, 2000)

NACHSTERN, Moritz /ARNTZEN, Ragnor—*Counterfeiters* (Osprey Publishing, 2008)

NIX, Phil /JEROME, Georges—*The Uniformed Police Forces of the Third Reich 1933–45* (Leandoer and Ekholm, 2006)

OERTLE, Vincenz—*Sollte ich aus Rußland nicht Zürückkehren: Swiss volunteers on German side 1939–1945* (Thesis-Verlag Zürich, 1997)

ORSKIEGO, Marka—*Filie Obozu Koncentracyjnego Stutthof w latach 1939-1945* (Gdańsk, 1999)

PANTENIUS, Hans-Jürgen—*Letzte Schlacht an der Ostfront: Von Döberitz bis Danzig* (Mittler und Sohn, 2002)

PIONTROWKSI, Piotr—*Trojmiasto Historia—Zapomniany obóz w Gdańsku Maćkowych Forgotten camp in Gdansk Madko* (No. 97 issue 25.4.2003)

GUTMAN, Yisrael—*Anatomy of the Auschwitz Death Camp* (Indiana University Press, 1998)

Padfield, Peter—*Himmler Reichsführer-SS* (Cassel & Co., 2001)

PENCZ, Rudolf—*For the Homeland* (Helion Publishing, 2002)

PINGEL, Falk—*Natzweiler-Struthof Encyclopaedia of the Holocaust* (New York: Macmillan, 1990)

REES, Lawrence—*Auschwitz: the Nazis and the Final Solution* (BBC Books, 2005)

READ, Anthony—*The Fall of Berlin* (Hutchinson, 1995)

REITLINGER, Gerald—*The SS, Alibi of a Nation: 1922–1945* (Book Club Associates London, 1981)

REYNOLDS, Micheal—*The Men of Steel* (Spellmount, 1999)

RICHARDI, Hans-Günther—*SS-Geiseln in der Alpenfestung* (Bozen Ed. Raetia 2005)

SCHULTE, Jan Eric—*Zwangsarbeit und Vernichtung; Das Wirtschaft Imperium der SS*, (Ferdinand Schöningh, 1999)

SCHULTE, Theo—*The German Army and Nazi Policies in Occupied Russia* (Berg Publishers 1988)

SCHUMANN, Heinz—*SS im Einsatz; eine Dokumentation über die Verbrechen der SS* (Deutscher Militarverlag, 1964)

SEIDLER, Franz. W.—*Die Militärgerichtsbarkeit der Deutschen Wehrmacht 1939–1945* (Ed. Verlag S. Bublies, 1999)

SEIDLER, Franz W.—*The Camp Danzig Matzkau* In: Damals, Heft 4, 24.Published(Back Then, issue 4, Jg. Gießen 1992.1992)

SIKORSKI, Gaby—*Kriechen hab ich nie Gelernt* (Mystory Verlag 2005)

SNYDER, David Raub—*Sex Crimes under the Wehrmacht* (University of Nebraska Press, 2007)

SKUTNIK, S. 355 - 363. Tadeusz—*Stutthof; Historic Guide* (1980)

STEIN, George H.—*The Waffen SS: Hitler's Elite Guard at War*, 1939–1945 (Cornell University Press, 1984)

STEINER, Felix—*Der Freiwilligen; Idee und Opfergang* (Schutz, 1973)

STRASSNER, Peter—*European Volunteers: the SS Panzer Division Wiking* (Fedorowicz (J. J.) Canada, 2006)

TESSIN, Georg—*Verbände und Truppen der Deutschen Wehrmacht & Waffen SS im WWII Band II* (Osnabrück, 1967 to 1998)

TIECKE, Wilhelm—*Das Ende Zwischen Oder und Elbe* (Motorbuch Verlag, 1995)

TISSIER, Tony Le—*Zhukov at the Oder*, (Praeger, 1996)

TISSIER, Tony Le—*Race for the Reichstag*, (Praeger, 1999)

TOTTEN, Samuel—*Centuries of Genocide: Essays and Eyewitness Accounts* (4. Edition)

TRANG, Charles—*Totenkopf* (Pictorial History, 2006)

UNGVARY, Krisztian—*Battle for Budapest* (I. B. Tauris, 2003)

VIEREGGE, Bianca—*Die Gerichtsbarkeit einer 'Elite'* (Nomos Verlagsgesellschaft Baden-Baden, 2002)

VOIGT, Horst—*Die 'Verlor'nen Haufen; Sondertruppen zur Frontbewährung im 2. Weltkrieg, Teil VIII* (BA NS 756/283a)

VOPERSAL, Wolfgang—*Soldaten, Marsch und Kampfe der SS Totenkopf Division* (Osnabrück, 1991)

WEDEKIND, Michael—*Nationalsozialistische Besatzungs-und Annexionspolitik in Nord Italien 1943–1945* (Oldenbourg Wissensch. Vlg München, 2003)

WEIMANN, Martin—*Das Nationalsozialistische Lagersystem* (Zweitausendeins Frankfurt, 1998)

WEIDINGER, Otto—*Das Reich part I* (Munin, 1990)

WERNER, Constanze—*Kreigswirtschaft und Zwangsarbeit bei BMW* (De Gruyter Oldenbourg, 2005)

WILDT, Michael—*Nachtrichendienst, Politische Elite und Mordeinheit. Der Sicherheitsdienst des Reichsführers SS* (Hamburg Edition, 2003)

WILDT, Michael—*Generation des Unbedingten: Das Führerkorps des Reichssicherheitshauptamtes* (Hamburg Edition, 2003)

WILLIAMSON, Gordon—*German Security and Police Soldier 1939–45* (Oxford: Osprey Publishing, 2002)

WILSON, Paul J.—*Himmler's Cavalry; the Equestrian SS 1930–45*, (Schiffer Military History, 2000)

WITTMANN, Anna M.—*Mutiny in the Balkans: Croat Volksdeutsche, the Waffen SS and Motherhood* (East European Quarterly, Vol. 36, 2002)

YERGER, Mark C.—*Waffen SS commanders part I* (Schiffer Military History, 1997)

YERGER, Mark C.—*Waffen SS commanders part II* (Schiffer Military History, 1999)

VORMBAUM, Thomas—*Euthanasie vor Gericht* (Berliner Wissenschafts-Verlag, 2005)

Eine „Säule des Erinnerns" macht auf diesen Platz aufmerksam.Die Zeit, 1.4.1994, p. 13 SS-*Straflager* article
Der Spiegel, 14/94, p. 94 SS-*Straflager* article

Institutions

Bundesarchiv Berlin

Archive of the former Berlin Document Centre (BDC)

Akte BArch / ehem. BDC: SS-Führer, SSO

SS-Unterführer- und Mannschaftsakten SSEM

Akte BArch / ehem. BDC: Rasse-und SS Siedlungshauptamt

NSDAP Parteikanzlei

NSDAP Ortskartei

Akte R 3001, (Reichsjustizministerium)

Bundesarchiv-Militärarchiv Freiburg (BA-MA)

Bundesarchiv Ludwigsburg (BAL)

Staatsarchiv München

Oberösterreichischen Landesarchiv

Instituts für Zeitgeschichte

DC 27.01 Bd1.

DC 01.06, page 36, 56.

DC 02.019, (SS-DBO).

Washington DC National Archives

Microfilm publication A3343, Records of SS officers from Berlin document centre, series SSO, (61, 000 officers of second lieutenant and above between 1932 and March 1945).

D.C NARA Washington Microfilm; T-580, roll 212.

D.C NARA Washington Microfilm; T-580 roll 213.

D.C NARA Washington Microfilm; T-580 roll 214.

D.C NARA Washington Microfilm; T-580 roll 215.

NARA—Records of the Army Staff (Record Group 319) investigative records repository (IRR) personal name files, 1939-1976, College park, Maryland; 270/84/01/01-270/84/19/07.

NARA—Records of the Central Intelligence Agency (Record Group 263).
SS-*Dienstaltersliste der Schutzstaffel der* N.S.D.A.P. stand vom 1.10.34 Berlin, *Personalkanzlei des* RFSS 1935
SS-*Dienstaltersliste der Schutzstaffel der* N.S.D.A.P. stand vom 1.7.35 Berlin, *Personalkanzlei des* RFSS 1935
SS-*Dienstaltersliste der Schutzstaffel der* N.S.D.A.P. stand vom 1.12.36 Berlin, *Personalkanzlei des* RFSS 1937
SS-*Dienstaltersliste der Schutzstaffel der* N.S.D.A.P. stand vom 1.12.37 Berlin, *Personalkanzlei des* RFSS 1938
SS-*Dienstaltersliste der Schutzstaffel der* N.S.D.A.P. stand vom 1.12.38 Berlin, *Personalkanzlei des* RFSS 1939
SS-*Dienstaltersliste der Schutzstaffel der* N.S.D.A.P. stand vom 1.11.44 Berlin, (reprinted by INFORA establishment, Vaduz Fürstentum, Lichtenstein 1985).
SS-*Dienstaltersliste der Schutzstaffel der* N.S.D.A.P (*Ostubaf. und Stubaf.*)—Stand vom 1.Oktober 1942.
SS-*Dienstaltersliste der Schutzstaffel der* N.S.D.A.P (*Ostubaf. und Stubaf.*)—Stand vom 1.Oktober 1943.
SS-*Dienstaltersliste der Schutzstaffel der* N.S.D.A.P (*Ostubaf. und Stubaf.*)—Stand vom 1.Oktober 1944.
SS-*Dienstaltersliste der Schutzstaffel der* N.S.D.A.P (*Oberst-Gruf. und Sta.*)—Stand vom 30.Januar 1944.
SS-*Dienstaltersliste der Schutzstaffel der* N.S.D.A.P (*Ogruf. bis Hstuf.*)—Stand vom 1.Juli 1944.

The Wiener Library for the Study of the Holocaust and Genocide

N.S.D.A.P. Main Archive
Document collection: MF Doc 29
29/3 Collection Streicher and collection Himmler
Reel 48A; Brieftagebuch: Geheim 1944. 1. Teil.
Reel 53A; Brieftagebuch 1942-1943. 1. Teil.
Reel 53A; Brieftagebuch ab 1.3.1940. 2.Teil.
Reel 54A; Brieftagebuch V geheim.

Vojenský Historický Archiv Praha, (VHA)

Internet Resources

http://www.angewandte-geologie.geol.uni-erlangen.de/doggerwe.htm
http://www.dws-xip.pl/reich/biografie/numery/numer110.html
http://fotoforum.gazeta.pl/72,2,736,50723790.html?v=2&wv.x=1
http://www.eksploracja.eu/tps/readarticle.php?article_id=24
http://www.its-arolsen.org (international tracing service)
http://www.juden-im-nuernberger-land.de/2_stationen/html/mahnmale/foerrenbach
http://www.trojmiasto.pl/wiadomosci/W-Gdansku-karano-SS-Mannow—(Marzena Sikorska)
http://www.dws-xip.pl/reich/biografie/numery/numer110.html
http://www.feldgrau.com/
http://www.wiadomosci24.pl/artykul/zapomniane_obozy_zaglady_aussenstelle_matzkau_137841.html
http://www.kz-gedenkstaette-dachau.de/
http://www.scrapbookpages.com/Dachauscrapbook/SScamp/AvenueSS.html
http://www.jewishvirtuallibrary.org/jsource/Holocaust/dachau.html
http://www.forum.dawnygdansk.pl—(forum for info on Matzkau)
http://www.kz-denk-neckarelz.de/—('Concentration camp Neckarelz')
http://www.gedenkstaetten-bw.de/gedenkstaetten
http://www.ifz-muenchen.de/heftarchiv/1962_3_2_auerbach.pdf (titled; 'Die einheit Dirlewanger')
http://www.goldenline.pl/jan-daniluk (historians own site) —instytut Pamieci narodowej w Gdansku
http://gztmdachau.de/4.3.1.1.html (death march from Dachau)

Private Archives

Mr John. P. Moore, *Führerliste der Waffen*-SS (Ed. May 2003).
Mr Phil Nix, biographical notes from the archive of Mr Nix Birmingham, England.
Vopersal Archive, *Kamerad wo bist du*, (*Polizei* SS division).
[Picture 002]